My Boyfriend is a VAMPiRE

Book 5 & 6

Yu-Rang Han

My Boyfriend is a VAMPIRE

BOOK 5 & 6

story & art by Yu-Rang Han

STAFF CREDITS

translation   ChanHee Grace Sung
adaptation   Bambi Eloriaga-Amago
lettering   Roland Amago
layout   Mheeya Wok
cover design   Nicky Lim
copy editor   Shanti Whitesides
editor   Adam Arnold

publisher   Jason DeAngelis
                  Seven Seas Entertainment

ISBN: 978-1-935934-77-6

Printed in the USA

First Printing: July 2012

10 9 8 7 6 5 4 3 2 1

Seven Sea

FOLLOW US ONLINE: www.gomanga.com

My Boyfrien VAMP

BOOK 5

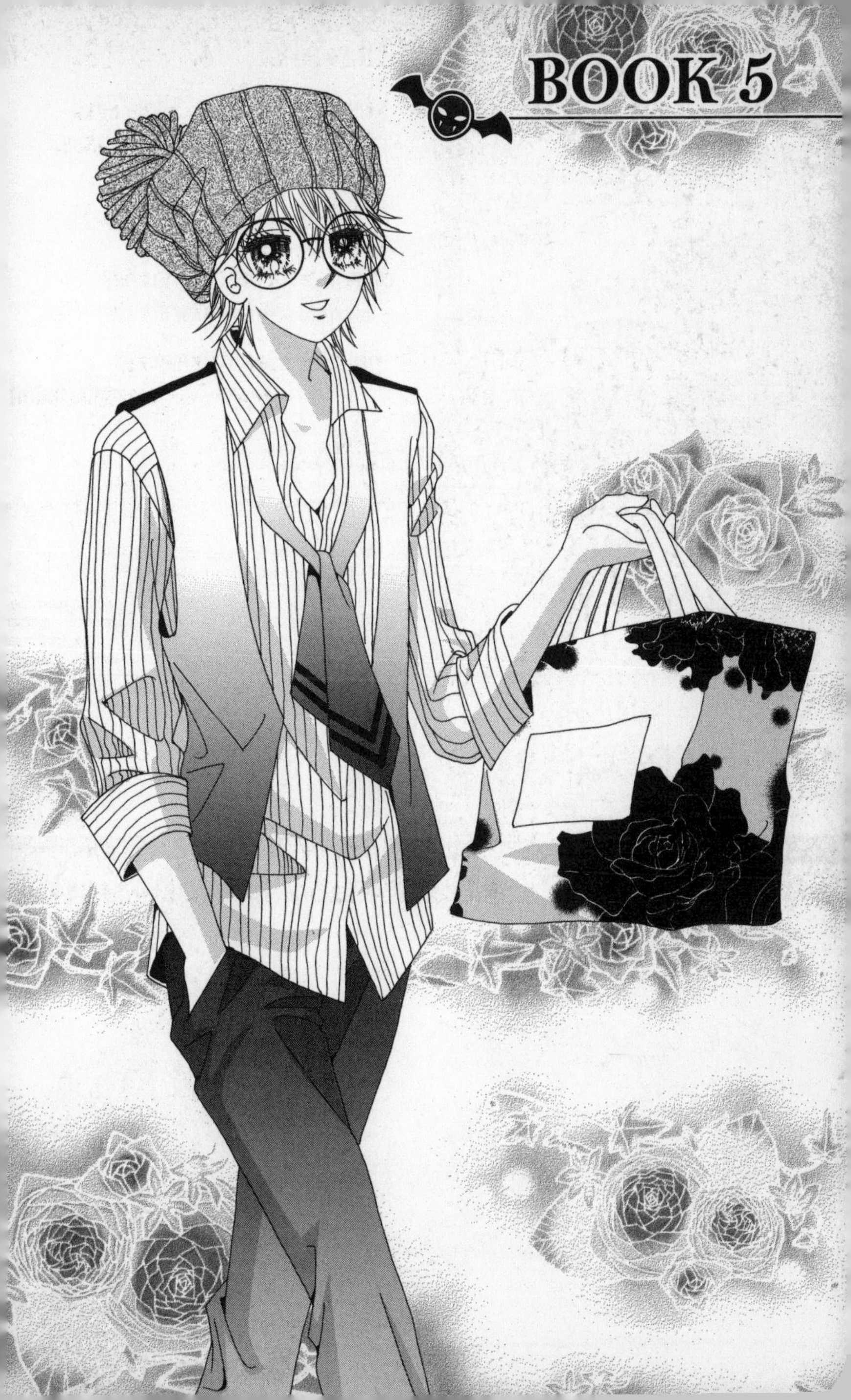

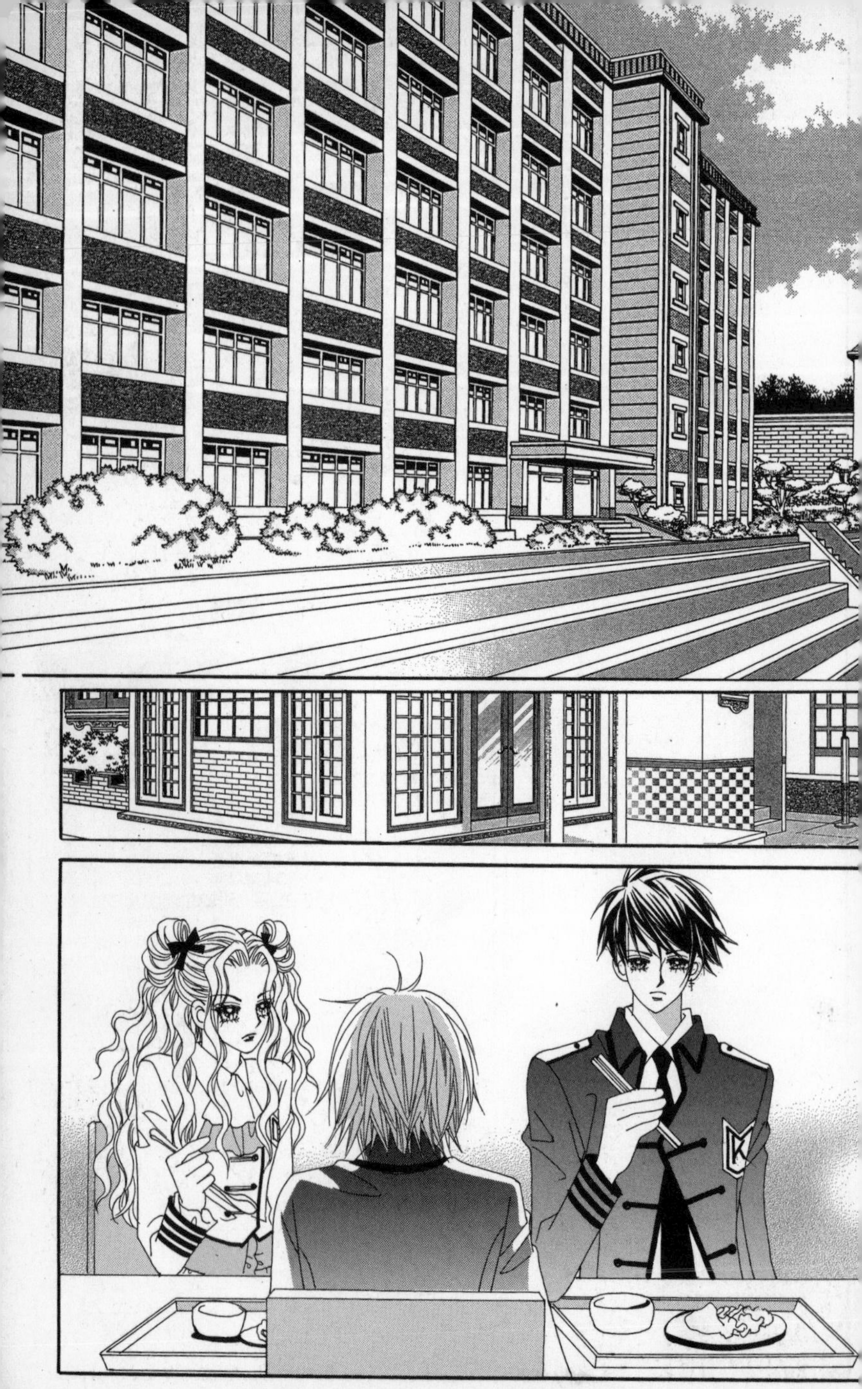

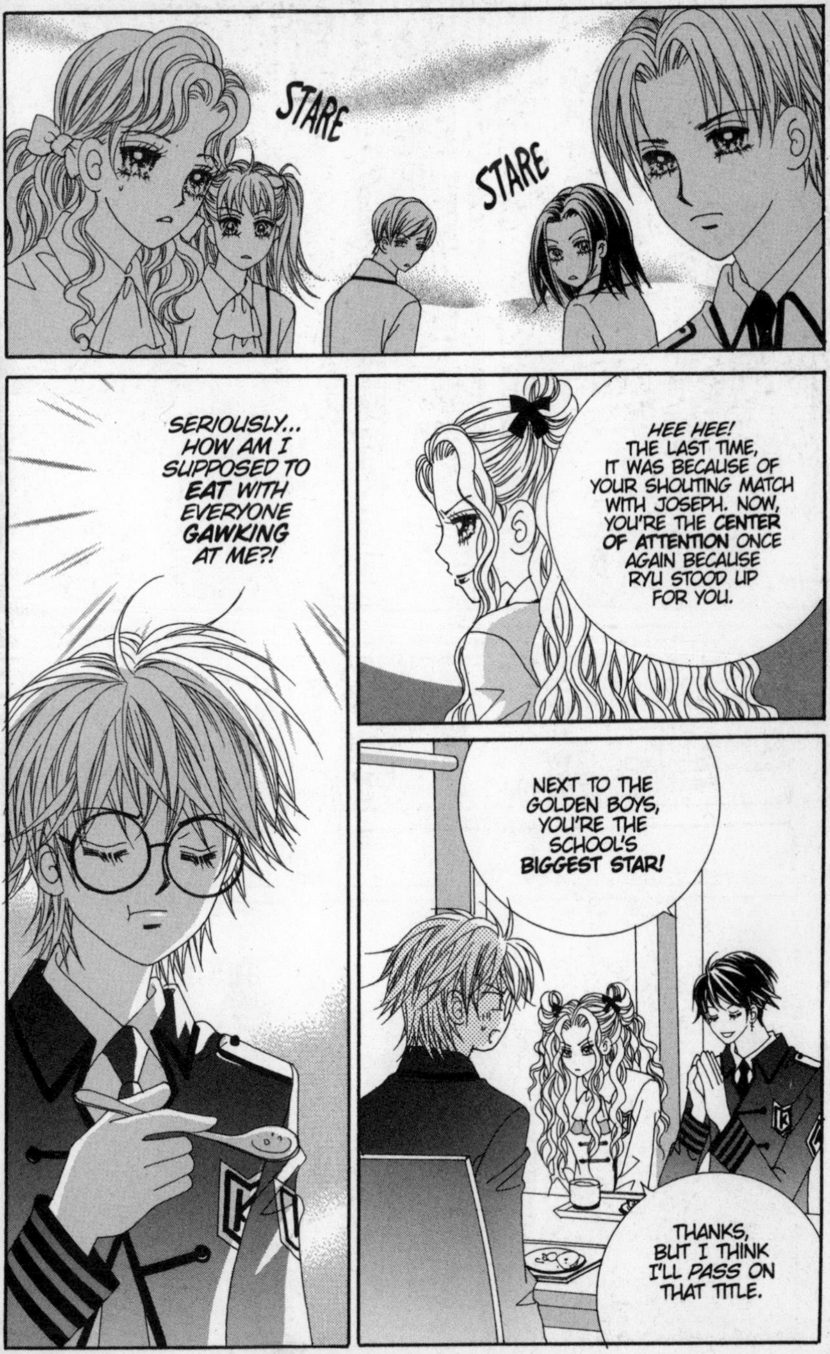
STARE
STARE
SERIOUSLY... HOW AM I SUPPOSED TO EAT WITH EVERYONE GAWKING AT ME?!
HEE HEE! THE LAST TIME, IT WAS BECAUSE OF YOUR SHOUTING MATCH WITH JOSEPH. NOW, YOU'RE THE CENTER OF ATTENTION ONCE AGAIN BECAUSE RYU STOOD UP FOR YOU.
NEXT TO THE GOLDEN BOYS, YOU'RE THE SCHOOL'S BIGGEST STAR!
THANKS, BUT I THINK I'LL PASS ON THAT TITLE.

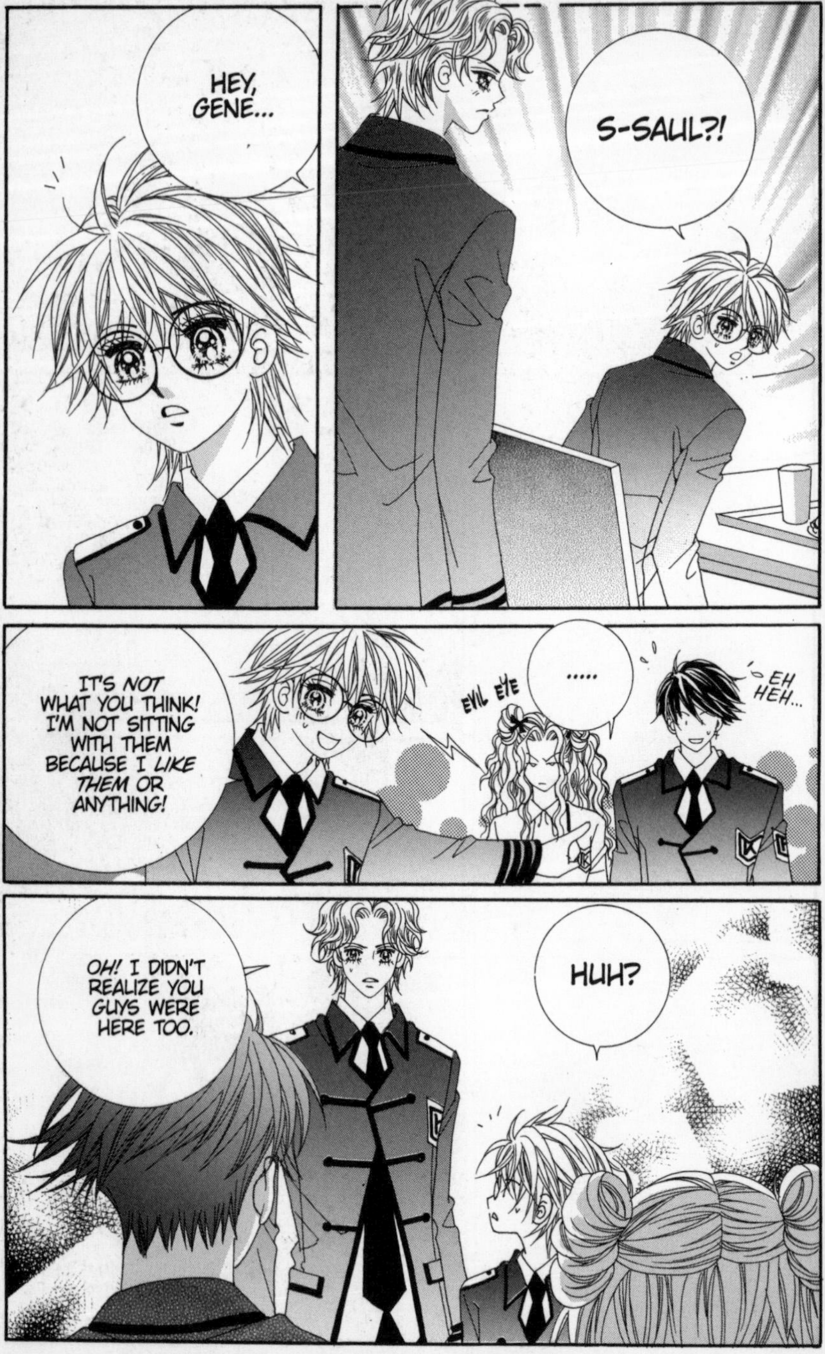
HEY, GENE...
S-SAUL?!
IT'S *NOT* WHAT YOU THINK! I'M NOT SITTING WITH THEM BECAUSE I *LIKE THEM* OR ANYTHING!
EVIL EYE
.....
EH HEH...
OH! I DIDN'T REALIZE YOU GUYS WERE HERE TOO.
HUH?

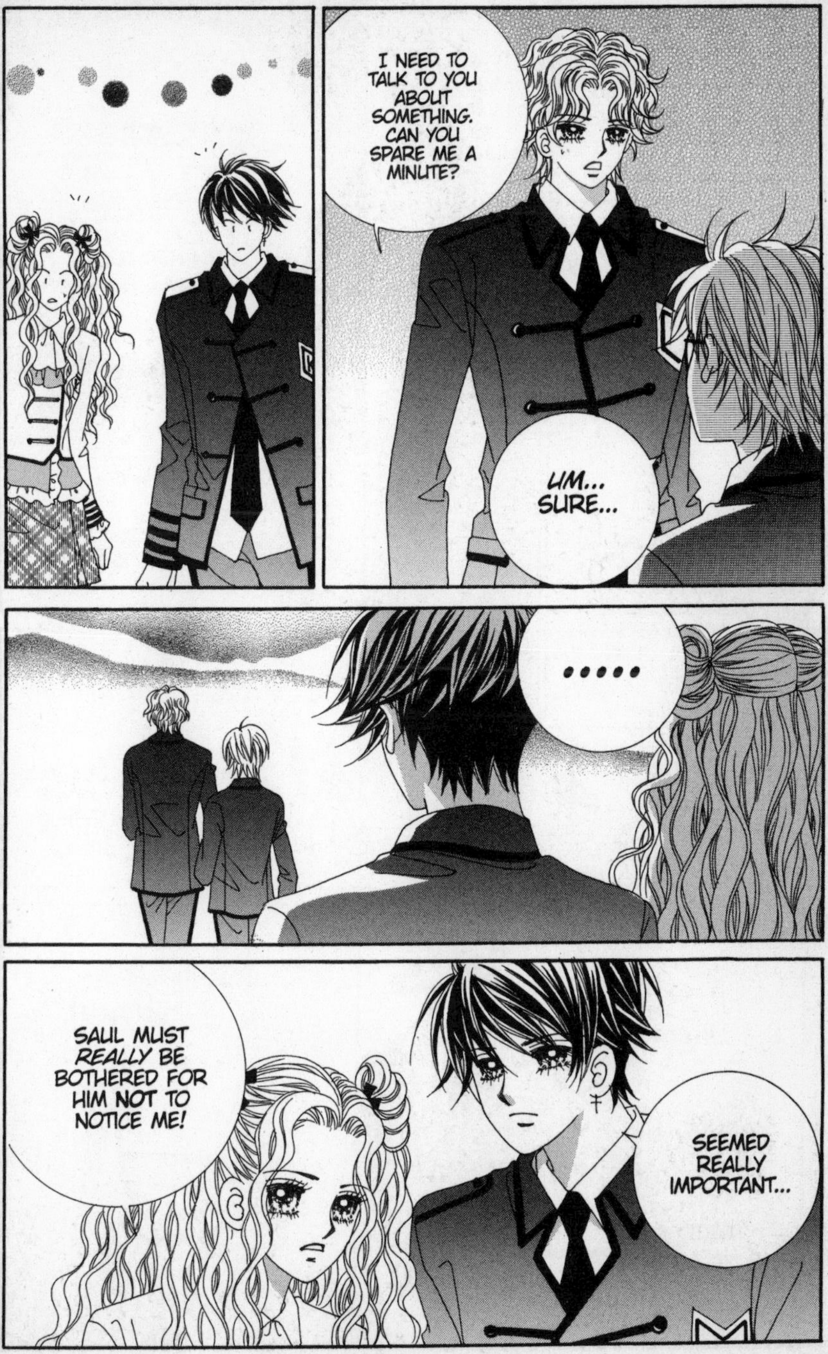
I NEED TO TALK TO YOU ABOUT SOMETHING. CAN YOU SPARE ME A MINUTE?
UM... SURE...
.....
SAUL MUST *REALLY* BE BOTHERED FOR HIM NOT TO NOTICE ME!
SEEMED REALLY IMPORTANT...

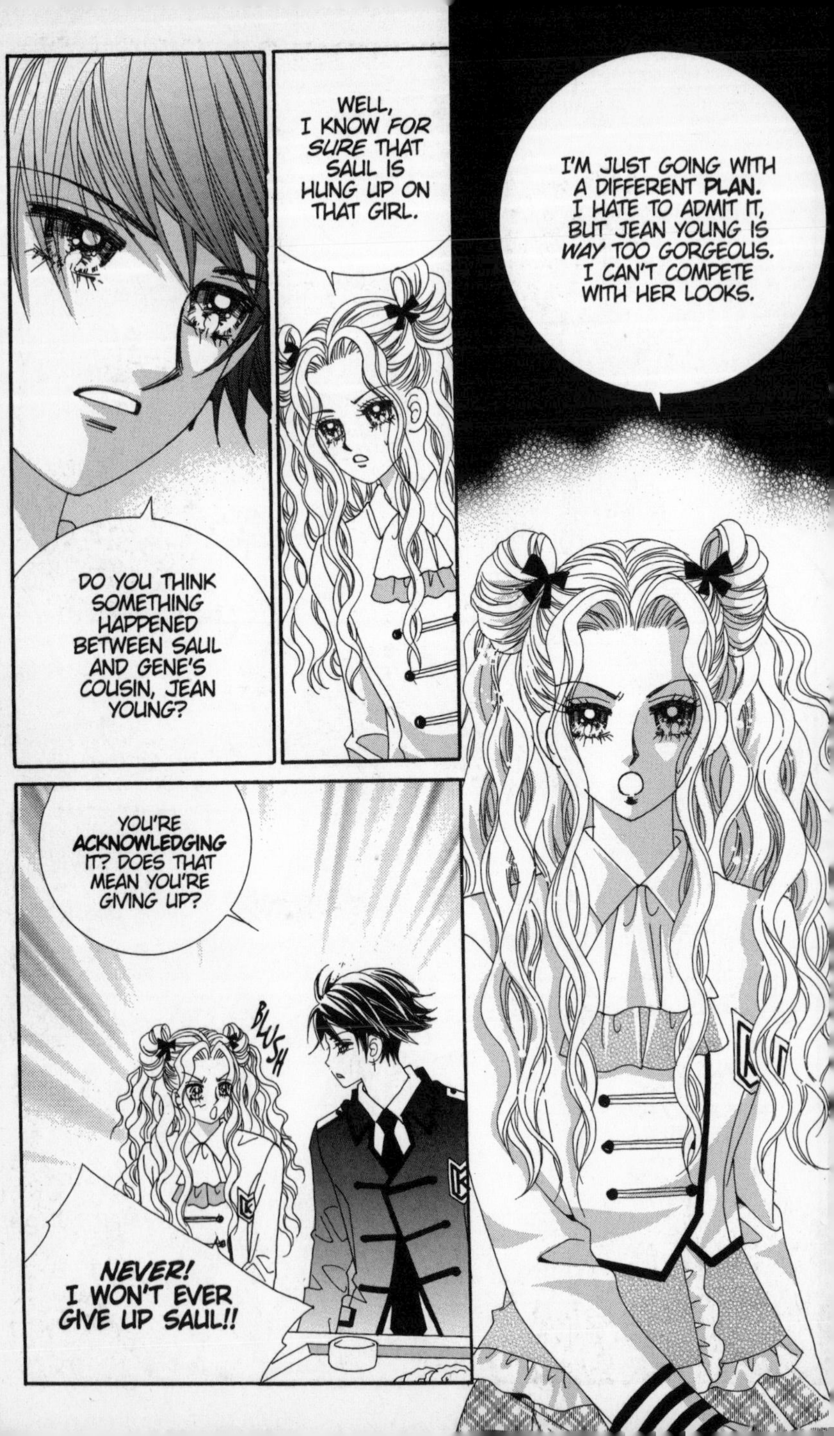
DO YOU THINK SOMETHING HAPPENED BETWEEN SAUL AND GENE'S COUSIN, JEAN YOUNG?
WELL, I KNOW *FOR SURE* THAT SAUL IS HUNG UP ON THAT GIRL.
YOU'RE ACKNOWLEDGING IT? DOES THAT MEAN YOU'RE GIVING UP?
BLUSH
NEVER! I WON'T EVER GIVE UP SAUL!!
I'M JUST GOING WITH A DIFFERENT PLAN. I HATE TO ADMIT IT, BUT JEAN YOUNG IS *WAY* TOO GORGEOUS. I CAN'T COMPETE WITH HER LOOKS.

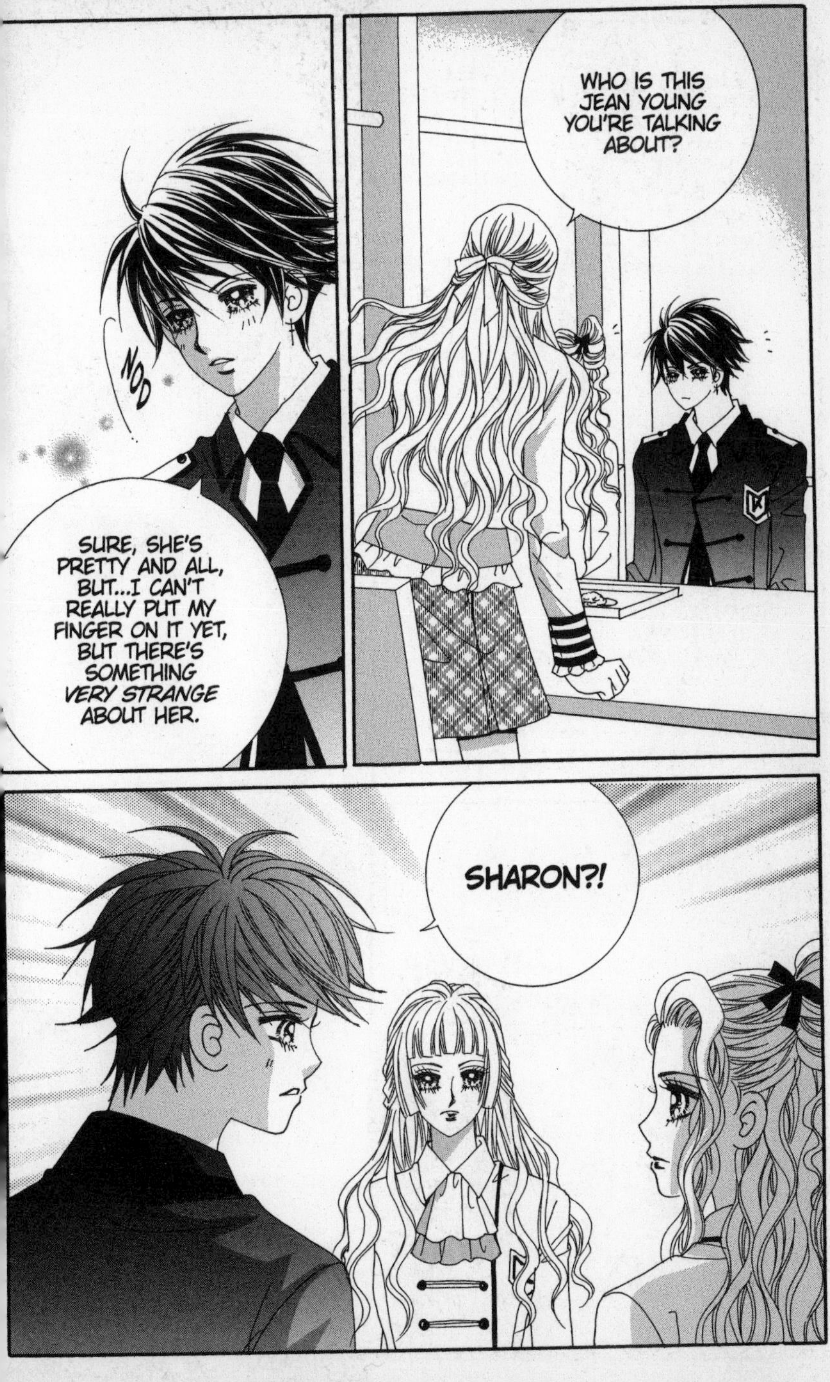
NOD
SURE, SHE'S PRETTY AND ALL, BUT...I CAN'T REALLY PUT MY FINGER ON IT YET, BUT THERE'S SOMETHING *VERY STRANGE* ABOUT HER.
WHO IS THIS JEAN YOUNG YOU'RE TALKING ABOUT?
SHARON?!

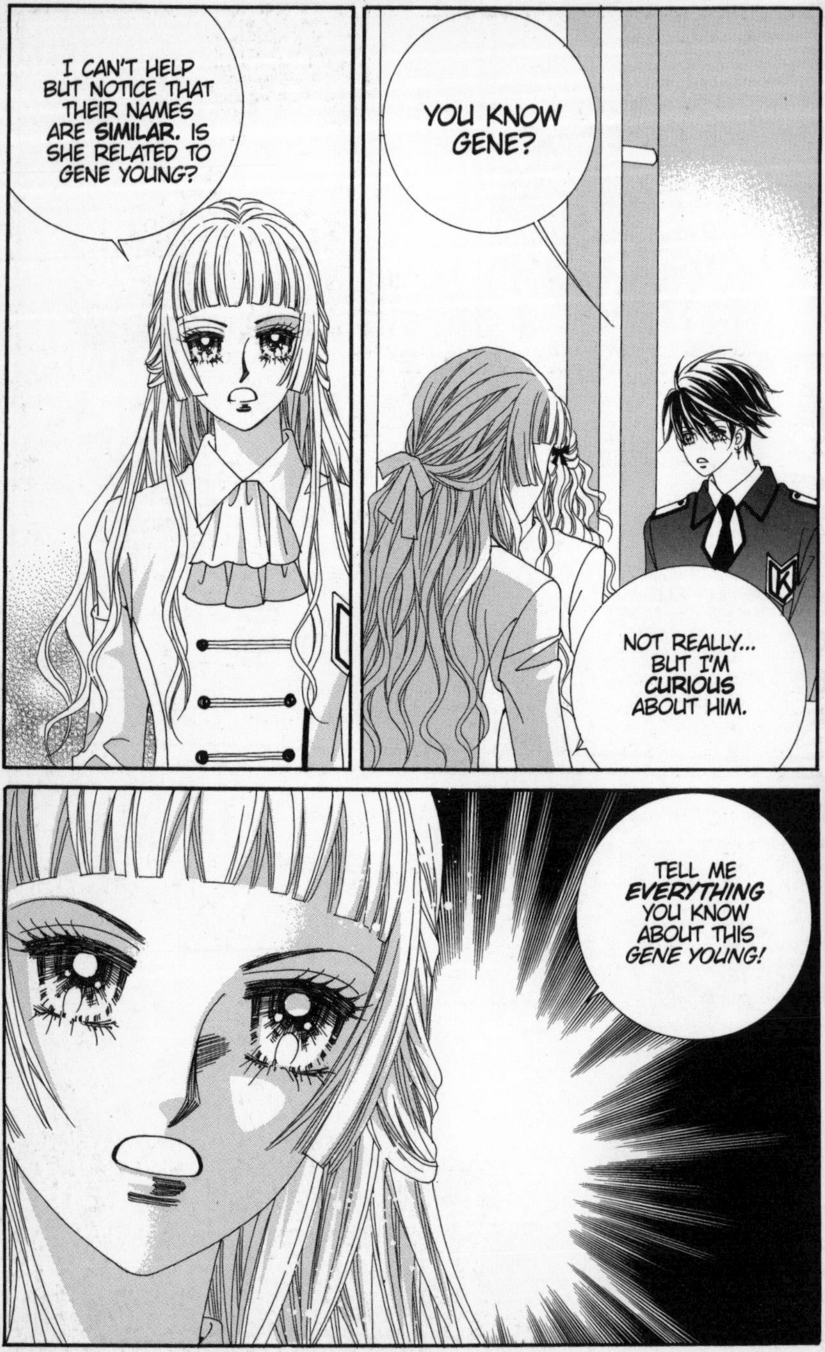
I CAN'T HELP BUT NOTICE THAT THEIR NAMES ARE **SIMILAR.** IS SHE RELATED TO GENE YOUNG?
YOU KNOW GENE?
NOT REALLY... BUT I'M **CURIOUS** ABOUT HIM.
TELL ME ***EVERYTHING*** YOU KNOW ABOUT THIS *GENE YOUNG!*

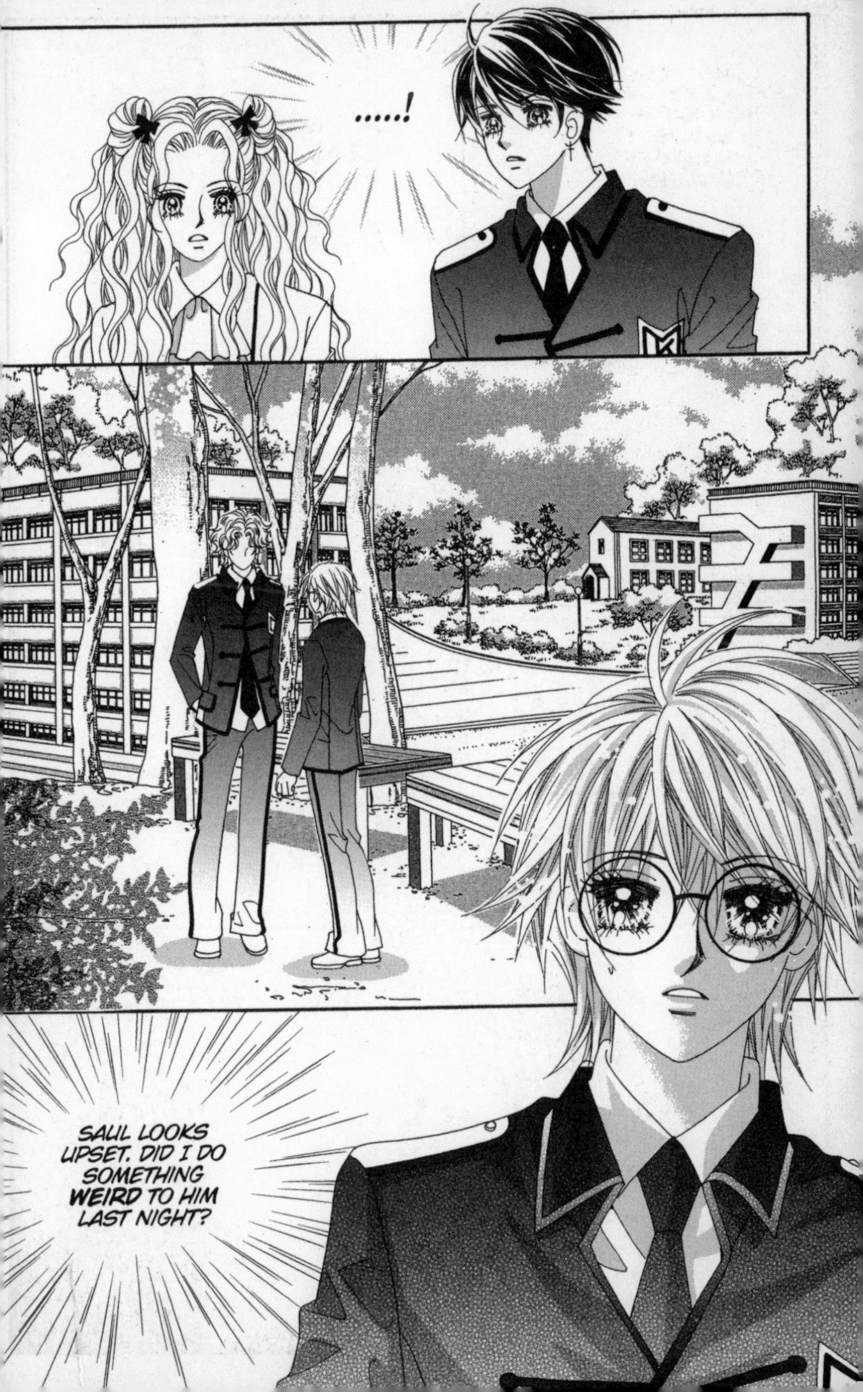
.....!
SAUL LOOKS UPSET. DID I DO SOMETHING **WEIRD** TO HIM LAST NIGHT?

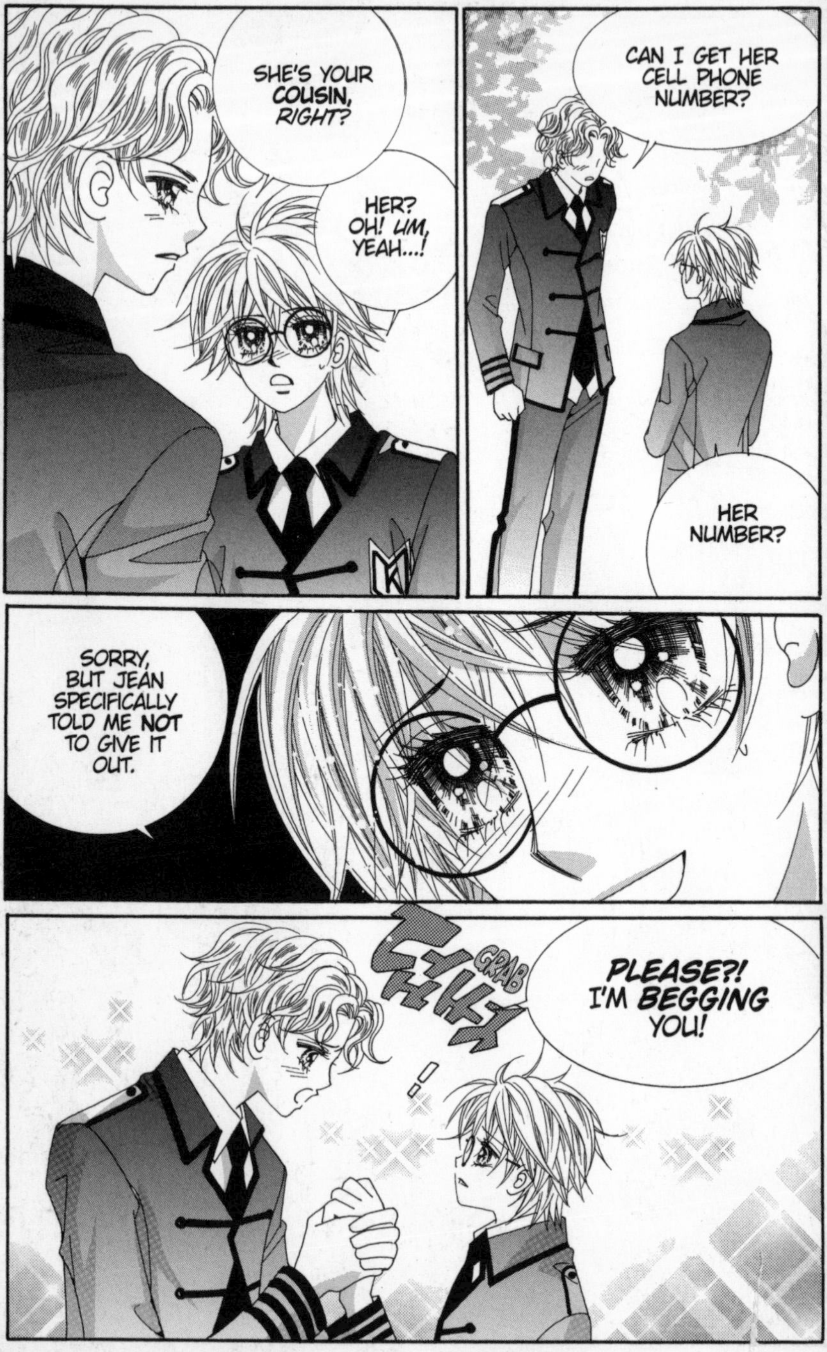
SHE'S YOUR COUSIN, RIGHT?
HER? OH! UM, YEAH...!
CAN I GET HER CELL PHONE NUMBER?
HER NUMBER?
SORRY, BUT JEAN SPECIFICALLY TOLD ME NOT TO GIVE IT OUT.
GRAB
PLEASE?! I'M BEGGING YOU!
!

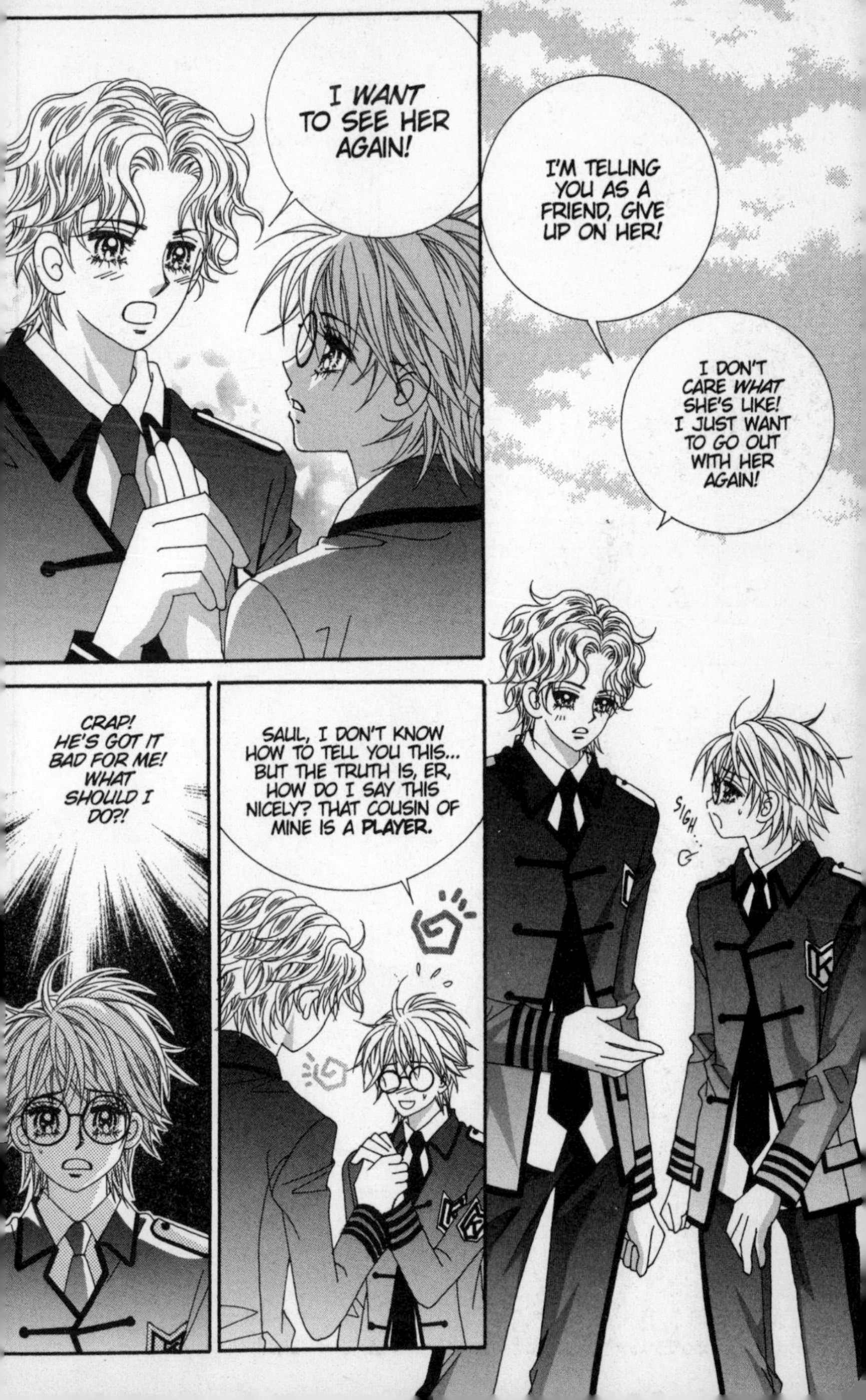
I WANT TO SEE HER AGAIN!
CRAP! HE'S GOT IT BAD FOR ME! WHAT SHOULD I DO?!
SAUL, I DON'T KNOW HOW TO TELL YOU THIS... BUT THE TRUTH IS, ER, HOW DO I SAY THIS NICELY? THAT COUSIN OF MINE IS A PLAYER.
I'M TELLING YOU AS A FRIEND, GIVE UP ON HER!
I DON'T CARE WHAT SHE'S LIKE! I JUST WANT TO GO OUT WITH HER AGAIN!
SIGH...

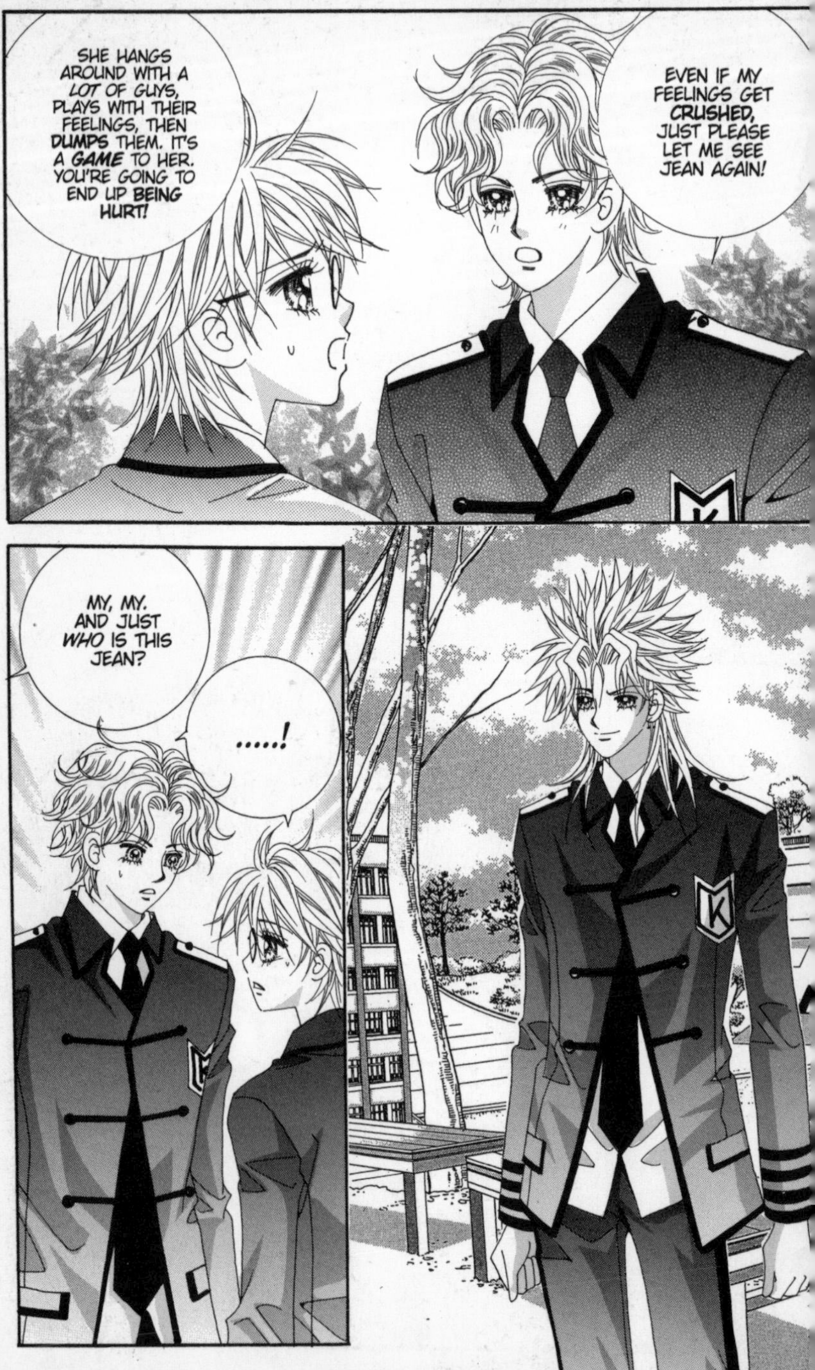
SHE HANGS AROUND WITH A LOT OF GUYS, PLAYS WITH THEIR FEELINGS, THEN DUMPS THEM. IT'S A GAME TO HER. YOU'RE GOING TO END UP BEING HURT!
EVEN IF MY FEELINGS GET CRUSHED, JUST PLEASE LET ME SEE JEAN AGAIN!
MY, MY. AND JUST WHO IS THIS JEAN?
.....!

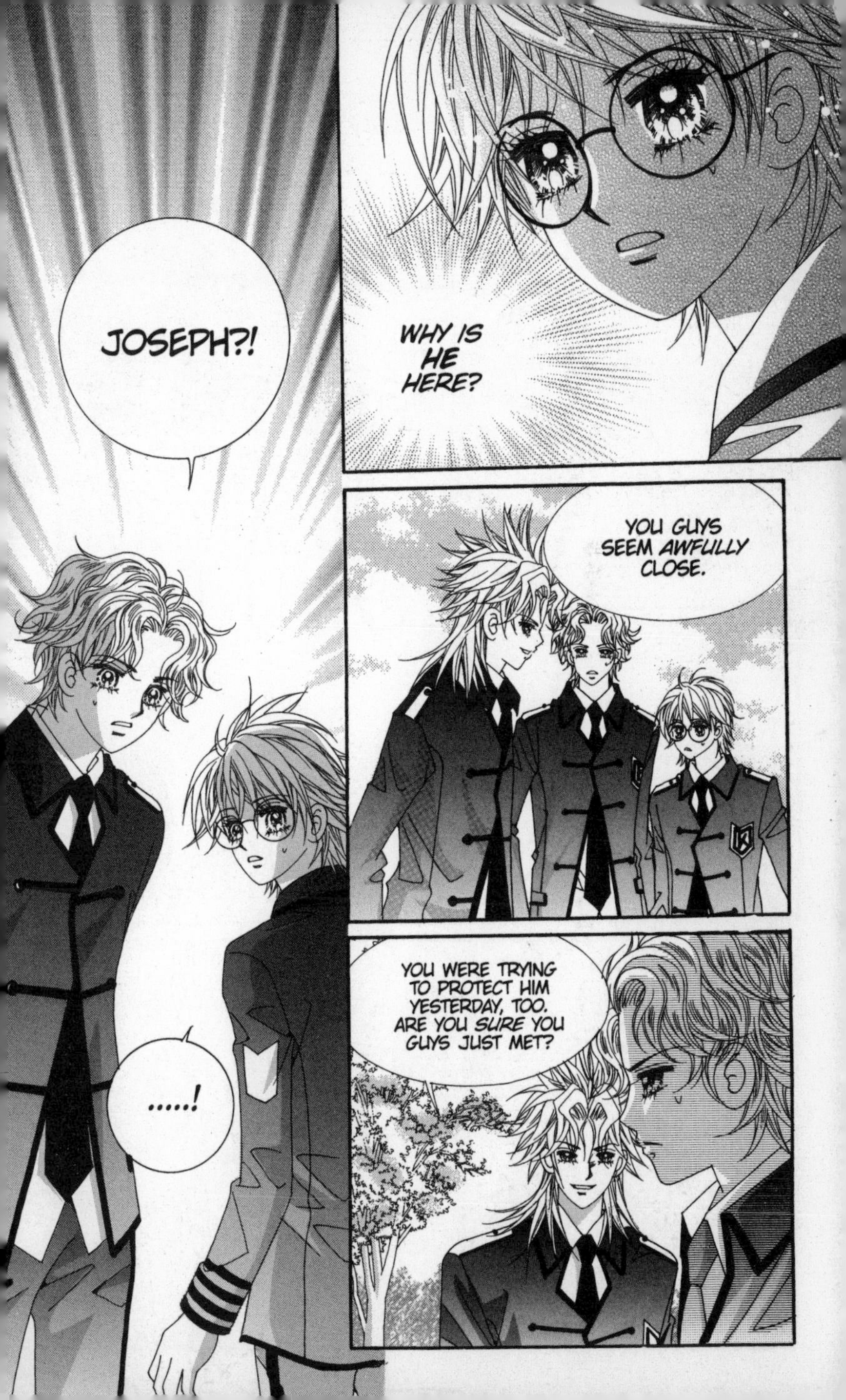
JOSEPH?!
.....!
WHY IS HE HERE?
YOU GUYS SEEM AWFULLY CLOSE.
YOU WERE TRYING TO PROTECT HIM YESTERDAY, TOO. ARE YOU *SURE* YOU GUYS JUST MET?

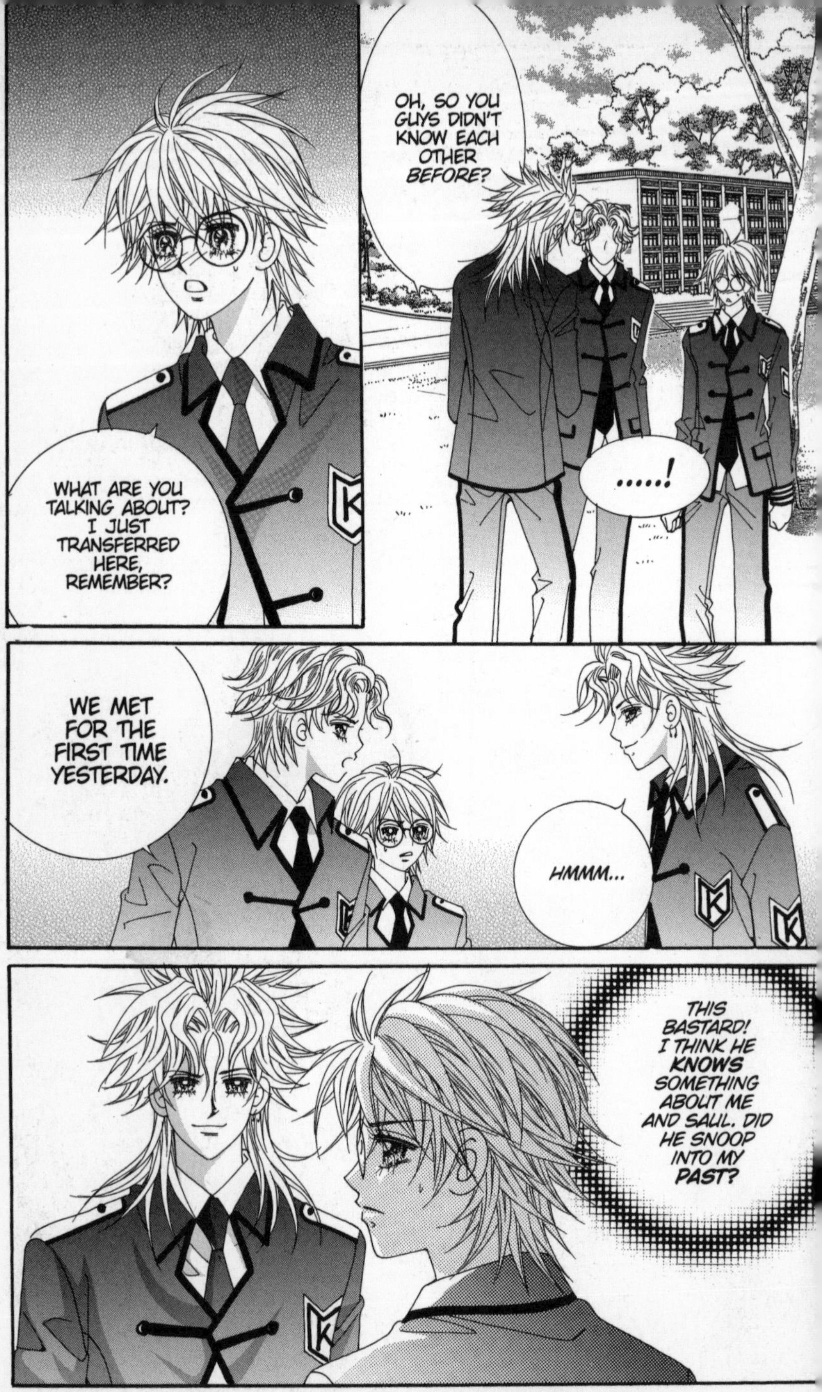
WHAT ARE YOU TALKING ABOUT? I JUST TRANSFERRED HERE, REMEMBER?
OH, SO YOU GUYS DIDN'T KNOW EACH OTHER BEFORE?
.....!
WE MET FOR THE FIRST TIME YESTERDAY.
HMMM...
THIS BASTARD! I THINK HE KNOWS SOMETHING ABOUT ME AND SAUL. DID HE SNOOP INTO MY PAST?

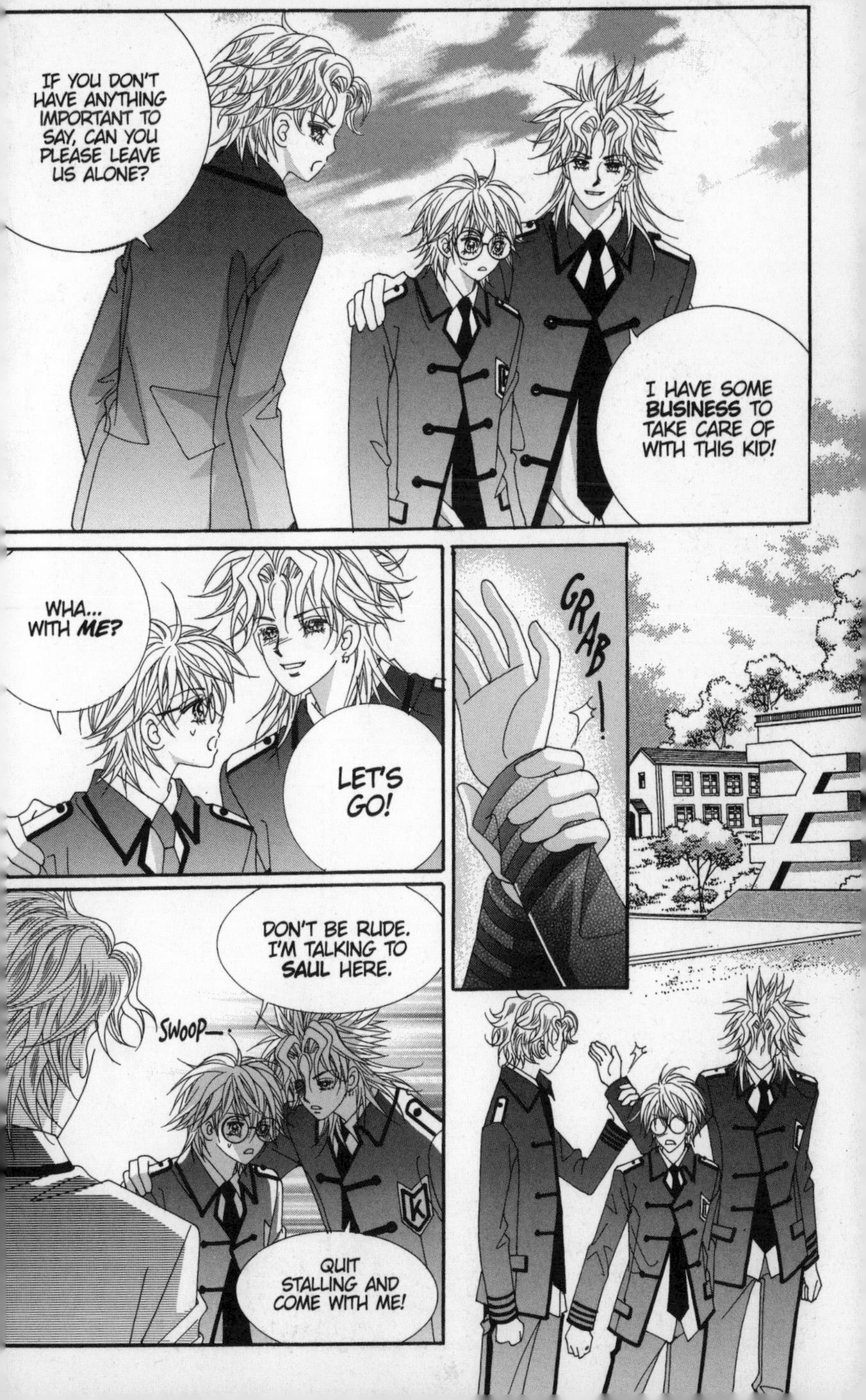
IF YOU DON'T HAVE ANYTHING IMPORTANT TO SAY, CAN YOU PLEASE LEAVE US ALONE?
I HAVE SOME BUSINESS TO TAKE CARE OF WITH THIS KID!
WHA... WITH ME?
LET'S GO!
GRAB!
DON'T BE RUDE. I'M TALKING TO SAUL HERE.
SWOOP—
QUIT STALLING AND COME WITH ME!

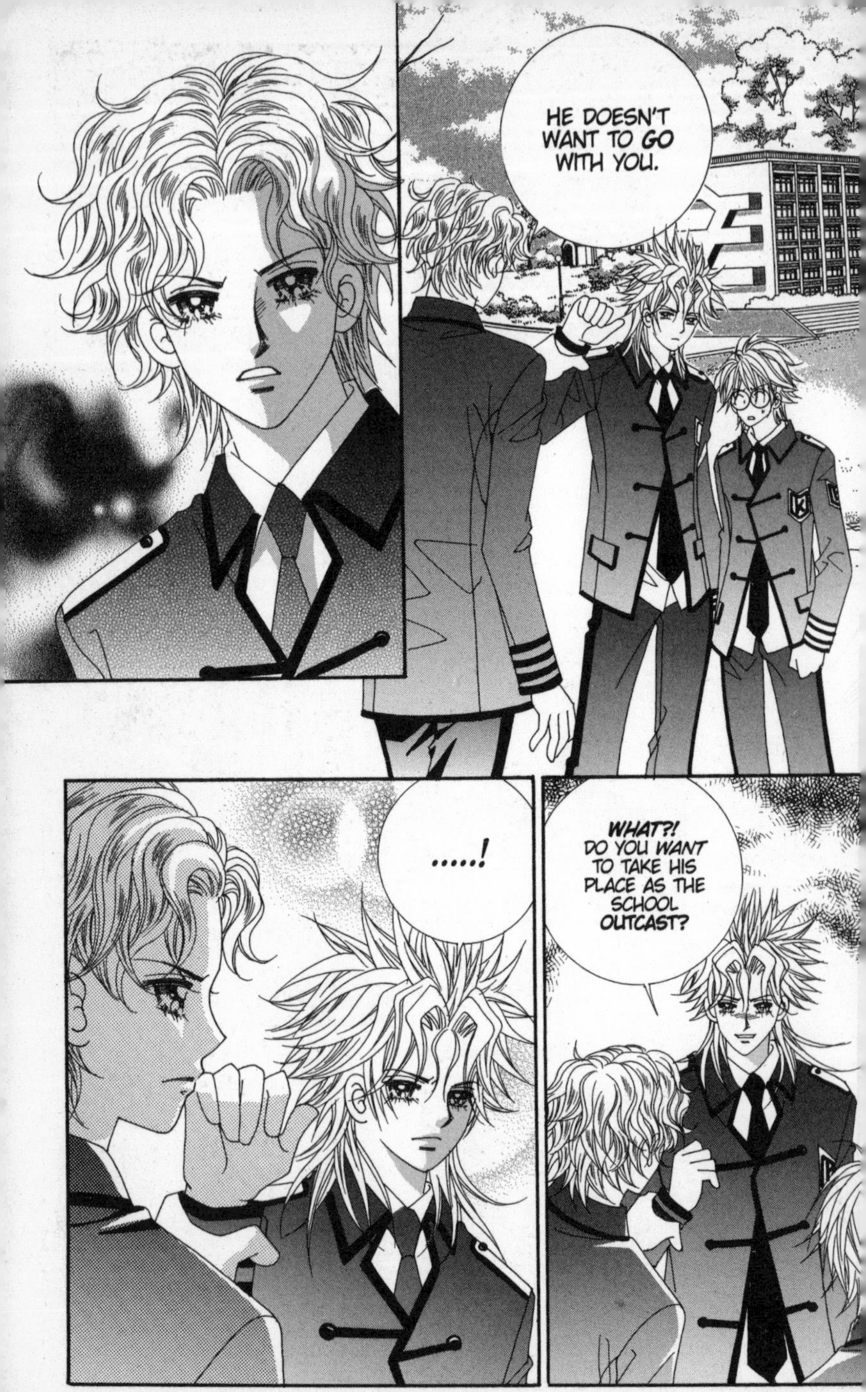
HE DOESN'T WANT TO GO WITH YOU.
.....!
WHAT?! DO YOU WANT TO TAKE HIS PLACE AS THE SCHOOL OUTCAST?

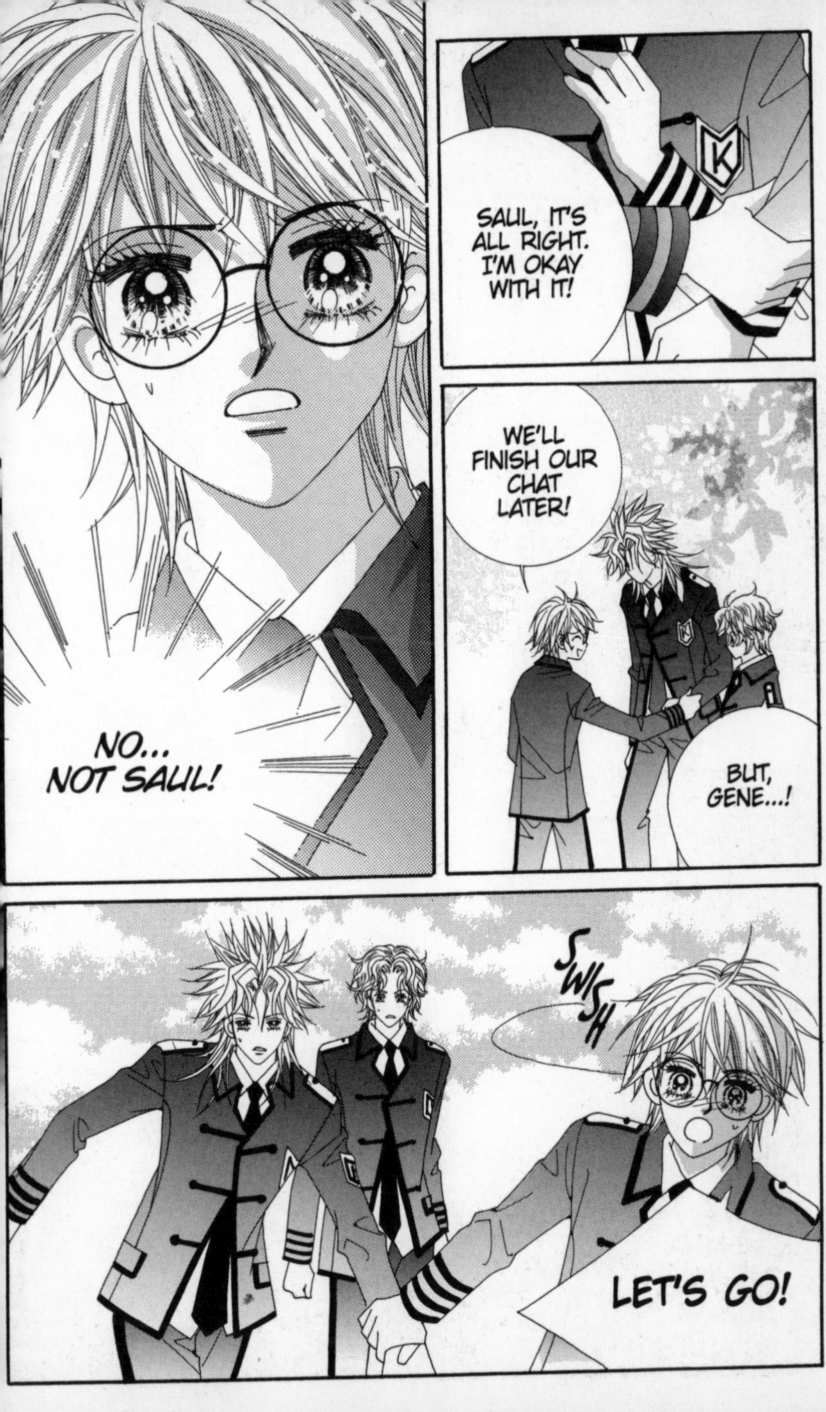
NO... NOT SAUL!
SAUL, IT'S ALL RIGHT. I'M OKAY WITH IT!
WE'LL FINISH OUR CHAT LATER!
BUT, GENE...!
SWISH
LET'S GO!

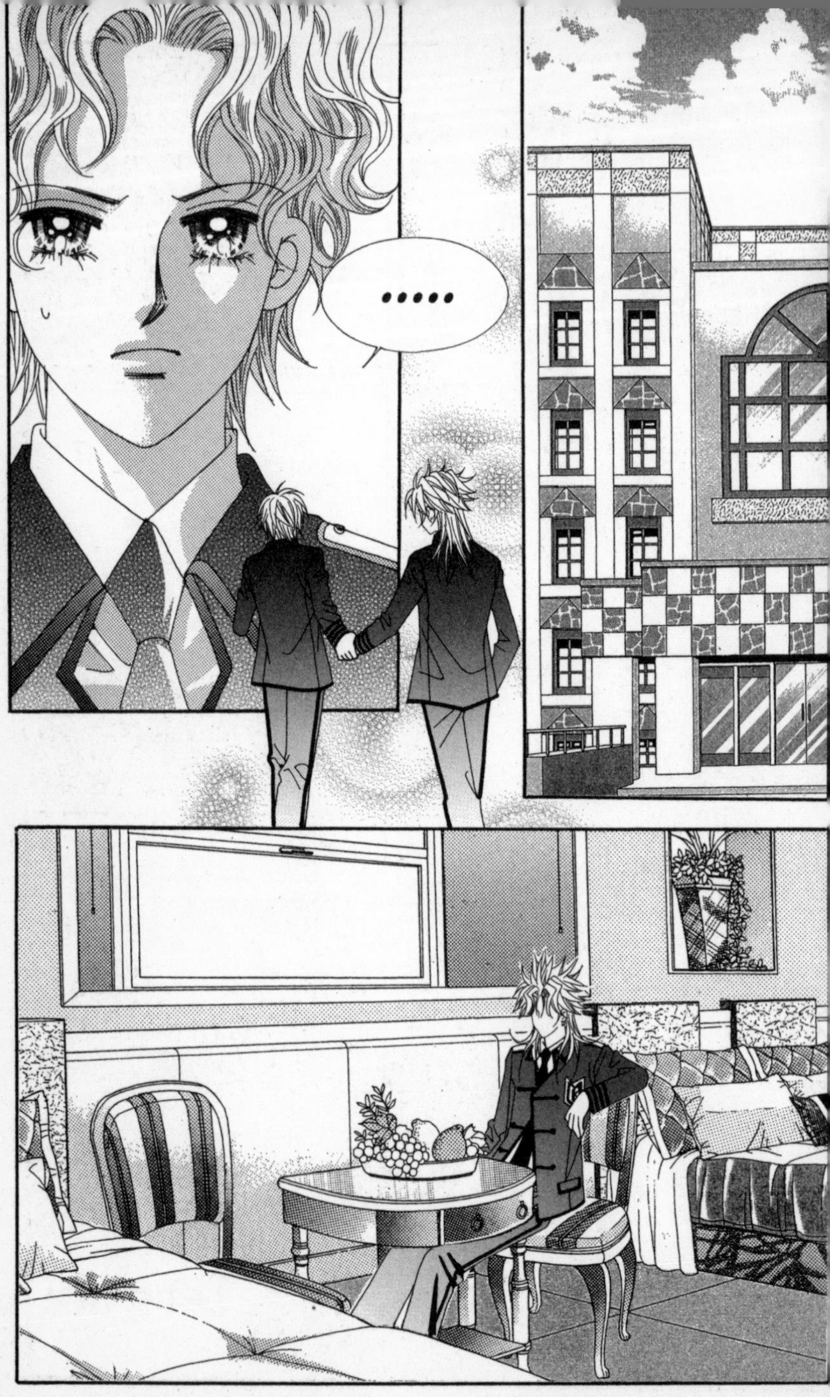
.....

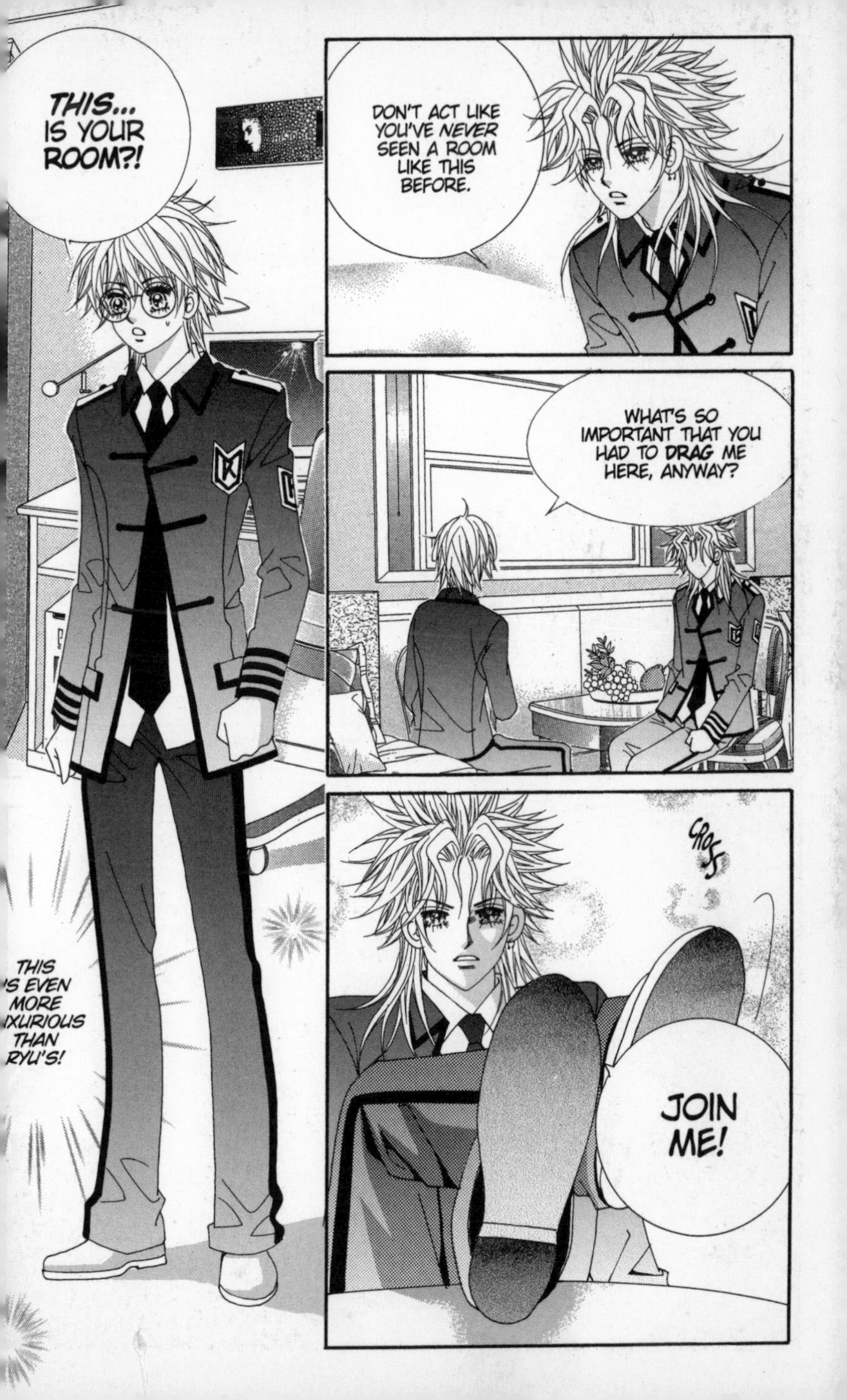
THIS... IS YOUR ROOM?!
THIS 'S EVEN MORE IXURIOUS THAN RYU'S!
DON'T ACT LIKE YOU'VE NEVER SEEN A ROOM LIKE THIS BEFORE.
WHAT'S SO IMPORTANT THAT YOU HAD TO DRAG ME HERE, ANYWAY?
CROSS
JOIN ME!

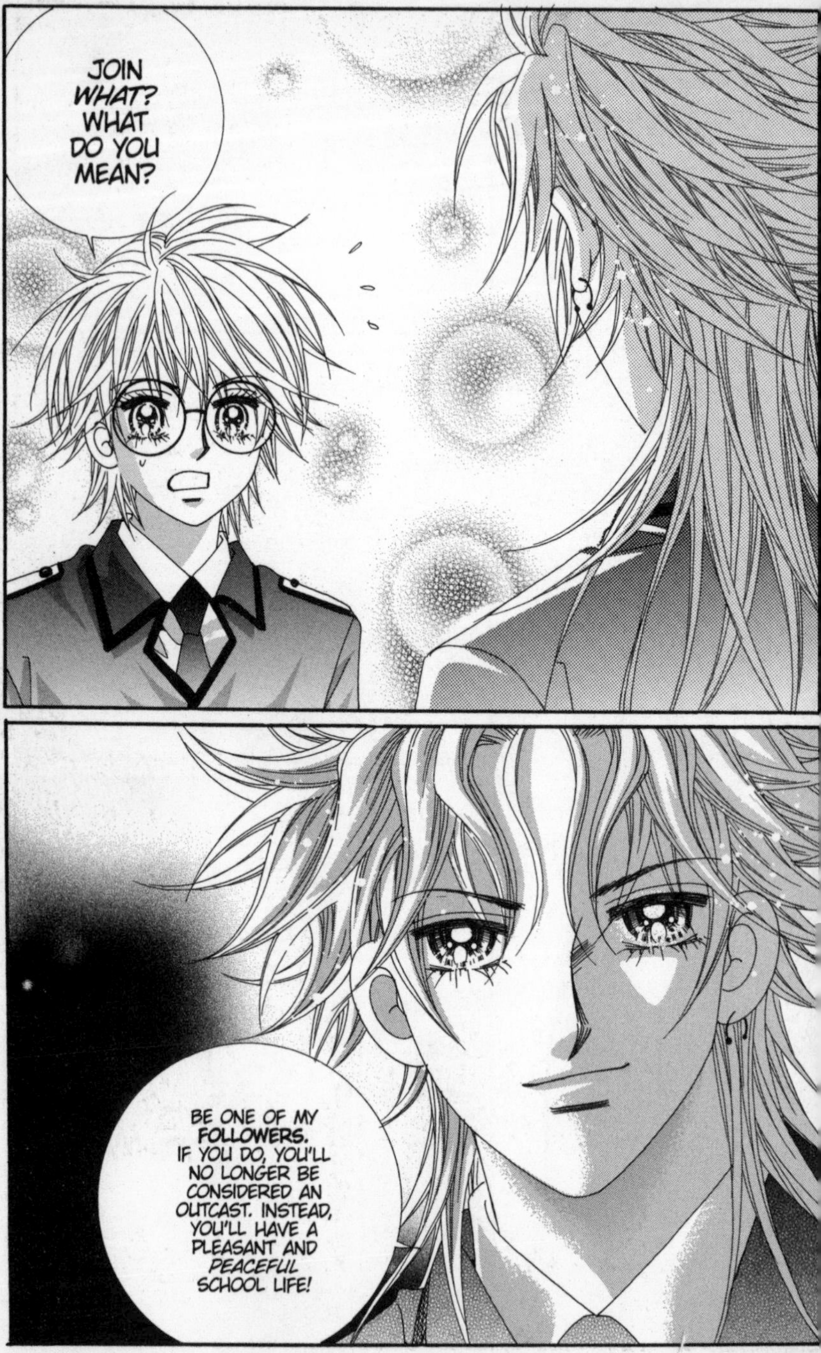
JOIN *WHAT?* WHAT DO YOU MEAN?
BE ONE OF MY **FOLLOWERS.** IF YOU DO, YOU'LL NO LONGER BE CONSIDERED AN OUTCAST. INSTEAD, YOU'LL HAVE A PLEASANT AND *PEACEFUL* SCHOOL LIFE!

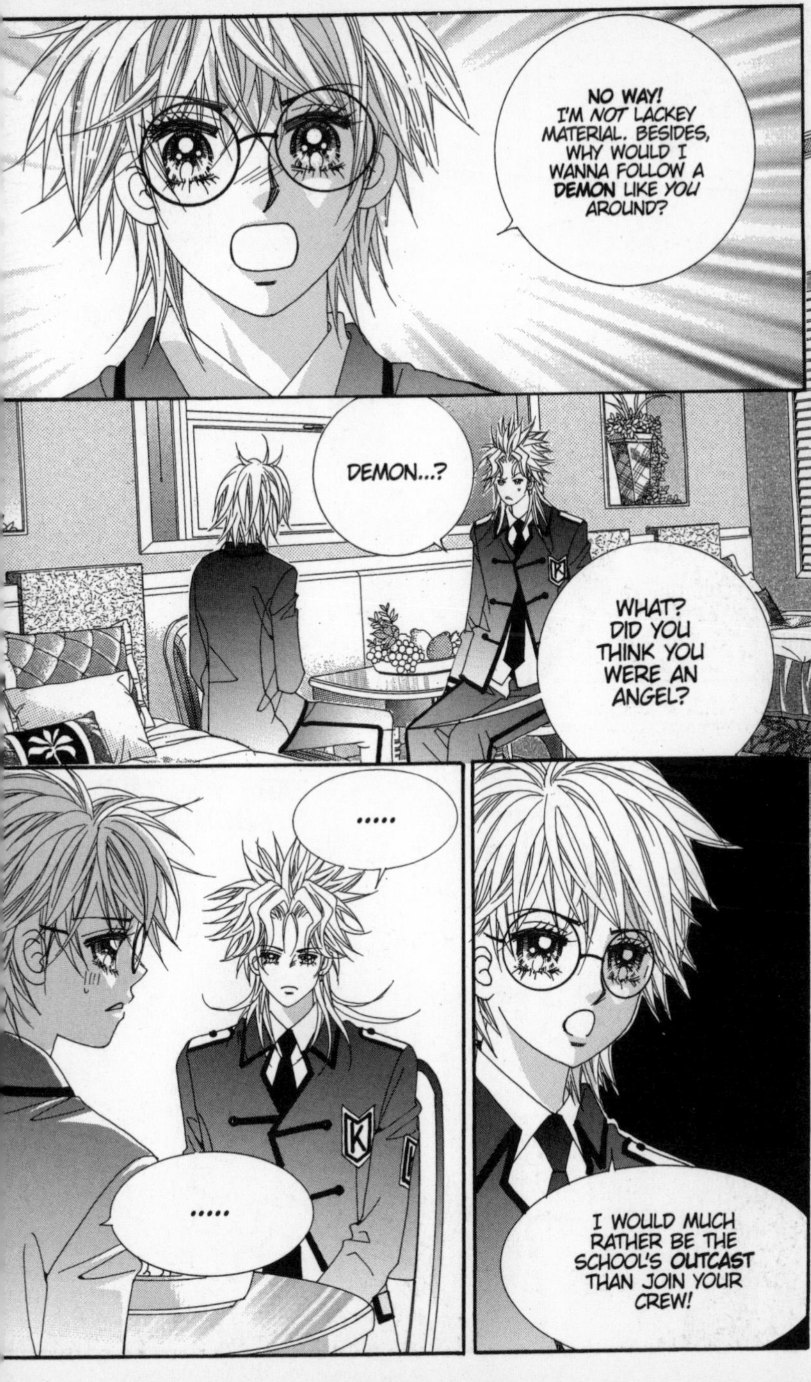
NO WAY! I'M NOT LACKEY MATERIAL. BESIDES, WHY WOULD I WANNA FOLLOW A DEMON LIKE YOU AROUND?
DEMON...?
WHAT? DID YOU THINK YOU WERE AN ANGEL?
.....
.....
I WOULD MUCH RATHER BE THE SCHOOL'S OUTCAST THAN JOIN YOUR CREW!

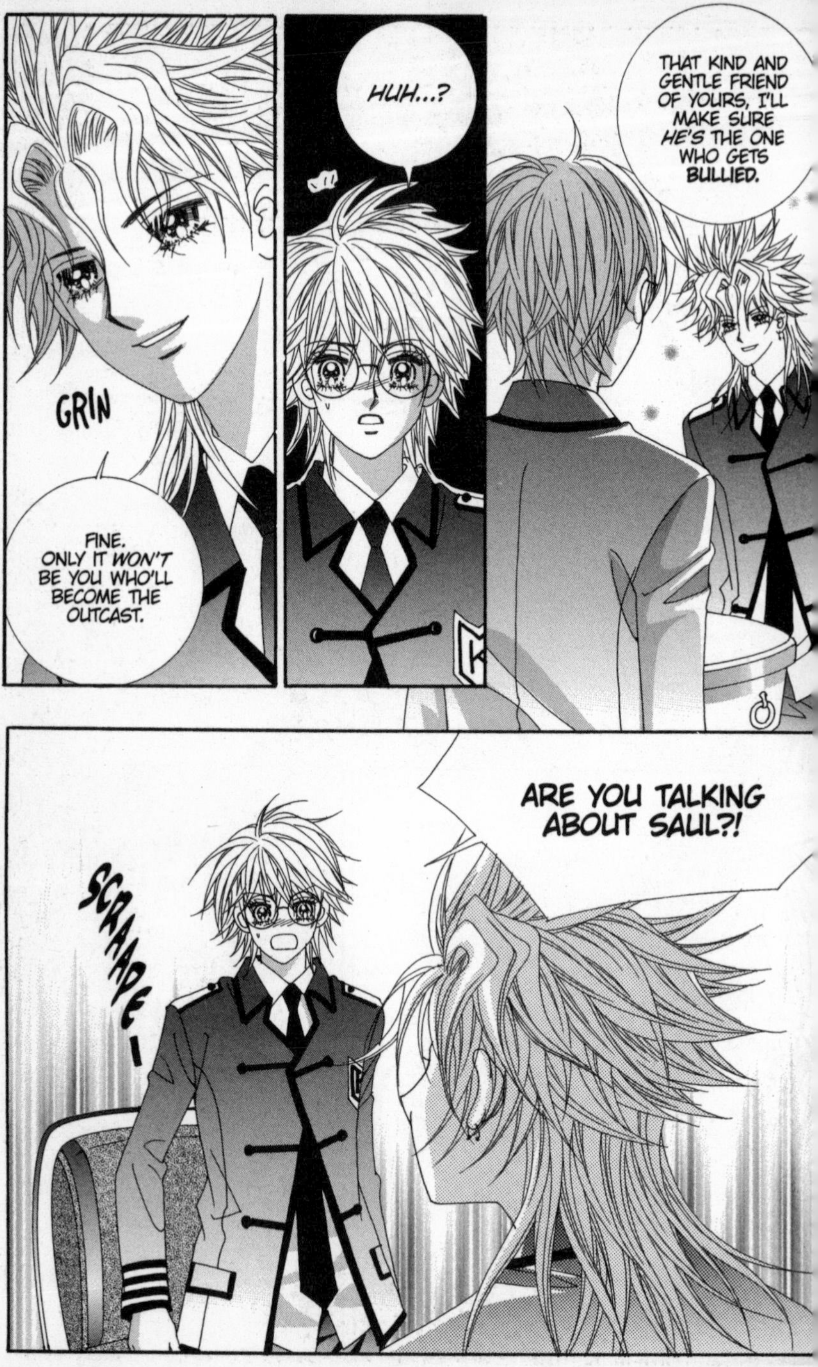
GRIN
FINE. ONLY IT WON'T BE YOU WHO'LL BECOME THE OUTCAST.
HUH...?
THAT KIND AND GENTLE FRIEND OF YOURS, I'LL MAKE SURE HE'S THE ONE WHO GETS BULLIED.
ARE YOU TALKING ABOUT SAUL?!
SCRAPE

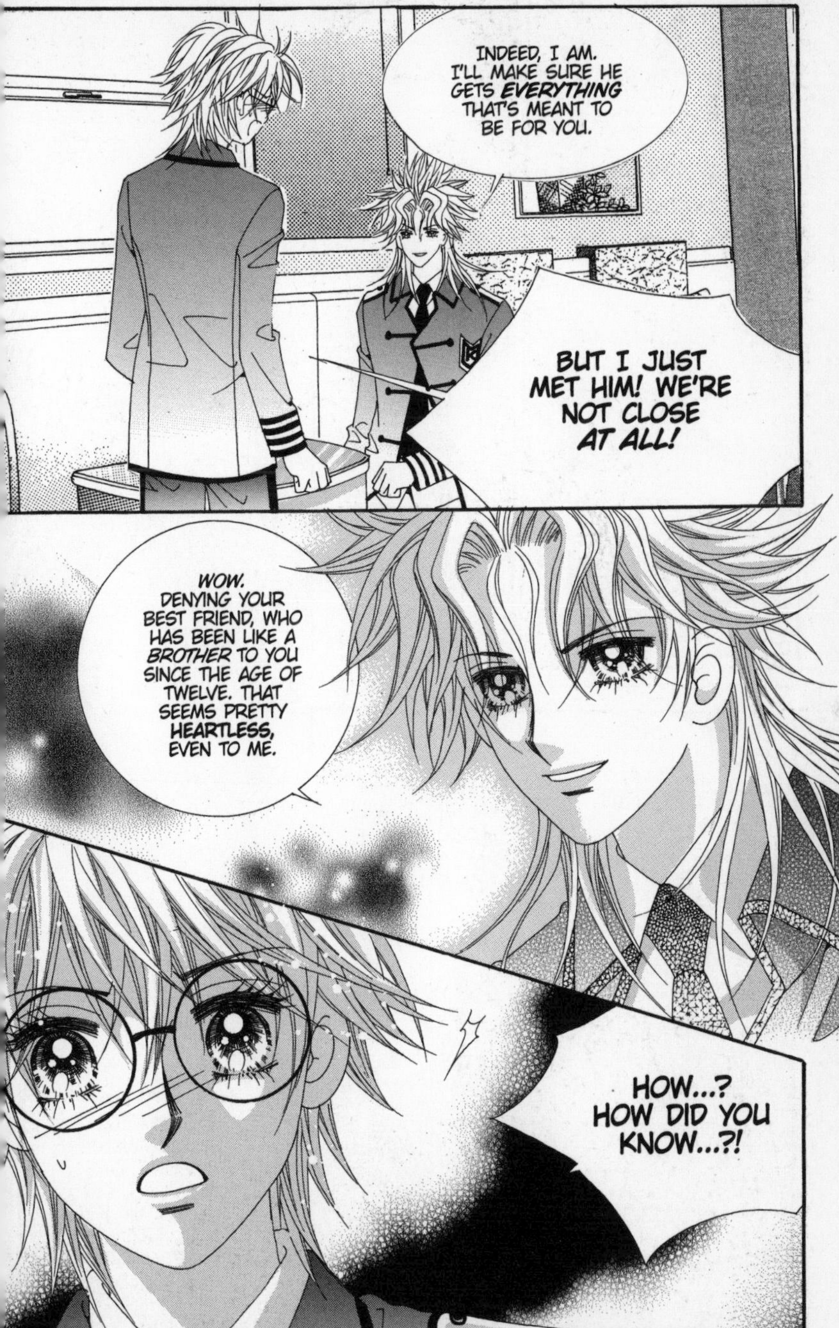
INDEED, I AM. I'LL MAKE SURE HE GETS *EVERYTHING* THAT'S MEANT TO BE FOR YOU.
BUT I JUST MET HIM! WE'RE NOT CLOSE *AT ALL!*
WOW. DENYING YOUR BEST FRIEND, WHO HAS BEEN LIKE A *BROTHER* TO YOU SINCE THE AGE OF TWELVE. THAT SEEMS PRETTY **HEARTLESS,** EVEN TO ME.
HOW...? HOW DID YOU KNOW...?!

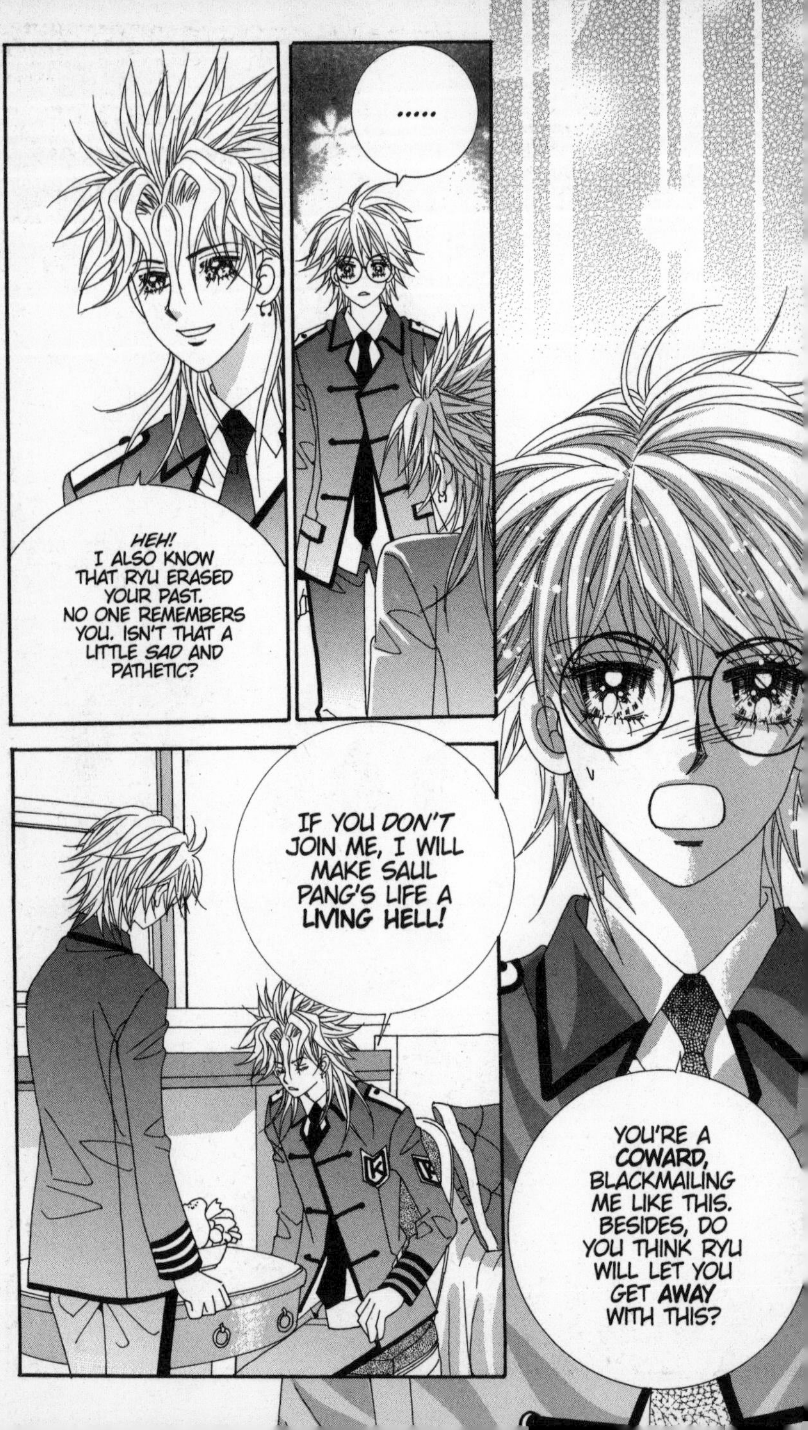
HEH!
I ALSO KNOW THAT RYU ERASED YOUR PAST. NO ONE REMEMBERS YOU. ISN'T THAT A LITTLE SAD AND PATHETIC?
......
IF YOU DON'T JOIN ME, I WILL MAKE SAUL PANG'S LIFE A LIVING HELL!
YOU'RE A COWARD, BLACKMAILING ME LIKE THIS. BESIDES, DO YOU THINK RYU WILL LET YOU GET AWAY WITH THIS?

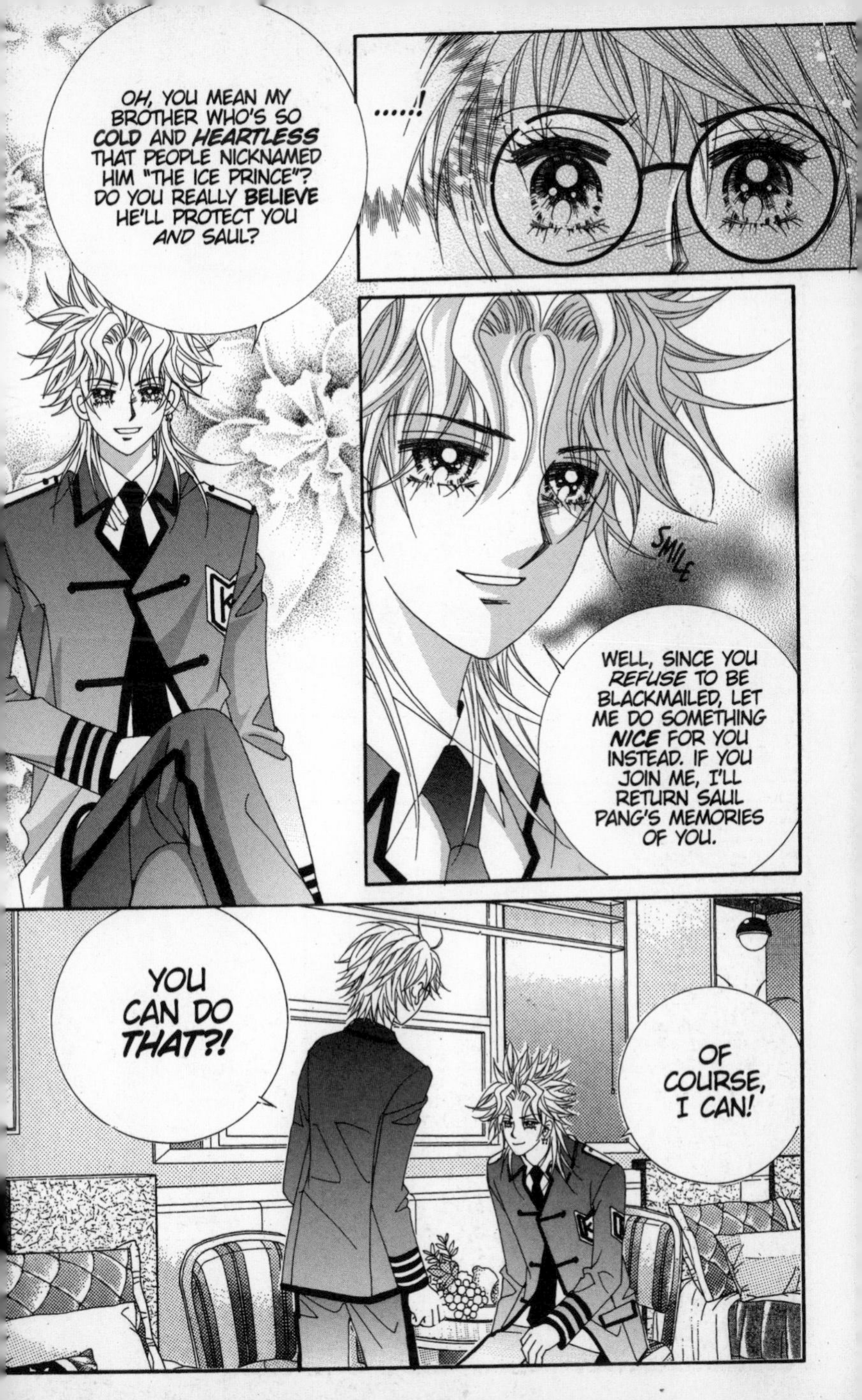
OH, YOU MEAN MY BROTHER WHO'S SO COLD AND HEARTLESS THAT PEOPLE NICKNAMED HIM "THE ICE PRINCE"? DO YOU REALLY BELIEVE HE'LL PROTECT YOU AND SAUL?
.....!
SMILE
WELL, SINCE YOU REFUSE TO BE BLACKMAILED, LET ME DO SOMETHING NICE FOR YOU INSTEAD. IF YOU JOIN ME, I'LL RETURN SAUL PANG'S MEMORIES OF YOU.
YOU CAN DO THAT?!
OF COURSE, I CAN!

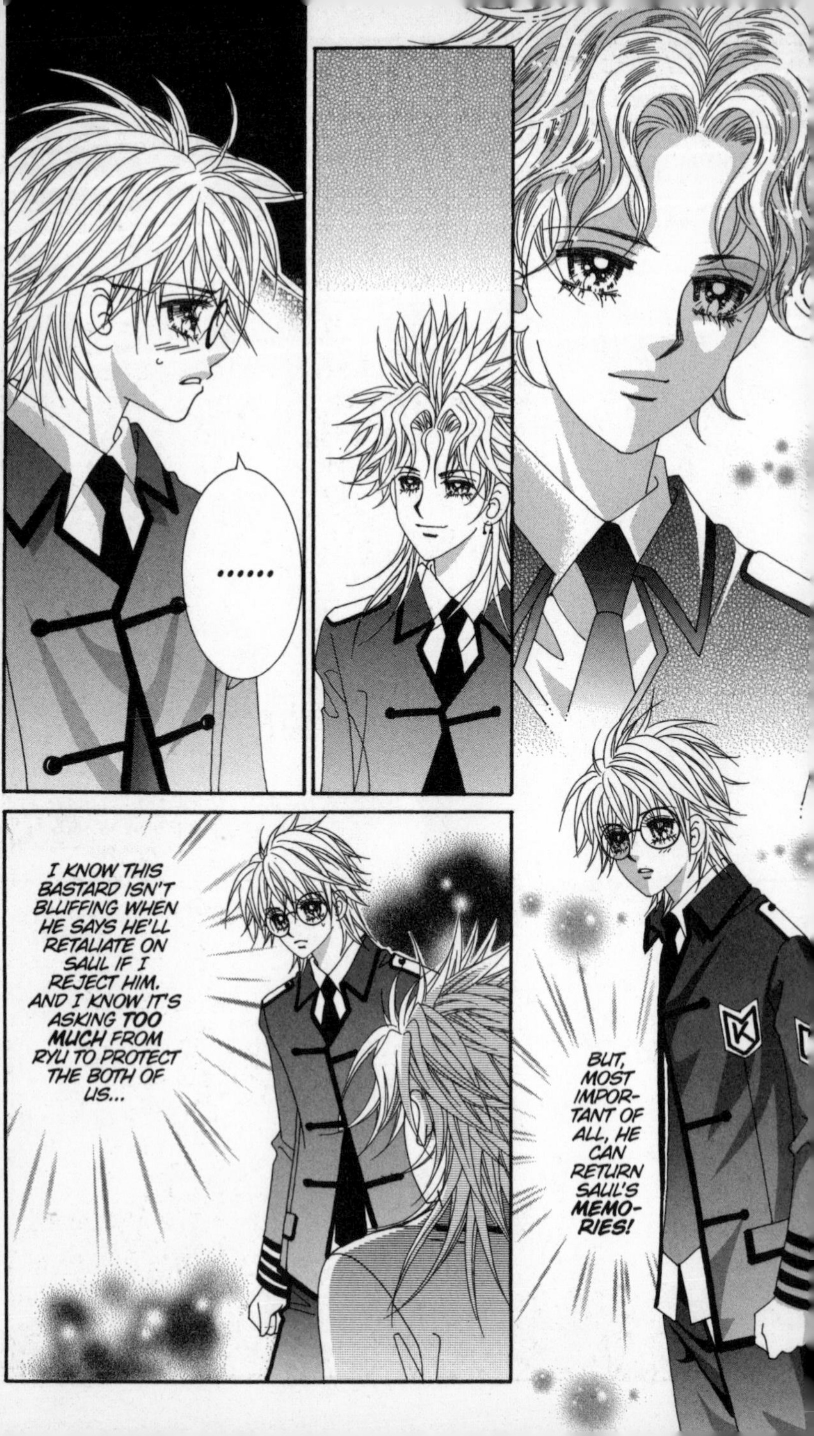
......
I KNOW THIS BASTARD ISN'T BLUFFING WHEN HE SAYS HE'LL RETALIATE ON SAUL IF I REJECT HIM. AND I KNOW IT'S ASKING TOO MUCH FROM RYU TO PROTECT THE BOTH OF US...
BUT, MOST IMPORTANT OF ALL, HE CAN RETURN SAUL'S MEMORIES!

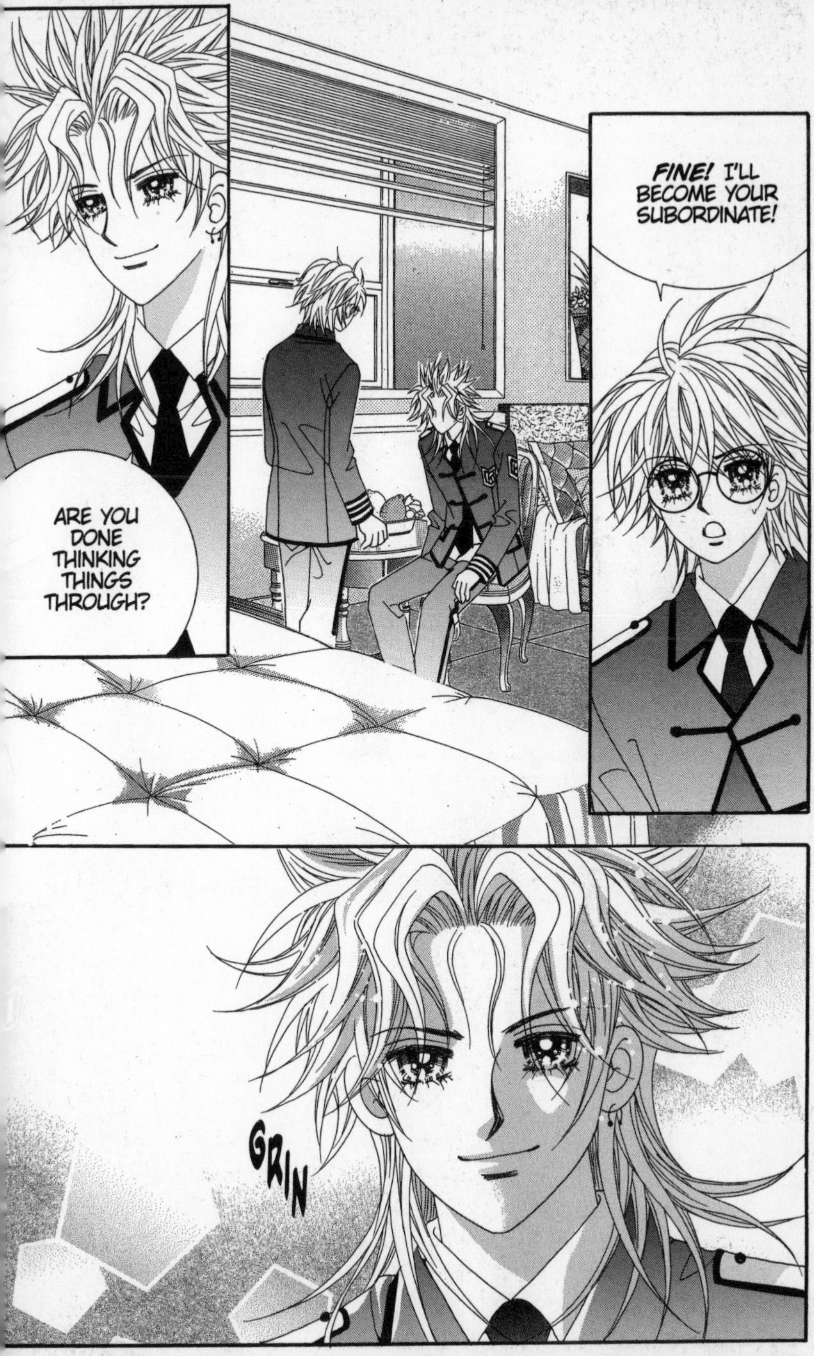
ARE YOU DONE THINKING THINGS THROUGH?
FINE! I'LL BECOME YOUR SUBORDINATE!
GRIN

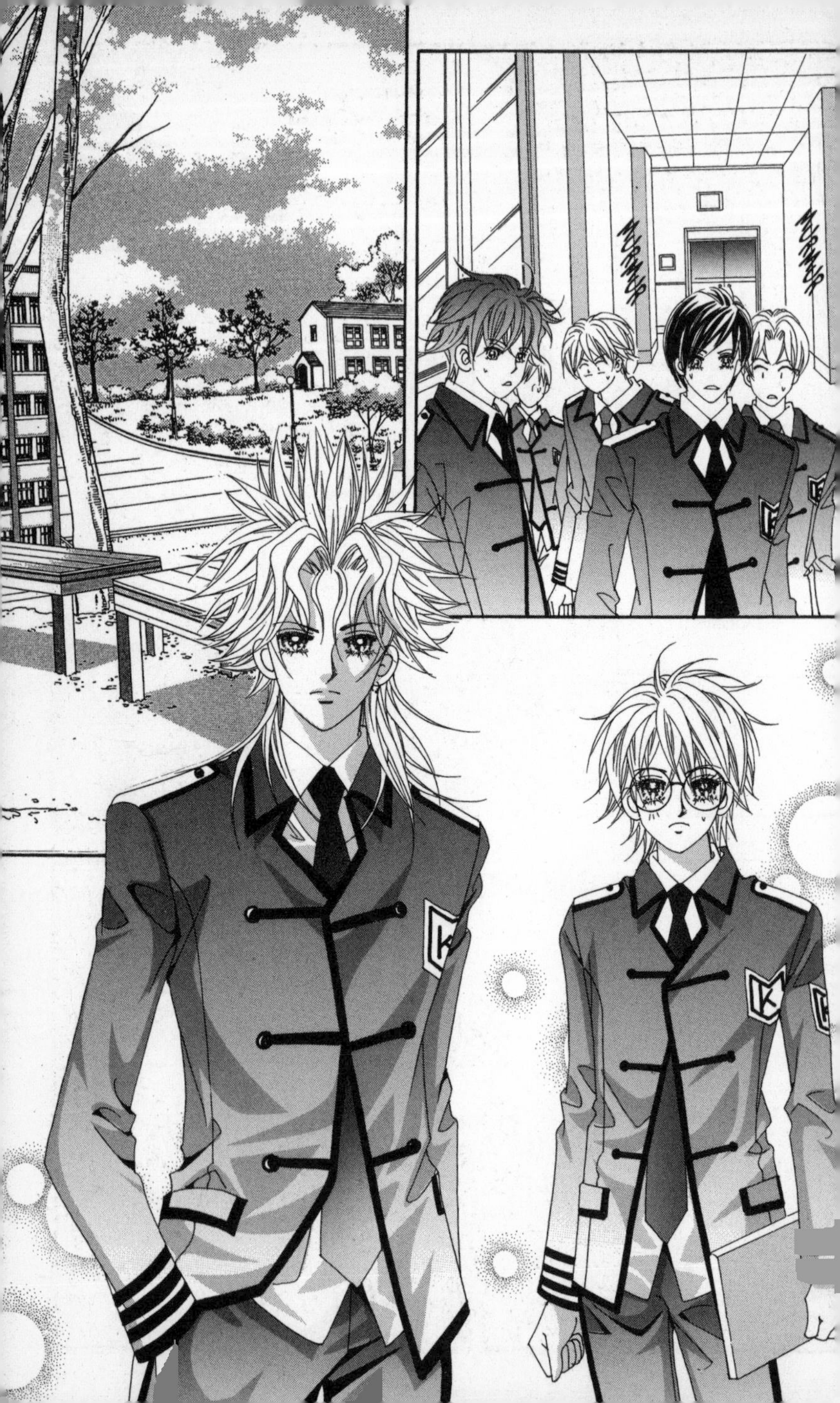
MURMUR
MURMUR

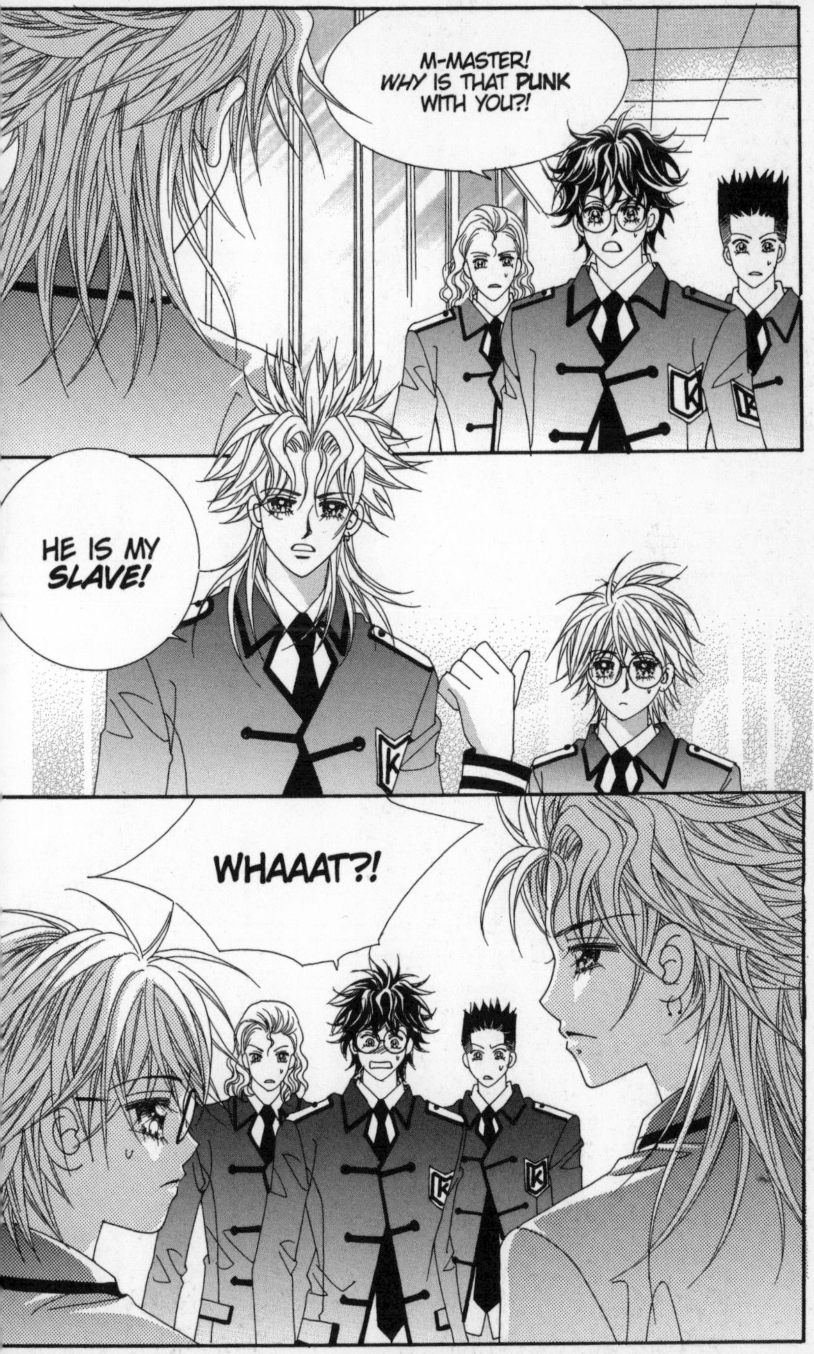
M-MASTER! WHY IS THAT PUNK WITH YOU?!
HE IS MY SLAVE!
WHAAAT?!

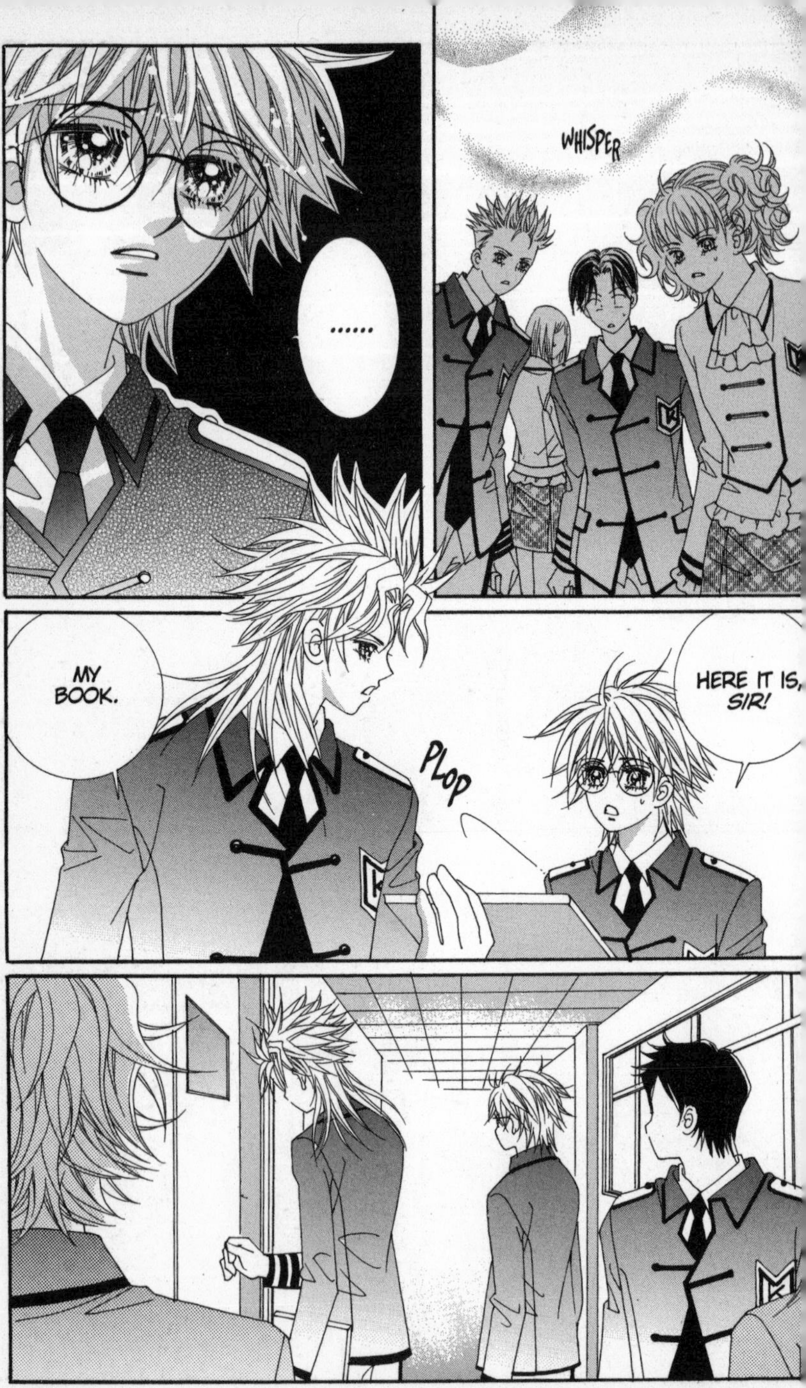
......
WHISPER
MY BOOK.
PLOP
HERE IT IS, SIR!

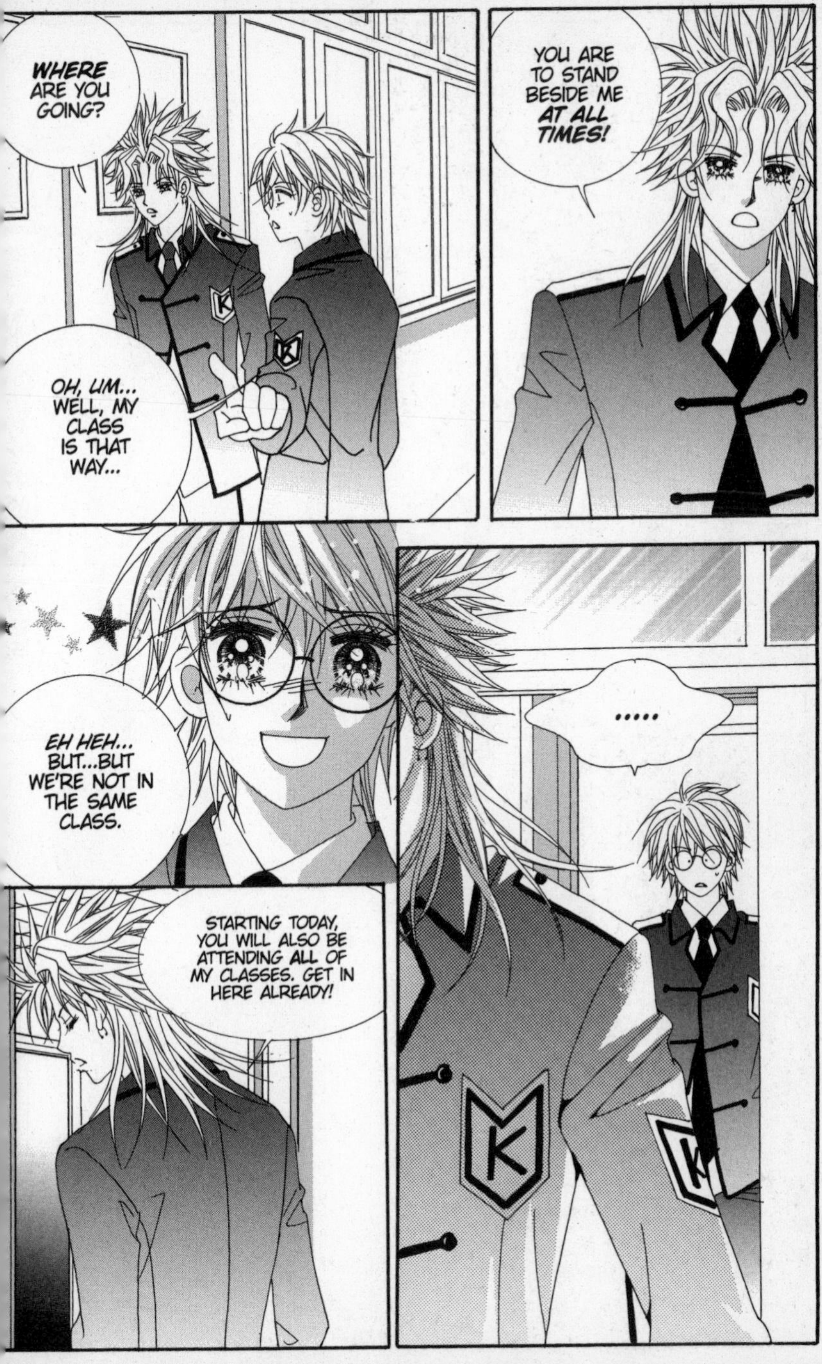
WHERE ARE YOU GOING?
OH, UM... WELL, MY CLASS IS THAT WAY...
YOU ARE TO STAND BESIDE ME AT ALL TIMES!
EH HEH... BUT...BUT WE'RE NOT IN THE SAME CLASS.
.....
STARTING TODAY, YOU WILL ALSO BE ATTENDING ALL OF MY CLASSES. GET IN HERE ALREADY!

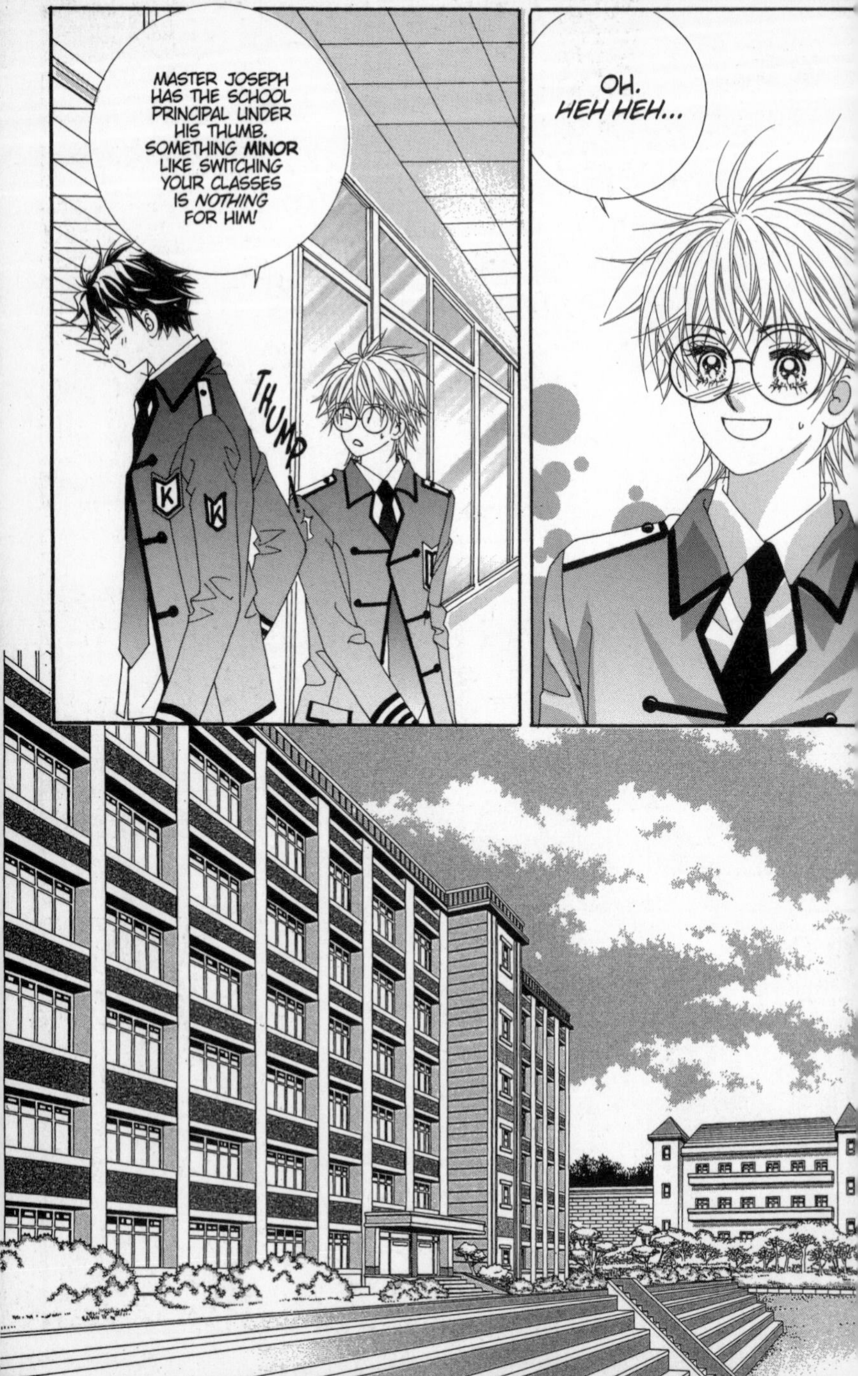
MASTER JOSEPH HAS THE SCHOOL PRINCIPAL UNDER HIS THUMB. SOMETHING **MINOR** LIKE SWITCHING YOUR CLASSES IS *NOTHING* FOR HIM!
THUMP
OH. *HEH HEH...*

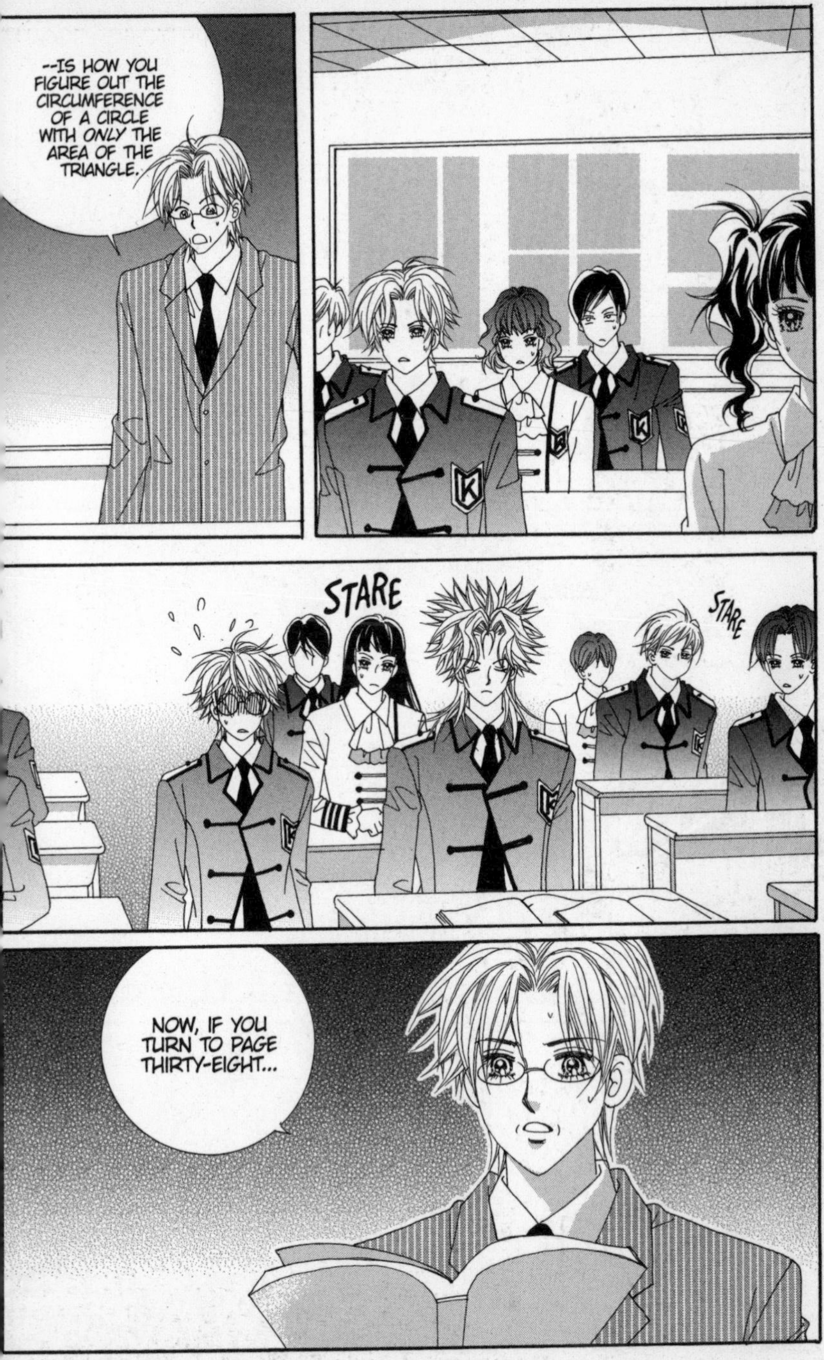
--IS HOW YOU FIGURE OUT THE CIRCUMFERENCE OF A CIRCLE WITH *ONLY* THE AREA OF THE TRIANGLE.
STARE
STARE
NOW, IF YOU TURN TO PAGE THIRTY-EIGHT...

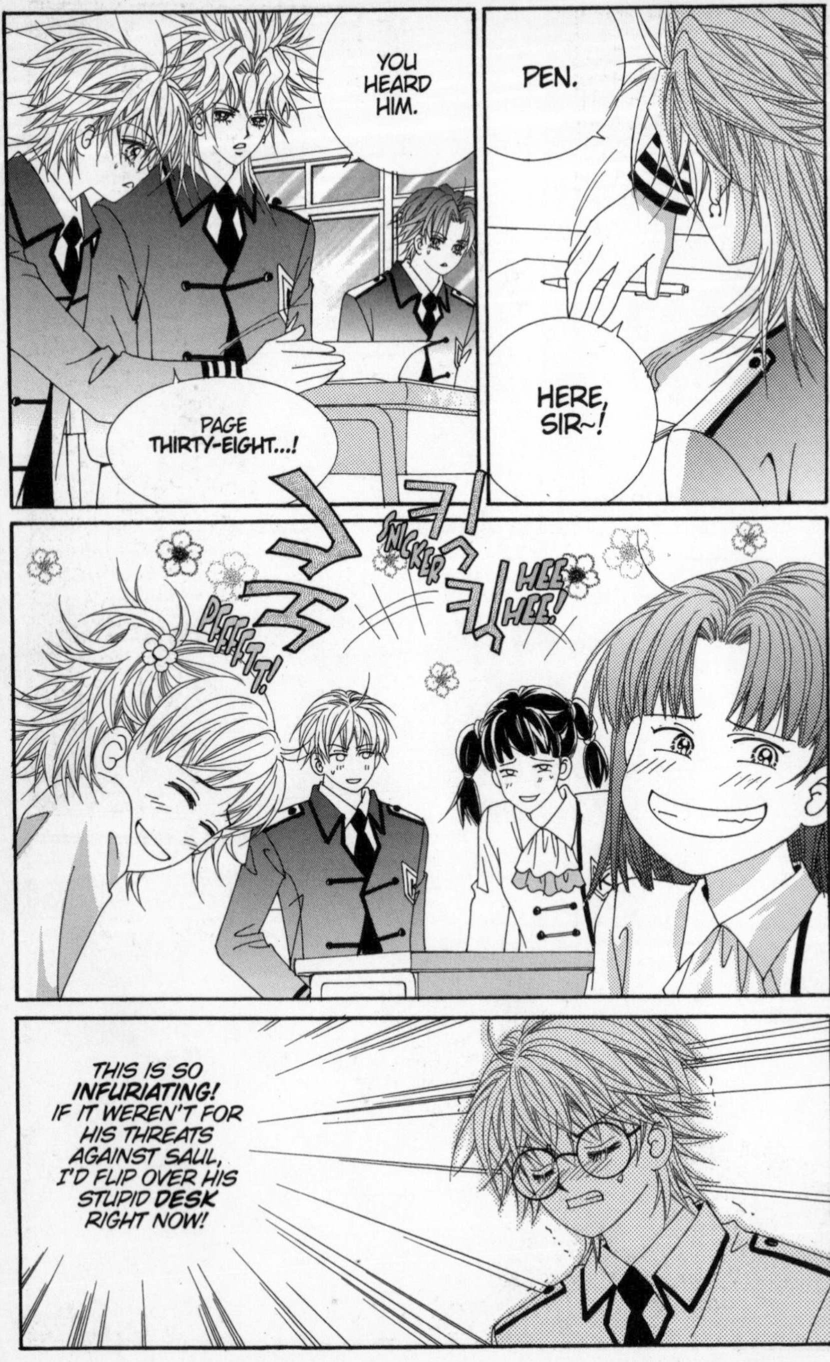
YOU HEARD HIM.
PAGE THIRTY-EIGHT...!
PEN.
HERE, SIR~!
PFFFFTT!
SNICKER
HEE HEE!
THIS IS SO INFURIATING! IF IT WEREN'T FOR HIS THREATS AGAINST SAUL, I'D FLIP OVER HIS STUPID DESK RIGHT NOW!

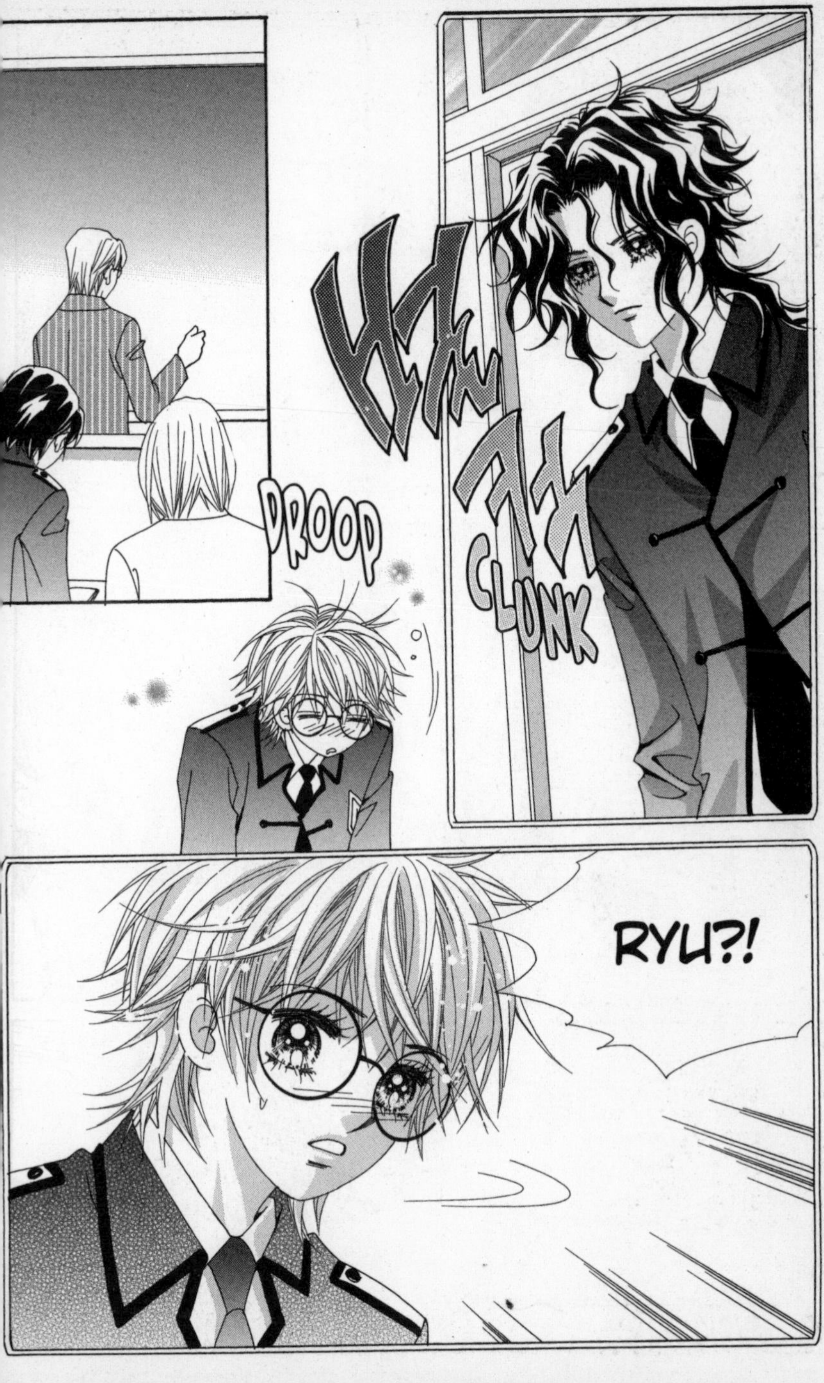
DROOP
CLUNK
RYU?!

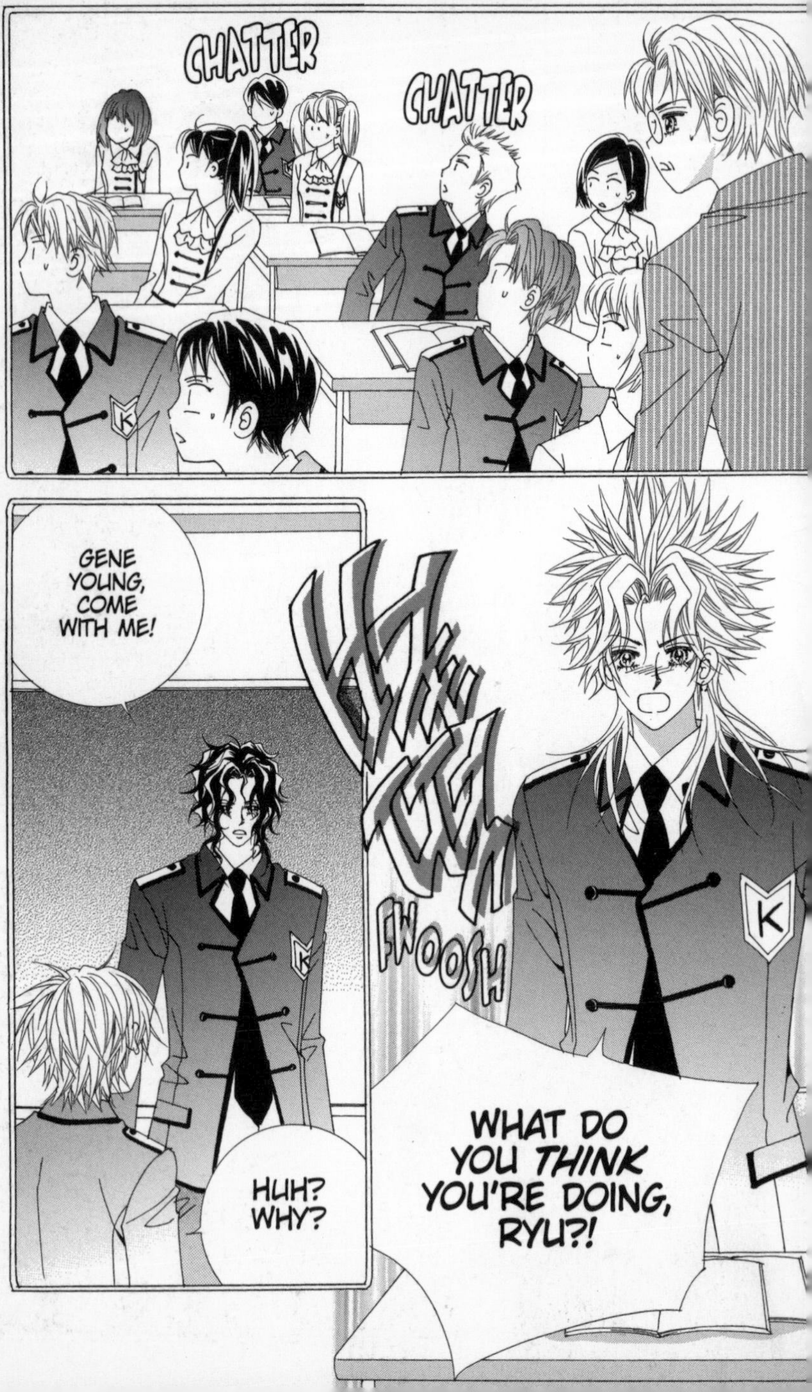
CHATTER
CHATTER
GENE YOUNG, COME WITH ME!
HUH? WHY?
FWOOSH
WHAT DO YOU THINK YOU'RE DOING, RYU?!

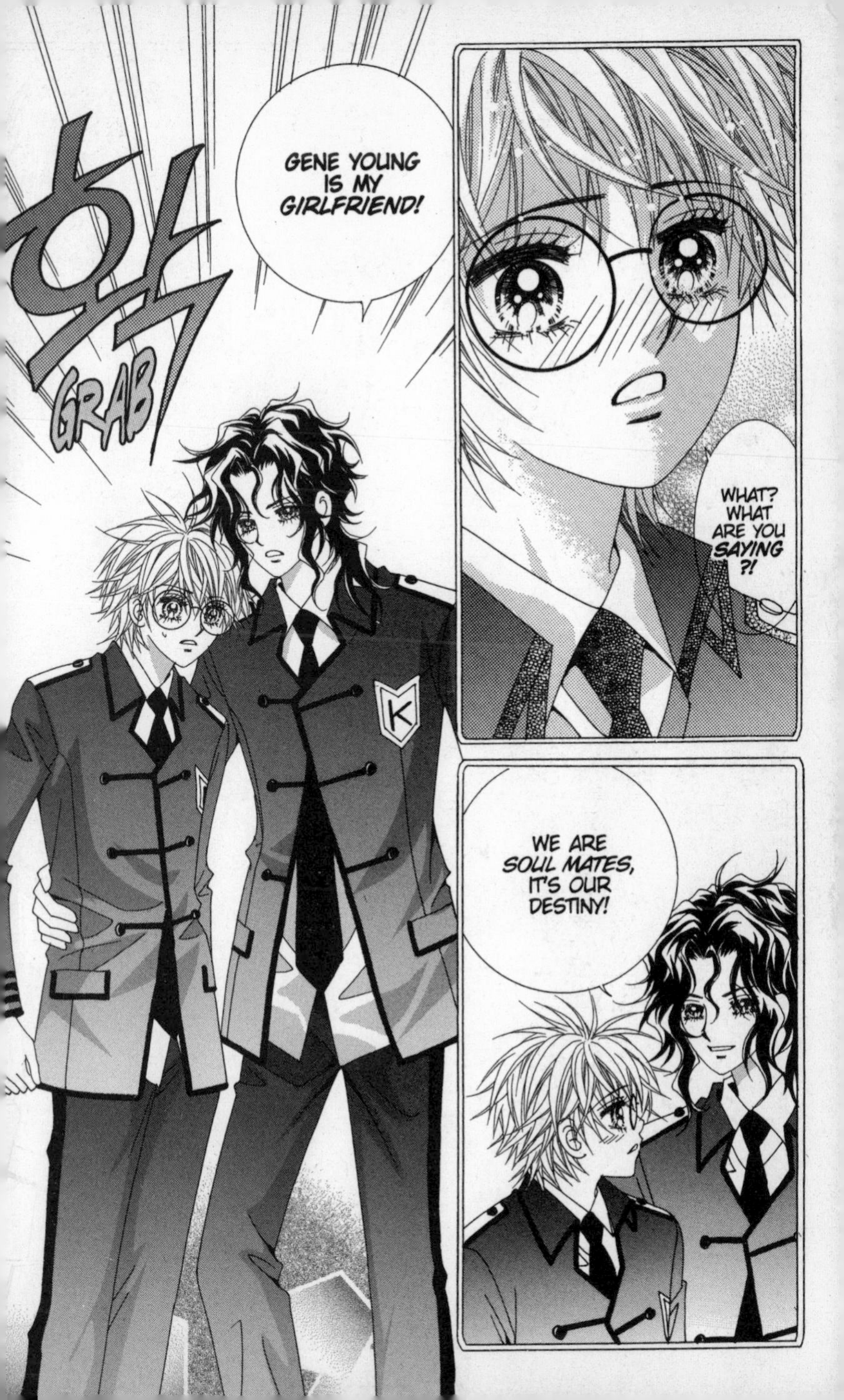
확
GRAB
GENE YOUNG IS MY GIRLFRIEND!
WHAT? WHAT ARE YOU SAYING ?!
WE ARE SOUL MATES, IT'S OUR DESTINY!

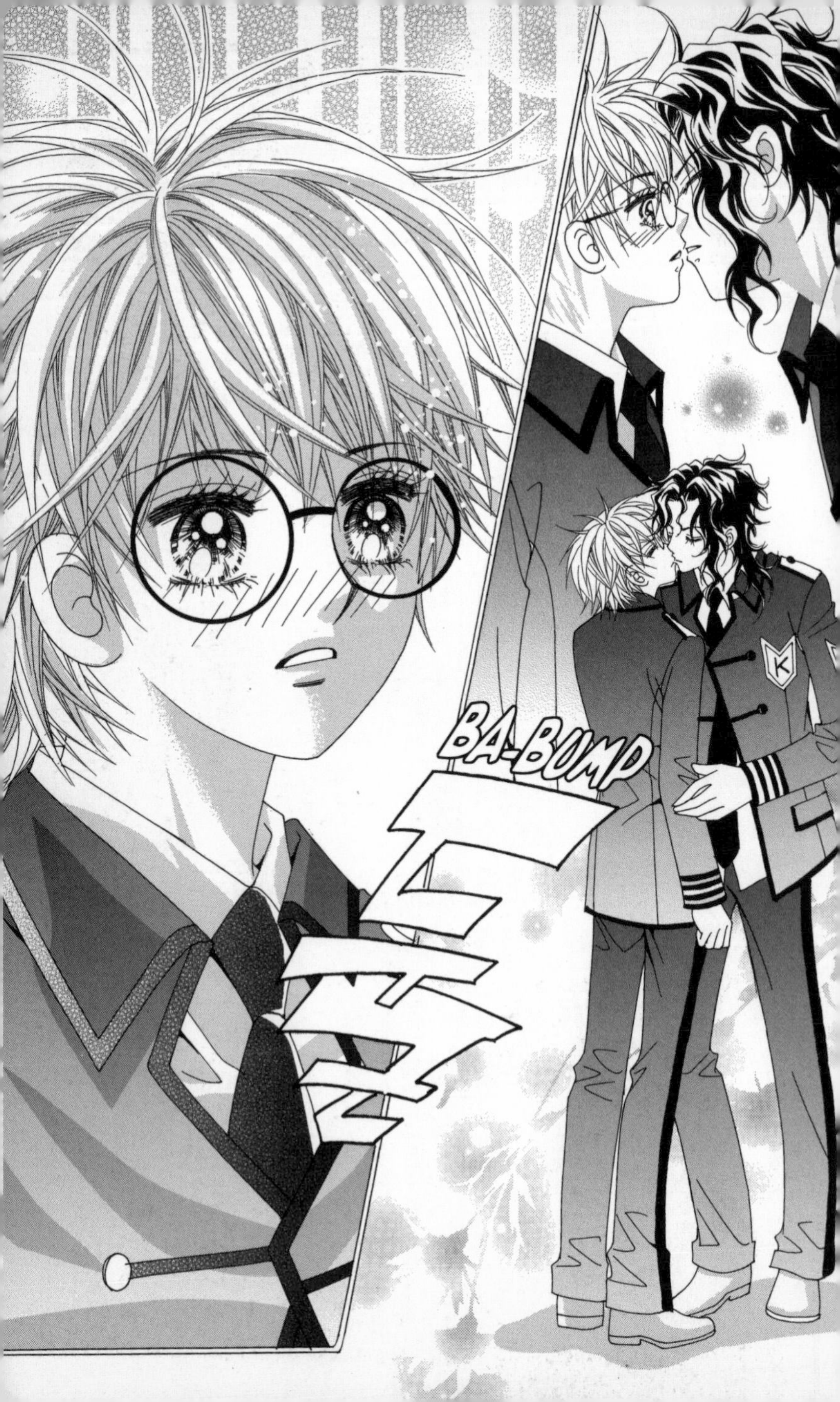
BA-BUMP

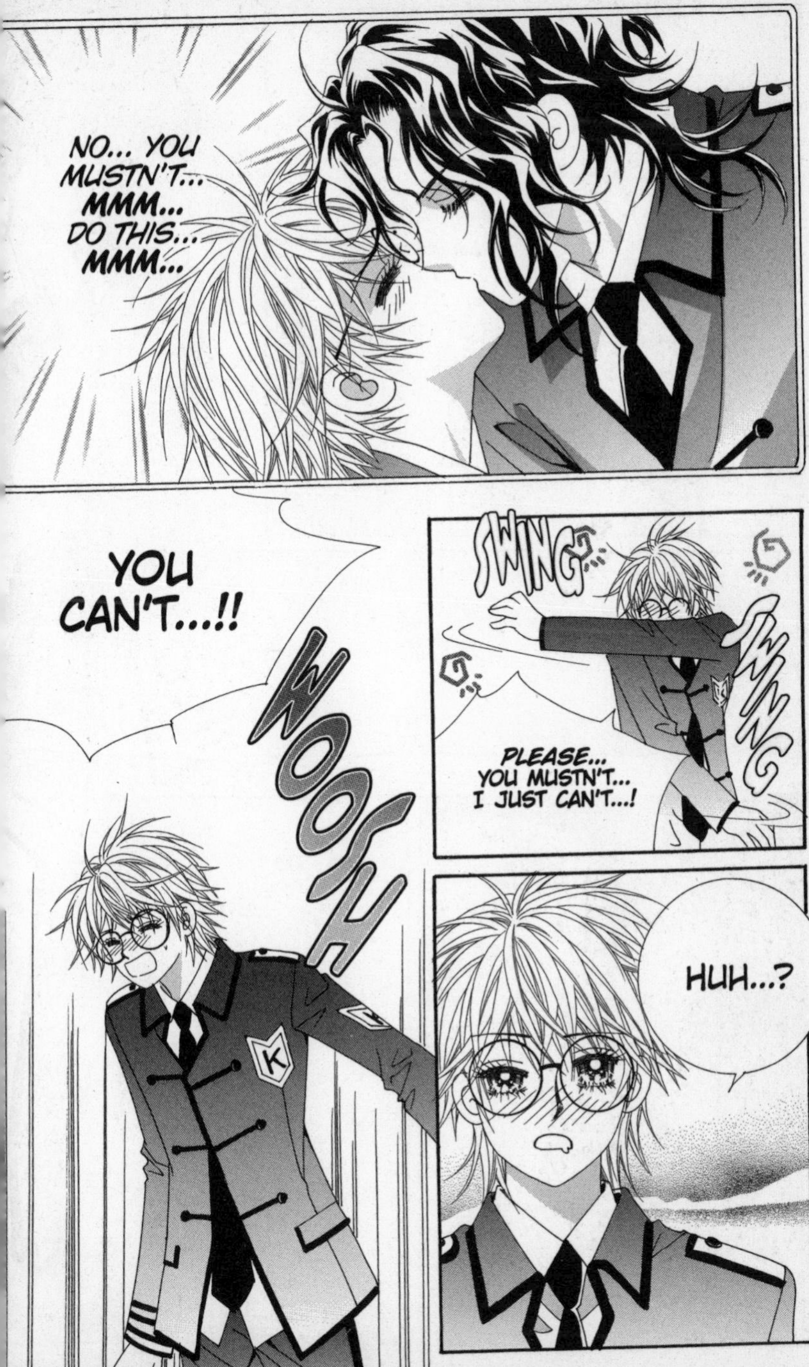

NO... YOU MUSTN'T... MMM... DO THIS... MMM...
YOU CAN'T...!!
WOOOSH
SWING
SWING
PLEASE... YOU MUSTN'T... I JUST CAN'T...!
HUH...?

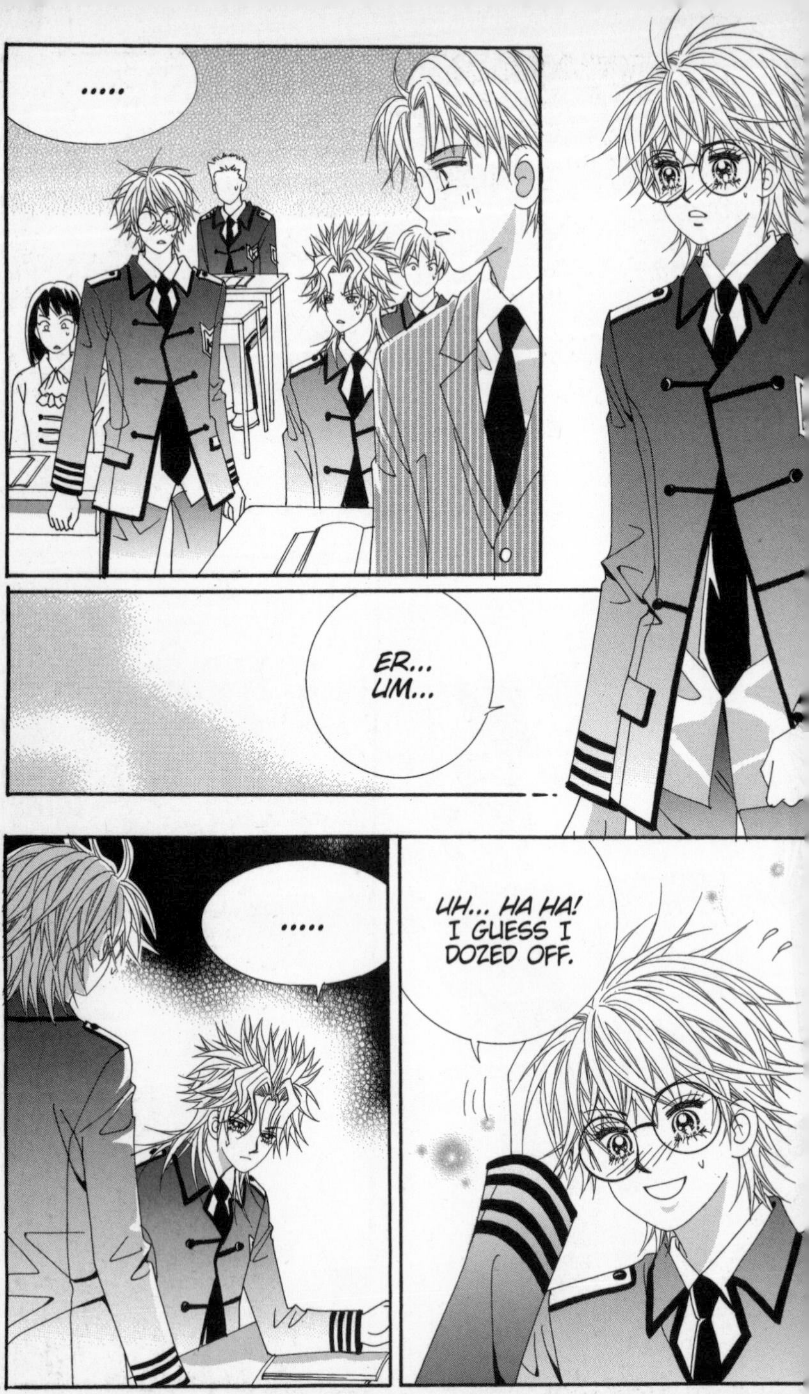
.....
ER... UM...
.....
UH... HA HA! I GUESS I DOZED OFF.

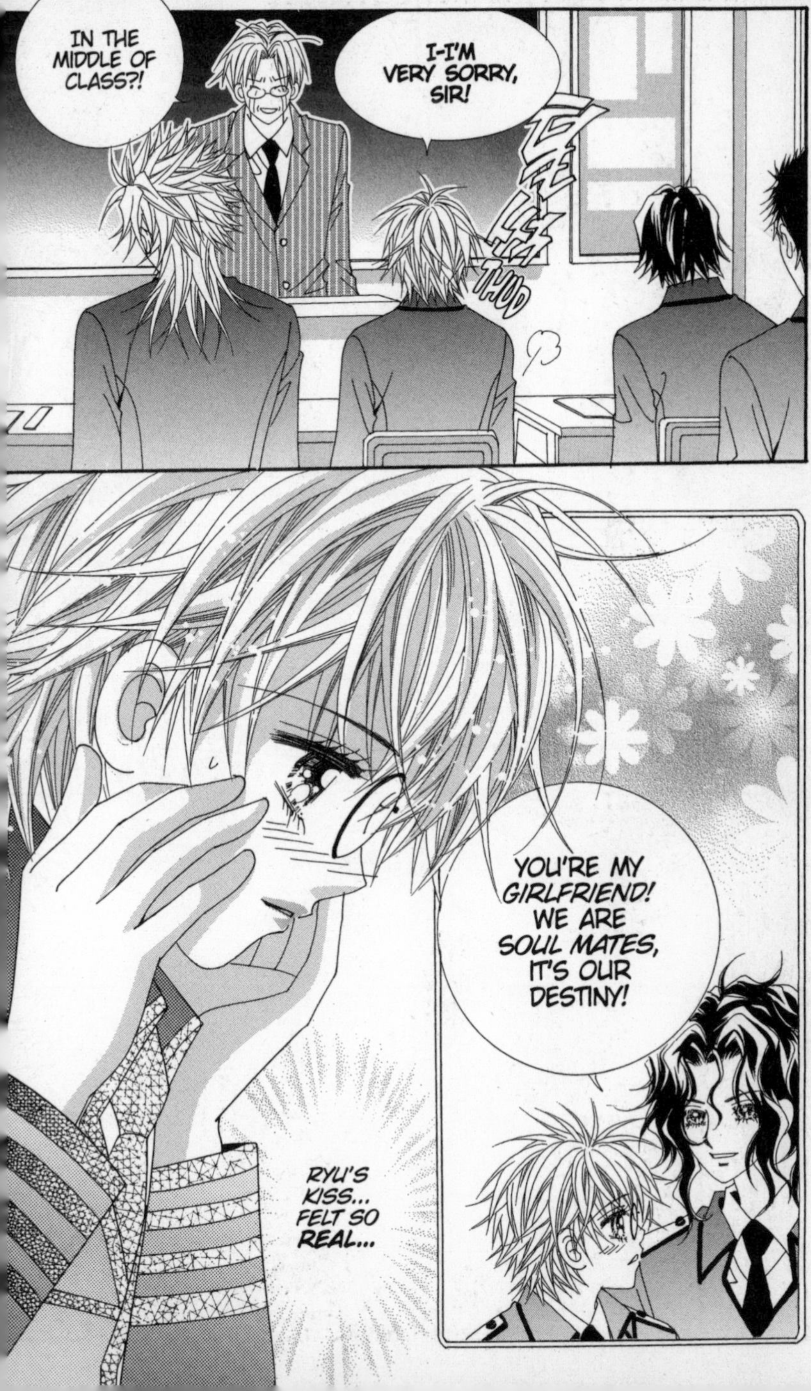
IN THE MIDDLE OF CLASS?!
I-I'M VERY SORRY, SIR!
THUD
RYU'S KISS... FELT SO REAL...
YOU'RE MY GIRLFRIEND! WE ARE SOUL MATES, IT'S OUR DESTINY!

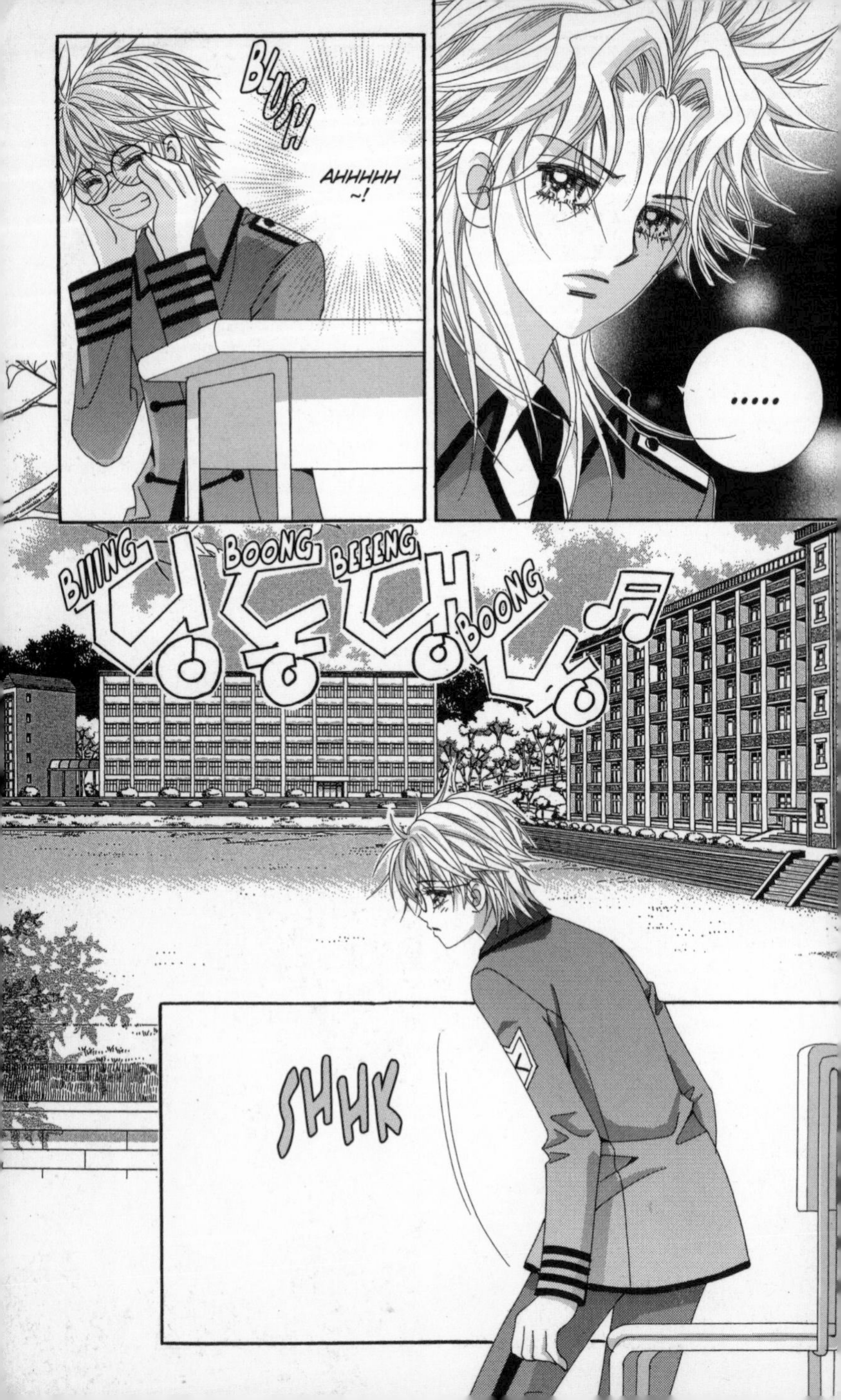
BLUSH
AHHHHH ~!
.....
BIIING
BOONG
BEEENG
BOONG
SHHK

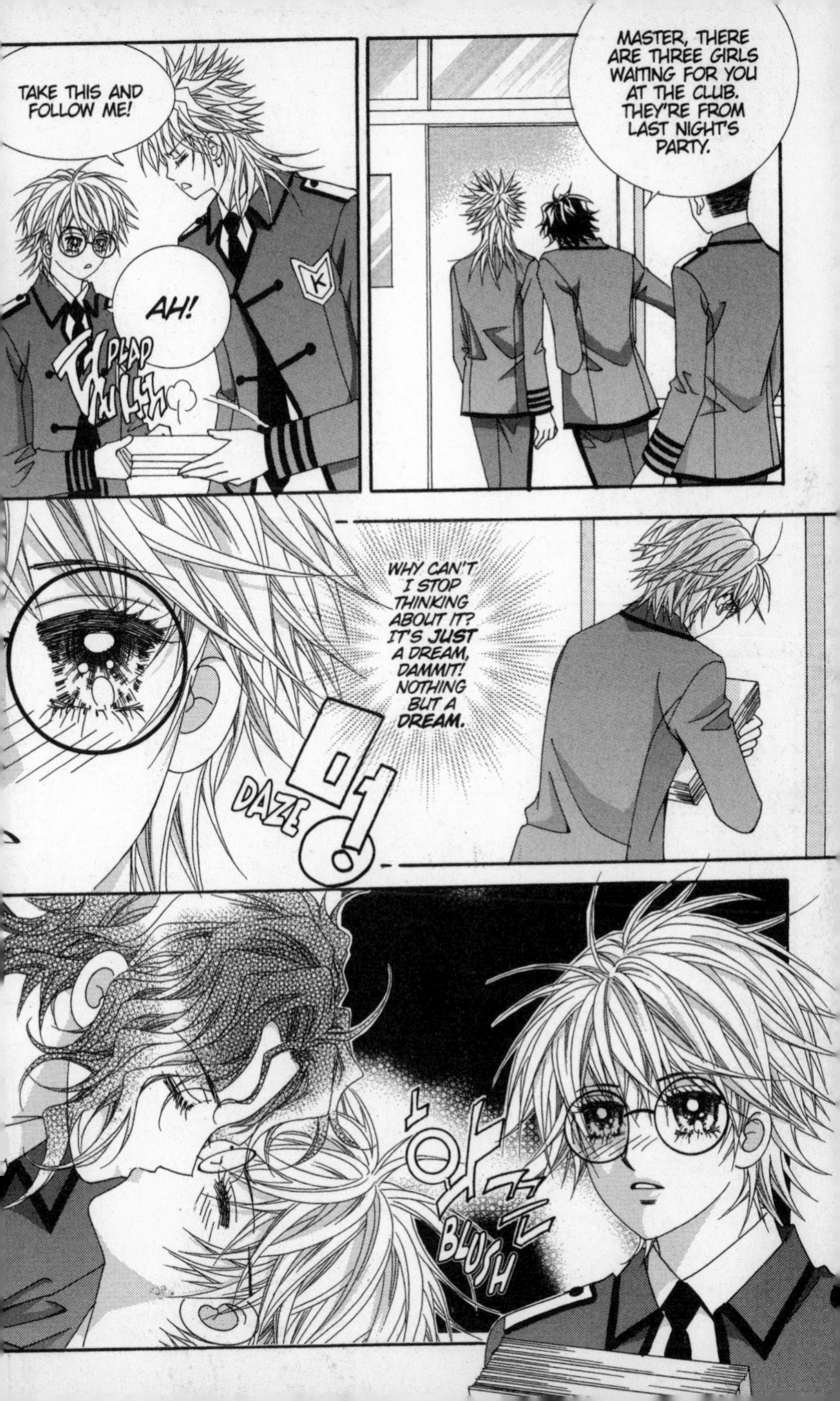

TAKE THIS AND FOLLOW ME!
AH!
PLAP
MASTER, THERE ARE THREE GIRLS WAITING FOR YOU AT THE CLUB. THEY'RE FROM LAST NIGHT'S PARTY.
DAZE
WHY CAN'T I STOP THINKING ABOUT IT? IT'S JUST A DREAM, DAMMIT! NOTHING BUT A DREAM.
BLUSH

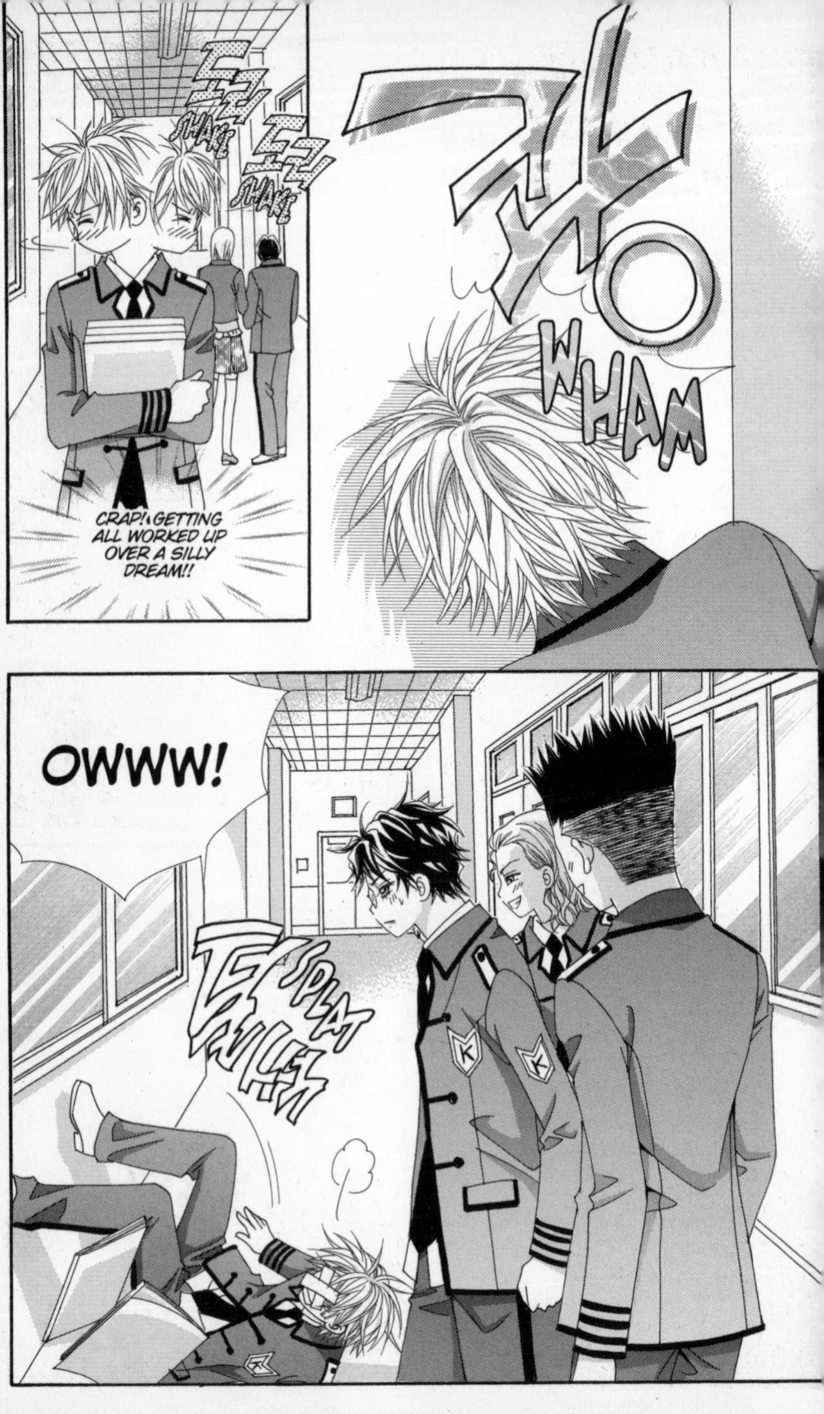
SHAKE
SHAKE
CRAP!! GETTING ALL WORKED UP OVER A SILLY DREAM!!
WHAM
OWWW!
SPLAT

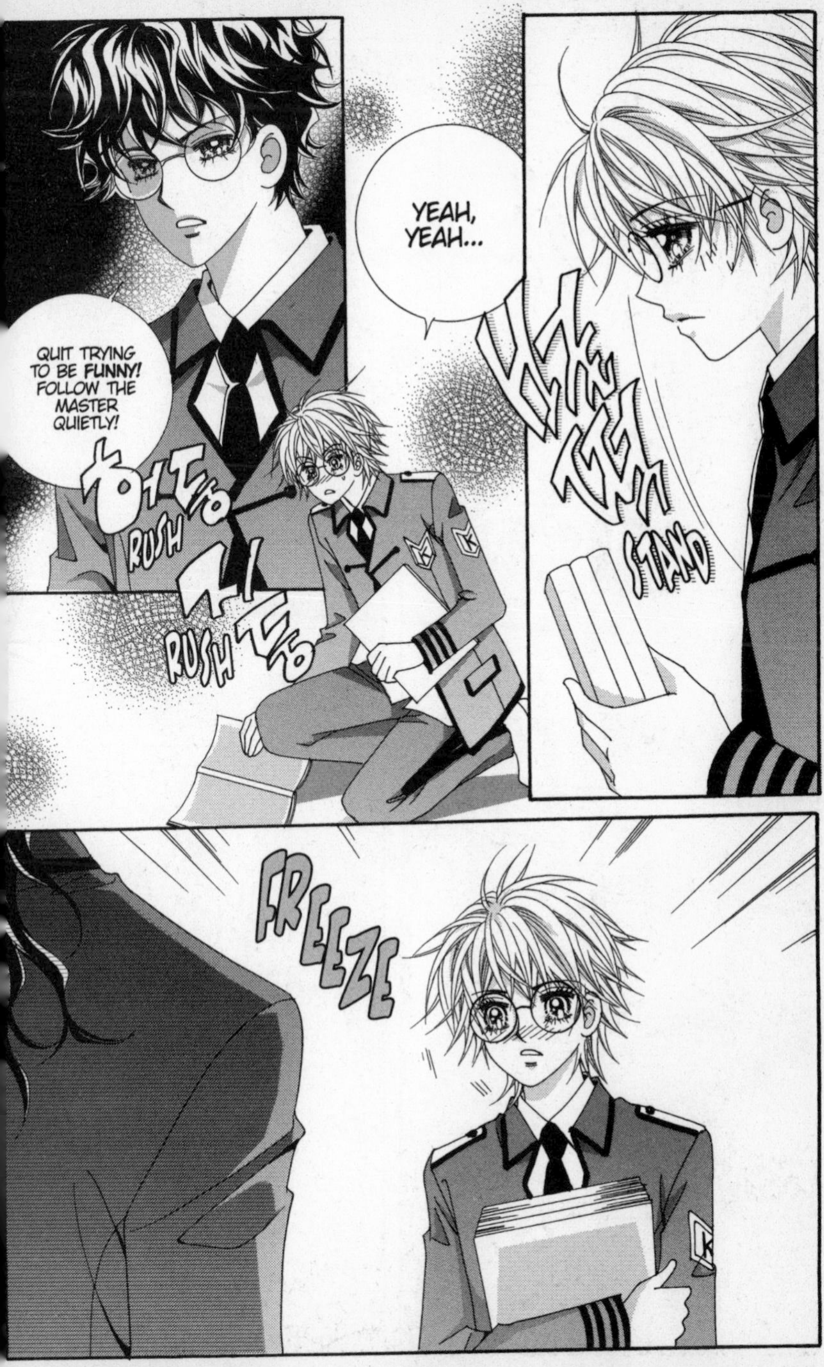
QUIT TRYING TO BE FUNNY! FOLLOW THE MASTER QUIETLY!
RUSH
YEAH, YEAH...
RUSH
STAND
FREEZE

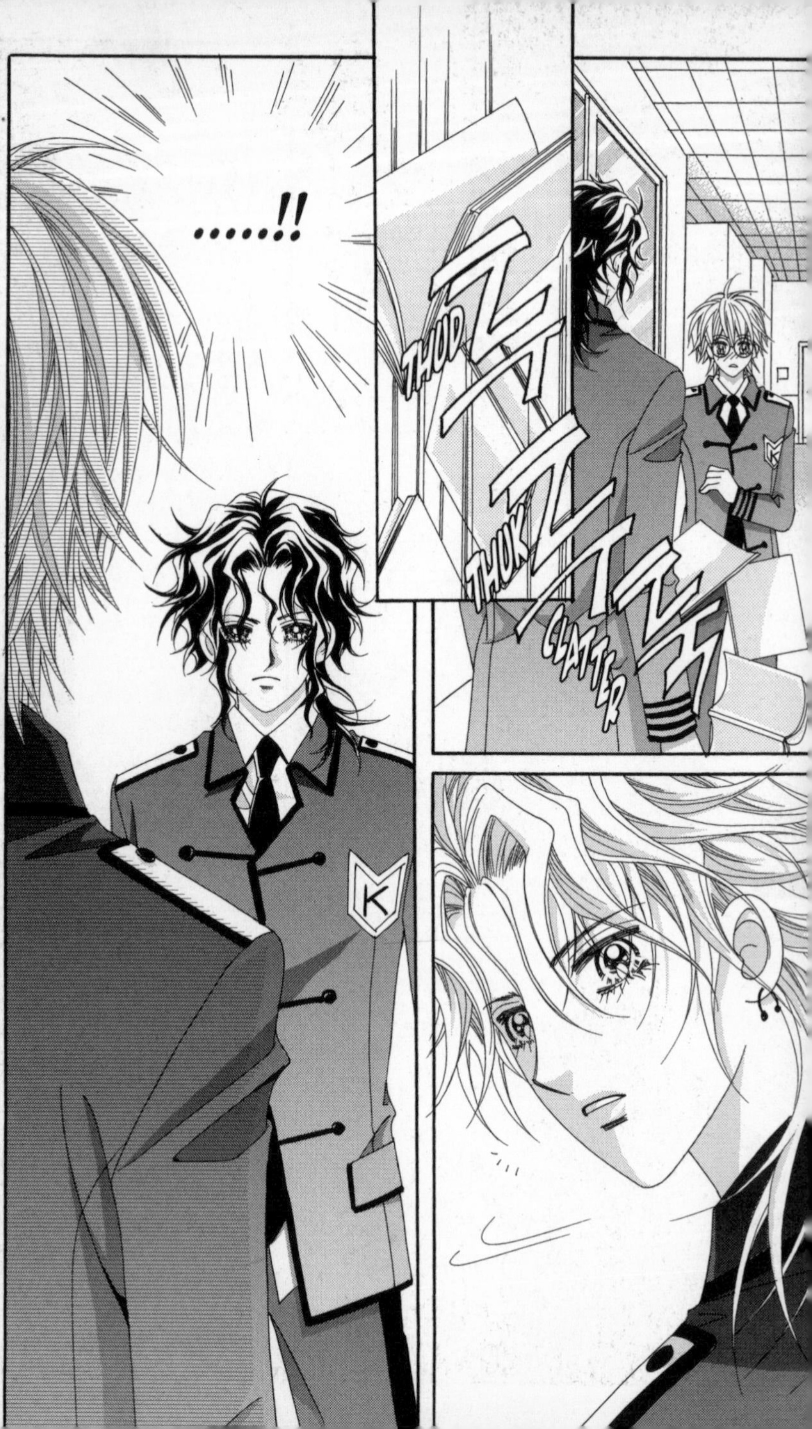
.....!!
THUD
THUK
CLATTER

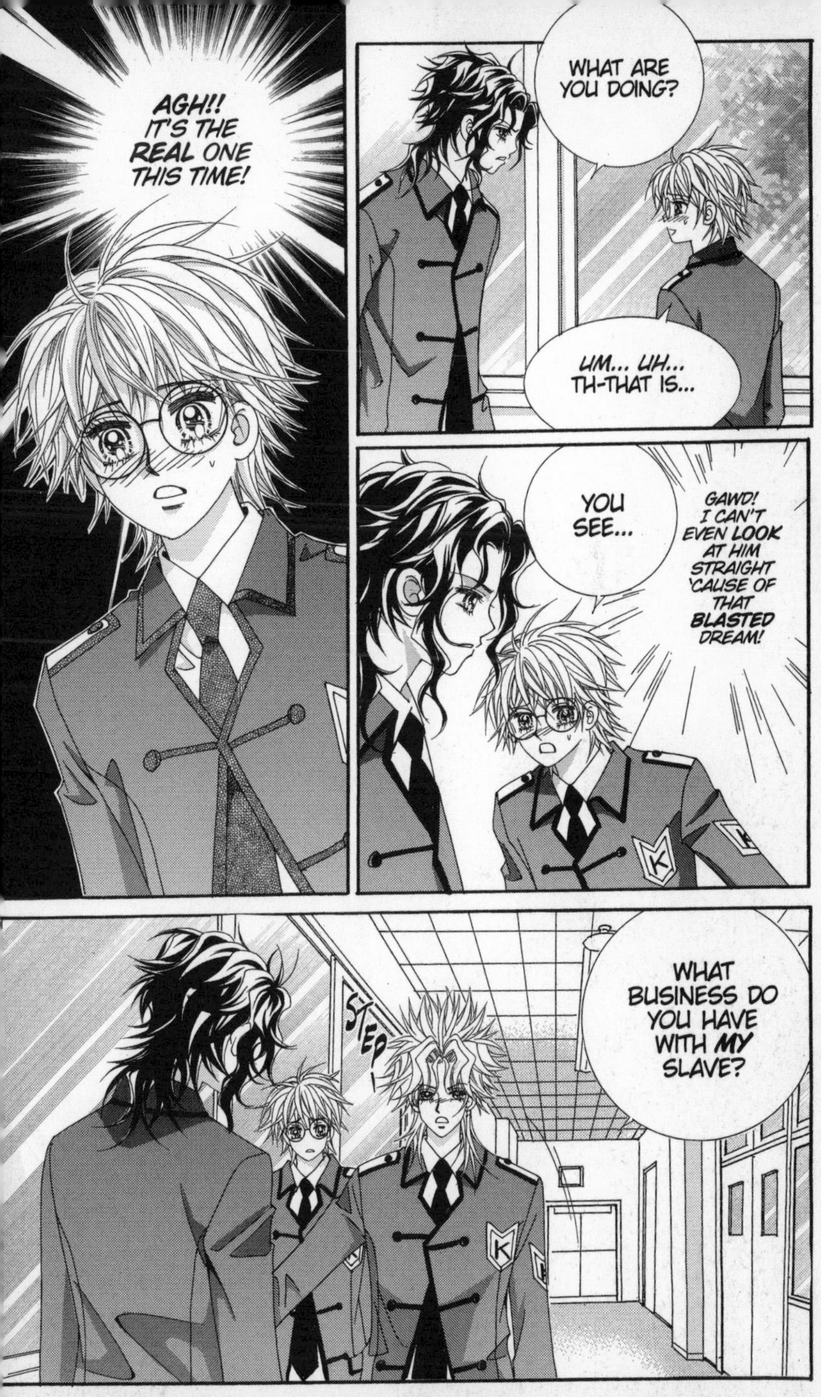
AGH!! IT'S THE REAL ONE THIS TIME!
WHAT ARE YOU DOING?
UM... UH... TH-THAT IS...
YOU SEE...
GAWD! I CAN'T EVEN LOOK AT HIM STRAIGHT 'CAUSE OF THAT BLASTED DREAM!
STEP
WHAT BUSINESS DO YOU HAVE WITH MY SLAVE?

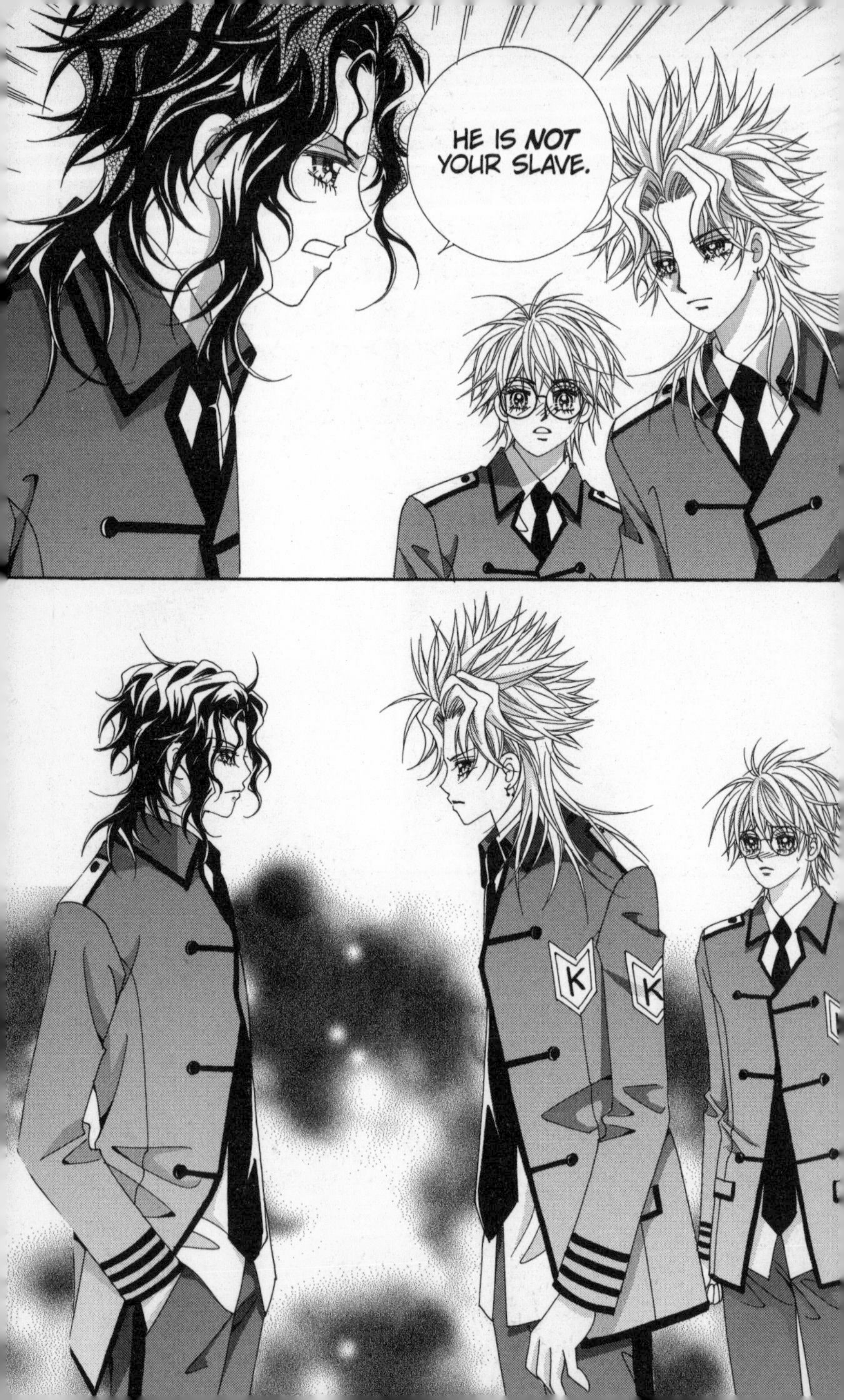
HE IS NOT YOUR SLAVE.

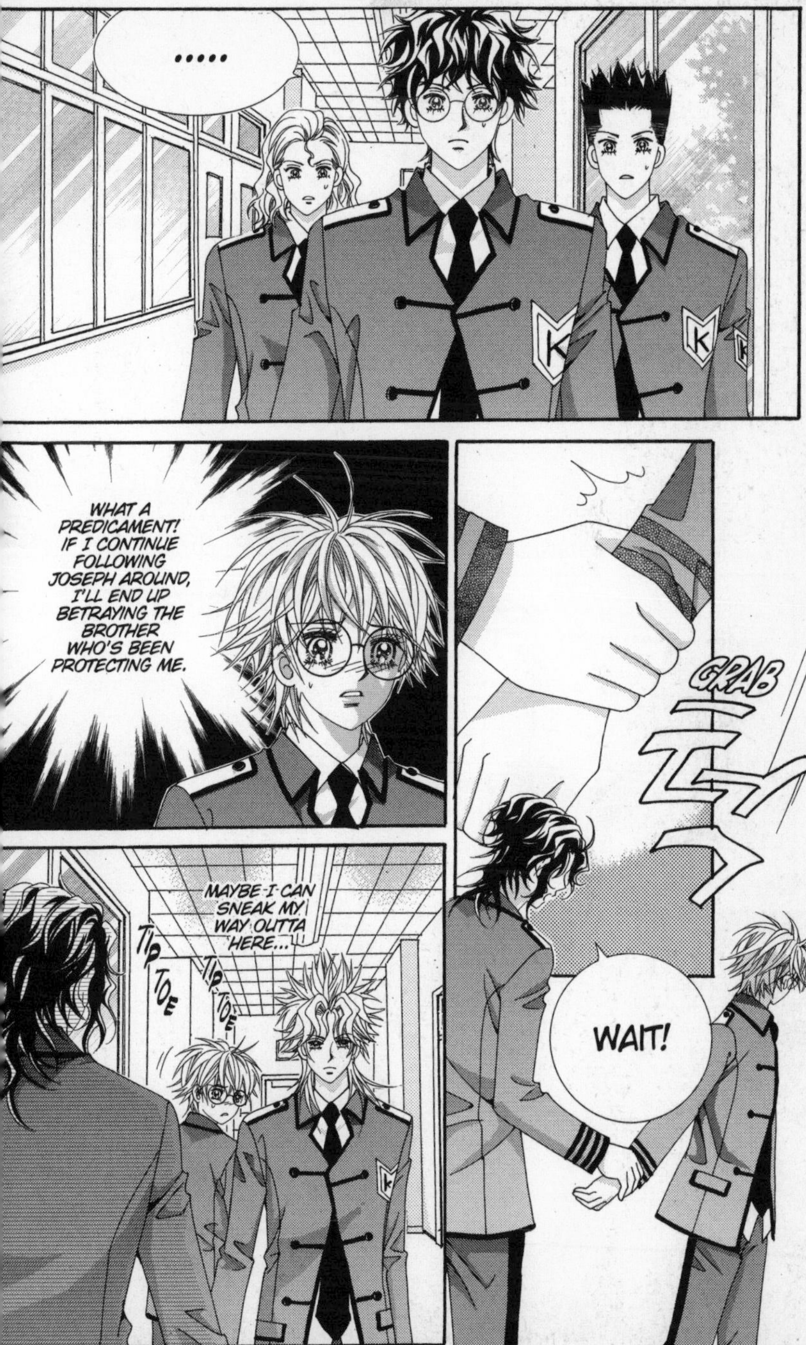
.....
WHAT A PREDICAMENT! IF I CONTINUE FOLLOWING JOSEPH AROUND, I'LL END UP BETRAYING THE BROTHER WHO'S BEEN PROTECTING ME.
GRAB
MAYBE I CAN SNEAK MY WAY OUTTA HERE...
TIP TOE
TIP TOE
WAIT!

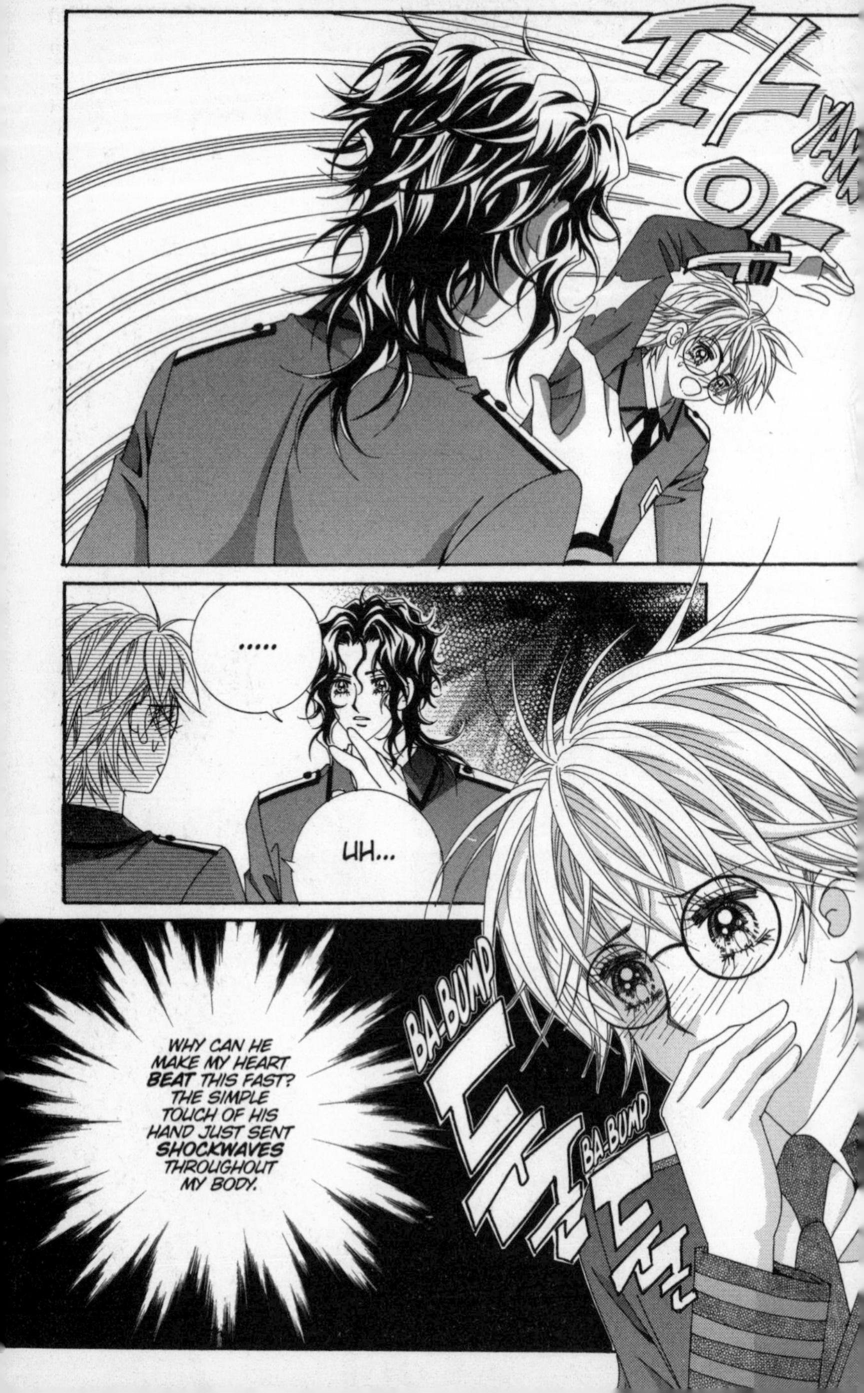
YANK
.....
UH...
WHY CAN HE MAKE MY HEART **BEAT** THIS FAST? THE SIMPLE TOUCH OF HIS HAND JUST SENT **SHOCKWAVES** THROUGHOUT MY BODY.
BA-BUMP
BA-BUMP

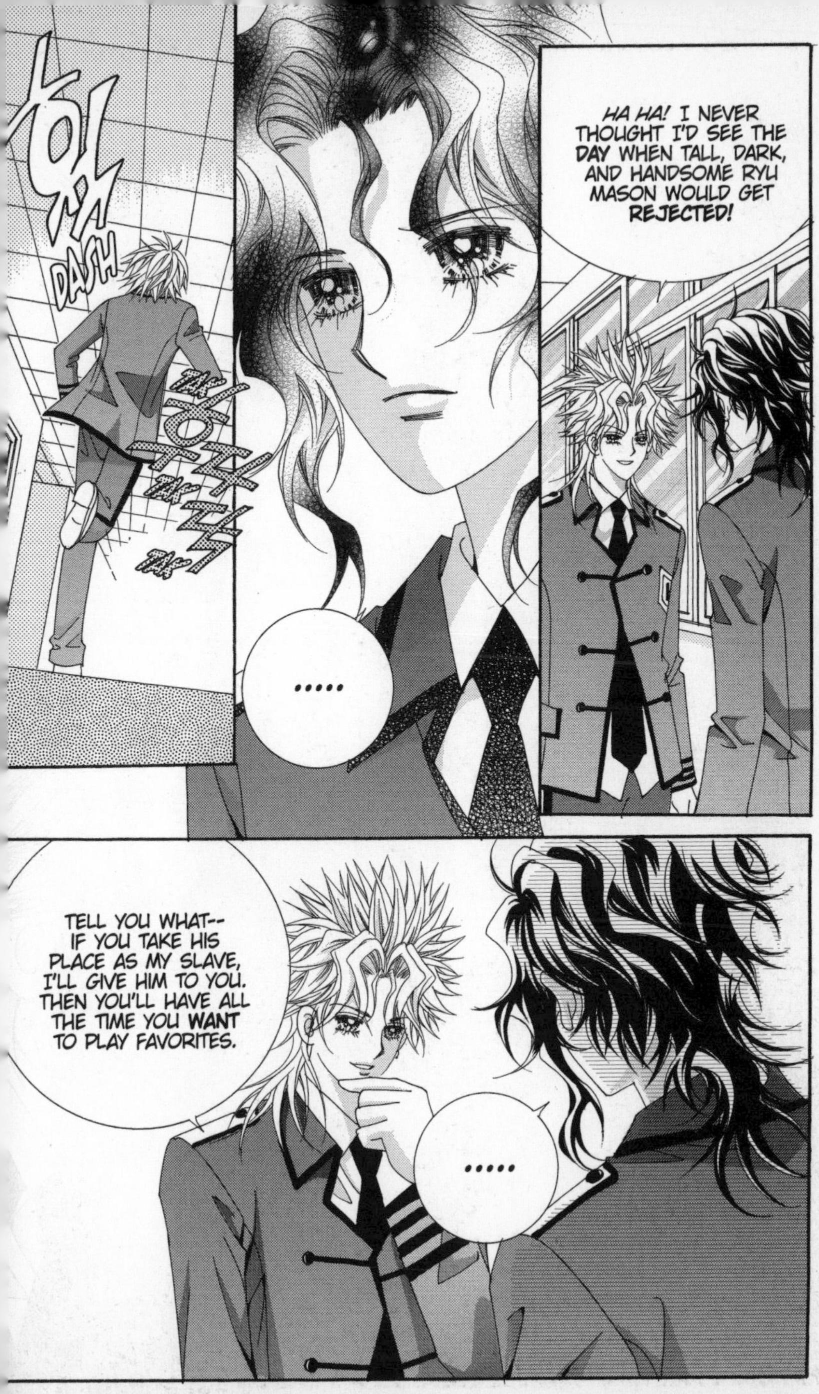

DASH
TAK TAK TAK
.....
HA HA! I NEVER THOUGHT I'D SEE THE DAY WHEN TALL, DARK, AND HANDSOME RYU MASON WOULD GET REJECTED!
TELL YOU WHAT-- IF YOU TAKE HIS PLACE AS MY SLAVE, I'LL GIVE HIM TO YOU. THEN YOU'LL HAVE ALL THE TIME YOU WANT TO PLAY FAVORITES.
.....

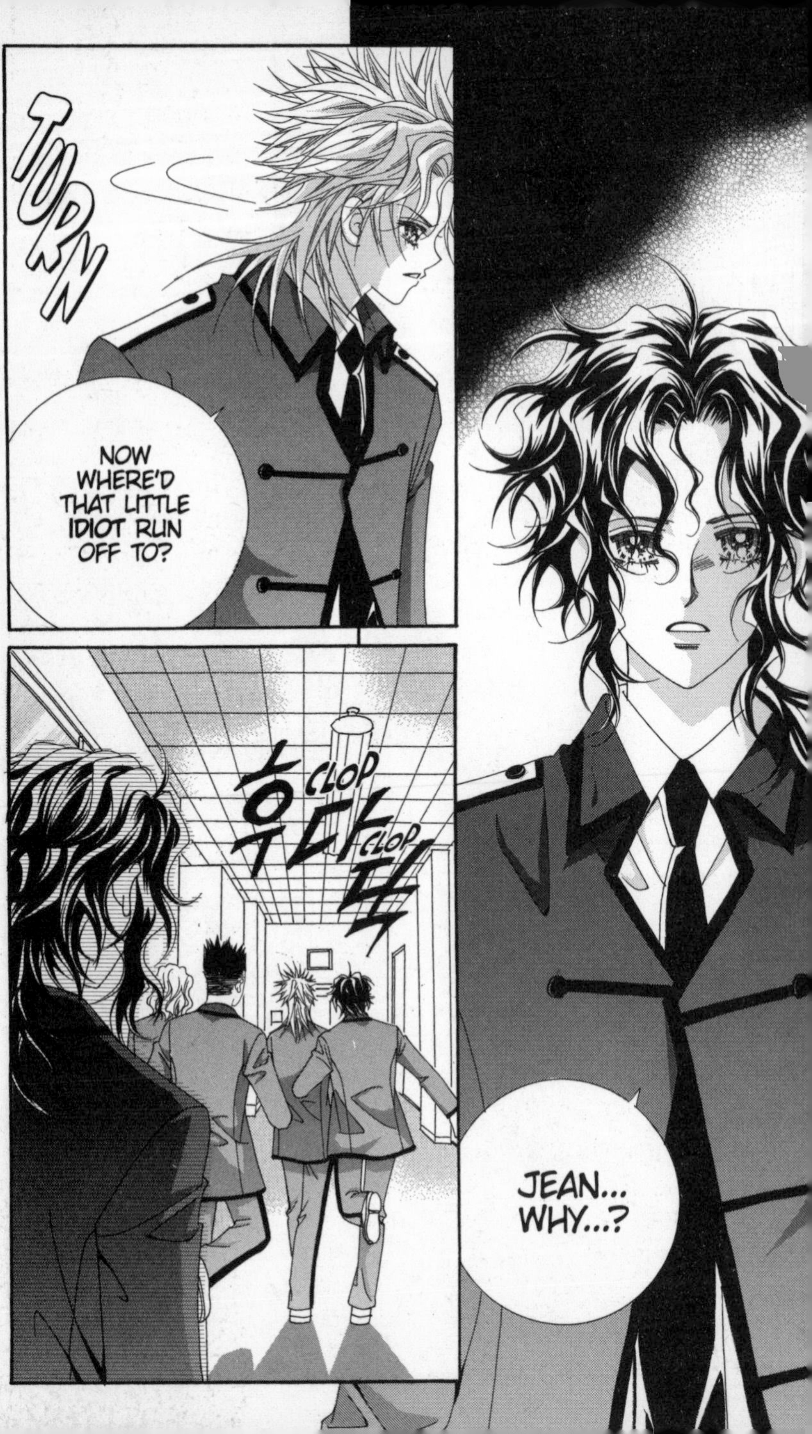
TURN
NOW WHERE'D THAT LITTLE IDIOT RUN OFF TO?
후다닥
CLOP
CLOP
JEAN... WHY...?

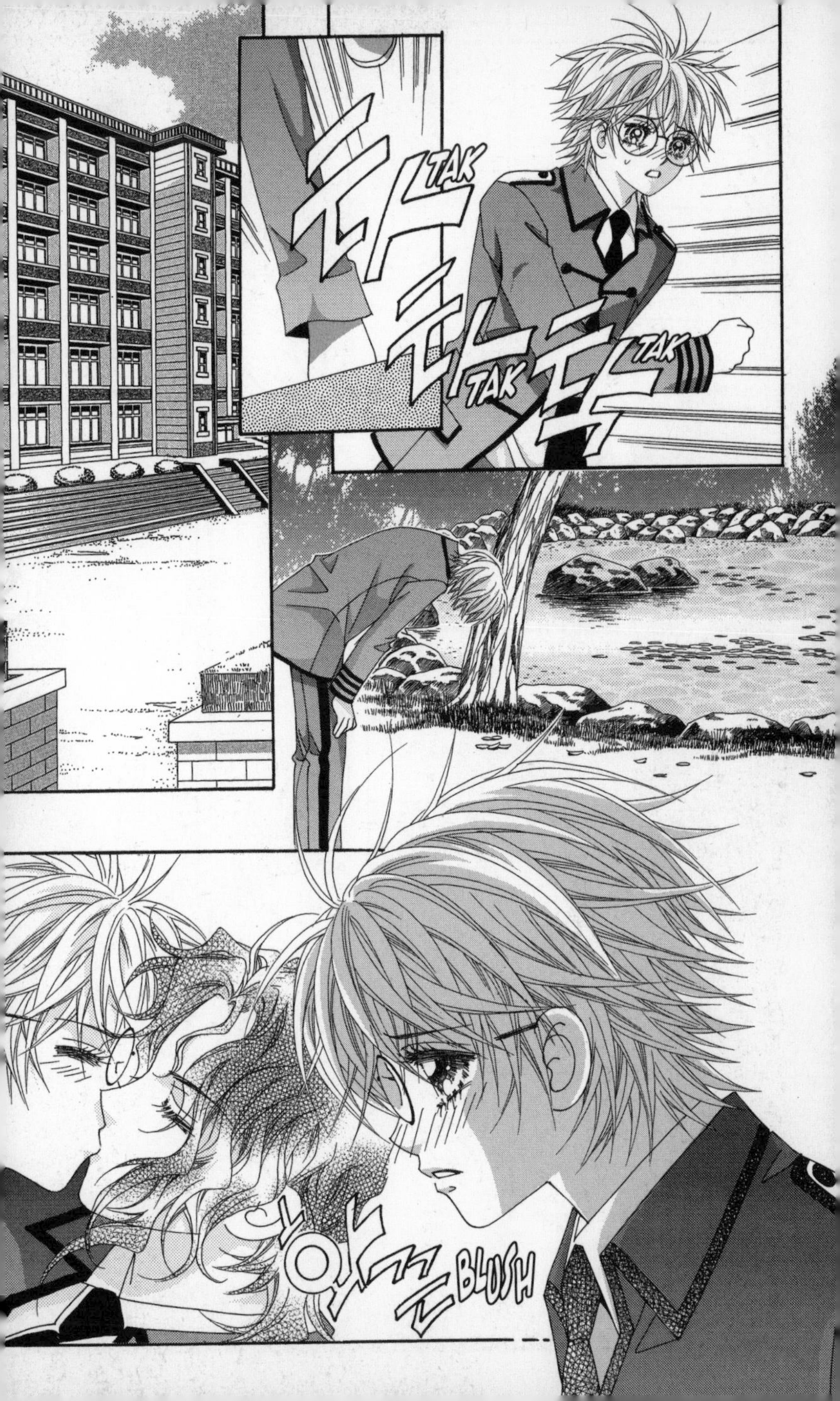
TAK
TAK
TAK
BLUSH

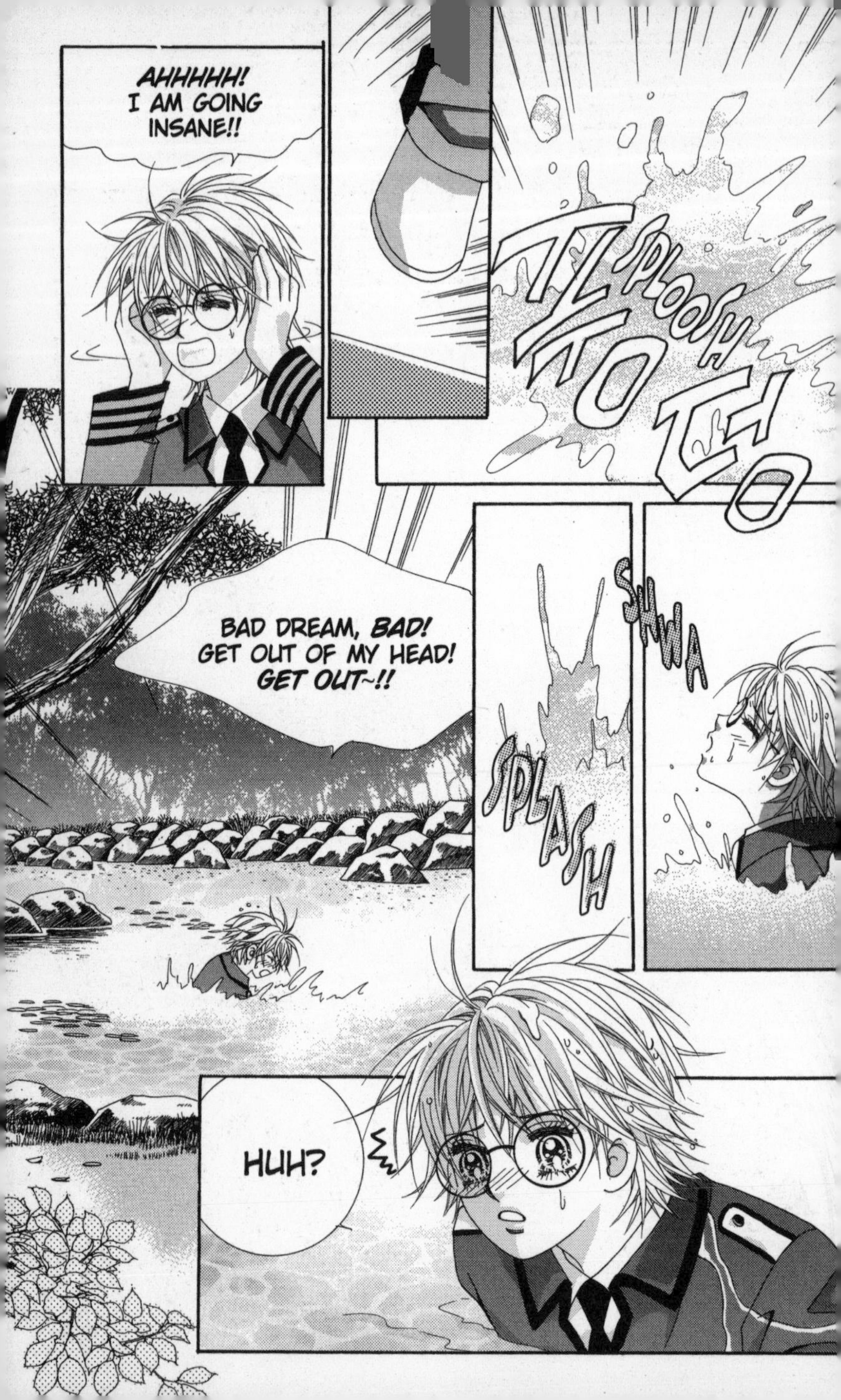
AHHHHH! I AM GOING INSANE!!
SPLOOSH
BAD DREAM, BAD! GET OUT OF MY HEAD! GET OUT~!!
SPLASH
SHWA
HUH?

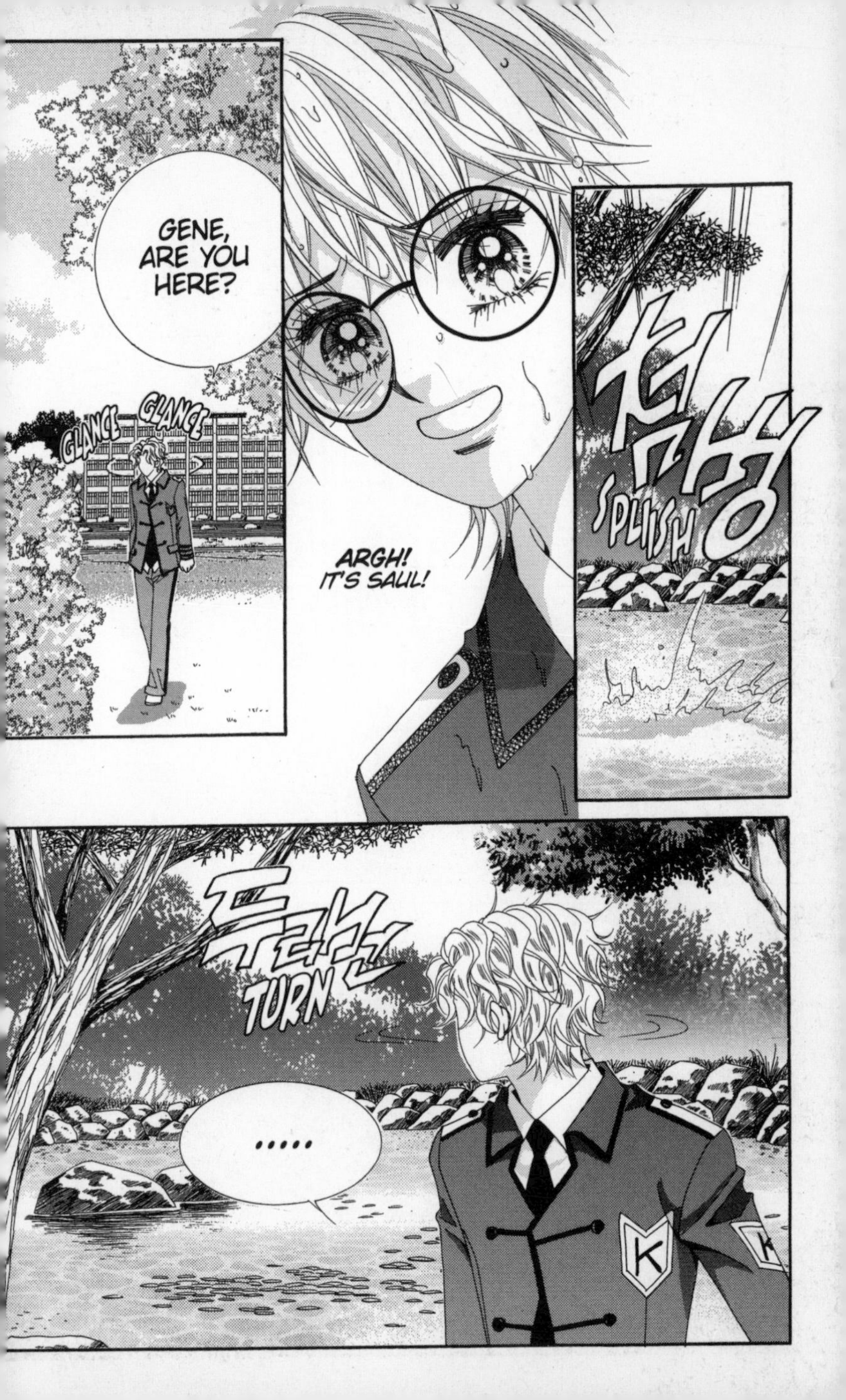
GENE, ARE YOU HERE?
GLANCE GLANCE
ARGH! IT'S SAUL!
첨벙
SPLISH
돌아선
TURN
.....

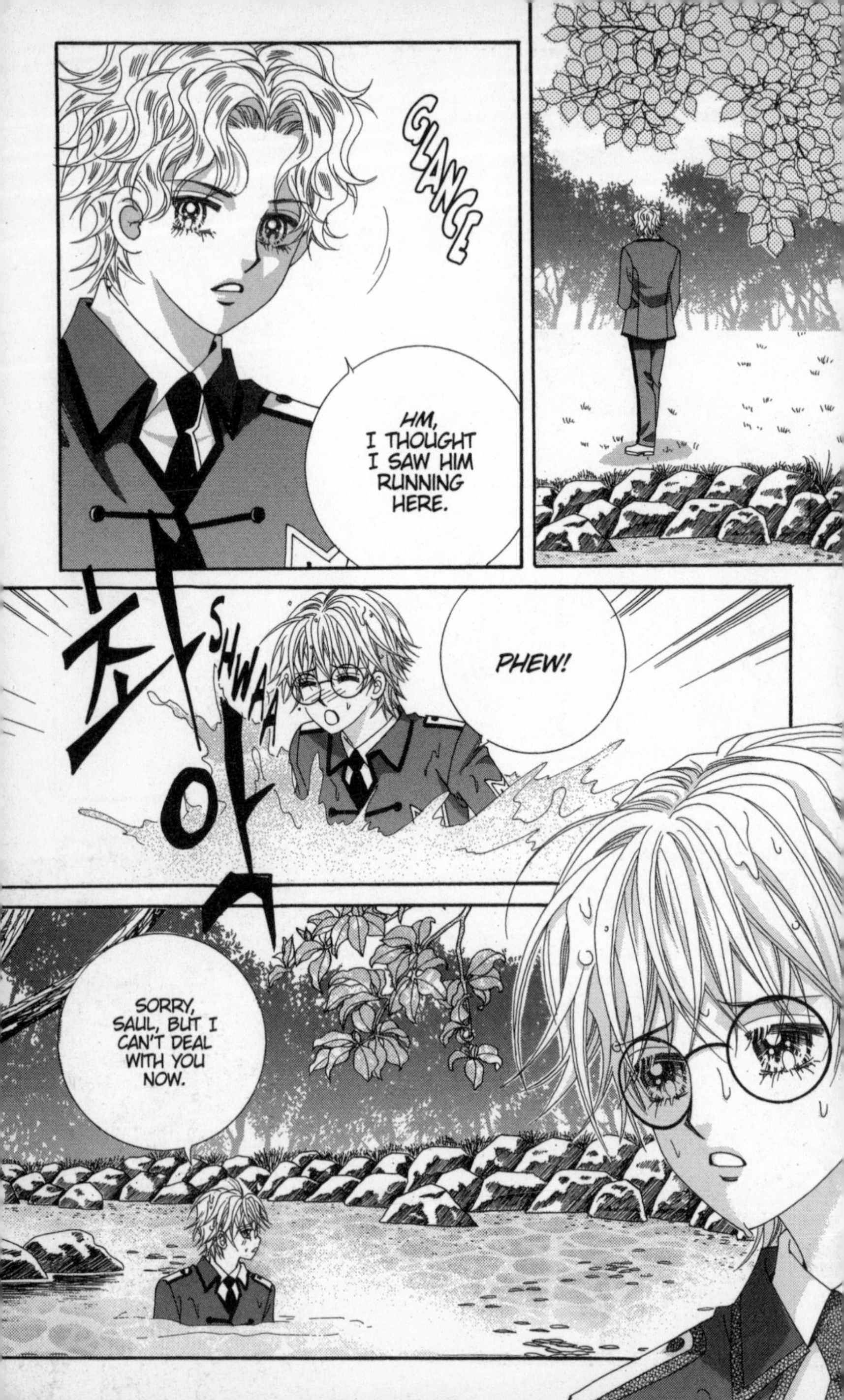

GLANCE
HM, I THOUGHT I SAW HIM RUNNING HERE.
SHWAA
PHEW!
SORRY, SAUL, BUT I CAN'T DEAL WITH YOU NOW.

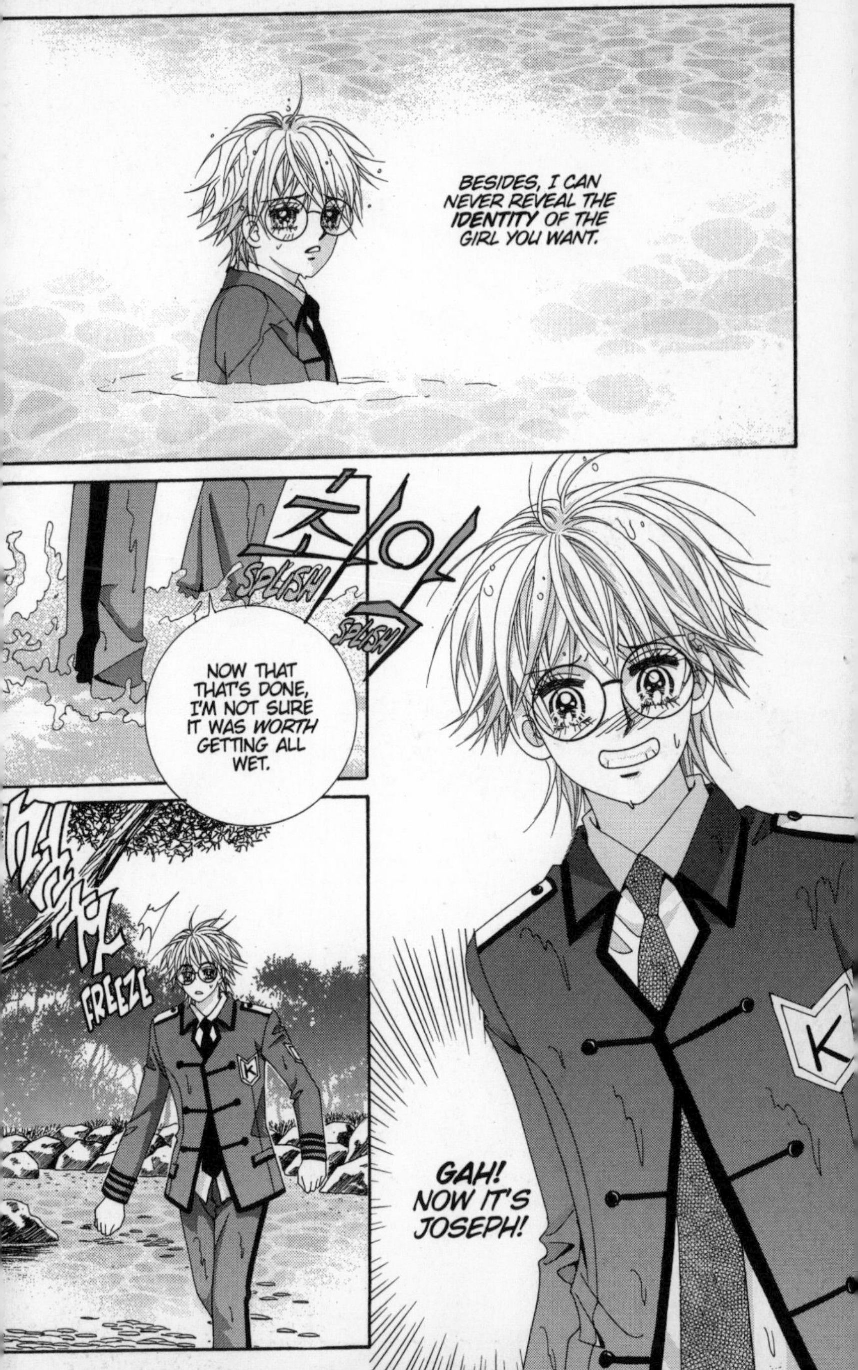
BESIDES, I CAN NEVER REVEAL THE IDENTITY OF THE GIRL YOU WANT.
SPLISH
SPLISH
NOW THAT THAT'S DONE, I'M NOT SURE IT WAS WORTH GETTING ALL WET.
FREEZE
GAH! NOW IT'S JOSEPH!

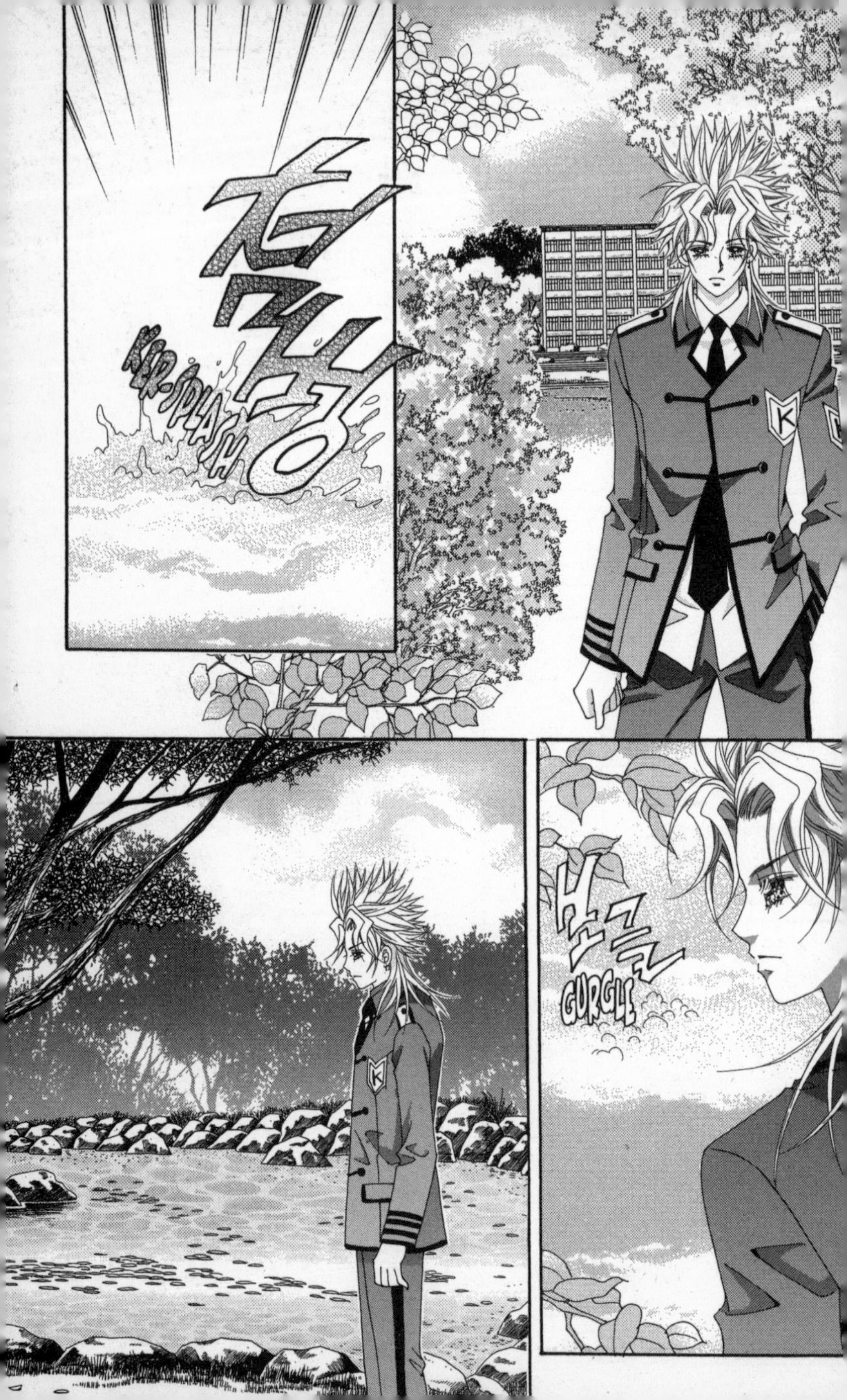
KER-SPLASH
GURGLE

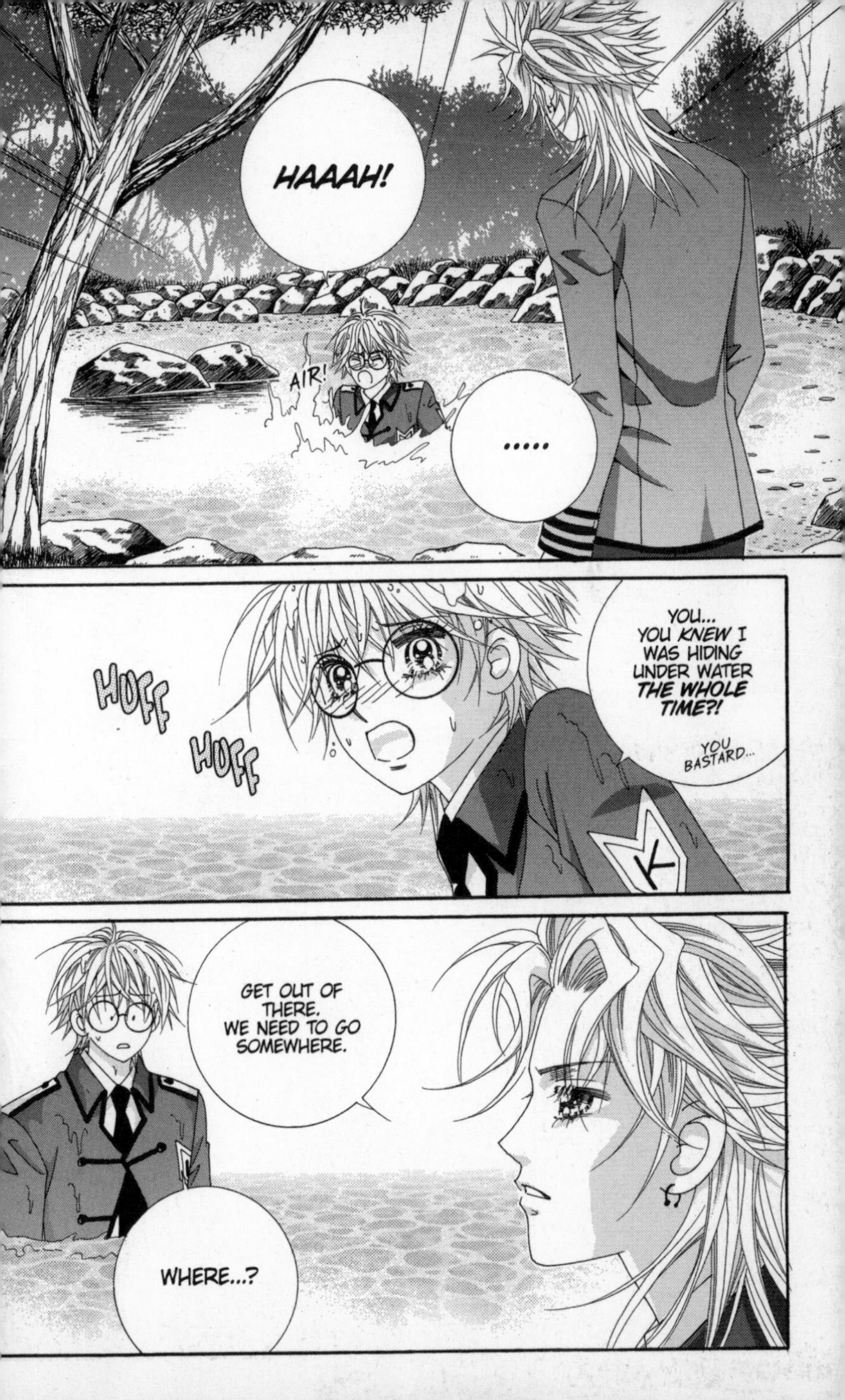
HAAAH!
AIR!
.....
HUFF
HUFF
YOU... YOU KNEW I WAS HIDING UNDER WATER THE WHOLE TIME?!
YOU BASTARD...
GET OUT OF THERE. WE NEED TO GO SOMEWHERE.
WHERE...?

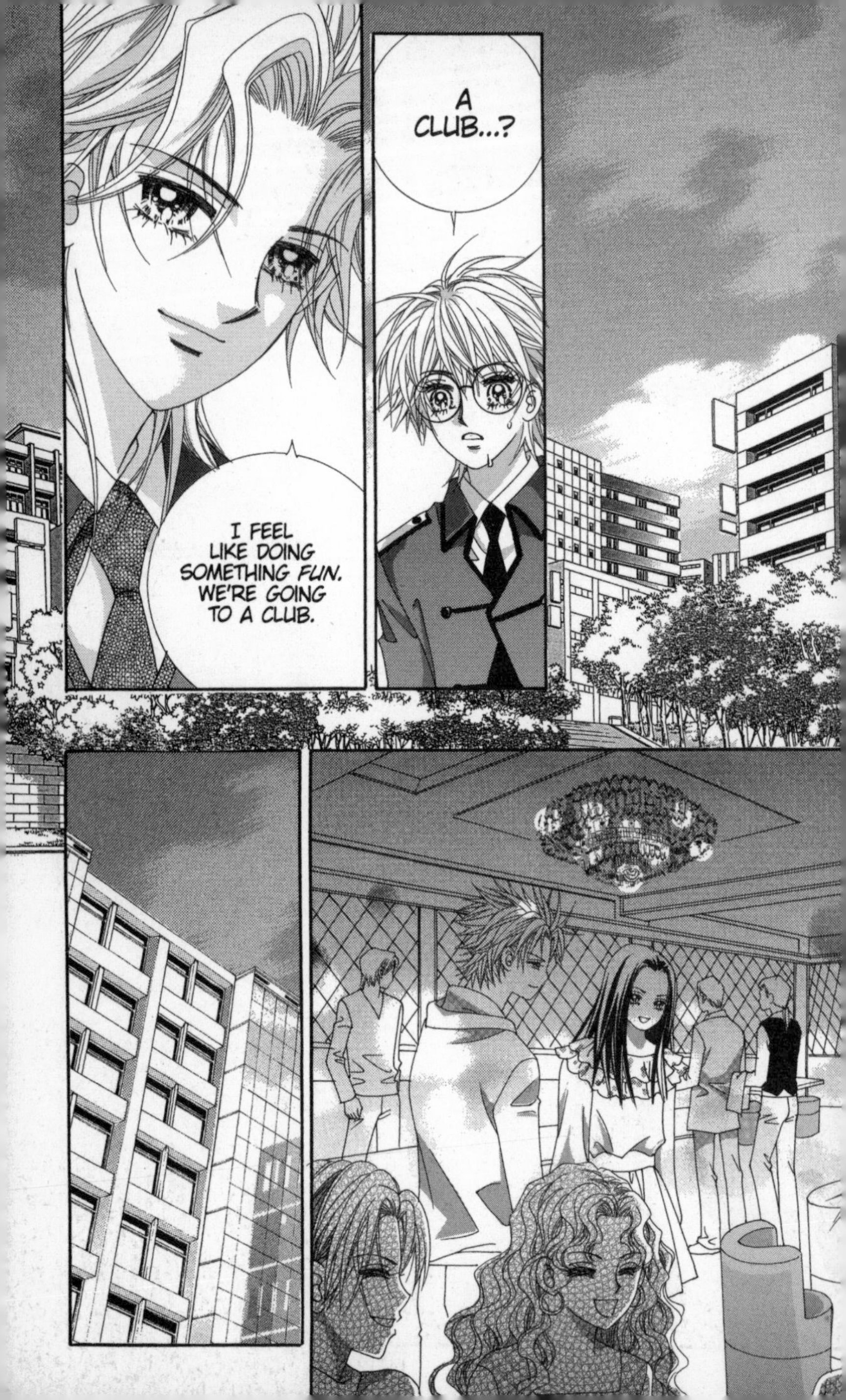
I FEEL LIKE DOING SOMETHING *FUN.* WE'RE GOING TO A CLUB.
A CLUB...?

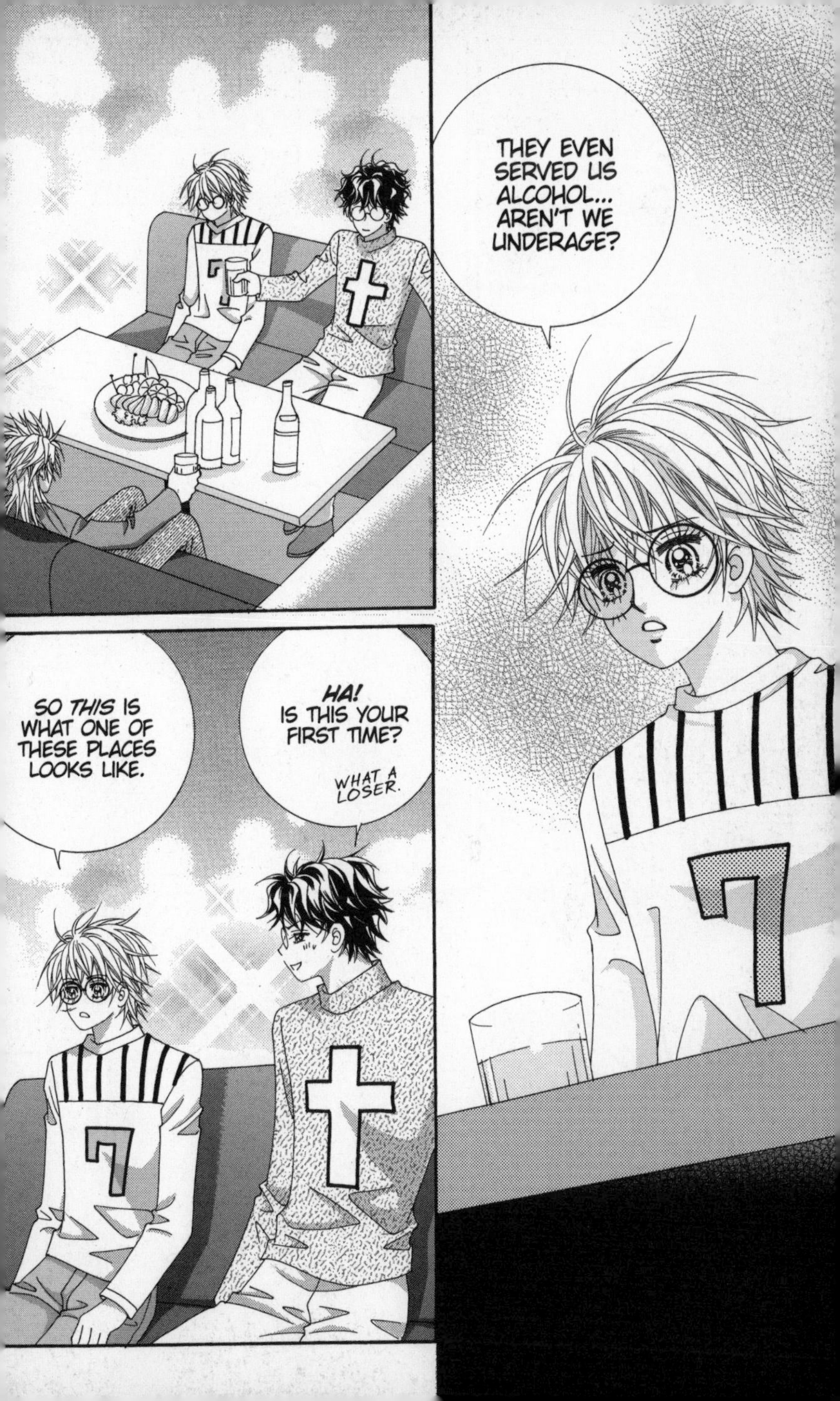
SO *THIS* IS WHAT ONE OF THESE PLACES LOOKS LIKE.
HA! IS THIS YOUR FIRST TIME?
WHAT A LOSER.
THEY EVEN SERVED US ALCOHOL... AREN'T WE UNDERAGE?

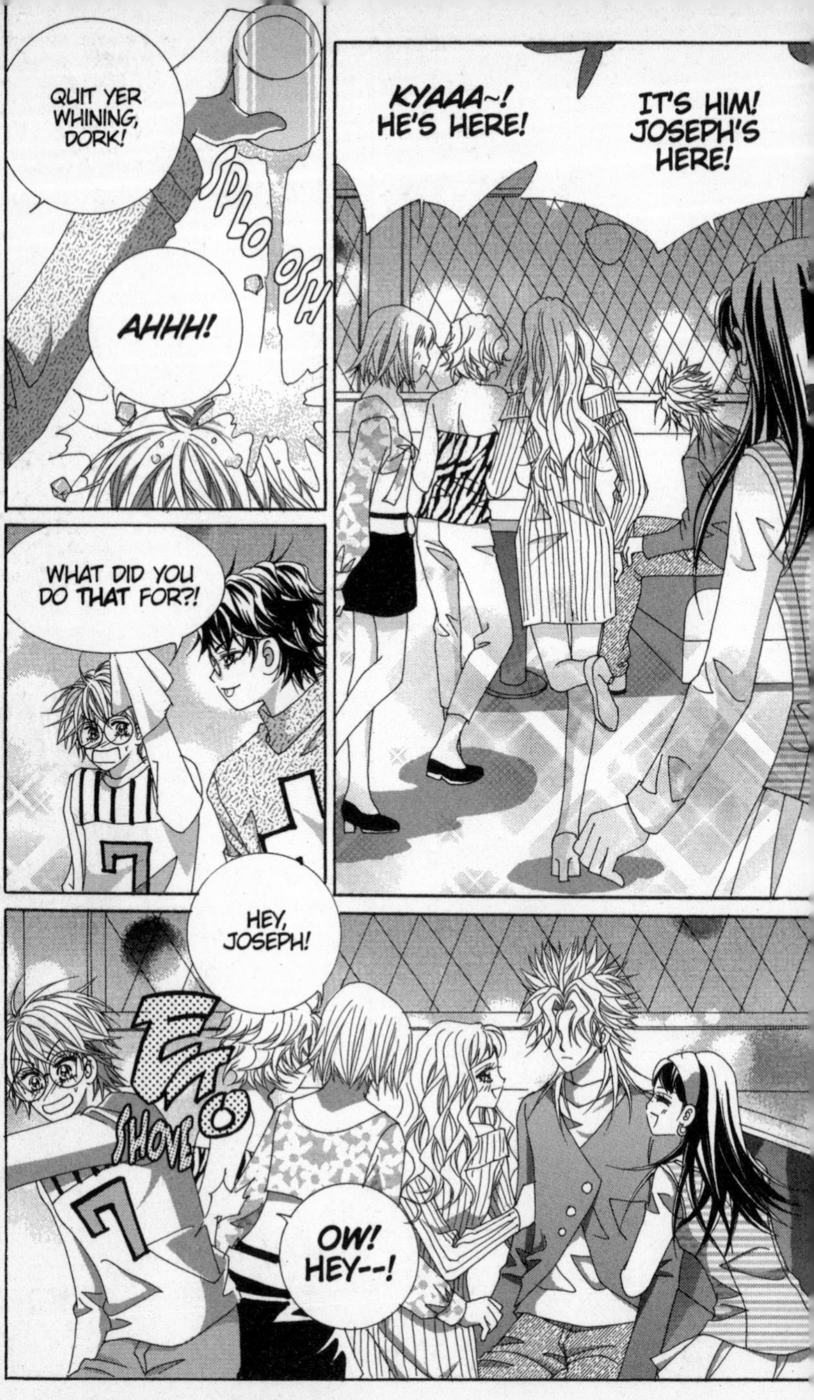
QUIT YER WHINING, DORK!
SPLOOSH
AHHH!
WHAT DID YOU DO THAT FOR?!
KYAAA~! HE'S HERE!
IT'S HIM! JOSEPH'S HERE!
HEY, JOSEPH!
SHOVE
OW! HEY--!

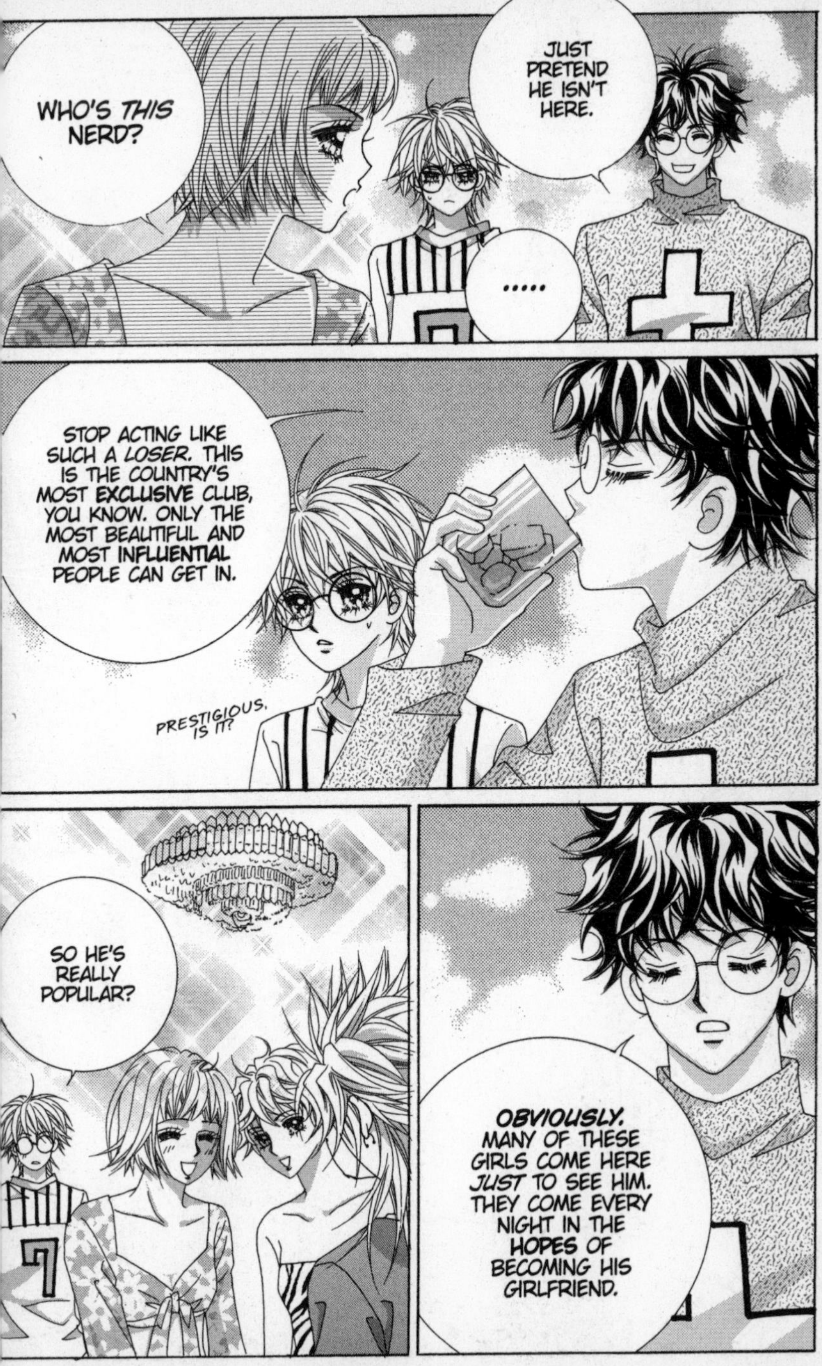
WHO'S *THIS* NERD?
JUST PRETEND HE ISN'T HERE.
.....
STOP ACTING LIKE SUCH A *LOSER*. THIS IS THE COUNTRY'S MOST **EXCLUSIVE** CLUB, YOU KNOW. ONLY THE MOST BEAUTIFUL AND MOST **INFLUENTIAL** PEOPLE CAN GET IN.
PRESTIGIOUS, IS IT?
SO HE'S REALLY POPULAR?
OBVIOUSLY. MANY OF THESE GIRLS COME HERE *JUST* TO SEE HIM. THEY COME EVERY NIGHT IN THE **HOPES** OF BECOMING HIS GIRLFRIEND.

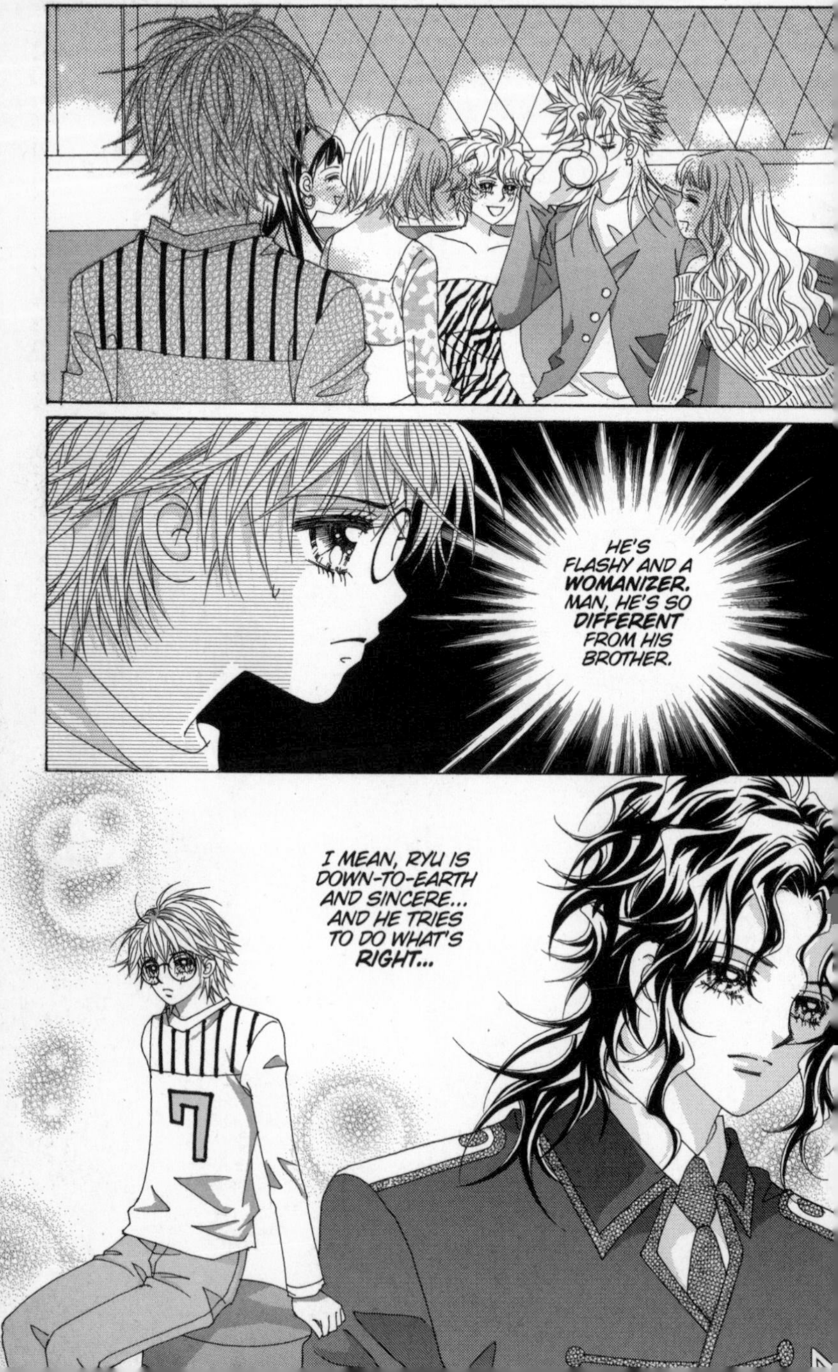
HE'S FLASHY AND A WOMANIZER. MAN, HE'S SO DIFFERENT FROM HIS BROTHER.
I MEAN, RYU IS DOWN-TO-EARTH AND SINCERE... AND HE TRIES TO DO WHAT'S RIGHT...

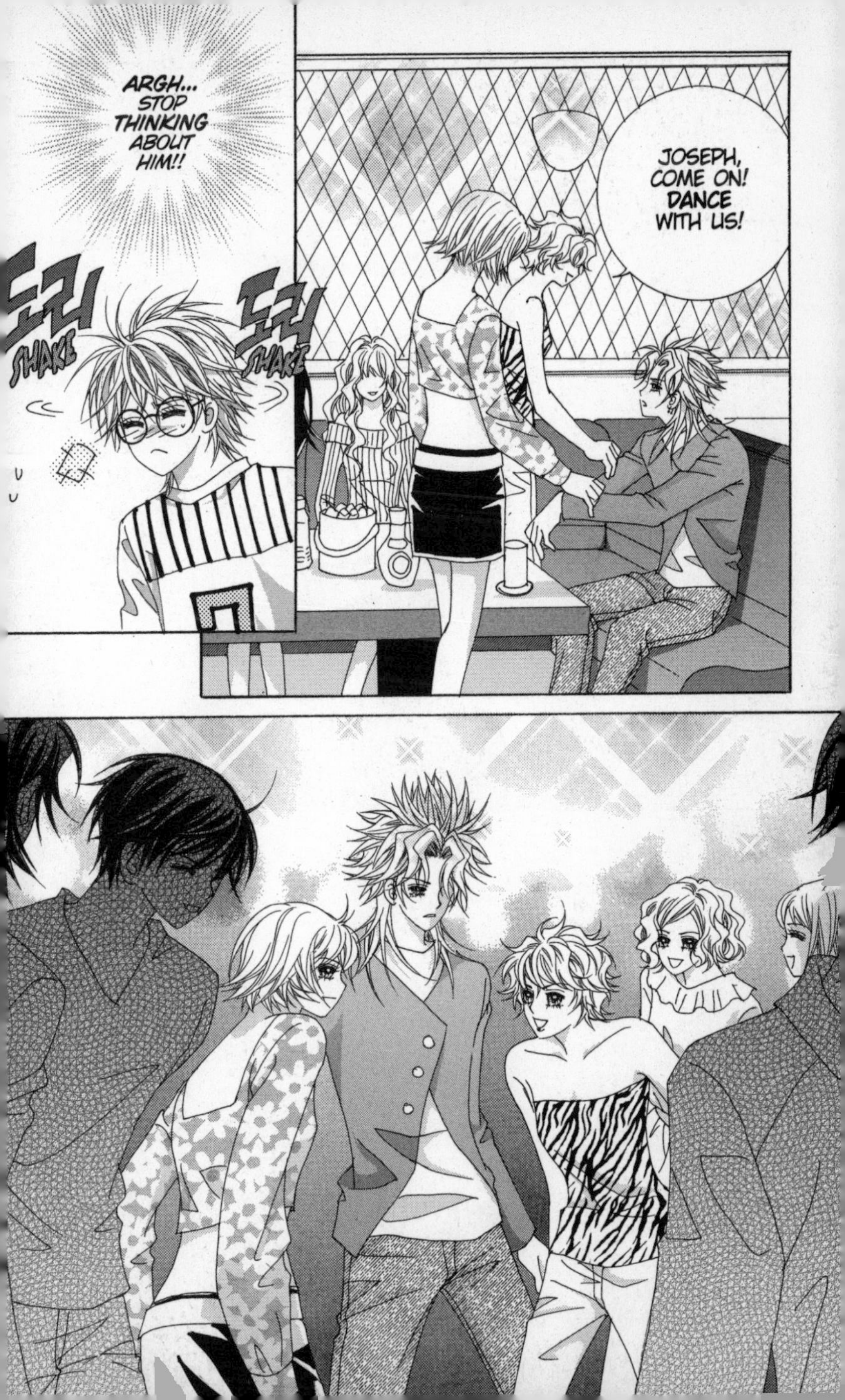
ARGH... STOP THINKING ABOUT HIM!!
SHAKE
SHAKE
JOSEPH, COME ON! DANCE WITH US!

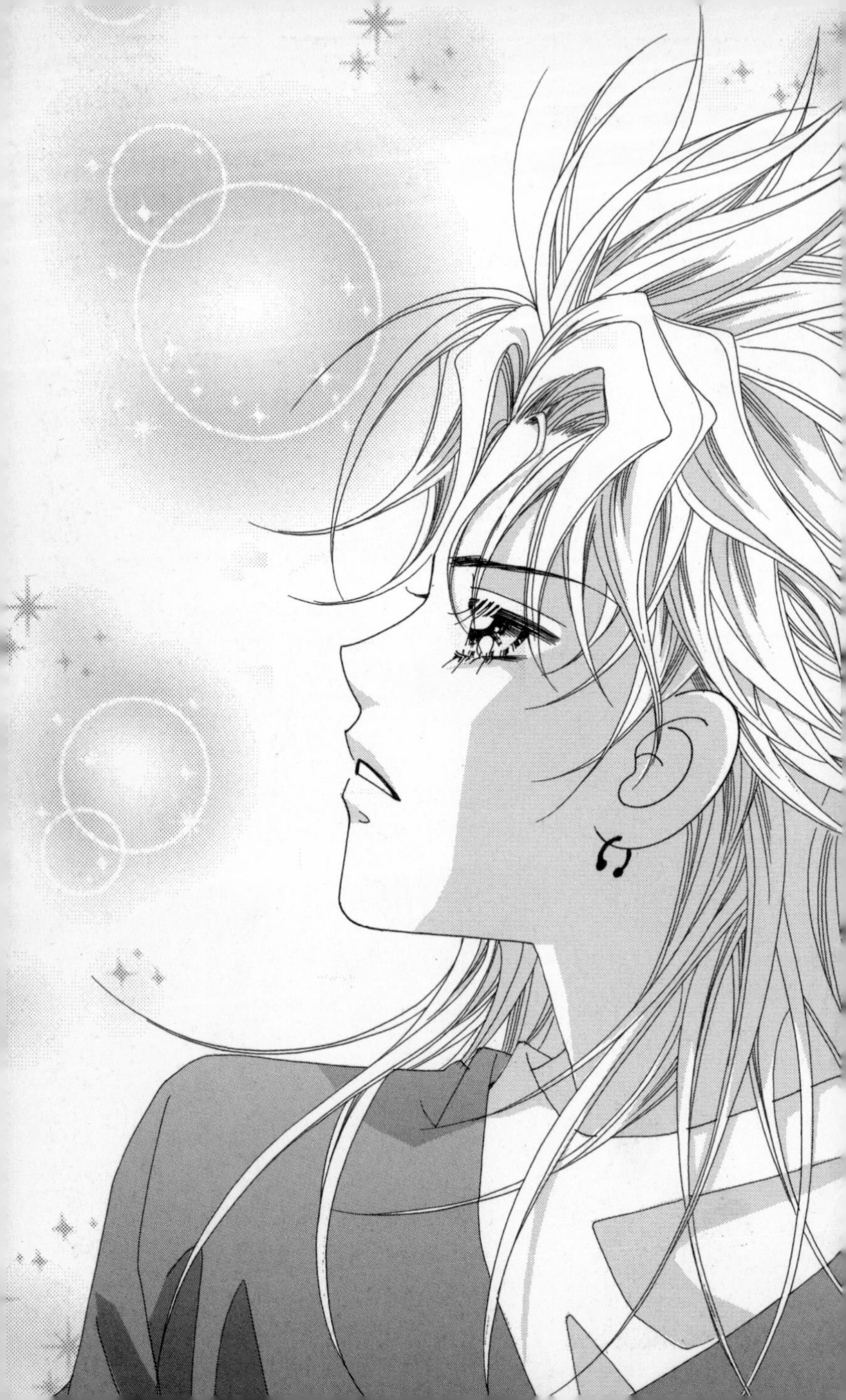

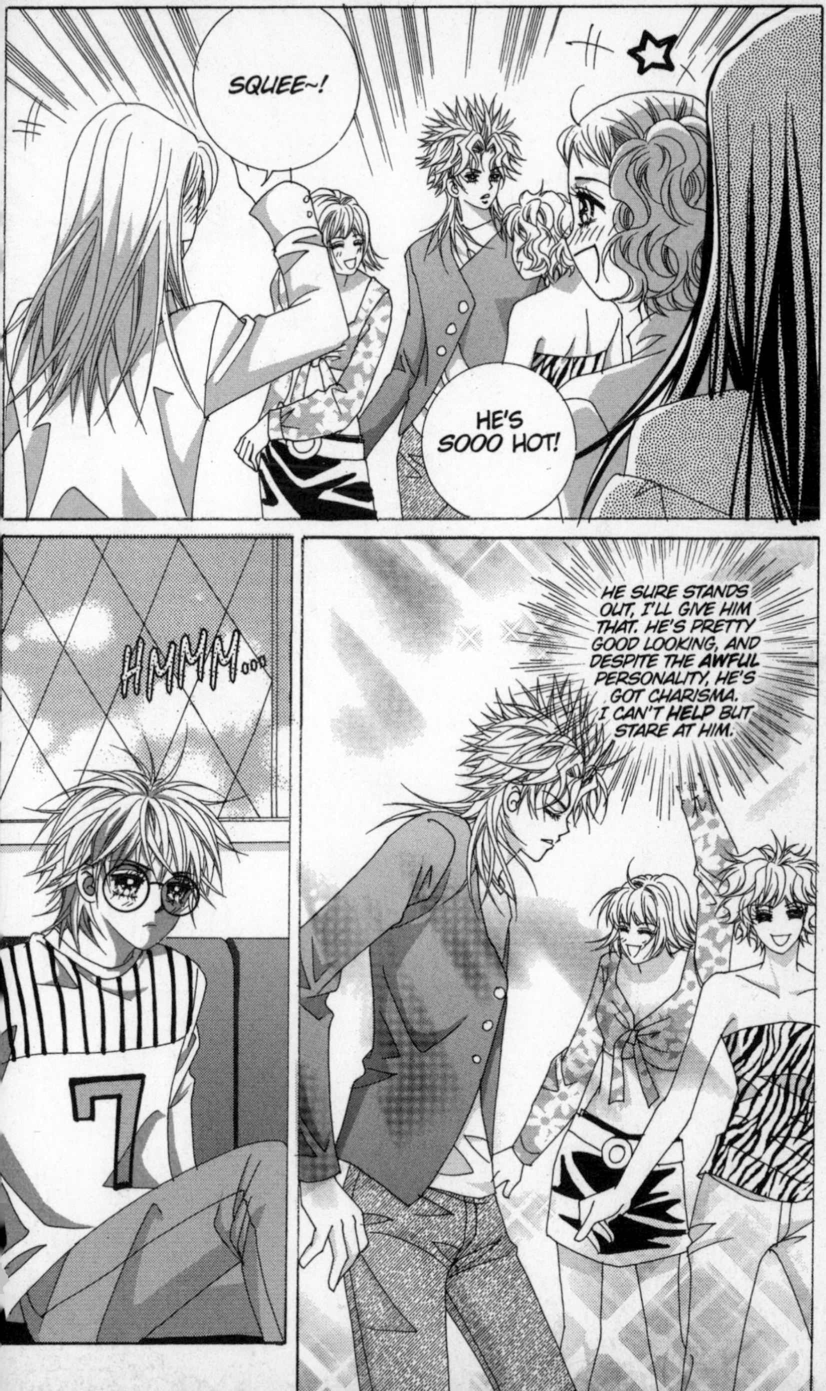
SQUEE~!
HE'S SOOO HOT!
HMMM...
HE SURE STANDS OUT, I'LL GIVE HIM THAT. HE'S PRETTY GOOD LOOKING, AND DESPITE THE AWFUL PERSONALITY, HE'S GOT CHARISMA. I CAN'T HELP BUT STARE AT HIM.

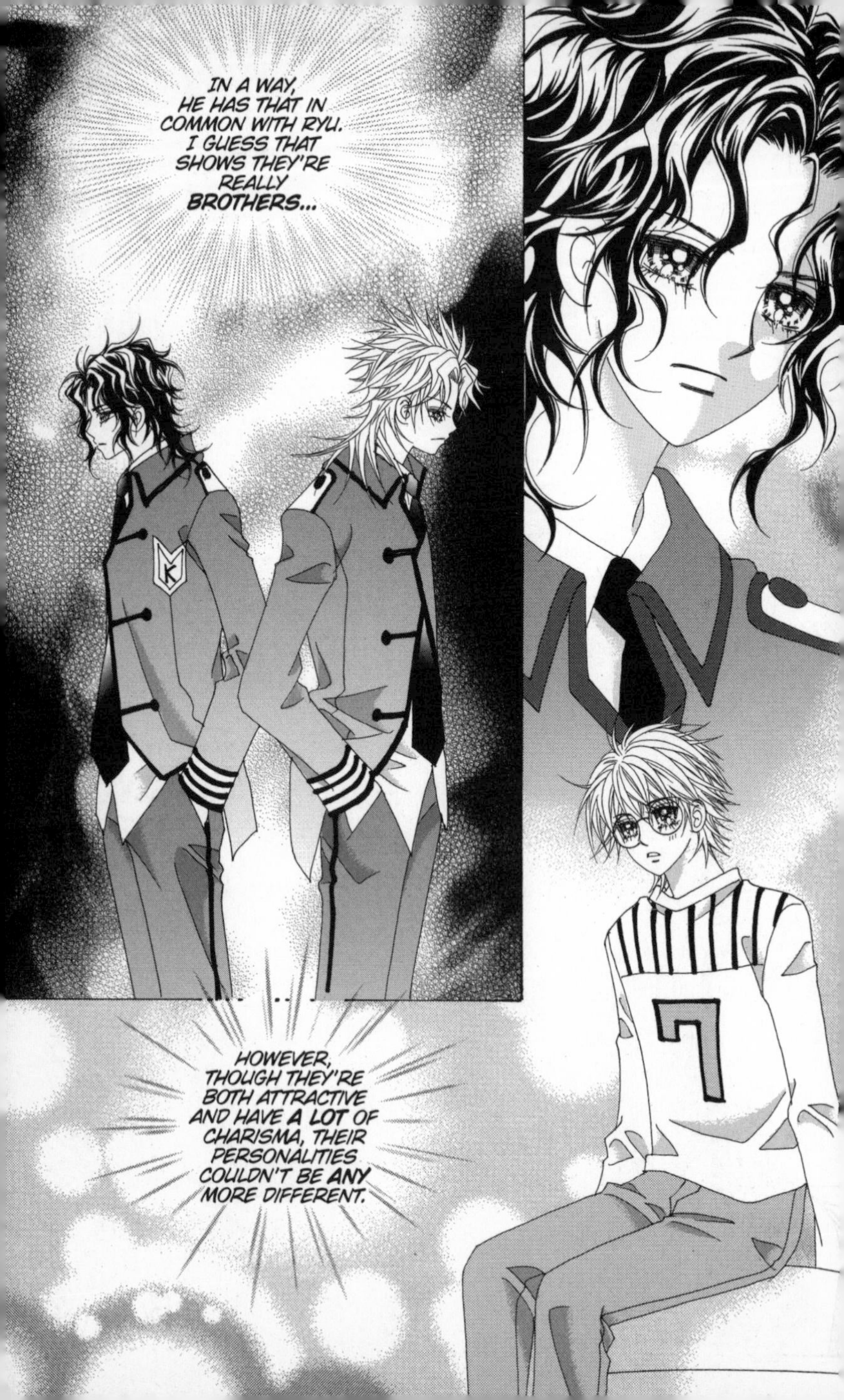
IN A WAY, HE HAS THAT IN COMMON WITH RYU. I GUESS THAT SHOWS THEY'RE REALLY BROTHERS...
HOWEVER, THOUGH THEY'RE BOTH ATTRACTIVE AND HAVE A LOT OF CHARISMA, THEIR PERSONALITIES COULDN'T BE ANY MORE DIFFERENT.

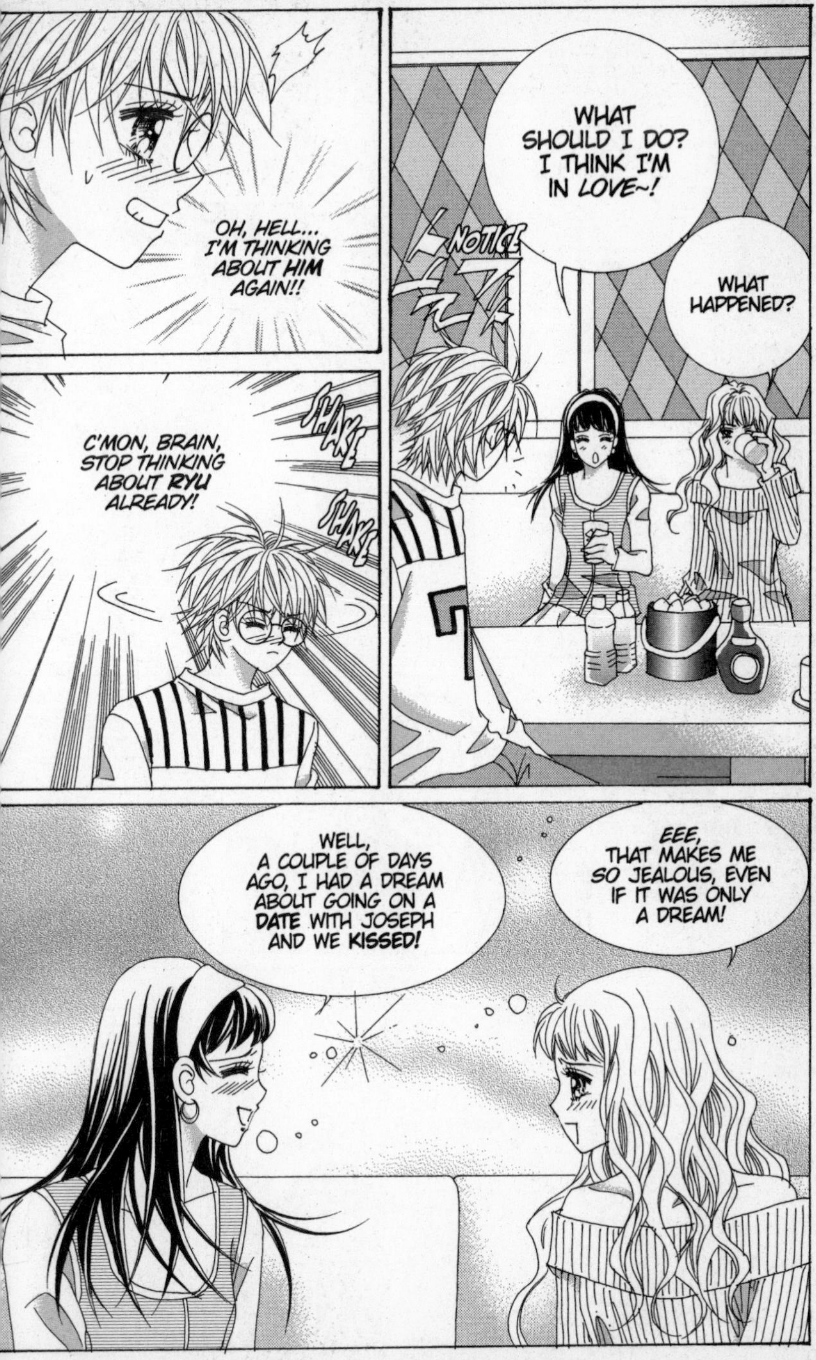
OH, HELL... I'M THINKING ABOUT HIM AGAIN!!
C'MON, BRAIN, STOP THINKING ABOUT RYU ALREADY!
SHAKE
SHAKE
WHAT SHOULD I DO? I THINK I'M IN LOVE~!
NOTICE
WHAT HAPPENED?
WELL, A COUPLE OF DAYS AGO, I HAD A DREAM ABOUT GOING ON A DATE WITH JOSEPH AND WE KISSED!
EEE, THAT MAKES ME SO JEALOUS, EVEN IF IT WAS ONLY A DREAM!

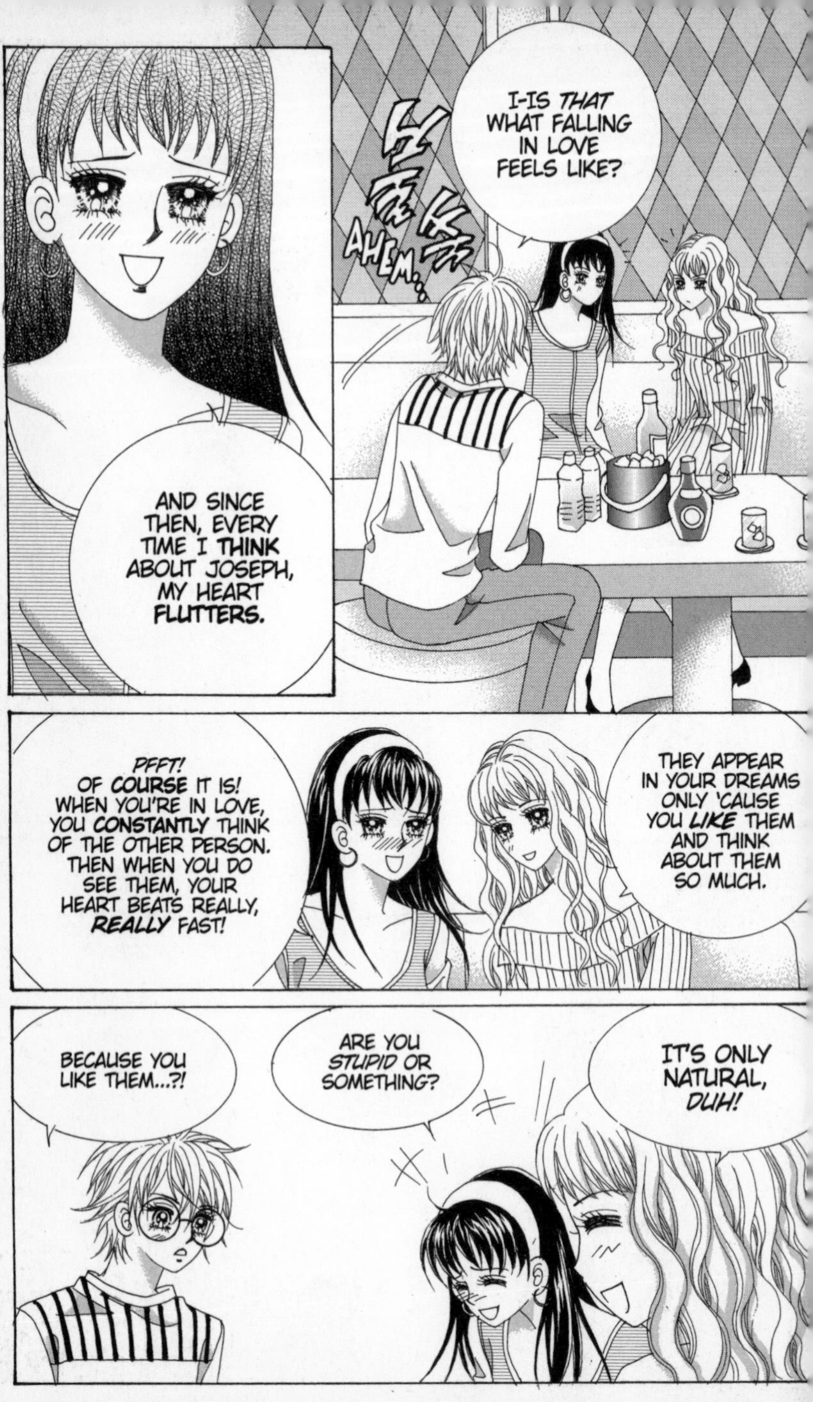

AND SINCE THEN, EVERY TIME I **THINK** ABOUT JOSEPH, MY HEART **FLUTTERS.**
I-IS *THAT* WHAT FALLING IN LOVE FEELS LIKE?
AHEM...
PFFT! OF **COURSE** IT IS! WHEN YOU'RE IN LOVE, YOU **CONSTANTLY** THINK OF THE OTHER PERSON. THEN WHEN YOU DO SEE THEM, YOUR HEART BEATS REALLY, ***REALLY*** FAST!
THEY APPEAR IN YOUR DREAMS ONLY 'CAUSE YOU ***LIKE*** THEM AND THINK ABOUT THEM SO MUCH.
BECAUSE YOU LIKE THEM...?!
ARE YOU *STUPID* OR SOMETHING?
IT'S ONLY NATURAL, *DUH!*

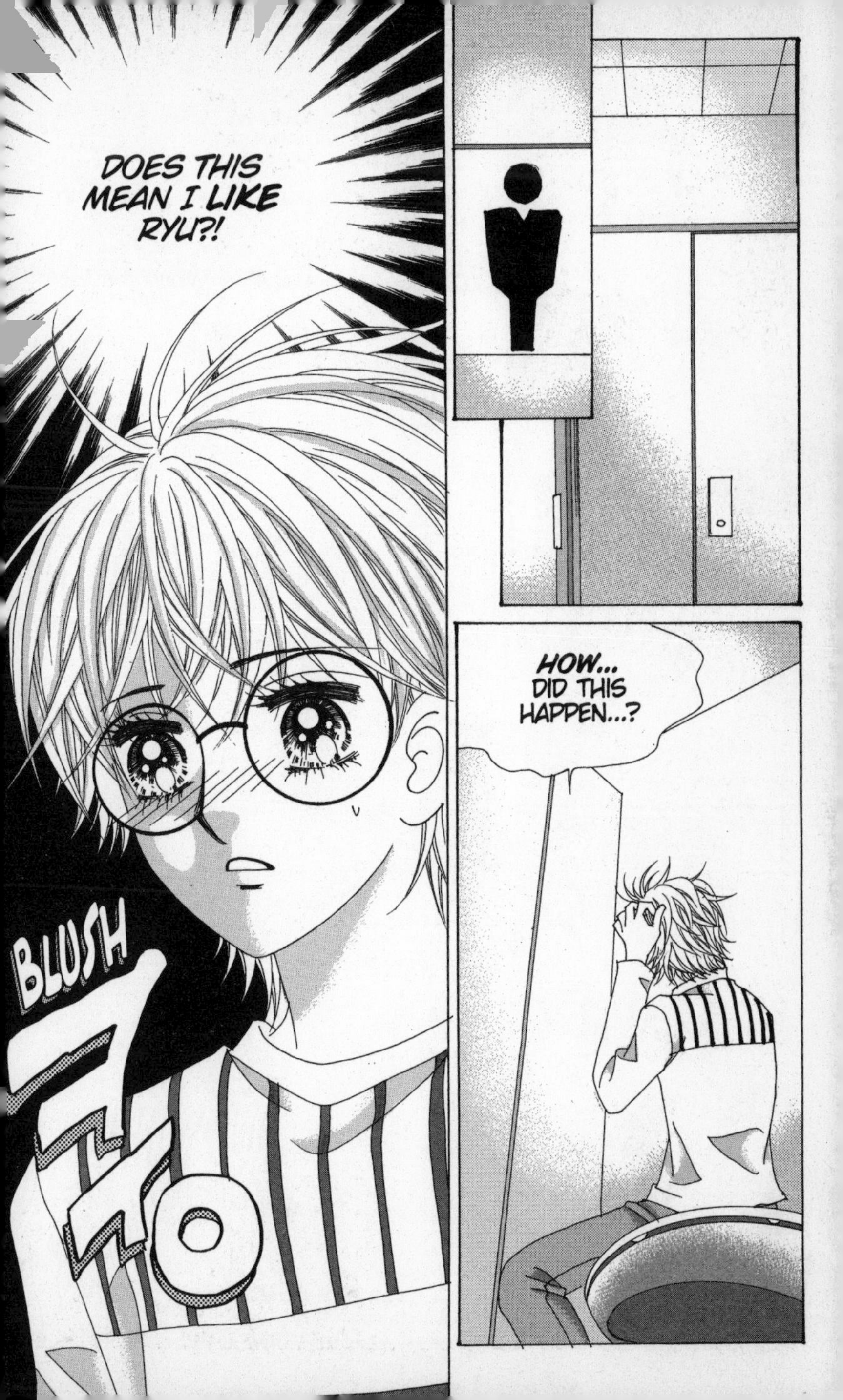
DOES THIS MEAN I LIKE RYU?!
BLUSH
HOW... DID THIS HAPPEN...?

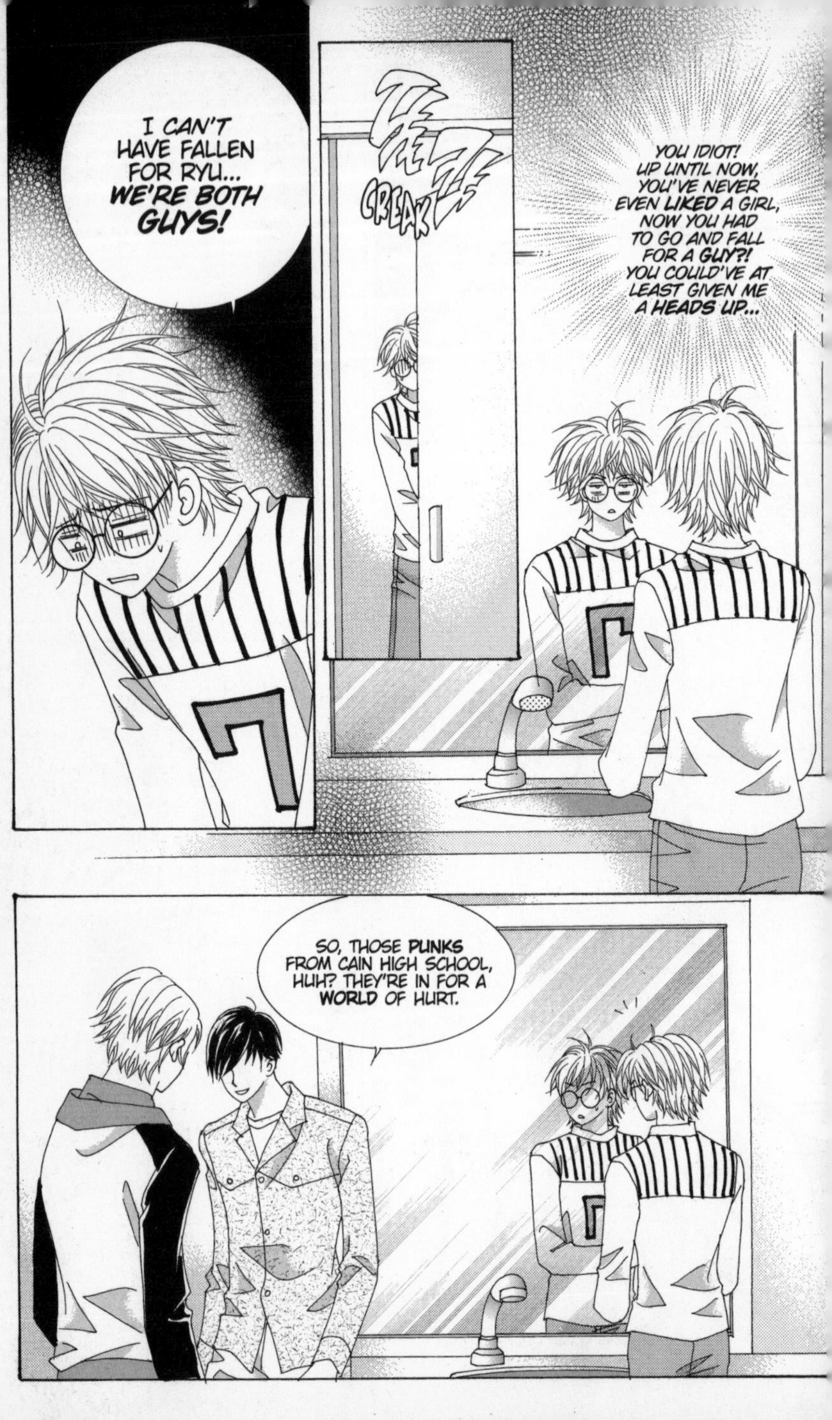
I CAN'T HAVE FALLEN FOR RYU... WE'RE BOTH GUYS!
CREAK
YOU IDIOT! UP UNTIL NOW, YOU'VE NEVER EVEN LIKED A GIRL, NOW YOU HAD TO GO AND FALL FOR A GUY?! YOU COULD'VE AT LEAST GIVEN ME A HEADS UP...
SO, THOSE PUNKS FROM CAIN HIGH SCHOOL, HUH? THEY'RE IN FOR A WORLD OF HURT.

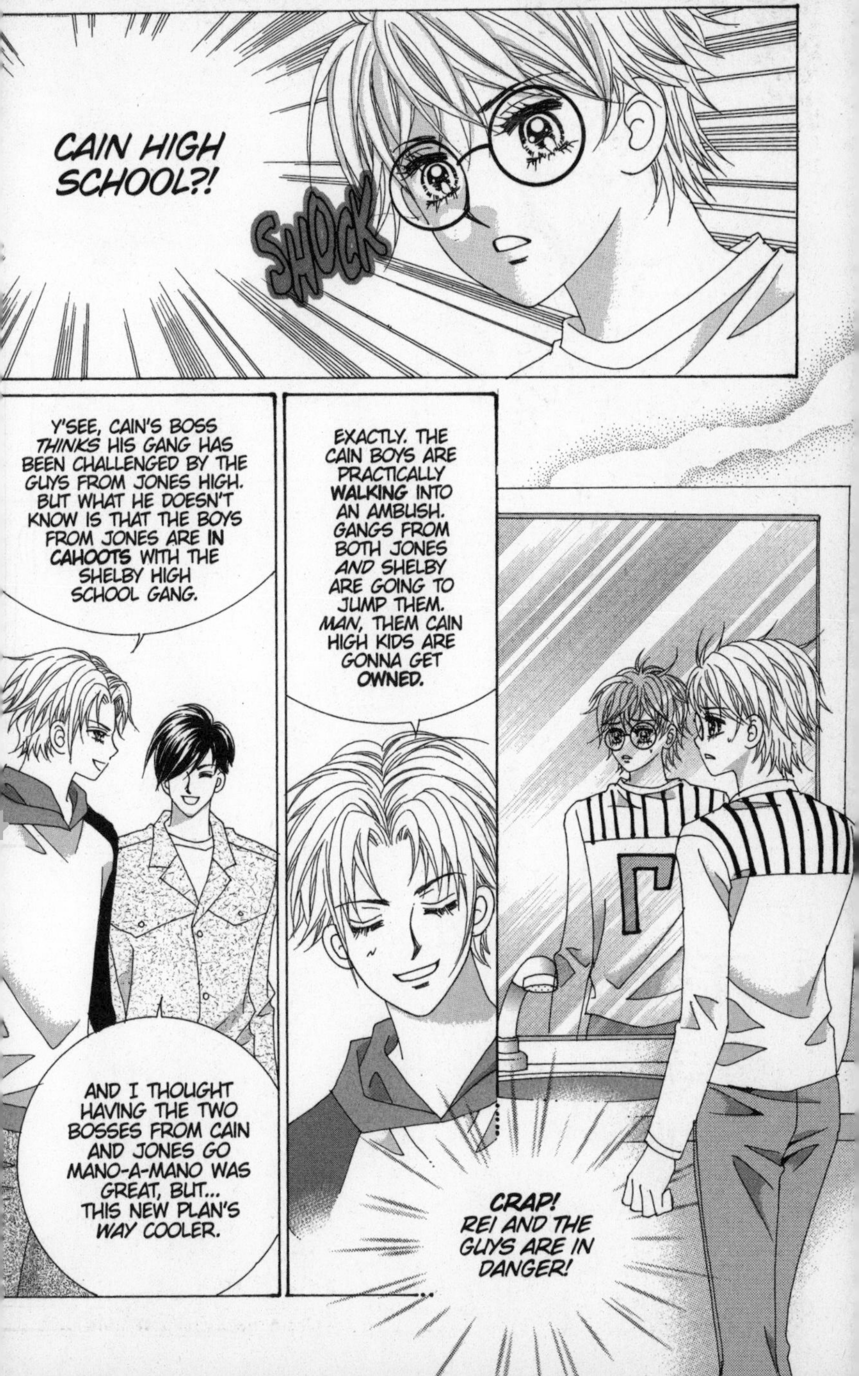
CAIN HIGH SCHOOL?!
SHOCK
Y'SEE, CAIN'S BOSS THINKS HIS GANG HAS BEEN CHALLENGED BY THE GUYS FROM JONES HIGH. BUT WHAT HE DOESN'T KNOW IS THAT THE BOYS FROM JONES ARE IN CAHOOTS WITH THE SHELBY HIGH SCHOOL GANG.
AND I THOUGHT HAVING THE TWO BOSSES FROM CAIN AND JONES GO MANO-A-MANO WAS GREAT, BUT... THIS NEW PLAN'S WAY COOLER.
EXACTLY. THE CAIN BOYS ARE PRACTICALLY WALKING INTO AN AMBUSH. GANGS FROM BOTH JONES AND SHELBY ARE GOING TO JUMP THEM. MAN, THEM CAIN HIGH KIDS ARE GONNA GET OWNED.
CRAP! REI AND THE GUYS ARE IN DANGER!

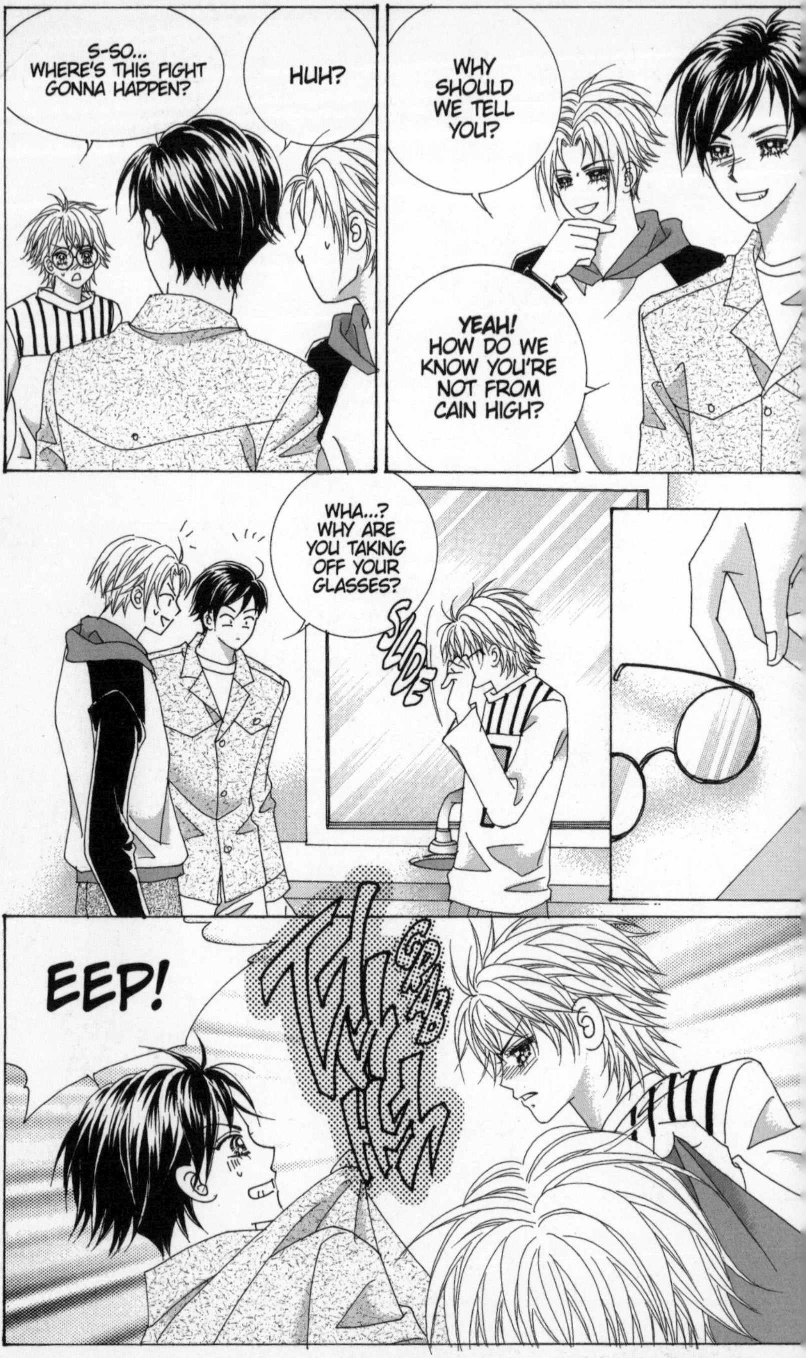
S-SO...
WHERE'S THIS FIGHT
GONNA HAPPEN?
HUH?
WHY
SHOULD
WE TELL
YOU?
YEAH!
HOW DO WE
KNOW YOU'RE
NOT FROM
CAIN HIGH?
WHA...?
WHY ARE
YOU TAKING
OFF YOUR
GLASSES?
SLIDE
EEP!

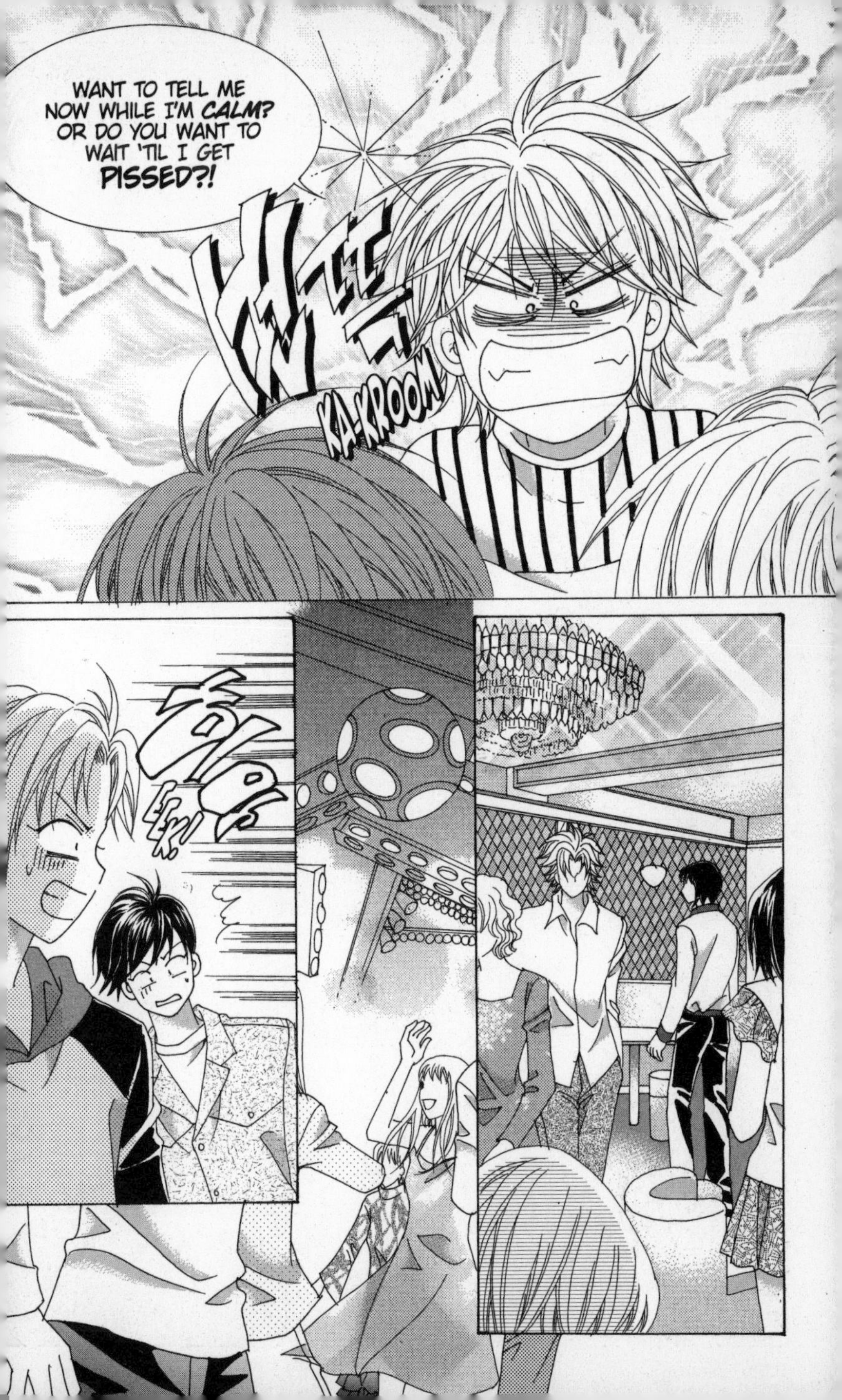
WANT TO TELL ME NOW WHILE I'M CALM? OR DO YOU WANT TO WAIT 'TIL I GET PISSED?!
KA-KROOM
EEK!

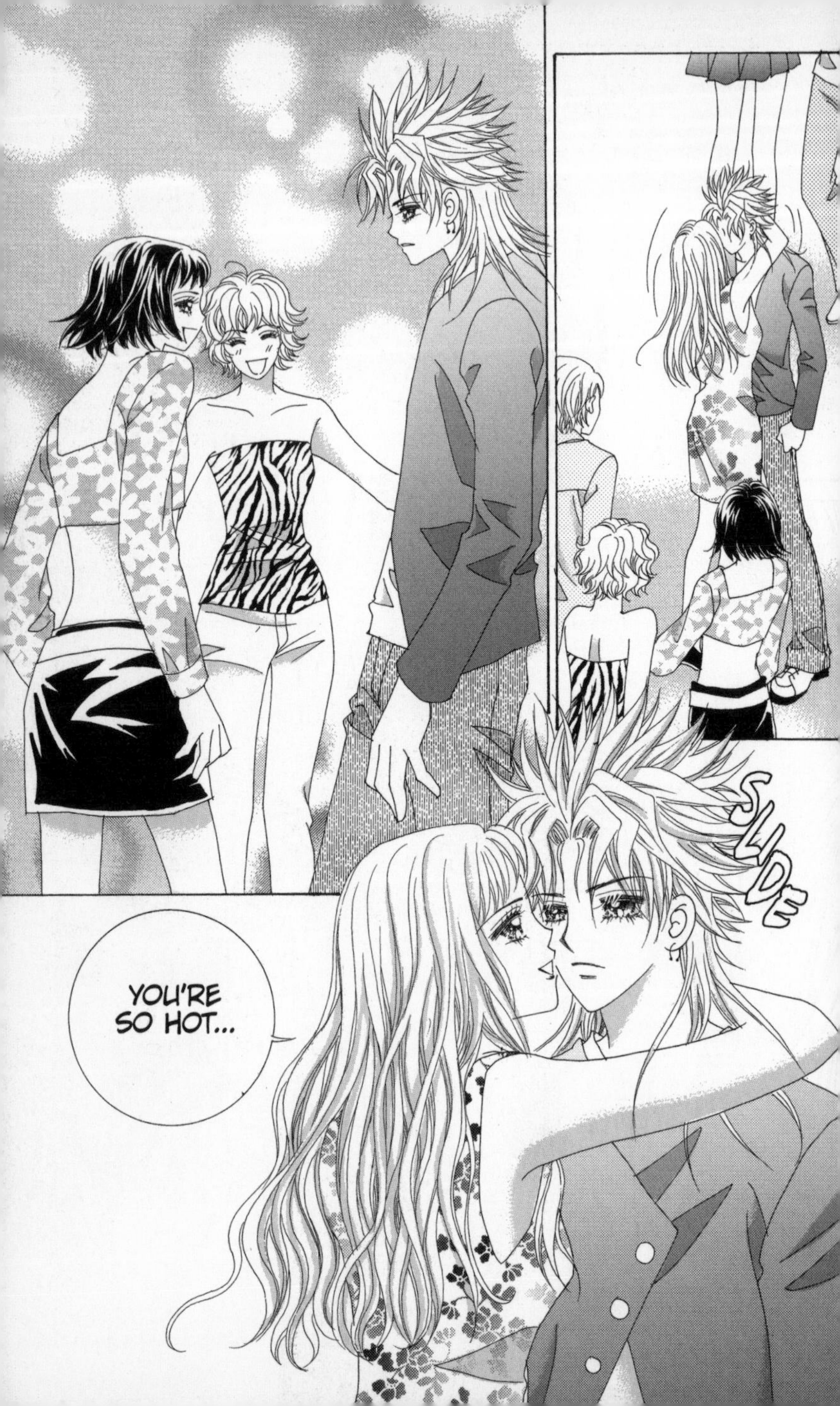
SLIDE
YOU'RE SO HOT...

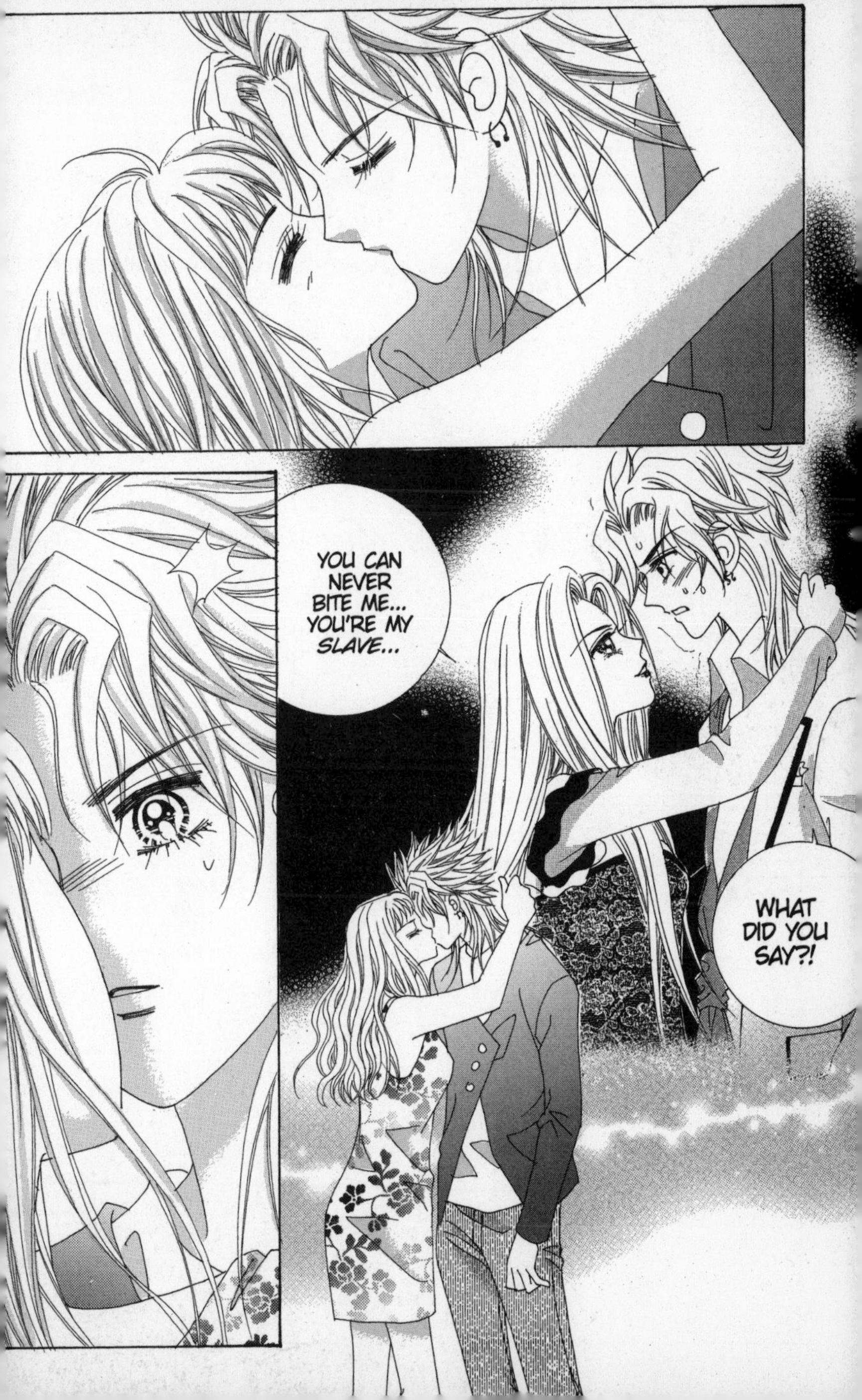
YOU CAN NEVER BITE ME... YOU'RE MY *SLAVE*...
WHAT DID YOU SAY?!

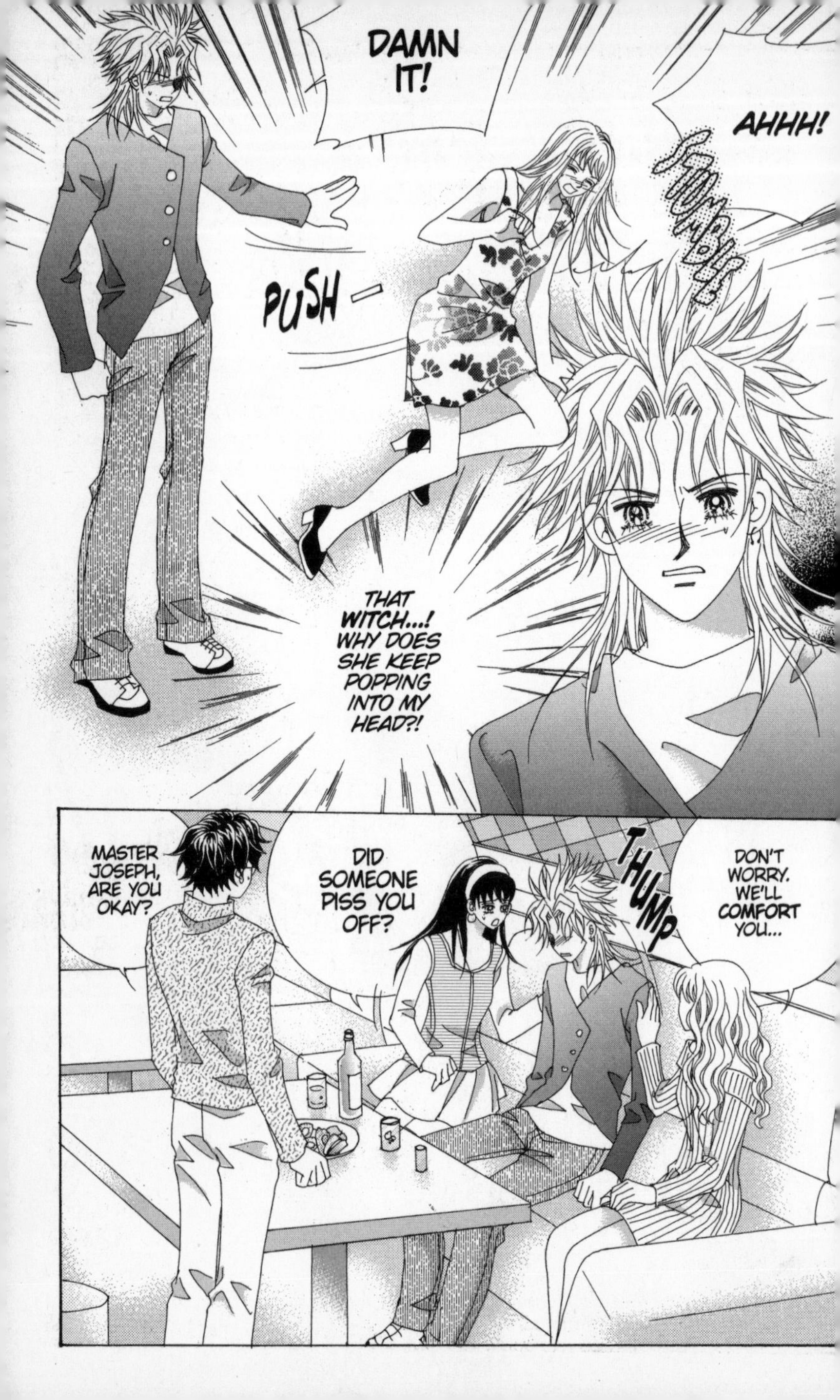
DAMN IT!
AHHH!
PUSH
THAT WITCH...! WHY DOES SHE KEEP POPPING INTO MY HEAD?!
MASTER JOSEPH, ARE YOU OKAY?
DID SOMEONE PISS YOU OFF?
THUMP
DON'T WORRY. WE'LL COMFORT YOU...

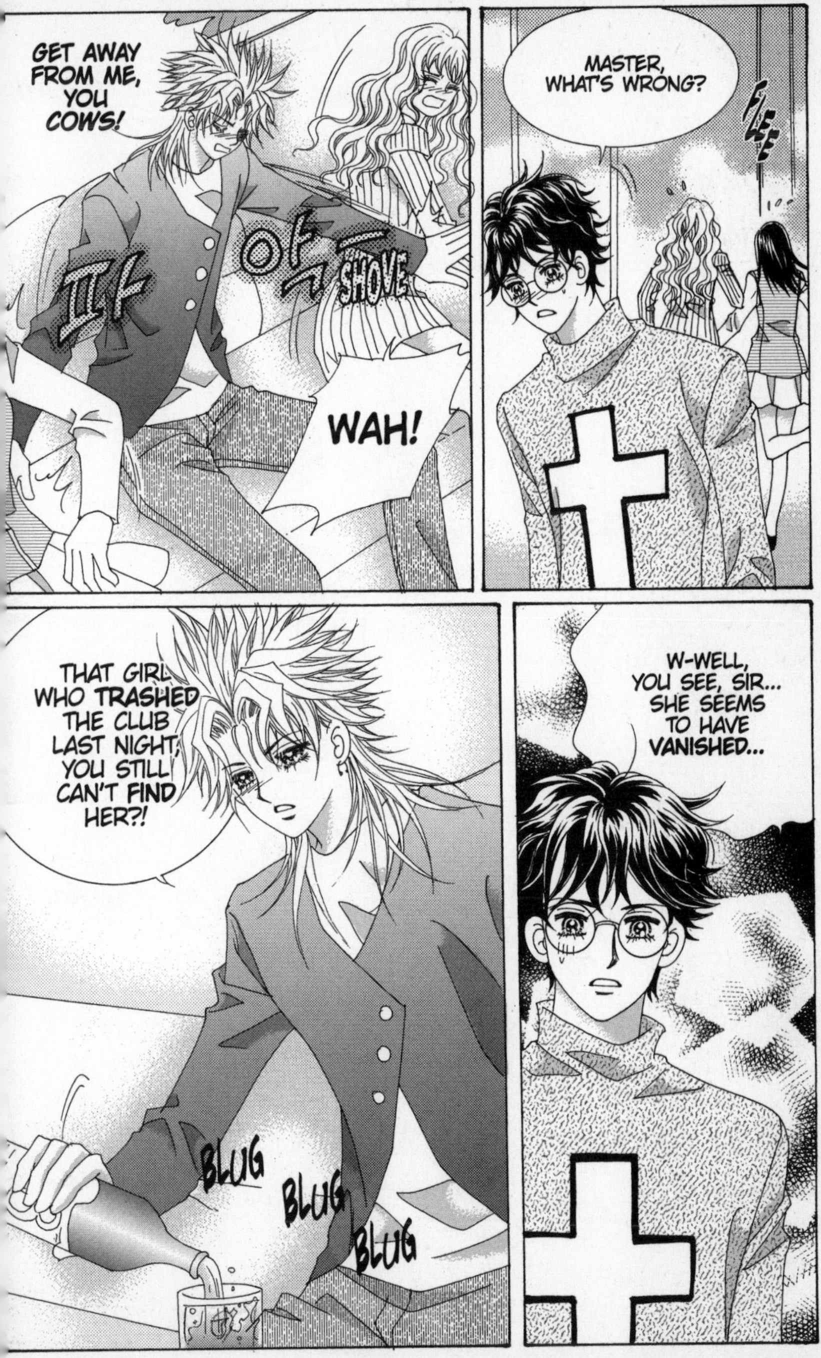
GET AWAY FROM ME, YOU COWS!
SHOVE
WAH!
MASTER, WHAT'S WRONG?
FLEE
THAT GIRL WHO TRASHED THE CLUB LAST NIGHT, YOU STILL CAN'T FIND HER?!
BLUG
BLUG
BLUG
W-WELL, YOU SEE, SIR... SHE SEEMS TO HAVE VANISHED...

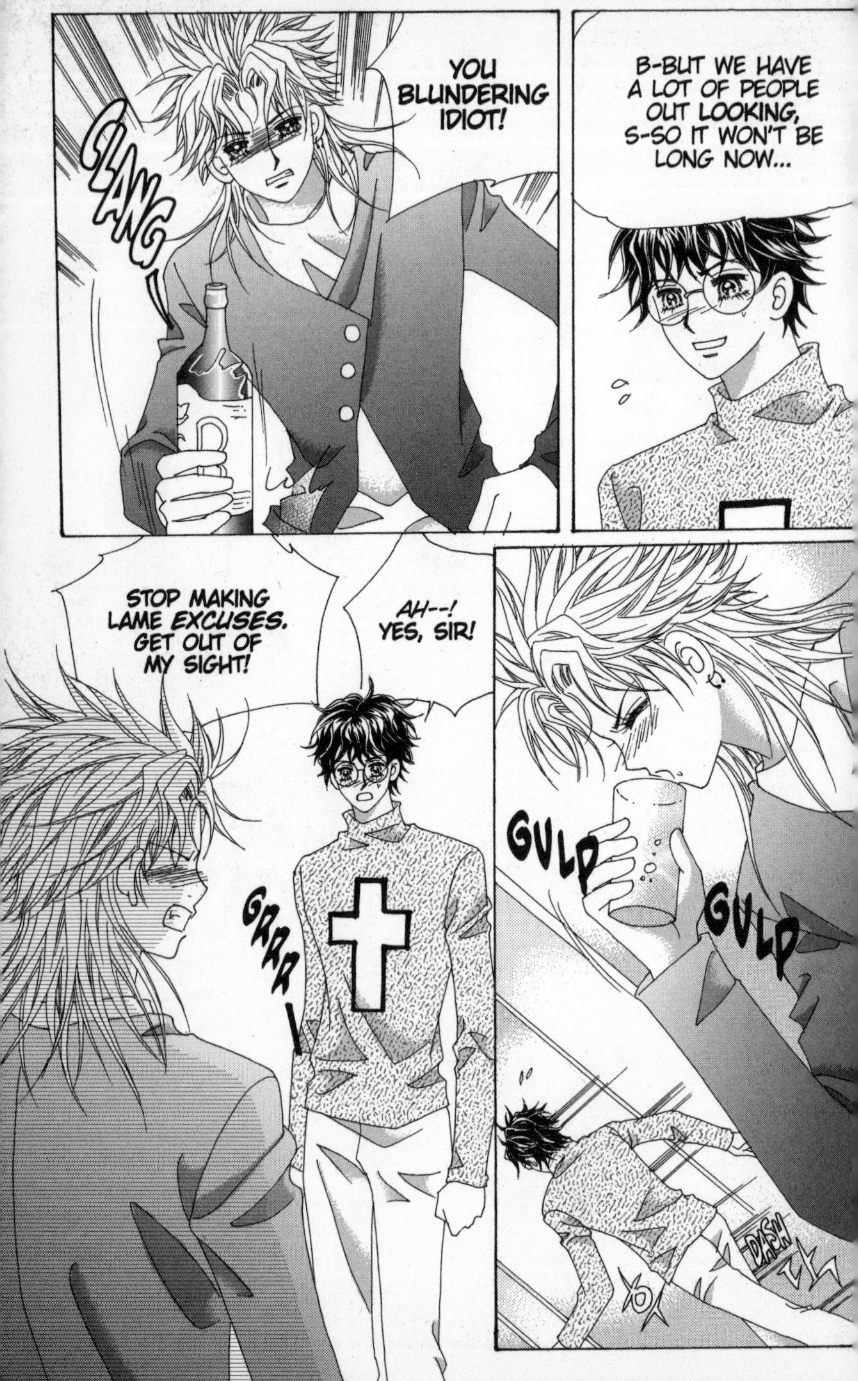
CLANG
YOU BLUNDERING IDIOT!
B-BUT WE HAVE A LOT OF PEOPLE OUT LOOKING, S-SO IT WON'T BE LONG NOW...
GULP
GULP
AH--! YES, SIR!
STOP MAKING LAME *EXCUSES.* GET OUT OF MY SIGHT!
GRRR
DASH

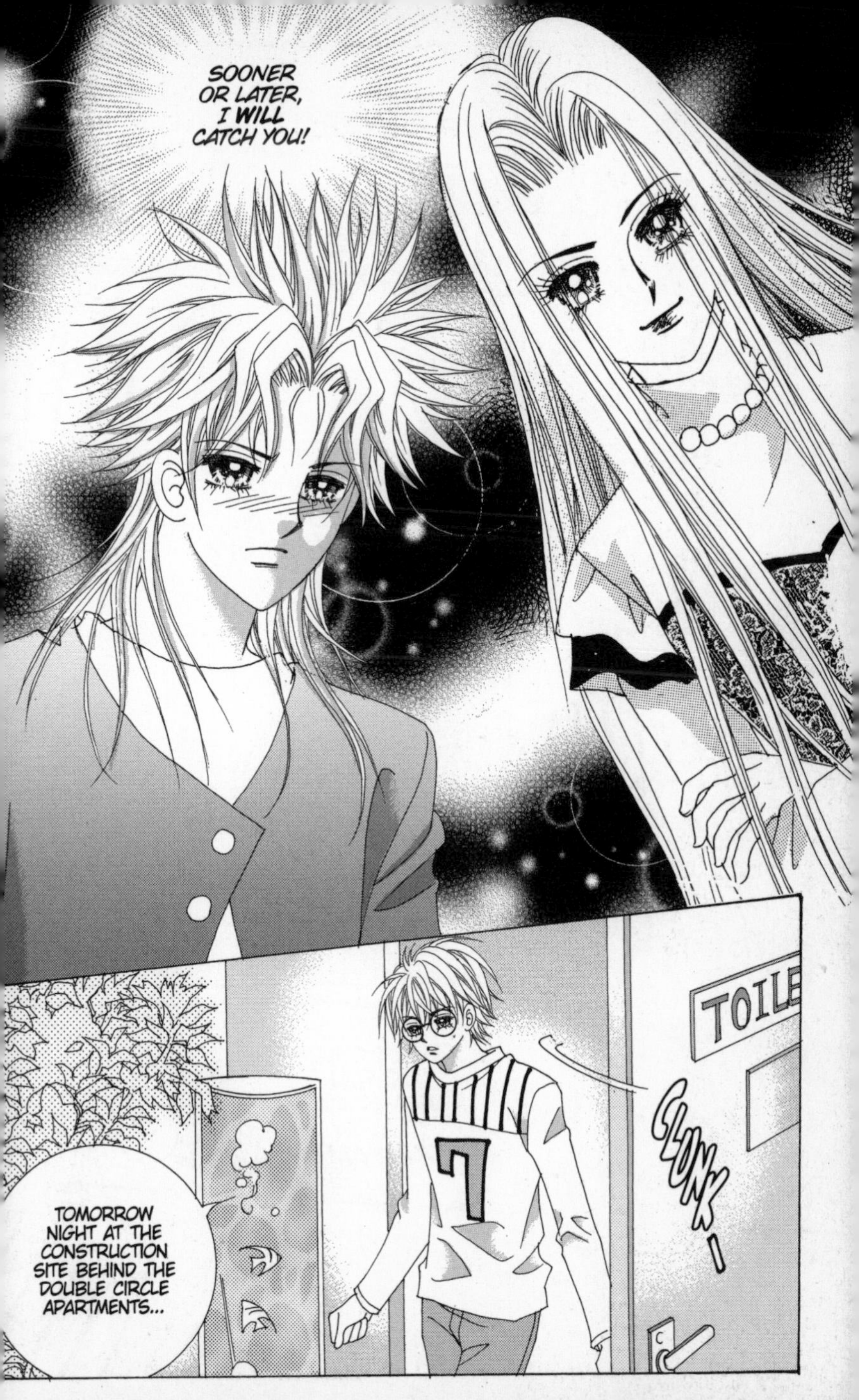
SOONER OR LATER, I WILL CATCH YOU!
TOMORROW NIGHT AT THE CONSTRUCTION SITE BEHIND THE DOUBLE CIRCLE APARTMENTS...
TOILE
CLONK-

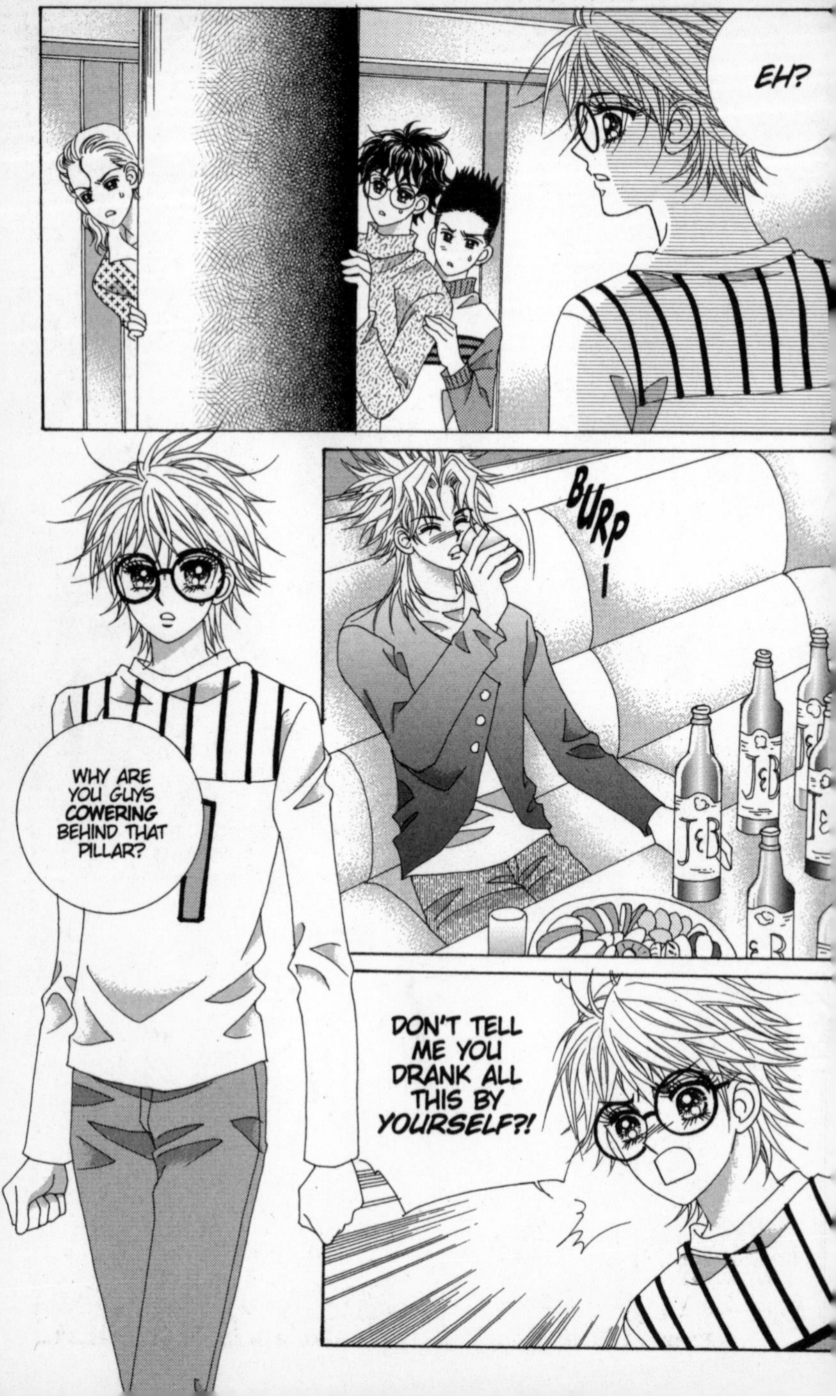
EH?
WHY ARE YOU GUYS COWERING BEHIND THAT PILLAR?
BURP
DON'T TELL ME YOU DRANK ALL THIS BY YOURSELF?!

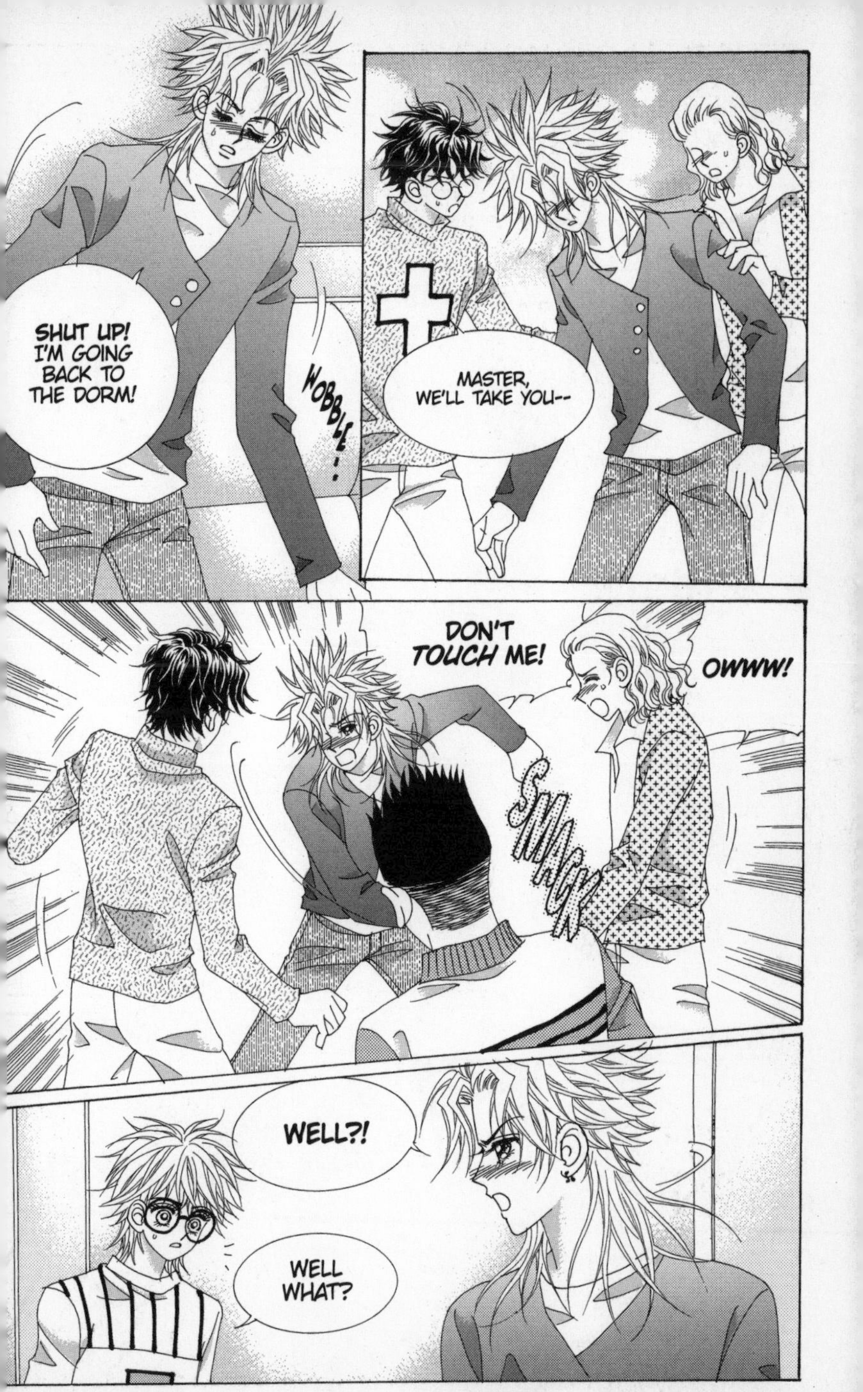
SHUT UP! I'M GOING BACK TO THE DORM!
WOBBLE...
MASTER, WE'LL TAKE YOU--
DON'T TOUCH ME!
OWWW!
SMACK
WELL?!
WELL WHAT?

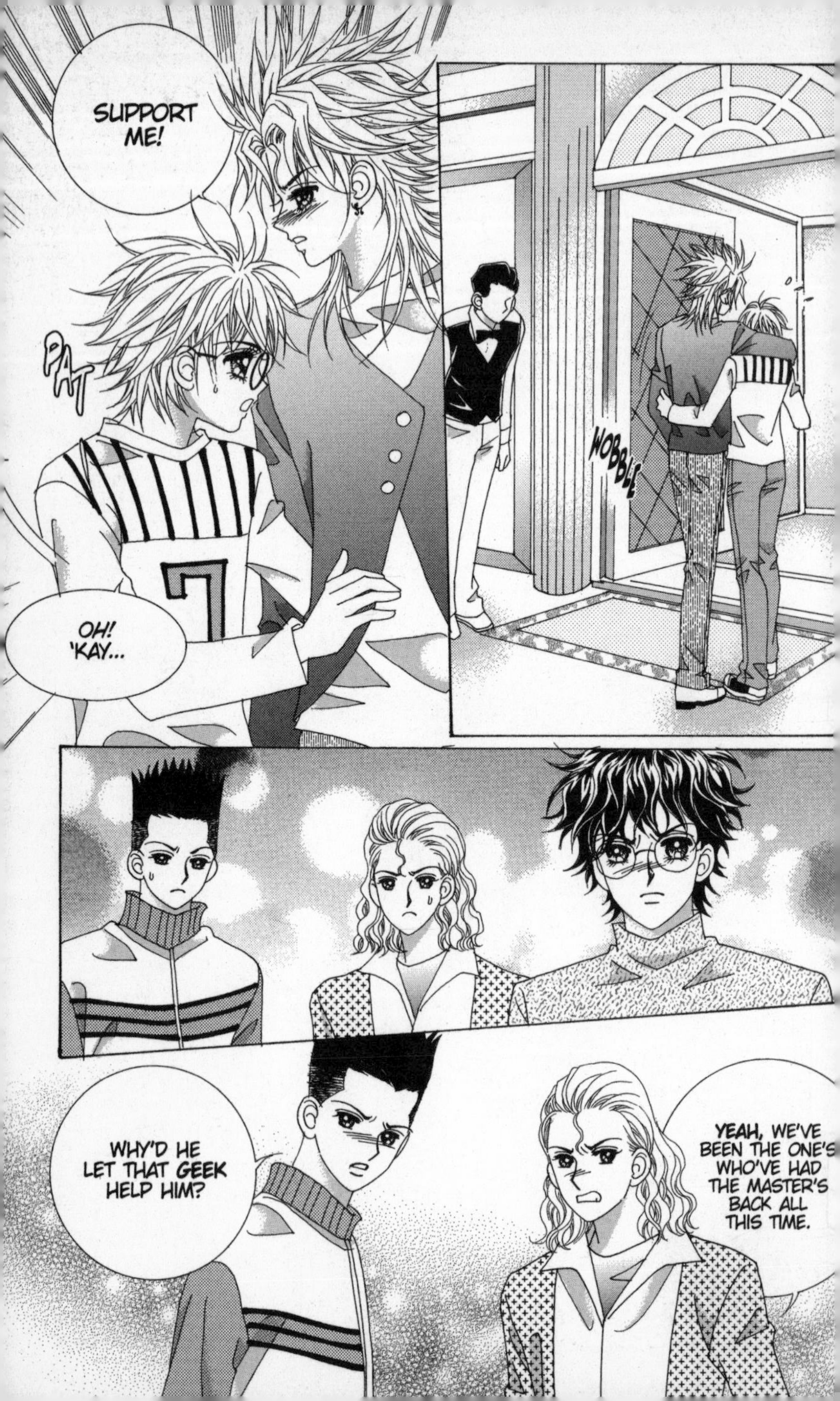

SUPPORT ME!
PAT
OH! 'KAY...
WOBBLE
WHY'D HE LET THAT GEEK HELP HIM?
YEAH, WE'VE BEEN THE ONE'S WHO'VE HAD THE MASTER'S BACK ALL THIS TIME.

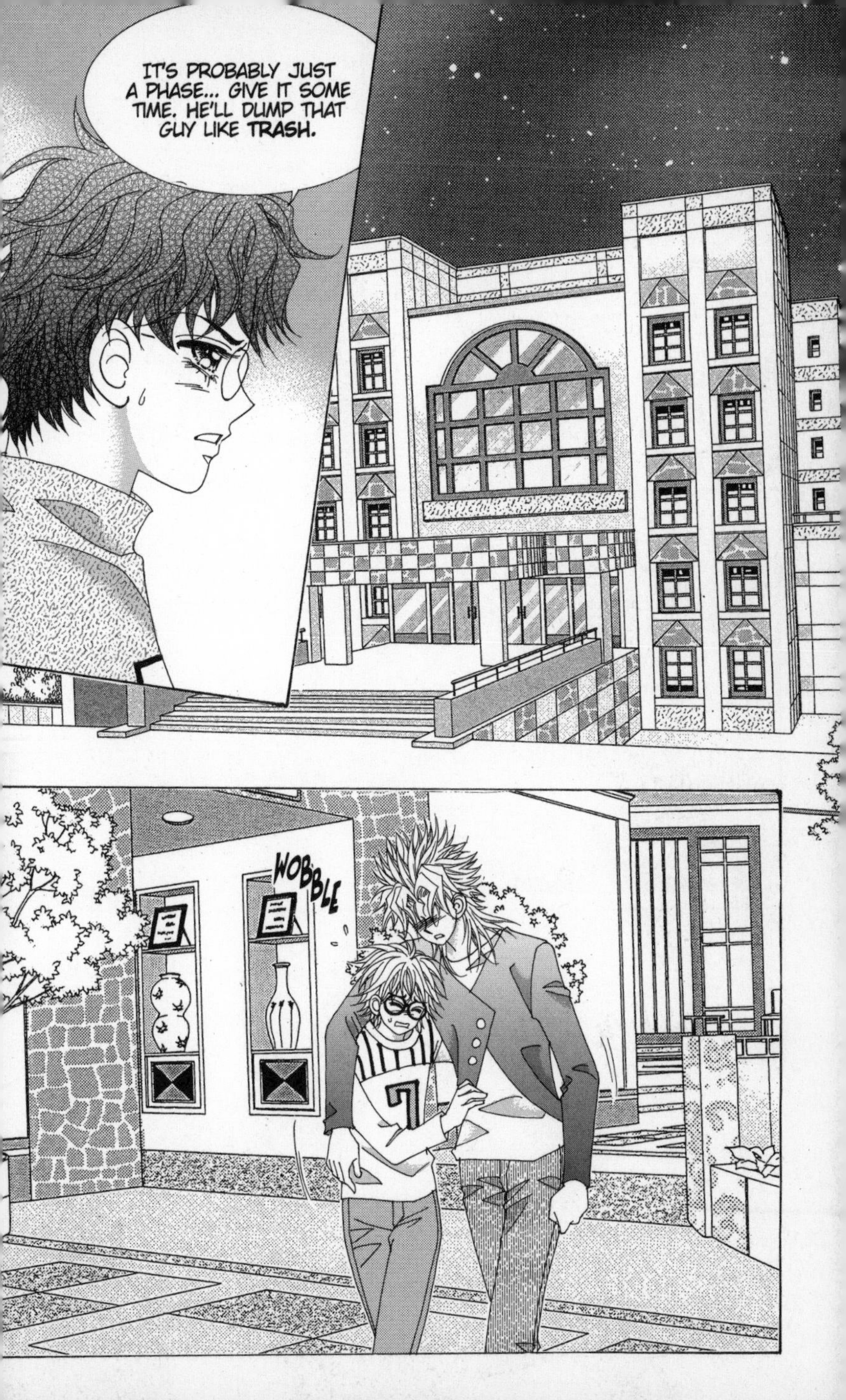
IT'S PROBABLY JUST A PHASE... GIVE IT SOME TIME. HE'LL DUMP THAT GUY LIKE TRASH.
WOBBLE

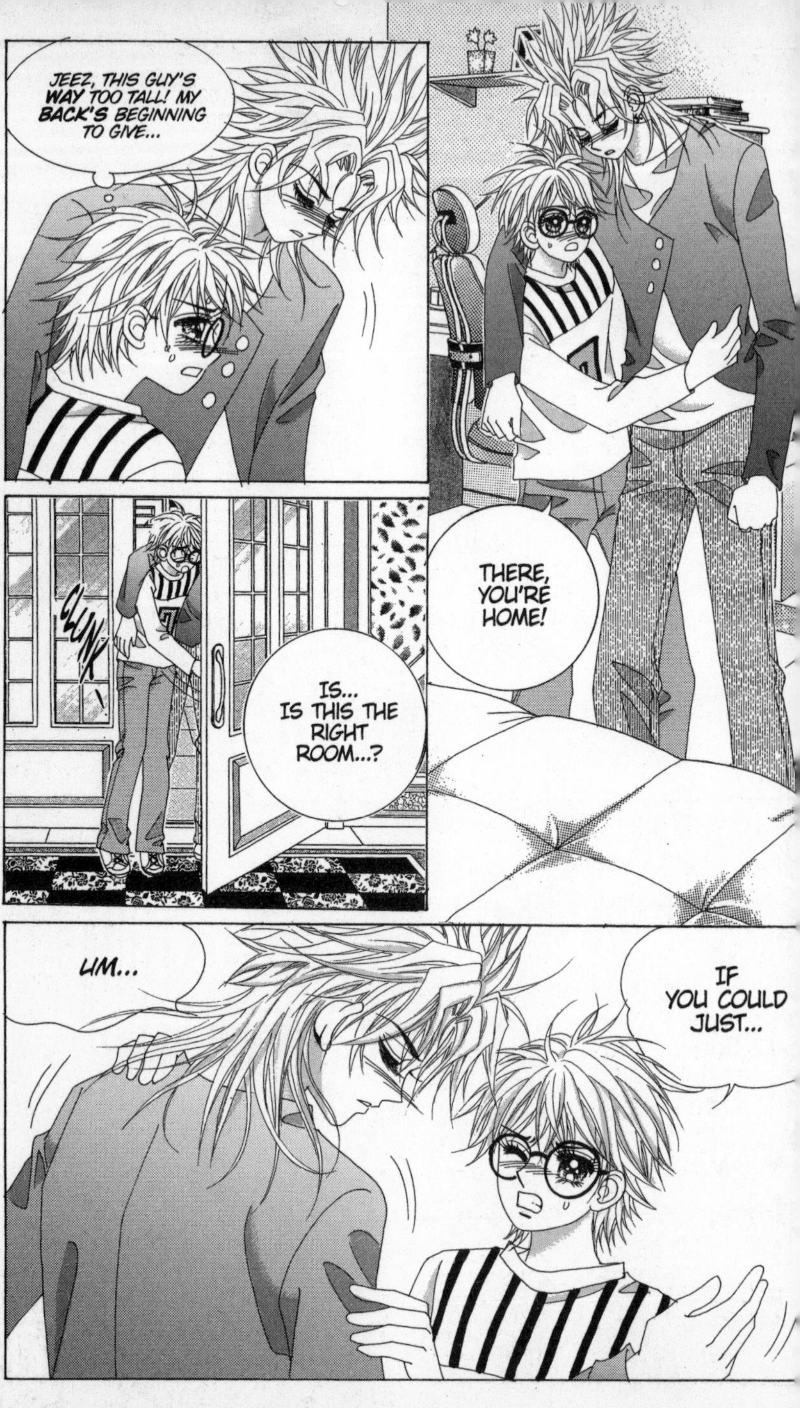

JEEZ, THIS GUY'S WAY TOO TALL! MY BACK'S BEGINNING TO GIVE...
CLUNK
IS... IS THIS THE RIGHT ROOM...?
THERE, YOU'RE HOME!
UM...
IF YOU COULD JUST...

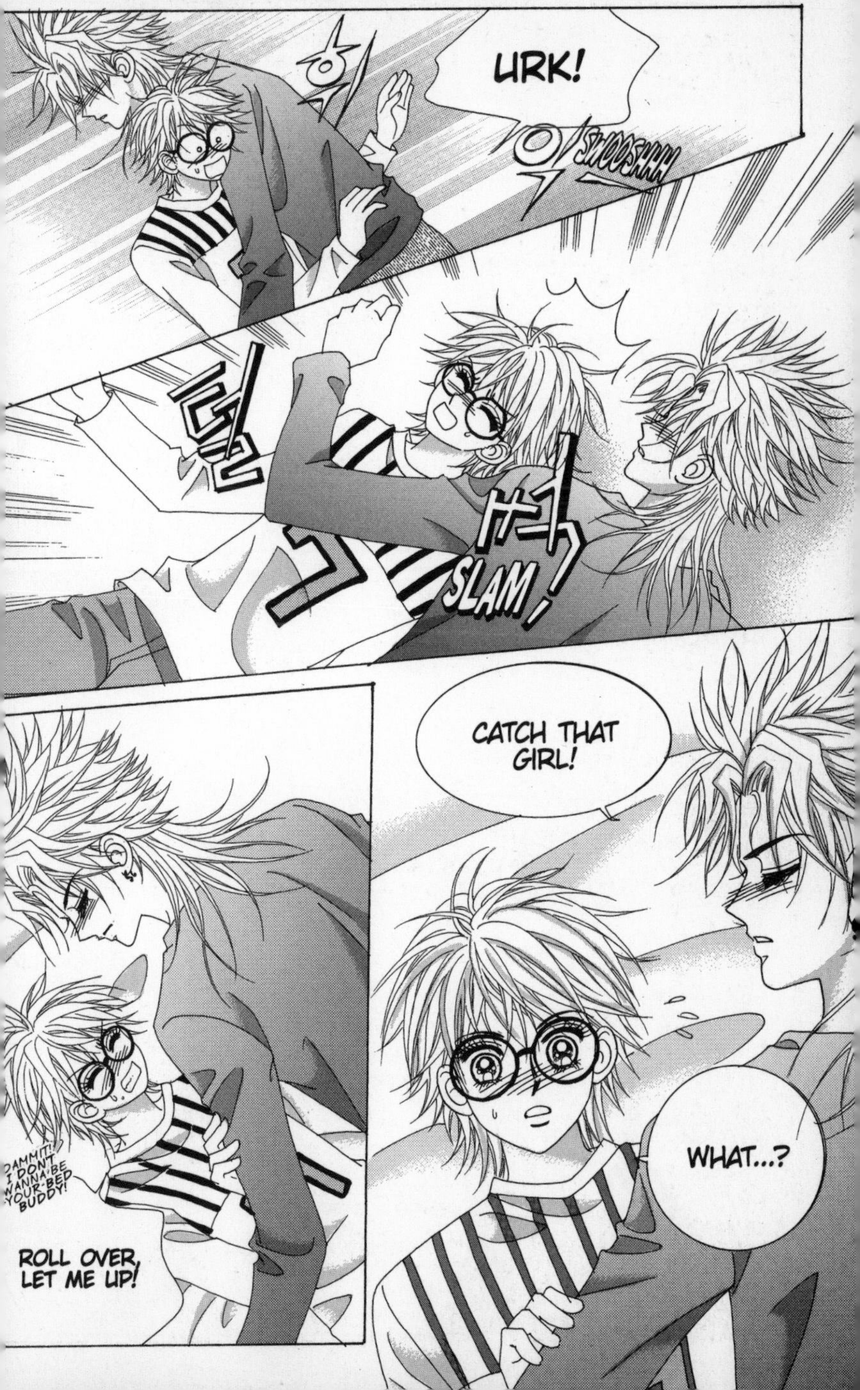
URK!
SWOOSHHH
SLAM!
DAMMIT! I DON'T WANNA BE YOUR BED BUDDY!
ROLL OVER, LET ME UP!
CATCH THAT GIRL!
WHAT...?

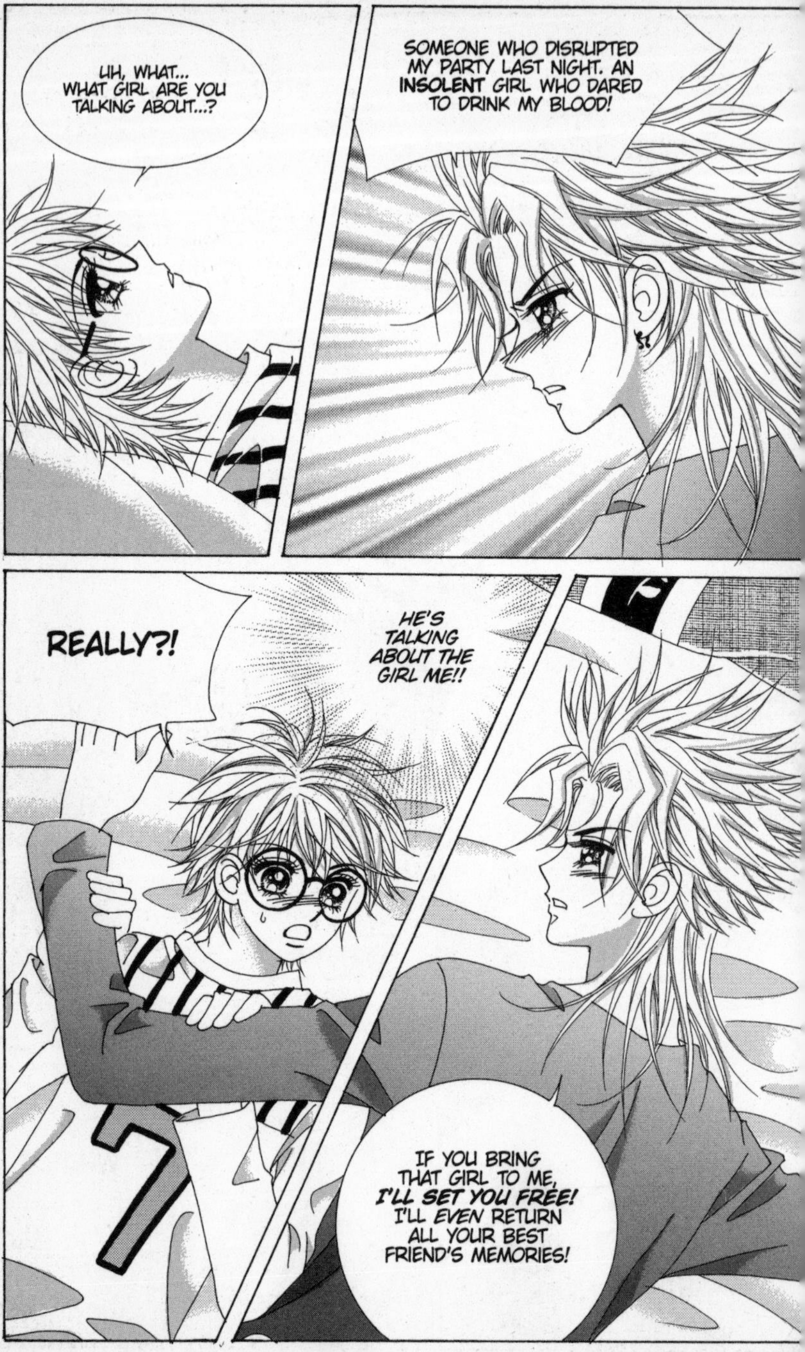
UH, WHAT... WHAT GIRL ARE YOU TALKING ABOUT...?
SOMEONE WHO DISRUPTED MY PARTY LAST NIGHT. AN **INSOLENT** GIRL WHO DARED TO DRINK MY BLOOD!
REALLY?!
HE'S TALKING ABOUT THE GIRL ME!!
IF YOU BRING THAT GIRL TO ME, ***I'LL SET YOU FREE!*** I'LL *EVEN* RETURN ALL YOUR BEST FRIEND'S MEMORIES!

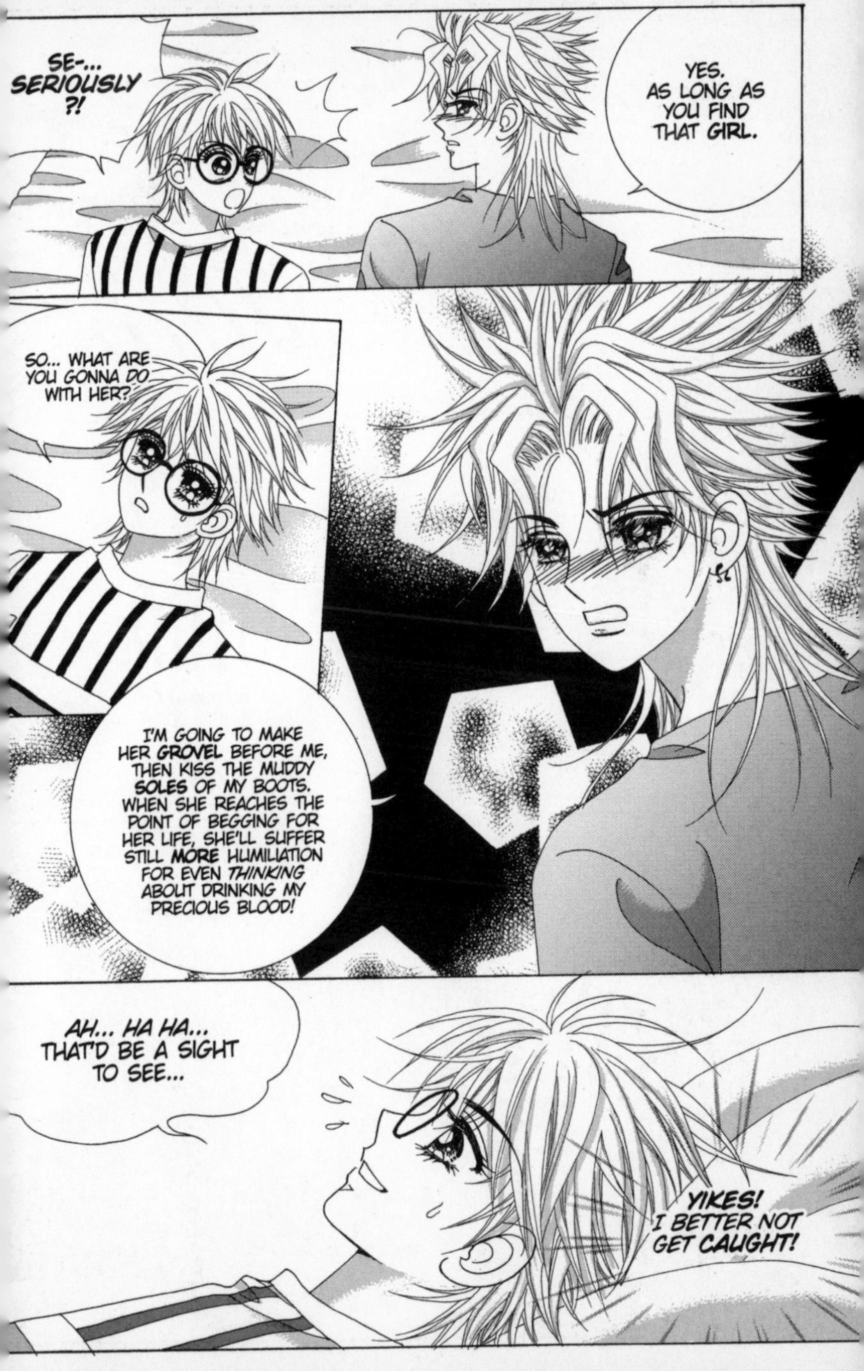

SE-... SERIOUSLY ?!
YES. AS LONG AS YOU FIND THAT GIRL.
SO... WHAT ARE YOU GONNA DO WITH HER?
I'M GOING TO MAKE HER GROVEL BEFORE ME, THEN KISS THE MUDDY SOLES OF MY BOOTS. WHEN SHE REACHES THE POINT OF BEGGING FOR HER LIFE, SHE'LL SUFFER STILL MORE HUMILIATION FOR EVEN THINKING ABOUT DRINKING MY PRECIOUS BLOOD!
AH... HA HA... THAT'D BE A SIGHT TO SEE...
YIKES! I BETTER NOT GET CAUGHT!

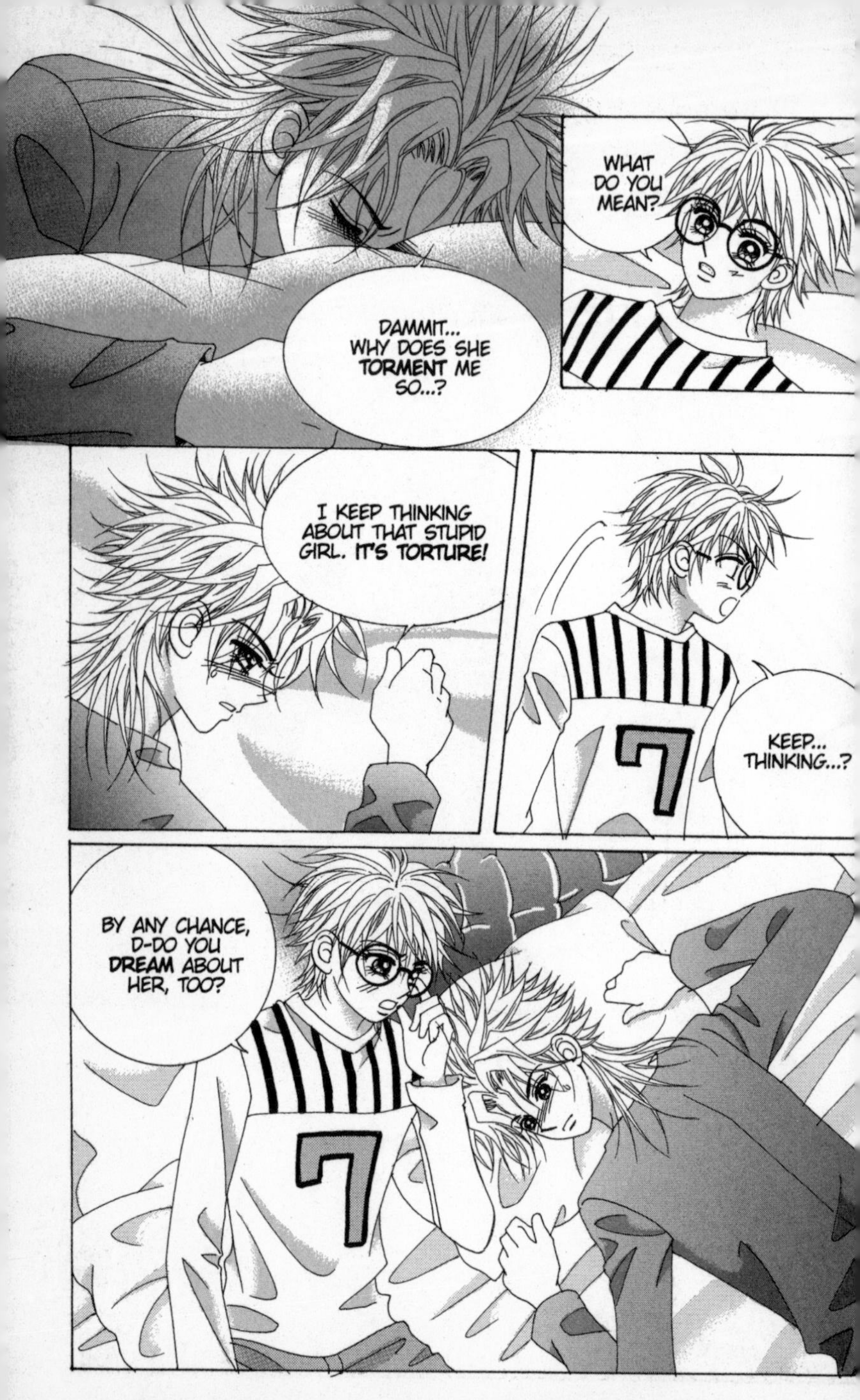
DAMMIT... WHY DOES SHE TORMENT ME SO...?
WHAT DO YOU MEAN?
I KEEP THINKING ABOUT THAT STUPID GIRL. IT'S TORTURE!
KEEP... THINKING...?
BY ANY CHANCE, D-DO YOU DREAM ABOUT HER, TOO?

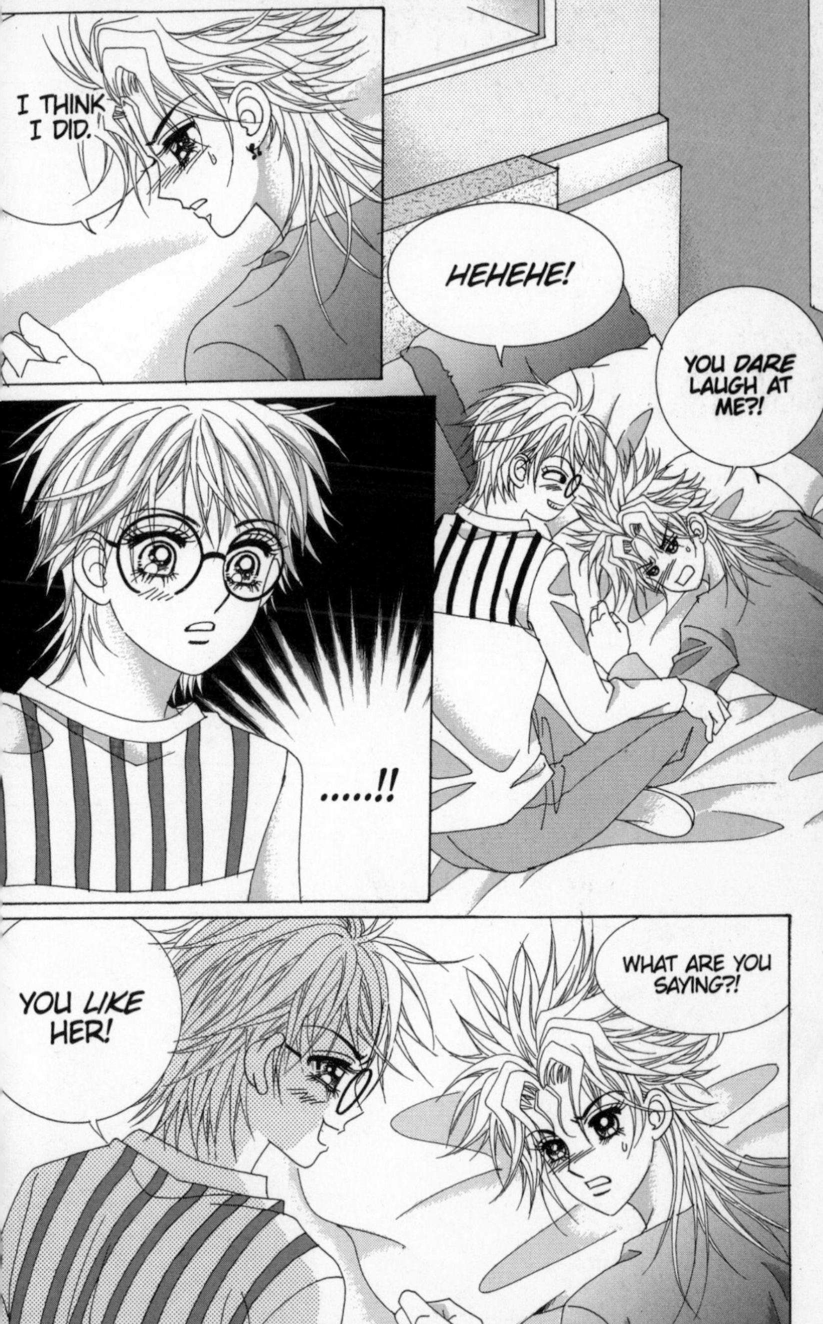
I THINK I DID.
.....!!
HEHEHE!
YOU DARE LAUGH AT ME?!
YOU LIKE HER!
WHAT ARE YOU SAYING?!

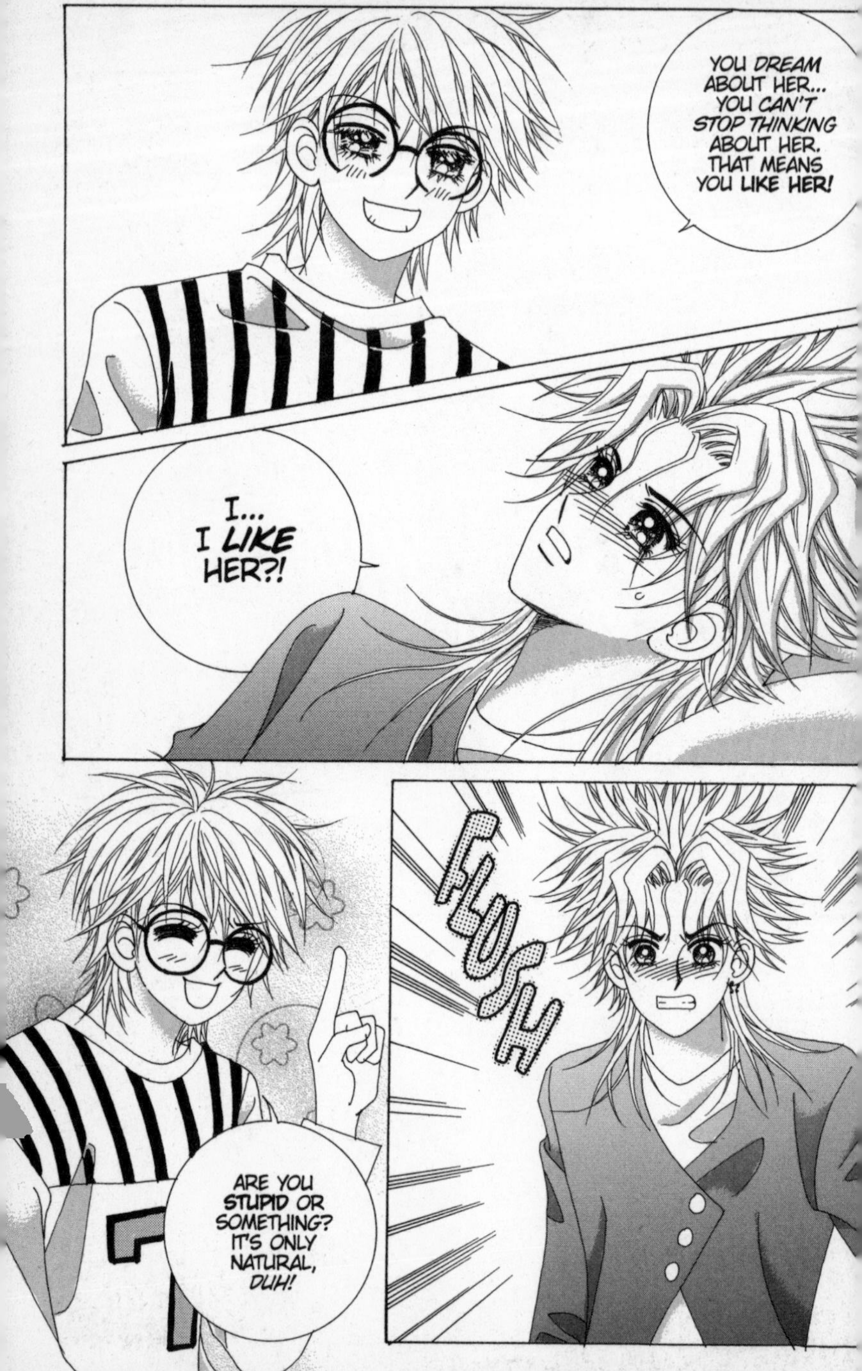
YOU DREAM ABOUT HER... YOU CAN'T STOP THINKING ABOUT HER. THAT MEANS YOU LIKE HER!
I... I LIKE HER?!
ARE YOU STUPID OR SOMETHING? IT'S ONLY NATURAL, DUH!
FLUSH

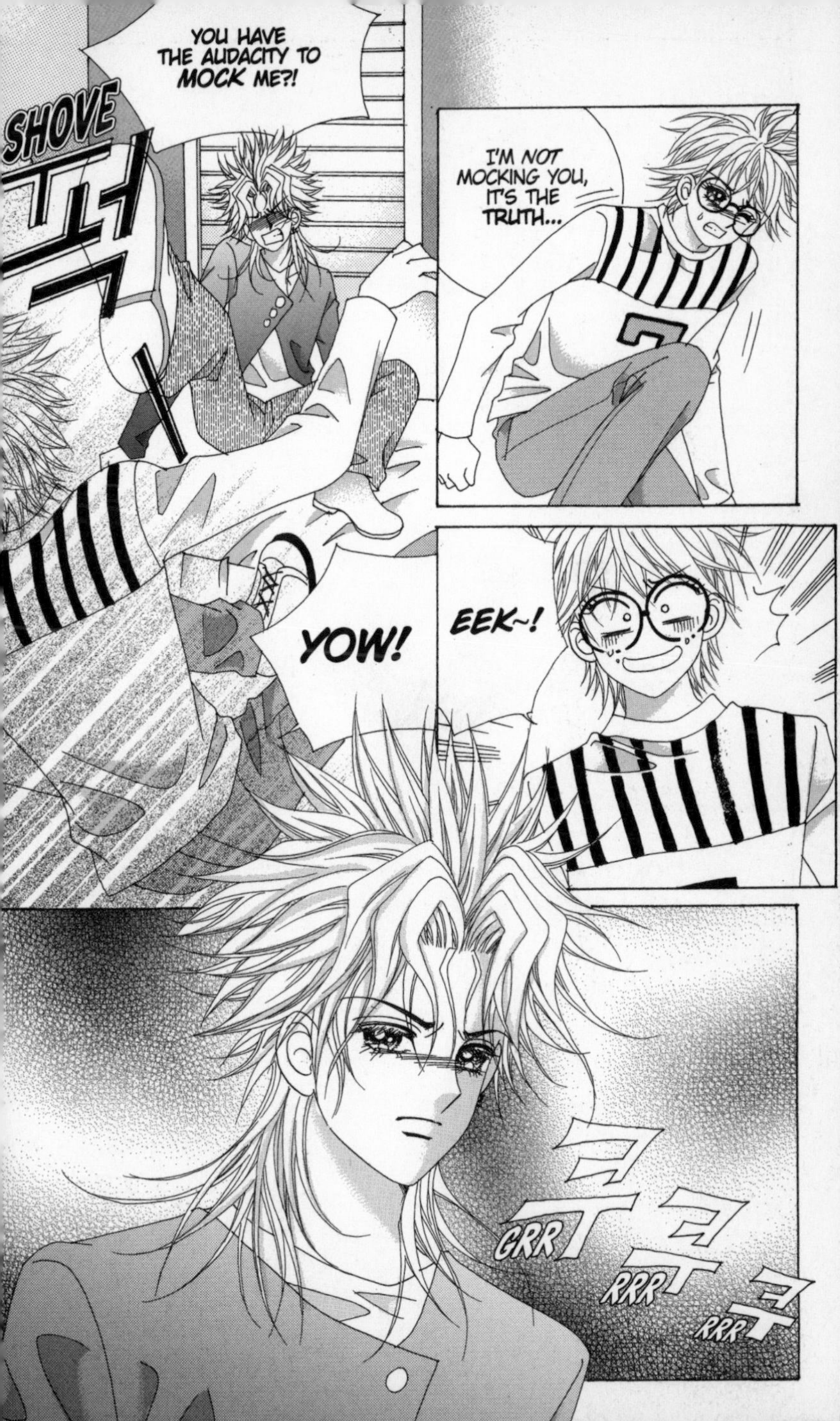
YOU HAVE THE AUDACITY TO MOCK ME?!
SHOVE
I'M NOT MOCKING YOU, IT'S THE TRUTH...
YOW!
EEK~!
GRR
RRR
RRR

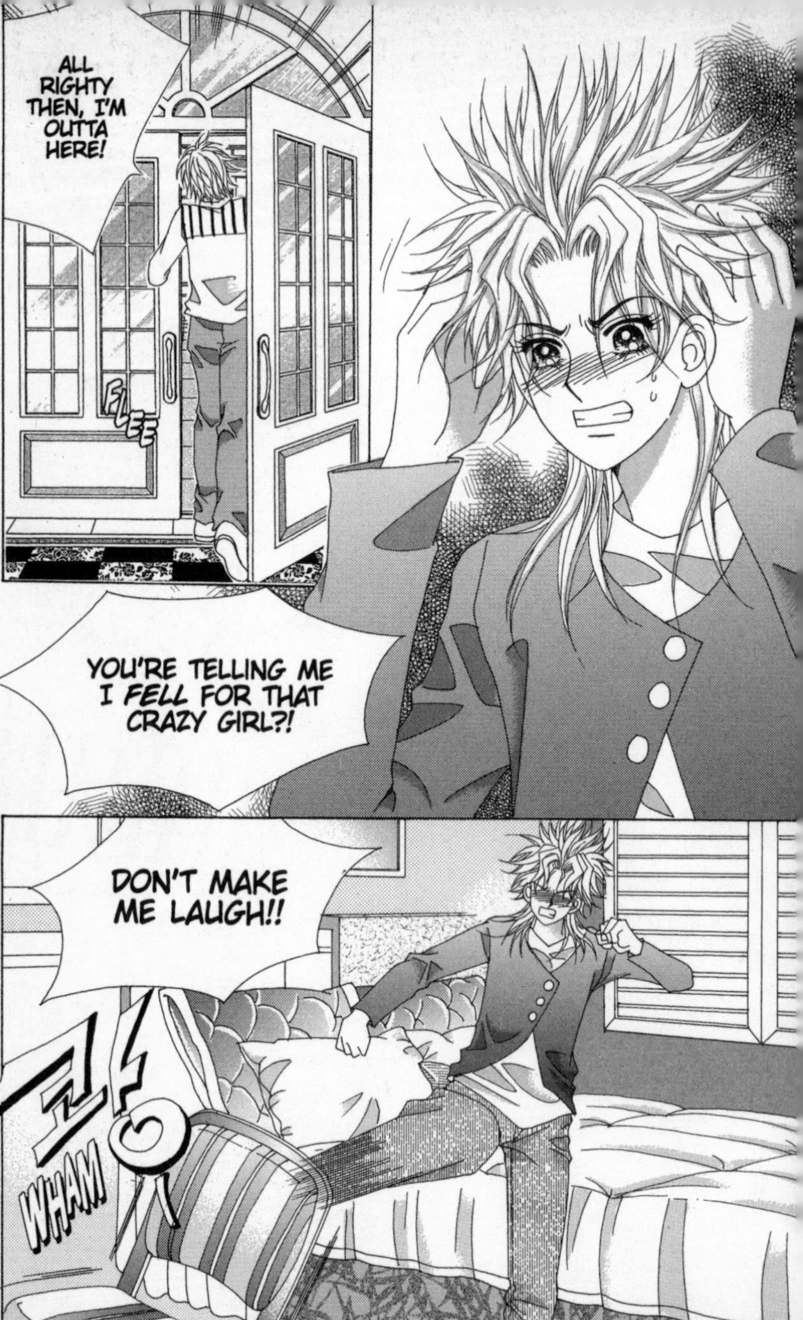
ALL RIGHTY THEN, I'M OUTTA HERE!
FLEE
YOU'RE TELLING ME I *FELL* FOR THAT CRAZY GIRL?!
DON'T MAKE ME LAUGH!!
WHAM

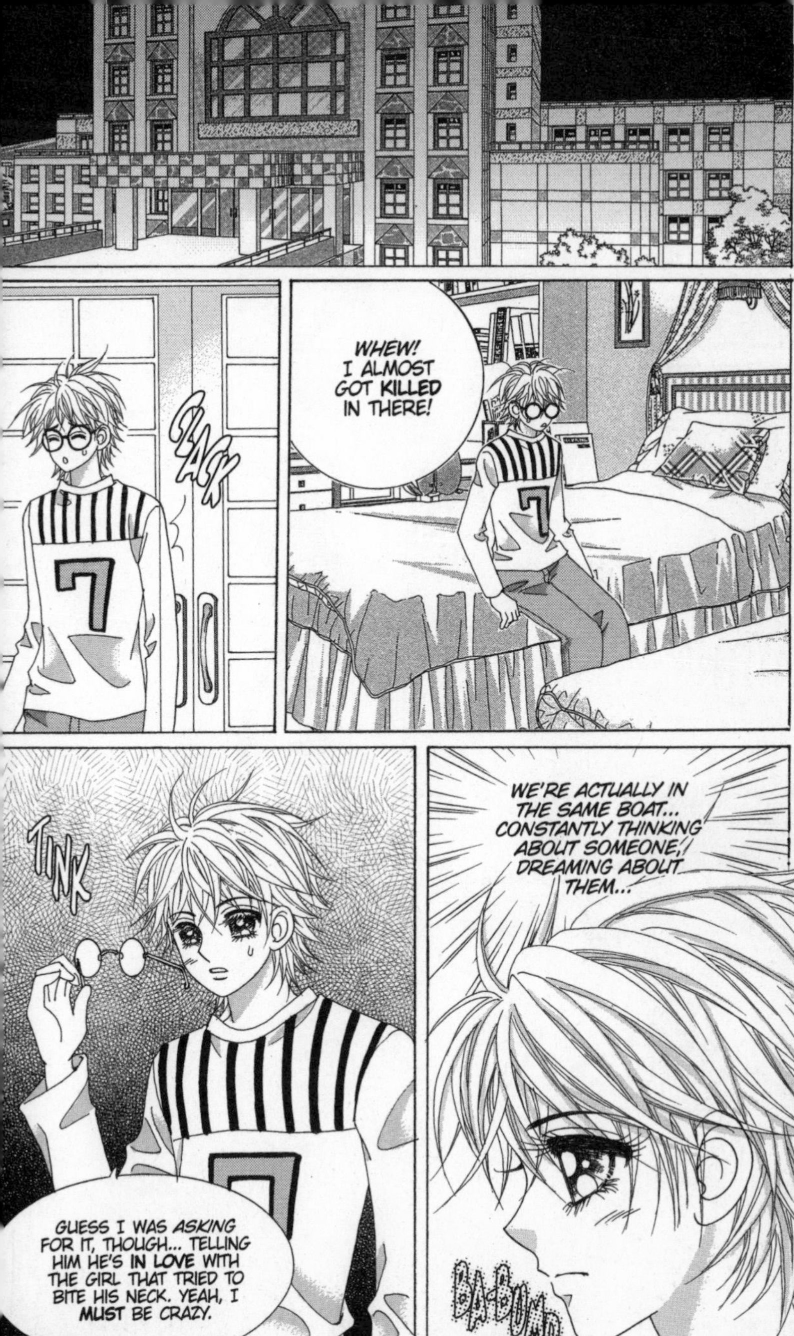
CLACK
WHEW! I ALMOST GOT KILLED IN THERE!
TINK
GUESS I WAS ASKING FOR IT, THOUGH... TELLING HIM HE'S IN LOVE WITH THE GIRL THAT TRIED TO BITE HIS NECK. YEAH, I MUST BE CRAZY.
WE'RE ACTUALLY IN THE SAME BOAT... CONSTANTLY THINKING ABOUT SOMEONE, DREAMING ABOUT THEM...
BA-BOMP

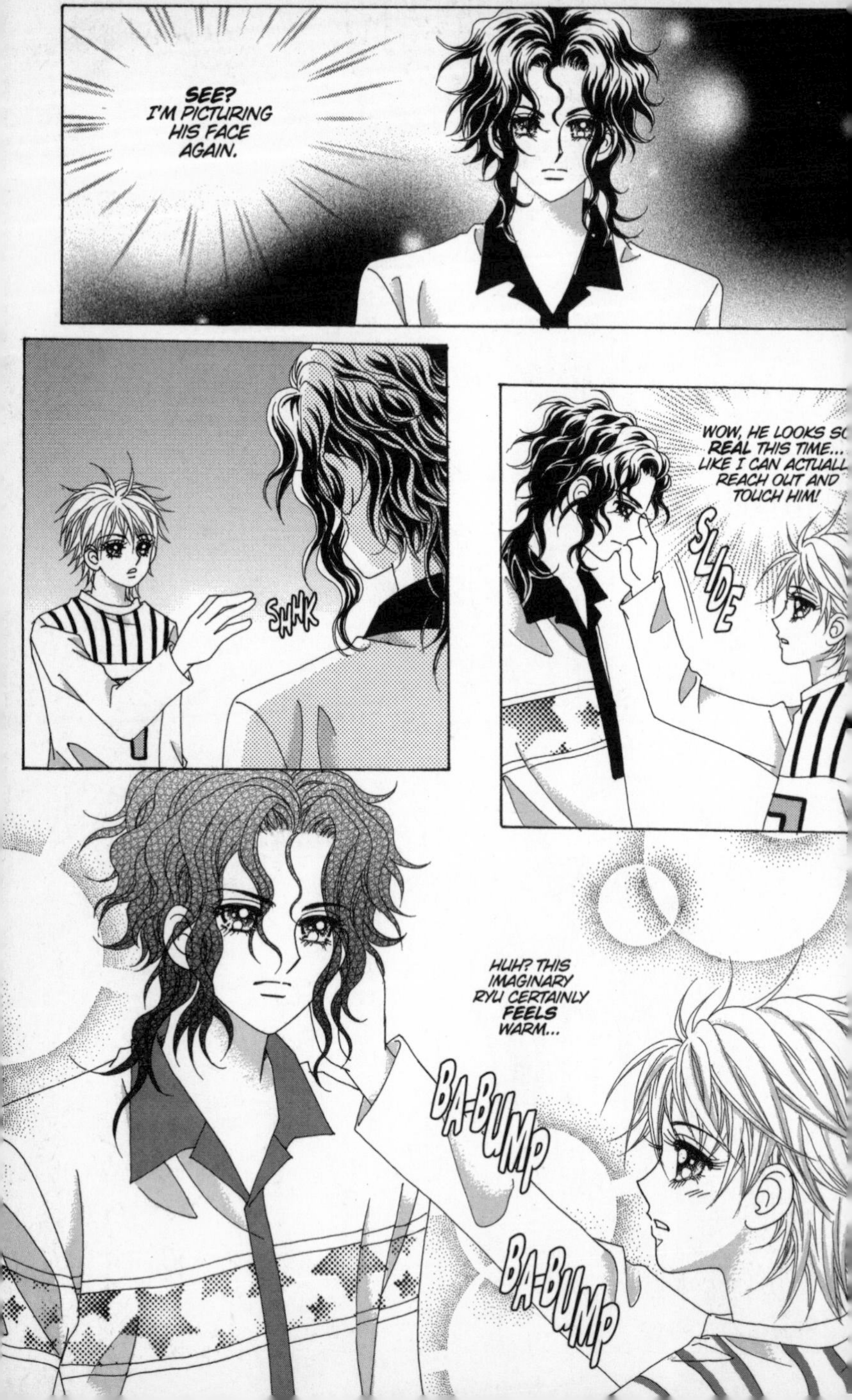
SEE? I'M PICTURING HIS FACE AGAIN.
SHHK
WOW, HE LOOKS S
REAL THIS TIME...
LIKE I CAN ACTUALL
REACH OUT AND TOUCH HIM!
SLIDE
HUH? THIS IMAGINARY RYU CERTAINLY FEELS WARM...
BA-BUMP
BA-BUMP

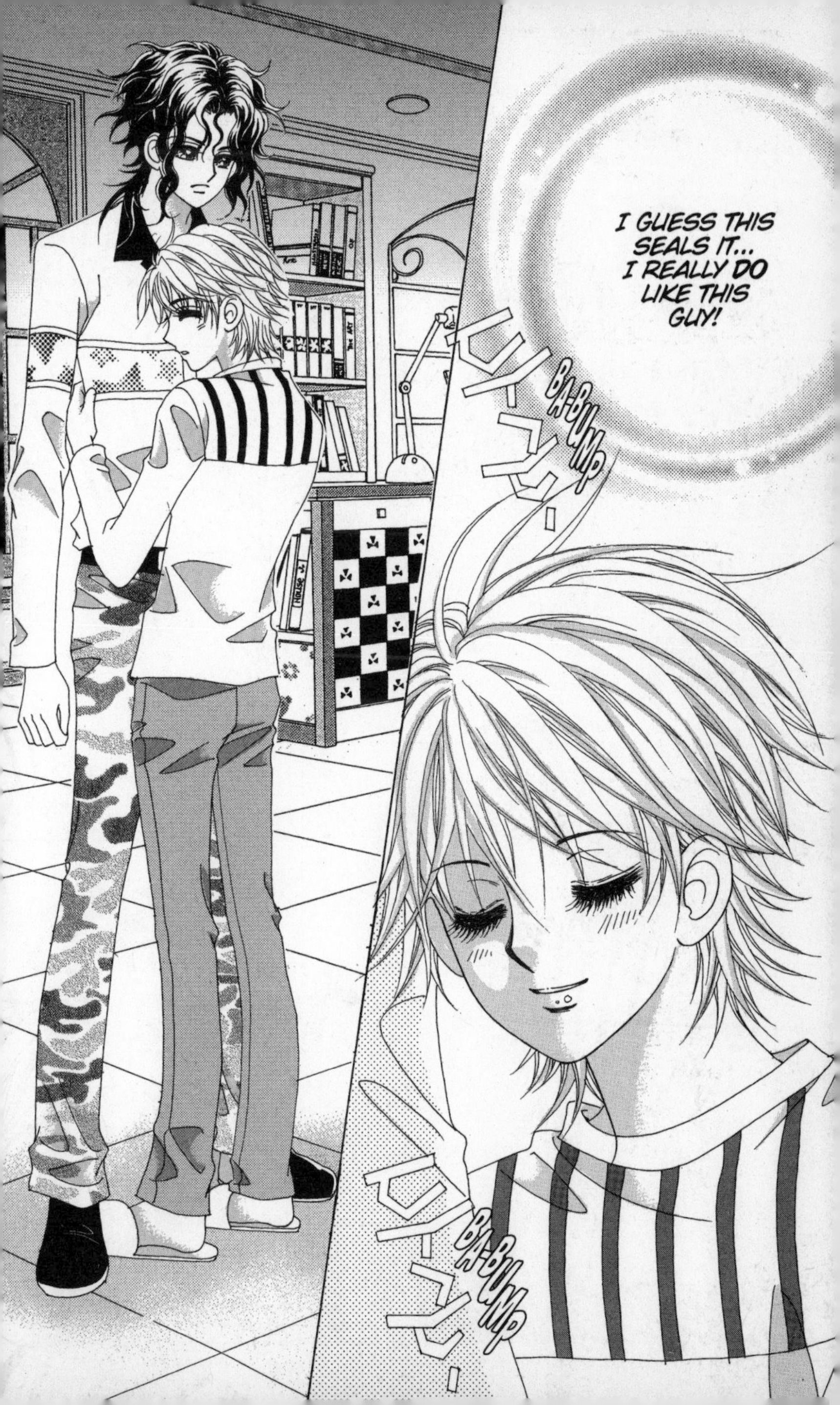
I GUESS THIS SEALS IT... I REALLY DO LIKE THIS GUY!
BA-BUMP
BA-BUMP

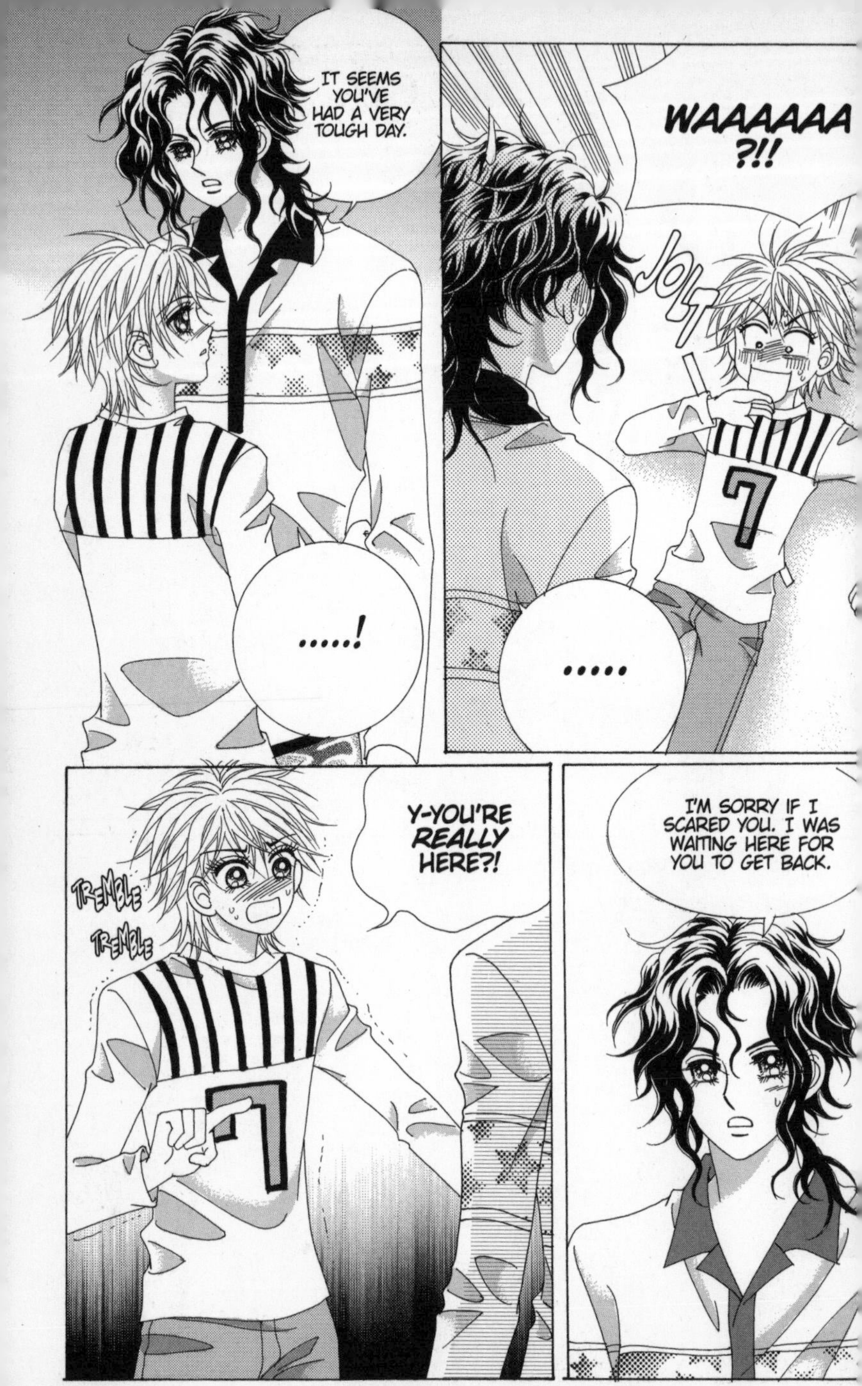

IT SEEMS YOU'VE HAD A VERY TOUGH DAY.
.....!
WAAAAAA ?!!
JOLT
.....
TREMBLE
TREMBLE
Y-YOU'RE REALLY HERE?!
I'M SORRY IF I SCARED YOU. I WAS WAITING HERE FOR YOU TO GET BACK.

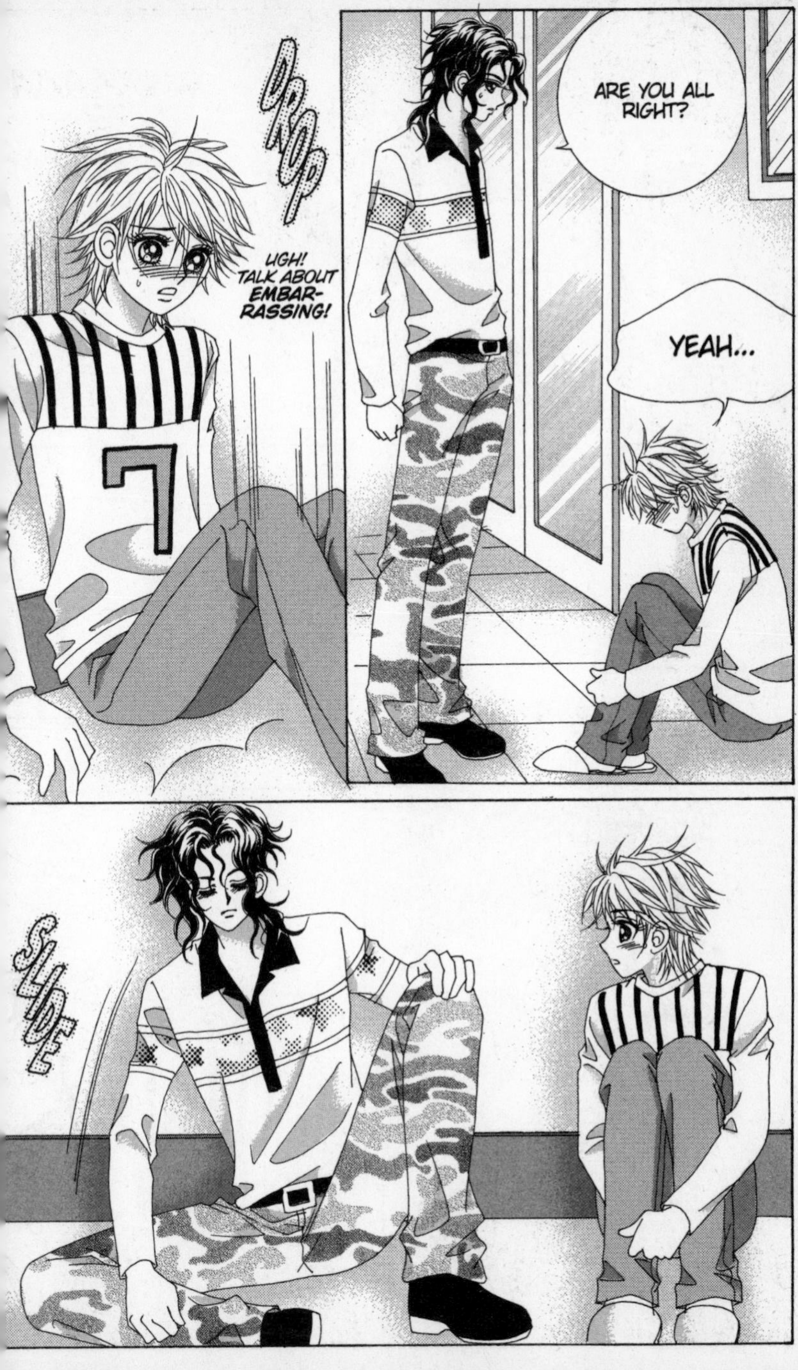
DROP
UGH! TALK ABOUT EMBARRASSING!
ARE YOU ALL RIGHT?
YEAH...
SLIDE

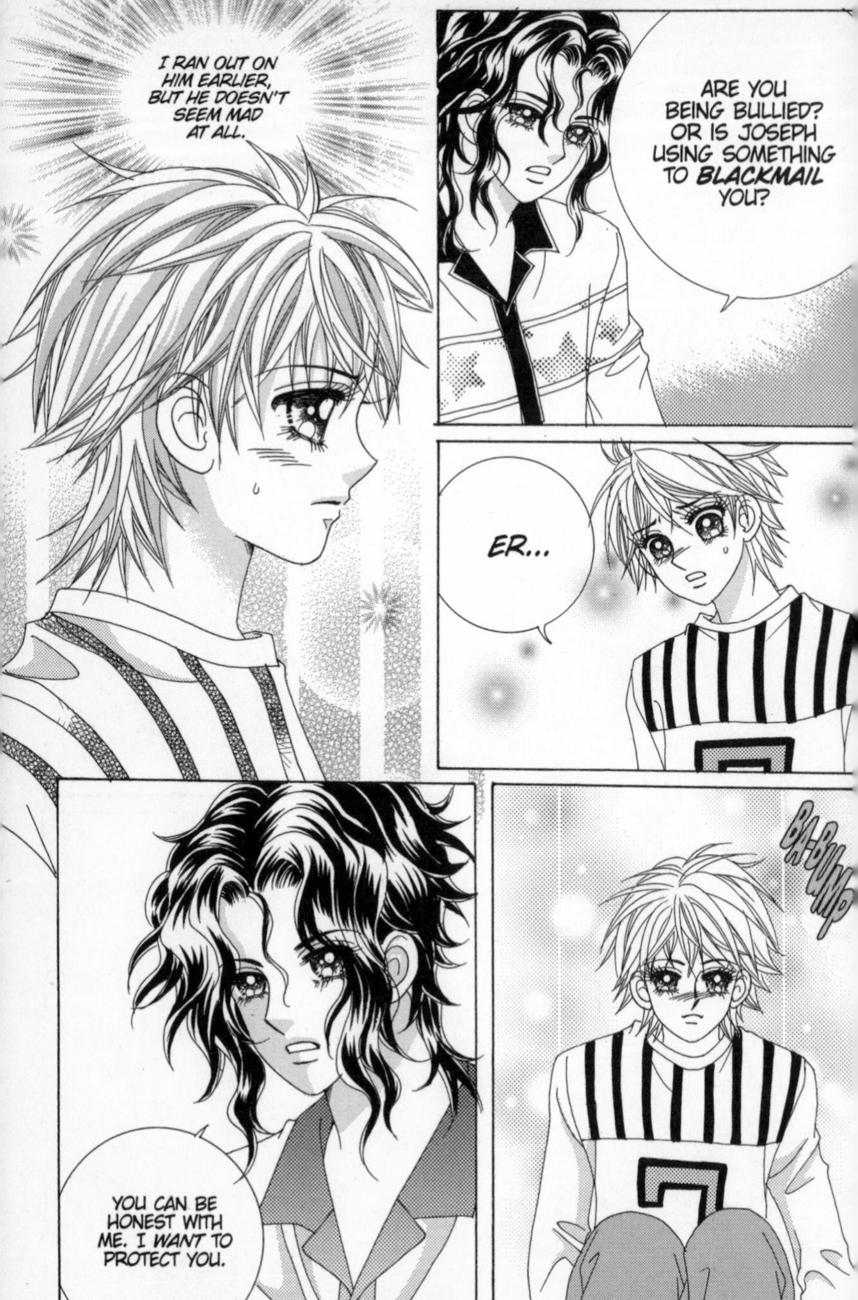
I RAN OUT ON HIM EARLIER, BUT HE DOESN'T SEEM MAD AT ALL.
ARE YOU BEING BULLIED? OR IS JOSEPH USING SOMETHING TO **BLACKMAIL** YOU?
ER...
YOU CAN BE HONEST WITH ME. I *WANT* TO PROTECT YOU.
BA-BUMP

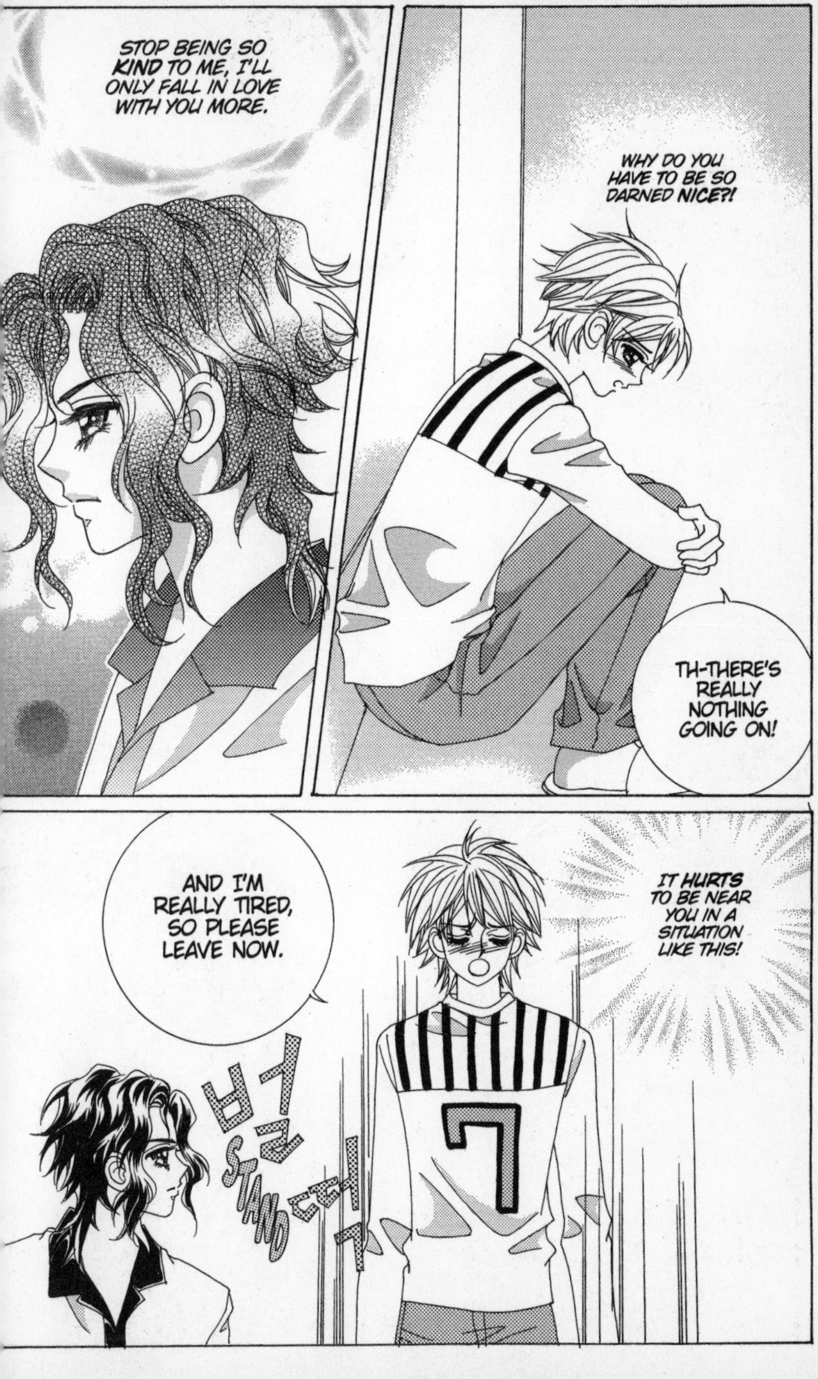
STOP BEING SO KIND TO ME, I'LL ONLY FALL IN LOVE WITH YOU MORE.
WHY DO YOU HAVE TO BE SO DARNED NICE?!
TH-THERE'S REALLY NOTHING GOING ON!
AND I'M REALLY TIRED, SO PLEASE LEAVE NOW.
STAND
IT HURTS TO BE NEAR YOU IN A SITUATION LIKE THIS!

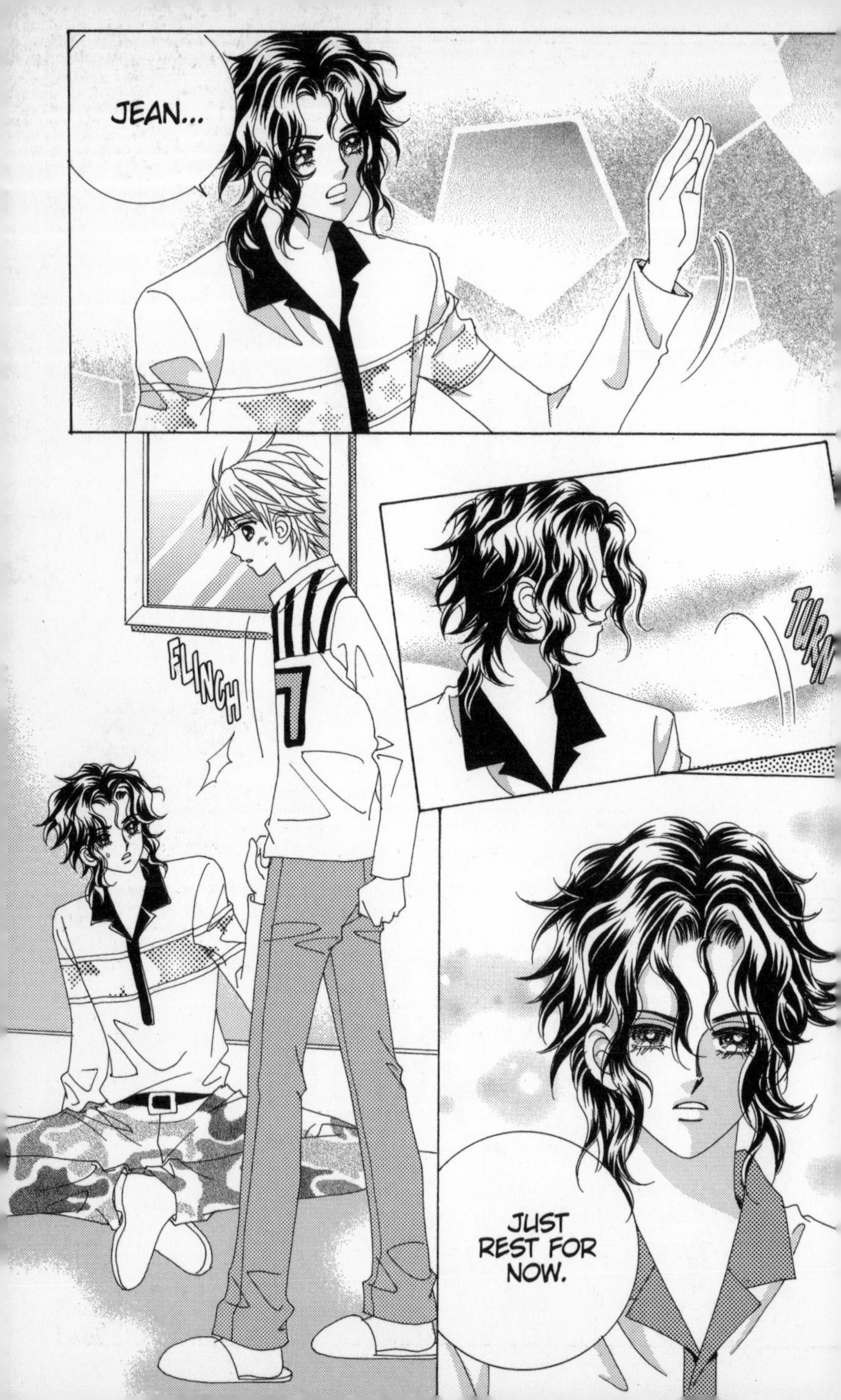
JEAN...
FLINCH
TURN
JUST REST FOR NOW.

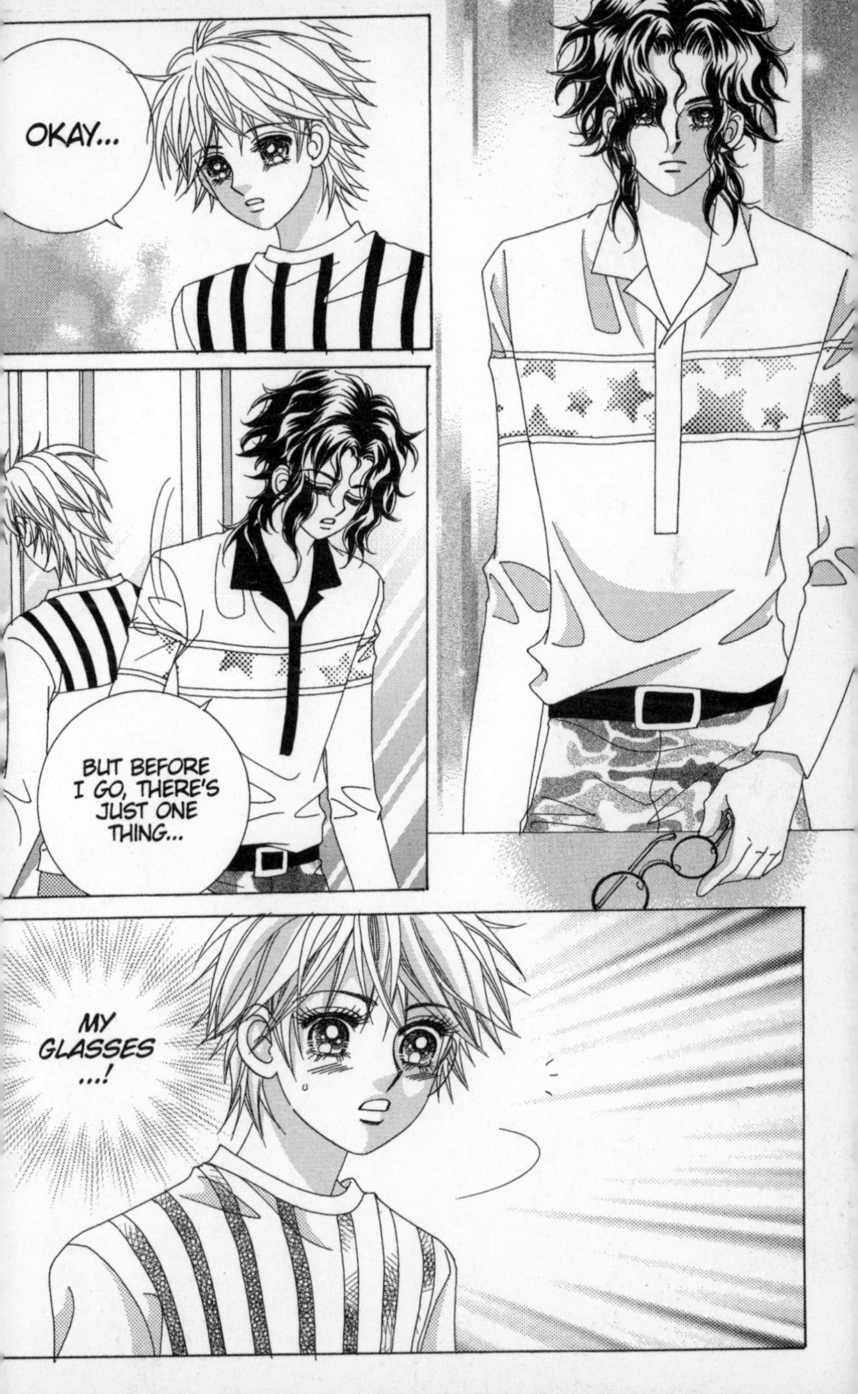
OKAY...
BUT BEFORE I GO, THERE'S JUST ONE THING...
MY GLASSES ...!

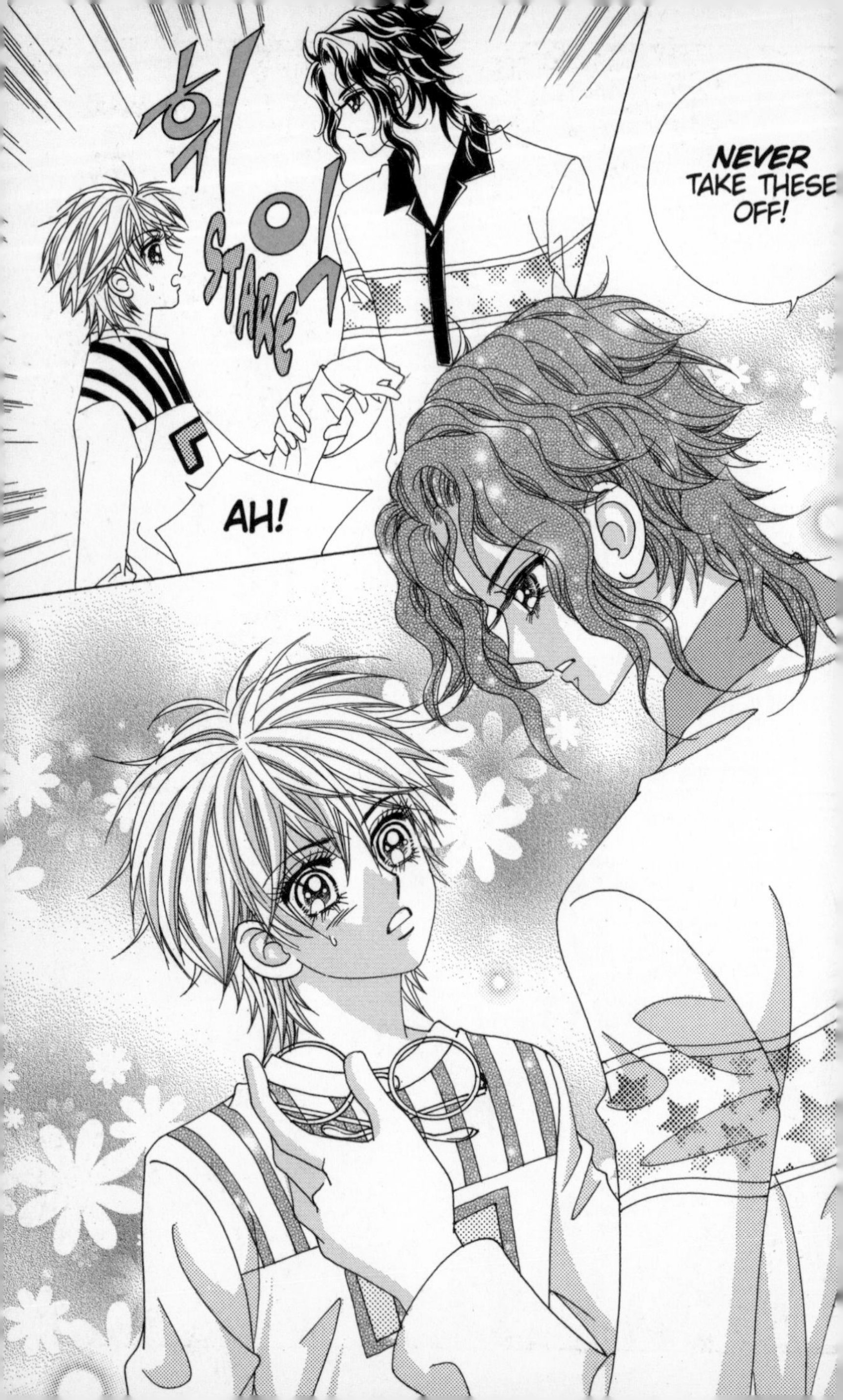
STARE
AH!
NEVER TAKE THESE OFF!

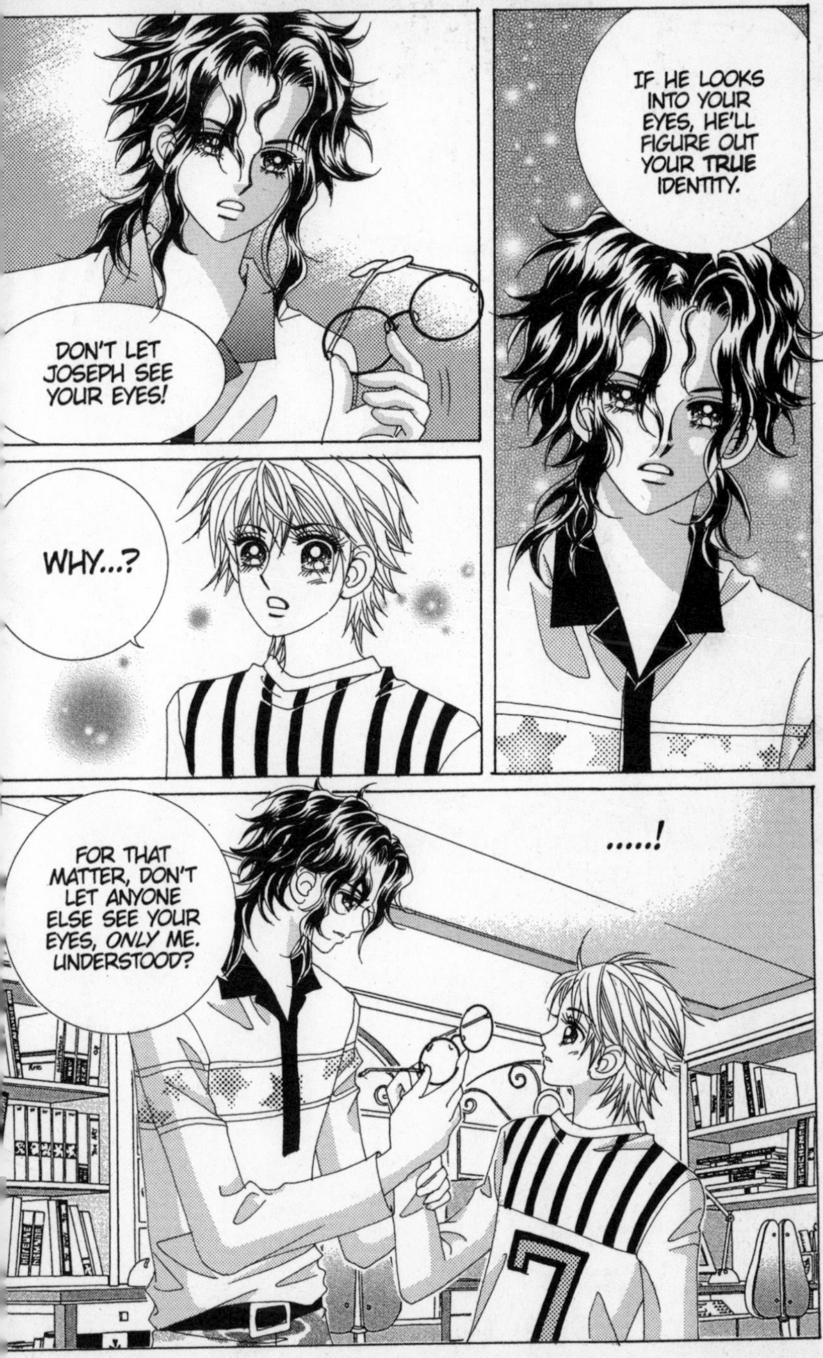
DON'T LET JOSEPH SEE YOUR EYES!
WHY...?
IF HE LOOKS INTO YOUR EYES, HE'LL FIGURE OUT YOUR TRUE IDENTITY.
FOR THAT MATTER, DON'T LET ANYONE ELSE SEE YOUR EYES, *ONLY* ME. UNDERSTOOD?
.....!

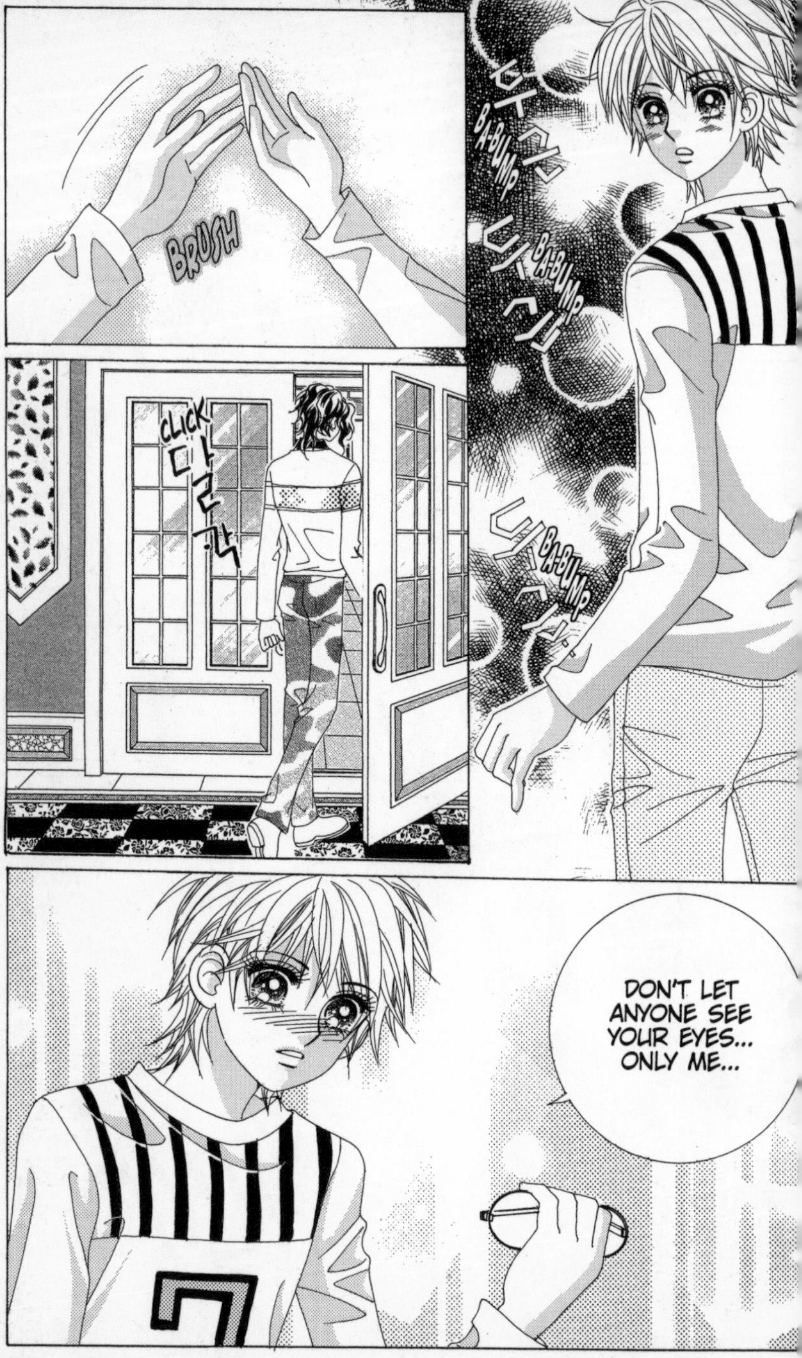
BRUSH
CLICK
BA-BUMP
BA-BUMP
BA-BUMP
DON'T LET ANYONE SEE YOUR EYES... ONLY ME...

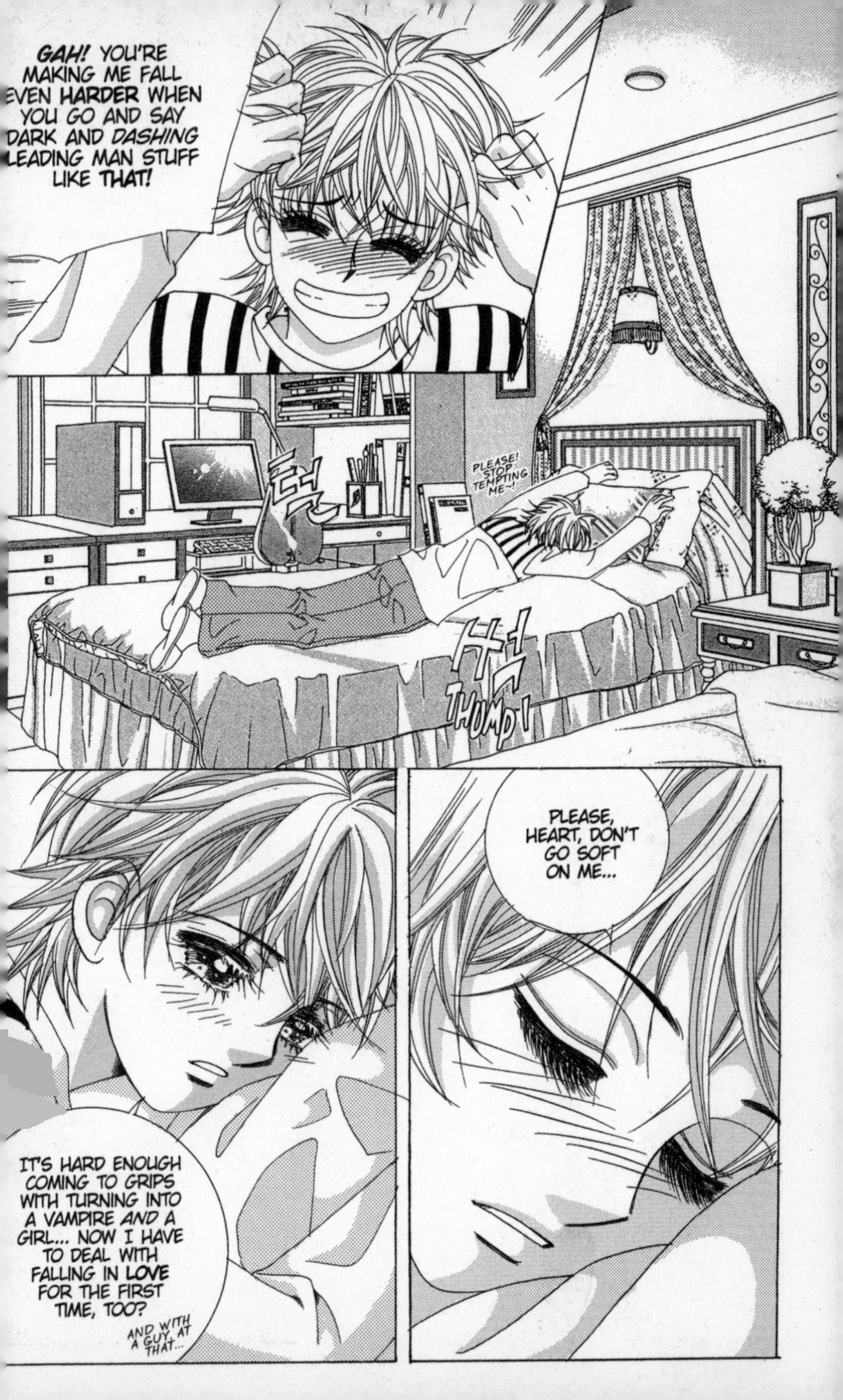
GAH! YOU'RE MAKING ME FALL EVEN HARDER WHEN YOU GO AND SAY DARK AND DASHING LEADING MAN STUFF LIKE THAT!
PLEASE! STOP TEMPTING ME~!
THUMP!
IT'S HARD ENOUGH COMING TO GRIPS WITH TURNING INTO A VAMPIRE AND A GIRL... NOW I HAVE TO DEAL WITH FALLING IN LOVE FOR THE FIRST TIME, TOO?
AND WITH A GUY, AT THAT...
PLEASE, HEART, DON'T GO SOFT ON ME...

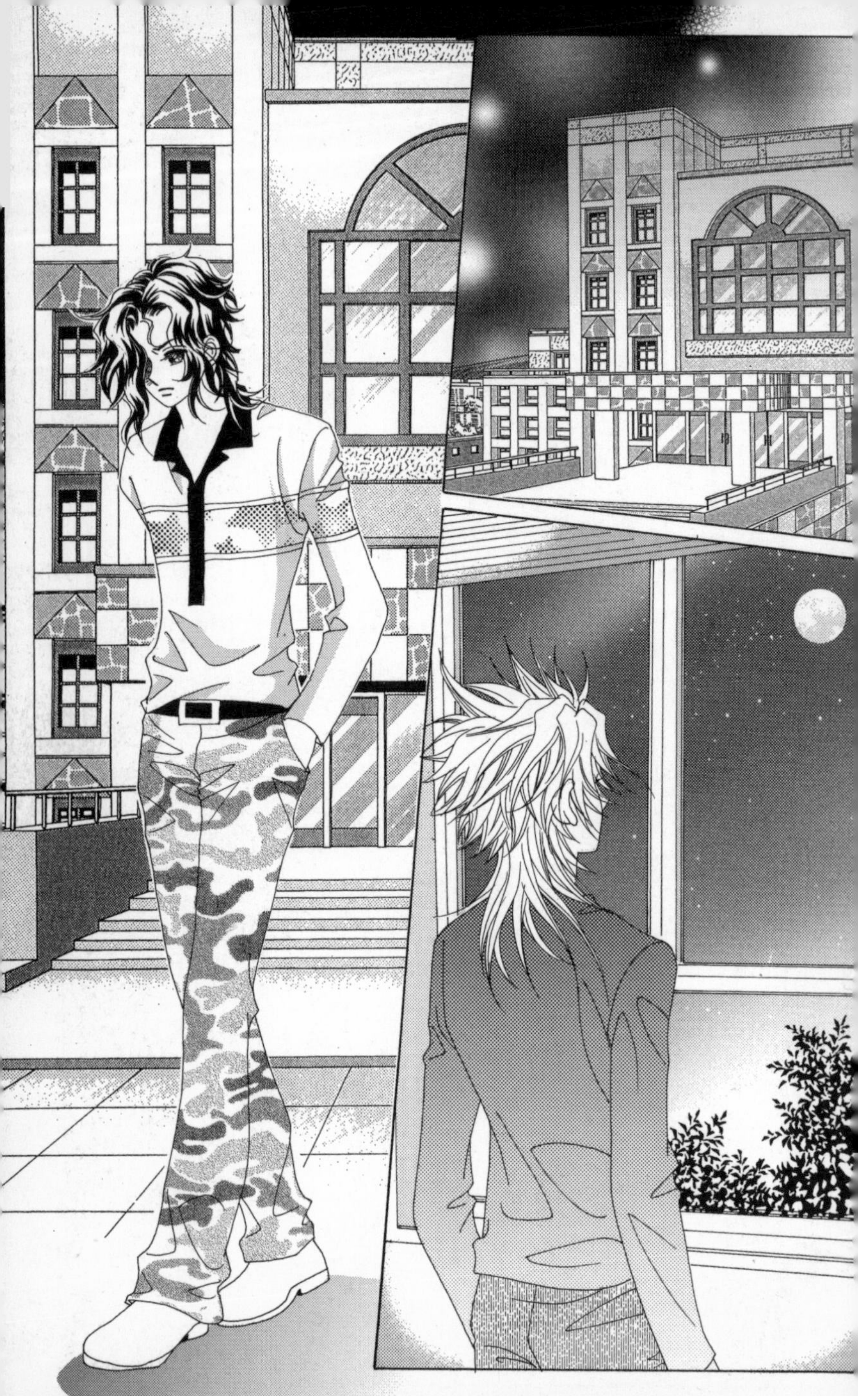

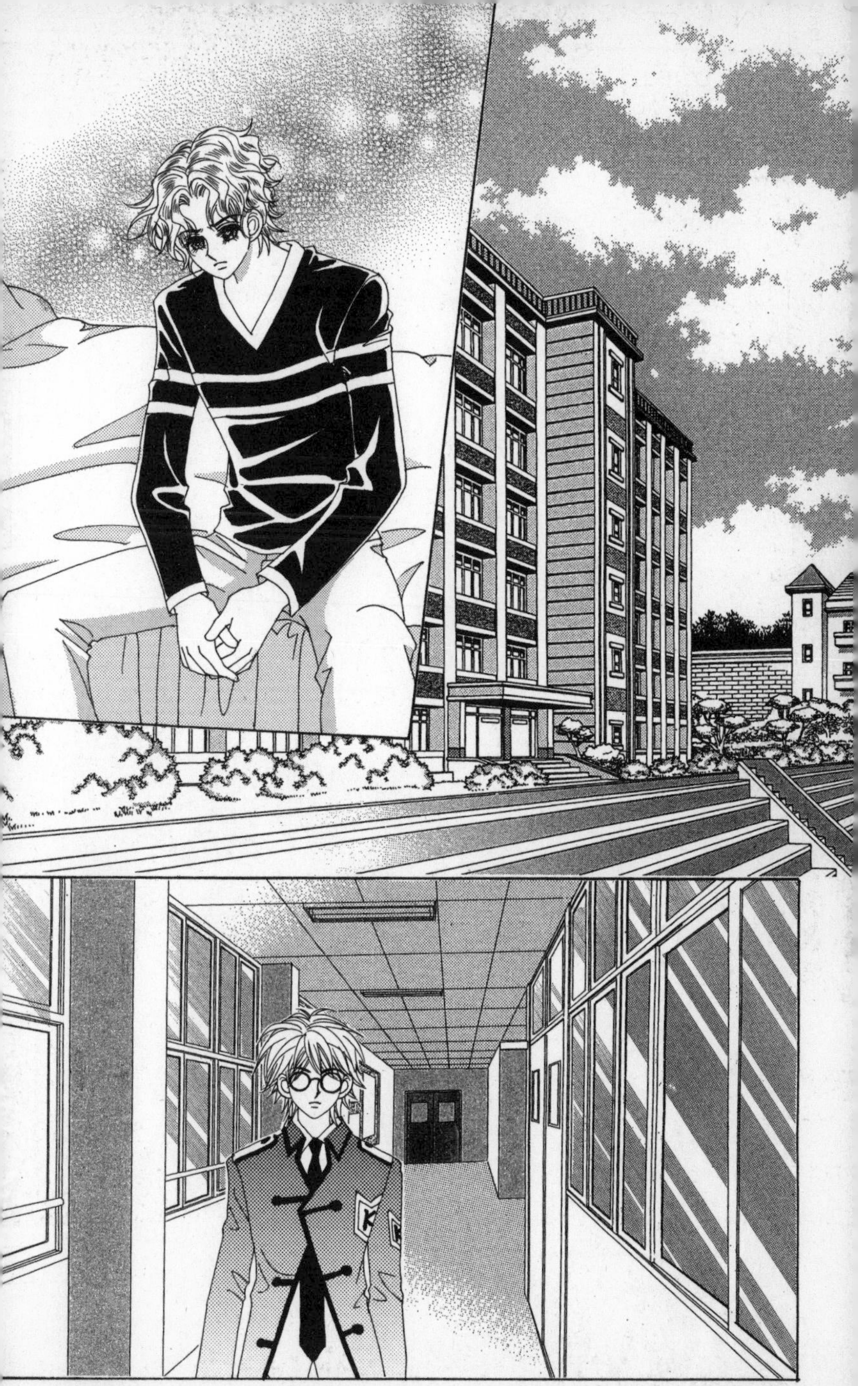

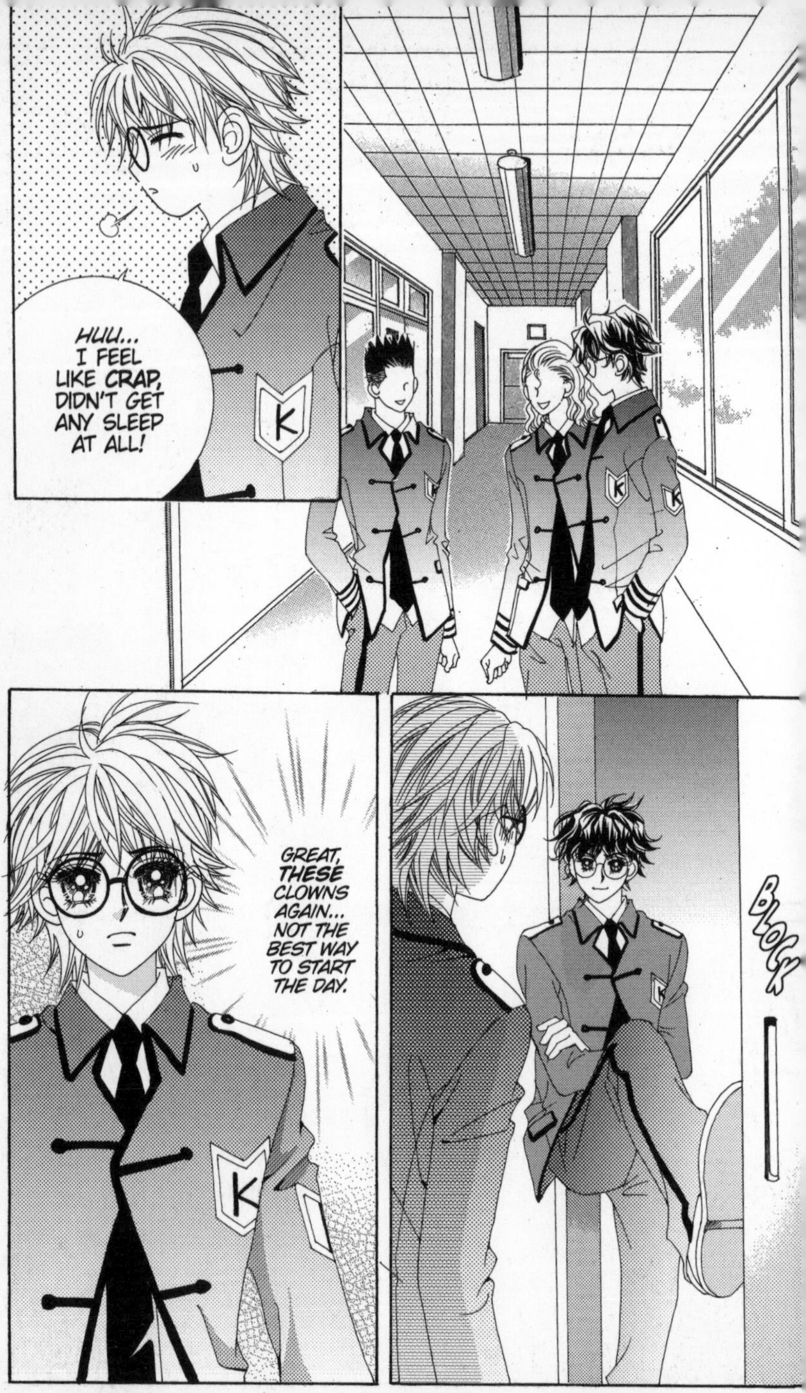
HUU... I FEEL LIKE CRAP, DIDN'T GET ANY SLEEP AT ALL!
GREAT, THESE CLOWNS AGAIN... NOT THE BEST WAY TO START THE DAY.
BLOCK

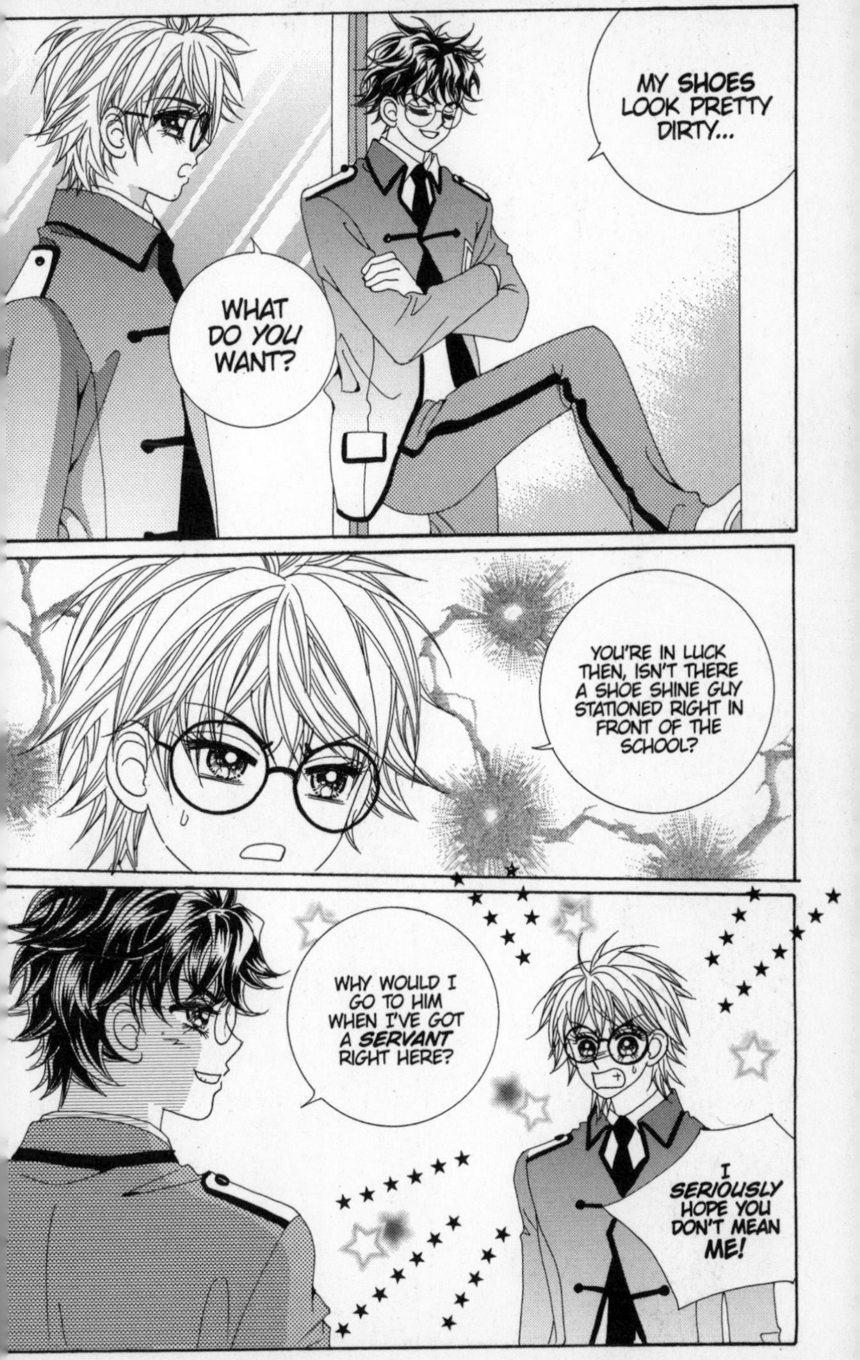
MY SHOES LOOK PRETTY DIRTY...
WHAT DO YOU WANT?
YOU'RE IN LUCK THEN, ISN'T THERE A SHOE SHINE GUY STATIONED RIGHT IN FRONT OF THE SCHOOL?
WHY WOULD I GO TO HIM WHEN I'VE GOT A SERVANT RIGHT HERE?
I SERIOUSLY HOPE YOU DON'T MEAN ME!

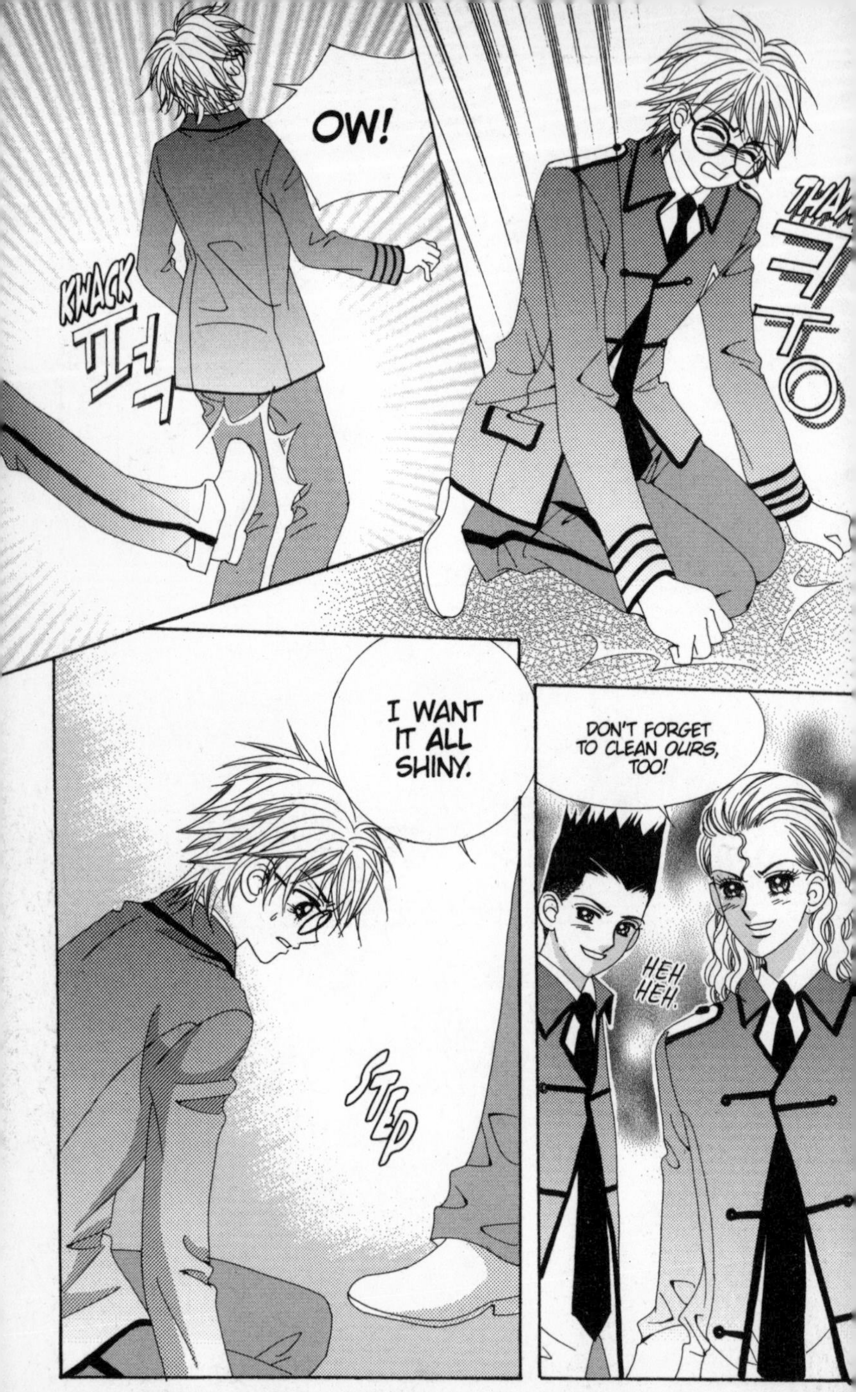
OW!
KWACK
I WANT IT ALL SHINY.
STEP
DON'T FORGET TO CLEAN OURS, TOO!
HEH HEH.

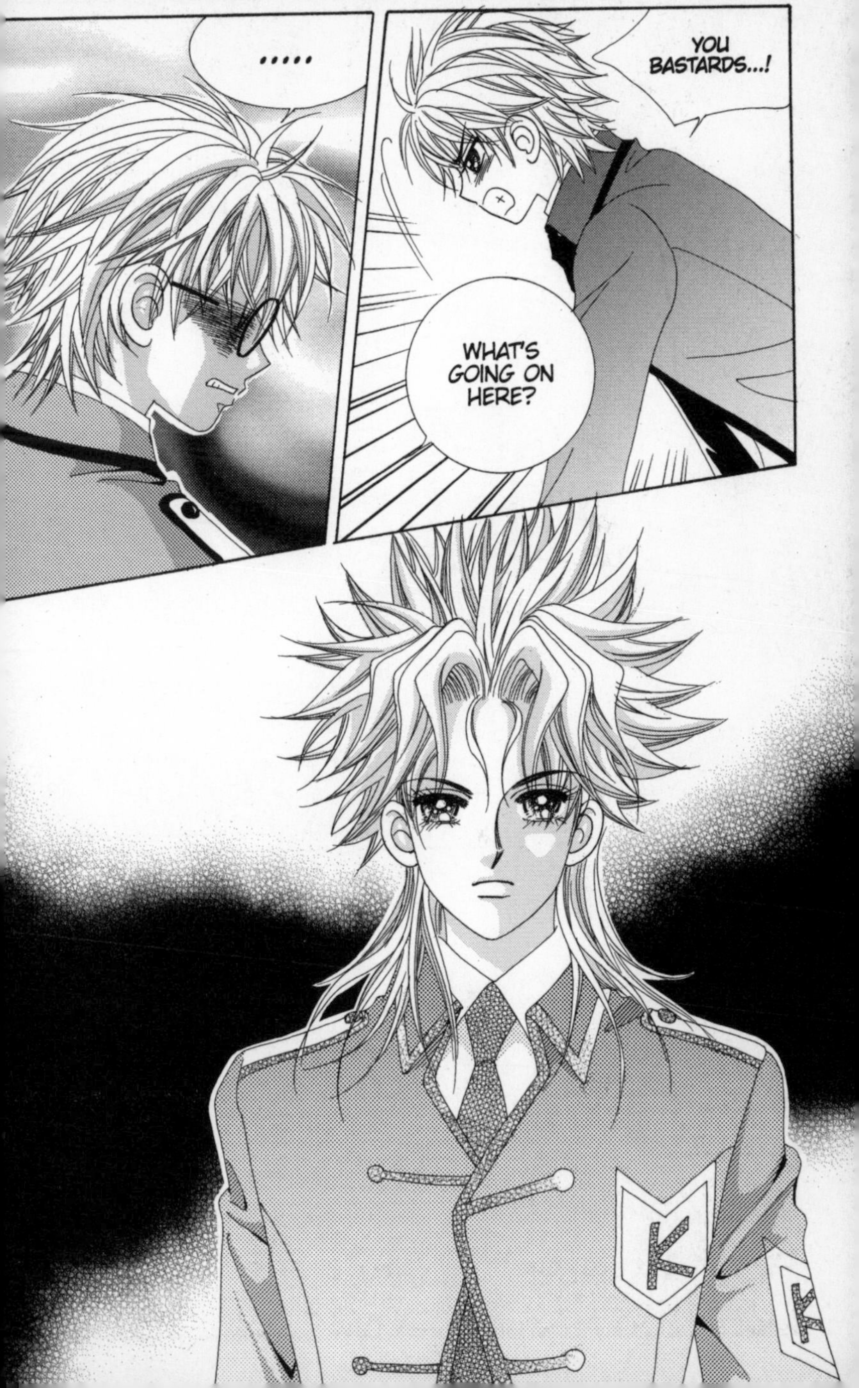
.....
YOU BASTARDS...!
WHAT'S GOING ON HERE?

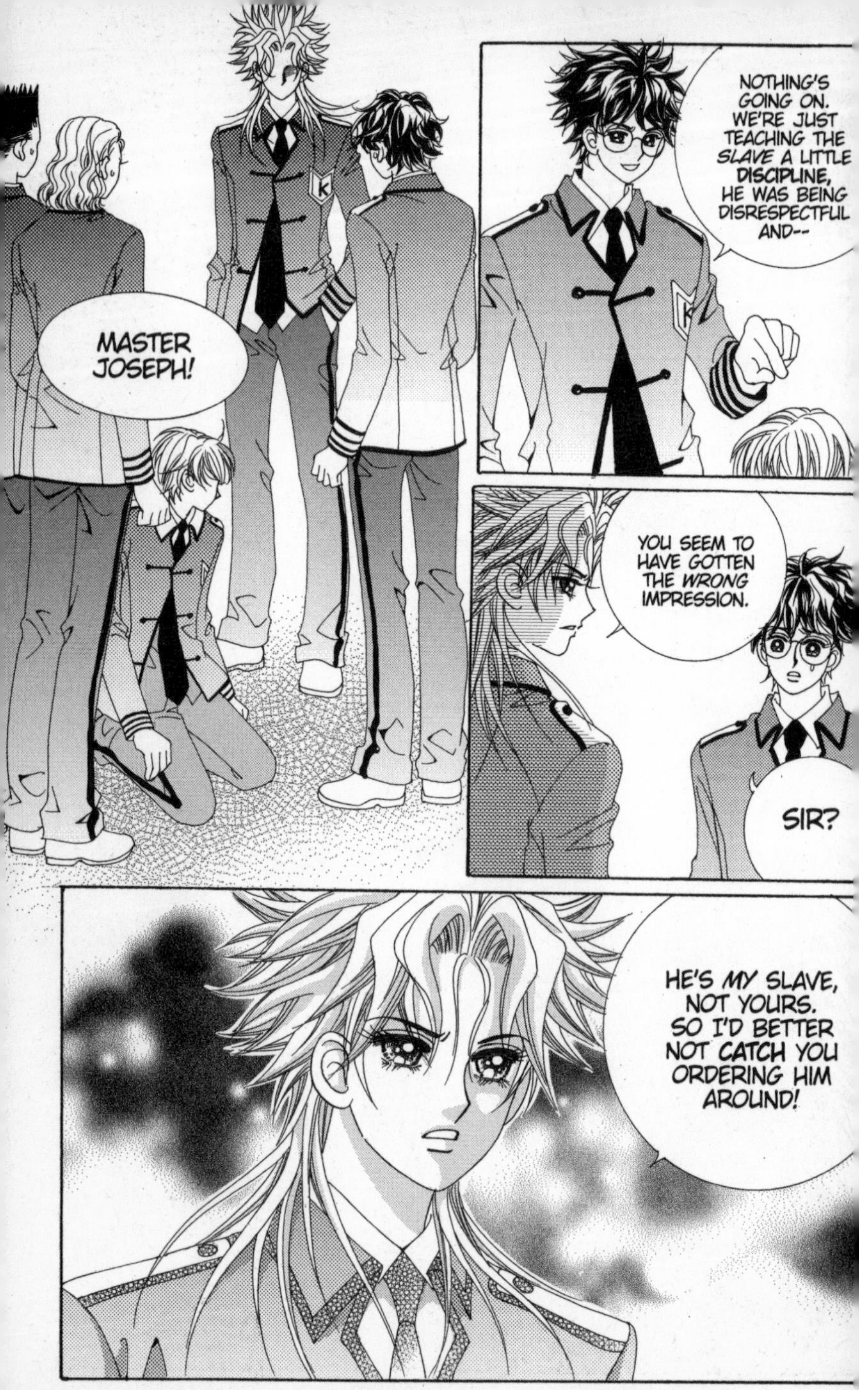
MASTER JOSEPH!
NOTHING'S GOING ON. WE'RE JUST TEACHING THE *SLAVE* A LITTLE DISCIPLINE, HE WAS BEING DISRESPECTFUL AND--
YOU SEEM TO HAVE GOTTEN THE *WRONG* IMPRESSION.
SIR?
HE'S *MY* SLAVE, NOT YOURS. SO I'D BETTER NOT CATCH YOU ORDERING HIM AROUND!

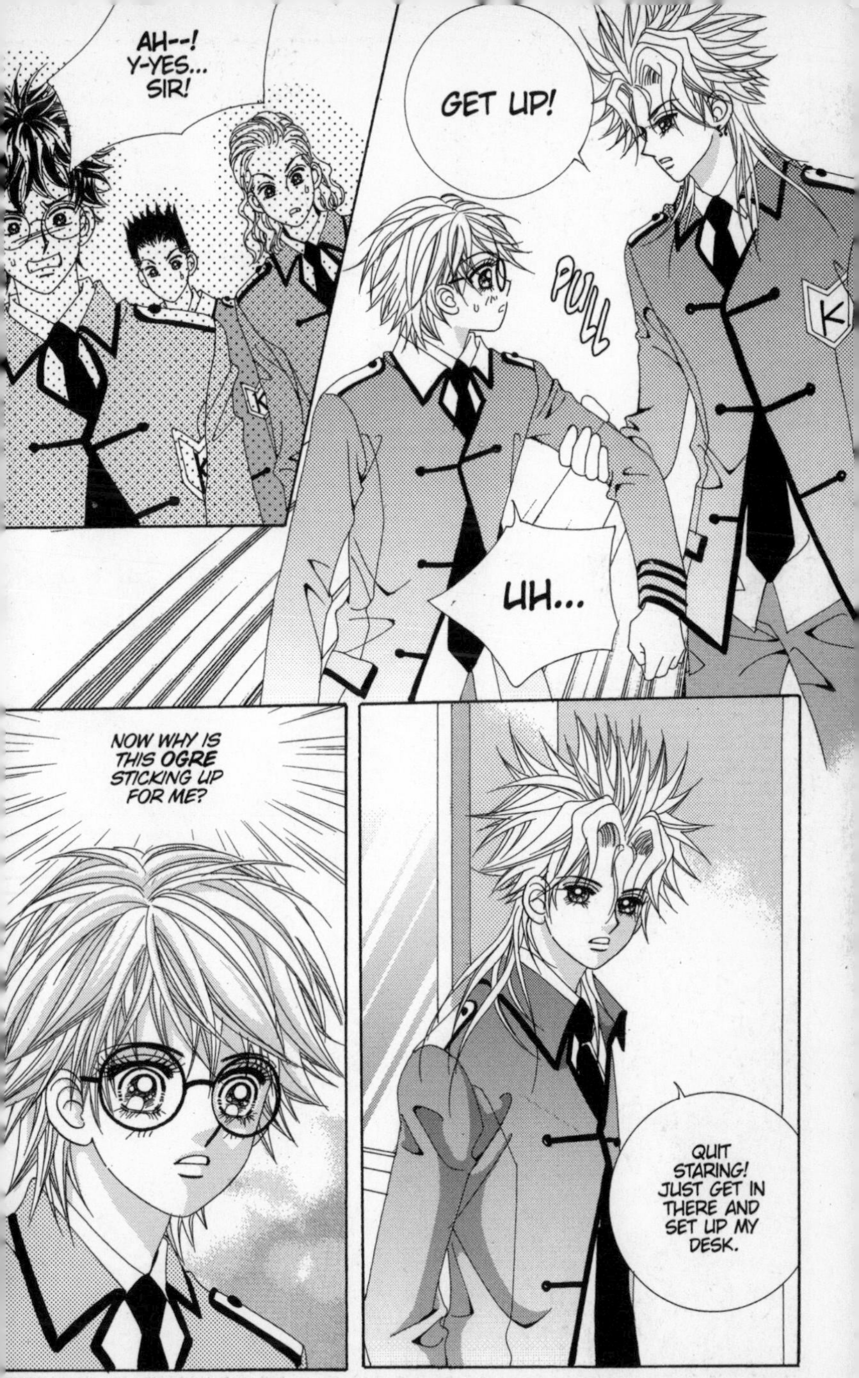
AH--! Y-YES... SIR!
GET UP!
PULL
UH...
NOW WHY IS THIS OGRE STICKING UP FOR ME?
QUIT STARING! JUST GET IN THERE AND SET UP MY DESK.

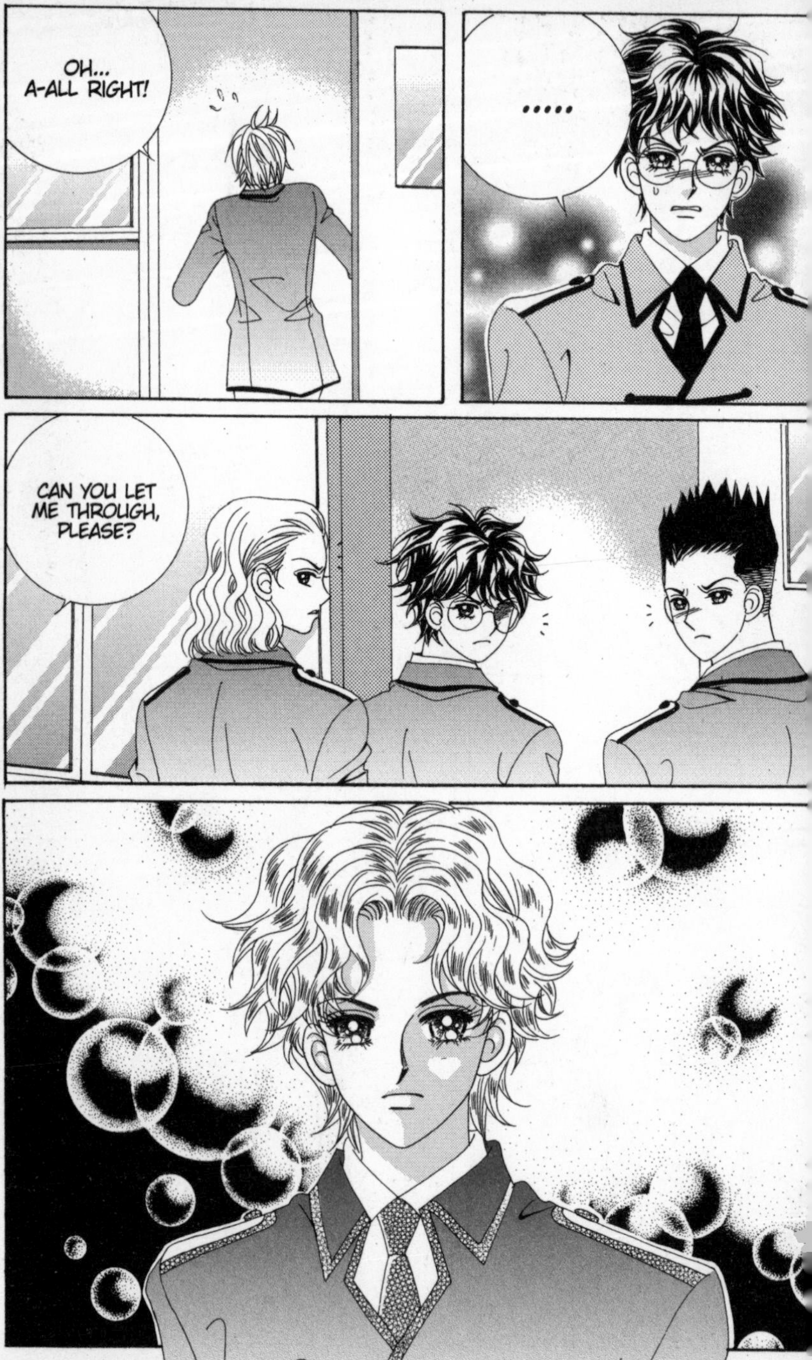
OH... A-ALL RIGHT!
.....
CAN YOU LET ME THROUGH, PLEASE?

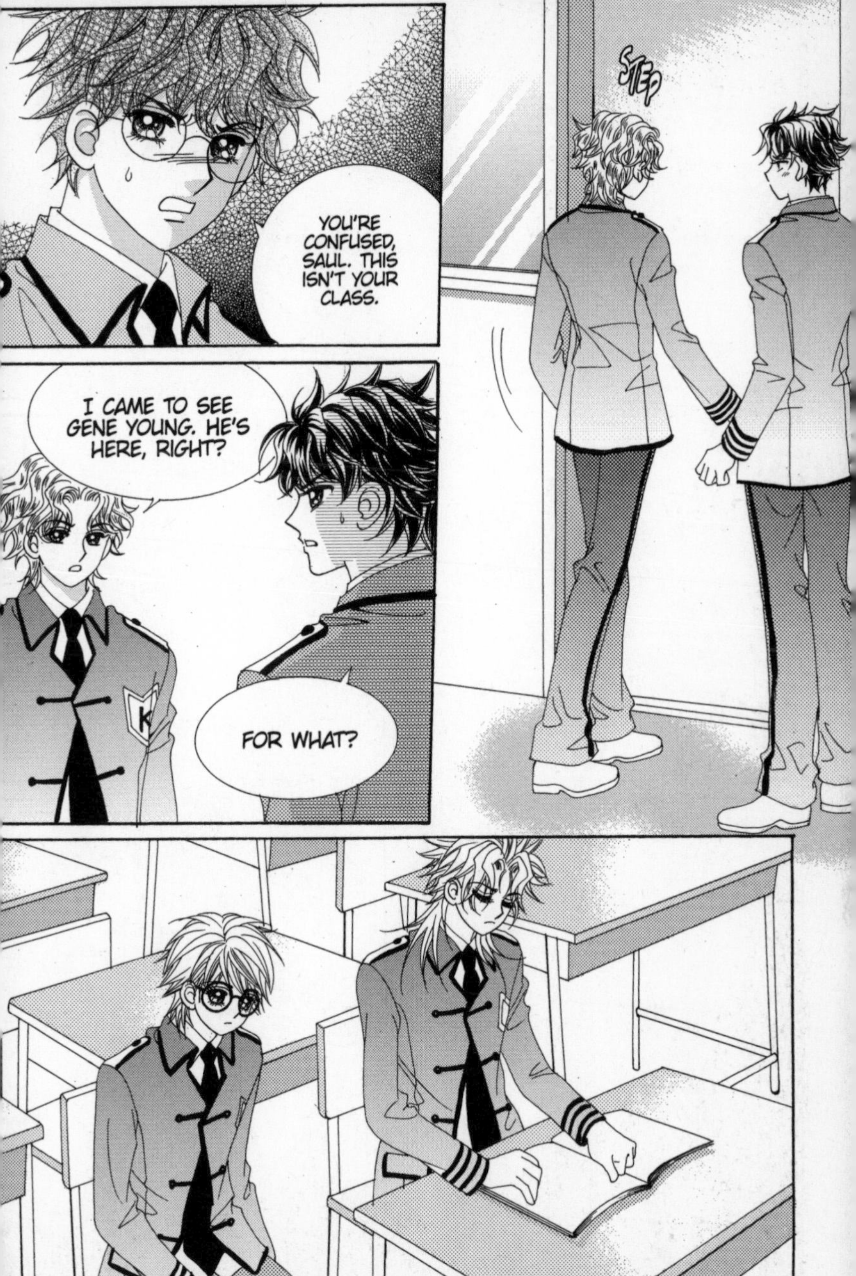
YOU'RE CONFUSED, SAUL. THIS ISN'T YOUR CLASS.
I CAME TO SEE GENE YOUNG. HE'S HERE, RIGHT?
FOR WHAT?
STEP

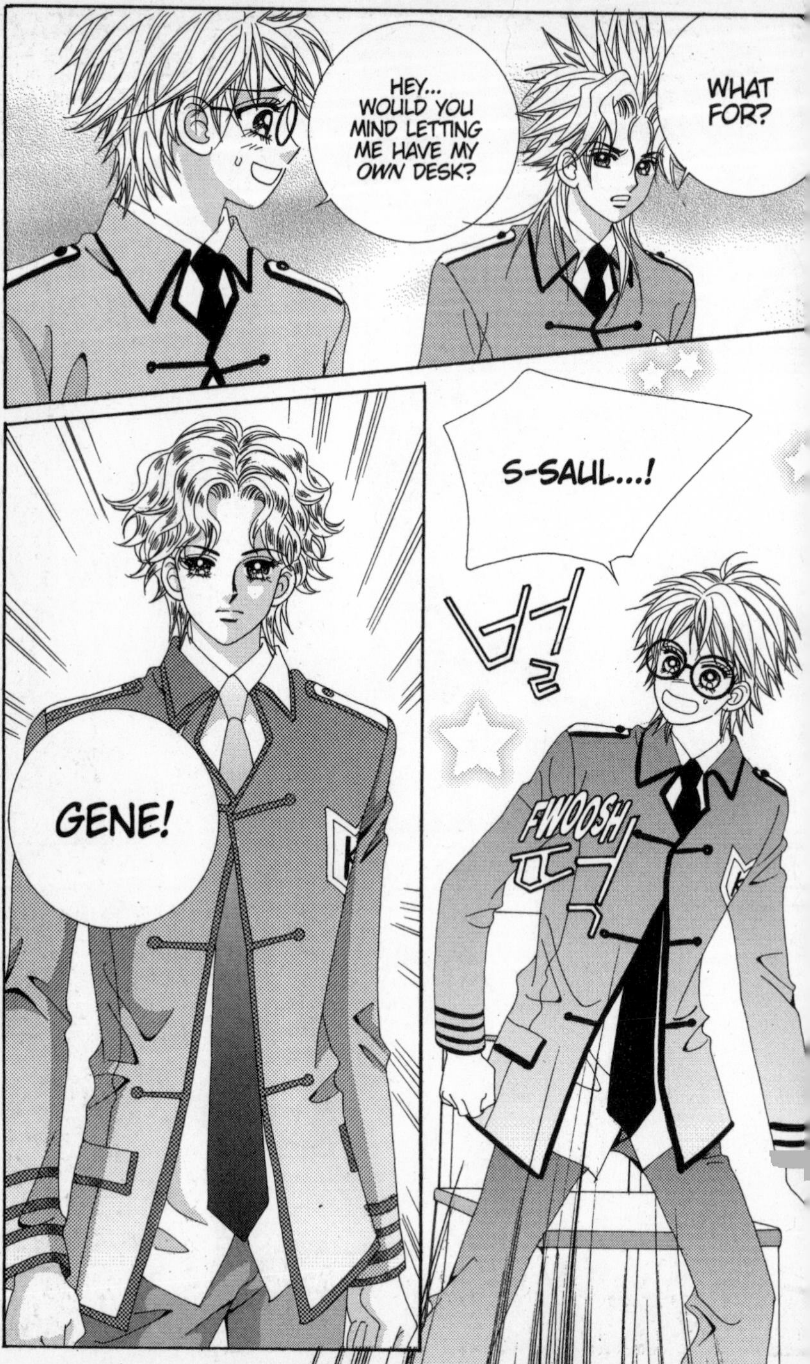
HEY... WOULD YOU MIND LETTING ME HAVE MY OWN DESK?
WHAT FOR?
GENE!
S-SAUL...!
FWOOSH

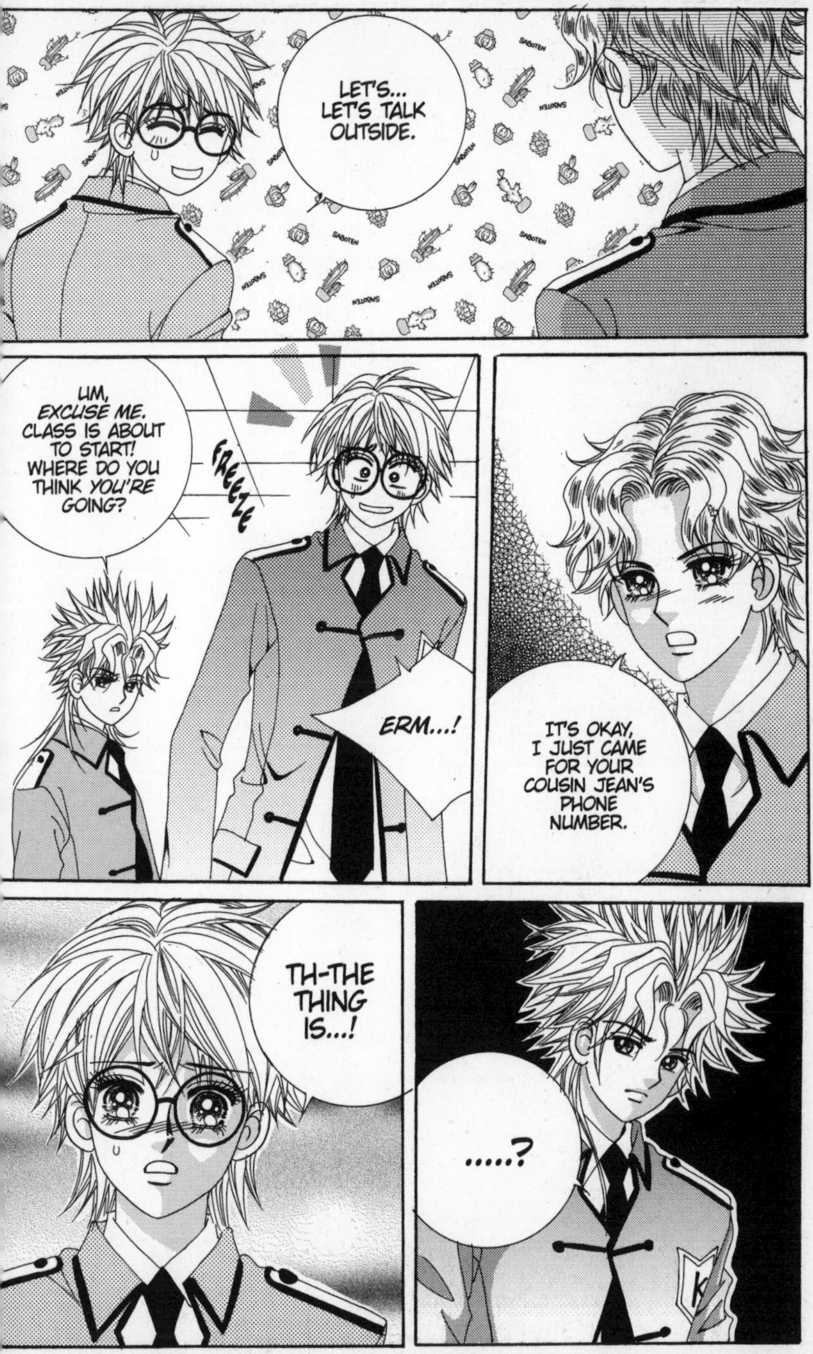
LET'S... LET'S TALK OUTSIDE.
SABOTEN
UM, *EXCUSE ME.* CLASS IS ABOUT TO START! WHERE DO YOU THINK *YOU'RE* GOING?
FREEZE
ERM...!
IT'S OKAY, I JUST CAME FOR YOUR COUSIN JEAN'S PHONE NUMBER.
TH-THE THING IS...!
.....?

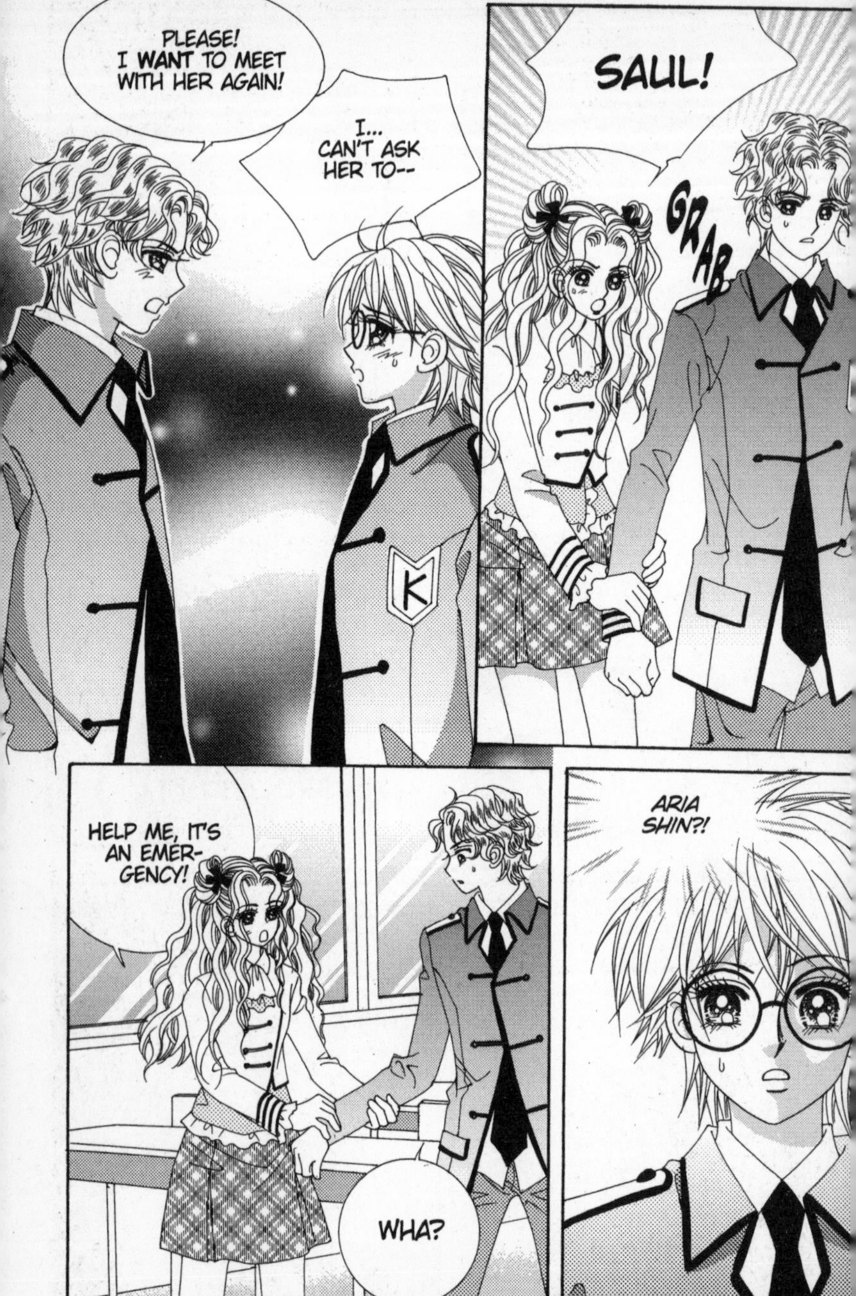
PLEASE! I WANT TO MEET WITH HER AGAIN!
I... CAN'T ASK HER TO--
SAUL!
GRAB
HELP ME, IT'S AN EMER-GENCY!
WHA?
ARIA SHIN?!

WHERE ARE WE GOING?

WHEW! SAVED BY ARIA! BUT HOW DO I SOLVE THIS ONCE AND FOR ALL? I'VE NEVER SEEN SAUL SO *GUNG-HO* OVER A GIRL BEFORE...

WHO IS THIS JEAN YOUNG PERSON?

......!

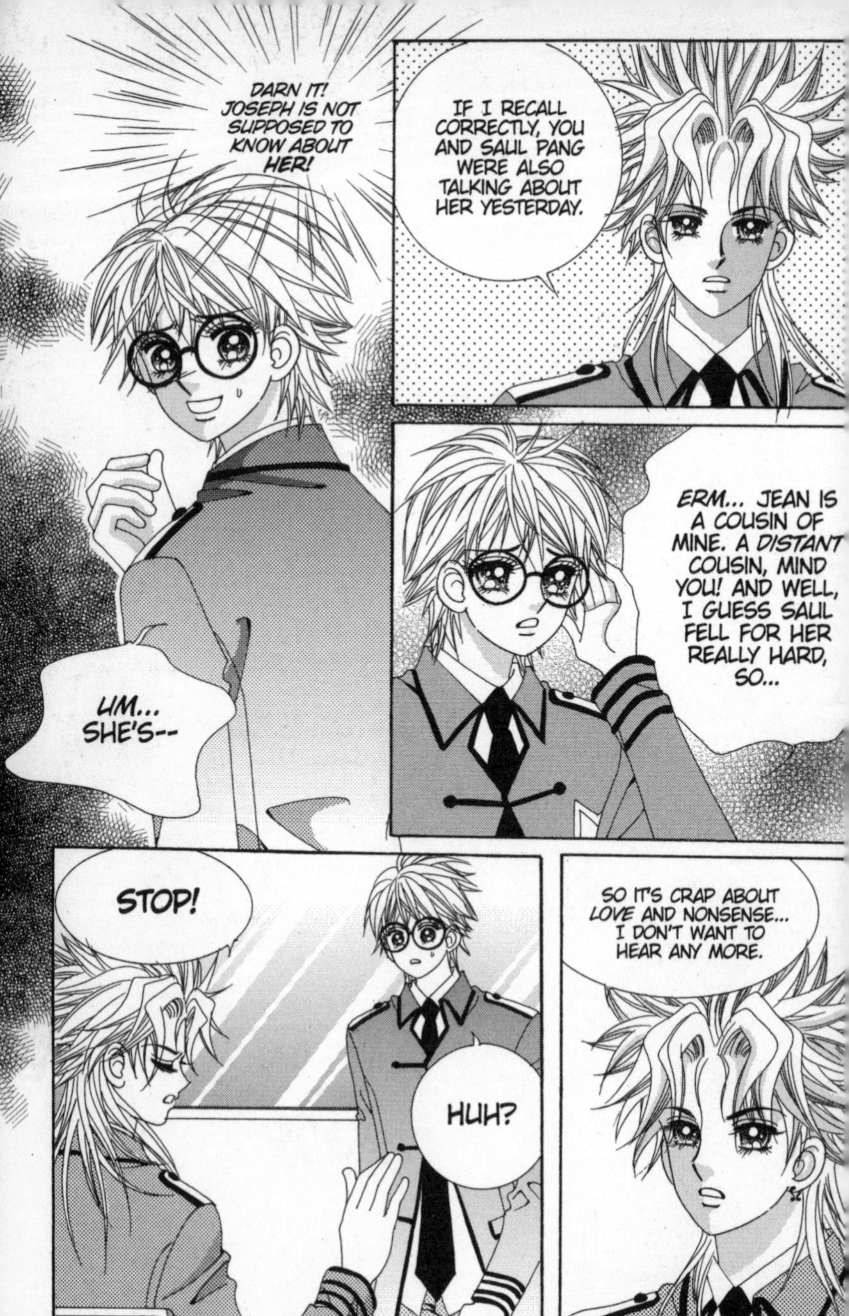
DARN IT! JOSEPH IS NOT SUPPOSED TO KNOW ABOUT HER!
UM... SHE'S--
IF I RECALL CORRECTLY, YOU AND SAUL PANG WERE ALSO TALKING ABOUT HER YESTERDAY.
ERM... JEAN IS A COUSIN OF MINE. A DISTANT COUSIN, MIND YOU! AND WELL, I GUESS SAUL FELL FOR HER REALLY HARD, SO...
STOP!
HUH?
SO IT'S CRAP ABOUT LOVE AND NONSENSE... I DON'T WANT TO HEAR ANY MORE.

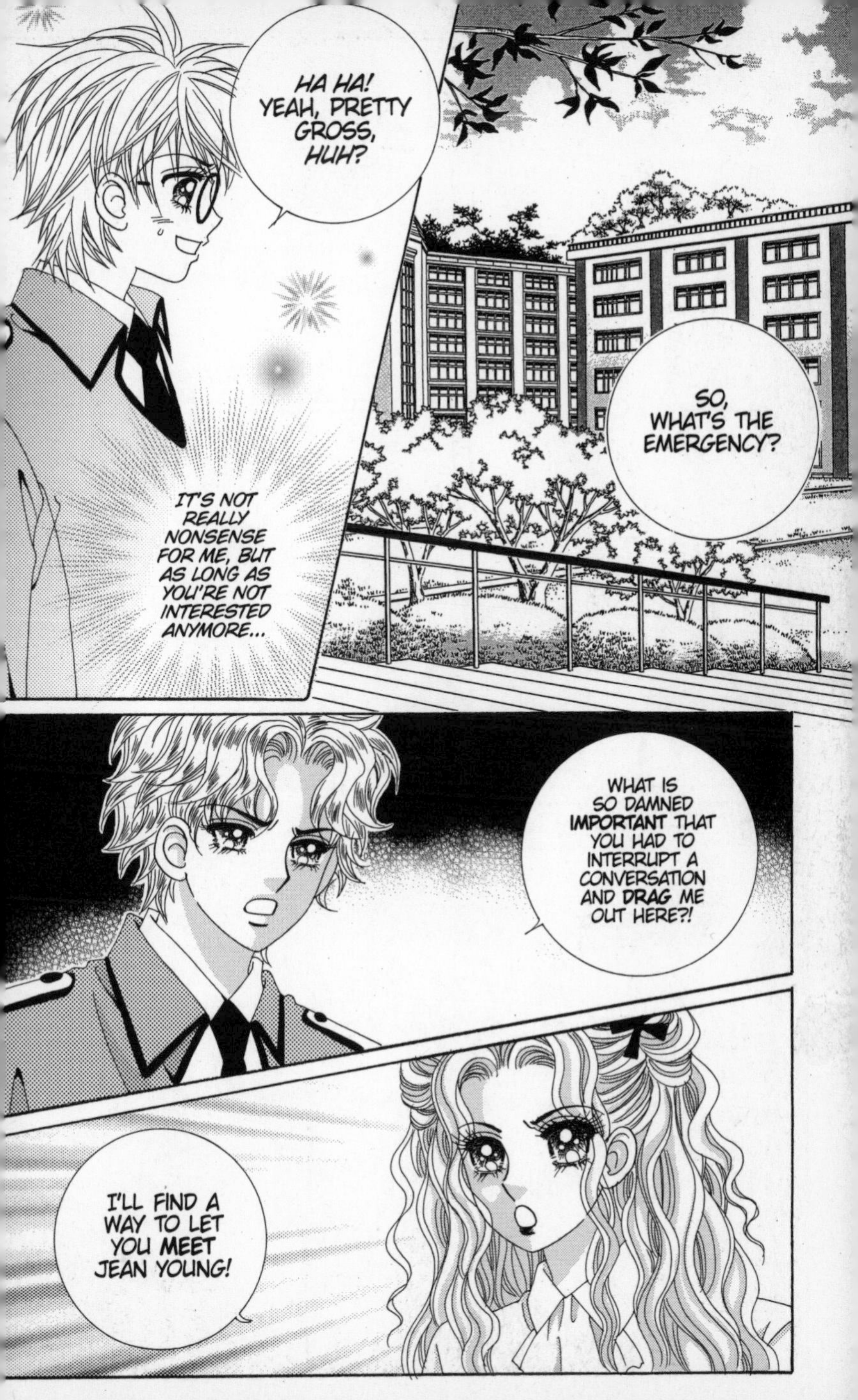
HA HA! YEAH, PRETTY GROSS, HUH?
IT'S NOT REALLY NONSENSE FOR ME, BUT AS LONG AS YOU'RE NOT INTERESTED ANYMORE...
SO, WHAT'S THE EMERGENCY?
WHAT IS SO DAMNED IMPORTANT THAT YOU HAD TO INTERRUPT A CONVERSATION AND DRAG ME OUT HERE?!
I'LL FIND A WAY TO LET YOU MEET JEAN YOUNG!

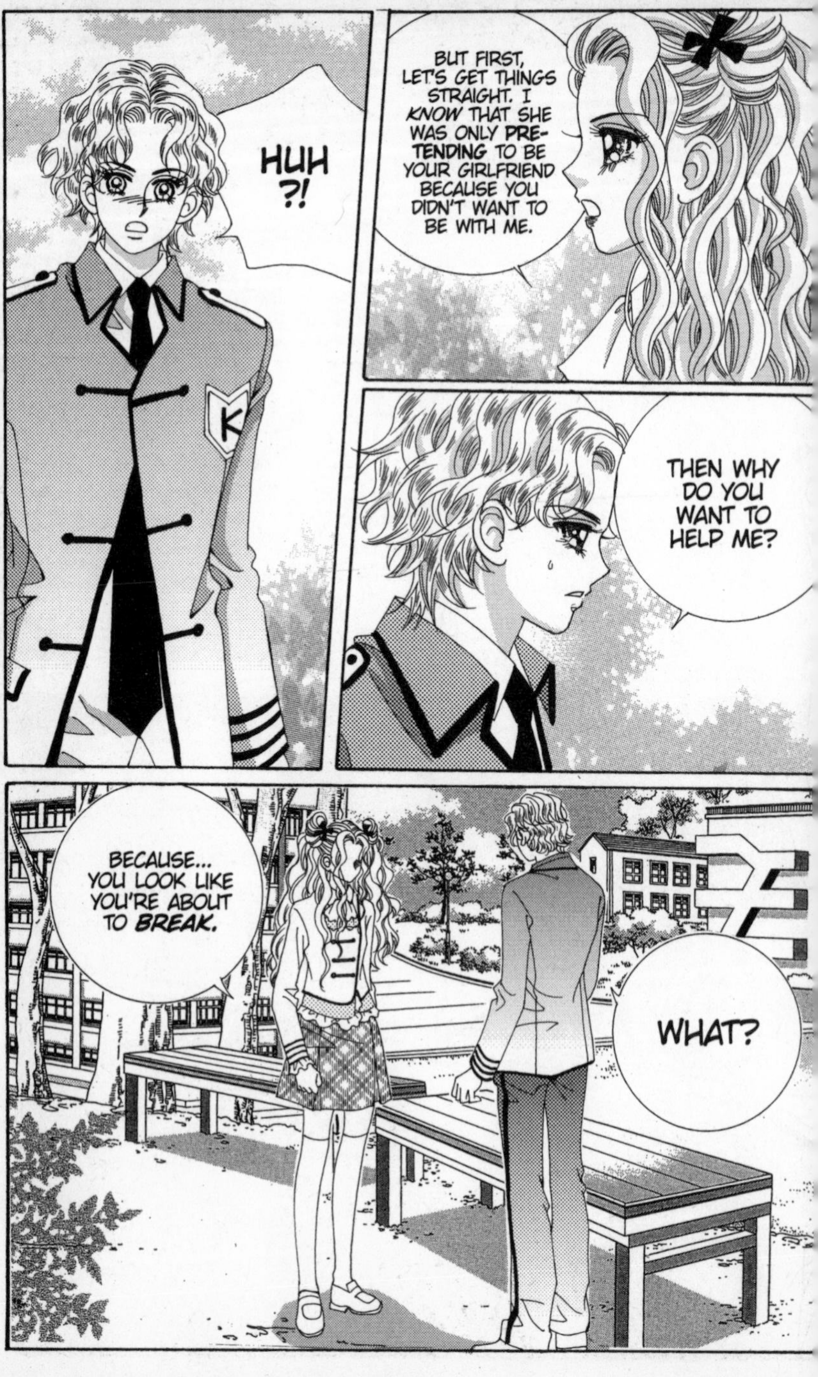
HUH ?!
BUT FIRST, LET'S GET THINGS STRAIGHT. I *KNOW* THAT SHE WAS ONLY **PRETENDING** TO BE YOUR GIRLFRIEND BECAUSE YOU DIDN'T WANT TO BE WITH ME.
THEN WHY DO YOU WANT TO HELP ME?
BECAUSE... YOU LOOK LIKE YOU'RE ABOUT TO ***BREAK.***
WHAT?

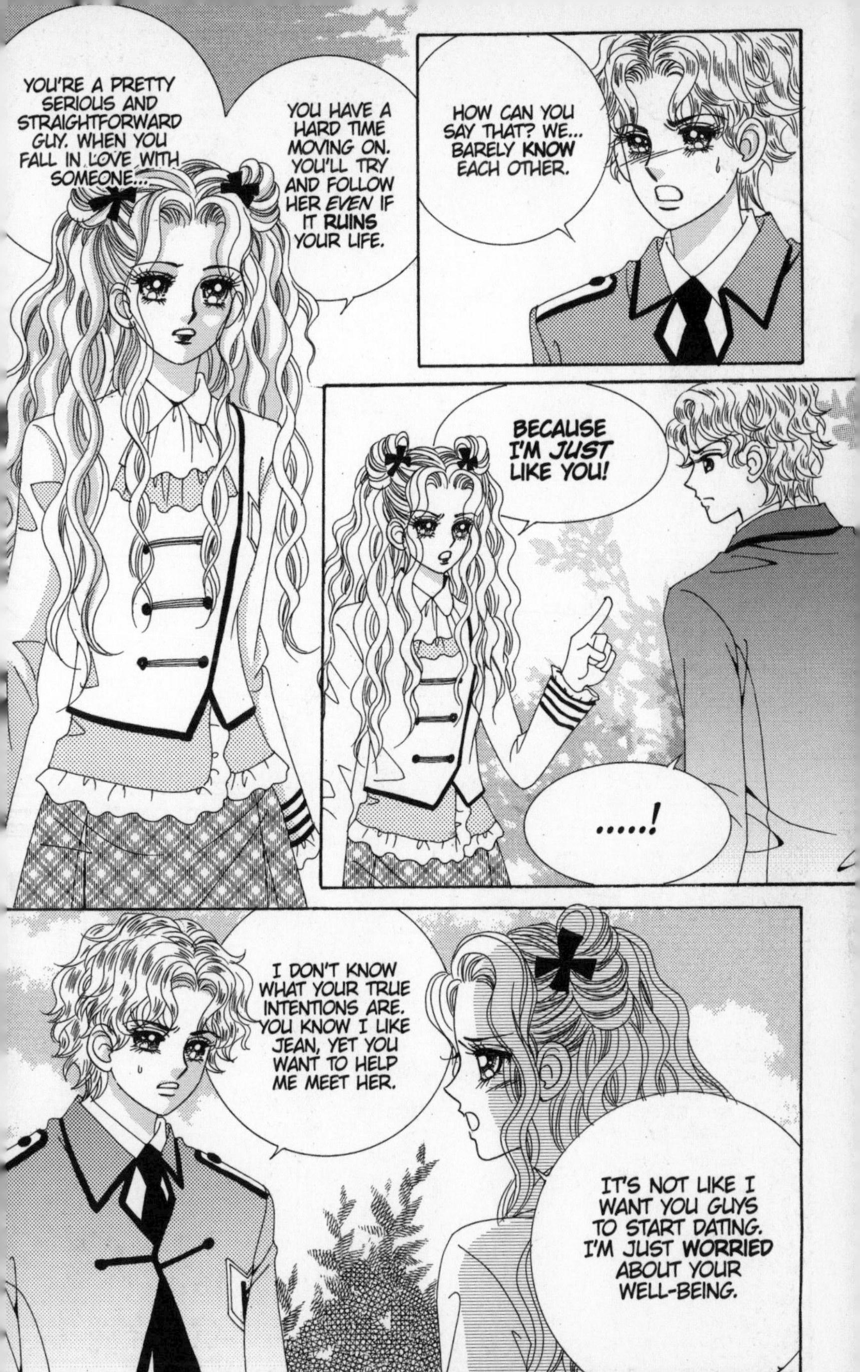
YOU'RE A PRETTY SERIOUS AND STRAIGHTFORWARD GUY. WHEN YOU FALL IN LOVE WITH SOMEONE...
YOU HAVE A HARD TIME MOVING ON. YOU'LL TRY AND FOLLOW HER *EVEN* IF IT **RUINS** YOUR LIFE.
HOW CAN YOU SAY THAT? WE... BARELY **KNOW** EACH OTHER.
BECAUSE I'M *JUST* LIKE YOU!
.....!
I DON'T KNOW WHAT YOUR TRUE INTENTIONS ARE. YOU KNOW I LIKE JEAN, YET YOU WANT TO HELP ME MEET HER.
IT'S NOT LIKE I WANT YOU GUYS TO START DATING. I'M JUST **WORRIED** ABOUT YOUR WELL-BEING.

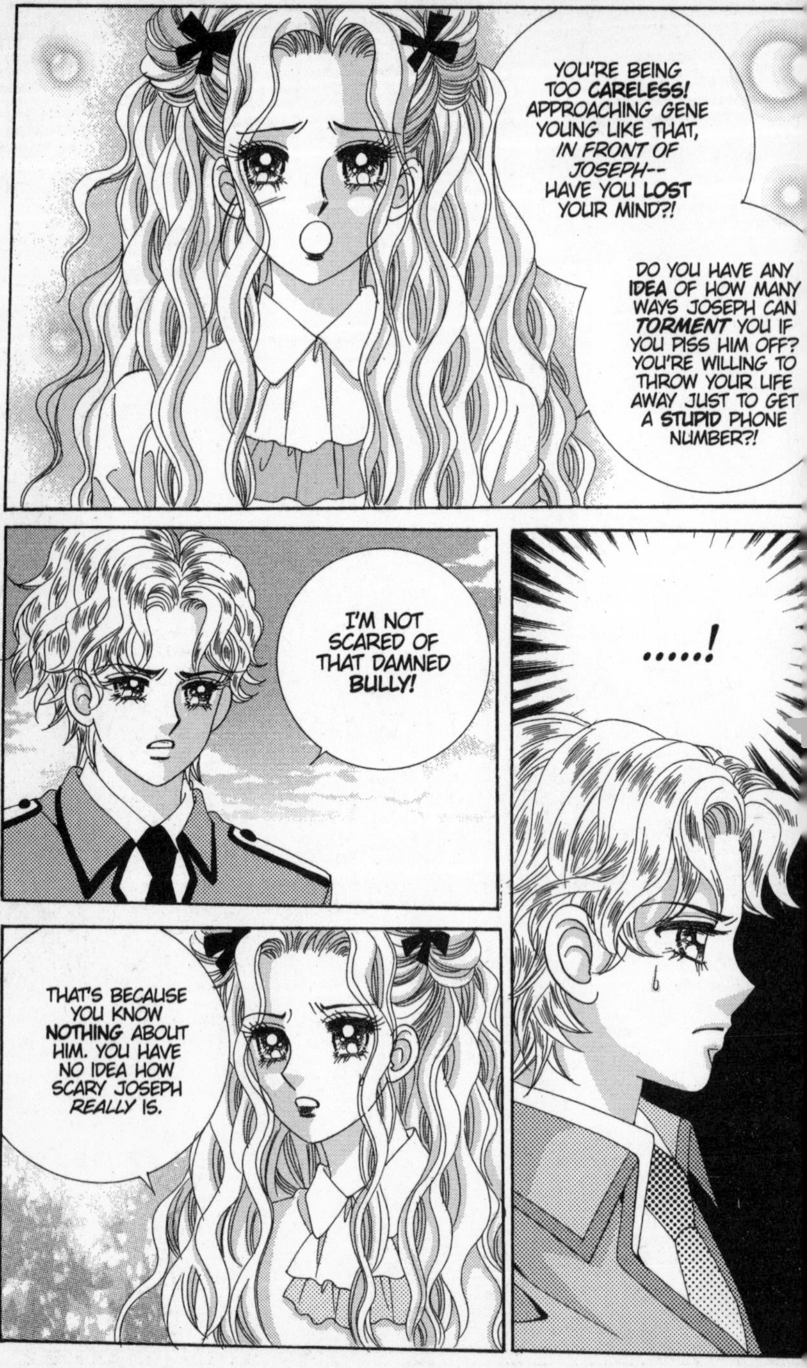

YOU'RE BEING TOO **CARELESS!** APPROACHING GENE YOUNG LIKE THAT, *IN FRONT OF JOSEPH--* HAVE YOU **LOST** YOUR MIND?!
DO YOU HAVE ANY **IDEA** OF HOW MANY WAYS JOSEPH CAN ***TORMENT*** YOU IF YOU PISS HIM OFF? YOU'RE WILLING TO THROW YOUR LIFE AWAY JUST TO GET A **STUPID** PHONE NUMBER?!
I'M NOT SCARED OF THAT DAMNED **BULLY!**
THAT'S BECAUSE YOU KNOW **NOTHING** ABOUT HIM. YOU HAVE NO IDEA HOW SCARY JOSEPH *REALLY* IS.
.....!

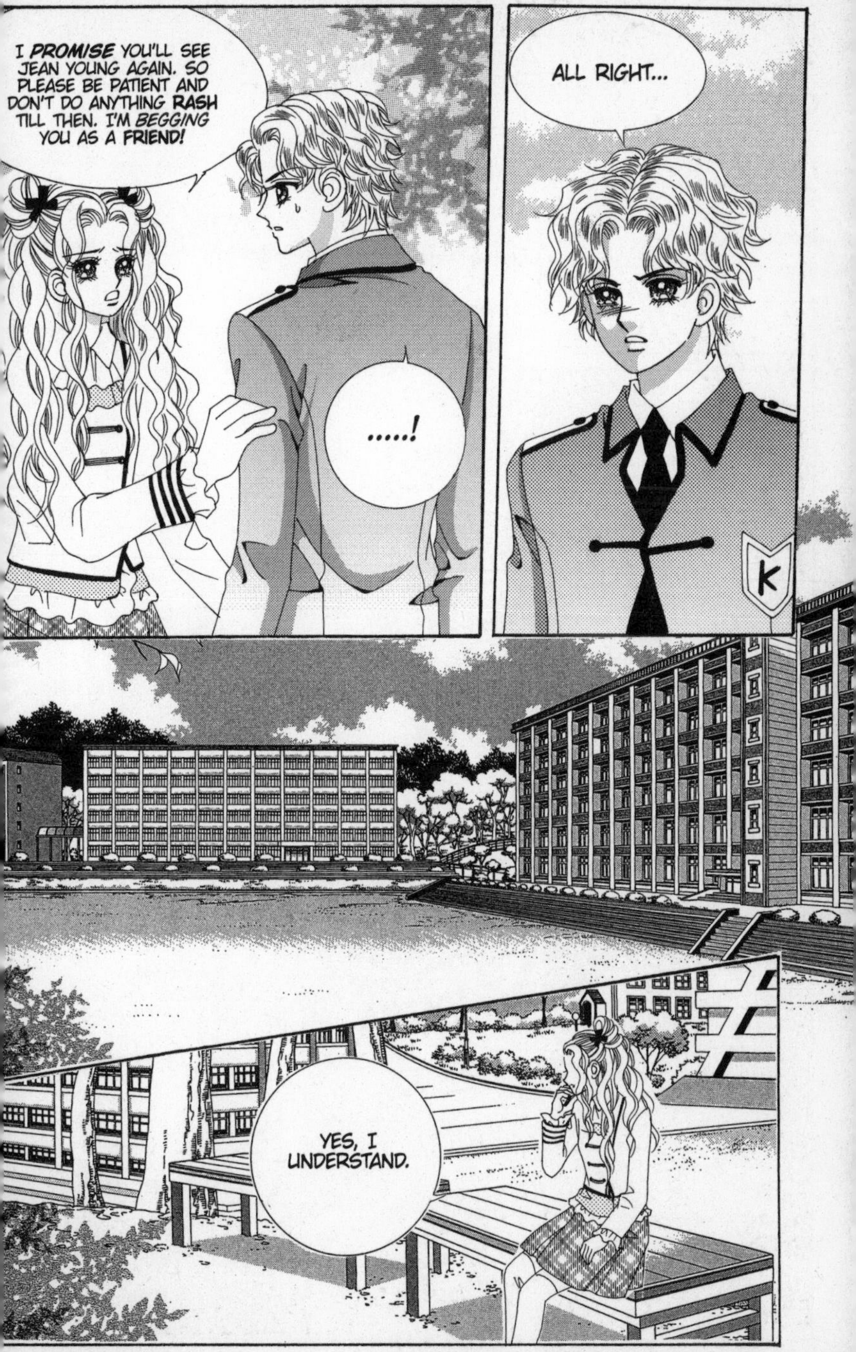
I PROMISE YOU'LL SEE JEAN YOUNG AGAIN. SO PLEASE BE PATIENT AND DON'T DO ANYTHING RASH TILL THEN. I'M BEGGING YOU AS A FRIEND!
.....!
ALL RIGHT...
YES, I UNDERSTAND.

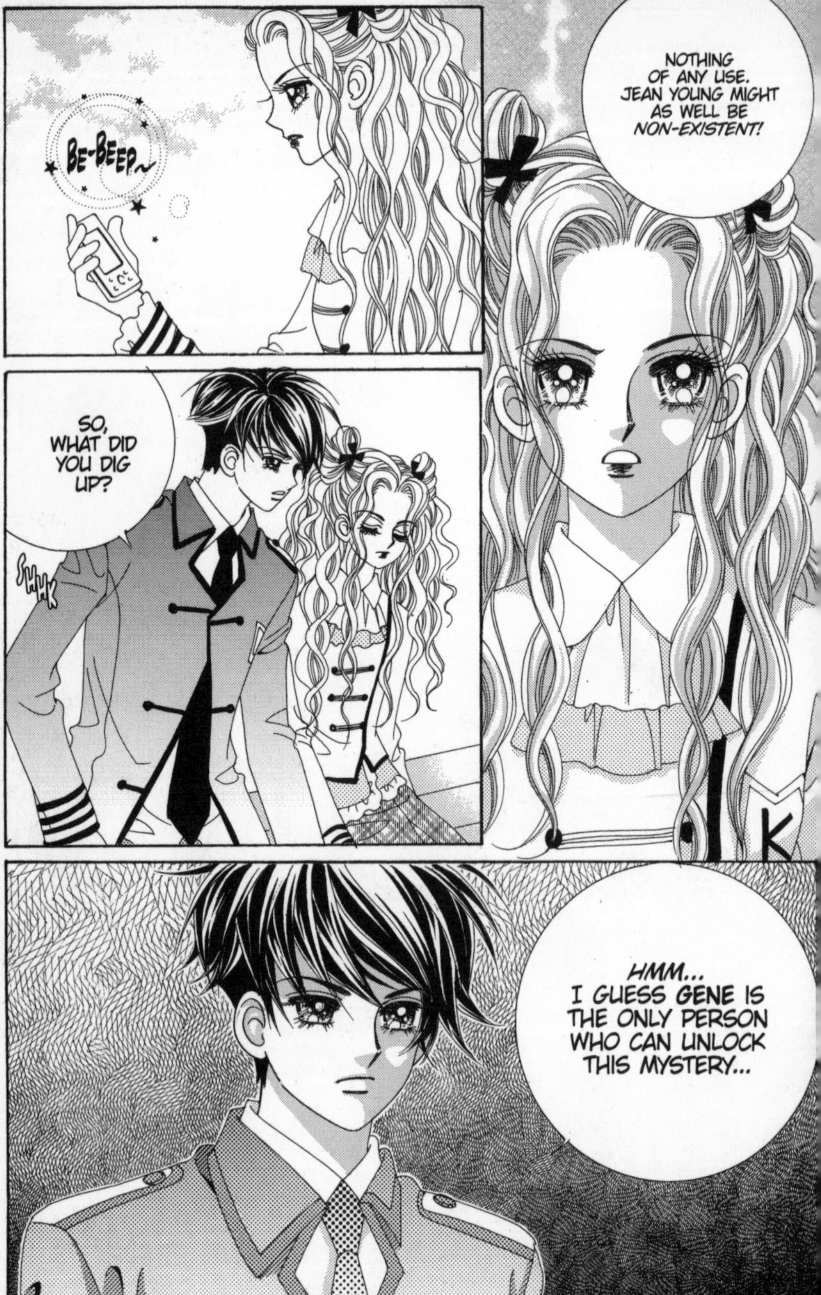
BE-BEEP~
SO, WHAT DID YOU DIG UP?
SHHK
NOTHING OF ANY USE. JEAN YOUNG MIGHT AS WELL BE *NON-EXISTENT!*
HMM... I GUESS GENE IS THE ONLY PERSON WHO CAN UNLOCK THIS MYSTERY...

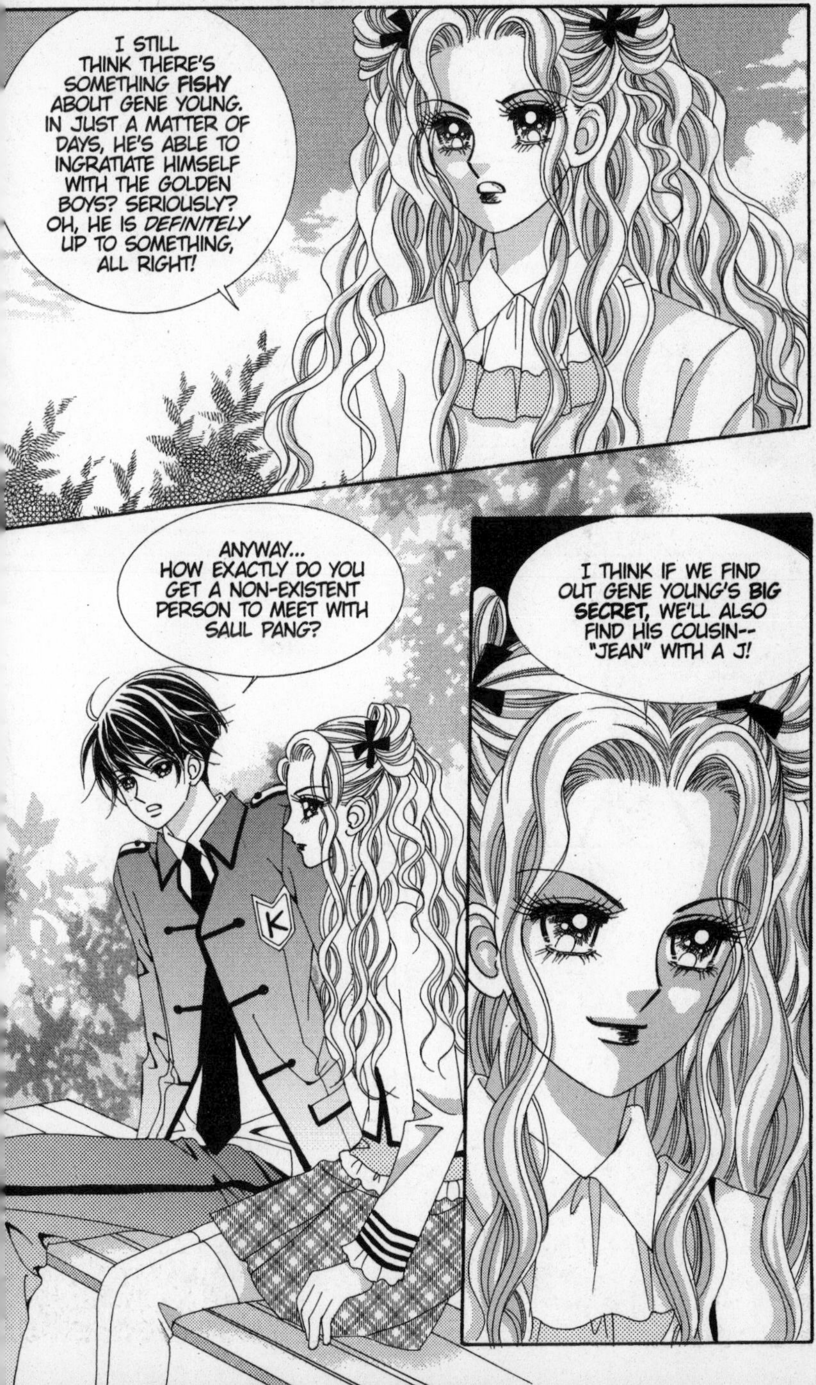
I STILL THINK THERE'S SOMETHING FISHY ABOUT GENE YOUNG. IN JUST A MATTER OF DAYS, HE'S ABLE TO INGRATIATE HIMSELF WITH THE GOLDEN BOYS? SERIOUSLY? OH, HE IS *DEFINITELY* UP TO SOMETHING, ALL RIGHT!
ANYWAY... HOW EXACTLY DO YOU GET A NON-EXISTENT PERSON TO MEET WITH SAUL PANG?
I THINK IF WE FIND OUT GENE YOUNG'S **BIG SECRET**, WE'LL ALSO FIND HIS COUSIN-- "JEAN" WITH A J!

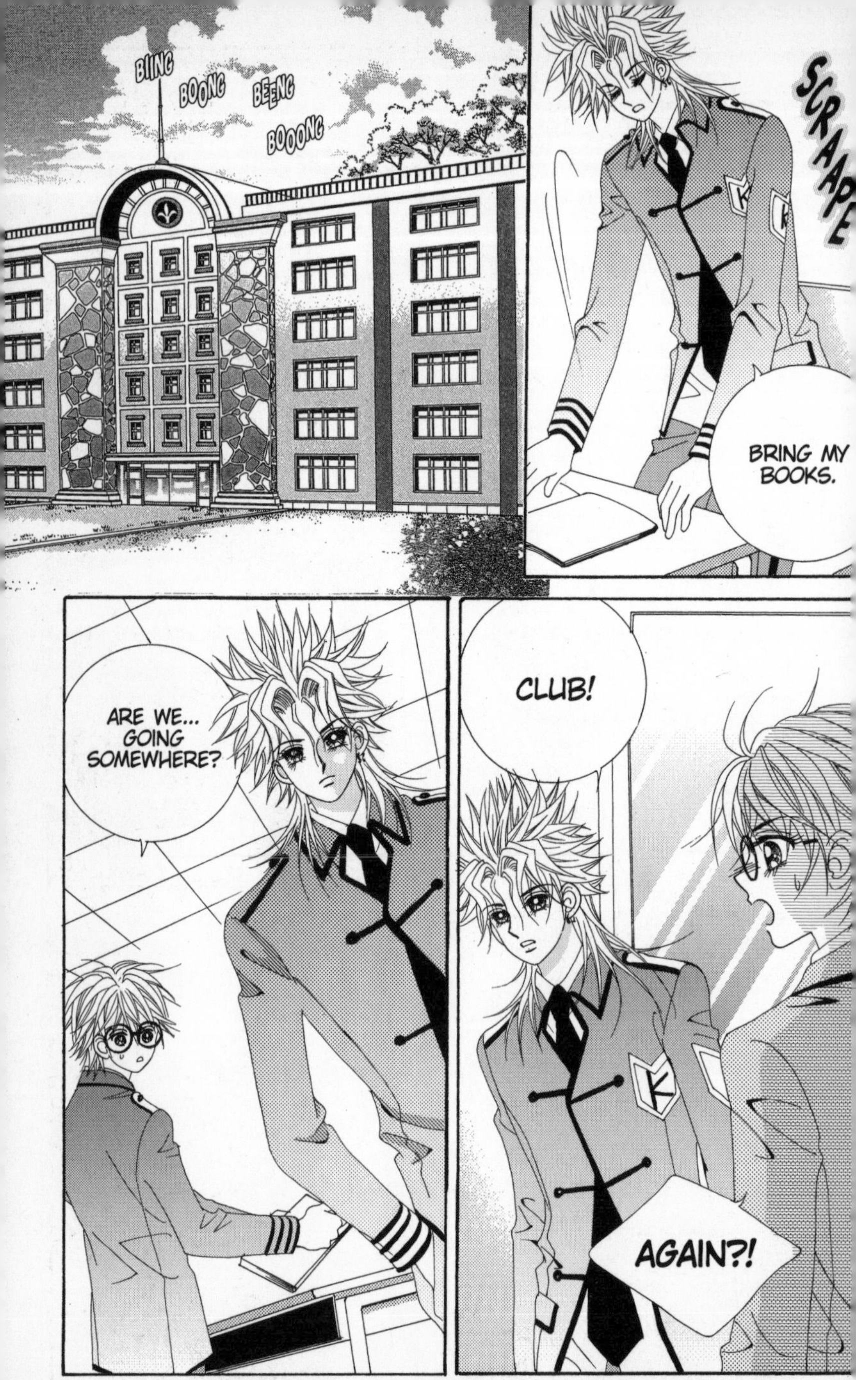
BIING
BOONG
BEENG
BOOONG
SCRAAAPE
BRING MY BOOKS.
ARE WE... GOING SOMEWHERE?
CLUB!
AGAIN?!

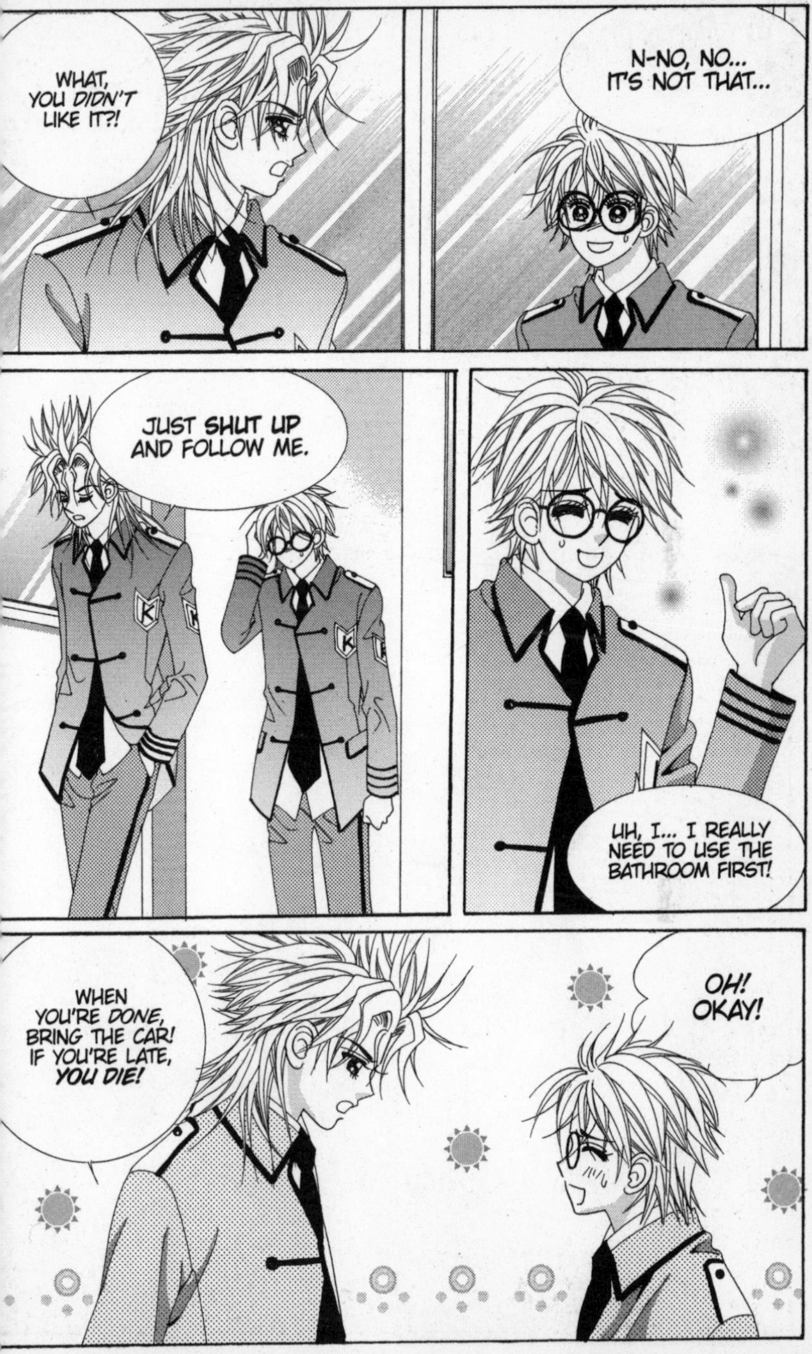
WHAT, YOU *DIDN'T* LIKE IT?!
N-NO, NO... IT'S NOT THAT...
JUST SHUT UP AND FOLLOW ME.
UH, I... I REALLY NEED TO USE THE BATHROOM FIRST!
WHEN YOU'RE *DONE*, BRING THE CAR! IF YOU'RE LATE, ***YOU DIE!***
OH! OKAY!

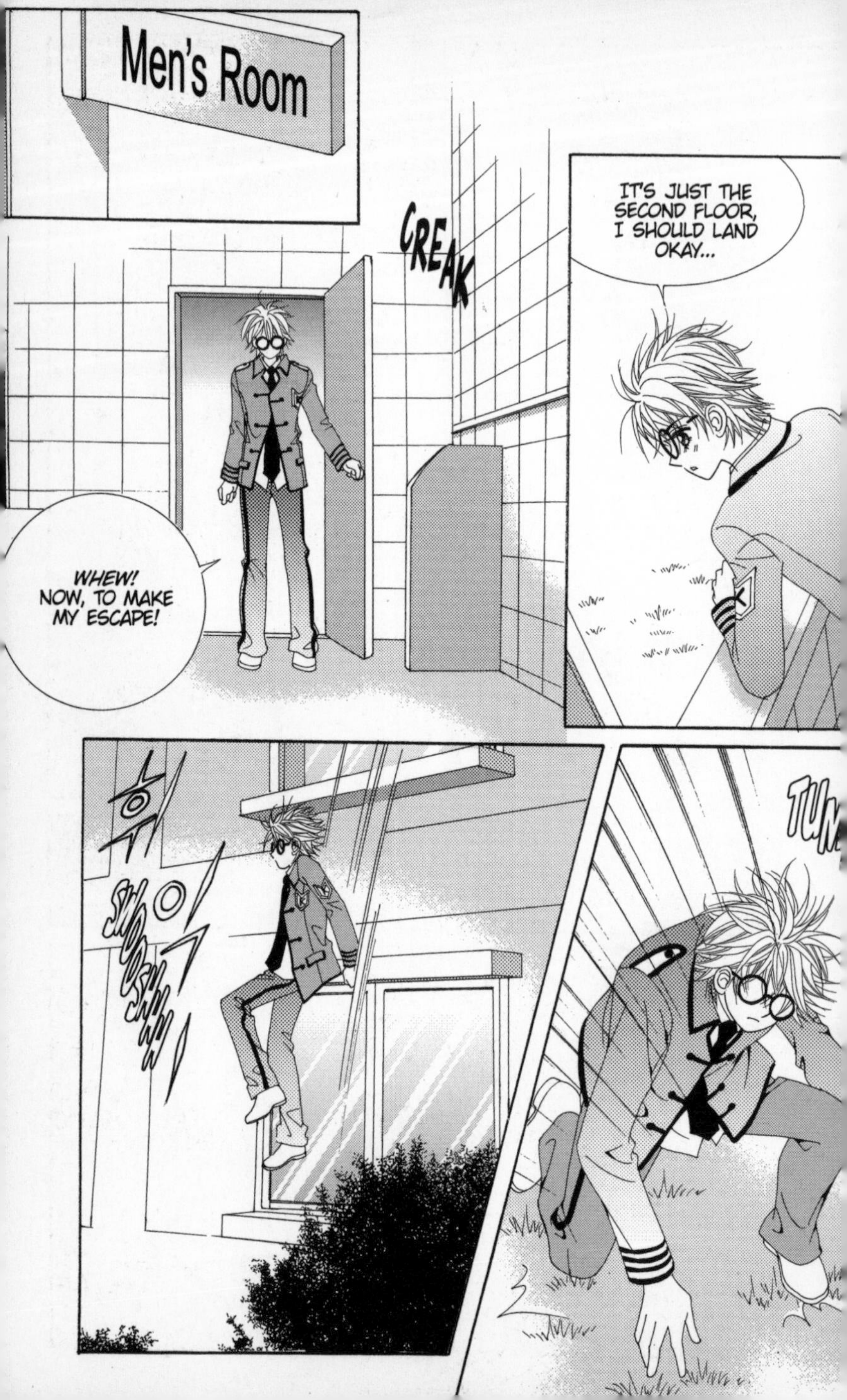
Men's Room
CREAK
WHEW! NOW, TO MAKE MY ESCAPE!
IT'S JUST THE SECOND FLOOR, I SHOULD LAND OKAY...
SWOOSH
TUN

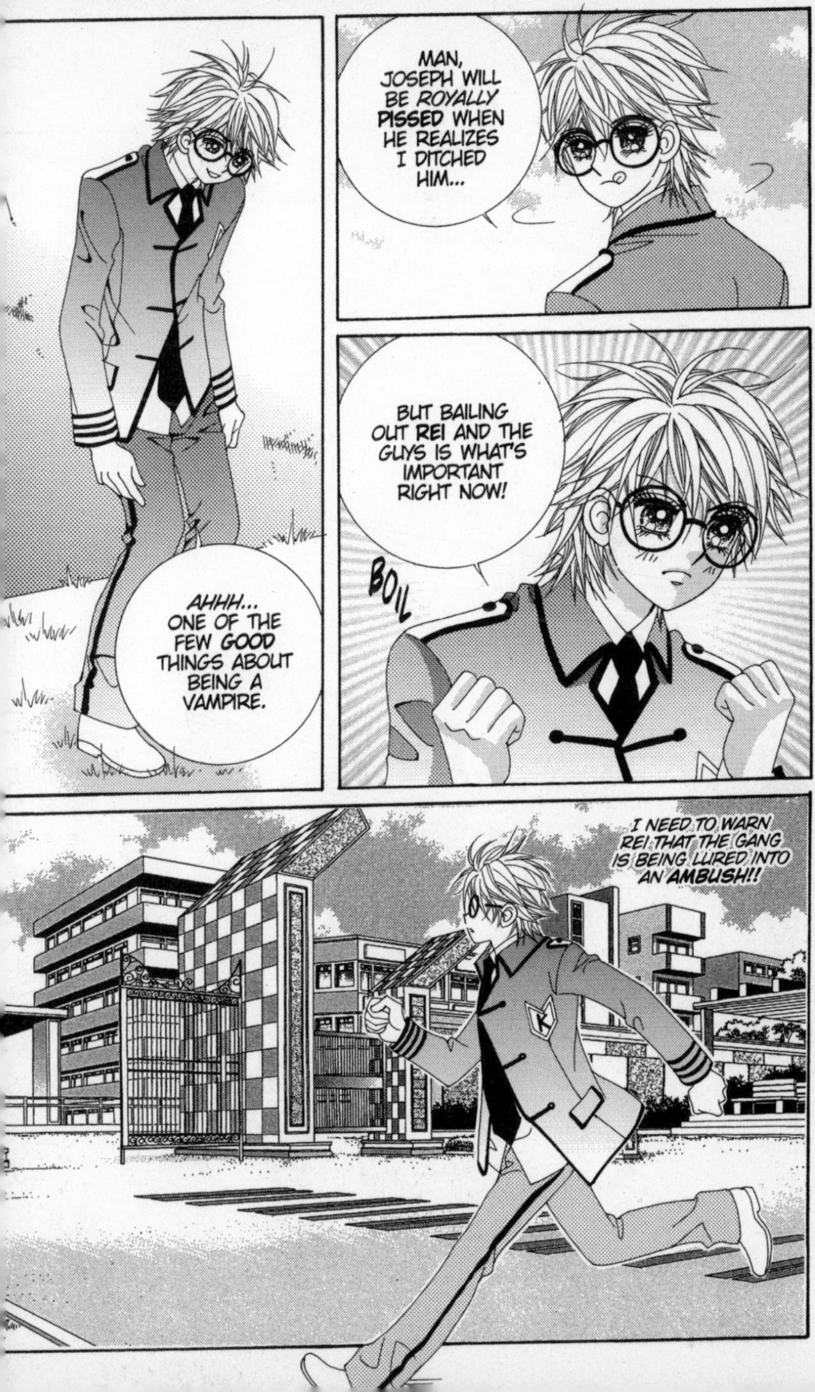
AHHH... ONE OF THE FEW GOOD THINGS ABOUT BEING A VAMPIRE.
MAN, JOSEPH WILL BE ROYALLY PISSED WHEN HE REALIZES I DITCHED HIM...
BUT BAILING OUT REI AND THE GUYS IS WHAT'S IMPORTANT RIGHT NOW!
BOIL
I NEED TO WARN REI THAT THE GANG IS BEING LURED INTO AN AMBUSH!!

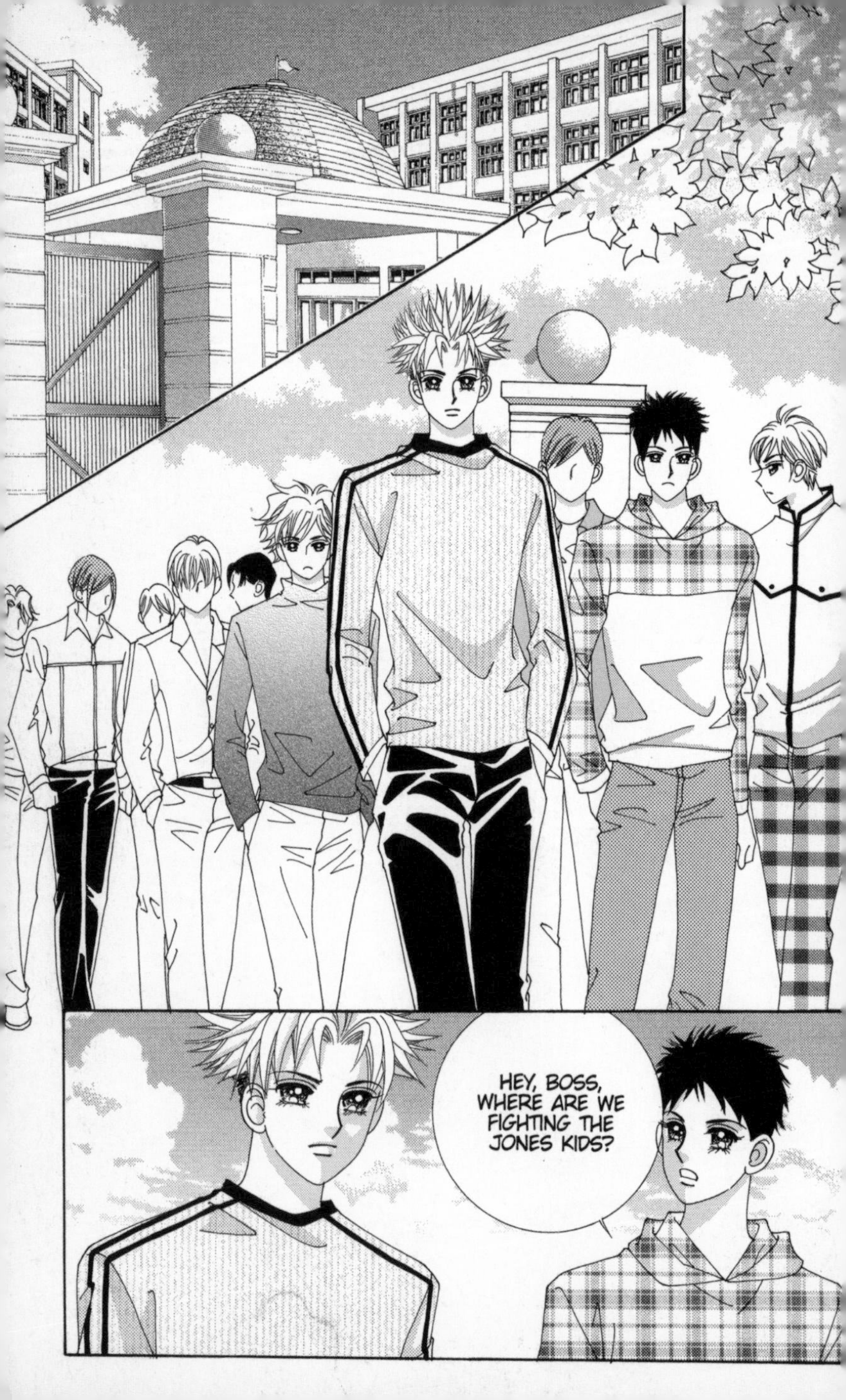
HEY, BOSS, WHERE ARE WE FIGHTING THE JONES KIDS?

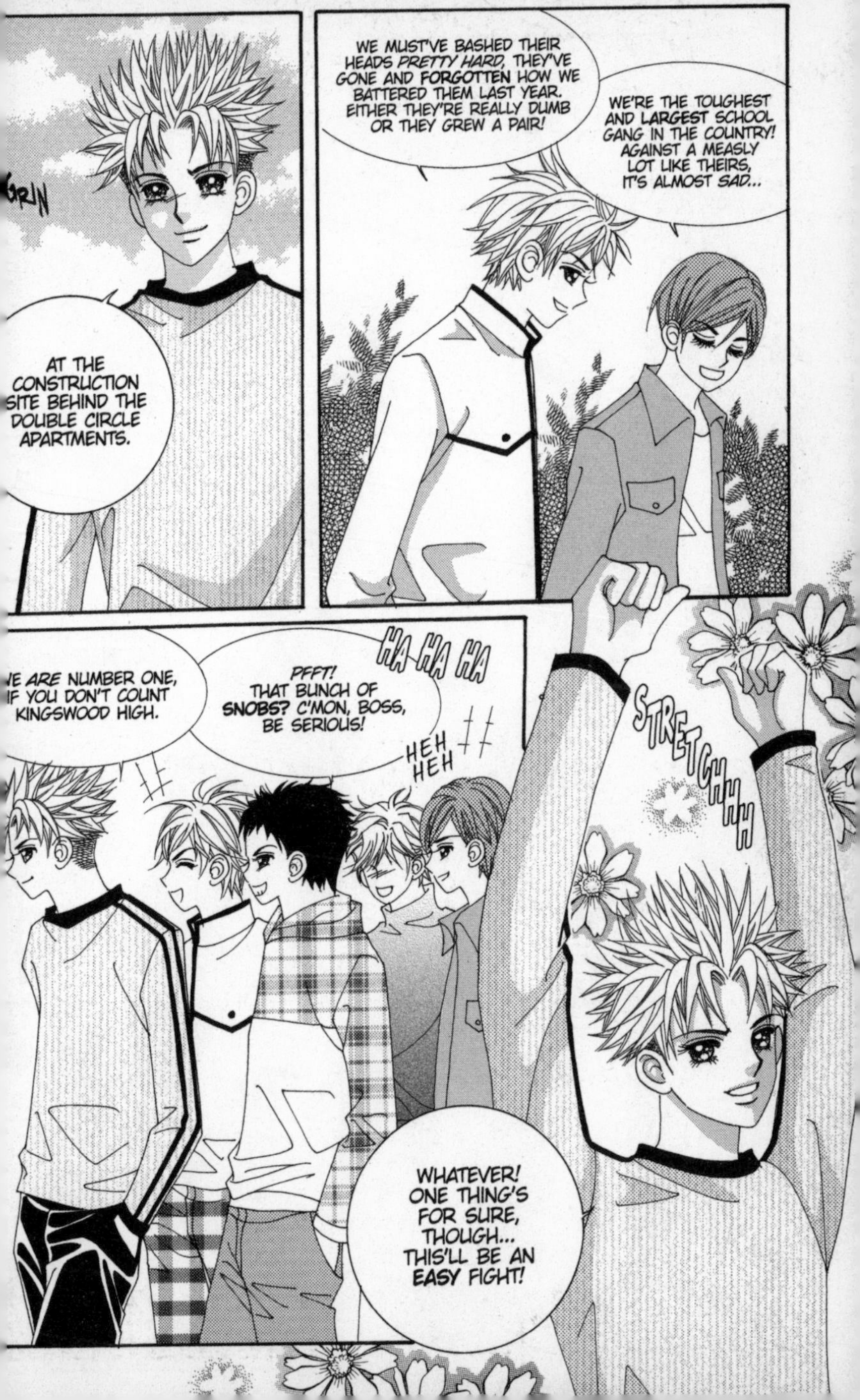
GRIN
AT THE CONSTRUCTION SITE BEHIND THE DOUBLE CIRCLE APARTMENTS.
WE MUST'VE BASHED THEIR HEADS PRETTY HARD, THEY'VE GONE AND FORGOTTEN HOW WE BATTERED THEM LAST YEAR. EITHER THEY'RE REALLY DUMB OR THEY GREW A PAIR!
WE'RE THE TOUGHEST AND LARGEST SCHOOL GANG IN THE COUNTRY! AGAINST A MEASLY LOT LIKE THEIRS, IT'S ALMOST SAD...
WE ARE NUMBER ONE, IF YOU DON'T COUNT KINGSWOOD HIGH.
PFFT! THAT BUNCH OF SNOBS? C'MON, BOSS, BE SERIOUS!
HA HA HA
HEH HEH
STRETCHHHH
WHATEVER! ONE THING'S FOR SURE, THOUGH... THIS'LL BE AN EASY FIGHT!

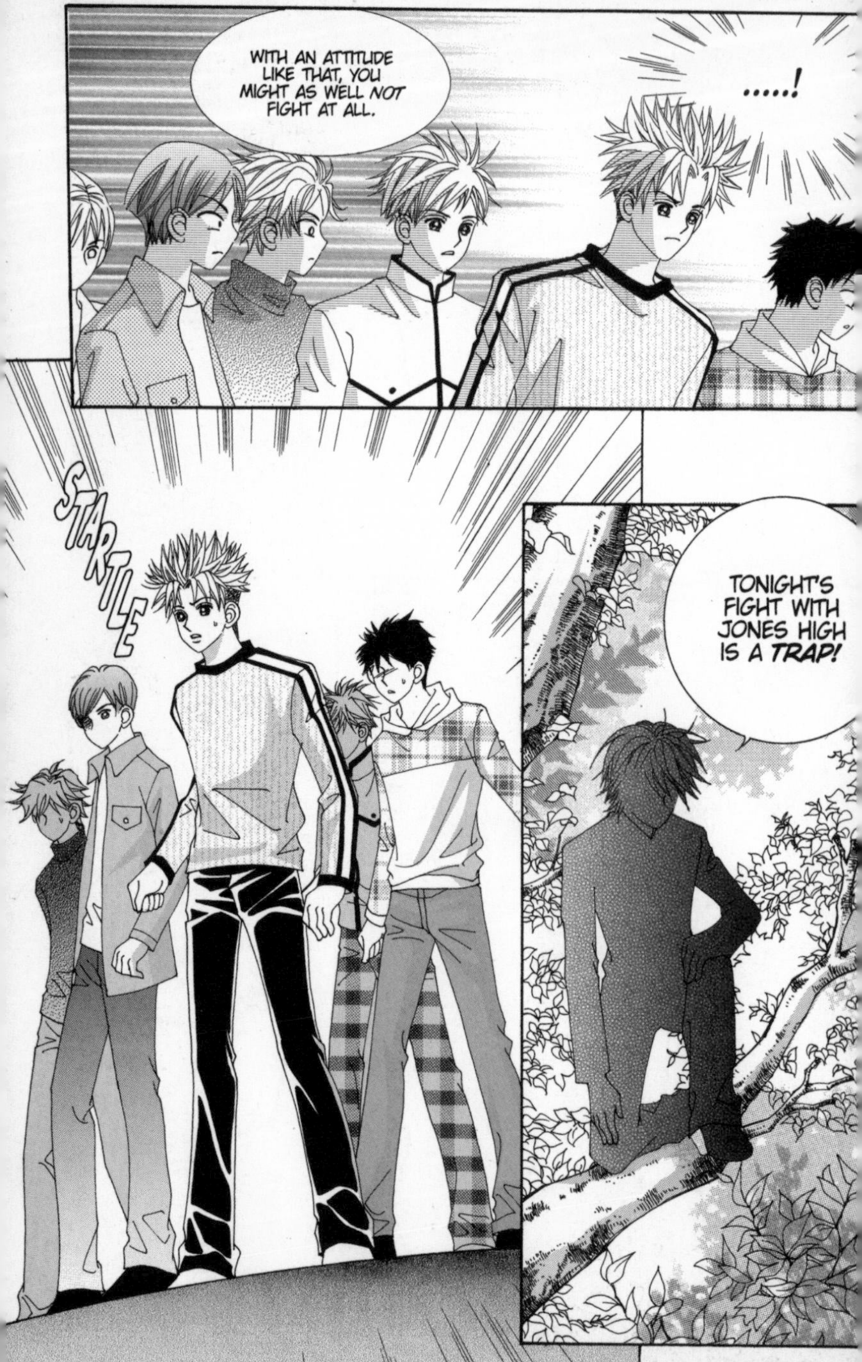
WITH AN ATTITUDE LIKE THAT, YOU MIGHT AS WELL NOT FIGHT AT ALL.
......!
STARTLE
TONIGHT'S FIGHT WITH JONES HIGH IS A TRAP!

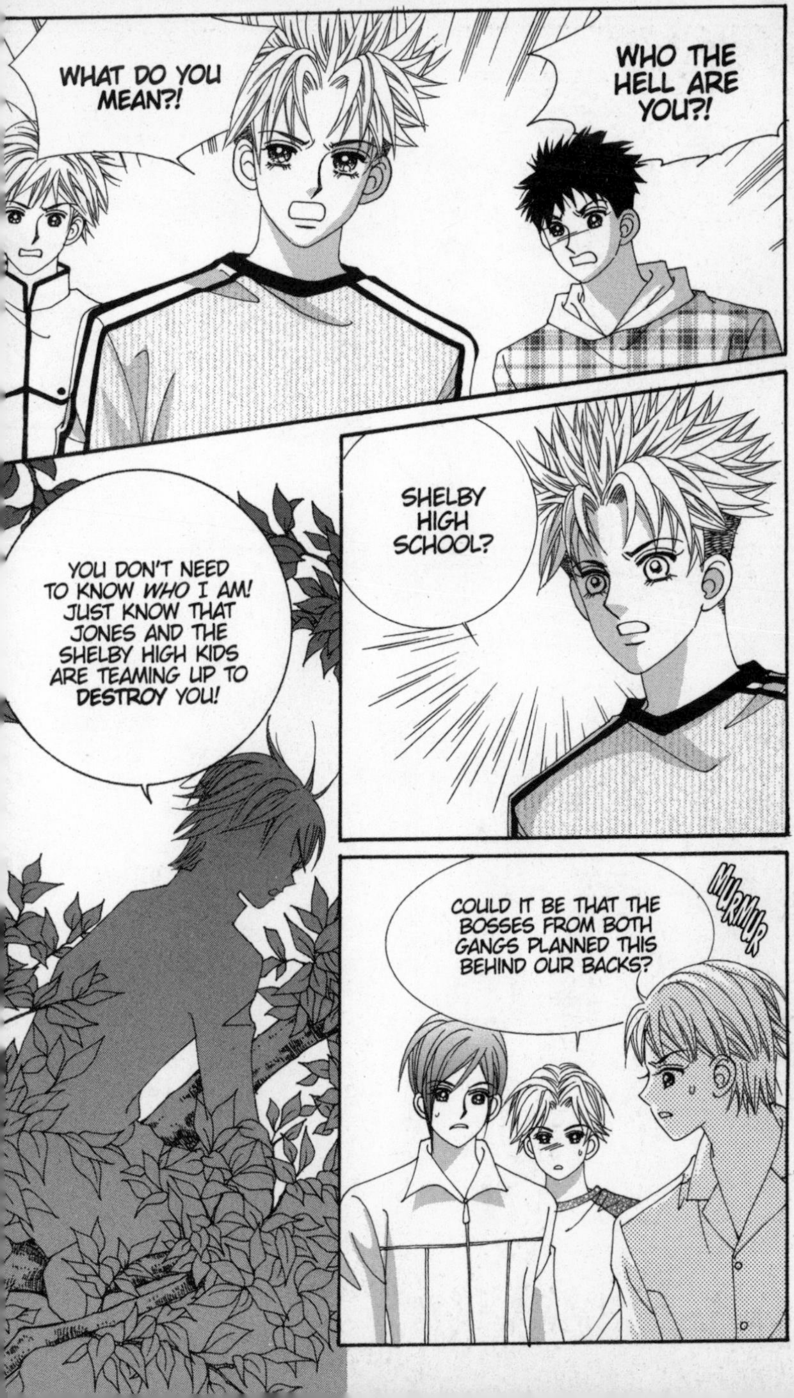
WHAT DO YOU MEAN?!
WHO THE HELL ARE YOU?!
YOU DON'T NEED TO KNOW *WHO* I AM! JUST KNOW THAT JONES AND THE SHELBY HIGH KIDS ARE TEAMING UP TO DESTROY YOU!
SHELBY HIGH SCHOOL?
COULD IT BE THAT THE BOSSES FROM BOTH GANGS PLANNED THIS BEHIND OUR BACKS?
MURMUR

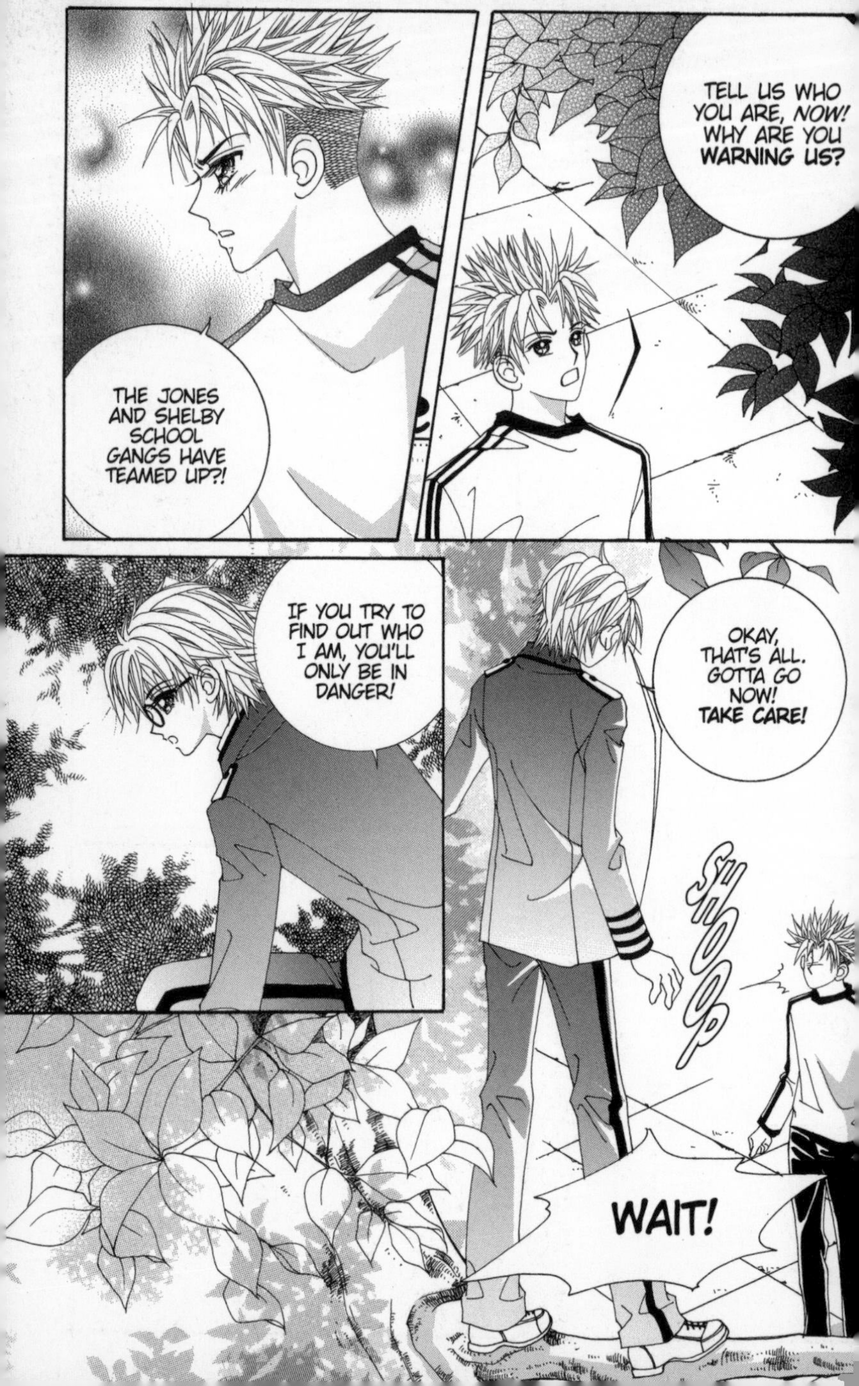
THE JONES AND SHELBY SCHOOL GANGS HAVE TEAMED UP?!
TELL US WHO YOU ARE, *NOW!* WHY ARE YOU WARNING US?
IF YOU TRY TO FIND OUT WHO I AM, YOU'LL ONLY BE IN DANGER!
OKAY, THAT'S ALL. GOTTA GO NOW! TAKE CARE!
SHOOP
WAIT!

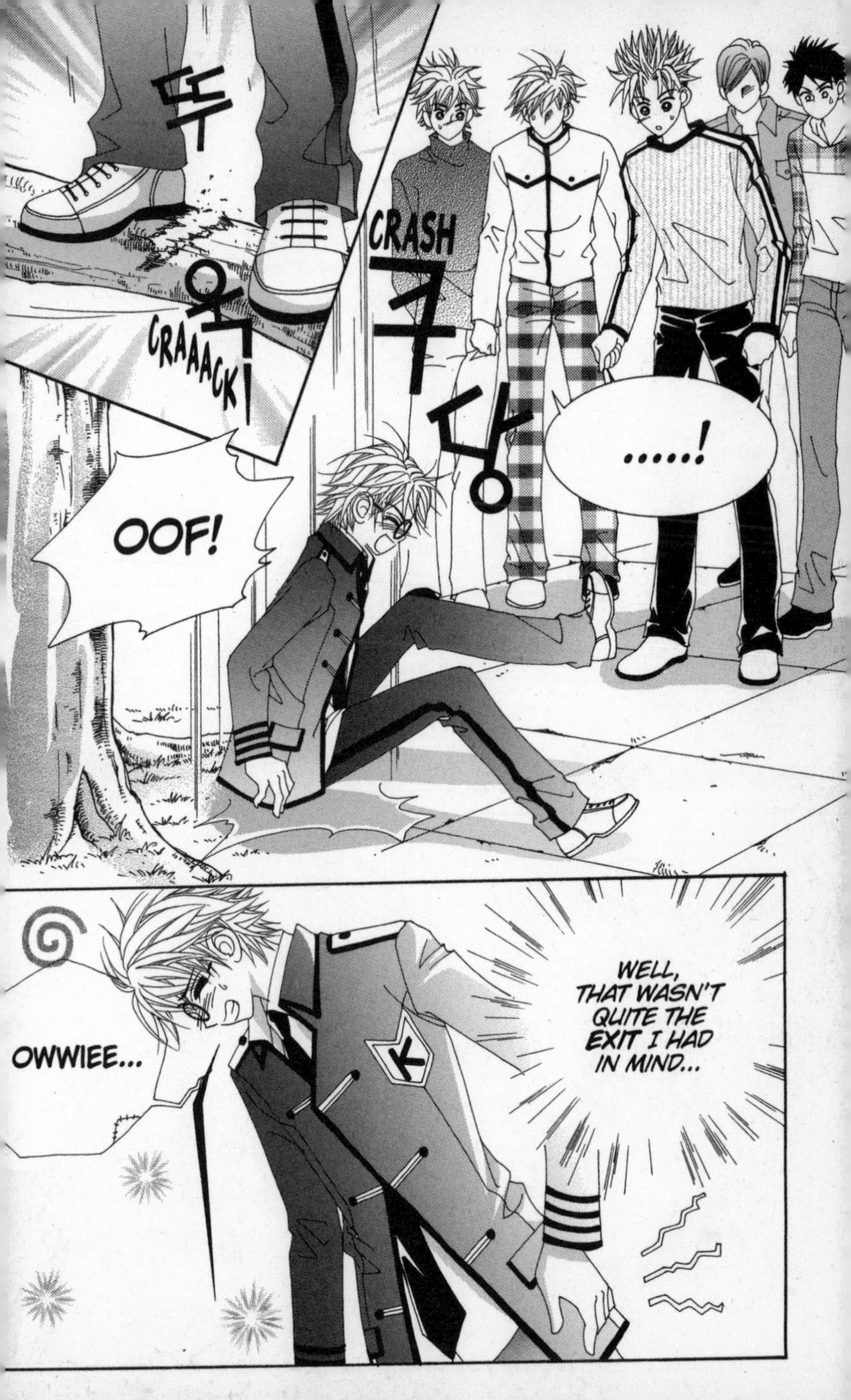

뚝
CRAAACK
CRASH
쿠당
......!
OOF!
OWWIEE...
WELL, THAT WASN'T QUITE THE EXIT I HAD IN MIND...

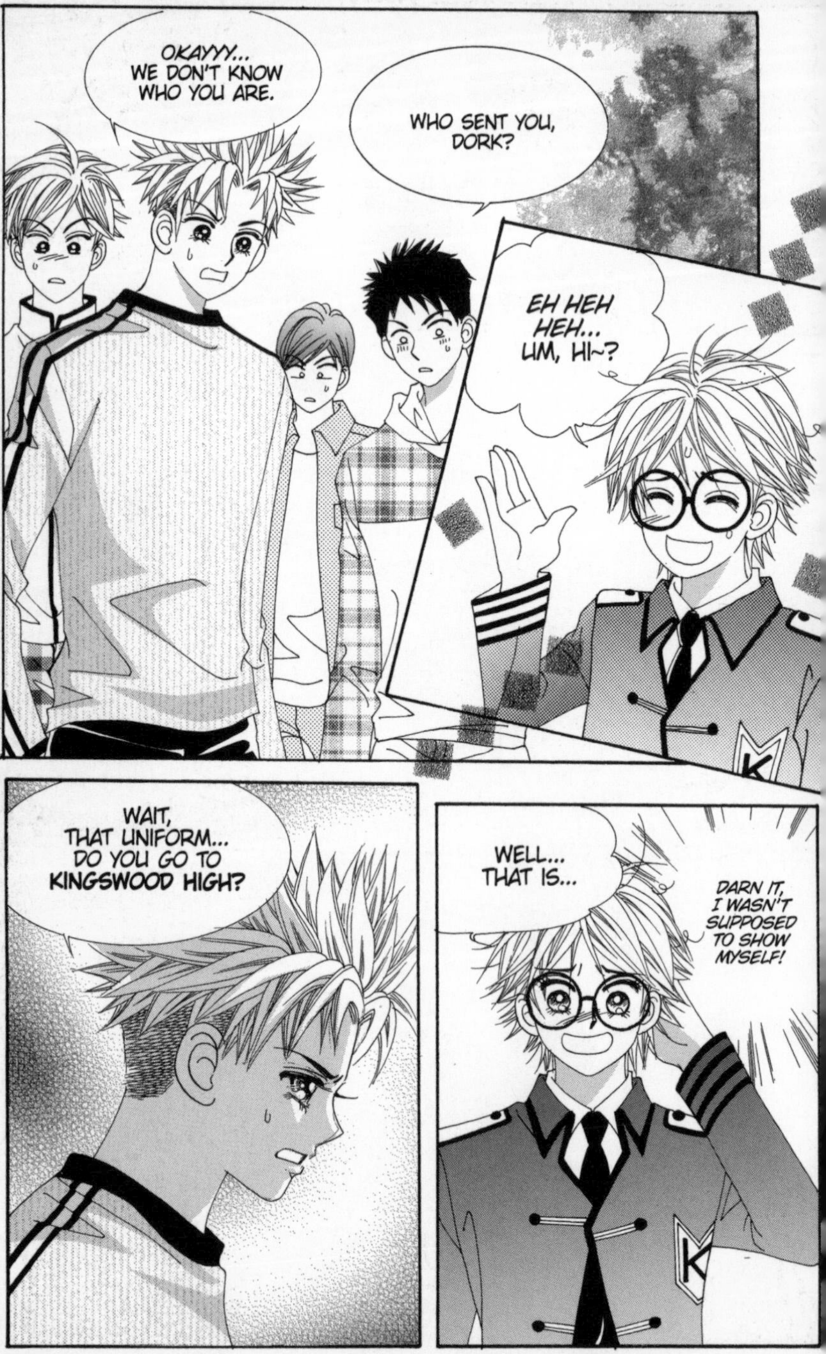
OKAYYY... WE DON'T KNOW WHO YOU ARE.
WHO SENT YOU, DORK?
EH HEH HEH... UM, HI~?
WAIT, THAT UNIFORM... DO YOU GO TO KINGSWOOD HIGH?
WELL... THAT IS...
DARN IT, I WASN'T SUPPOSED TO SHOW MYSELF!

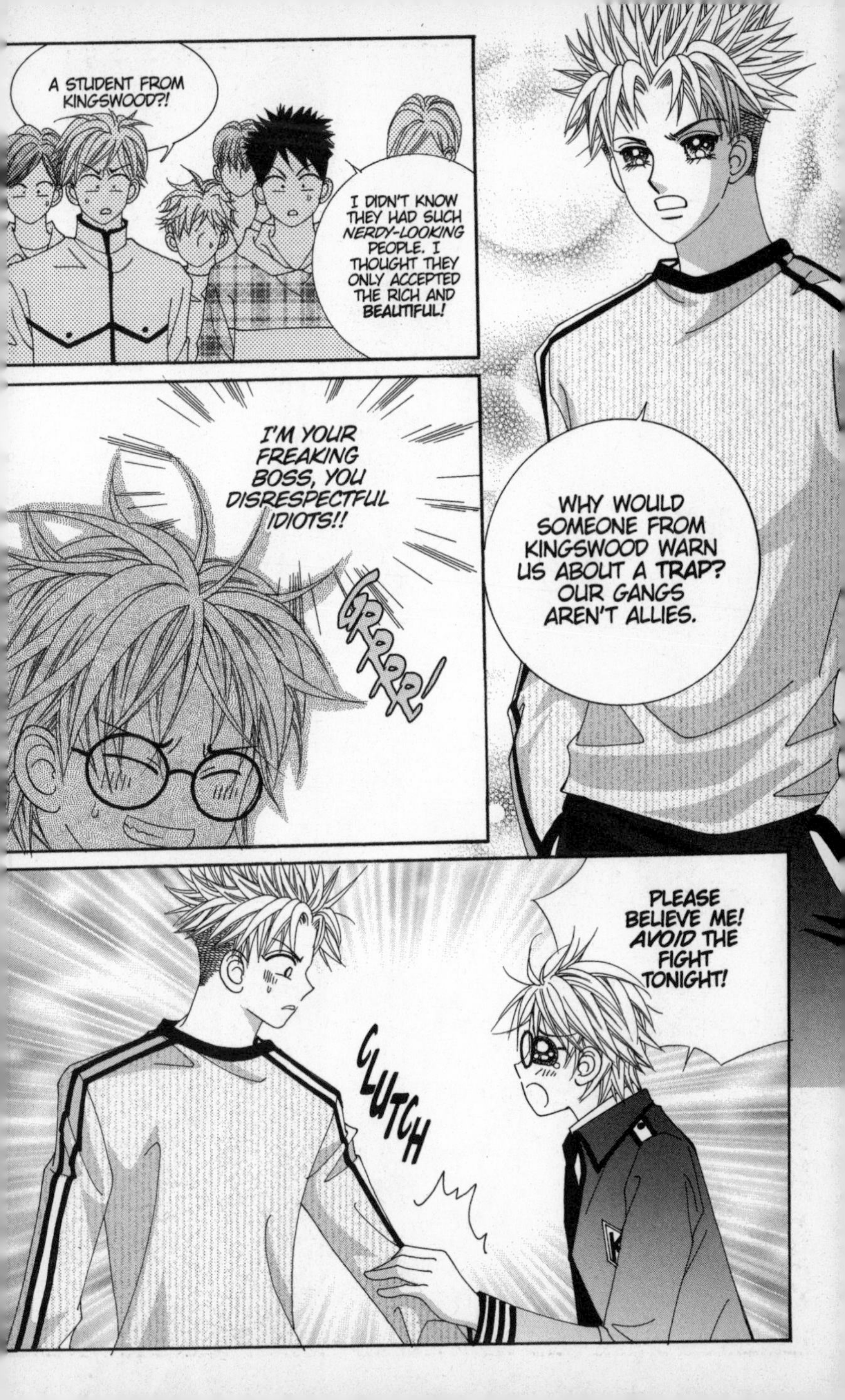

A STUDENT FROM KINGSWOOD?!
I DIDN'T KNOW THEY HAD SUCH NERDY-LOOKING PEOPLE. I THOUGHT THEY ONLY ACCEPTED THE RICH AND BEAUTIFUL!
I'M YOUR FREAKING BOSS, YOU DISRESPECTFUL IDIOTS!!
GRRRR!
WHY WOULD SOMEONE FROM KINGSWOOD WARN US ABOUT A TRAP? OUR GANGS AREN'T ALLIES.
PLEASE BELIEVE ME! AVOID THE FIGHT TONIGHT!
CLUTCH

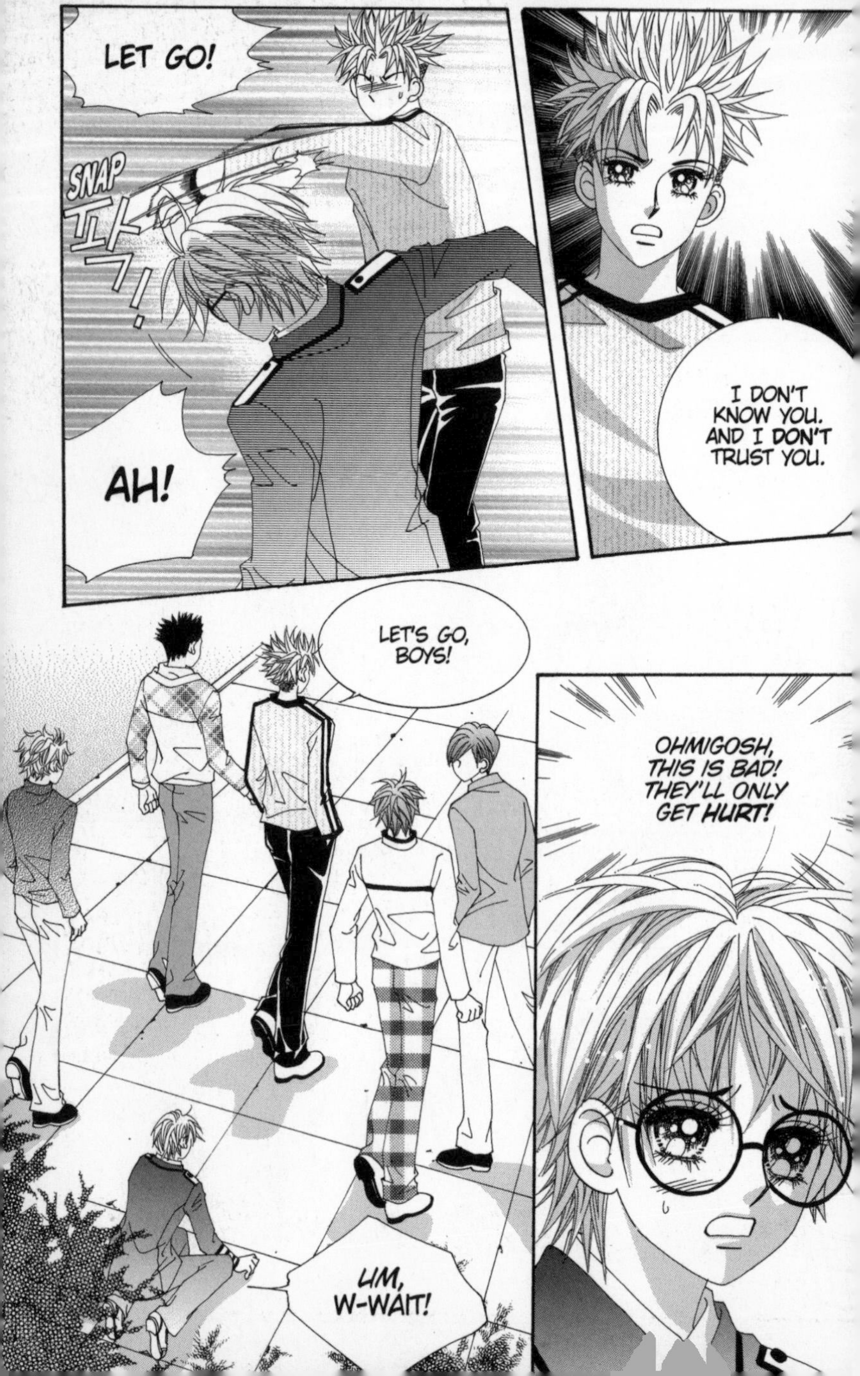
LET GO!
SNAP
AH!
I DON'T KNOW YOU. AND I DON'T TRUST YOU.
LET'S GO, BOYS!
UM, W-WAIT!
OHMIGOSH, THIS IS BAD! THEY'LL ONLY GET HURT!

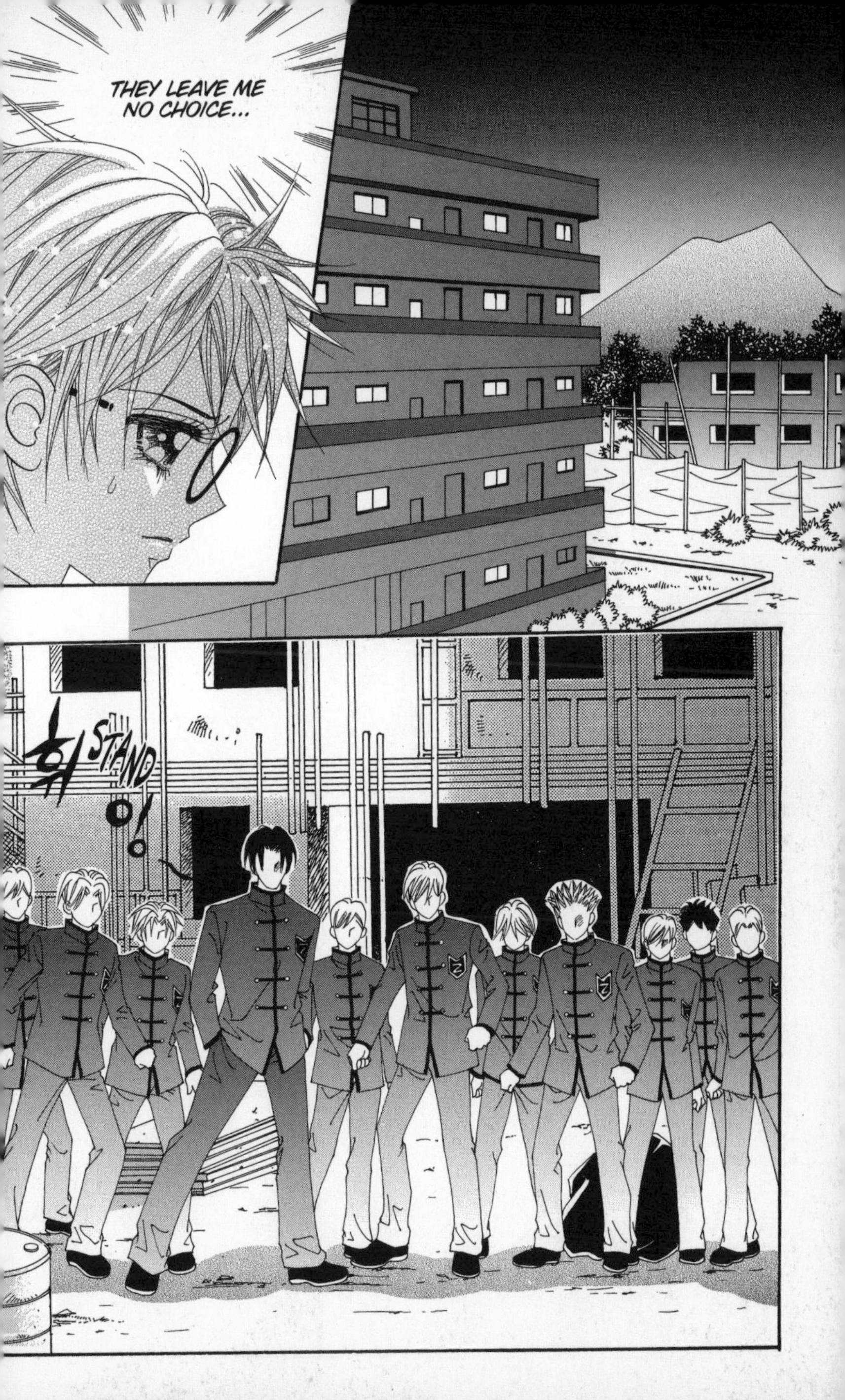
THEY LEAVE ME NO CHOICE...
STAND

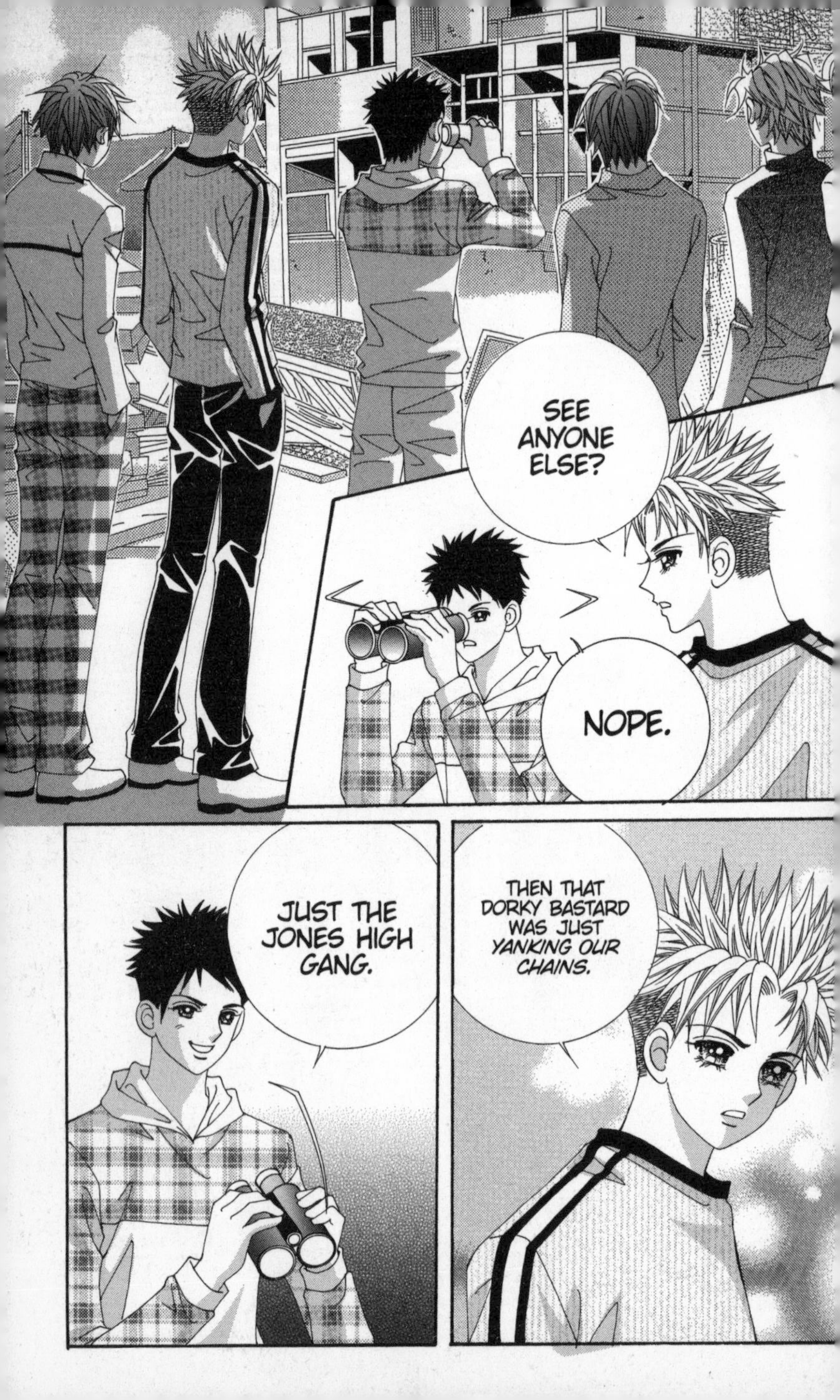
SEE ANYONE ELSE?
NOPE.
JUST THE JONES HIGH GANG.
THEN THAT DORKY BASTARD WAS JUST *YANKING OUR CHAINS.*

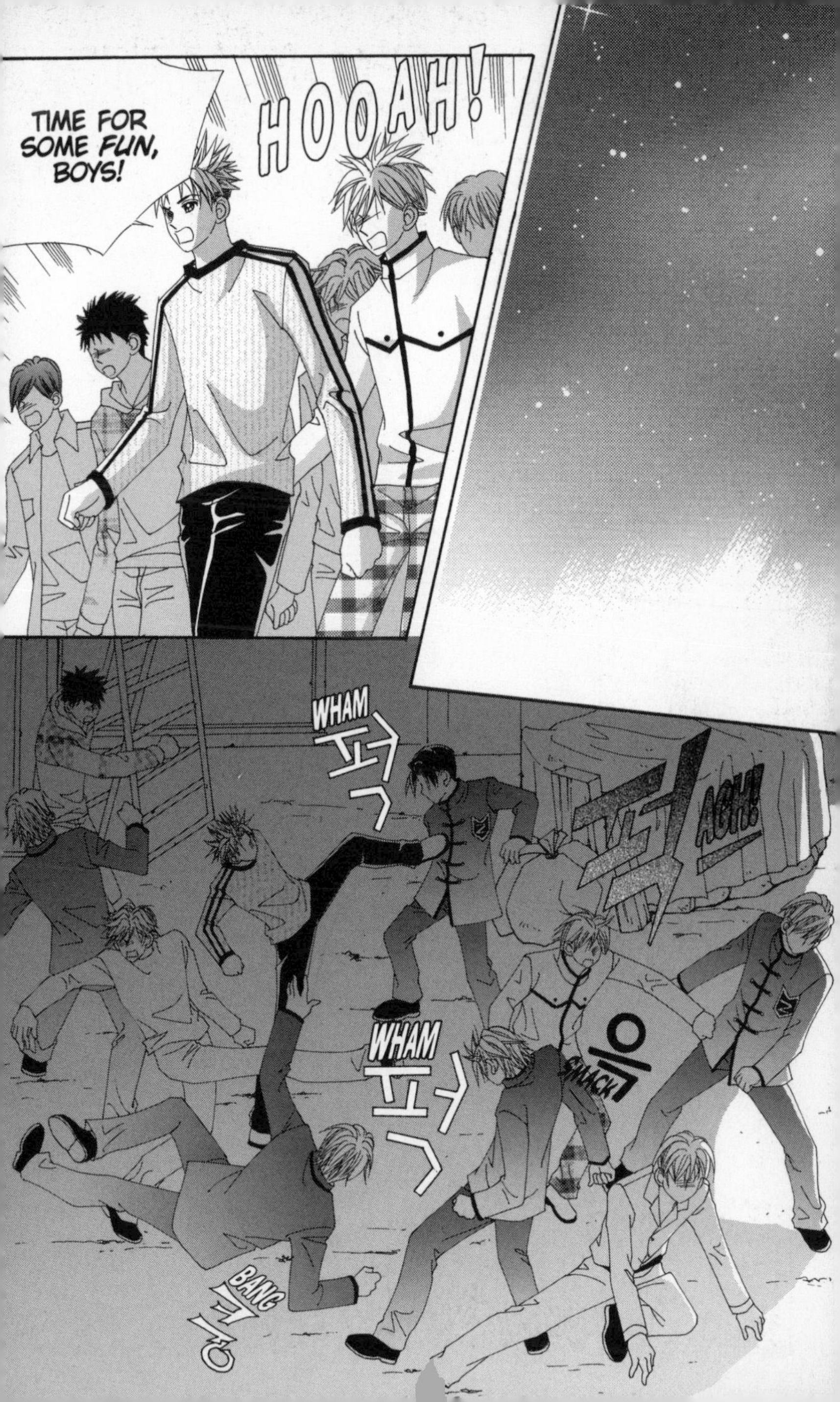
TIME FOR SOME FUN, BOYS!
HOOAH!
WHAM
ACH!
WHAM
SMACK
BANG

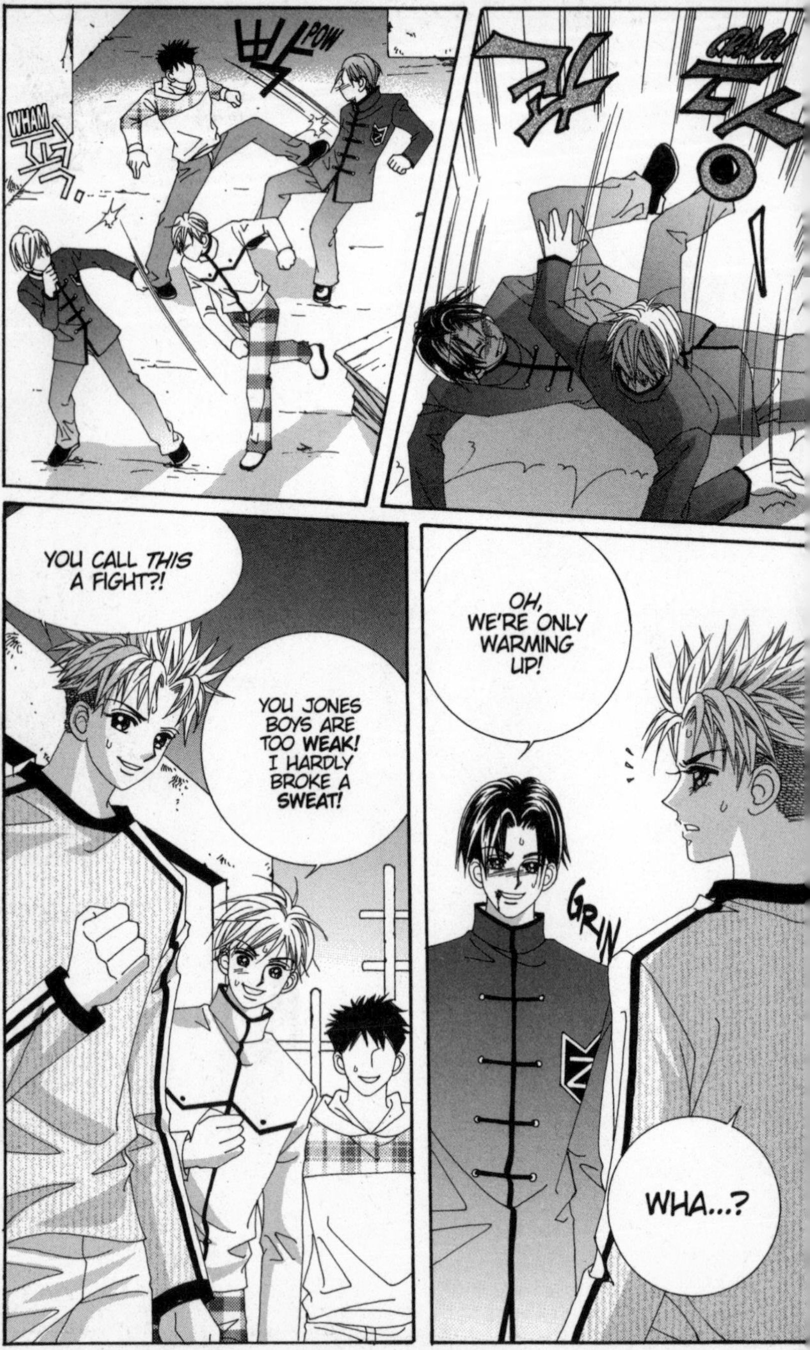
WHAM
POW
CRASH
YOU CALL THIS A FIGHT?!
YOU JONES BOYS ARE TOO WEAK! I HARDLY BROKE A SWEAT!
OH, WE'RE ONLY WARMING UP!
GRIN
WHA...?

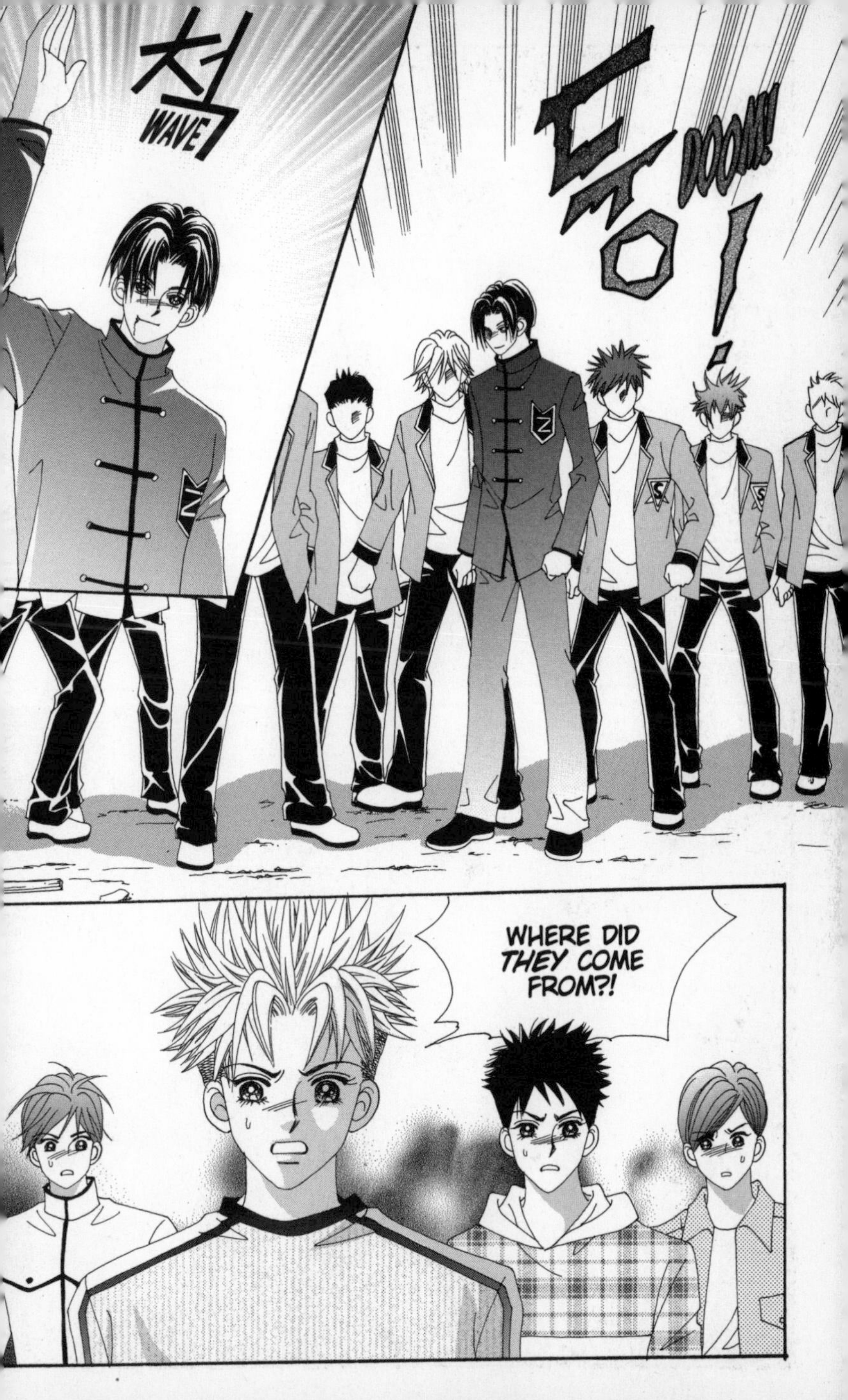
척
WAVE
둥!
DOOM!
WHERE DID THEY COME FROM?!

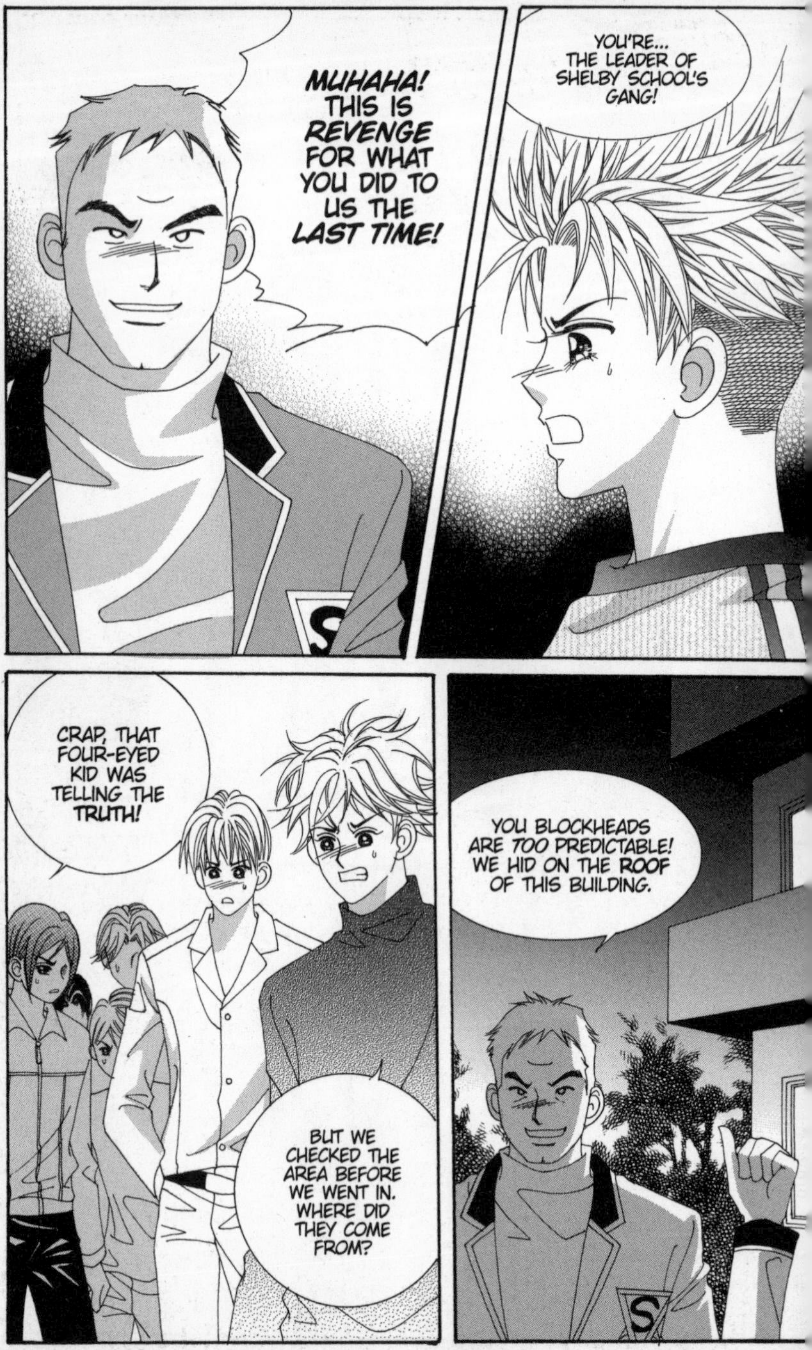
MUHAHA! THIS IS REVENGE FOR WHAT YOU DID TO US THE LAST TIME!
YOU'RE... THE LEADER OF SHELBY SCHOOL'S GANG!
CRAP, THAT FOUR-EYED KID WAS TELLING THE TRUTH!
BUT WE CHECKED THE AREA BEFORE WE WENT IN. WHERE DID THEY COME FROM?
YOU BLOCKHEADS ARE TOO PREDICTABLE! WE HID ON THE ROOF OF THIS BUILDING.

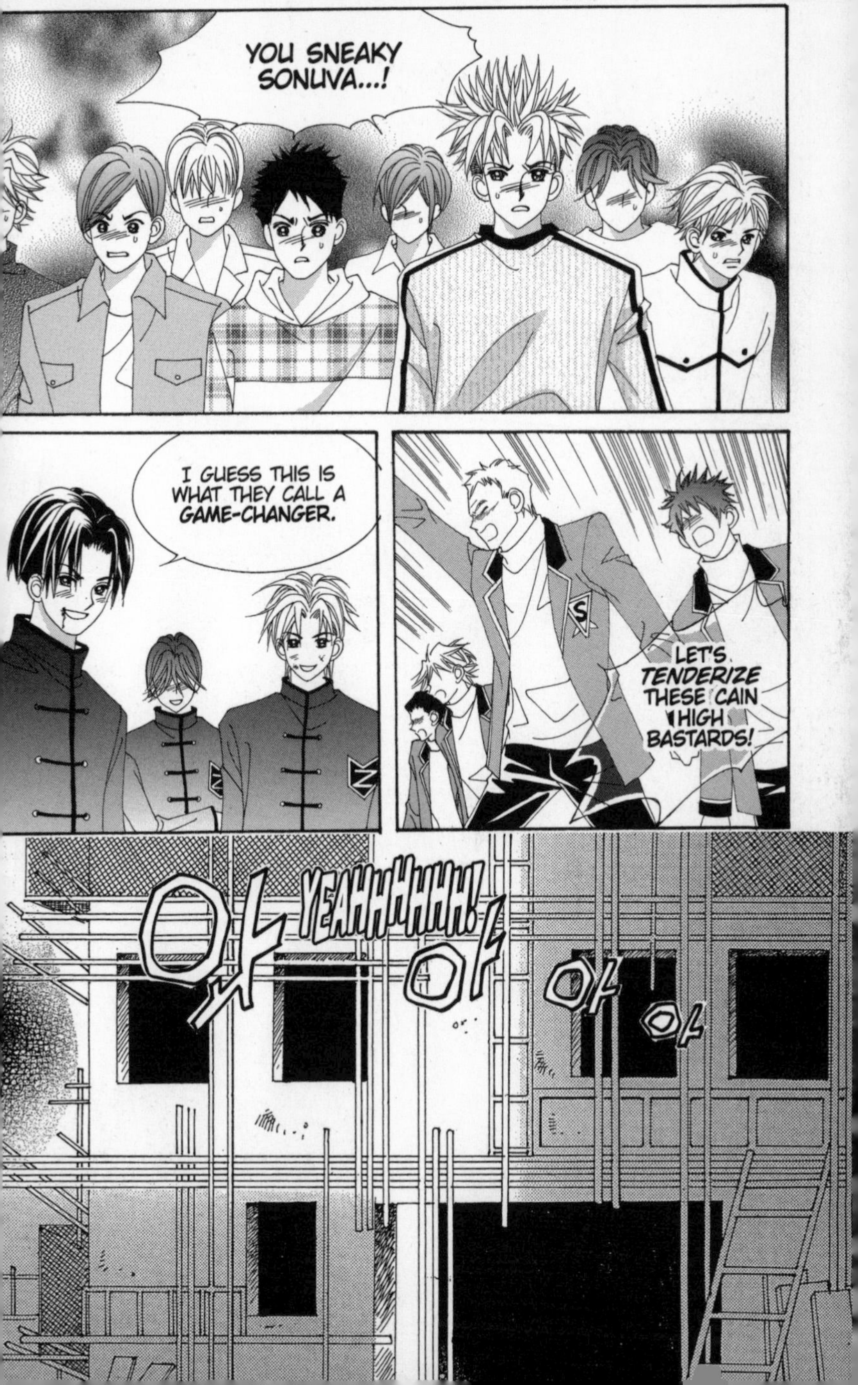
YOU SNEAKY SONUVA...!
I GUESS THIS IS WHAT THEY CALL A GAME-CHANGER.
LET'S TENDERIZE THESE CAIN HIGH BASTARDS!
YEAHHHHHH!

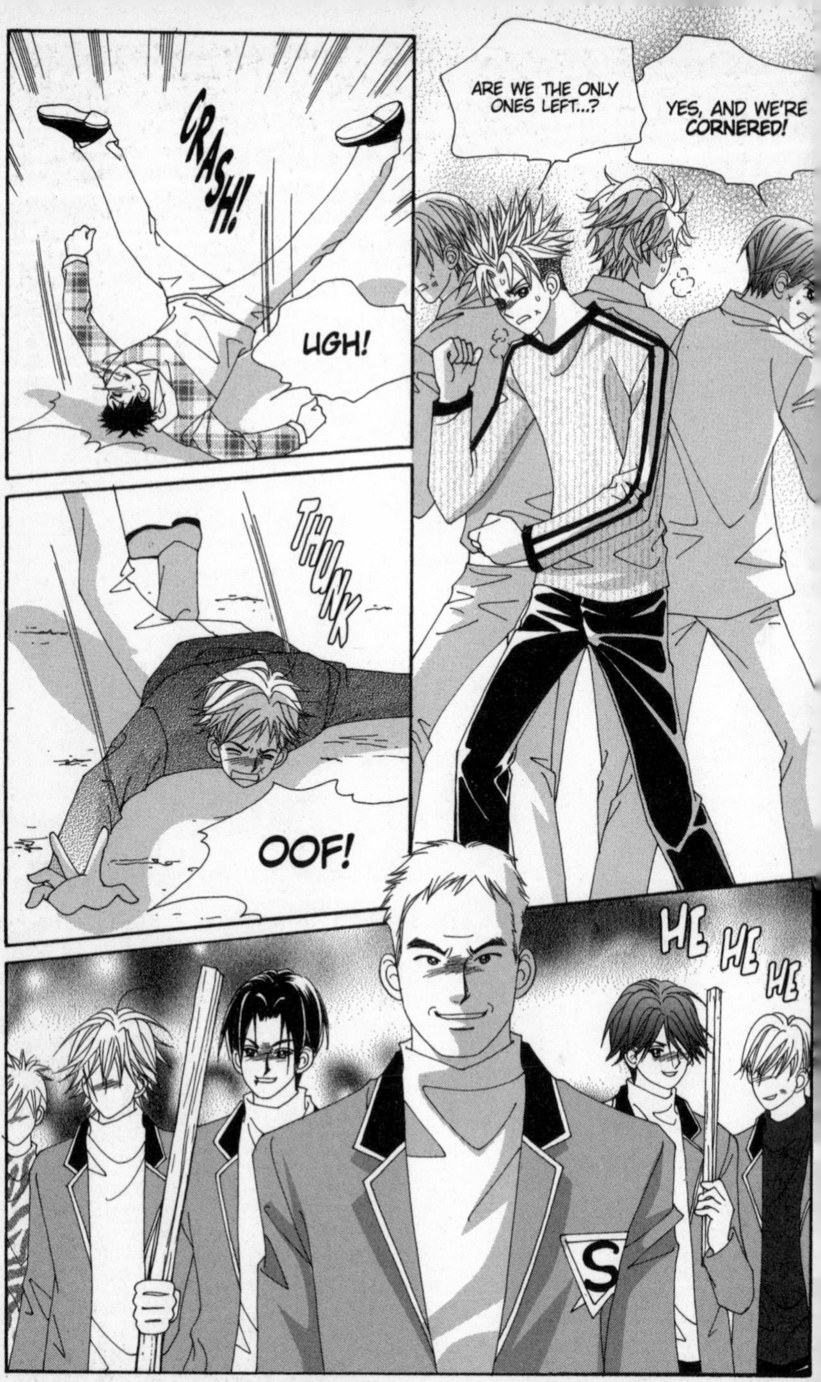
CRASH!
UGH!
THUNK
OOF!
ARE WE THE ONLY ONES LEFT...?
YES, AND WE'RE CORNERED!
HE HE HE

HUFF HUFF HUFF

HUFF

TOO MANY... NO WAY WE CAN TAKE 'EM!

MAN, I'VE BEEN DREAMING OF THIS MOMENT!

CRUNCH

CRUNCH

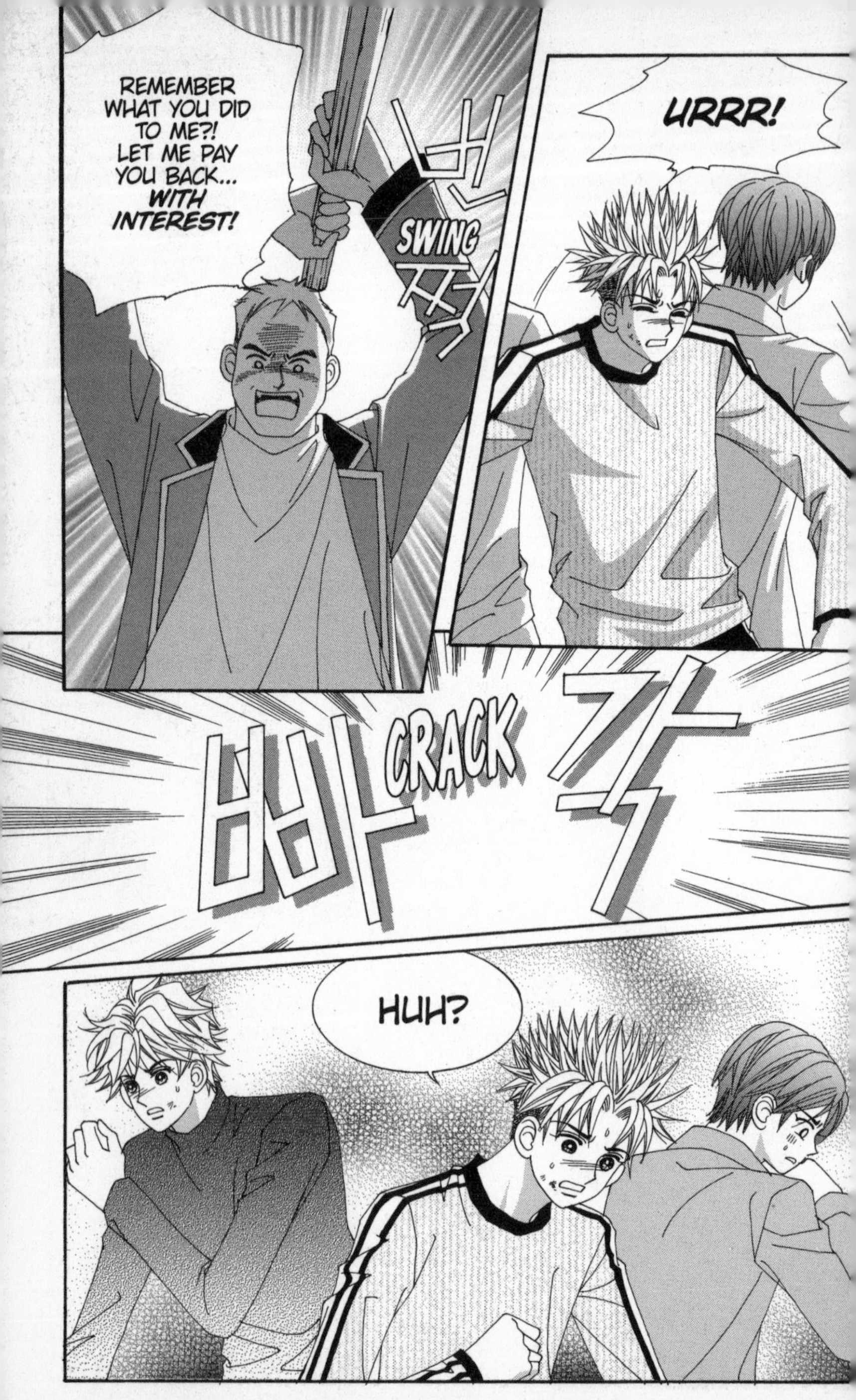
REMEMBER WHAT YOU DID TO ME?! LET ME PAY YOU BACK... WITH INTEREST!
SWING
URRR!
CRACK
HUH?

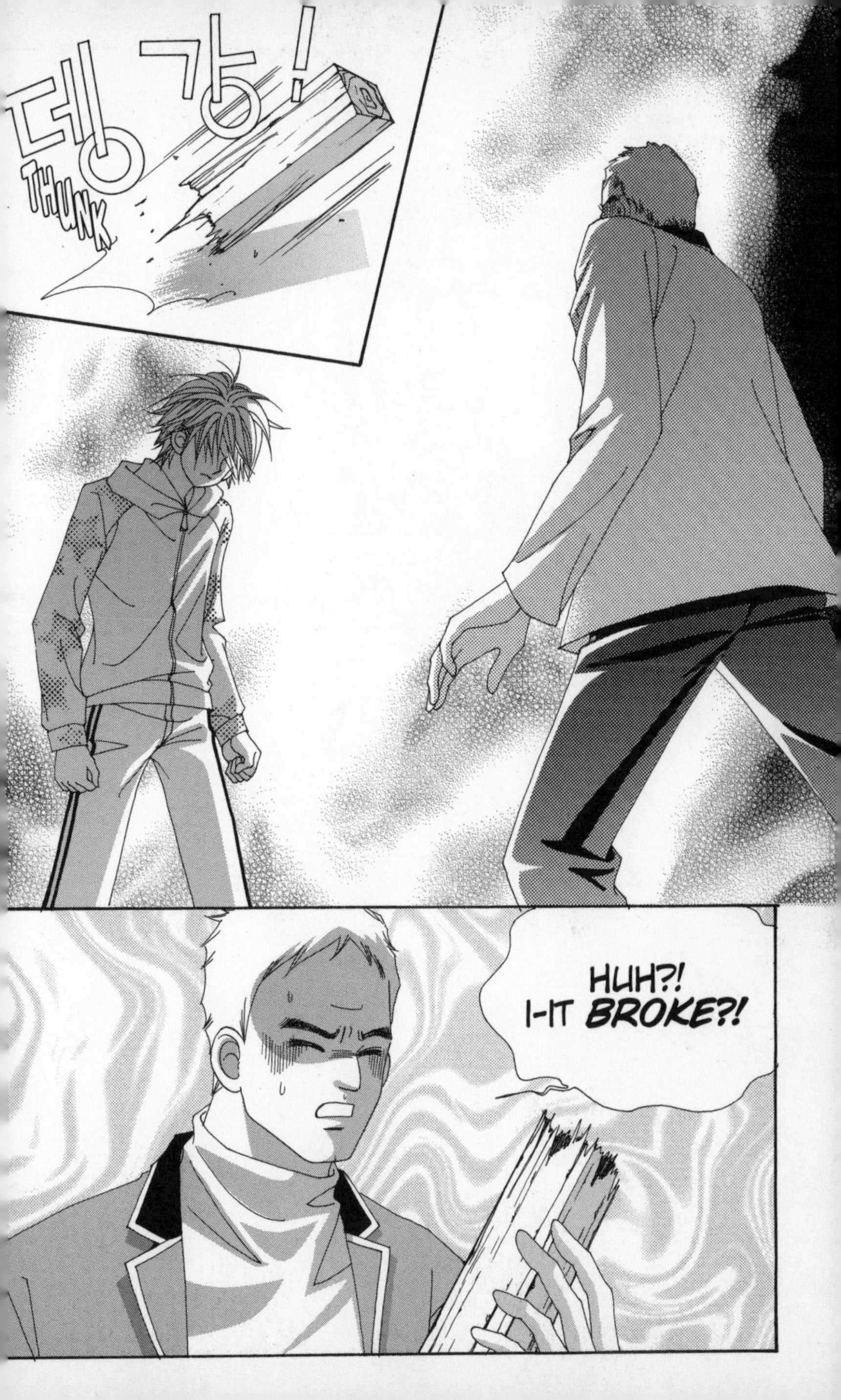
THUNK
HUH?!
I-IT BROKE?!

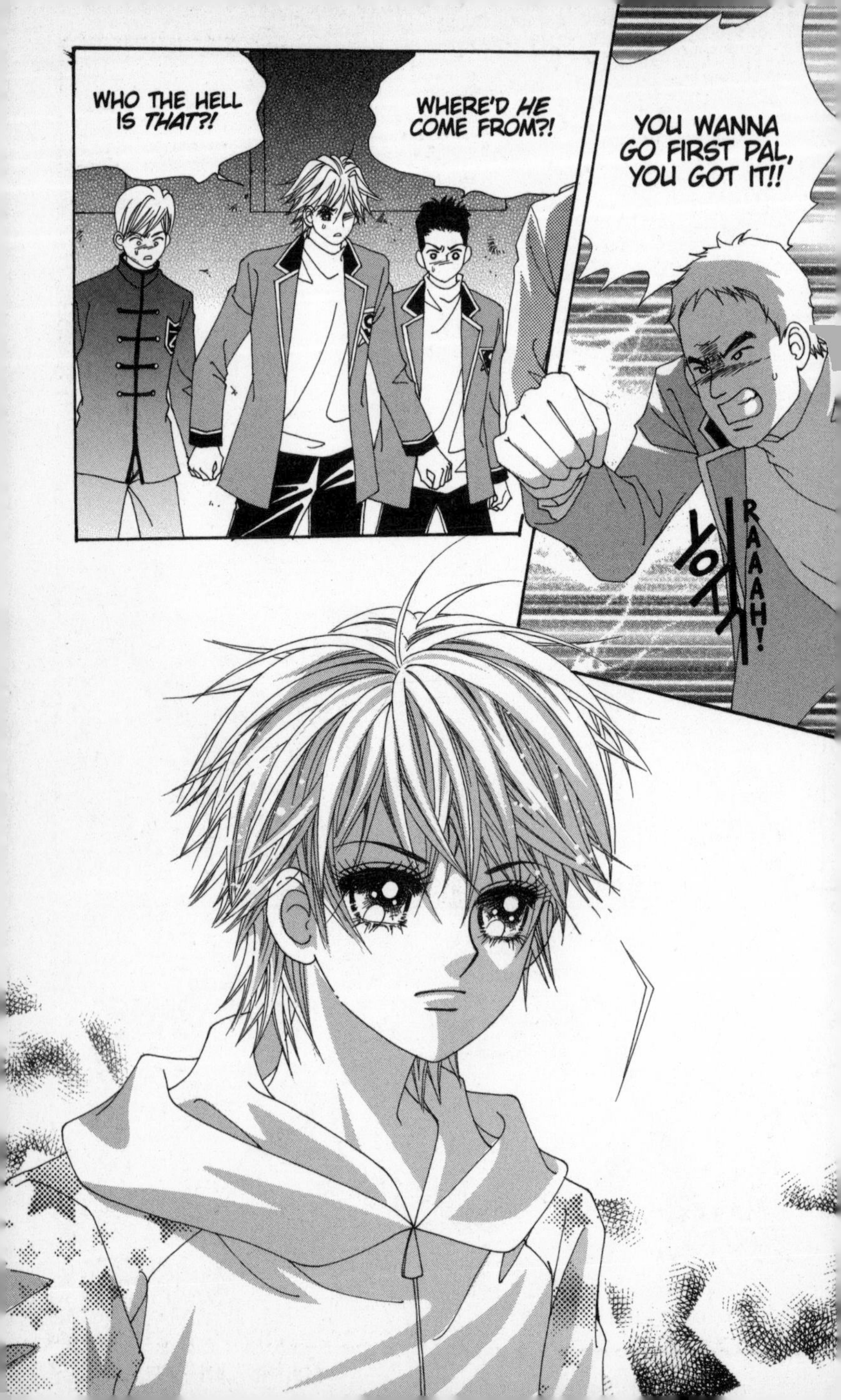
WHO THE HELL IS THAT?!
WHERE'D HE COME FROM?!
YOU WANNA GO FIRST PAL, YOU GOT IT!!
YO
RAAAH!

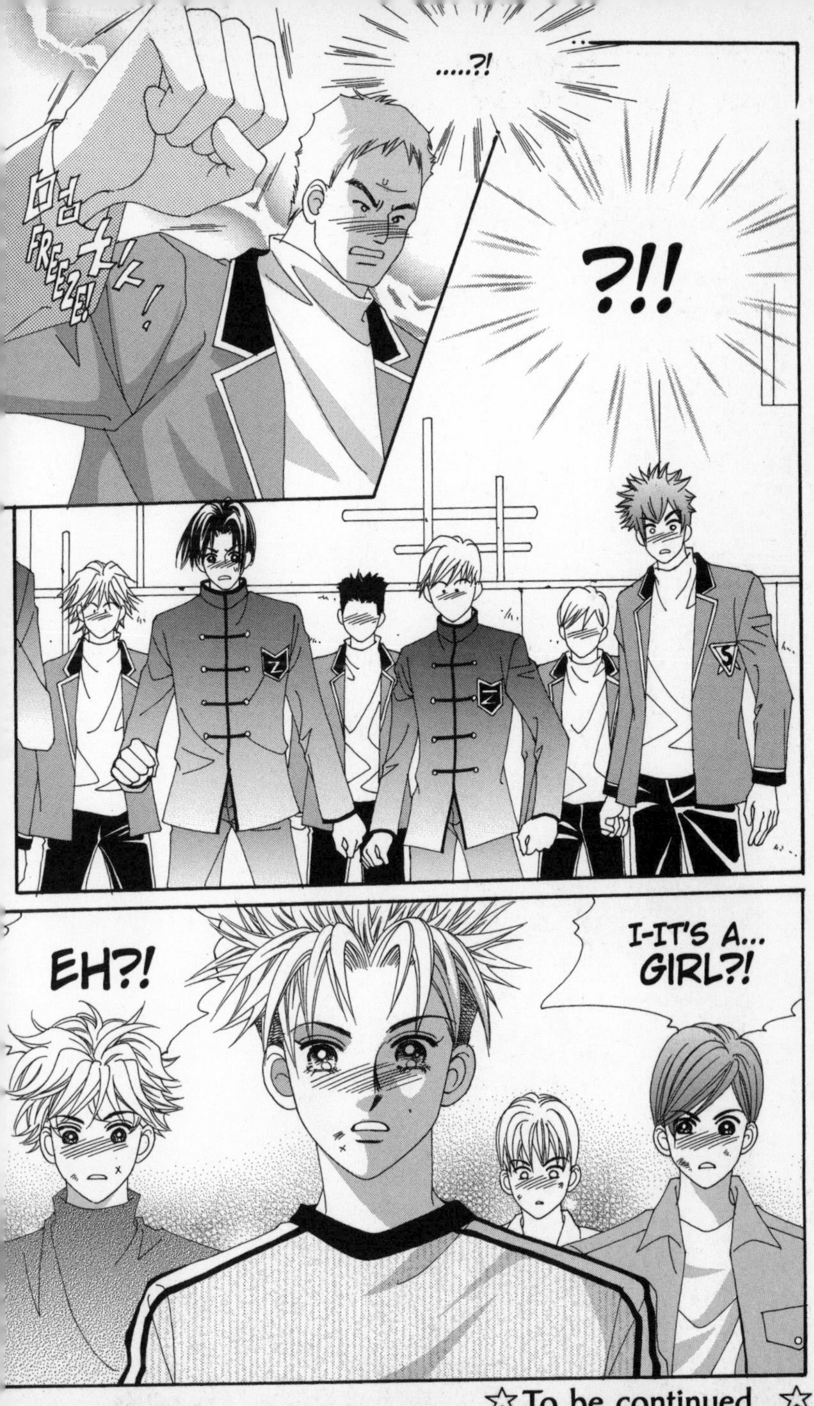

멈칫!
FREEZE!
.....?!
?!!
EH?!
I-IT'S A...
GIRL?!

☆To be continued...☆

My Boyfriend is a
VAMPIRE

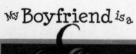

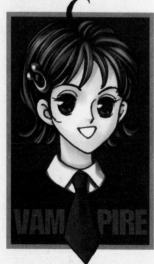

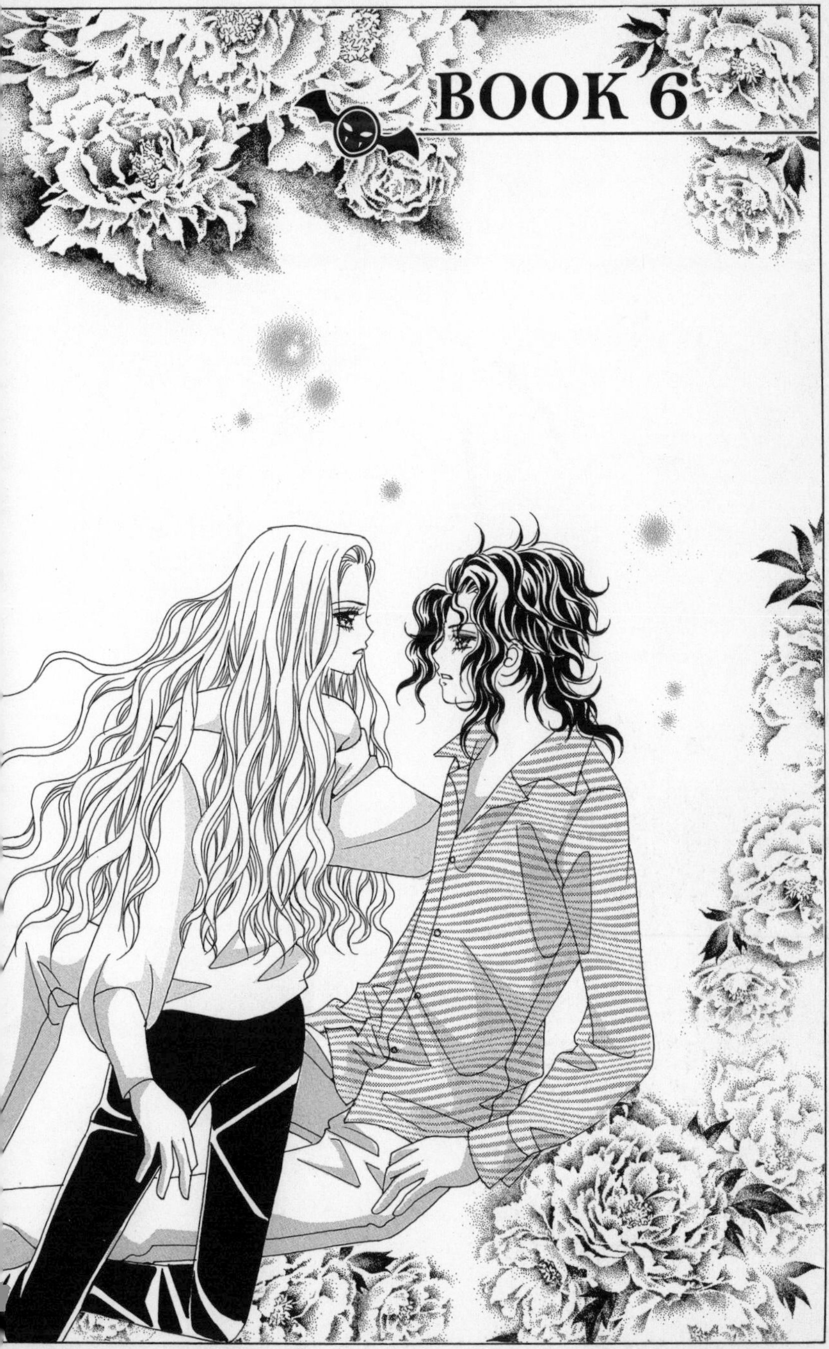
BOOK 6

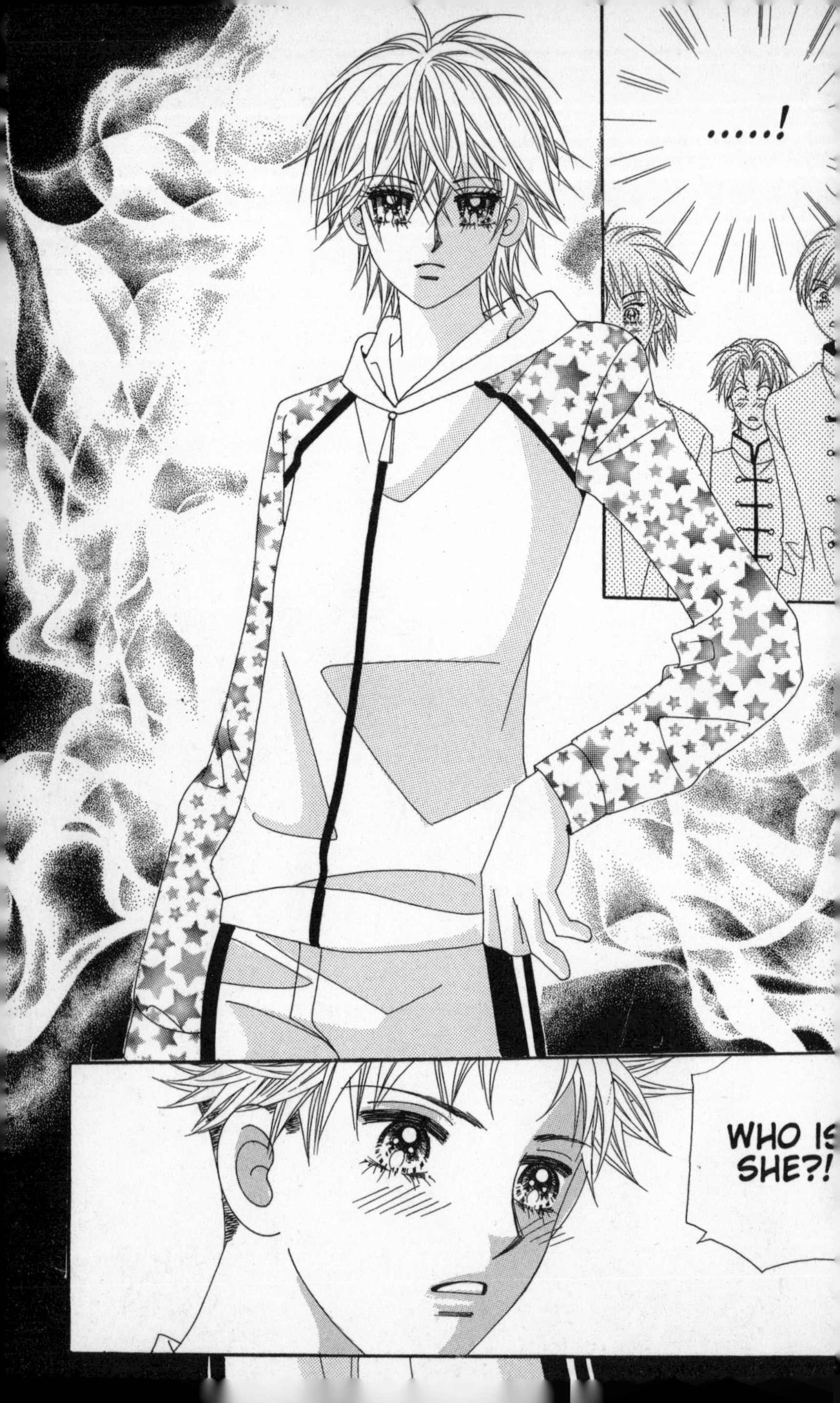

.....!
WHO IS SHE?!

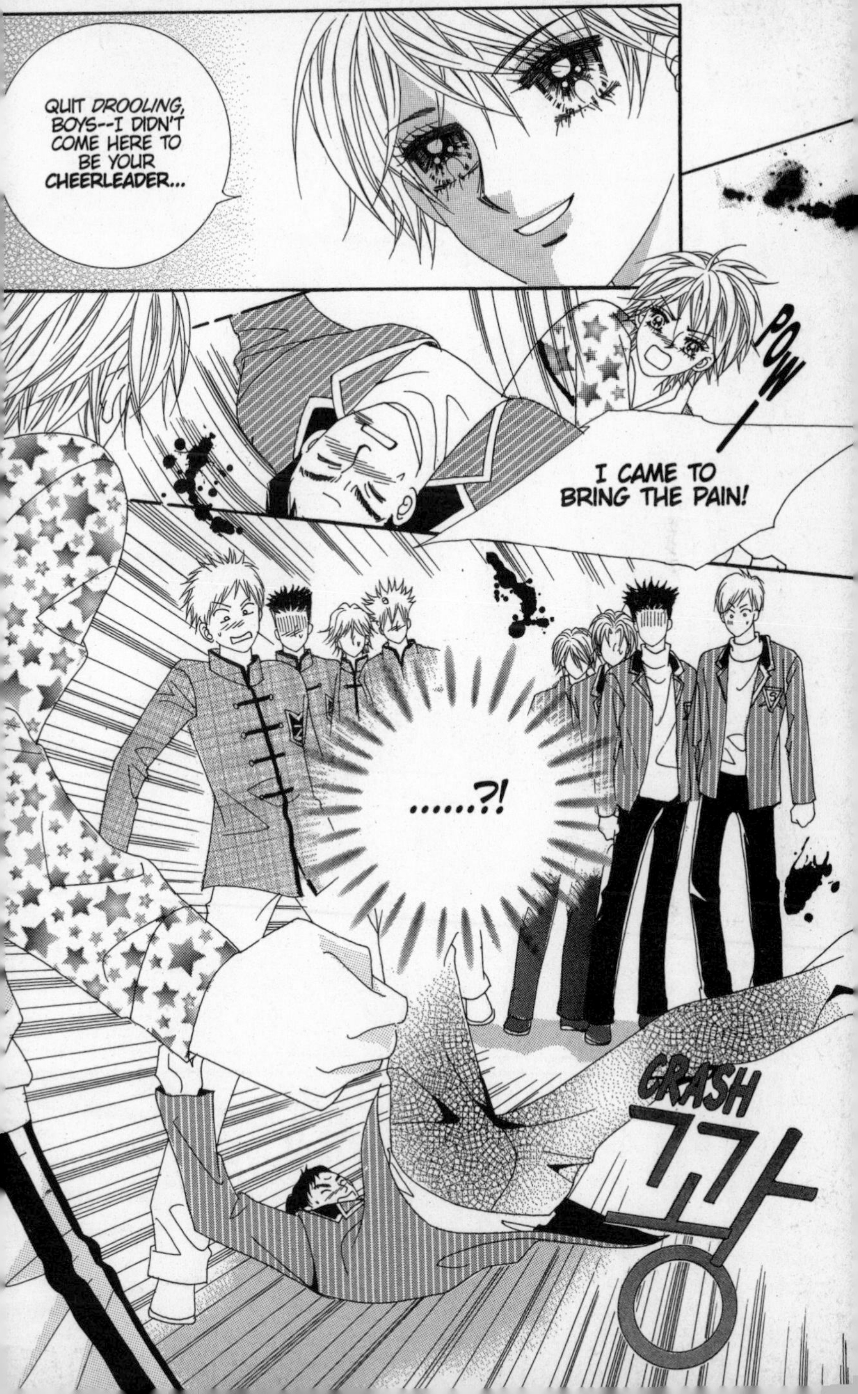
QUIT *DROOLING*, BOYS--I DIDN'T COME HERE TO BE YOUR CHEERLEADER...
POW
I CAME TO BRING THE PAIN!
......?!
CRASH
꽝

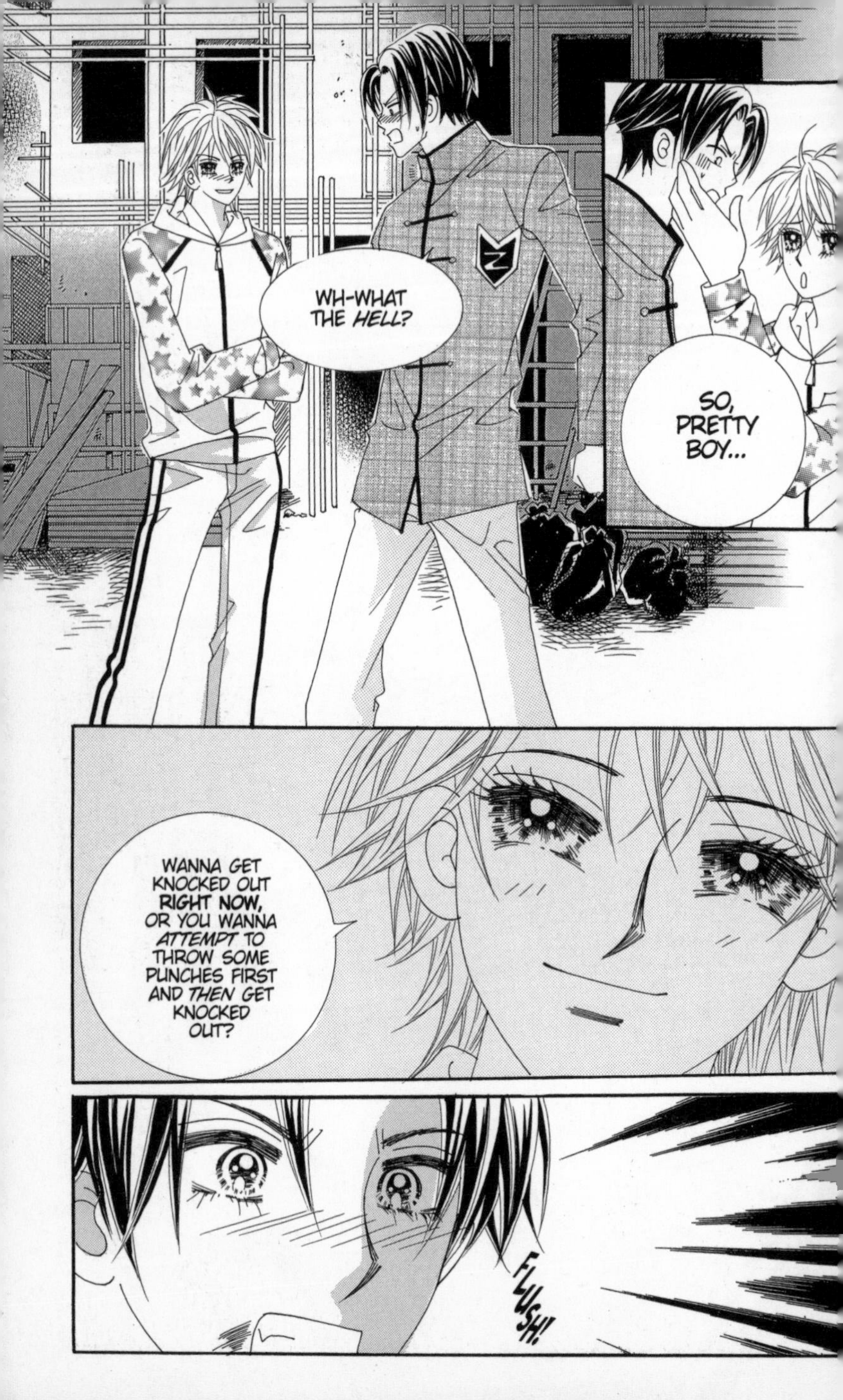
WH-WHAT THE *HELL*?
SO, PRETTY BOY...
WANNA GET KNOCKED OUT **RIGHT NOW**, OR YOU WANNA *ATTEMPT* TO THROW SOME PUNCHES FIRST AND *THEN* GET KNOCKED OUT?
FLUSH!

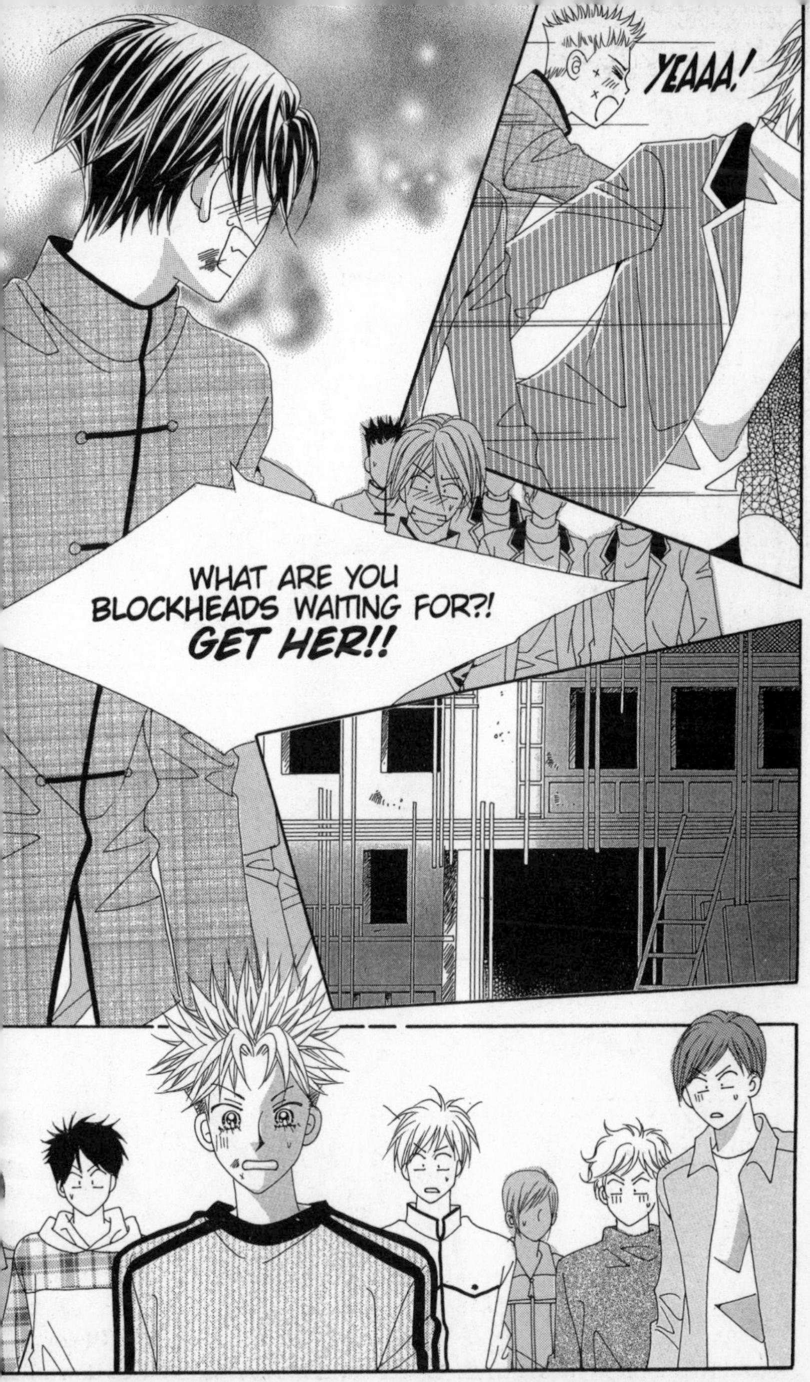
WHAT ARE YOU BLOCKHEADS WAITING FOR?! GET HER!!
YEAAA!

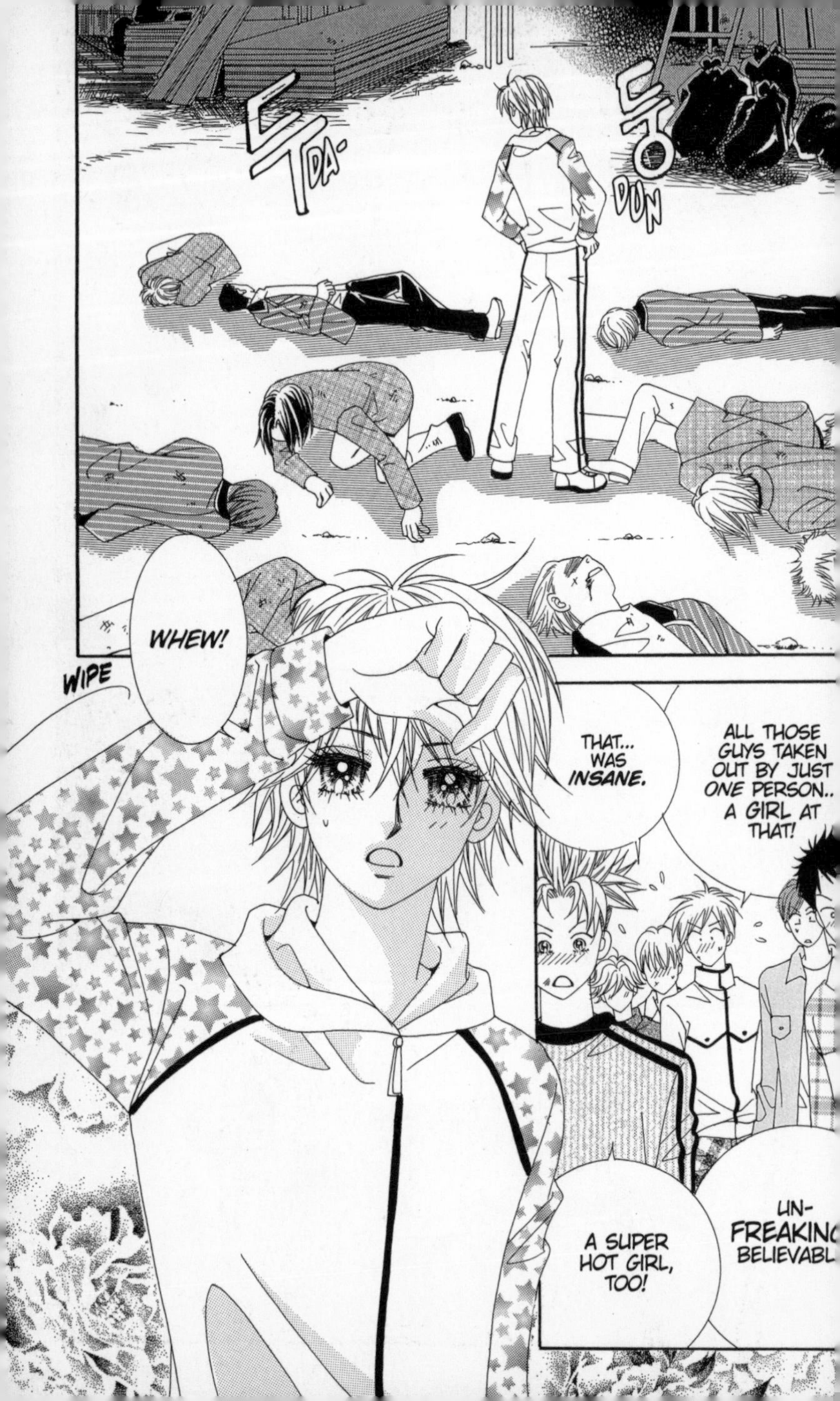

드
DA-
둥
DUN
WHEW!
WIPE
THAT... WAS INSANE.
ALL THOSE GUYS TAKEN OUT BY JUST ONE PERSON.. A GIRL AT THAT!
A SUPER HOT GIRL, TOO!
UN-FREAKIN BELIEVABL

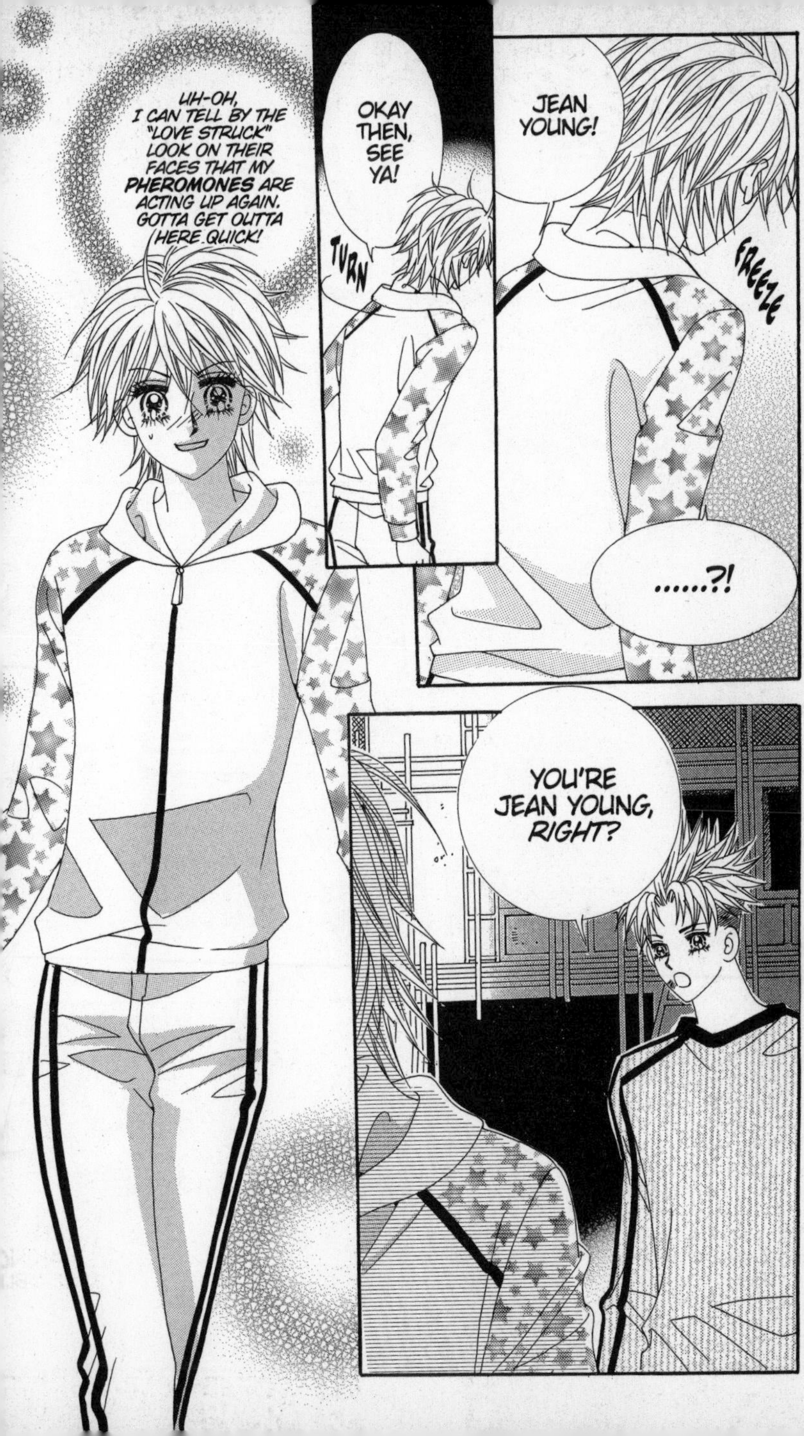
UH-OH, I CAN TELL BY THE "LOVE STRUCK" LOOK ON THEIR FACES THAT MY PHEROMONES ARE ACTING UP AGAIN. GOTTA GET OUTTA HERE QUICK!
OKAY THEN, SEE YA!
TURN
JEAN YOUNG!
FREEZE
......?!
YOU'RE JEAN YOUNG, RIGHT?

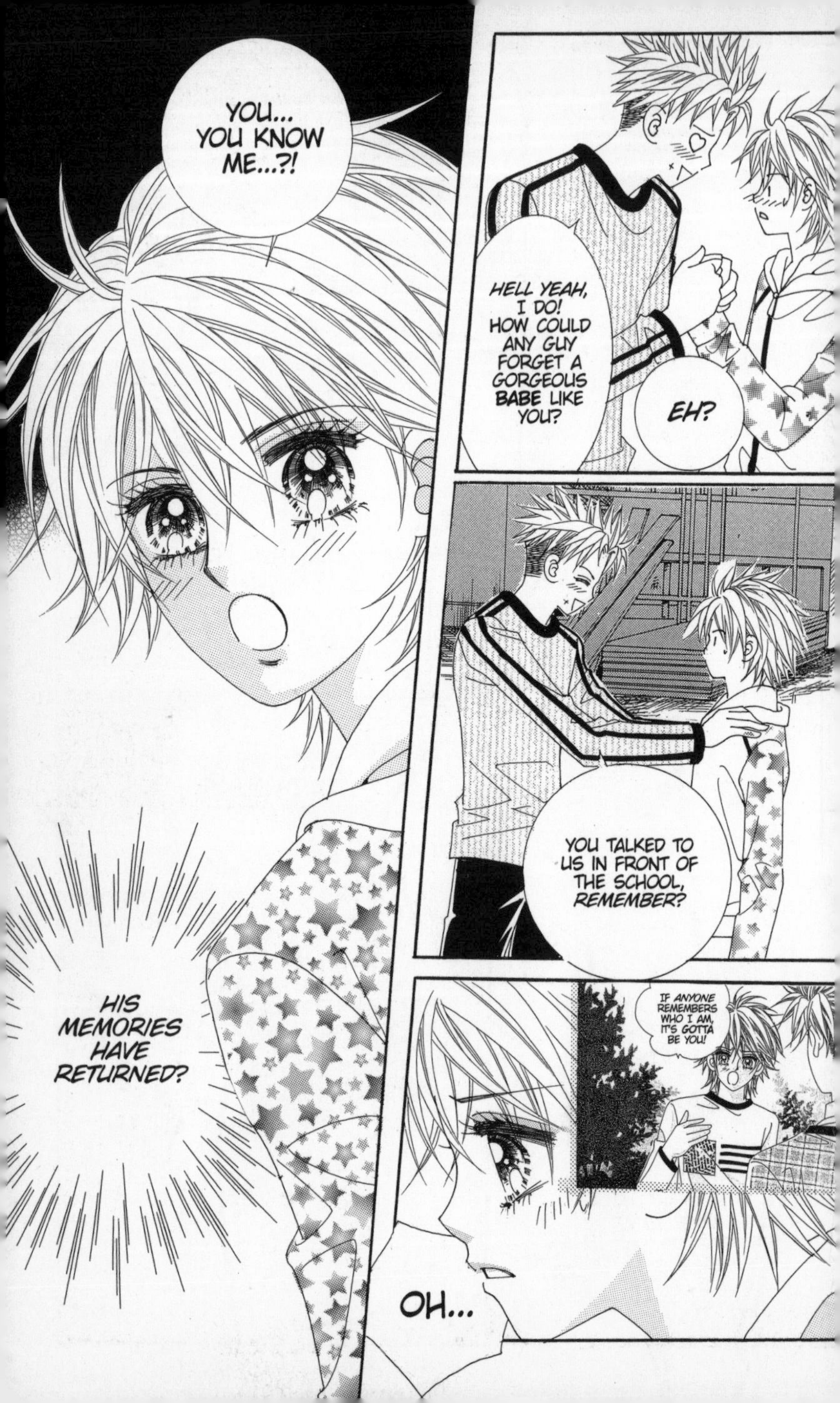
YOU... YOU KNOW ME...?!
HIS MEMORIES HAVE RETURNED?
HELL YEAH, I DO! HOW COULD ANY GUY FORGET A GORGEOUS BABE LIKE YOU?
EH?
YOU TALKED TO US IN FRONT OF THE SCHOOL, REMEMBER?
IF ANYONE REMEMBERS WHO I AM, IT'S GOTTA BE YOU!
OH...

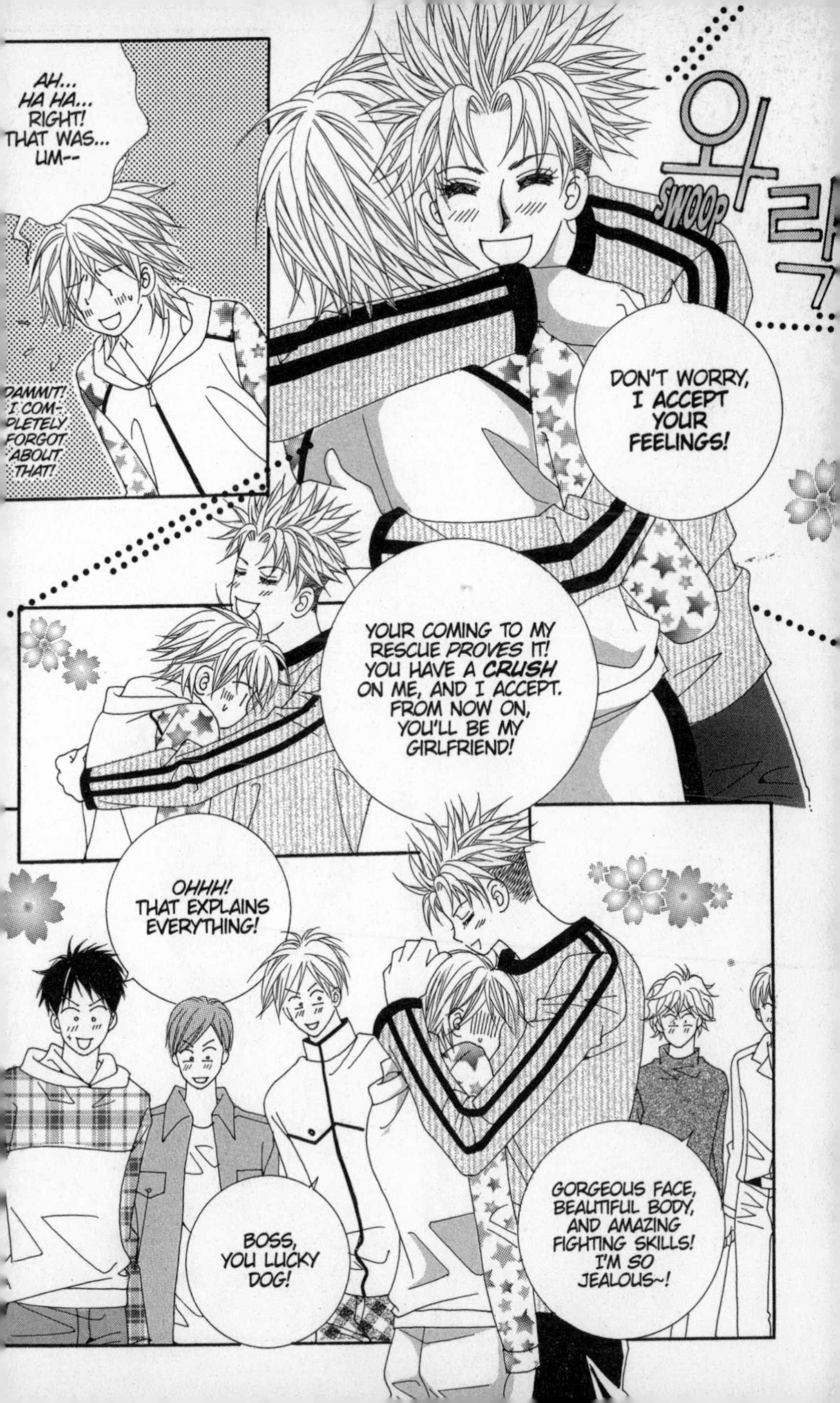
AH... HA HA... RIGHT! THAT WAS... UM--
DAMMIT! I COMPLETELY FORGOT ABOUT THAT!
와락
SWOOP
DON'T WORRY, I ACCEPT YOUR FEELINGS!
YOUR COMING TO MY RESCUE PROVES IT! YOU HAVE A CRUSH ON ME, AND I ACCEPT. FROM NOW ON, YOU'LL BE MY GIRLFRIEND!
OHHH! THAT EXPLAINS EVERYTHING!
BOSS, YOU LUCKY DOG!
GORGEOUS FACE, BEAUTIFUL BODY, AND AMAZING FIGHTING SKILLS! I'M SO JEALOUS~!

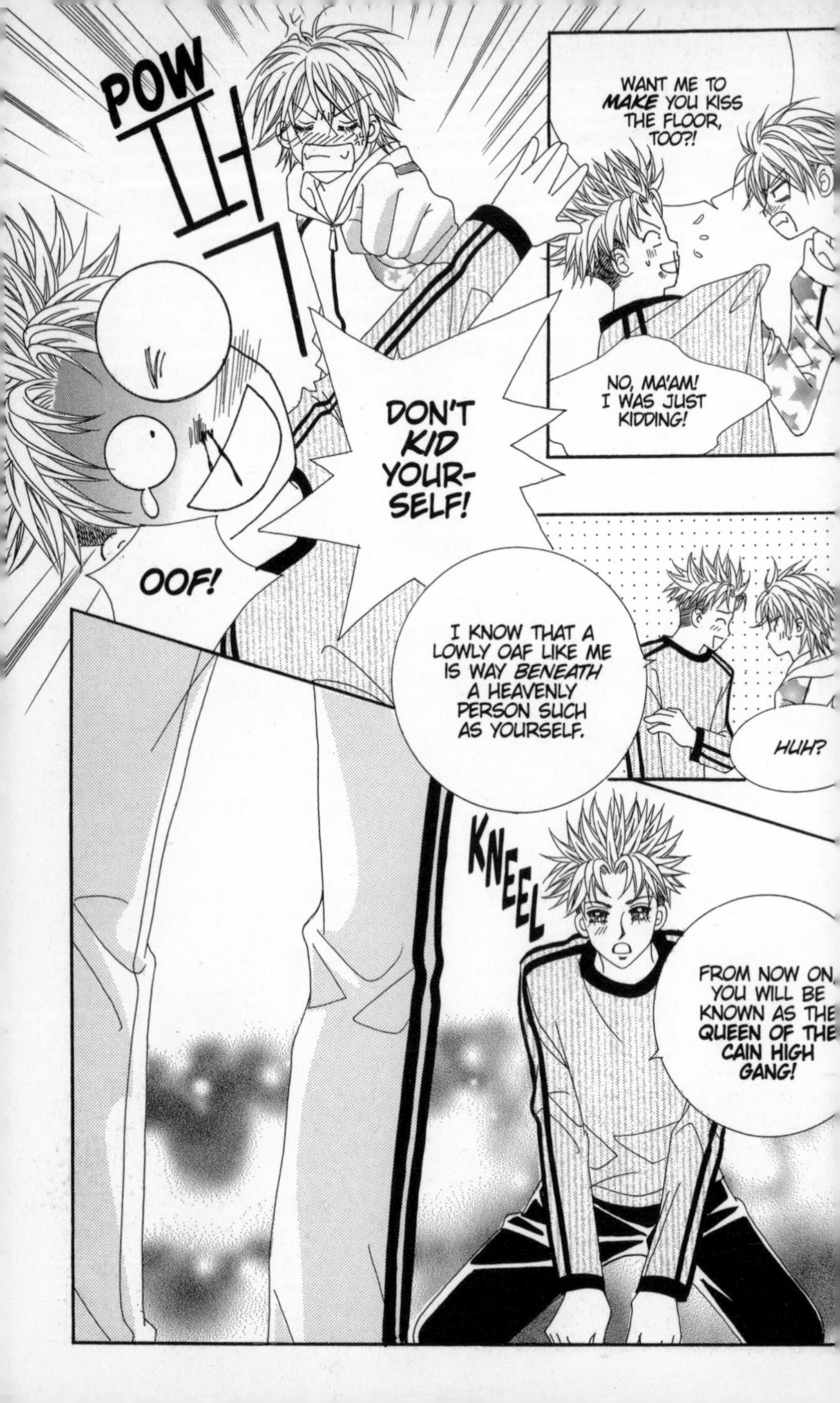

WANT ME TO MAKE YOU KISS THE FLOOR, TOO?!
NO, MA'AM! I WAS JUST KIDDING!
POW
DON'T KID YOURSELF!
OOF!
I KNOW THAT A LOWLY OAF LIKE ME IS WAY BENEATH A HEAVENLY PERSON SUCH AS YOURSELF.
HUH?
KNEEL
FROM NOW ON, YOU WILL BE KNOWN AS THE QUEEN OF THE CAIN HIGH GANG!

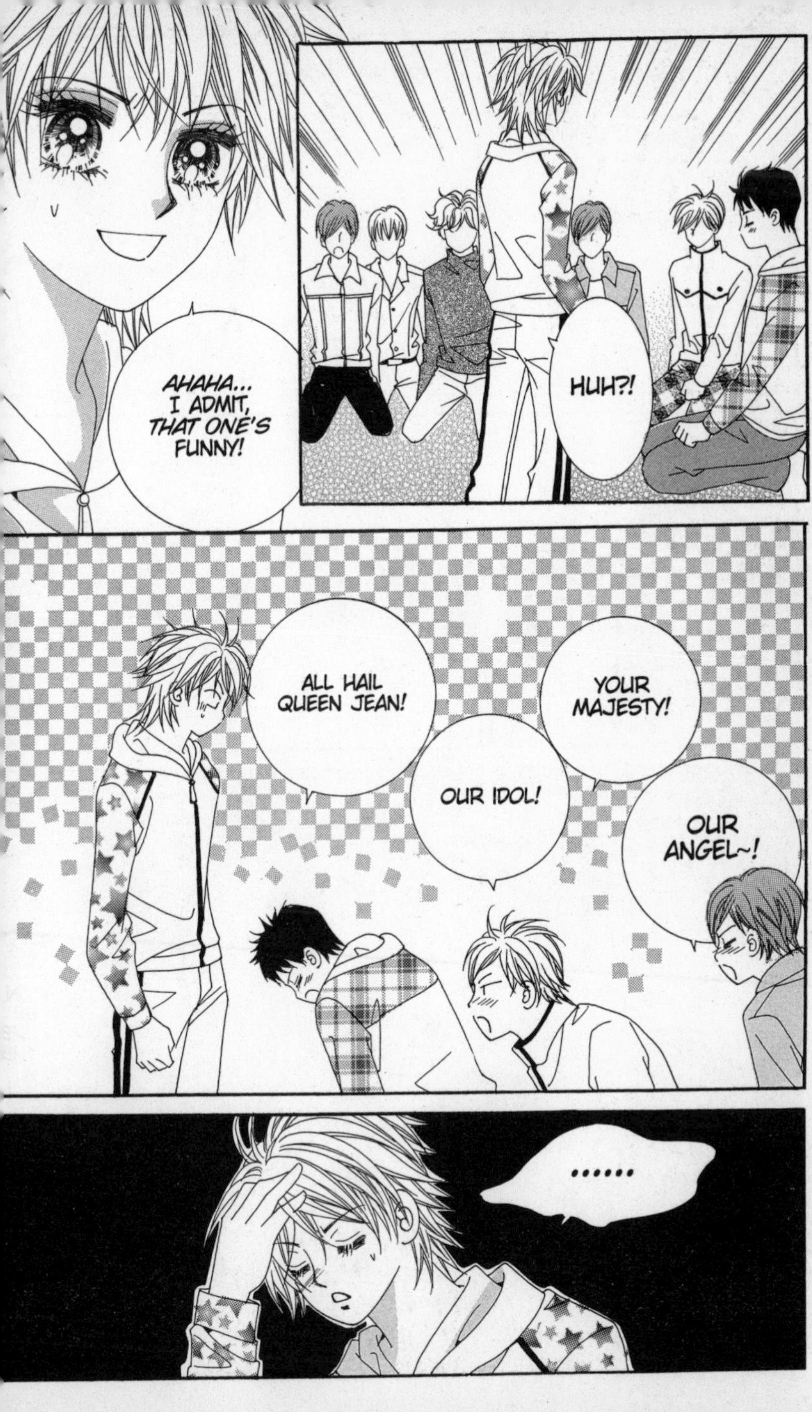
AHAHA... I ADMIT, THAT ONE'S FUNNY!
HUH?!
ALL HAIL QUEEN JEAN!
YOUR MAJESTY!
OUR IDOL!
OUR ANGEL~!
......

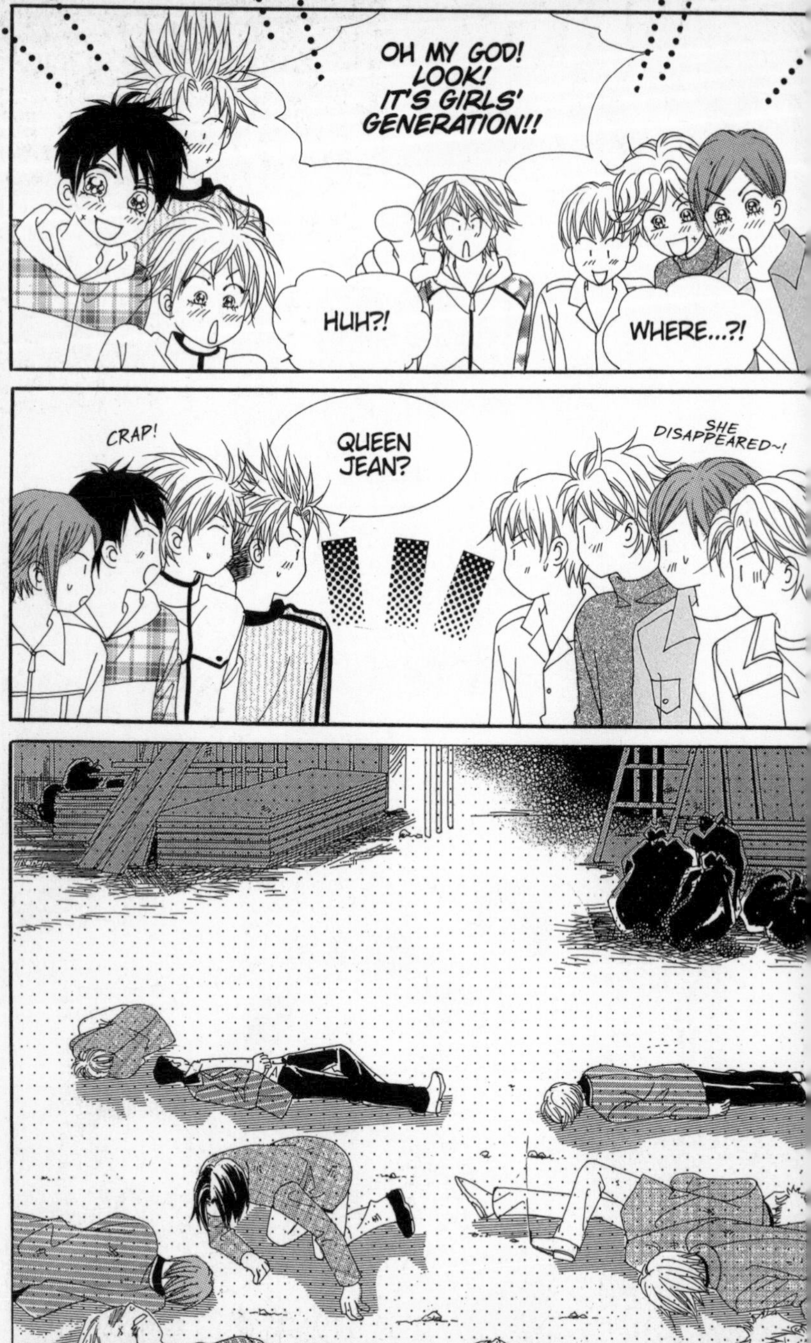
OH MY GOD! LOOK! IT'S GIRLS' GENERATION!!
HUH?!
WHERE...?!
CRAP!
QUEEN JEAN?
SHE DISAPPEARED~!

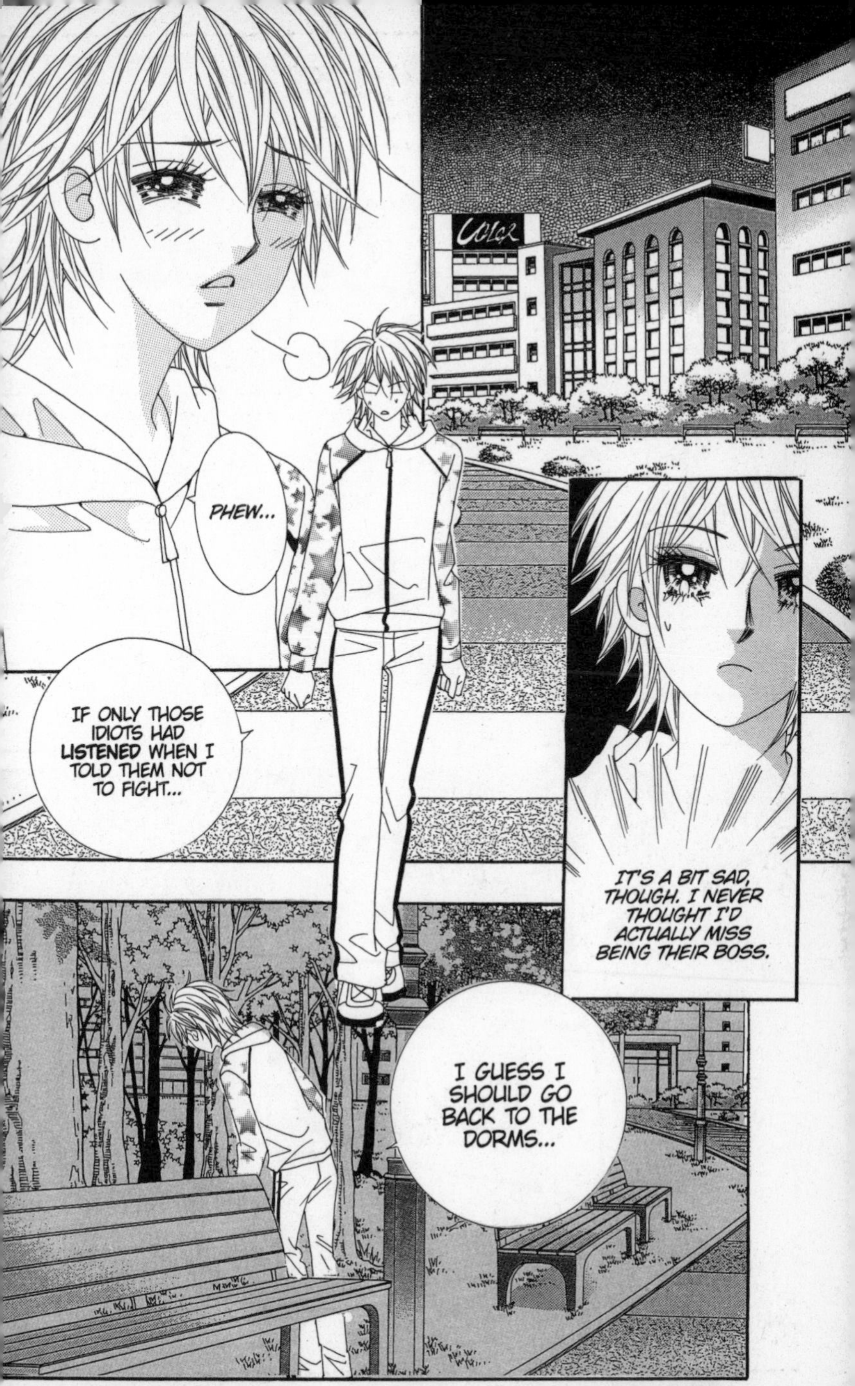
PHEW...
IF ONLY THOSE IDIOTS HAD LISTENED WHEN I TOLD THEM NOT TO FIGHT...
IT'S A BIT SAD, THOUGH. I NEVER THOUGHT I'D ACTUALLY MISS BEING THEIR BOSS.
I GUESS I SHOULD GO BACK TO THE DORMS...

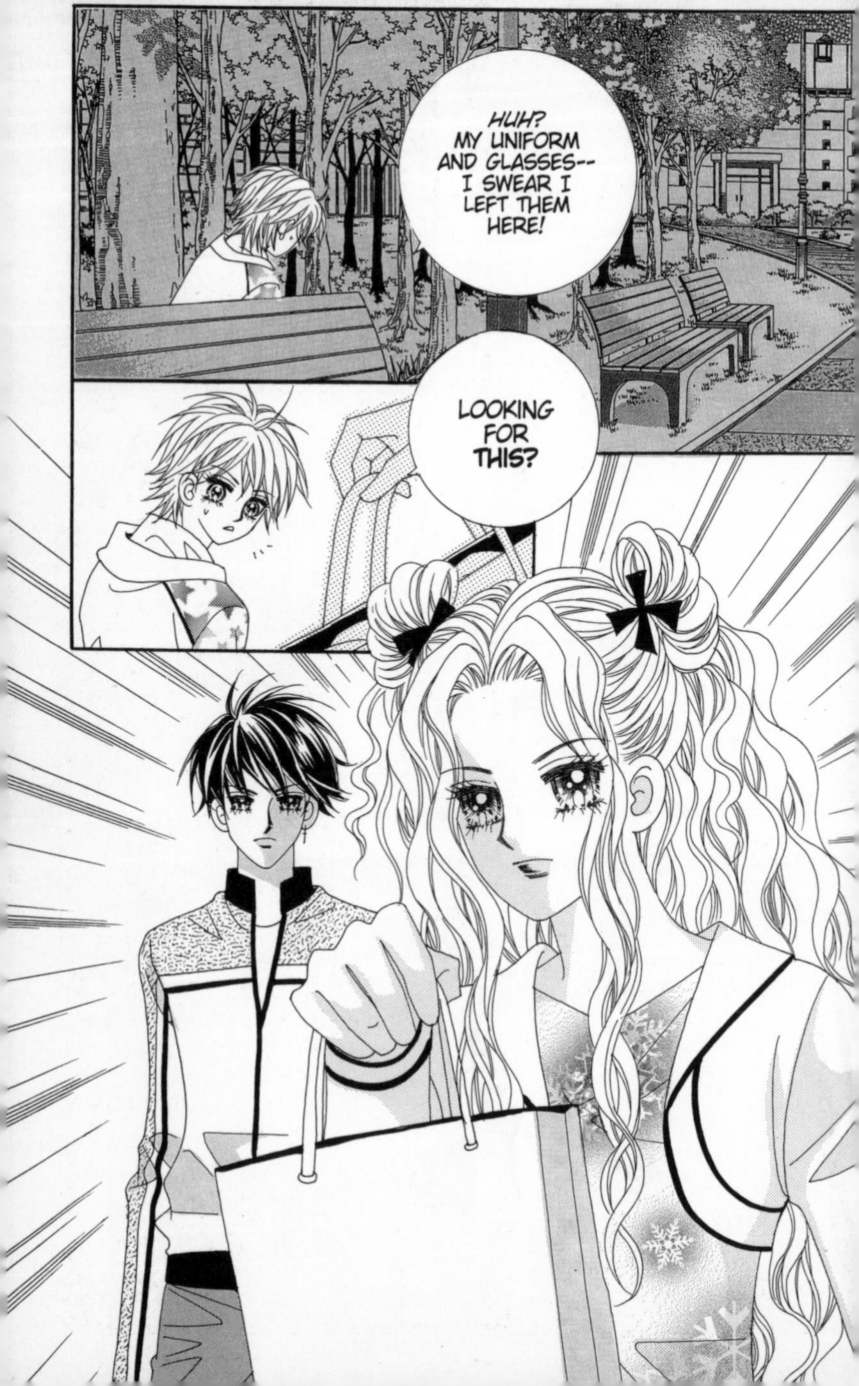
HUH? MY UNIFORM AND GLASSES-- I SWEAR I LEFT THEM HERE!
LOOKING FOR THIS?

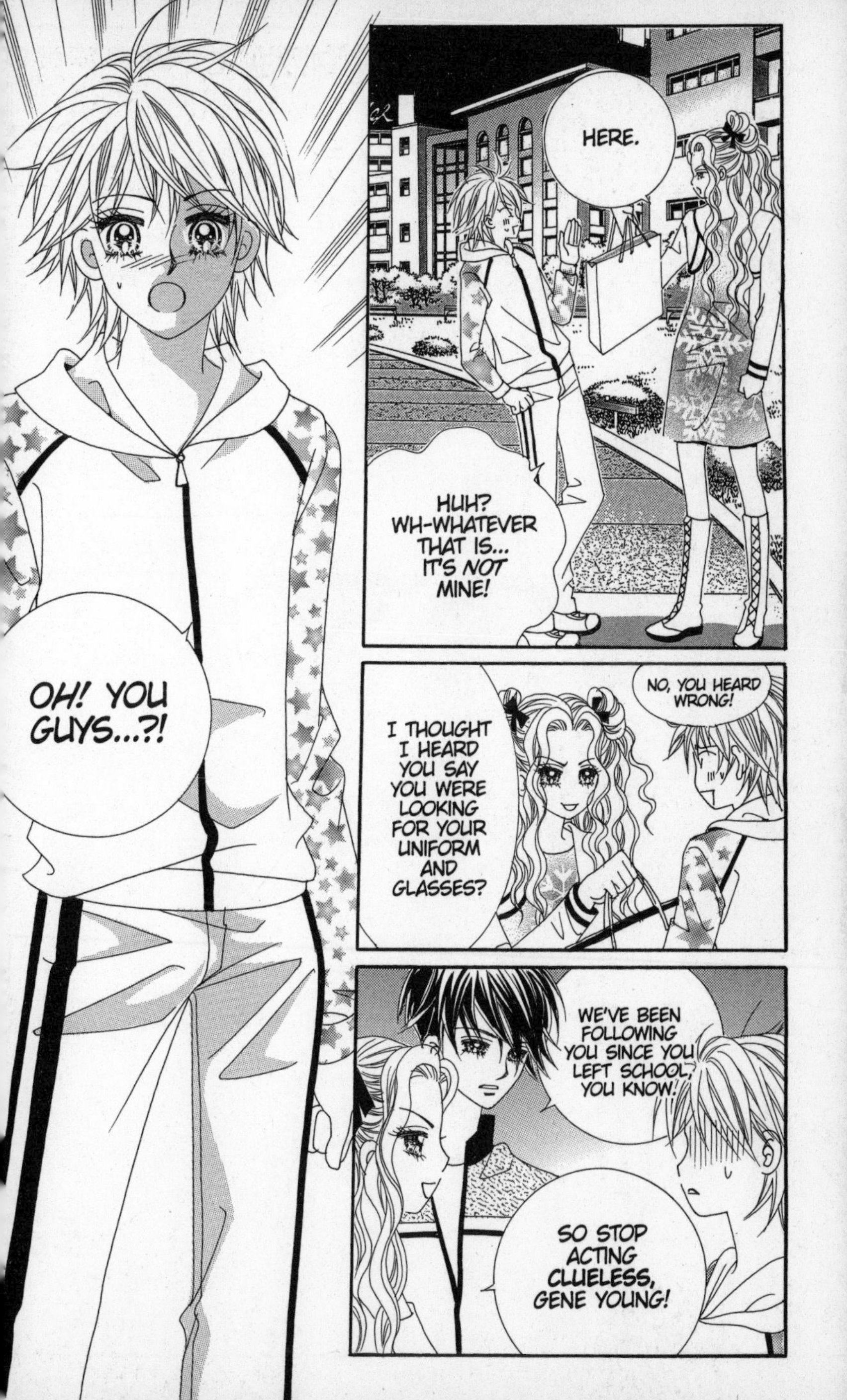
OH! YOU GUYS...?!
HERE.
HUH? WH-WHATEVER THAT IS... IT'S *NOT* MINE!
I THOUGHT I HEARD YOU SAY YOU WERE LOOKING FOR YOUR UNIFORM AND GLASSES?
NO, YOU HEARD WRONG!
WE'VE BEEN FOLLOWING YOU SINCE YOU LEFT SCHOOL, YOU KNOW!
SO STOP ACTING CLUELESS, GENE YOUNG!

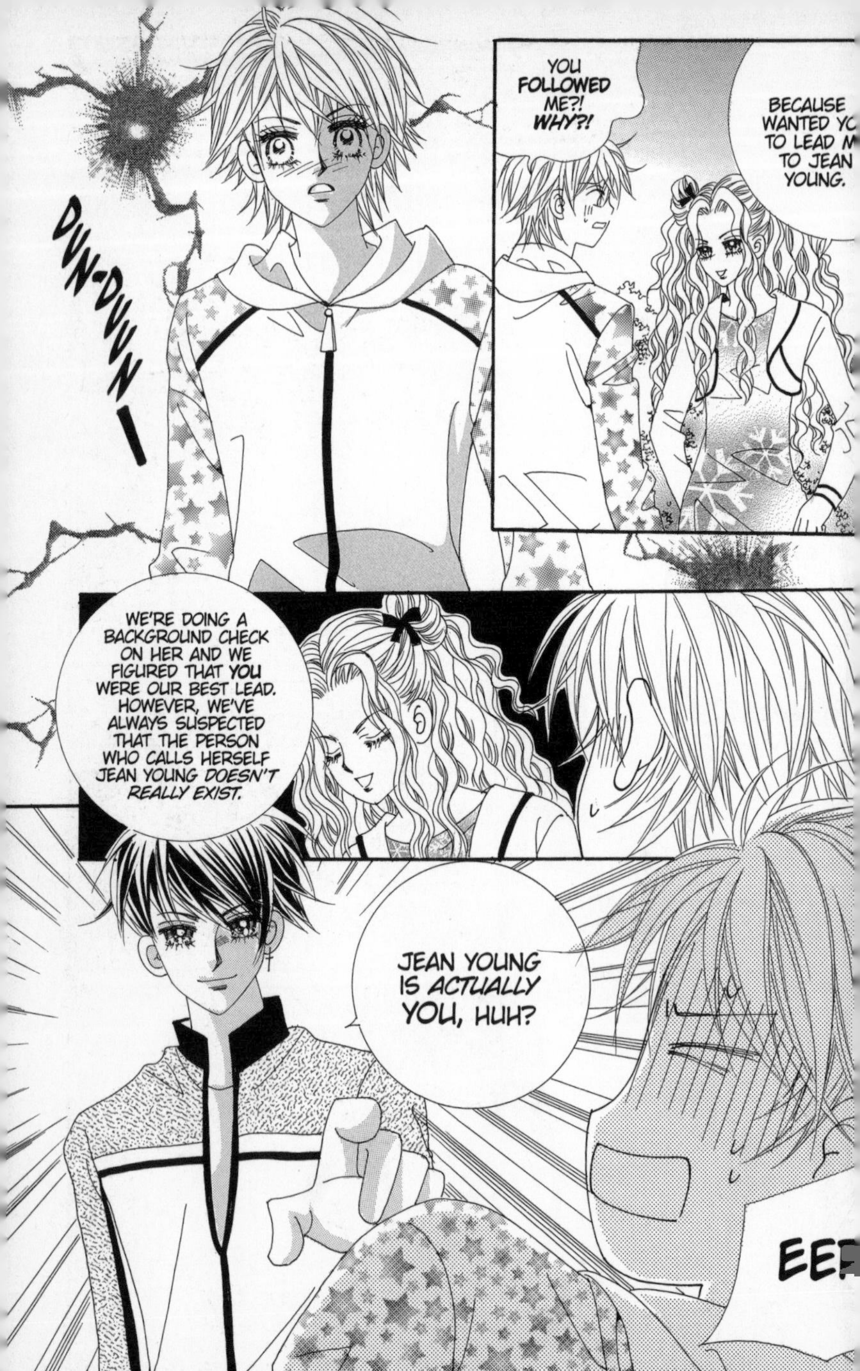
DUN-DUUN—
YOU FOLLOWED ME?! WHY?!
BECAUSE WANTED YO TO LEAD M TO JEAN YOUNG.
WE'RE DOING A BACKGROUND CHECK ON HER AND WE FIGURED THAT YOU WERE OUR BEST LEAD. HOWEVER, WE'VE ALWAYS SUSPECTED THAT THE PERSON WHO CALLS HERSELF JEAN YOUNG DOESN'T REALLY EXIST.
JEAN YOUNG IS ACTUALLY YOU, HUH?
EEP

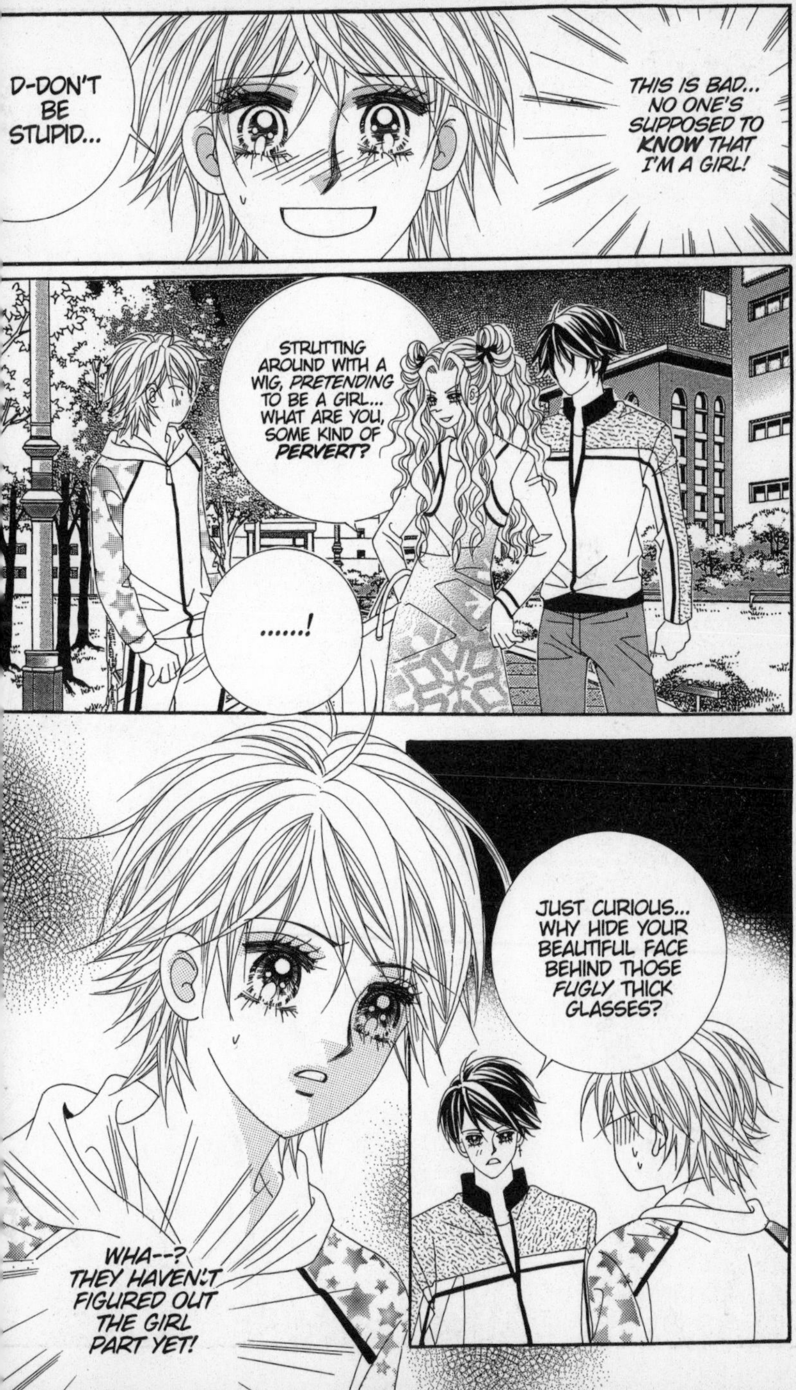
D-DON'T BE STUPID...
THIS IS BAD... NO ONE'S SUPPOSED TO **KNOW** THAT I'M A GIRL!
STRUTTING AROUND WITH A WIG, *PRETENDING* TO BE A GIRL... WHAT ARE YOU, SOME KIND OF ***PERVERT?***
......!
WHA--? THEY HAVEN'T FIGURED OUT THE GIRL PART YET!
JUST CURIOUS... WHY HIDE YOUR BEAUTIFUL FACE BEHIND THOSE *FUGLY* THICK GLASSES?

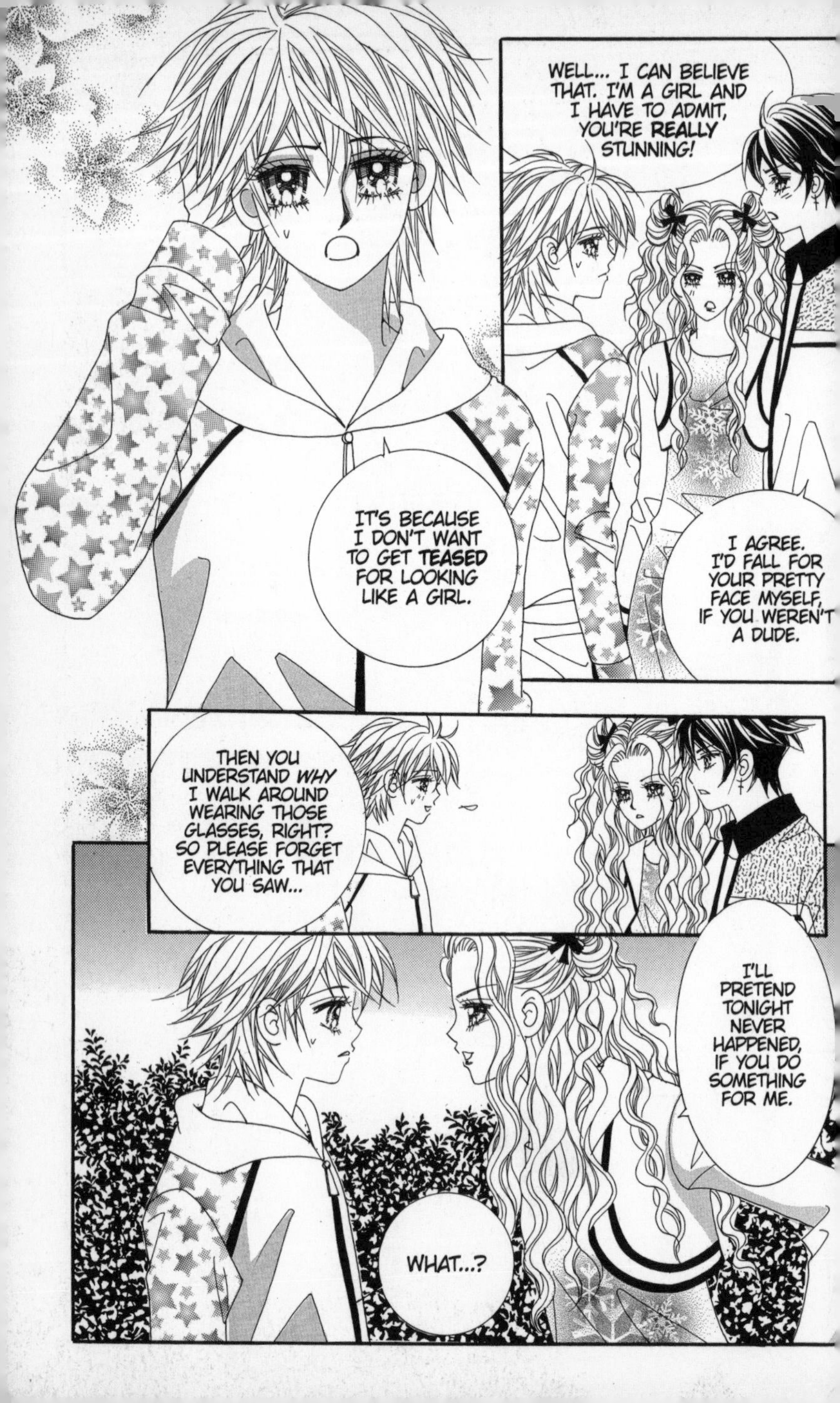
IT'S BECAUSE I DON'T WANT TO GET TEASED FOR LOOKING LIKE A GIRL.
WELL... I CAN BELIEVE THAT. I'M A GIRL AND I HAVE TO ADMIT, YOU'RE REALLY STUNNING!
I AGREE. I'D FALL FOR YOUR PRETTY FACE MYSELF, IF YOU WEREN'T A DUDE.
THEN YOU UNDERSTAND WHY I WALK AROUND WEARING THOSE GLASSES, RIGHT? SO PLEASE FORGET EVERYTHING THAT YOU SAW...
I'LL PRETEND TONIGHT NEVER HAPPENED, IF YOU DO SOMETHING FOR ME.
WHAT...?

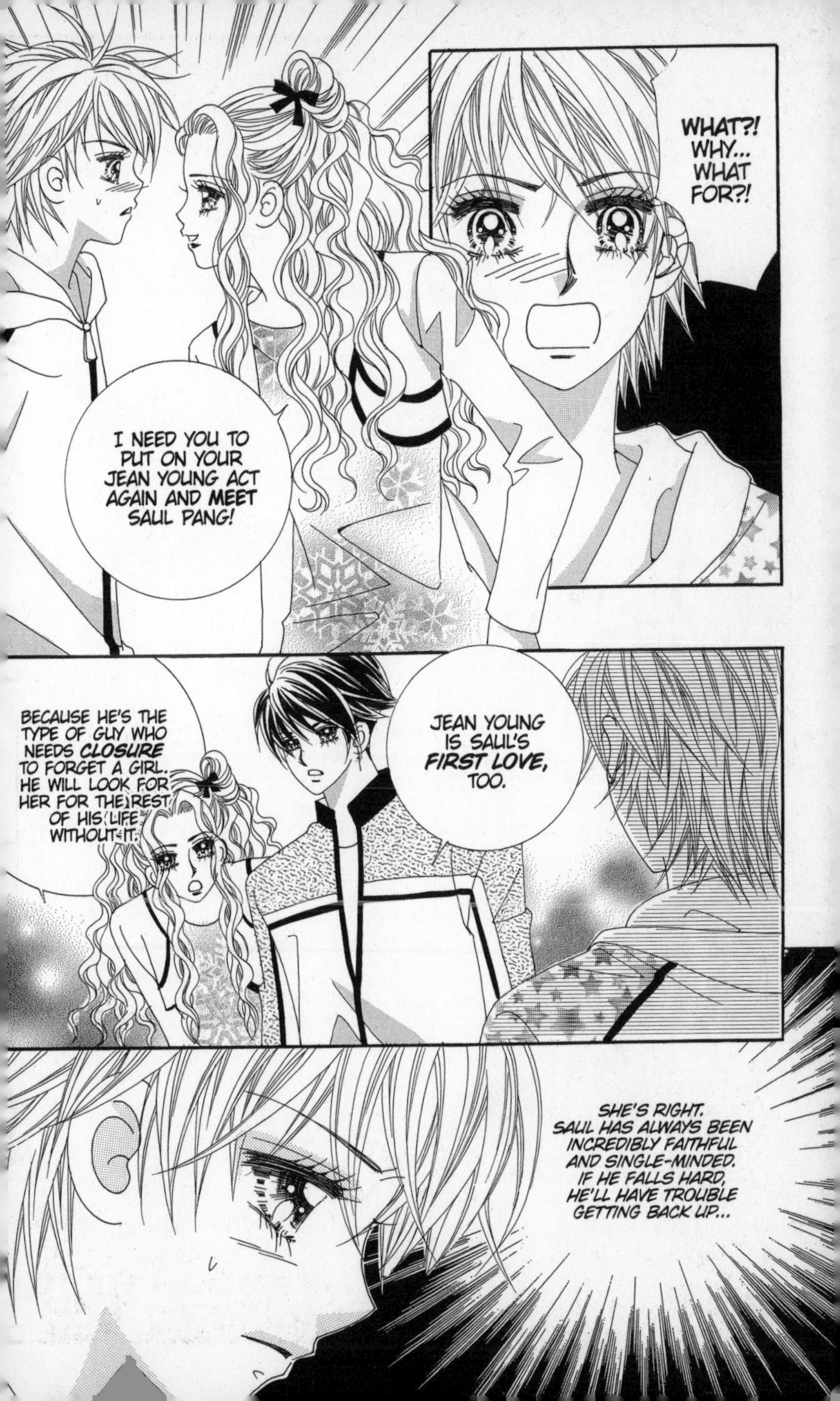
I NEED YOU TO PUT ON YOUR JEAN YOUNG ACT AGAIN AND MEET SAUL PANG!
WHAT?! WHY... WHAT FOR?!
BECAUSE HE'S THE TYPE OF GUY WHO NEEDS CLOSURE TO FORGET A GIRL. HE WILL LOOK FOR HER FOR THE REST OF HIS LIFE WITHOUT IT.
JEAN YOUNG IS SAUL'S FIRST LOVE, TOO.
SHE'S RIGHT. SAUL HAS ALWAYS BEEN INCREDIBLY FAITHFUL AND SINGLE-MINDED. IF HE FALLS HARD, HE'LL HAVE TROUBLE GETTING BACK UP...

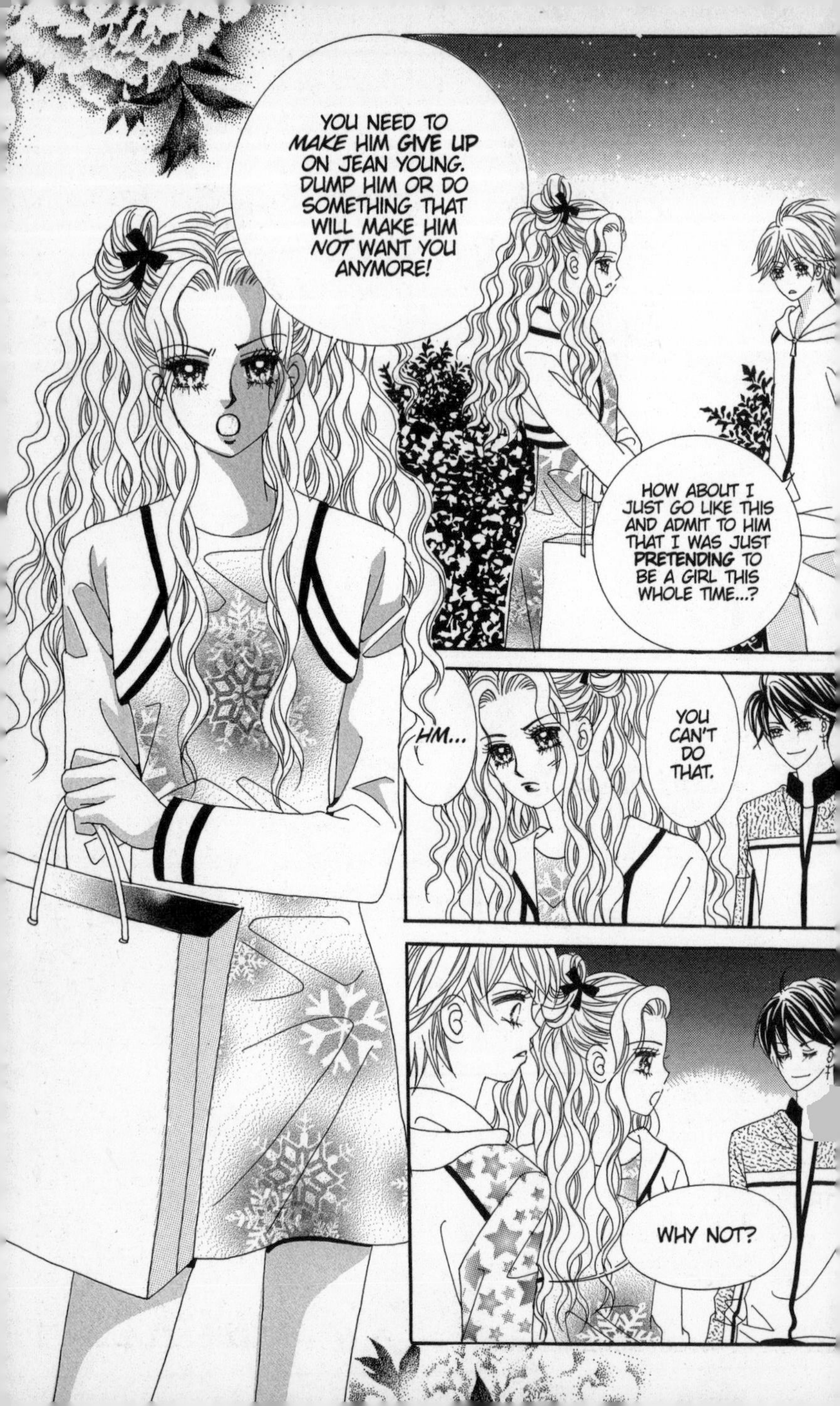
YOU NEED TO MAKE HIM GIVE UP ON JEAN YOUNG. DUMP HIM OR DO SOMETHING THAT WILL MAKE HIM NOT WANT YOU ANYMORE!
HOW ABOUT I JUST GO LIKE THIS AND ADMIT TO HIM THAT I WAS JUST PRETENDING TO BE A GIRL THIS WHOLE TIME...?
HM...
YOU CAN'T DO THAT.
WHY NOT?

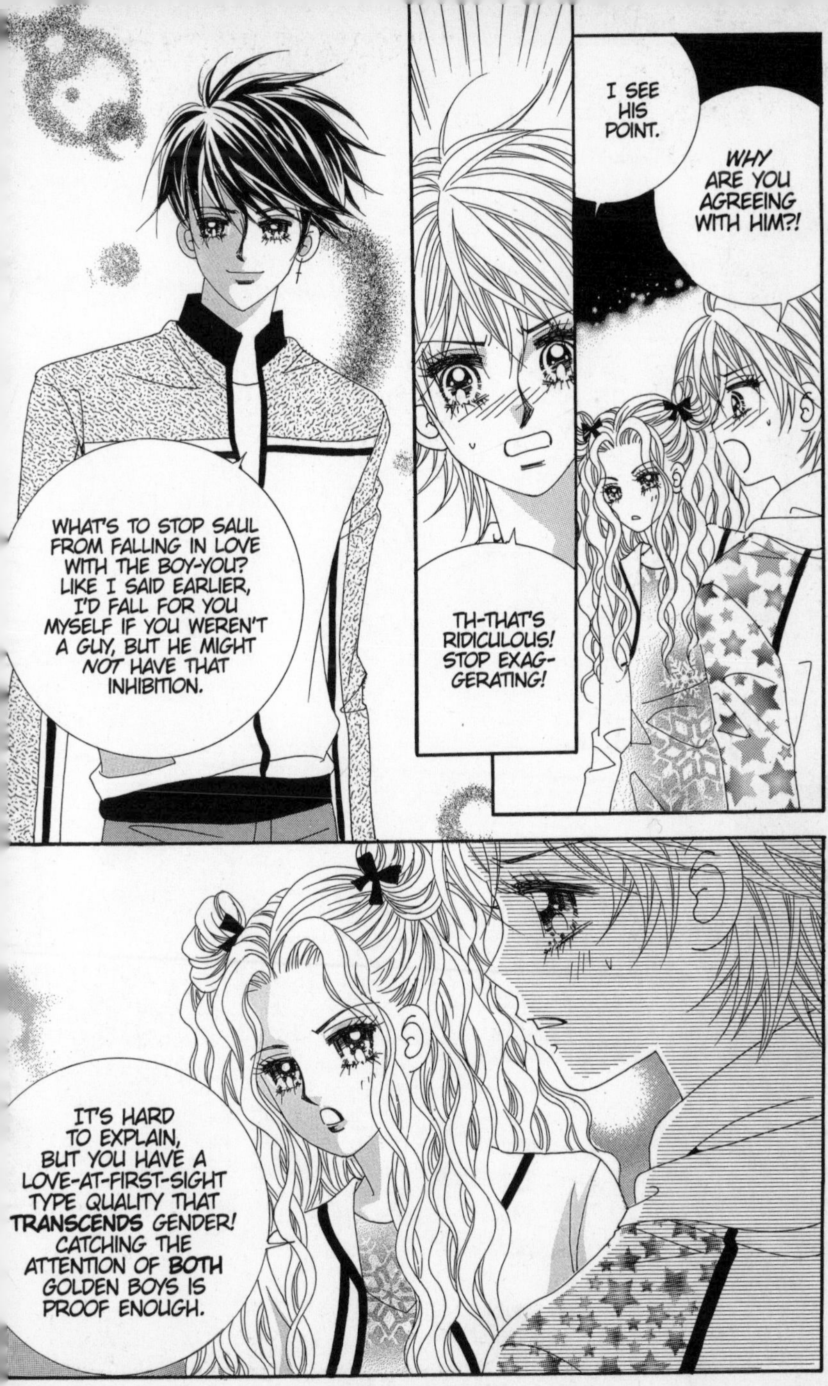
WHAT'S TO STOP SAUL FROM FALLING IN LOVE WITH THE BOY-YOU? LIKE I SAID EARLIER, I'D FALL FOR YOU MYSELF IF YOU WEREN'T A GUY, BUT HE MIGHT *NOT* HAVE THAT INHIBITION.
TH-THAT'S RIDICULOUS! STOP EXAG-GERATING!
I SEE HIS POINT.
WHY ARE YOU AGREEING WITH HIM?!
IT'S HARD TO EXPLAIN, BUT YOU HAVE A LOVE-AT-FIRST-SIGHT TYPE QUALITY THAT **TRANSCENDS** GENDER! CATCHING THE ATTENTION OF **BOTH** GOLDEN BOYS IS PROOF ENOUGH.

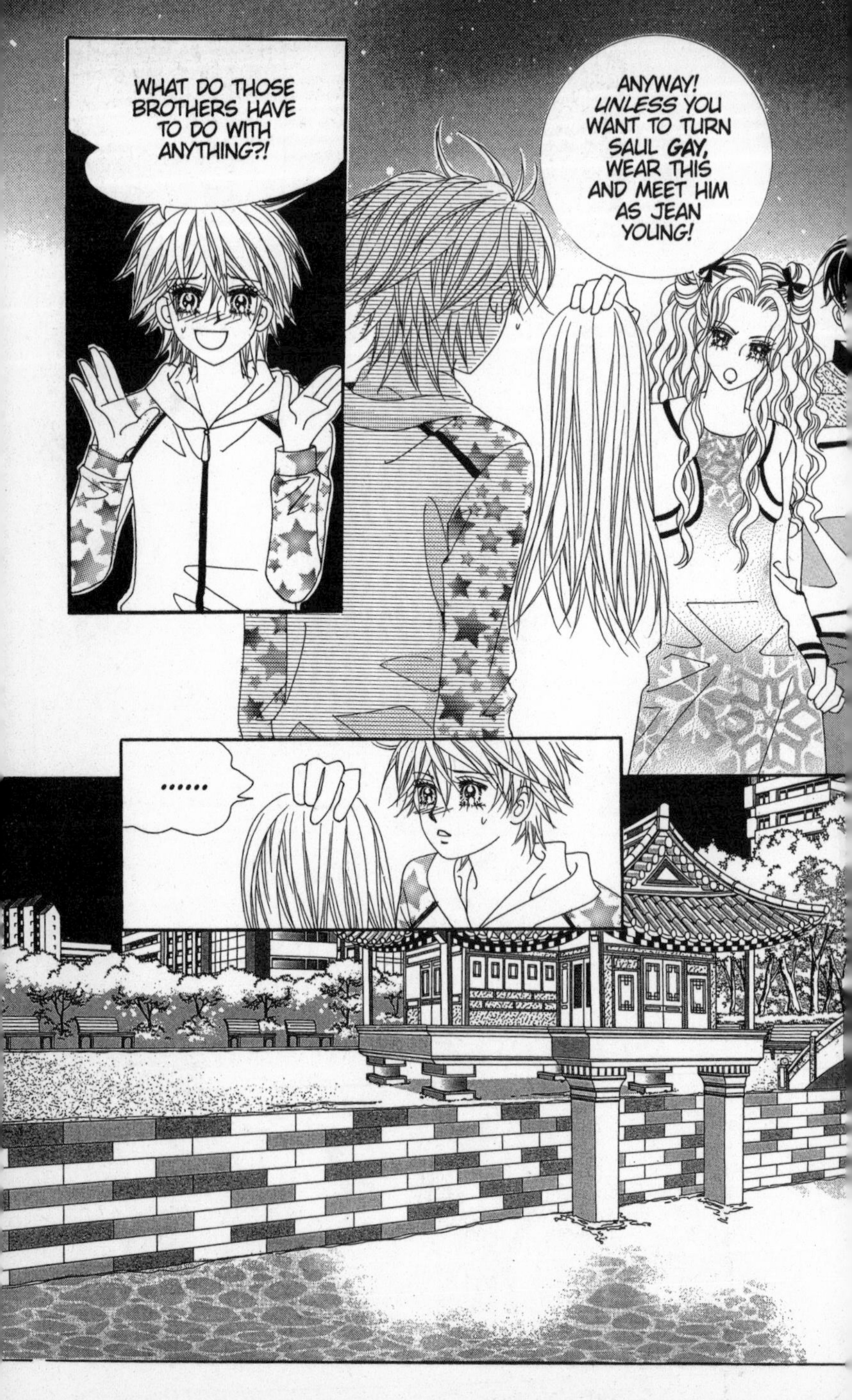
WHAT DO THOSE BROTHERS HAVE TO DO WITH ANYTHING?!
ANYWAY! UNLESS YOU WANT TO TURN SAUL GAY, WEAR THIS AND MEET HIM AS JEAN YOUNG!
......

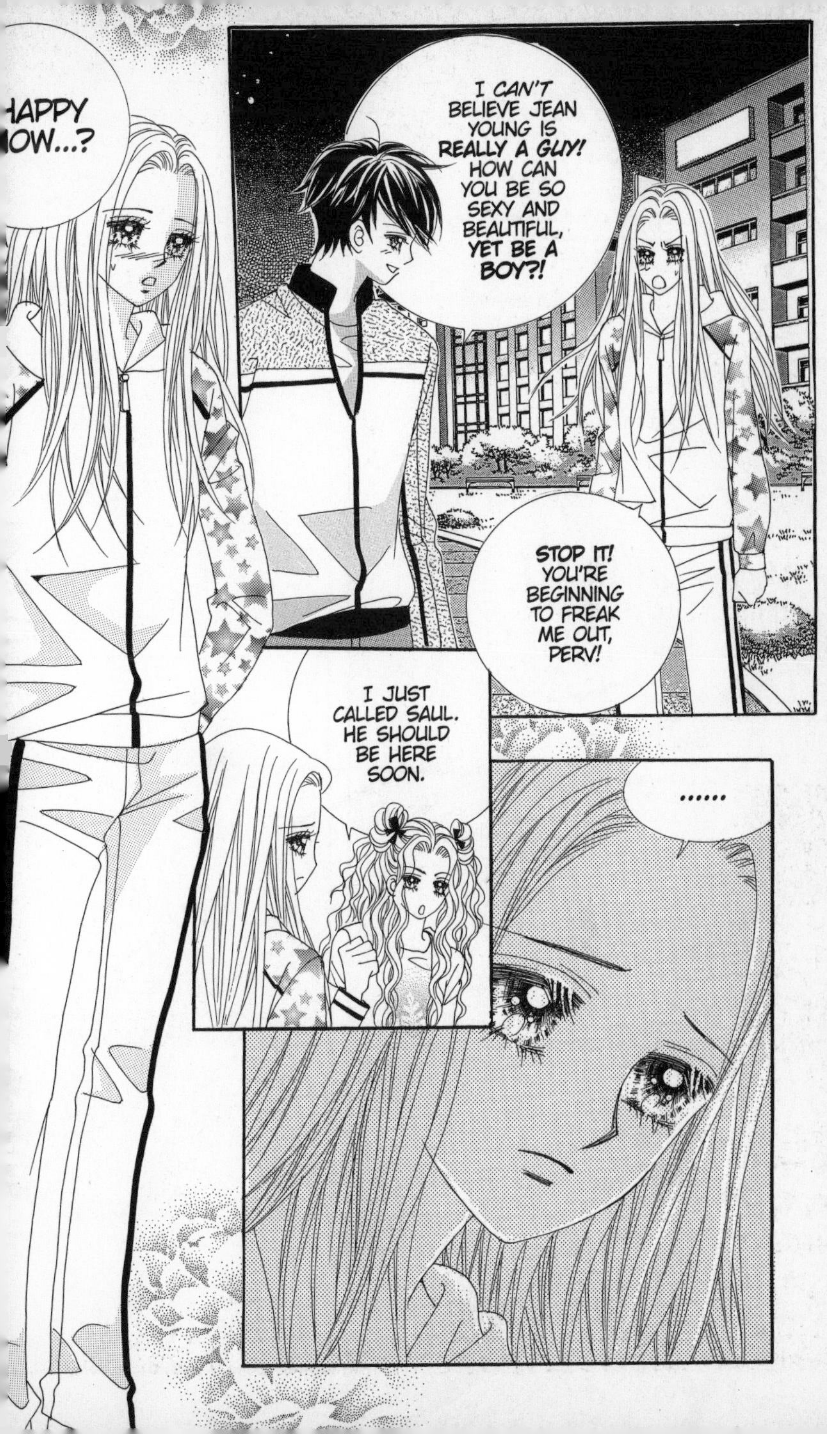
HAPPY NOW...?
I CAN'T BELIEVE JEAN YOUNG IS REALLY A GUY! HOW CAN YOU BE SO SEXY AND BEAUTIFUL, YET BE A BOY?!
STOP IT! YOU'RE BEGINNING TO FREAK ME OUT, PERV!
I JUST CALLED SAUL. HE SHOULD BE HERE SOON.
......

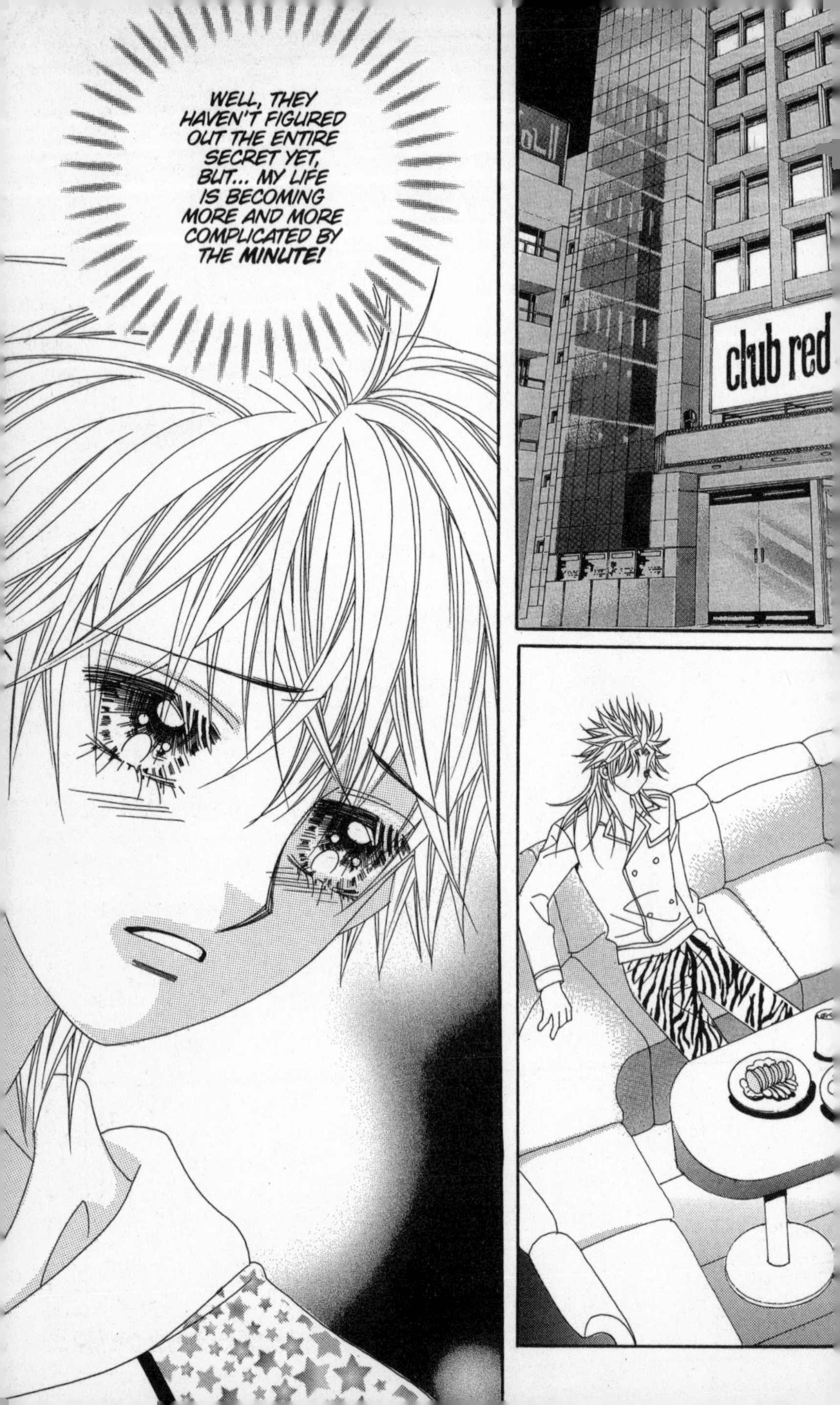
WELL, THEY HAVEN'T FIGURED OUT THE ENTIRE SECRET YET, BUT... MY LIFE IS BECOMING MORE AND MORE COMPLICATED BY THE MINUTE!
club red

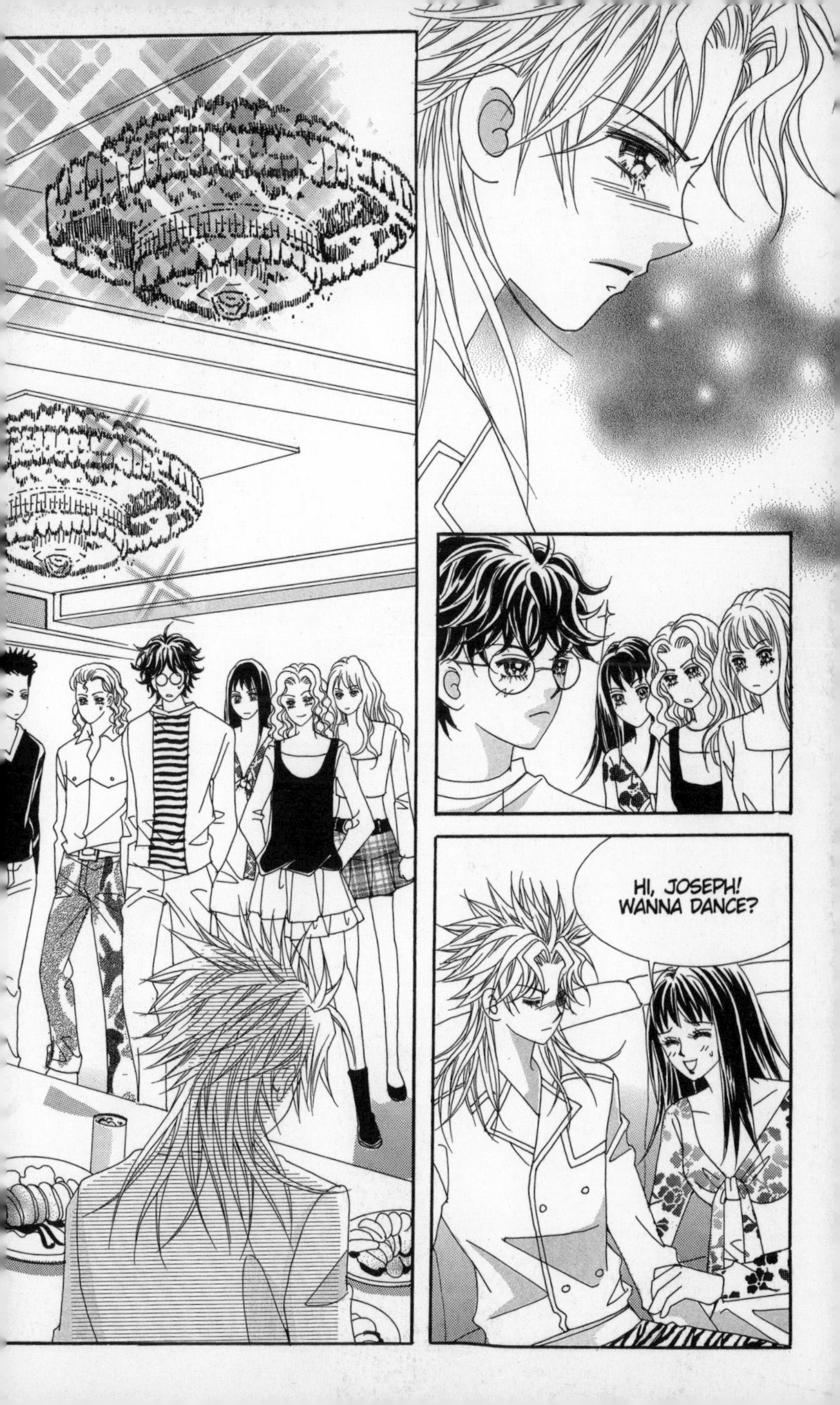
HI, JOSEPH!
WANNA DANCE?

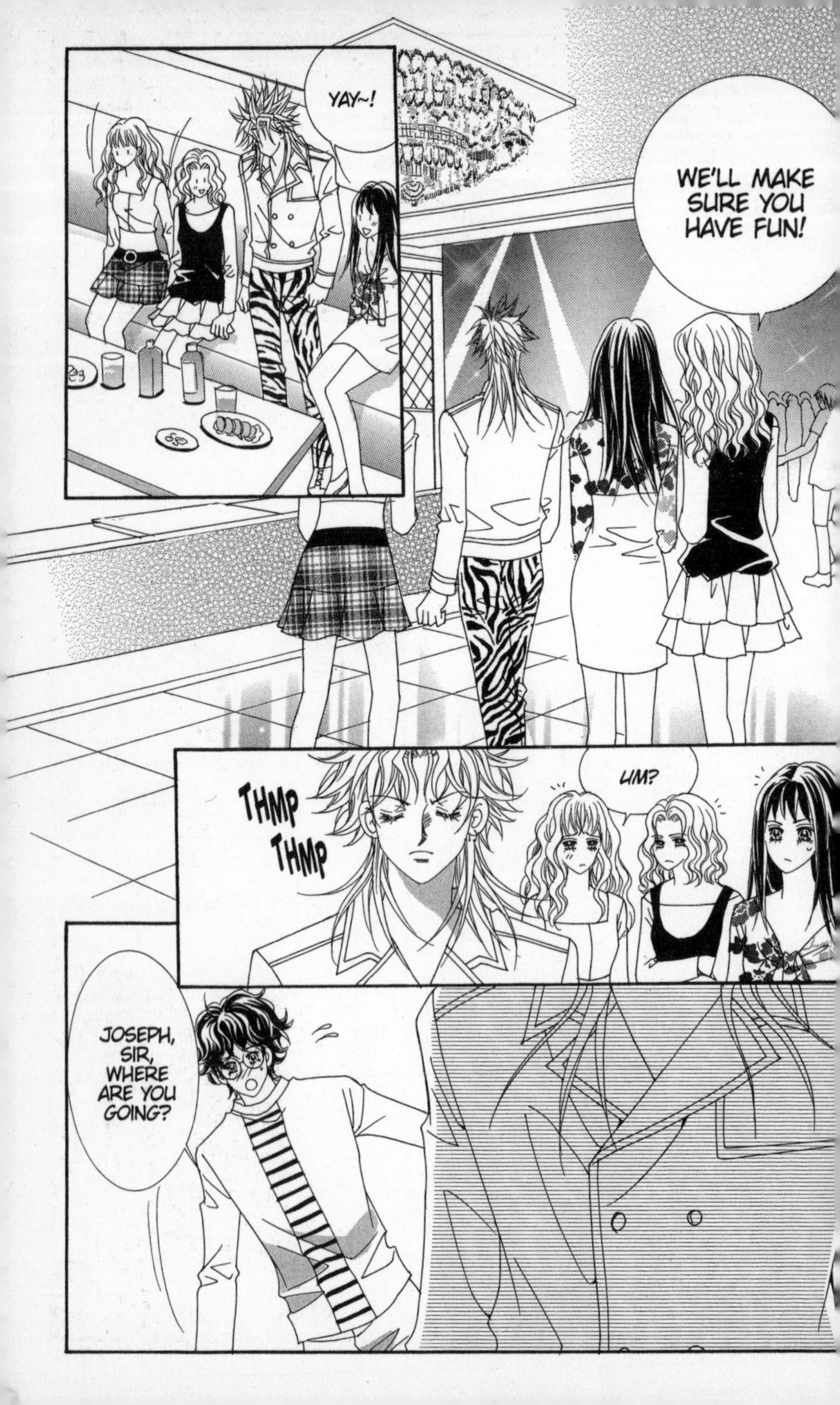
YAY~!
WE'LL MAKE SURE YOU HAVE FUN!
THMP THMP
UM?
JOSEPH, SIR, WHERE ARE YOU GOING?

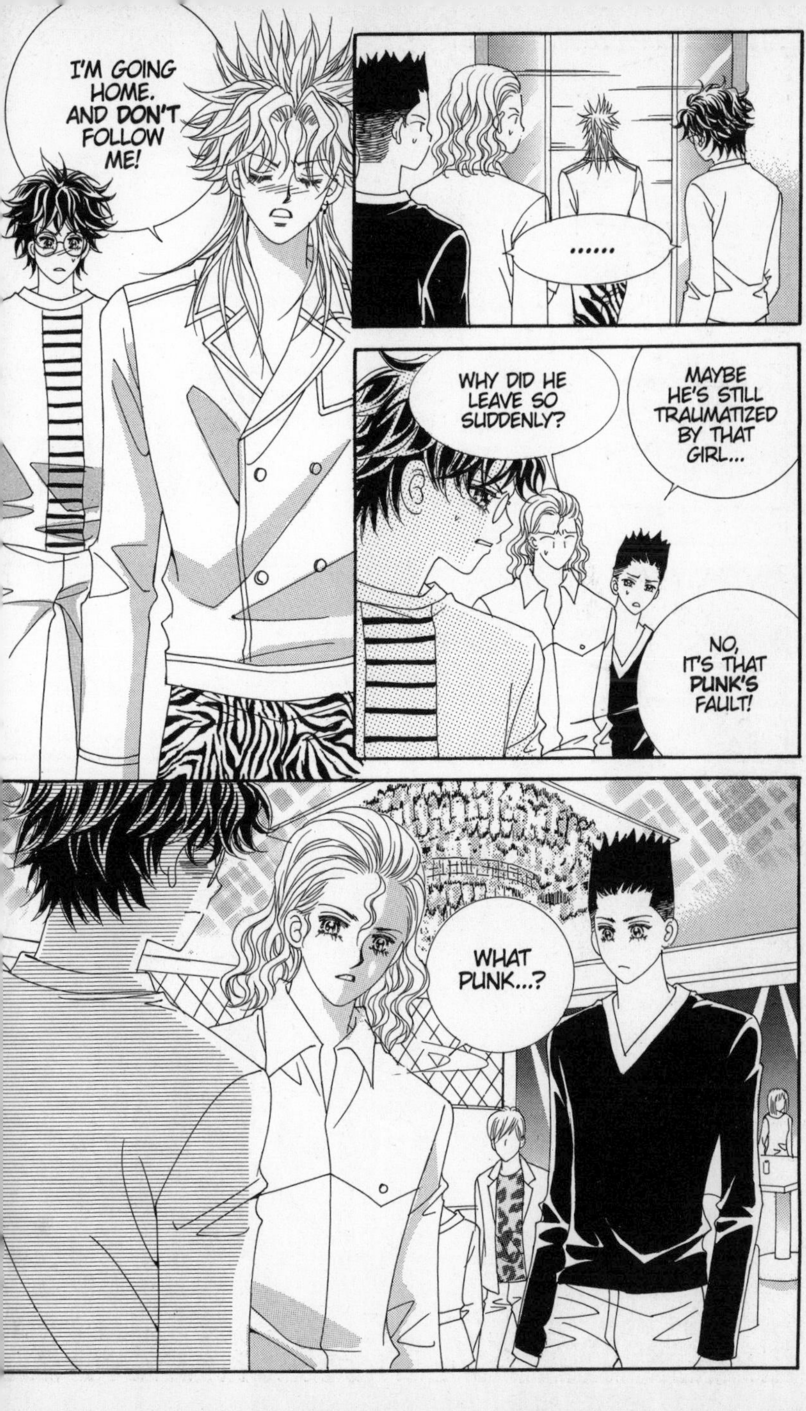
I'M GOING HOME. AND DON'T FOLLOW ME!
......
WHY DID HE LEAVE SO SUDDENLY?
MAYBE HE'S STILL TRAUMATIZED BY THAT GIRL...
NO, IT'S THAT PUNK'S FAULT!
WHAT PUNK...?

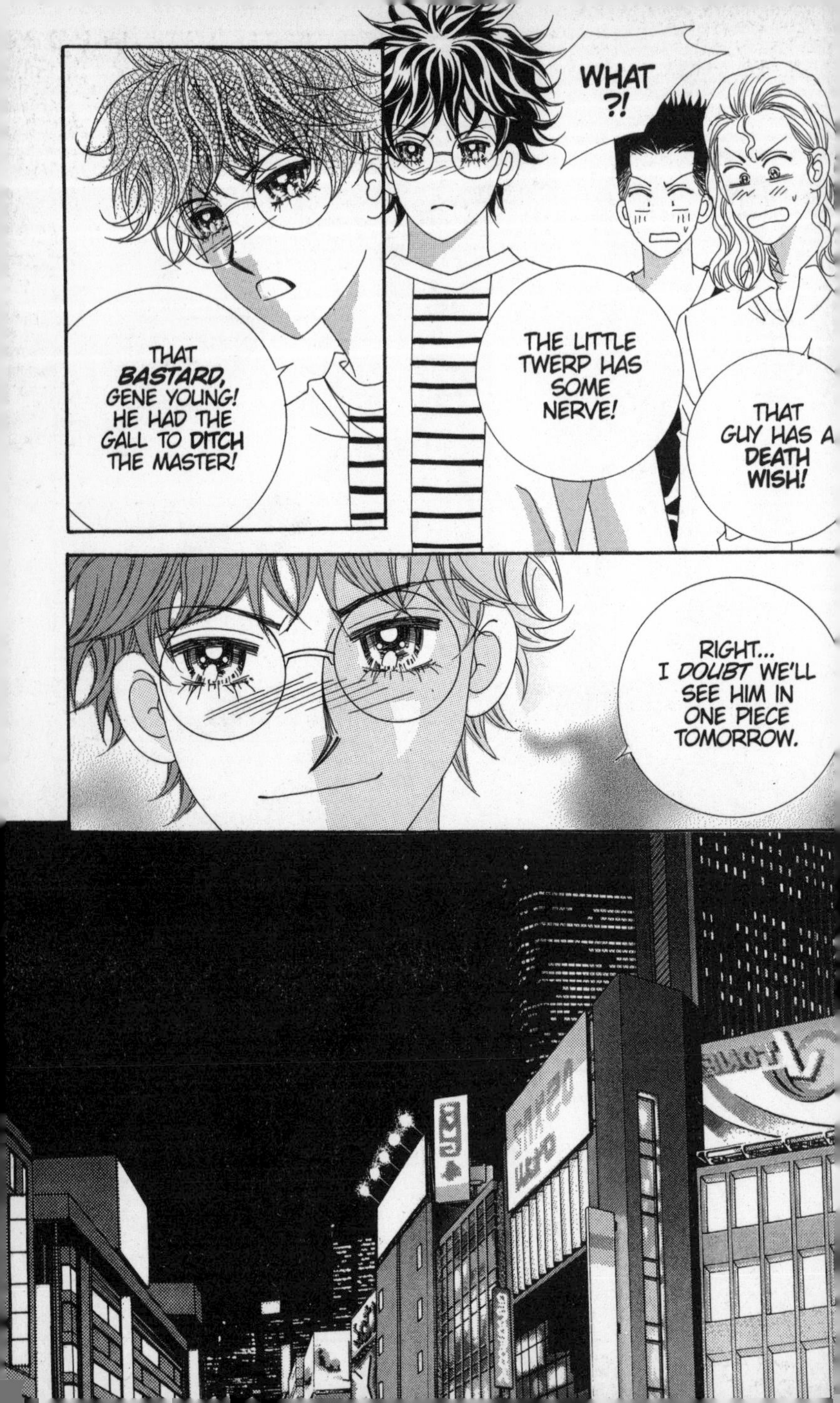
THAT BASTARD, GENE YOUNG! HE HAD THE GALL TO DITCH THE MASTER!
WHAT ?!
THE LITTLE TWERP HAS SOME NERVE!
THAT GUY HAS A DEATH WISH!
RIGHT... I DOUBT WE'LL SEE HIM IN ONE PIECE TOMORROW.

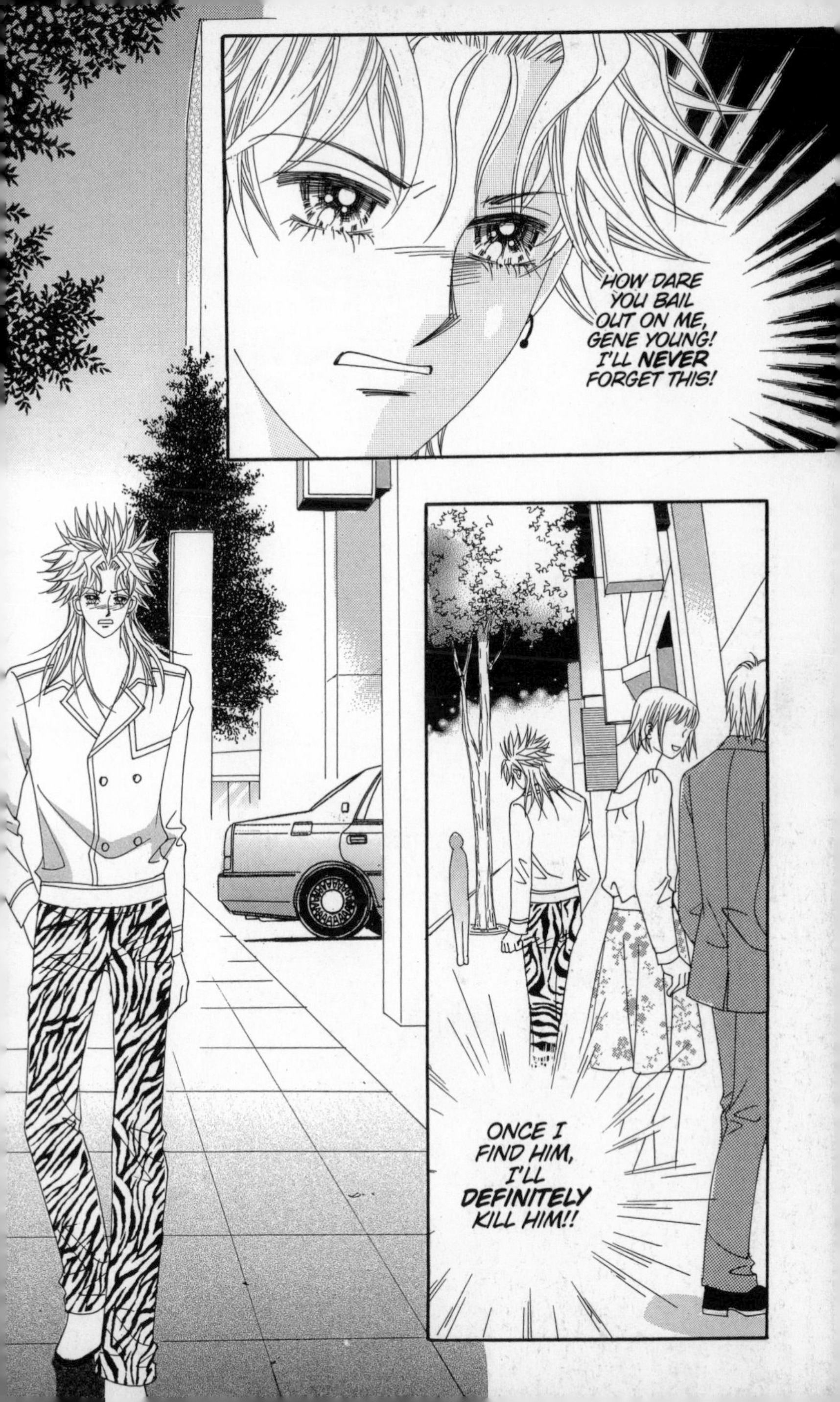
HOW DARE YOU BAIL OUT ON ME, GENE YOUNG! I'LL **NEVER** FORGET THIS!
ONCE I FIND HIM, I'LL **DEFINITELY** KILL HIM!!

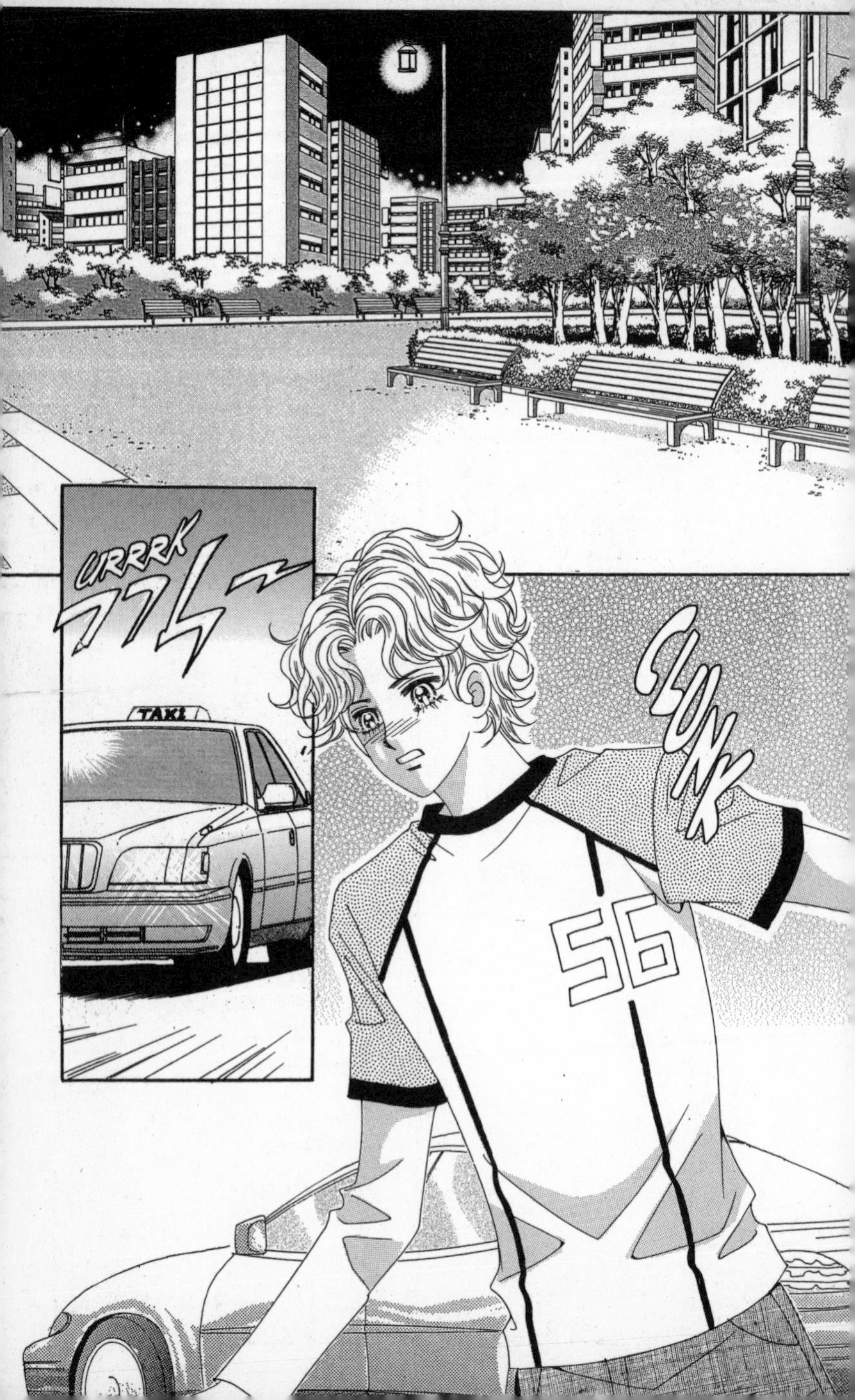
URRRK
TAXI
CLUNK

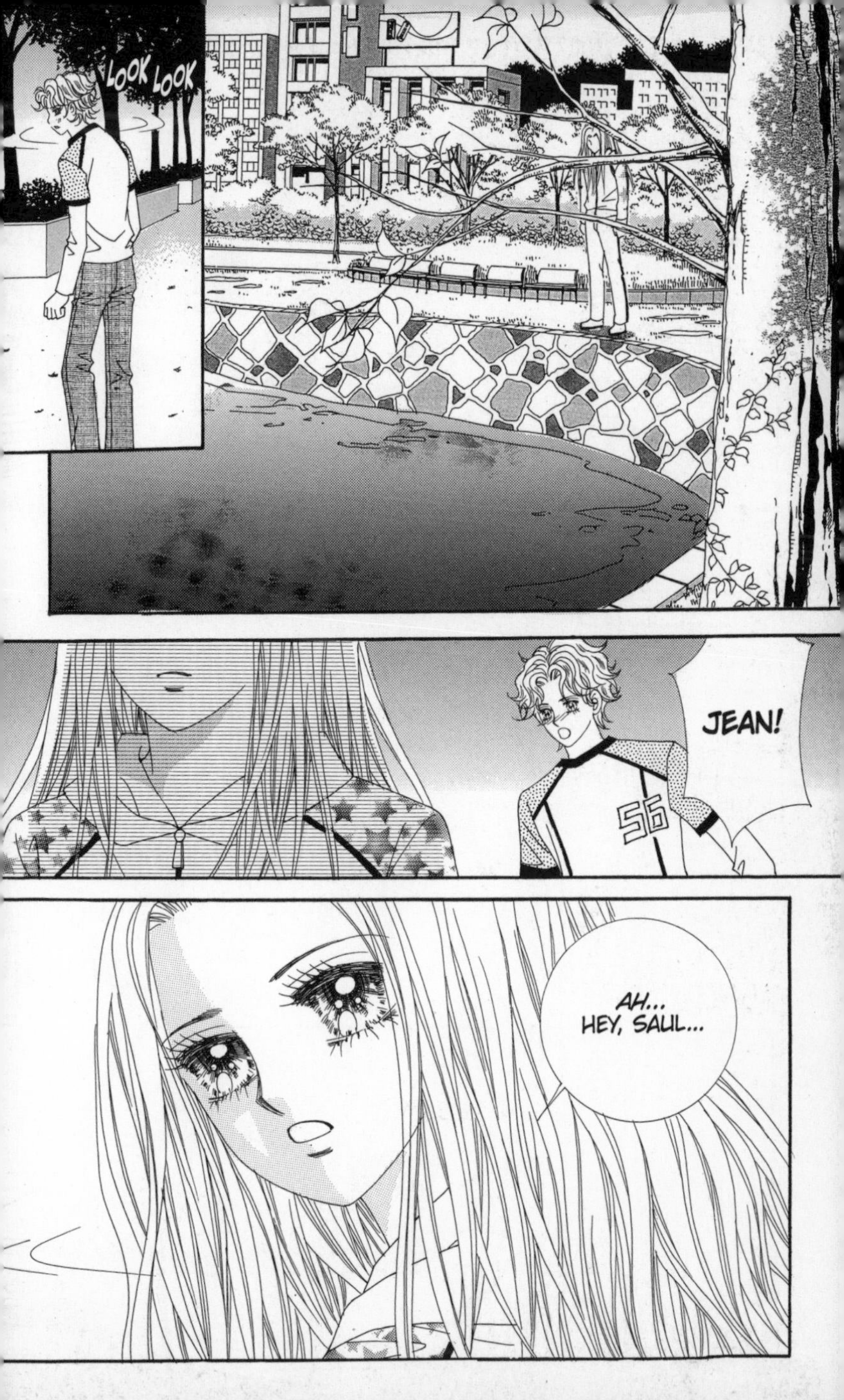
LOOK LOOK
JEAN!
AH... HEY, SAUL...

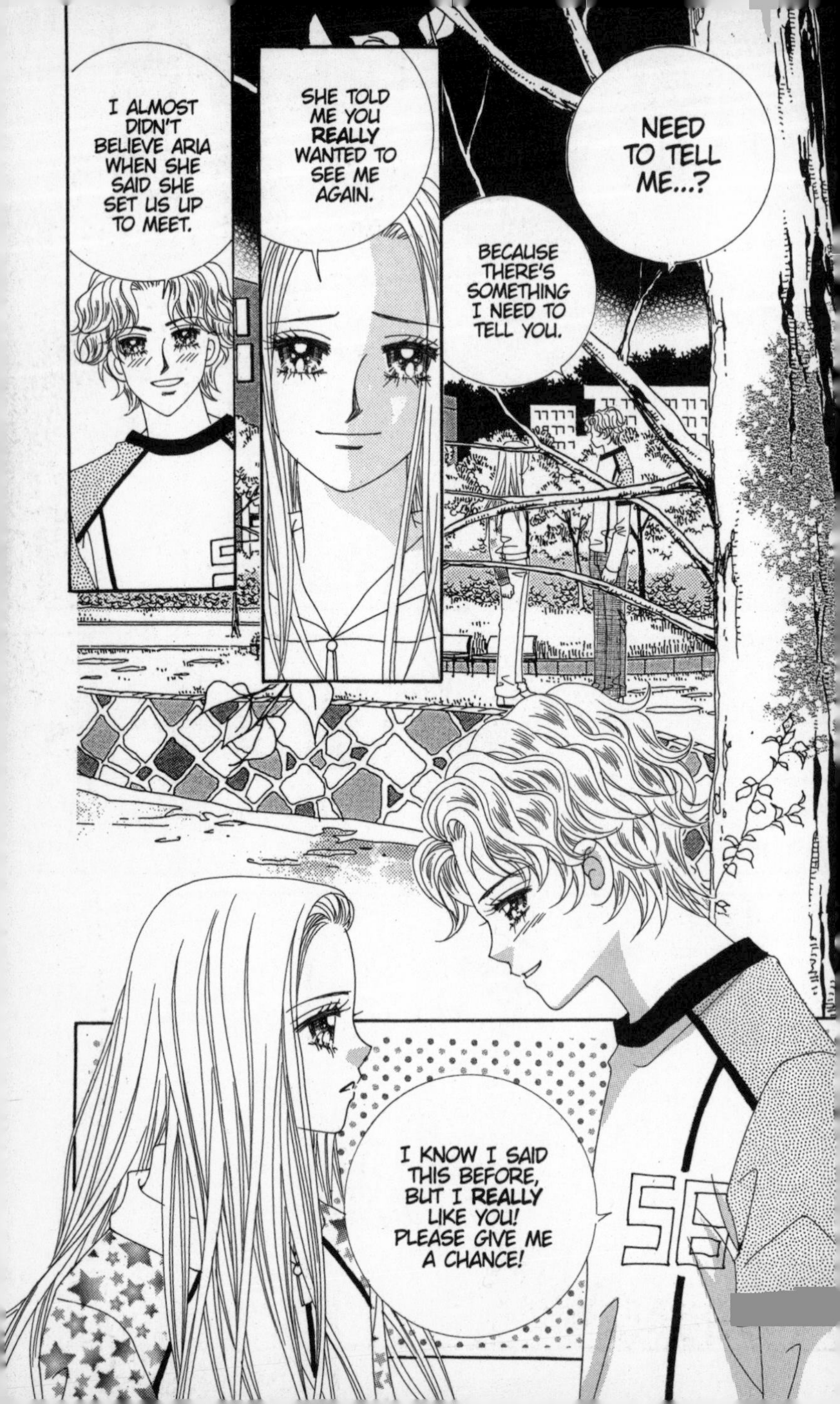
I ALMOST DIDN'T BELIEVE ARIA WHEN SHE SAID SHE SET US UP TO MEET.
SHE TOLD ME YOU REALLY WANTED TO SEE ME AGAIN.
BECAUSE THERE'S SOMETHING I NEED TO TELL YOU.
NEED TO TELL ME...?
I KNOW I SAID THIS BEFORE, BUT I REALLY LIKE YOU! PLEASE GIVE ME A CHANCE!

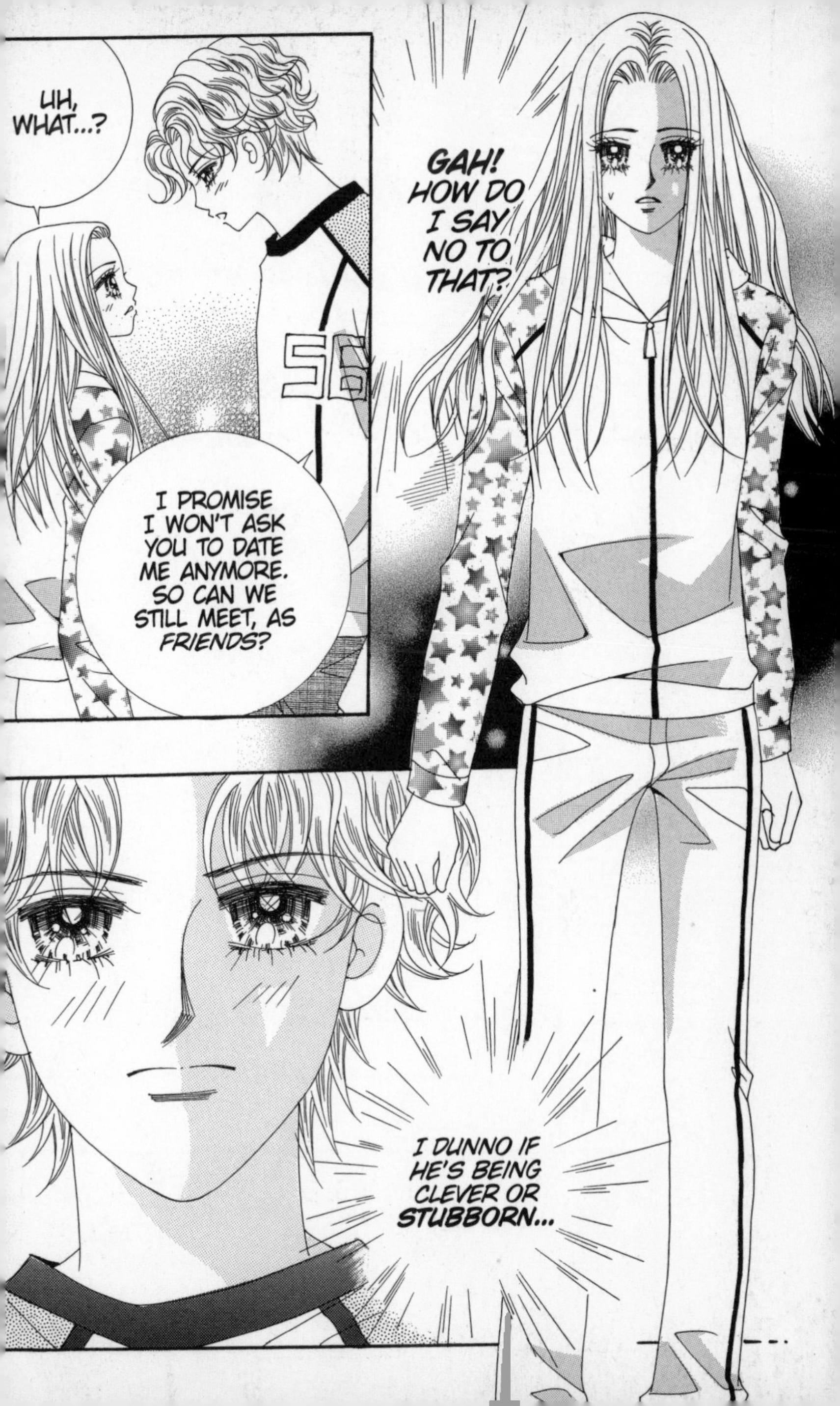
UH, WHAT...?
I PROMISE I WON'T ASK YOU TO DATE ME ANYMORE. SO CAN WE STILL MEET, AS *FRIENDS?*
I DUNNO IF HE'S BEING CLEVER OR STUBBORN...
GAH! HOW DO I SAY NO TO THAT?

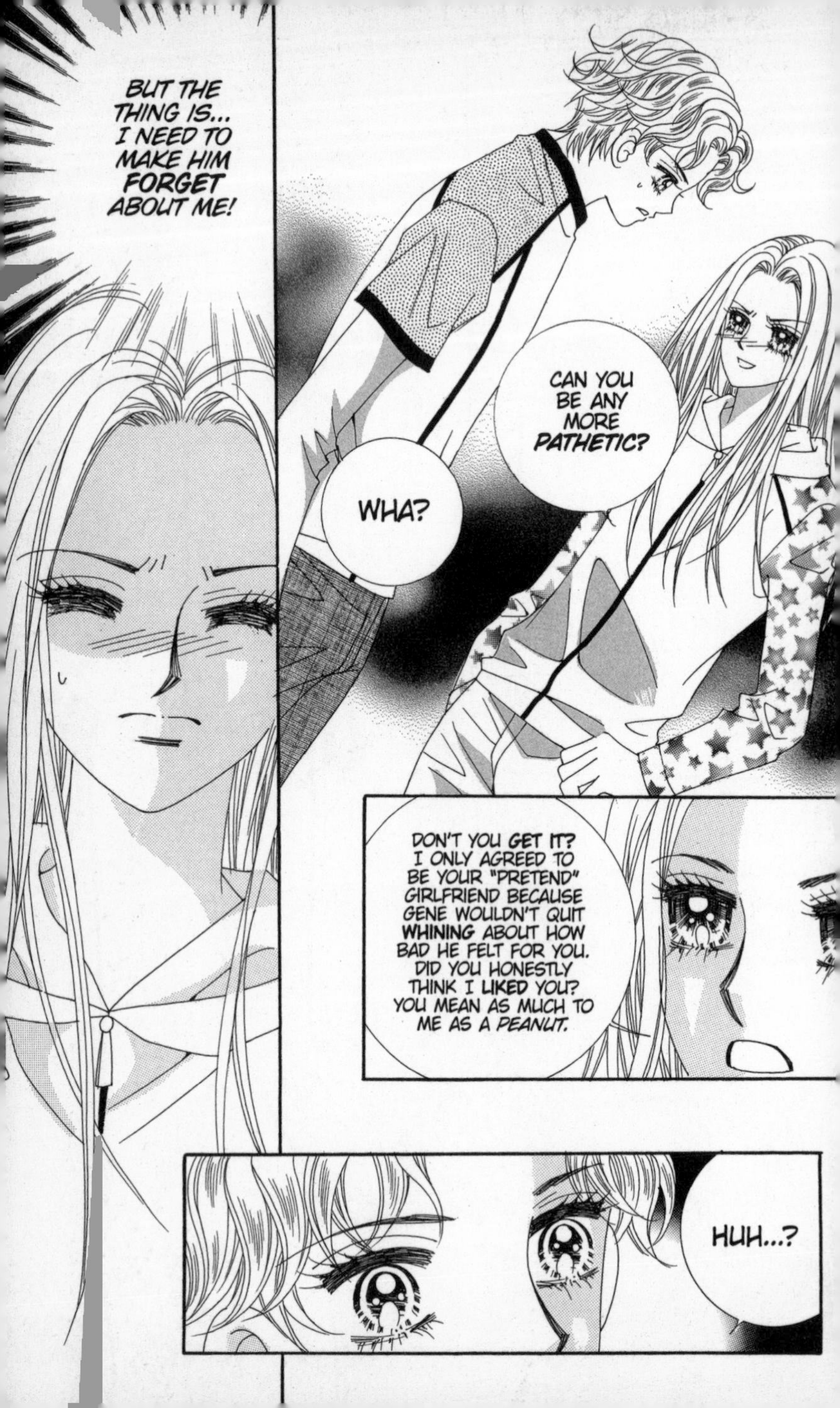
BUT THE THING IS... I NEED TO MAKE HIM FORGET ABOUT ME!
CAN YOU BE ANY MORE PATHETIC?
WHA?
DON'T YOU GET IT? I ONLY AGREED TO BE YOUR "PRETEND" GIRLFRIEND BECAUSE GENE WOULDN'T QUIT WHINING ABOUT HOW BAD HE FELT FOR YOU. DID YOU HONESTLY THINK I LIKED YOU? YOU MEAN AS MUCH TO ME AS A PEANUT.
HUH...?

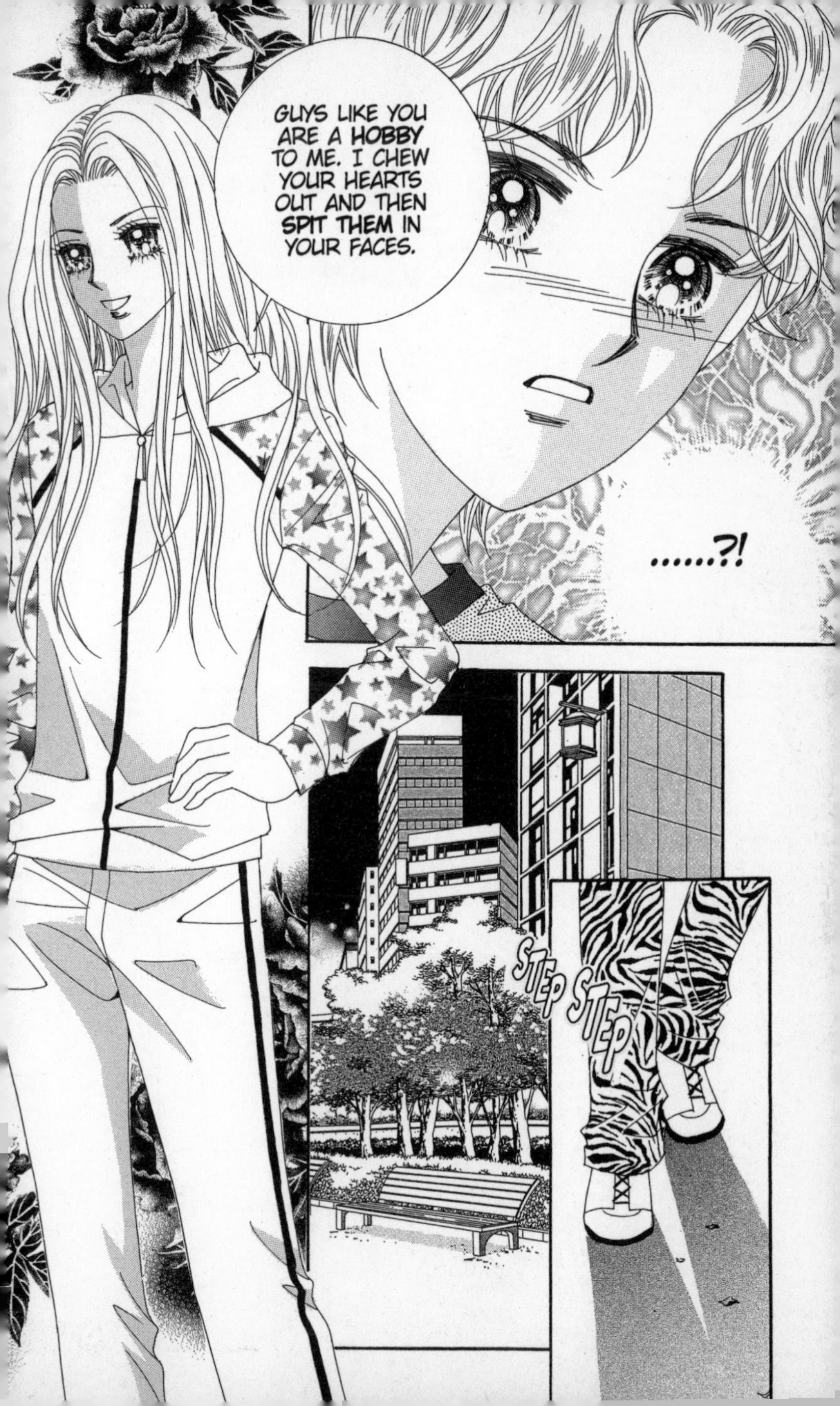
GUYS LIKE YOU ARE A HOBBY TO ME. I CHEW YOUR HEARTS OUT AND THEN SPIT THEM IN YOUR FACES.
......?!
STEP STEP

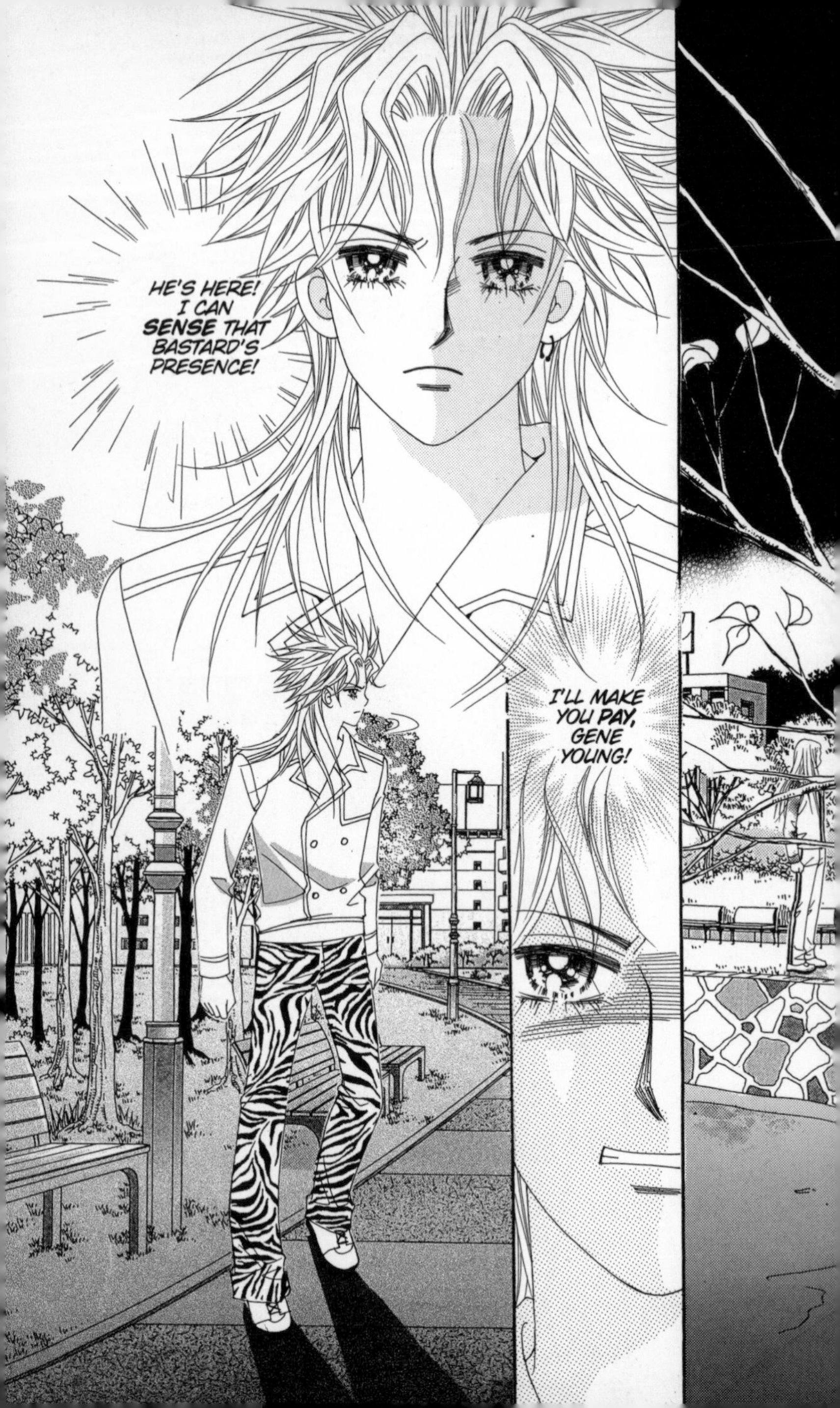
HE'S HERE! I CAN SENSE THAT BASTARD'S PRESENCE!
I'LL MAKE YOU PAY, GENE YOUNG!

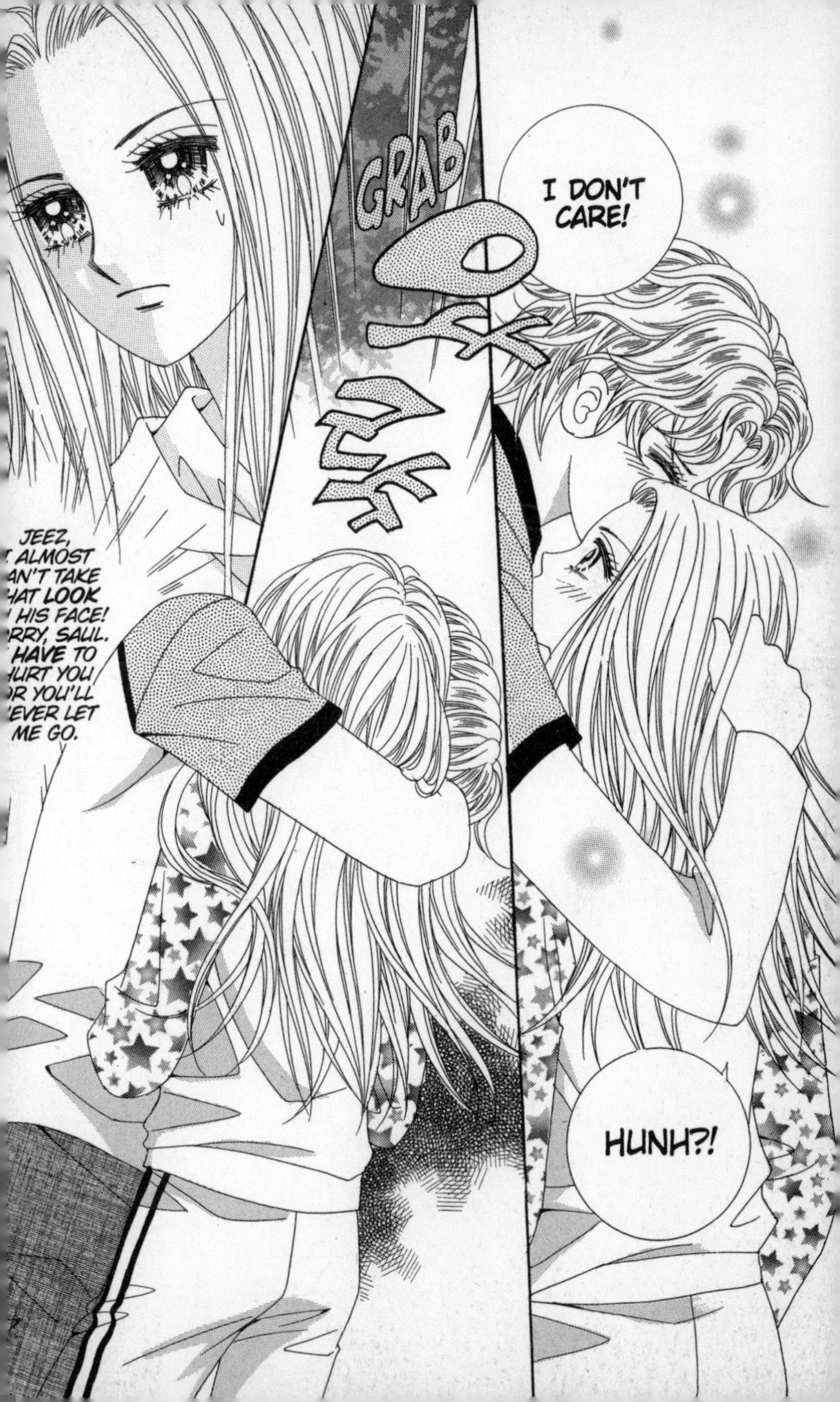

JEEZ, ALMOST AN'T TAKE HAT LOOK HIS FACE! RRY, SAUL. HAVE TO HURT YOU OR YOU'LL EVER LET ME GO.
GRAB
I DON'T CARE!
HUNH?!

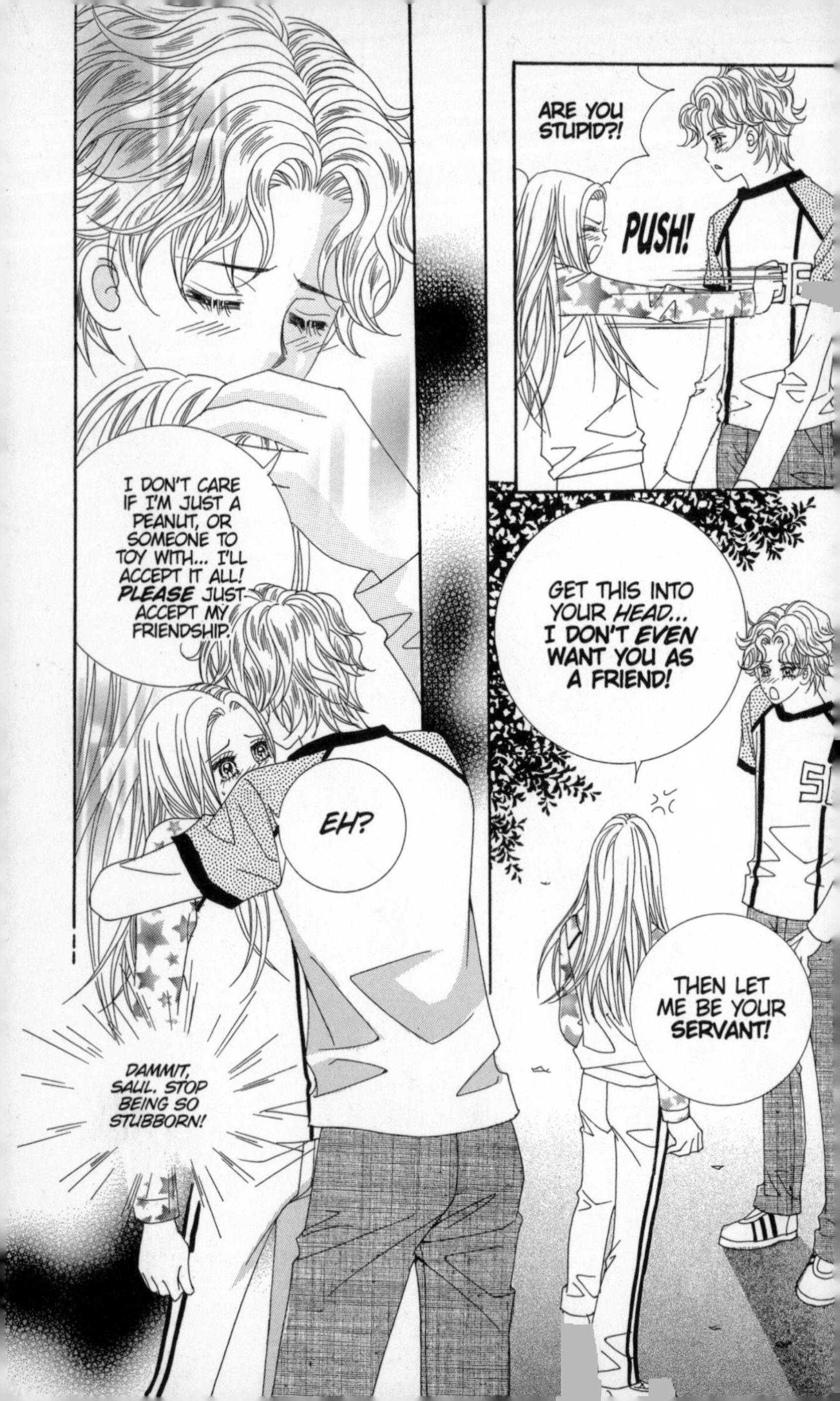
I DON'T CARE IF I'M JUST A PEANUT, OR SOMEONE TO TOY WITH... I'LL ACCEPT IT ALL! PLEASE JUST ACCEPT MY FRIENDSHIP.
EH?
DAMMIT, SAUL. STOP BEING SO STUBBORN!
ARE YOU STUPID?!
PUSH!
GET THIS INTO YOUR HEAD... I DON'T EVEN WANT YOU AS A FRIEND!
THEN LET ME BE YOUR SERVANT!

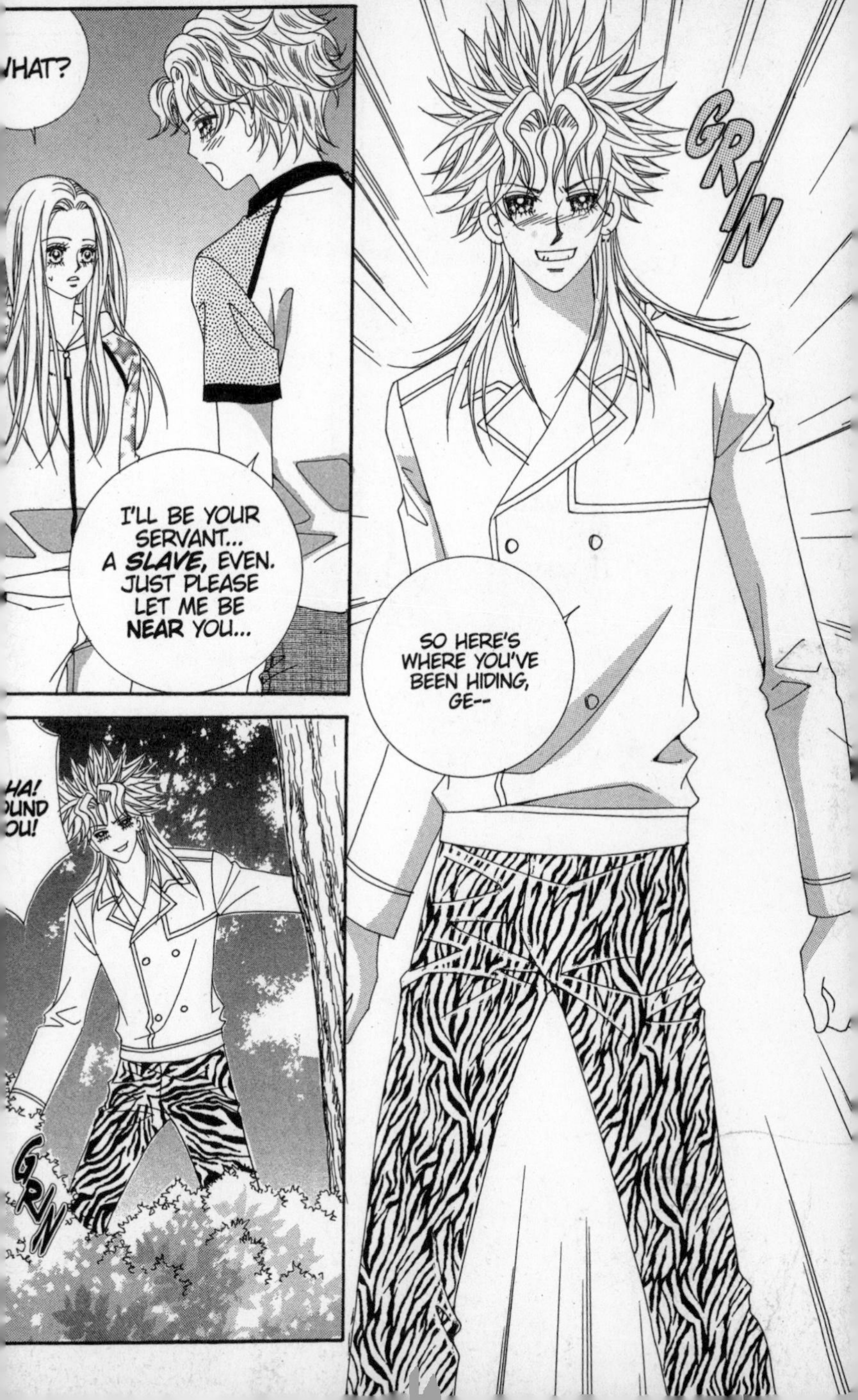
WHAT?
I'LL BE YOUR SERVANT... A ***SLAVE,*** EVEN. JUST PLEASE LET ME BE **NEAR** YOU...
HA! OUND OU!
GRIN
GRIN
SO HERE'S WHERE YOU'VE BEEN HIDING, GE--

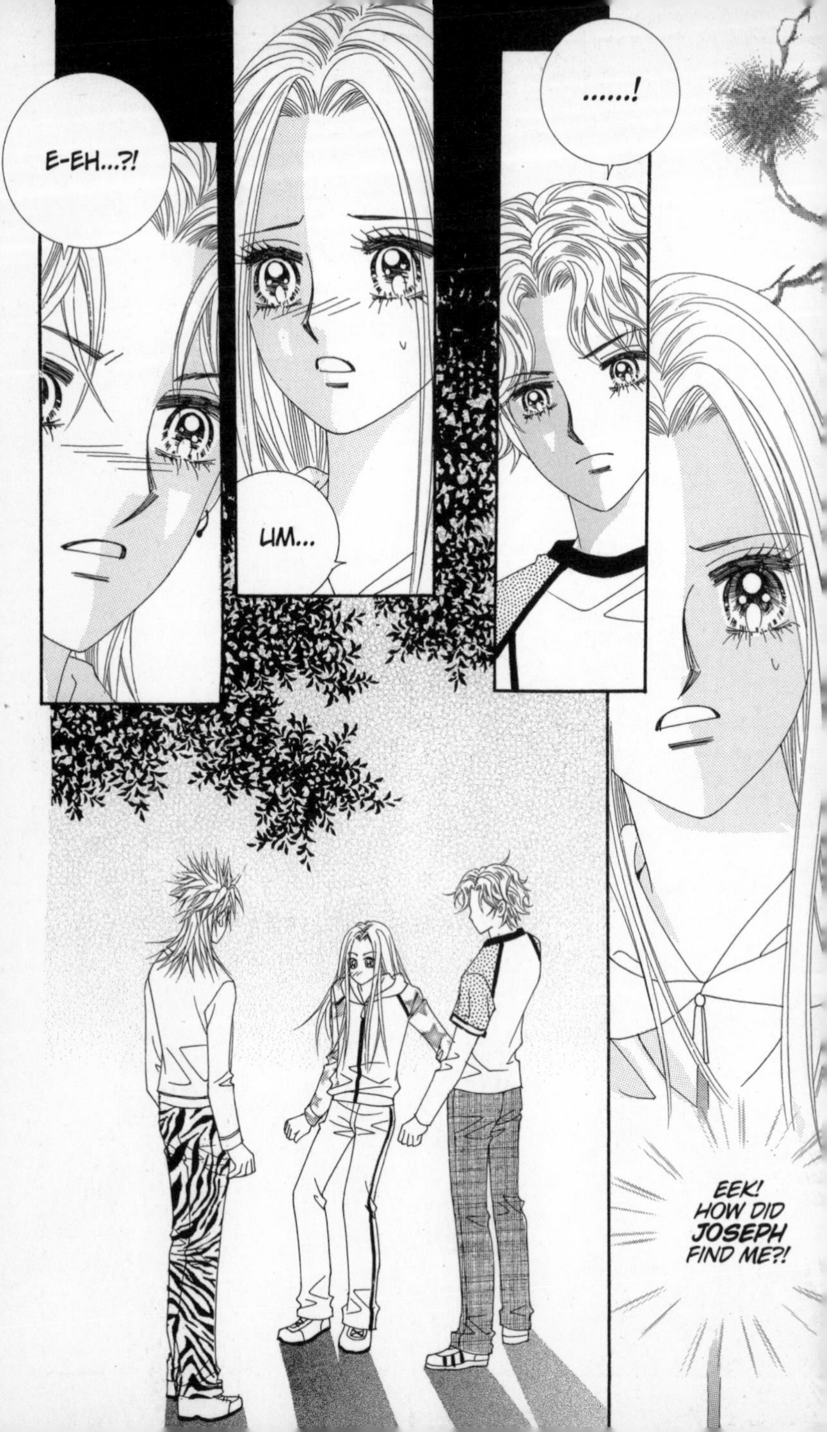
E-EH...?!
UM...
......!
EEK! HOW DID JOSEPH FIND ME?!

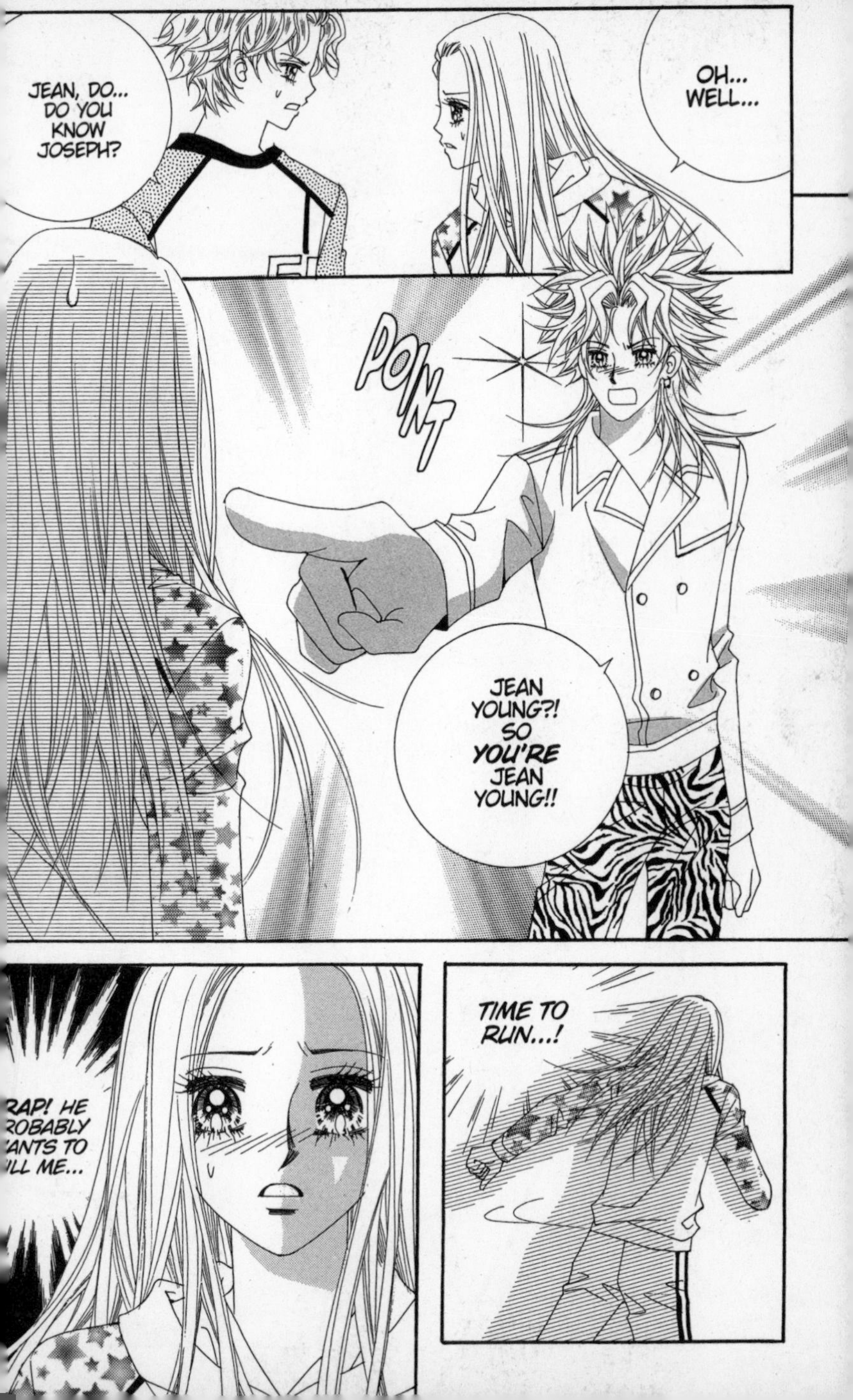
JEAN, DO... DO YOU KNOW JOSEPH?
OH... WELL...
POINT
JEAN YOUNG?! SO *YOU'RE* JEAN YOUNG!!
RAP! HE ROBABLY ANTS TO ILL ME...
TIME TO RUN...!

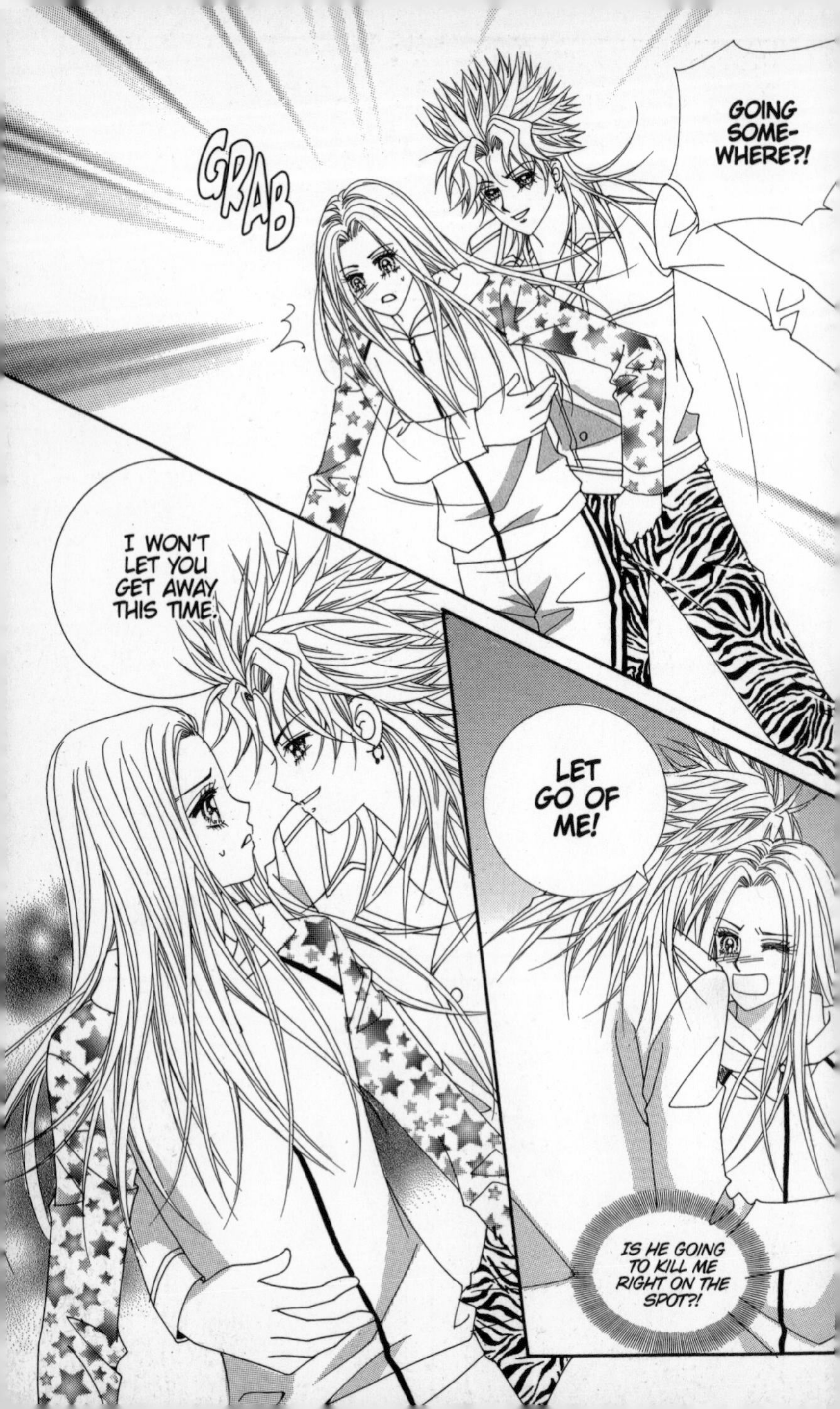
GRAB
GOING SOME-WHERE?!
I WON'T LET YOU GET AWAY THIS TIME.
LET GO OF ME!
IS HE GOING TO KILL ME RIGHT ON THE SPOT?!

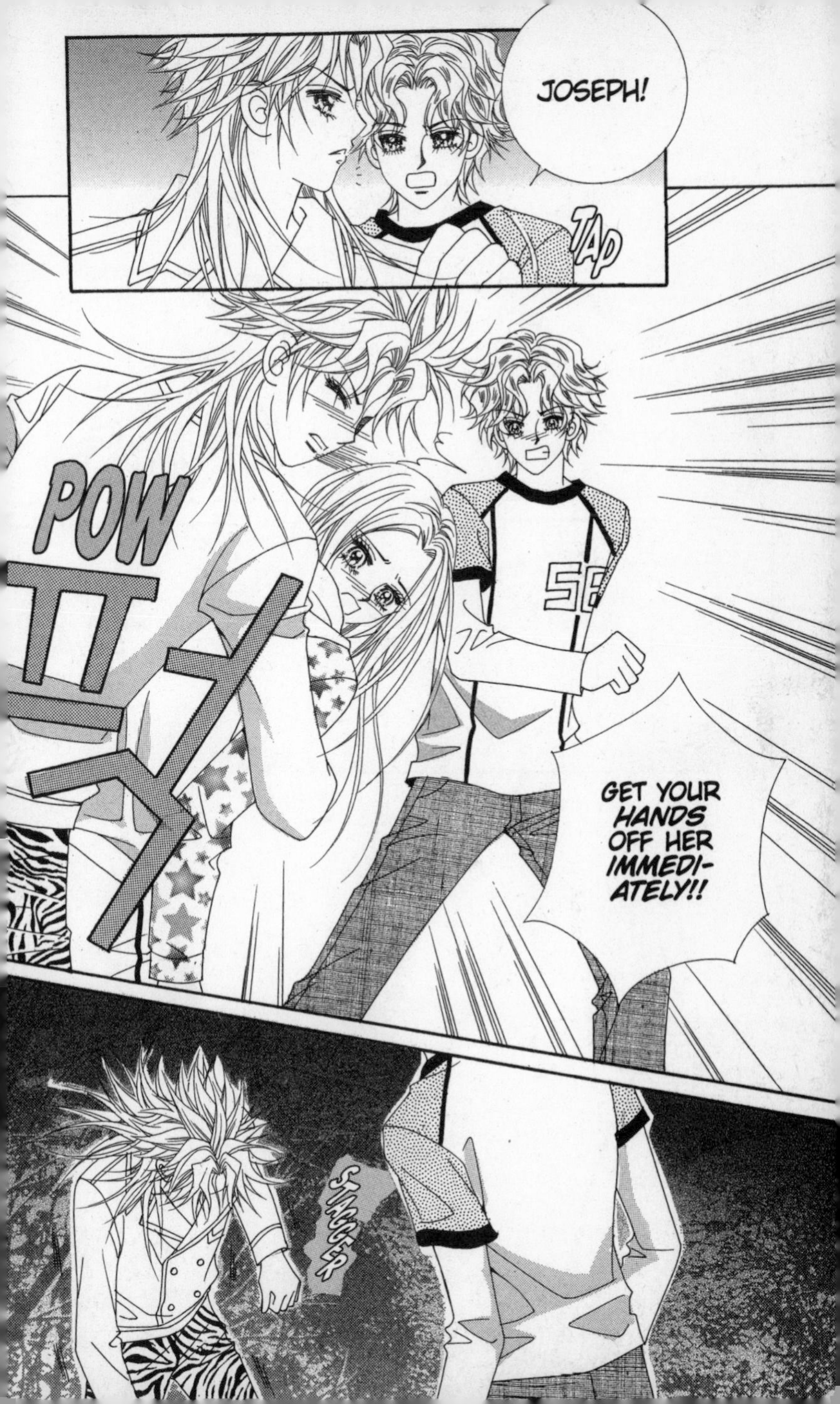
JOSEPH!
TAP
POW
GET YOUR HANDS OFF HER IMMEDI-ATELY!!
STAGGER

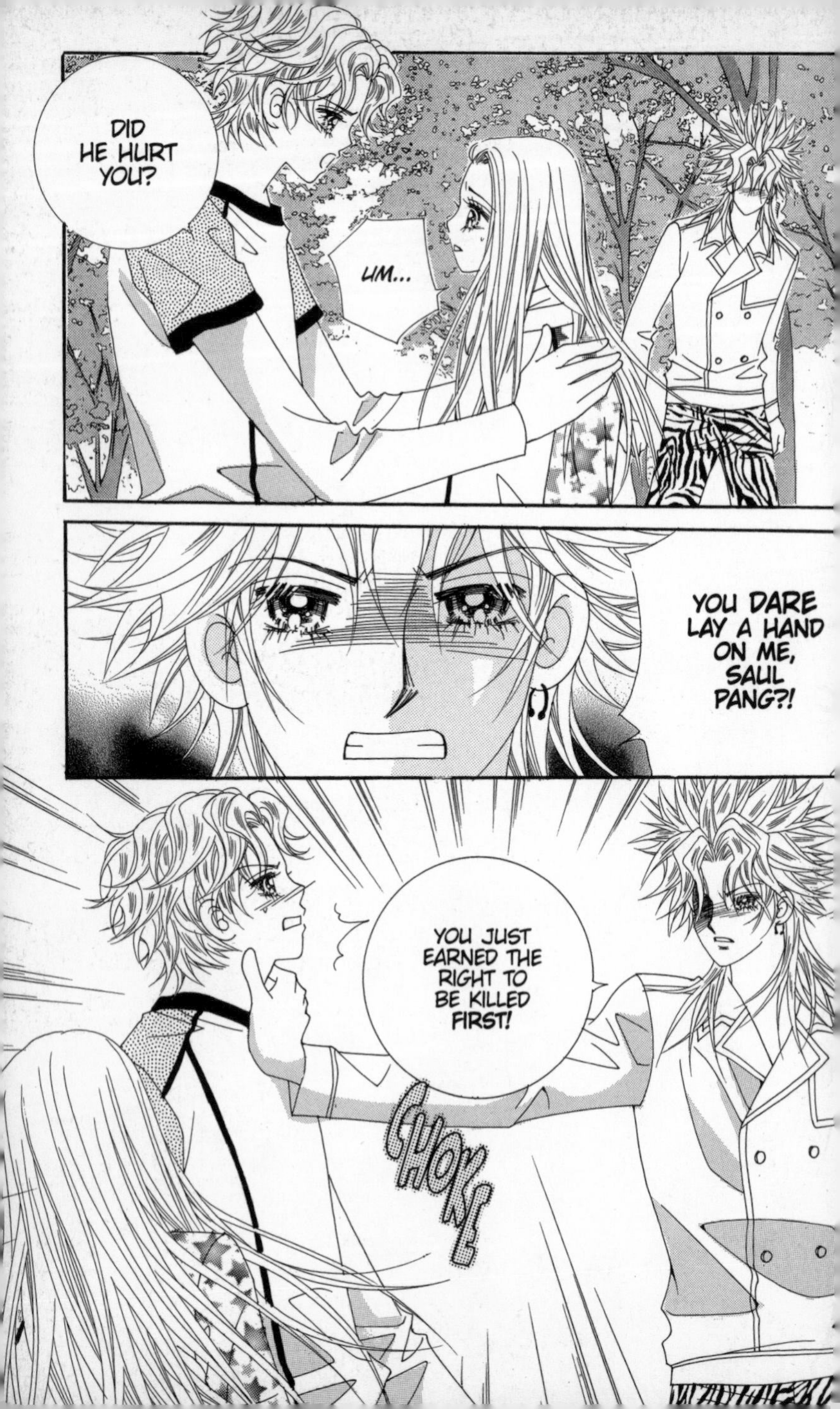
DID HE HURT YOU?
UM...
YOU DARE LAY A HAND ON ME, SAUL PANG?!
YOU JUST EARNED THE RIGHT TO BE KILLED FIRST!
CHOKE!

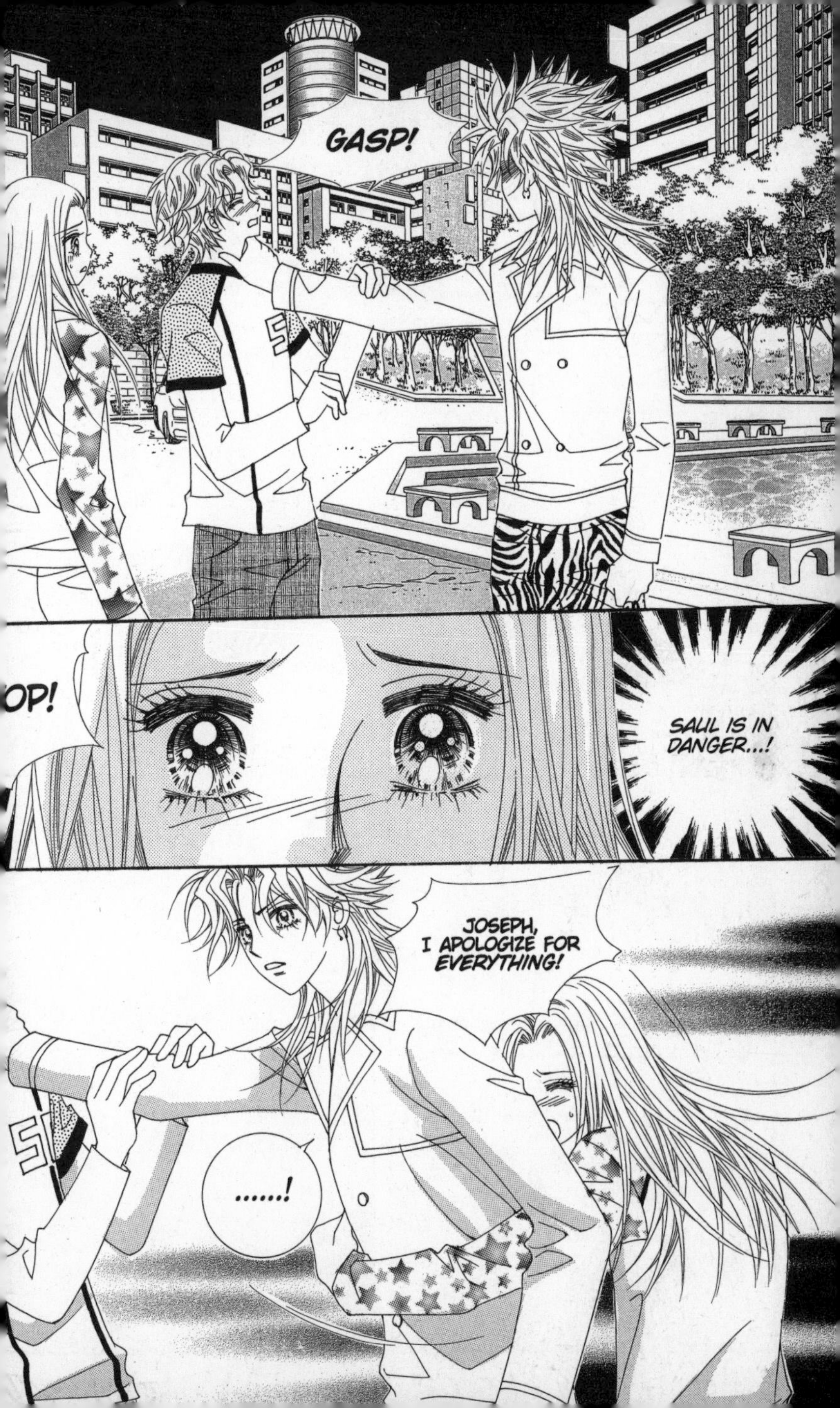
GASP!
OP!
SAUL IS IN DANGER...!
JOSEPH, I APOLOGIZE FOR EVERYTHING!
......!

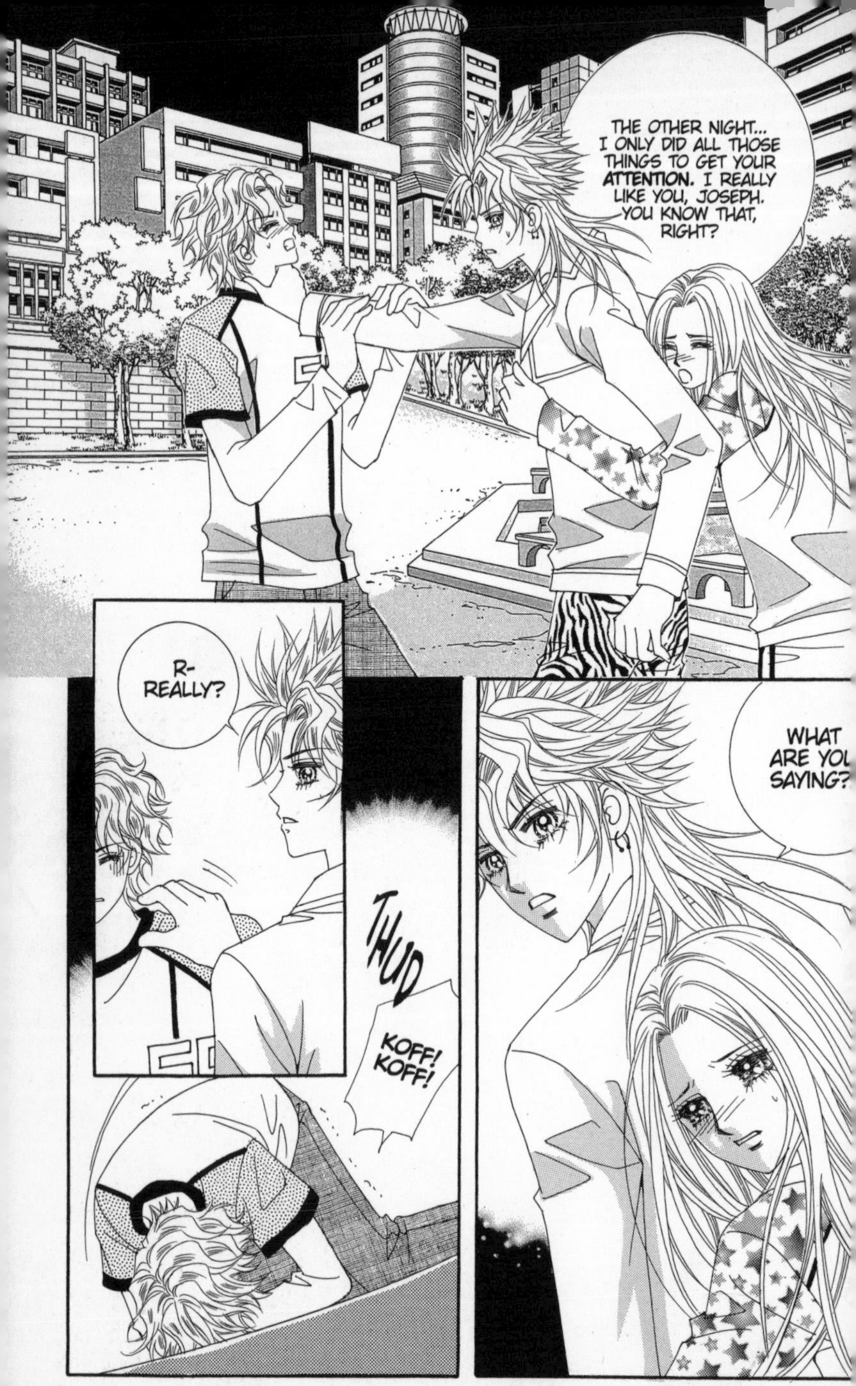
THE OTHER NIGHT... I ONLY DID ALL THOSE THINGS TO GET YOUR ATTENTION. I REALLY LIKE YOU, JOSEPH. YOU KNOW THAT, RIGHT?
R- REALLY?
THUD
KOFF! KOFF!
WHAT ARE YOU SAYING?

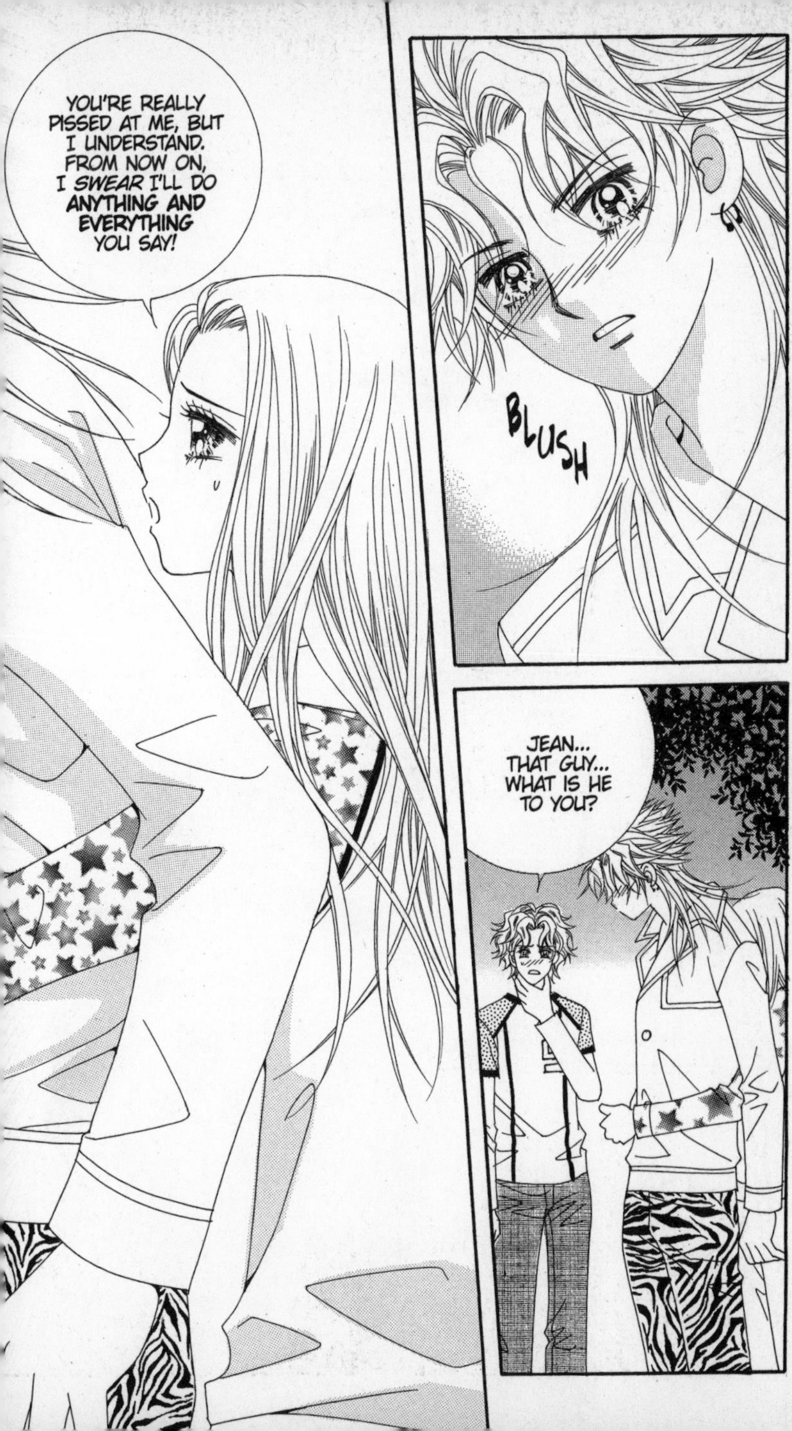
YOU'RE REALLY PISSED AT ME, BUT I UNDERSTAND. FROM NOW ON, I *SWEAR* I'LL DO ANYTHING AND EVERYTHING YOU SAY!
BLUSH
JEAN... THAT GUY... WHAT IS HE TO YOU?

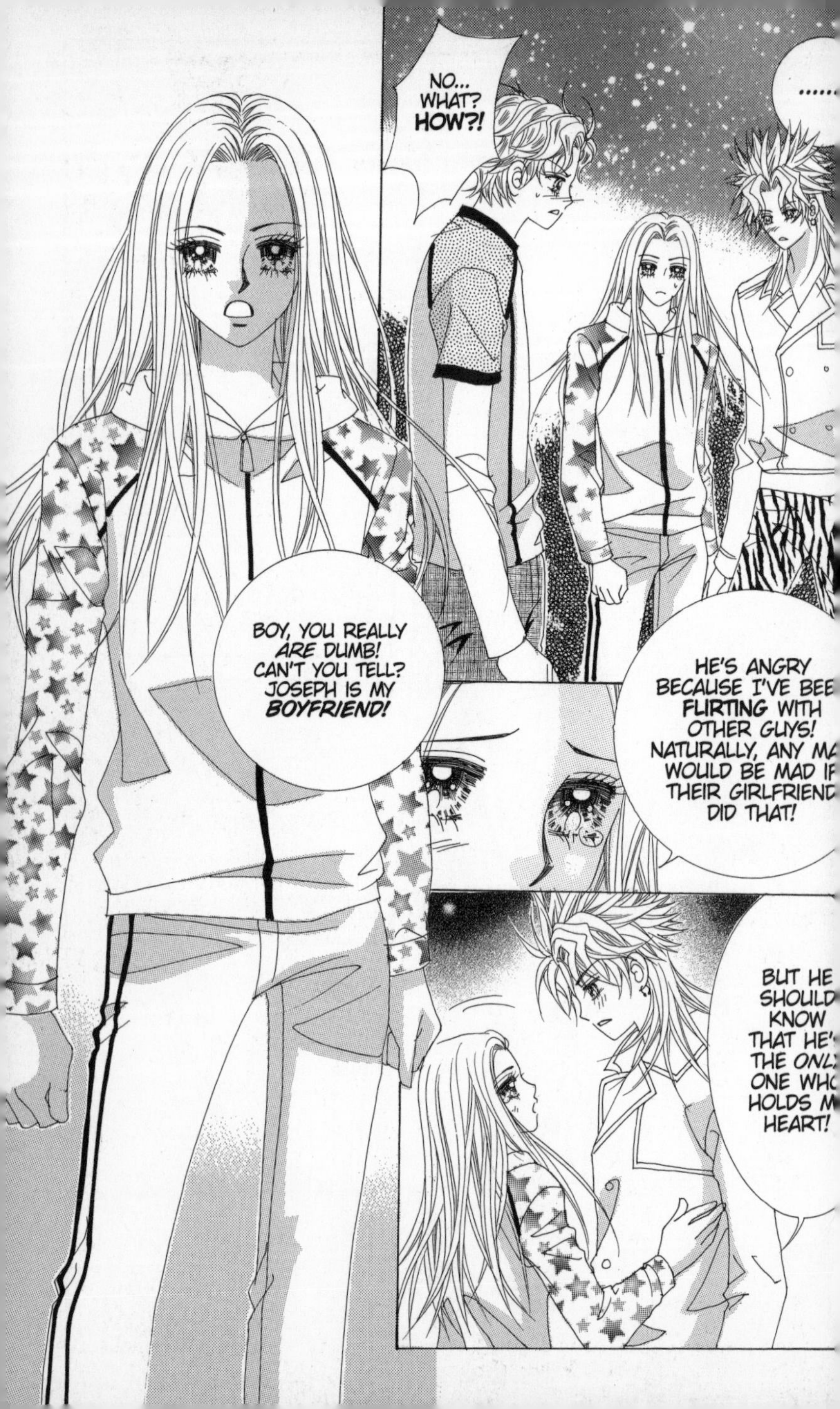

BOY, YOU REALLY *ARE* DUMB! CAN'T YOU TELL? JOSEPH IS MY ***BOYFRIEND!***
NO... WHAT? **HOW?!**
......
HE'S ANGRY BECAUSE I'VE BEE **FLIRTING** WITH OTHER GUYS! NATURALLY, ANY MA WOULD BE MAD IF THEIR GIRLFRIEND DID THAT!
BUT HE SHOULD KNOW THAT HE' THE *ONL* ONE WHC HOLDS M HEART!

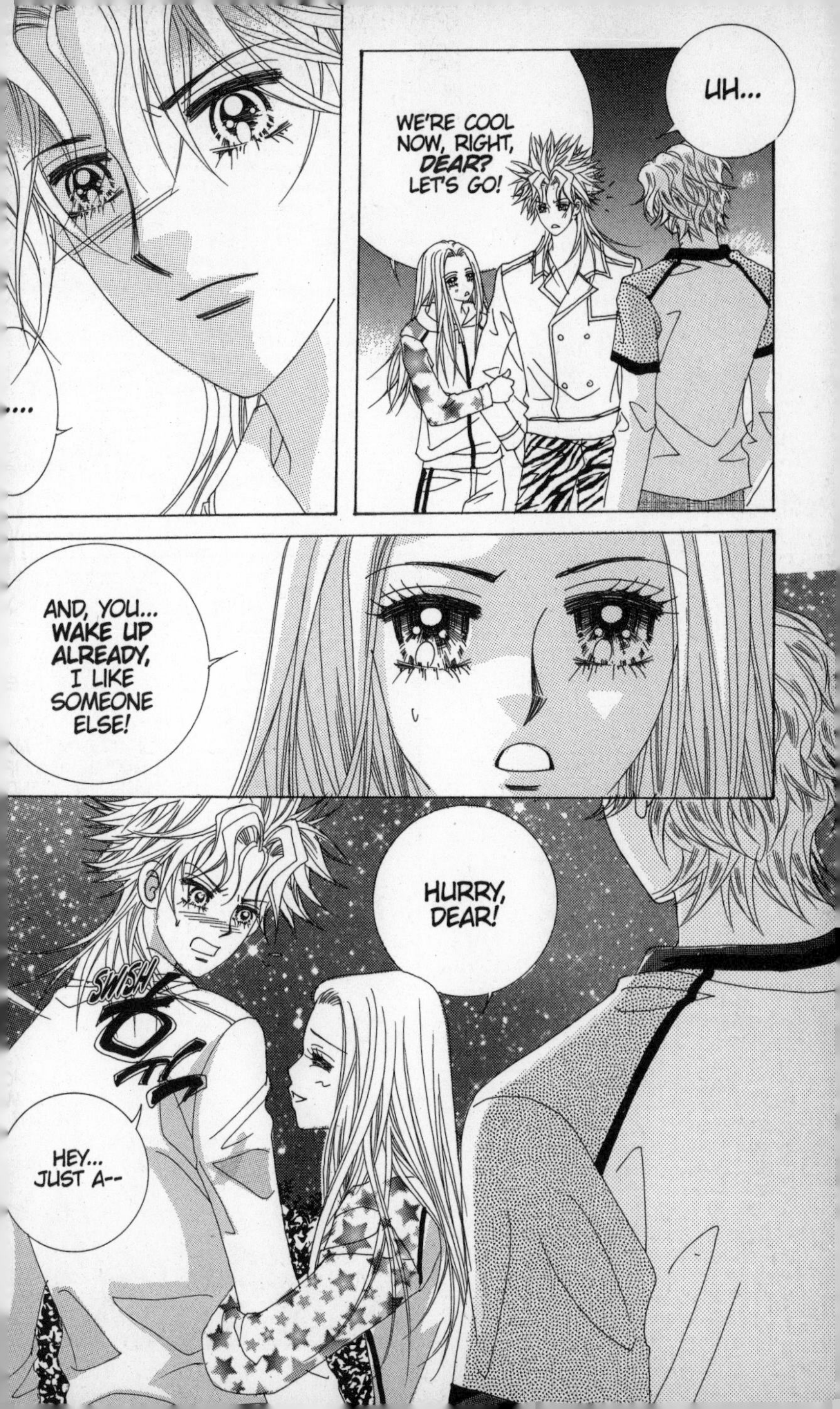
....
WE'RE COOL NOW, RIGHT, DEAR? LET'S GO!
UH...
AND, YOU... WAKE UP ALREADY, I LIKE SOMEONE ELSE!
HURRY, DEAR!
SWISH
FOM
HEY... JUST A--

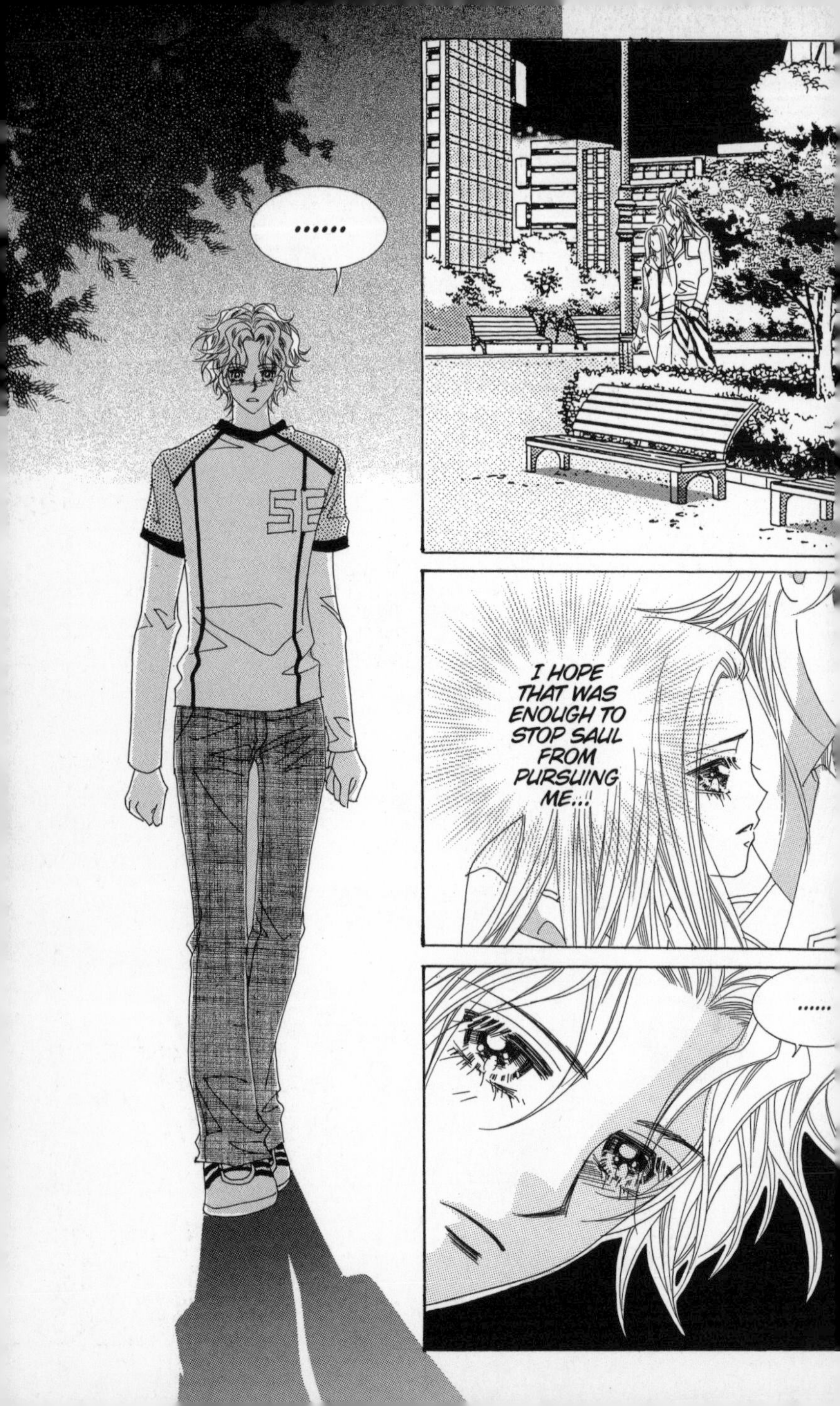
......
I HOPE THAT WAS ENOUGH TO STOP SAUL FROM PURSUING ME...!
......

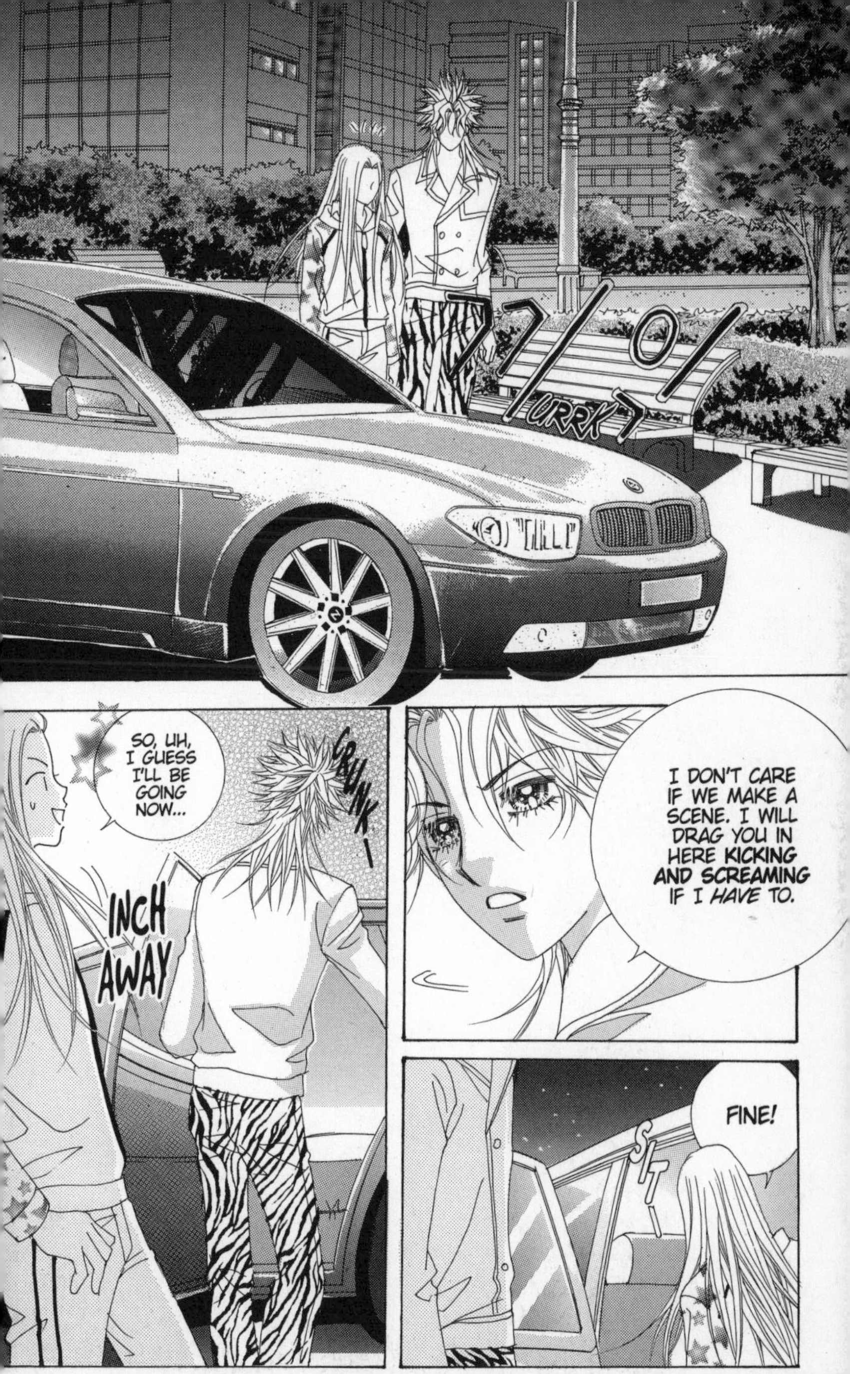
URRK
SO, UH, I GUESS I'LL BE GOING NOW...
CRUNK
INCH AWAY
I DON'T CARE IF WE MAKE A SCENE. I WILL DRAG YOU IN HERE **KICKING AND SCREAMING** IF I *HAVE* TO.
FINE!
SIT

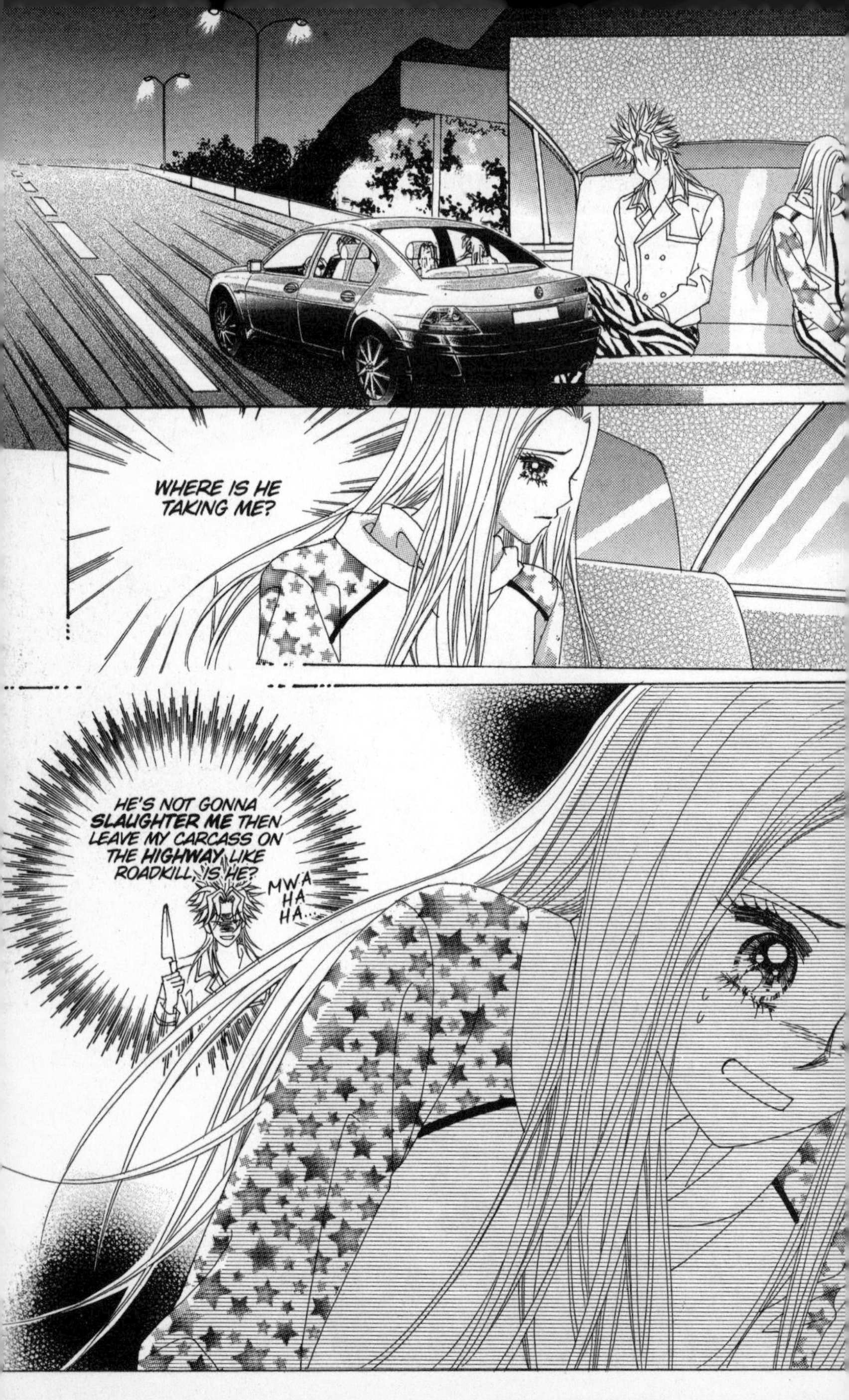
WHERE IS HE TAKING ME?
HE'S NOT GONNA SLAUGHTER ME THEN LEAVE MY CARCASS ON THE HIGHWAY LIKE ROADKILL, IS HE?
MWA HA HA...

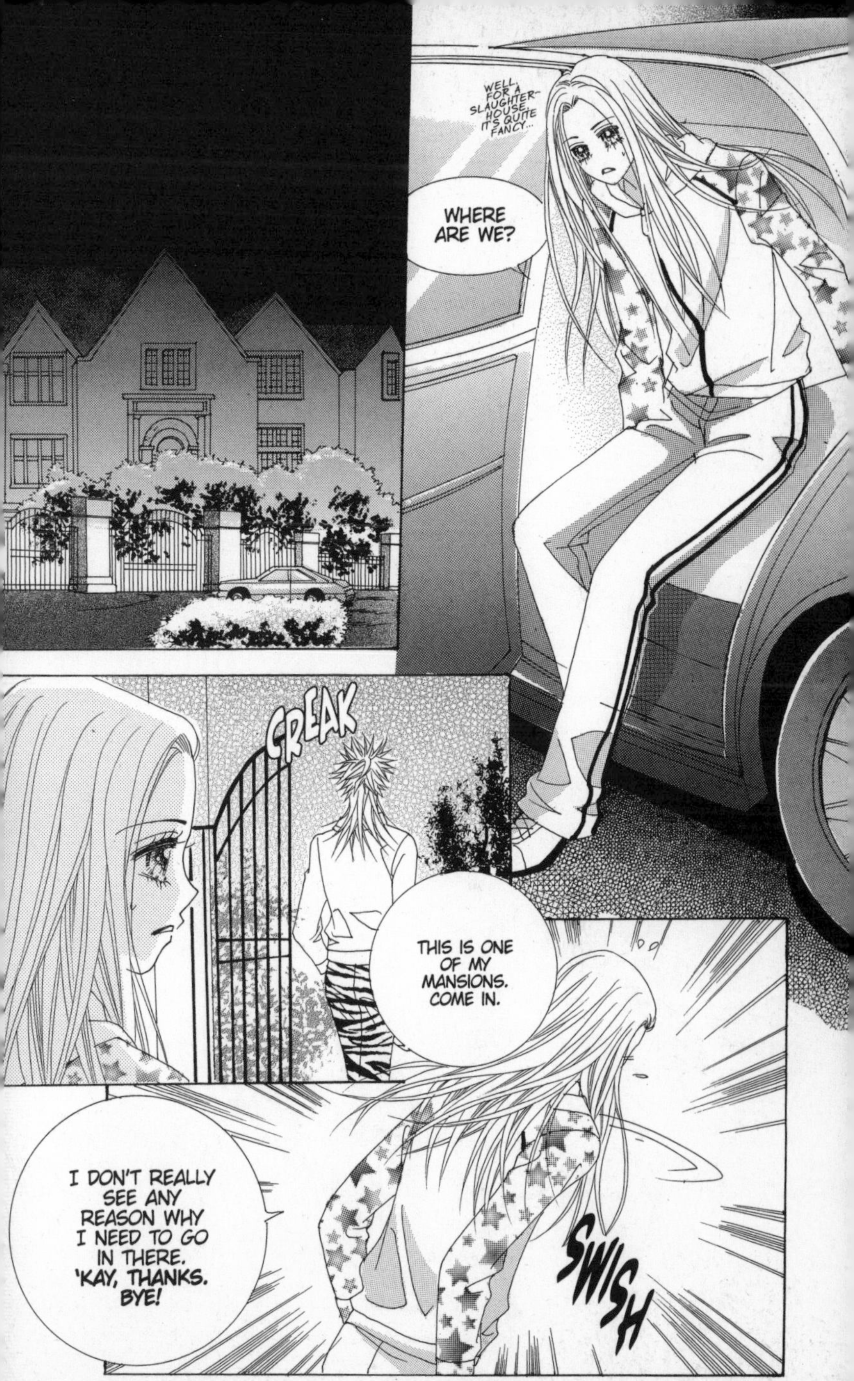
WELL, FOR A SLAUGHTER-HOUSE, IT'S QUITE FANCY...
WHERE ARE WE?
CREAK
THIS IS ONE OF MY MANSIONS. COME IN.
I DON'T REALLY SEE ANY REASON WHY I NEED TO GO IN THERE. 'KAY, THANKS. BYE!
SWISH

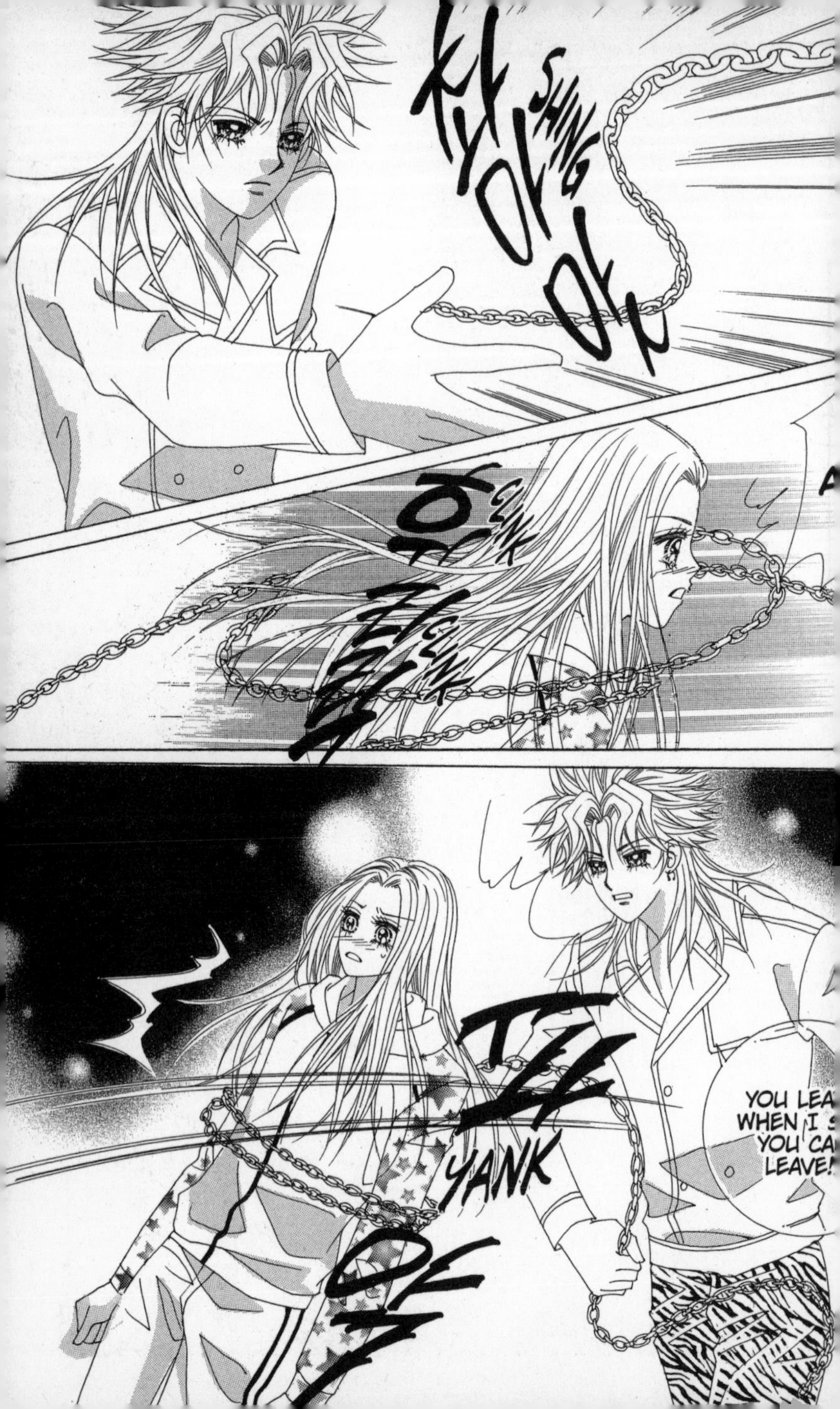
SHING
CLINK
CLINK
YANK
YOU LEA
WHEN I S
YOU CA
LEAVE!

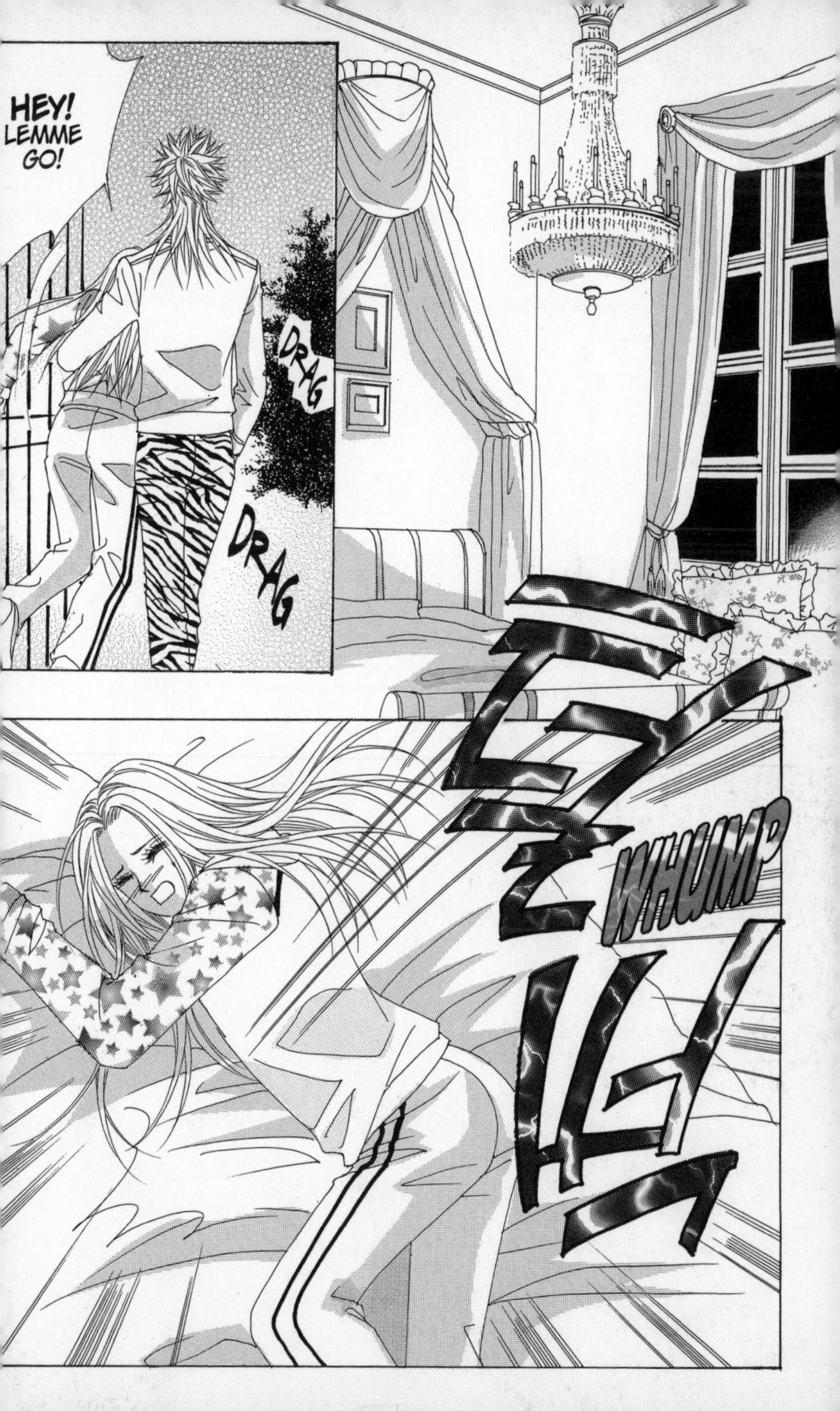
HEY! LEMME GO!
DRAG
DRAG
WHUMP

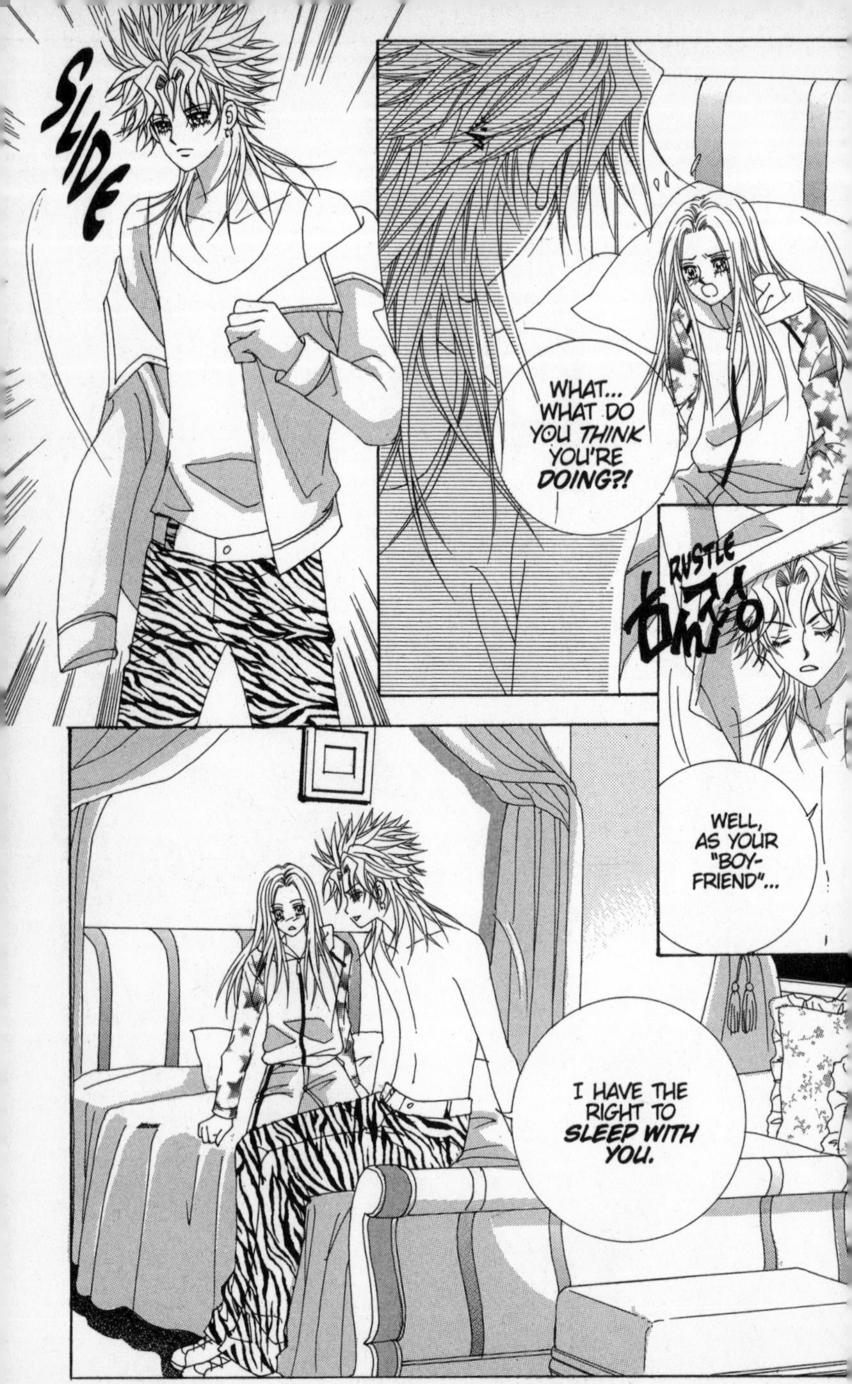
SLIDE
WHAT... WHAT DO YOU THINK YOU'RE DOING?!
RUSTLE
WELL, AS YOUR "BOY-FRIEND"...
I HAVE THE RIGHT TO SLEEP WITH YOU.

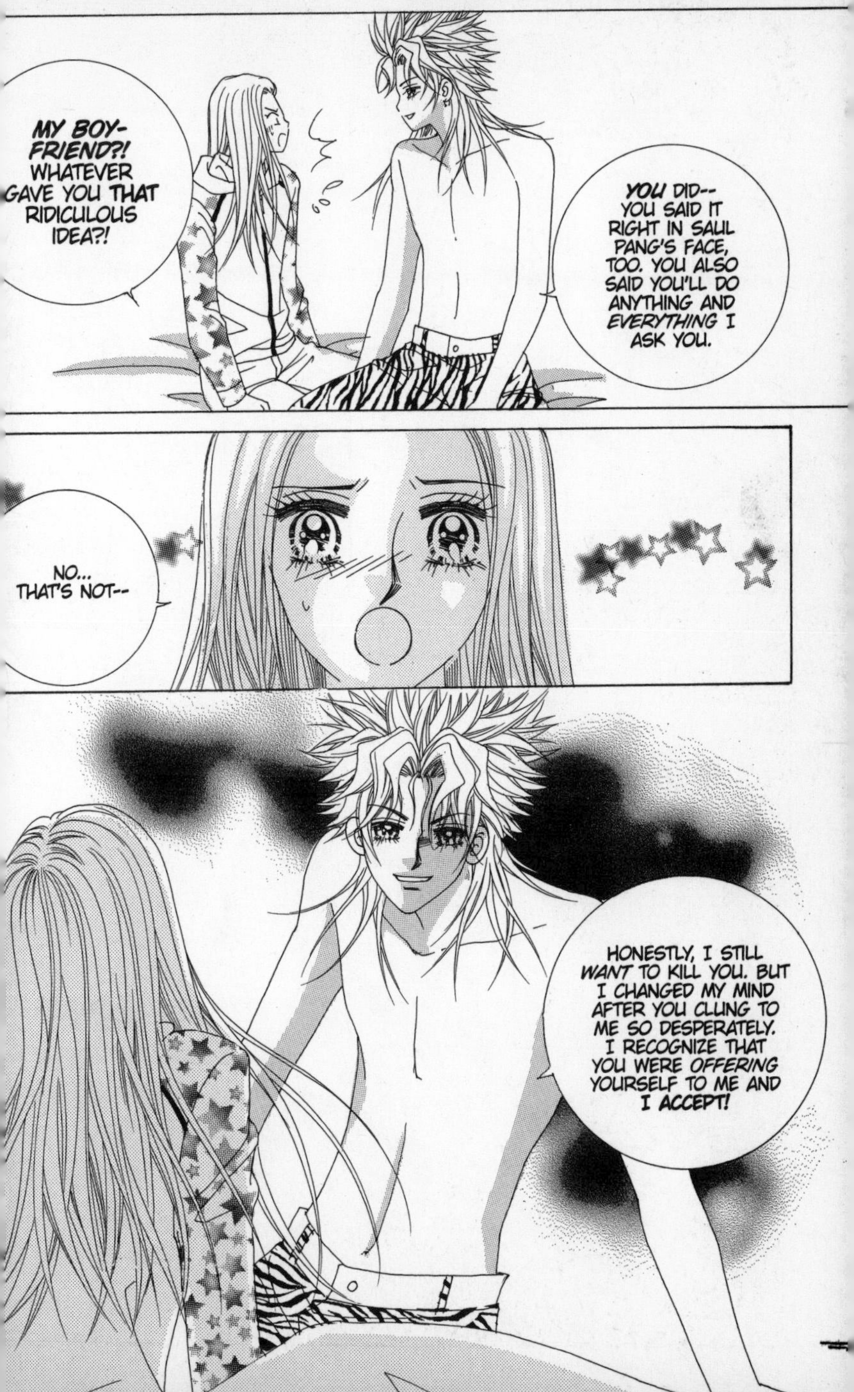

MY BOY-FRIEND?! WHATEVER GAVE YOU THAT RIDICULOUS IDEA?!
YOU DID-- YOU SAID IT RIGHT IN SAUL PANG'S FACE, TOO. YOU ALSO SAID YOU'LL DO ANYTHING AND EVERYTHING I ASK YOU.
NO... THAT'S NOT--
HONESTLY, I STILL WANT TO KILL YOU. BUT I CHANGED MY MIND AFTER YOU CLUNG TO ME SO DESPERATELY. I RECOGNIZE THAT YOU WERE OFFERING YOURSELF TO ME AND I ACCEPT!

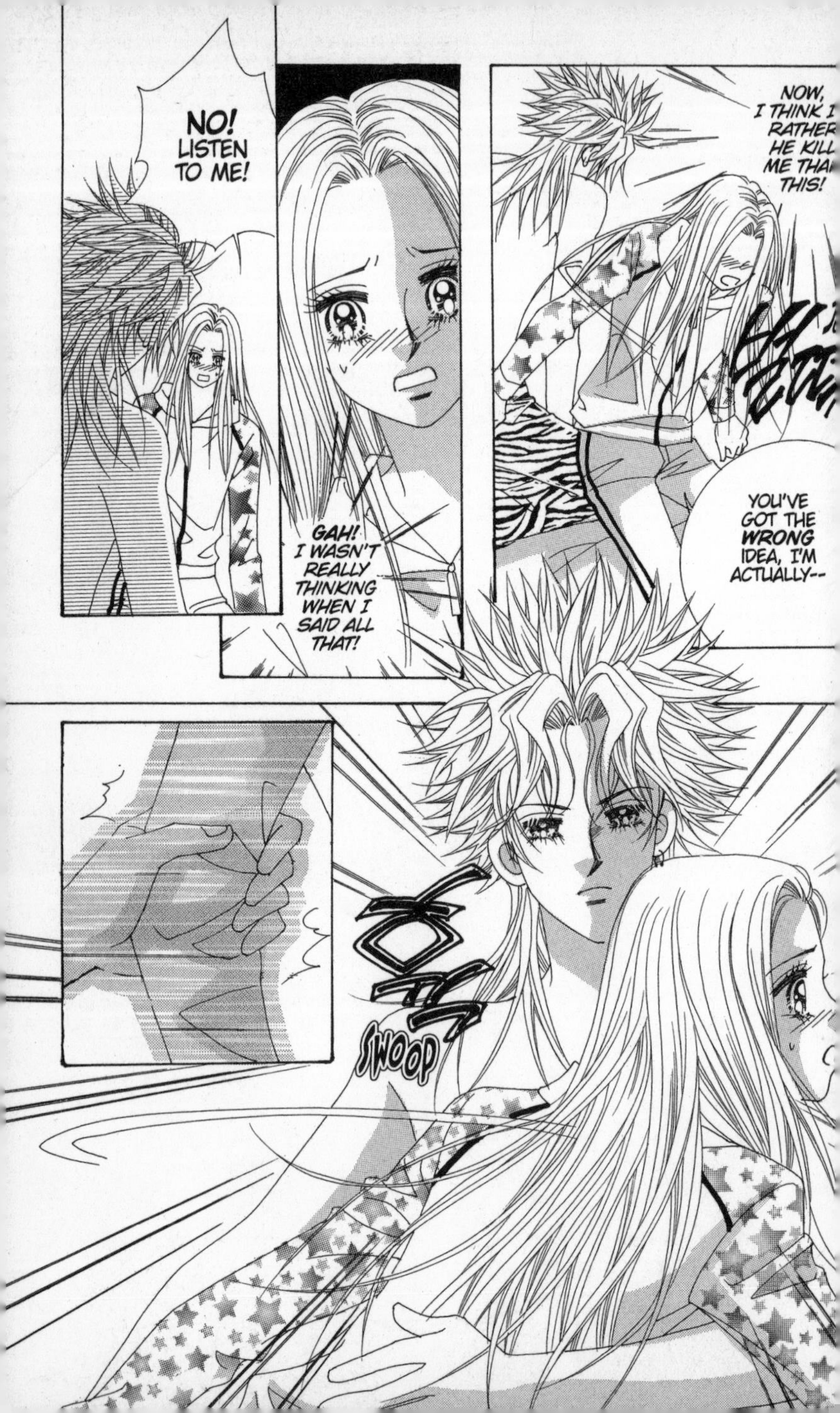
NO! LISTEN TO ME!
GAH! I WASN'T REALLY THINKING WHEN I SAID ALL THAT!
NOW, I THINK I RATHER HE KILL ME THA THIS!
YOU'VE GOT THE WRONG IDEA, I'M ACTUALLY--
SWOOP

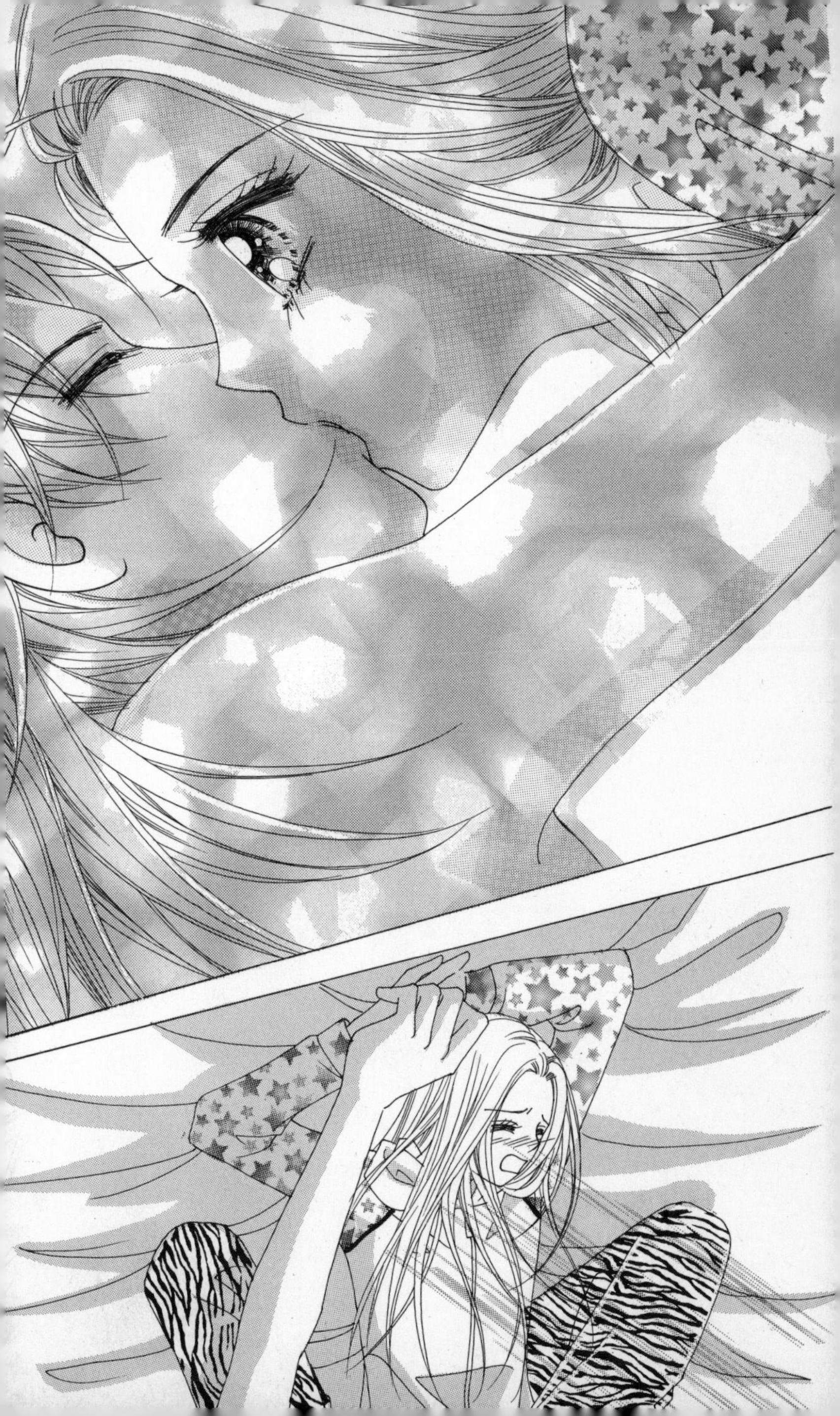

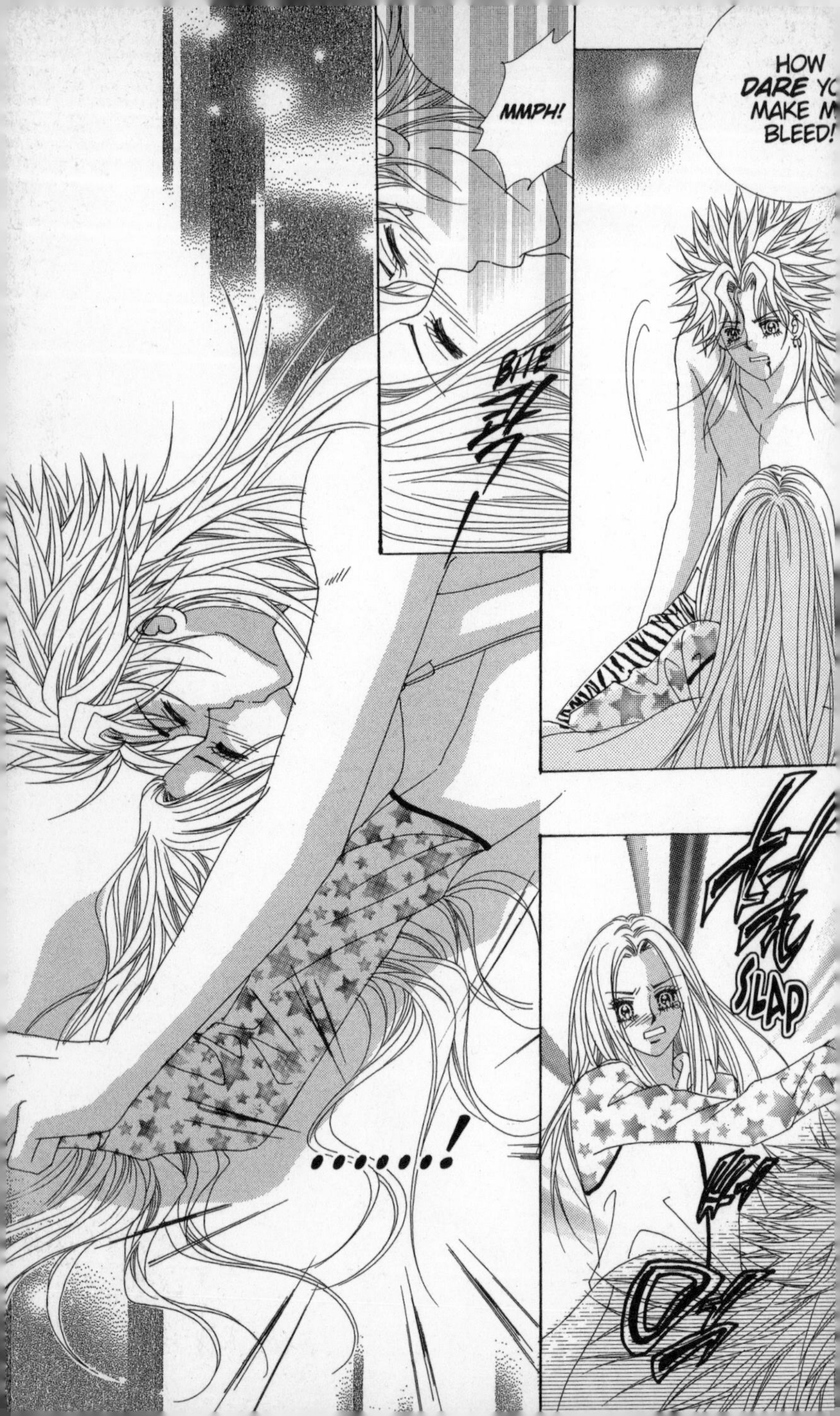
......!
MMPH!
BITE
HOW DARE YO MAKE M BLEED!
SLAP

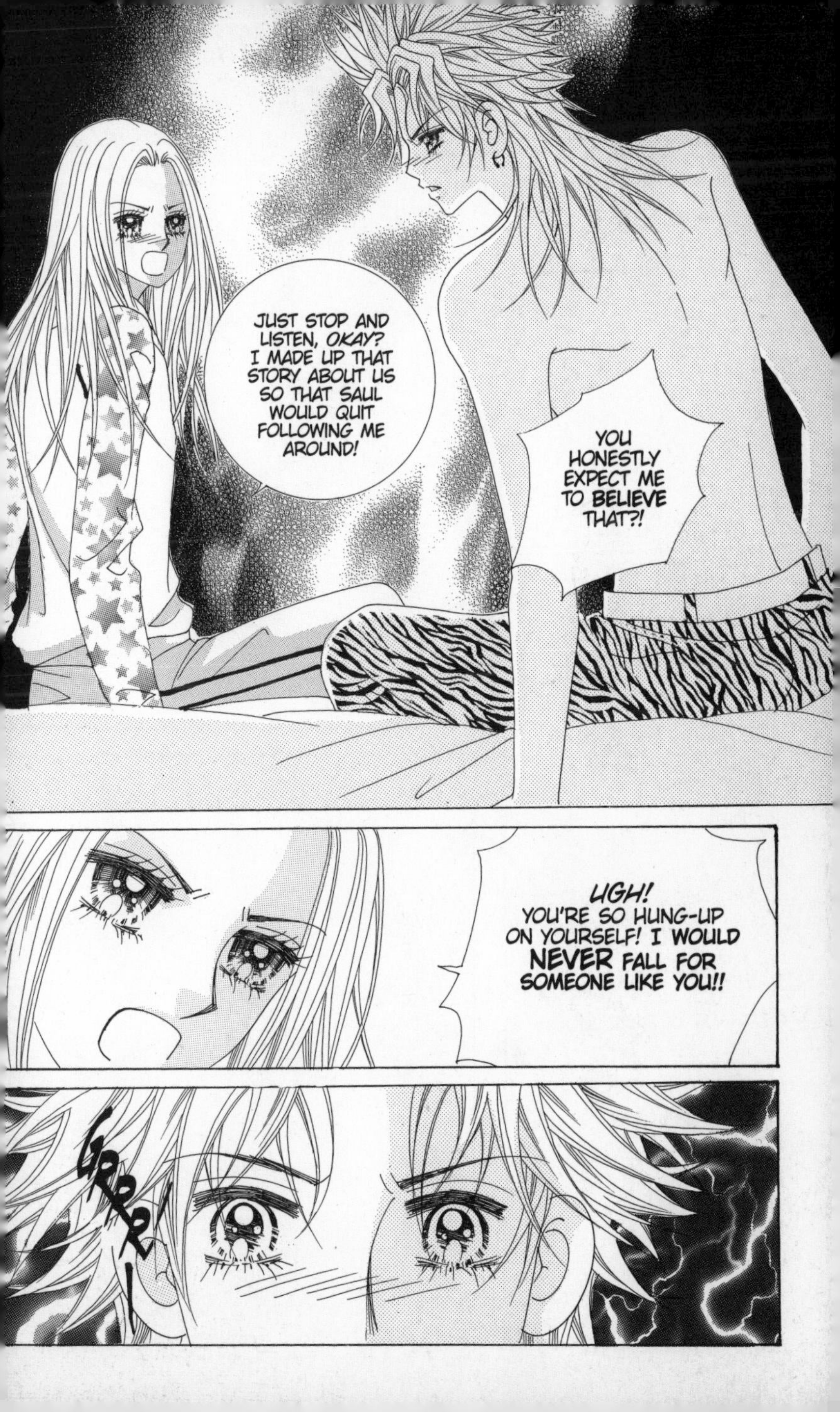
JUST STOP AND LISTEN, *OKAY?* I MADE UP THAT STORY ABOUT US SO THAT SAUL WOULD QUIT FOLLOWING ME AROUND!
YOU HONESTLY EXPECT ME TO **BELIEVE** THAT?!
UGH! YOU'RE SO HUNG-UP ON YOURSELF! I WOULD **NEVER** FALL FOR SOMEONE LIKE YOU!!
GRRR!

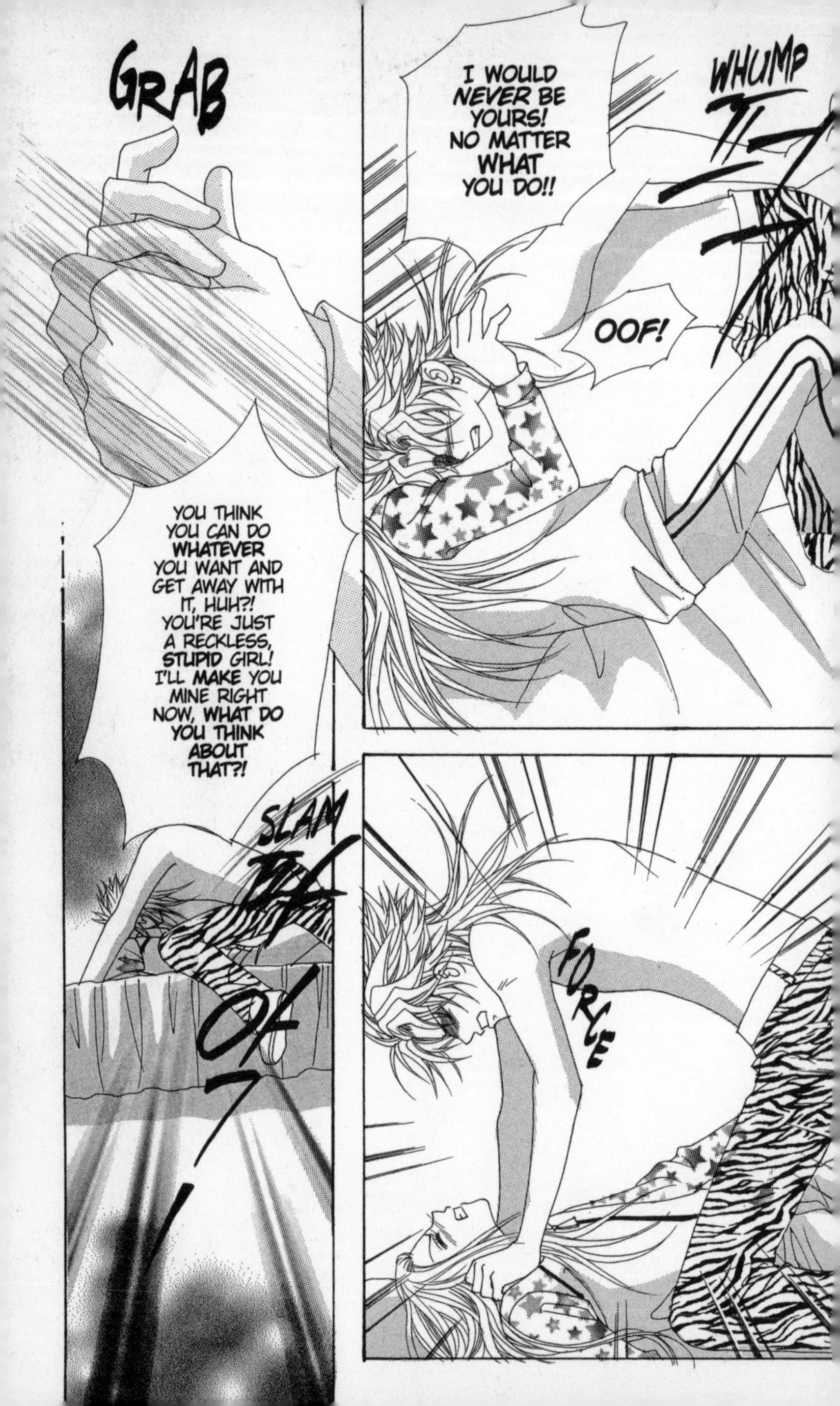

GRAB
YOU THINK YOU CAN DO WHATEVER YOU WANT AND GET AWAY WITH IT, HUH?! YOU'RE JUST A RECKLESS, STUPID GIRL! I'LL MAKE YOU MINE RIGHT NOW, WHAT DO YOU THINK ABOUT THAT?!
SLAM
I WOULD NEVER BE YOURS! NO MATTER WHAT YOU DO!!
WHUMP
OOF!
FORCE

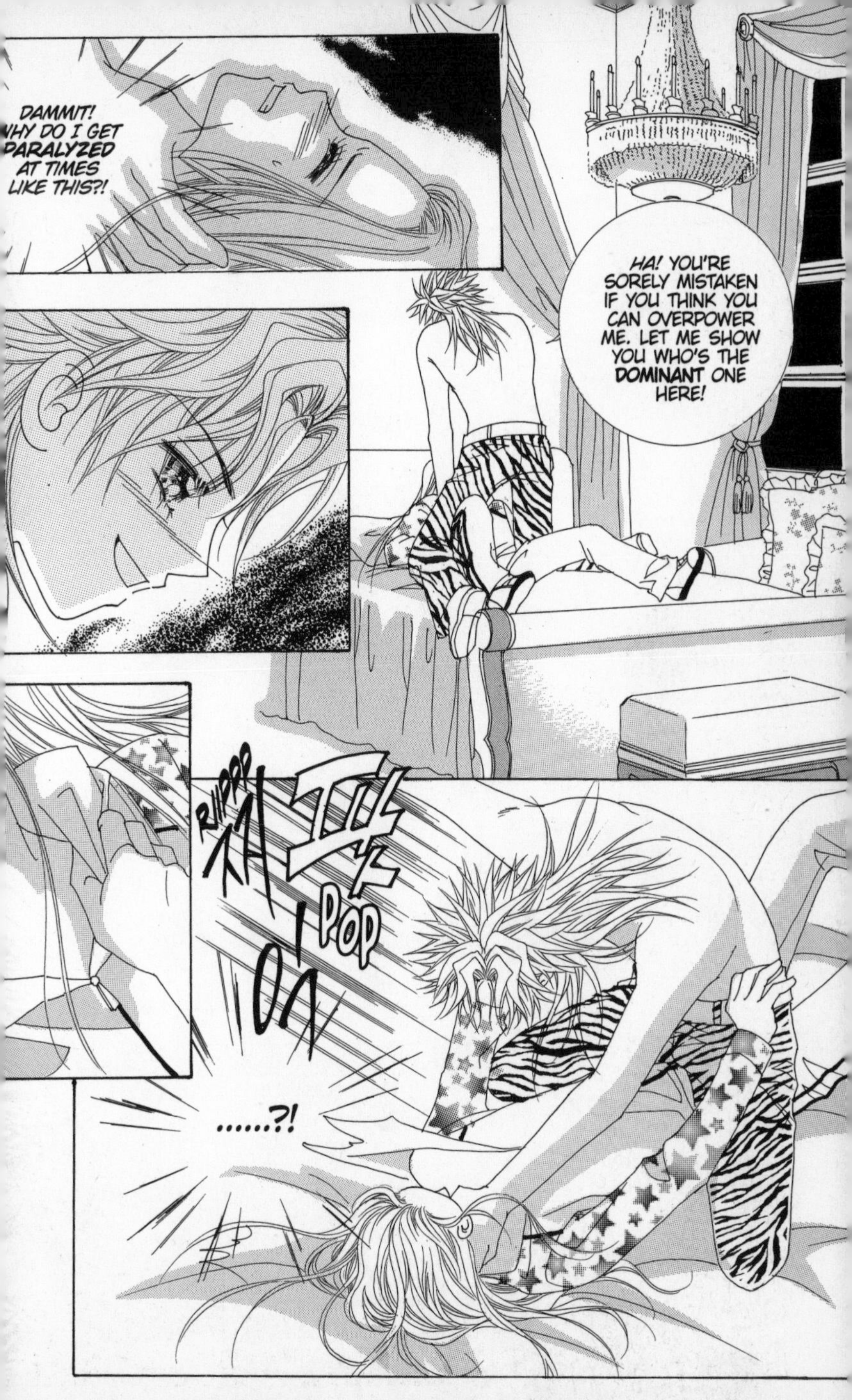
DAMMIT! WHY DO I GET PARALYZED AT TIMES LIKE THIS?!
HA! YOU'RE SORELY MISTAKEN IF YOU THINK YOU CAN OVERPOWER ME. LET ME SHOW YOU WHO'S THE **DOMINANT** ONE HERE!
RIPPP
POP
......?!

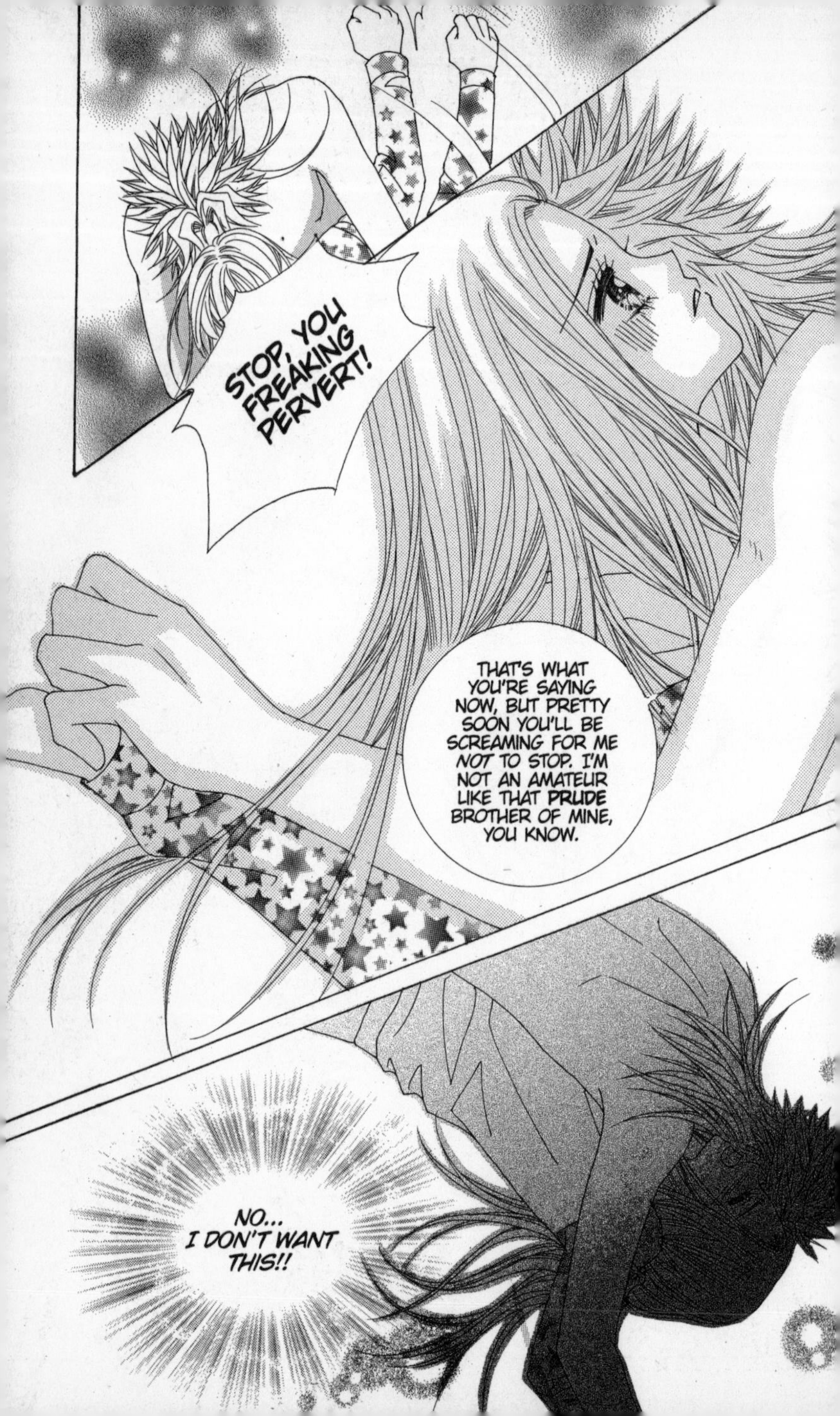
STOP, YOU FREAKING PERVERT!
THAT'S WHAT YOU'RE SAYING NOW, BUT PRETTY SOON YOU'LL BE SCREAMING FOR ME *NOT* TO STOP. I'M NOT AN AMATEUR LIKE THAT **PRUDE** BROTHER OF MINE, YOU KNOW.
NO... I DON'T WANT THIS!!

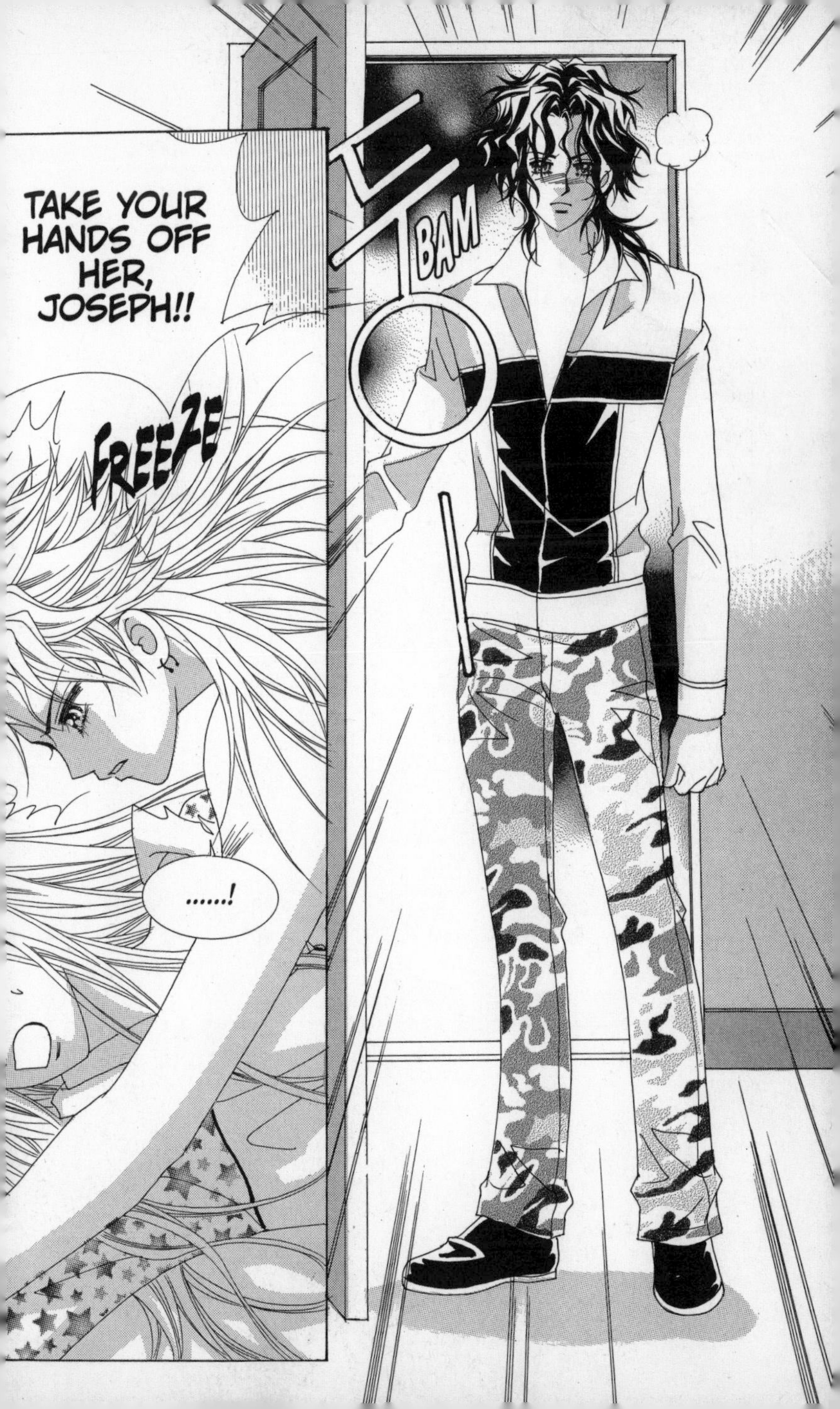
TAKE YOUR HANDS OFF HER, JOSEPH!!
BAM
FREEZE
......!

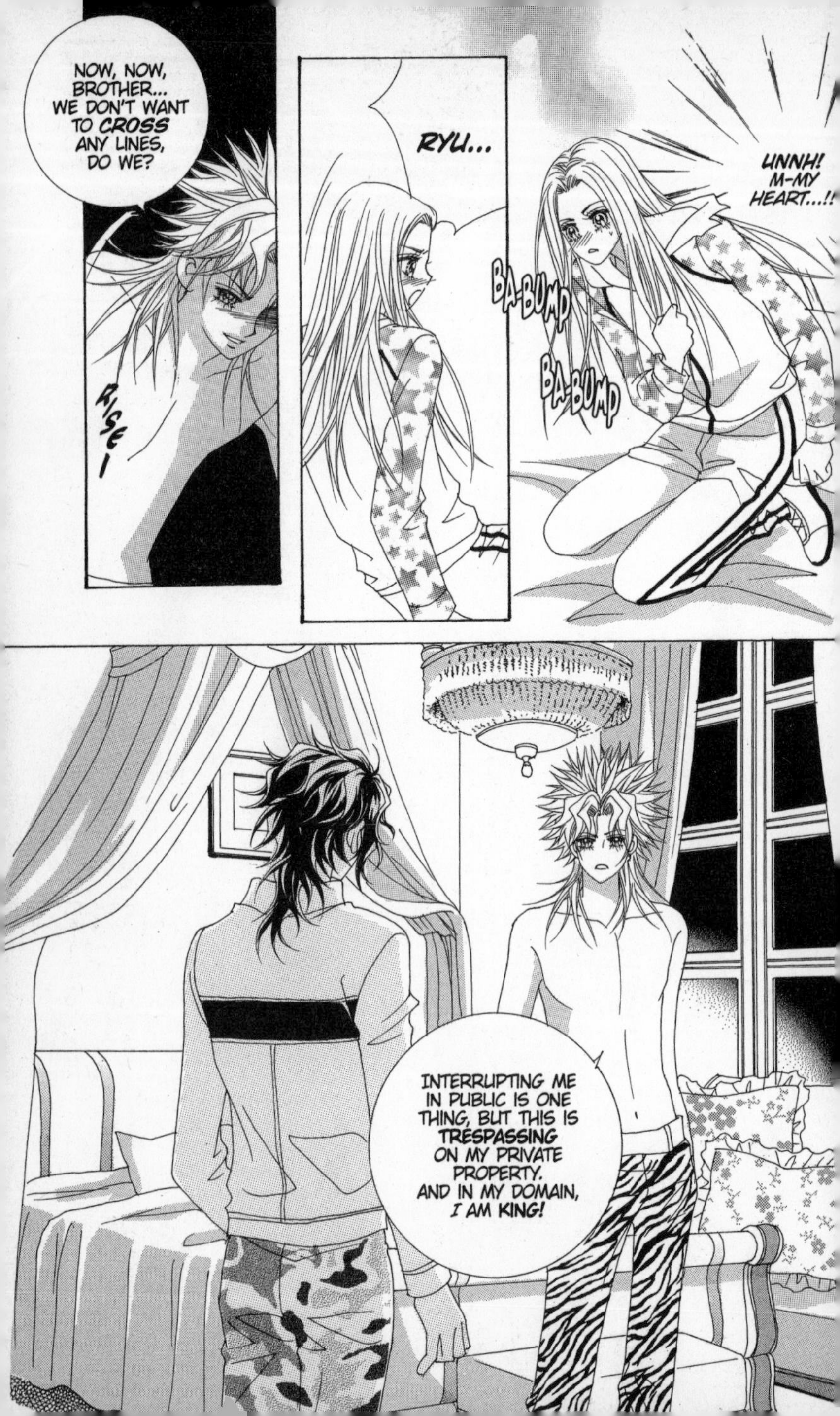
NOW, NOW, BROTHER... WE DON'T WANT TO CROSS ANY LINES, DO WE?
RISE
RYU...
UNNH! M-MY HEART...!!
BA-BUMP
BA-BUMP
INTERRUPTING ME IN PUBLIC IS ONE THING, BUT THIS IS TRESPASSING ON MY PRIVATE PROPERTY. AND IN MY DOMAIN, I AM KING!

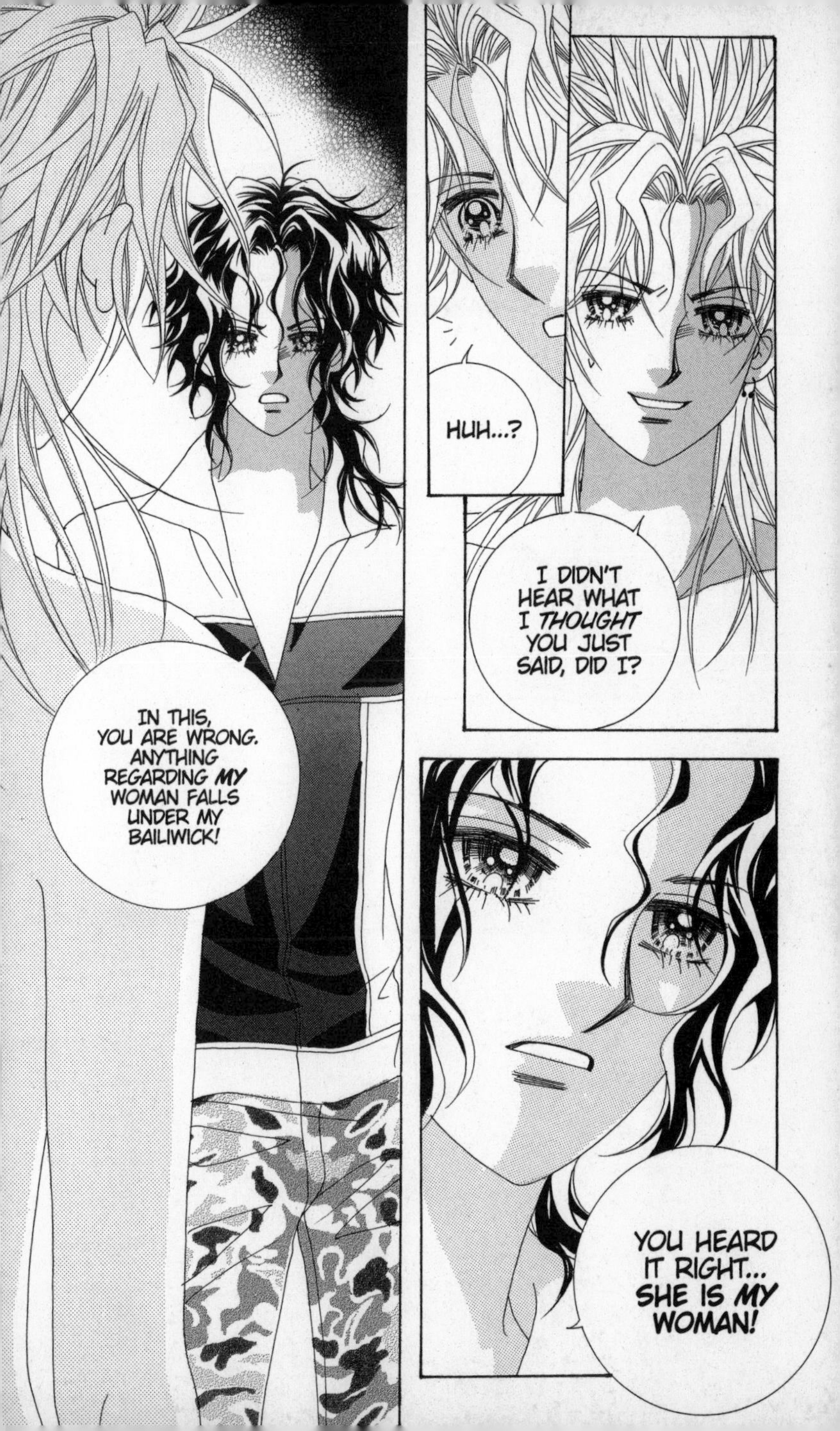
IN THIS, YOU ARE WRONG. ANYTHING REGARDING *MY* WOMAN FALLS UNDER MY BAILIWICK!
HUH...?
I DIDN'T HEAR WHAT I *THOUGHT* YOU JUST SAID, DID I?
YOU HEARD IT RIGHT... SHE IS *MY* WOMAN!

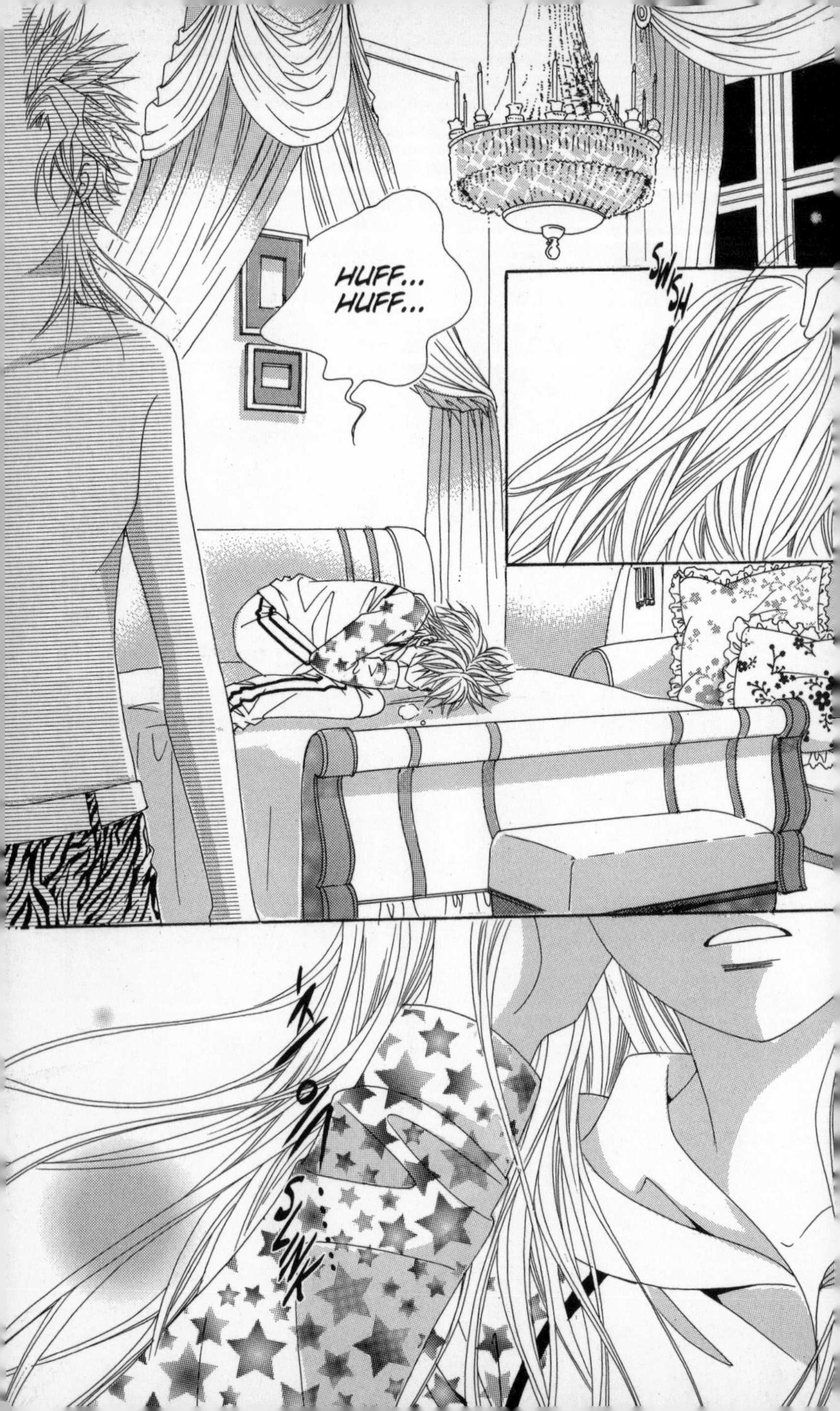
HUFF... HUFF...
SWISH
SLINK...

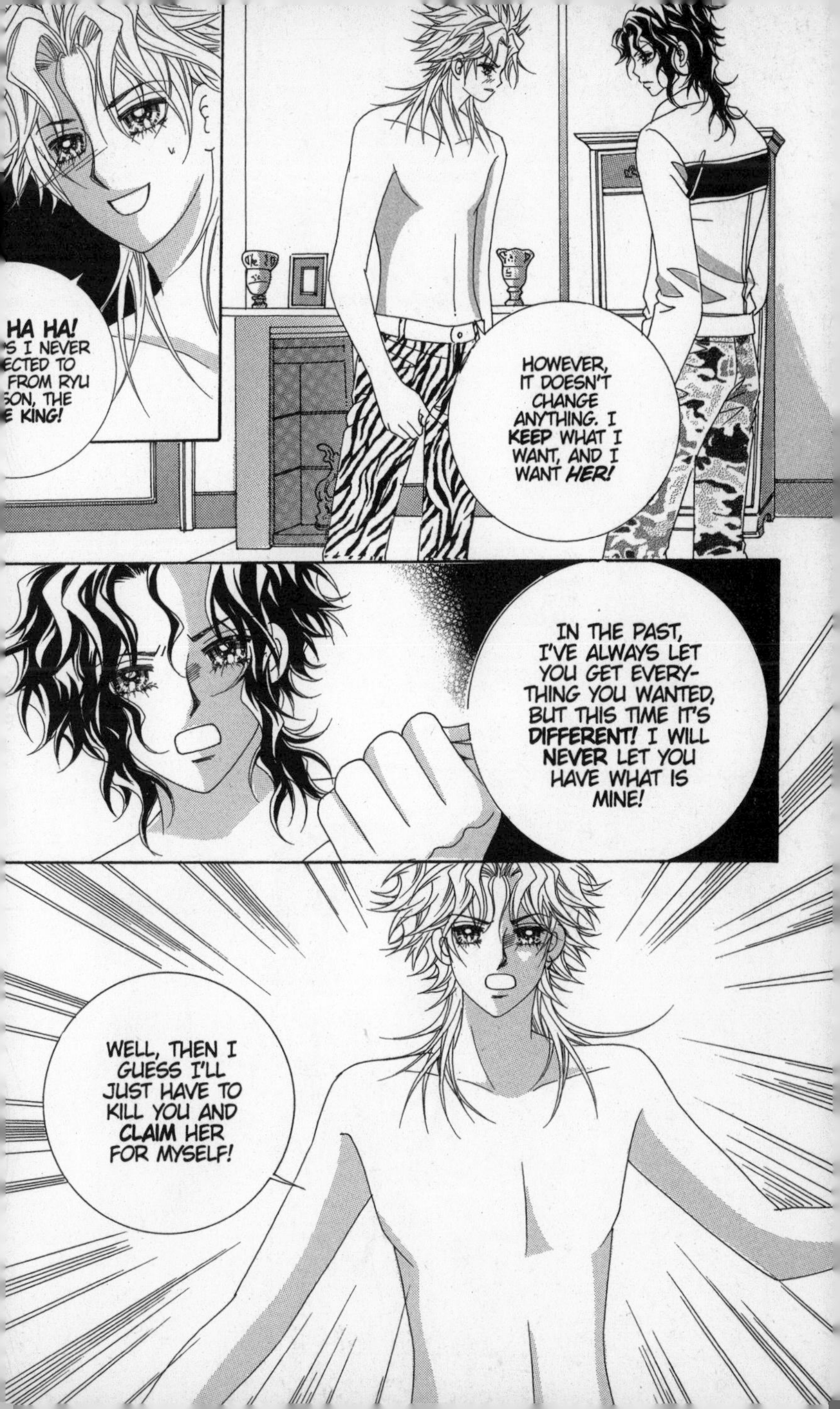
HA HA! ...S I NEVER ...ECTED TO ... FROM RYU ...SON, THE ...E KING!
HOWEVER, IT DOESN'T CHANGE ANYTHING. I KEEP WHAT I WANT, AND I WANT HER!
IN THE PAST, I'VE ALWAYS LET YOU GET EVERY-THING YOU WANTED, BUT THIS TIME IT'S DIFFERENT! I WILL NEVER LET YOU HAVE WHAT IS MINE!
WELL, THEN I GUESS I'LL JUST HAVE TO KILL YOU AND CLAIM HER FOR MYSELF!

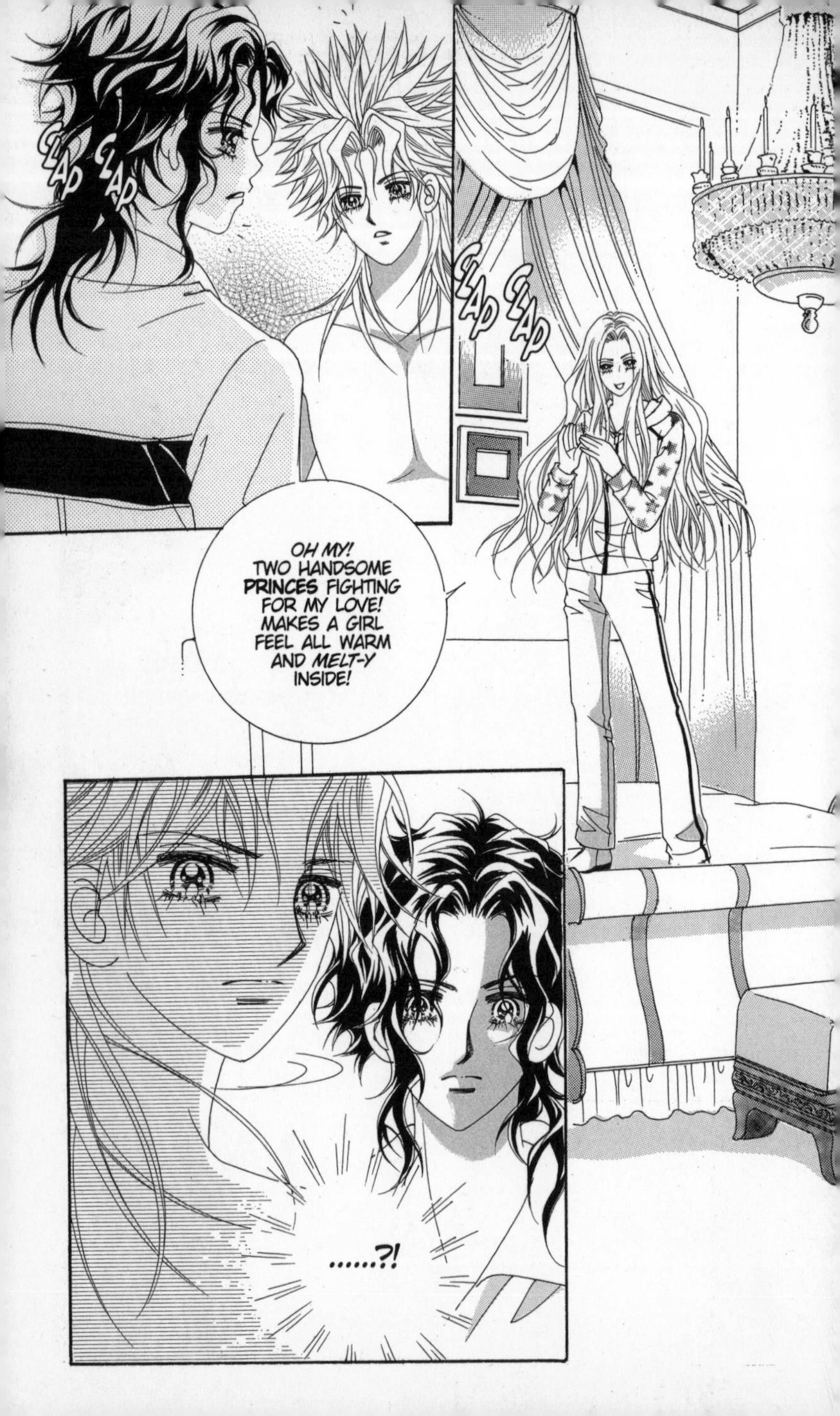
CLAP CLAP
CLAP CLAP
OH MY! TWO HANDSOME PRINCES FIGHTING FOR MY LOVE! MAKES A GIRL FEEL ALL WARM AND MELT-Y INSIDE!
......?!

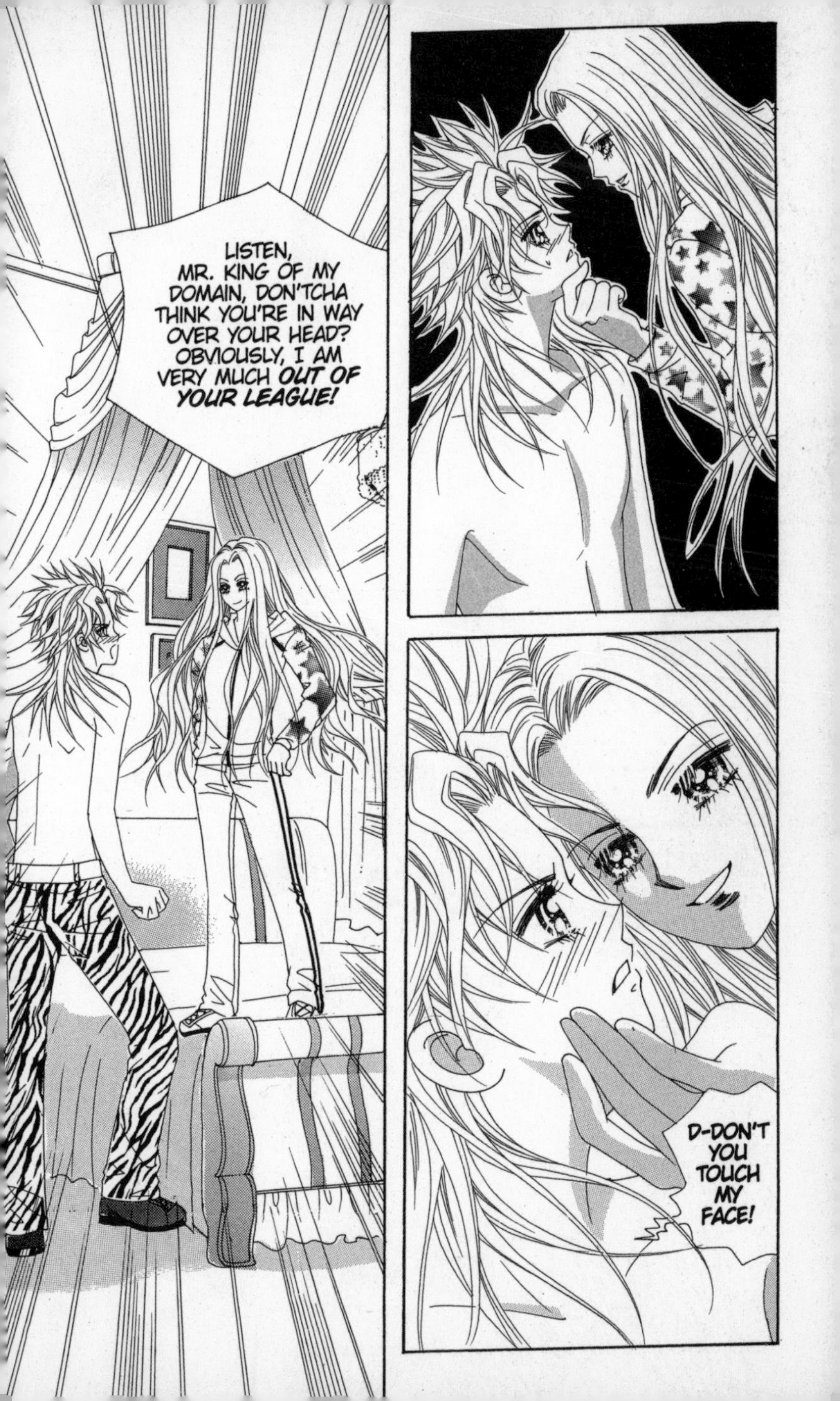
LISTEN, MR. KING OF MY DOMAIN, DON'TCHA THINK YOU'RE IN WAY OVER YOUR HEAD? OBVIOUSLY, I AM VERY MUCH ***OUT OF YOUR LEAGUE!***
D-DON'T YOU TOUCH MY FACE!

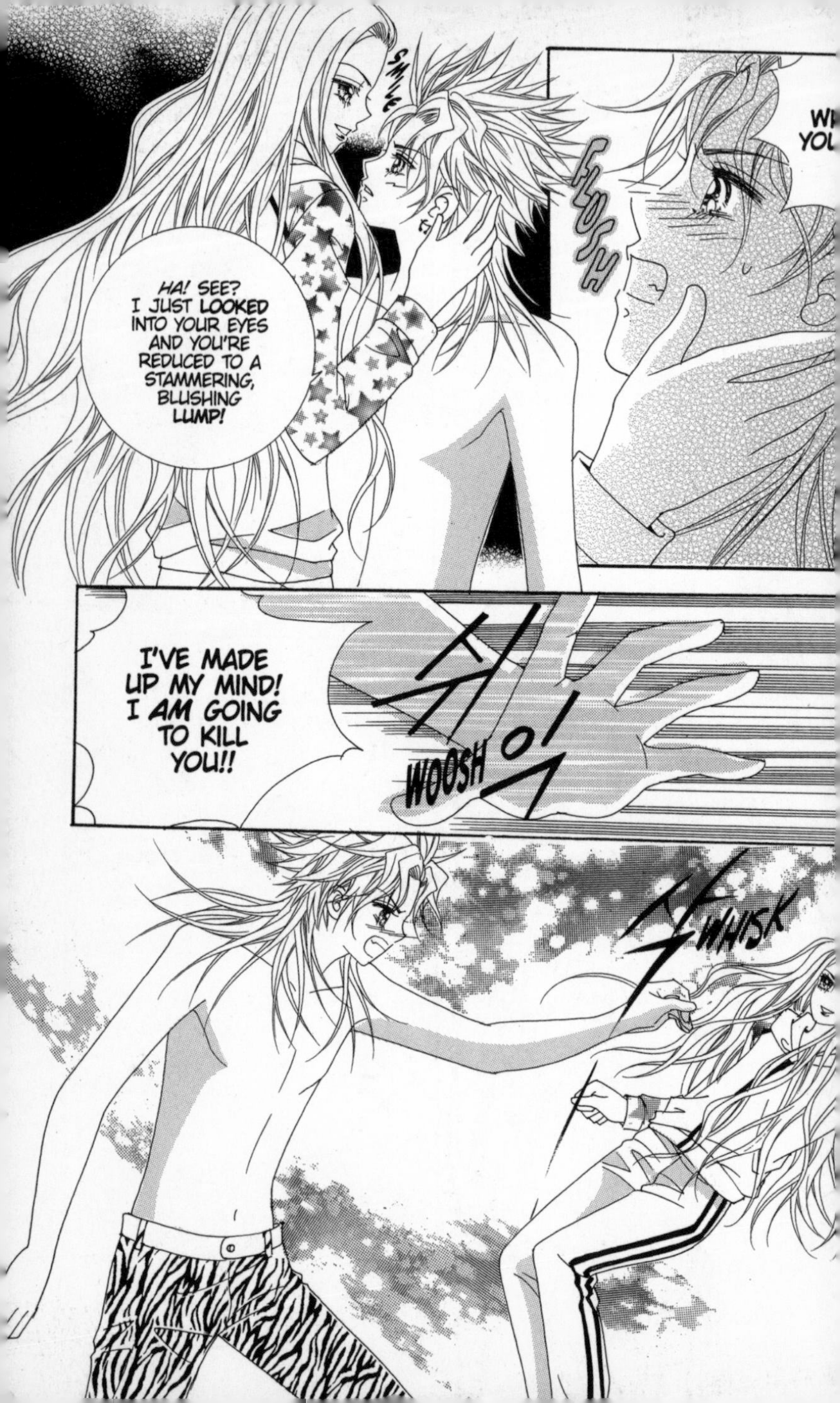
SMILE
HA! SEE? I JUST LOOKED INTO YOUR EYES AND YOU'RE REDUCED TO A STAMMERING, BLUSHING LUMP!
FLUSH
I'VE MADE UP MY MIND! I AM GOING TO KILL YOU!!
WOOSH
WHISK

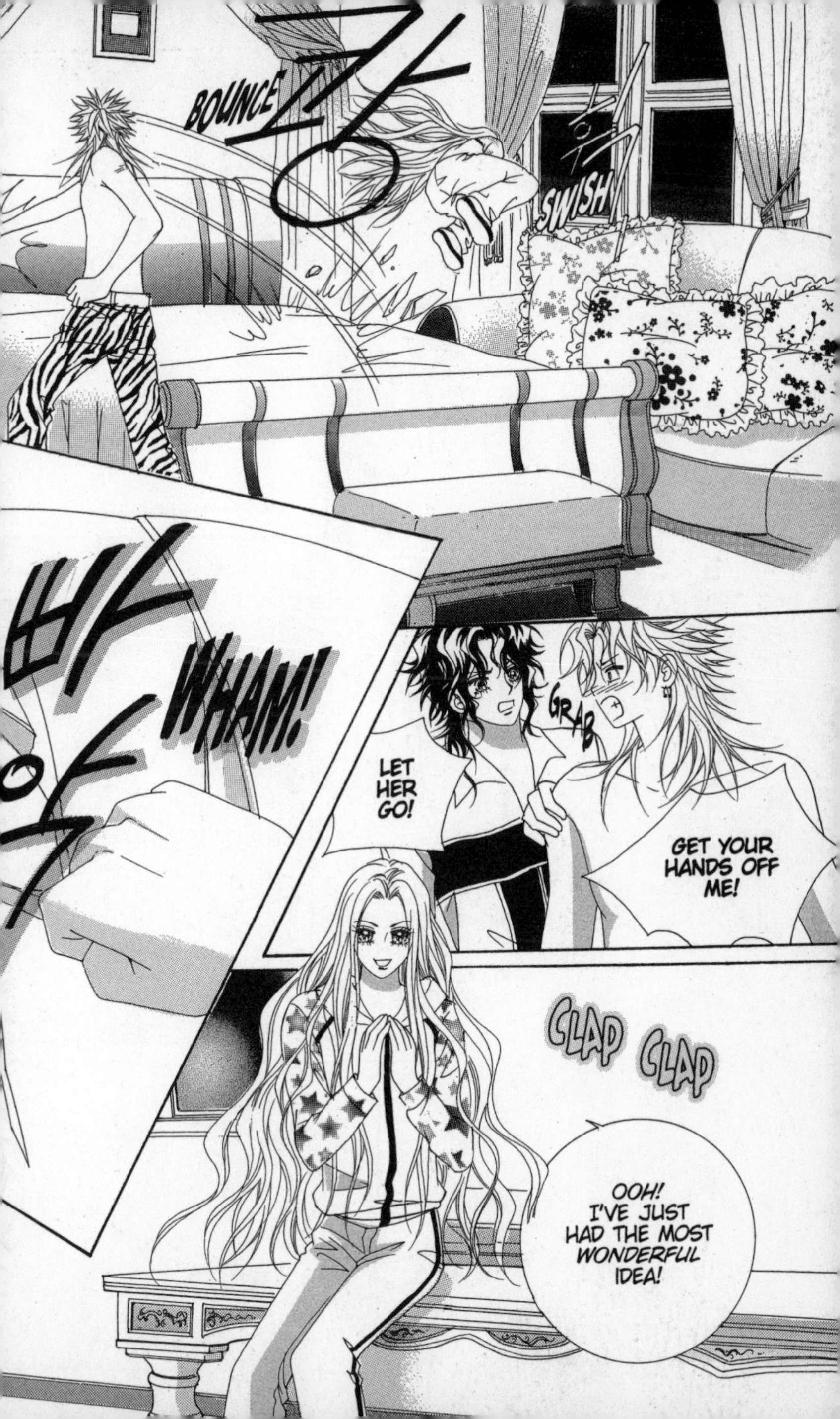
BOUNCE
SWISH
WHAM!
LET HER GO!
GRAB
GET YOUR HANDS OFF ME!
CLAP CLAP
OOH! I'VE JUST HAD THE MOST WONDERFUL IDEA!

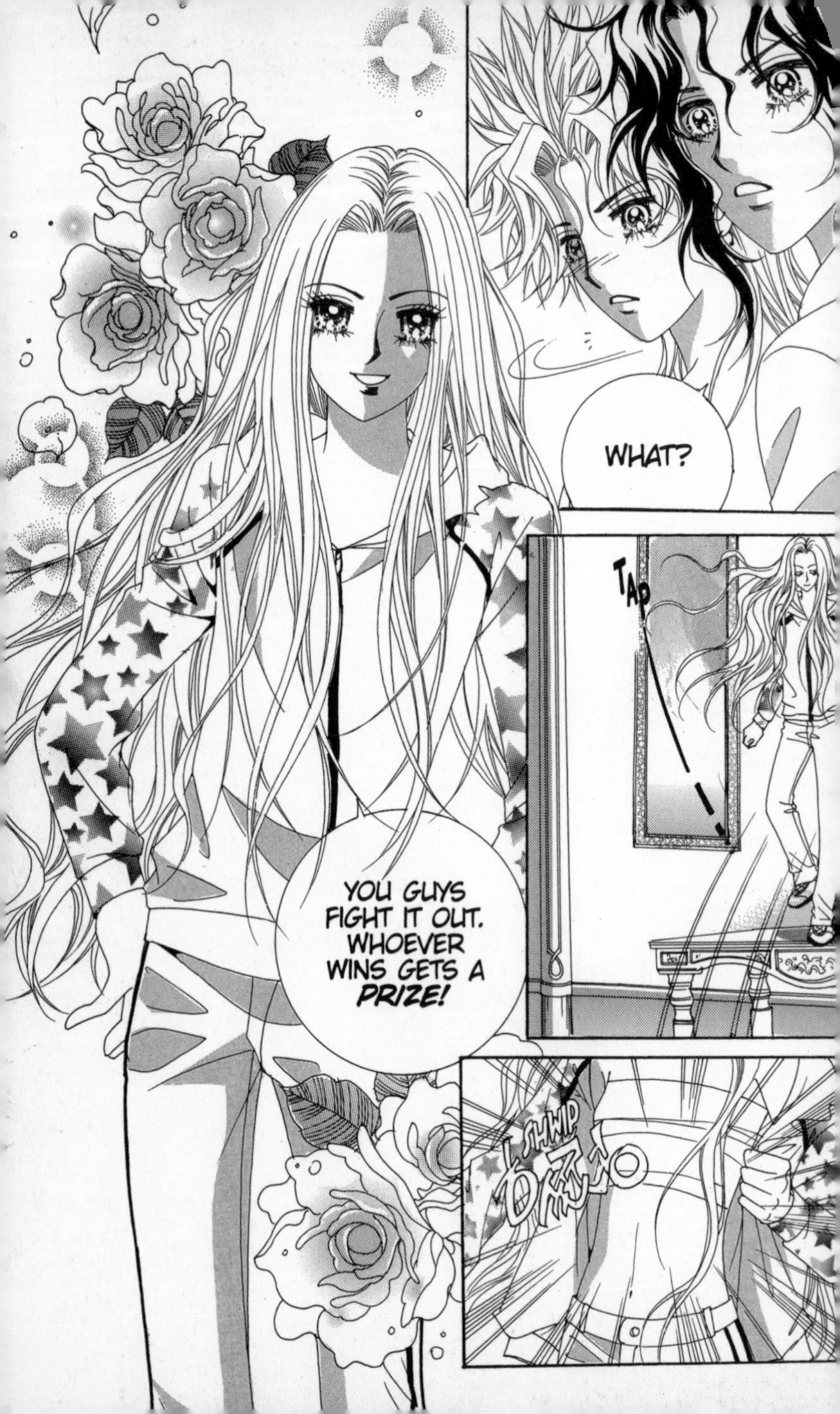
YOU GUYS FIGHT IT OUT. WHOEVER WINS GETS A *PRIZE!*
WHAT?
TAP
SHWIP

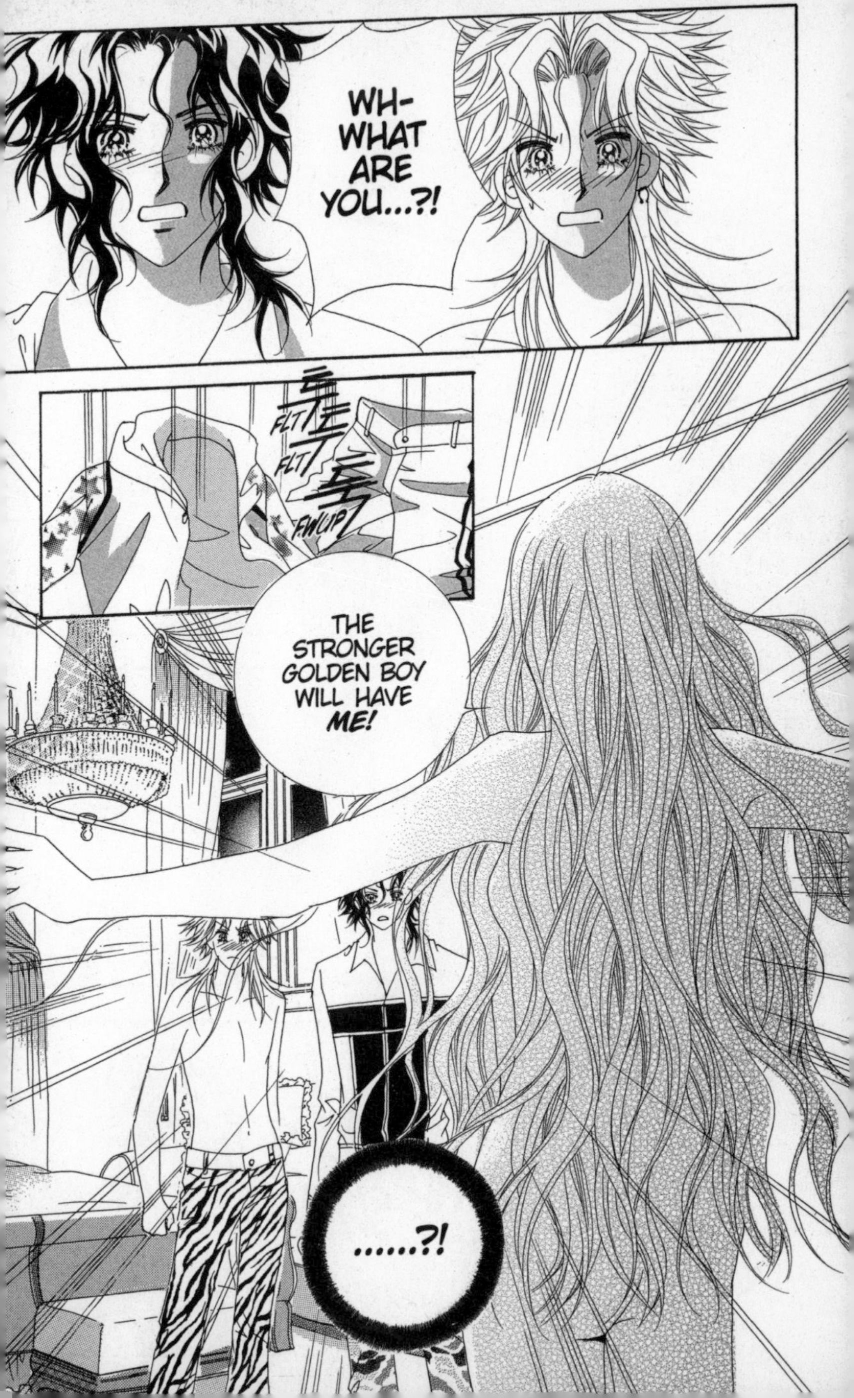
WH-WHAT ARE YOU...?!
FLT FLT
FWUP
THE STRONGER GOLDEN BOY WILL HAVE *ME!*
......?!

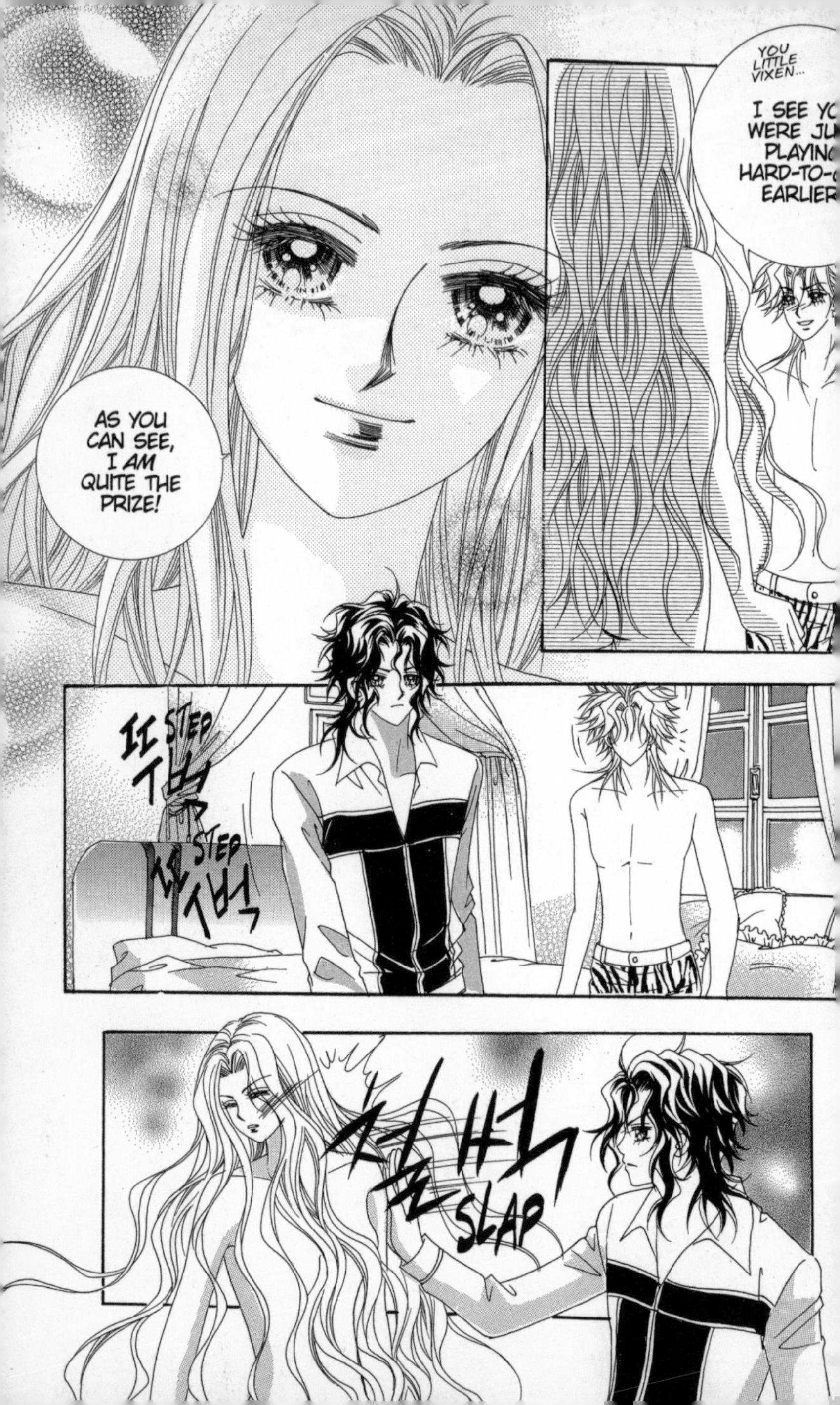
AS YOU CAN SEE, I AM QUITE THE PRIZE!
YOU LITTLE VIXEN...
I SEE YO
WERE JU
PLAYIN
HARD-TO-
EARLIER
STEP
STEP
SLAP

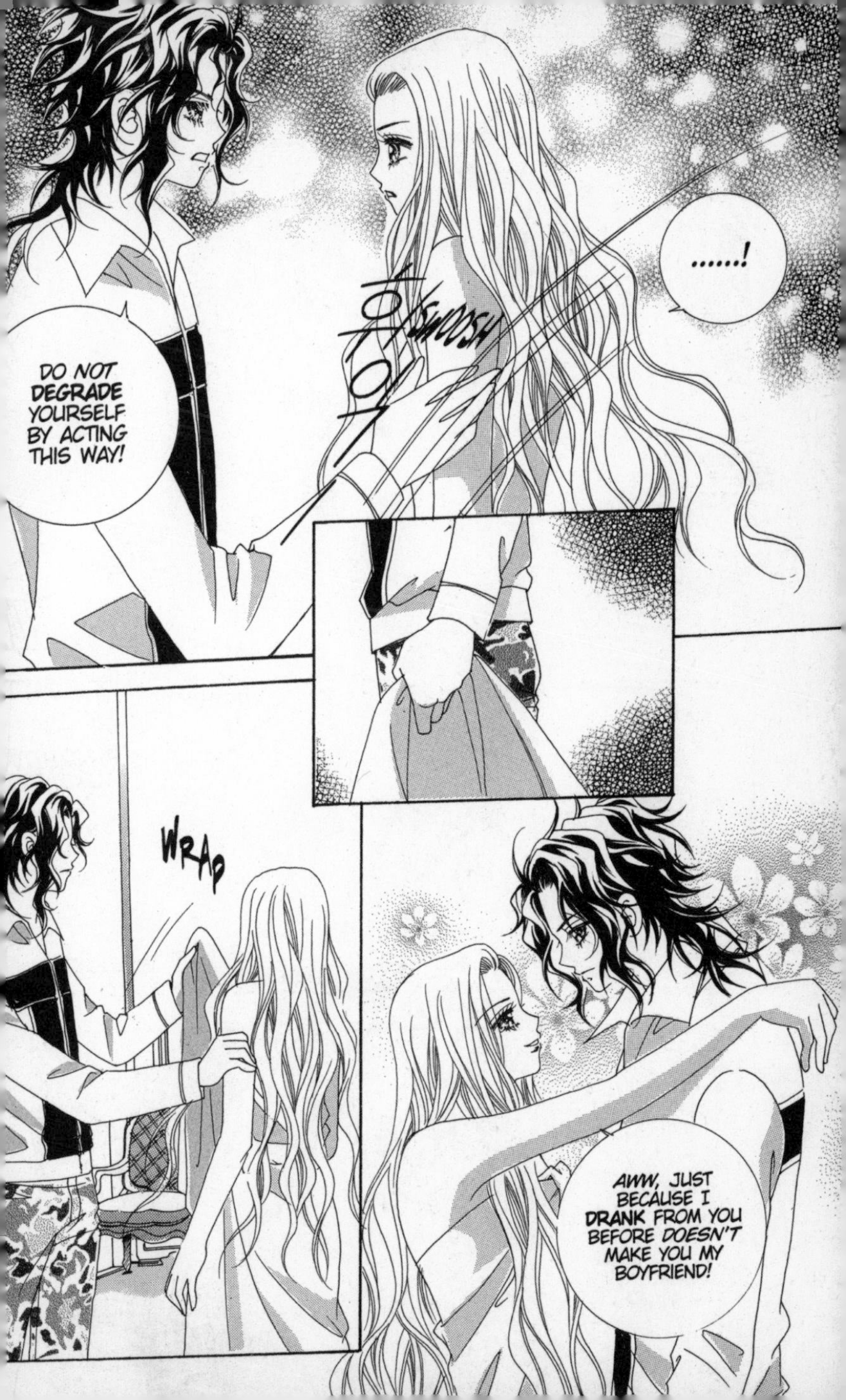
DO NOT DEGRADE YOURSELF BY ACTING THIS WAY!
SWOOSH
......!
WRAP
AWW, JUST BECAUSE I DRANK FROM YOU BEFORE DOESN'T MAKE YOU MY BOYFRIEND!

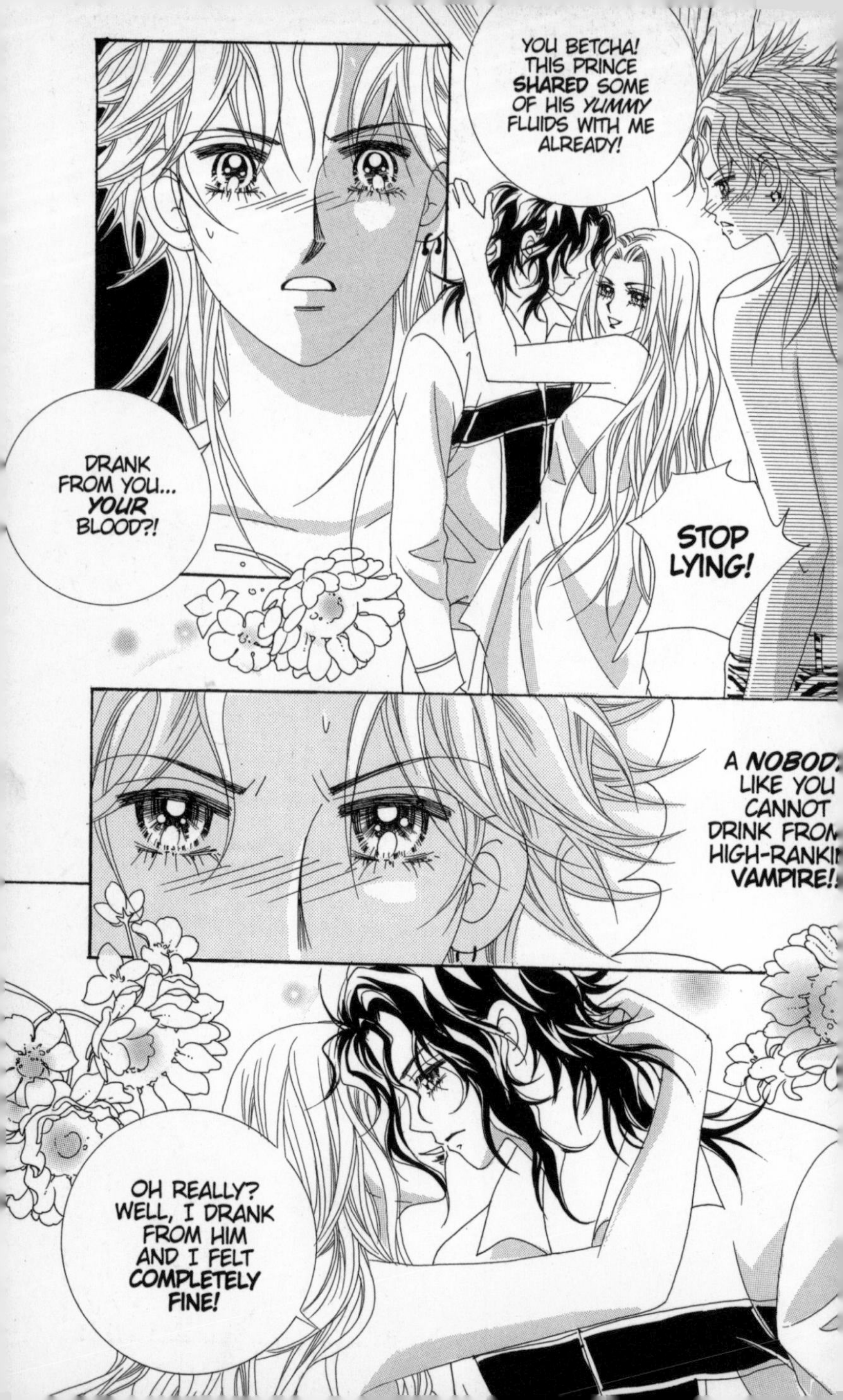
YOU BETCHA! THIS PRINCE SHARED SOME OF HIS YUMMY FLUIDS WITH ME ALREADY!
DRANK FROM YOU... YOUR BLOOD?!
STOP LYING!
A NOBOD LIKE YOU CANNOT DRINK FROM HIGH-RANKI VAMPIRE!
OH REALLY? WELL, I DRANK FROM HIM AND I FELT COMPLETELY FINE!

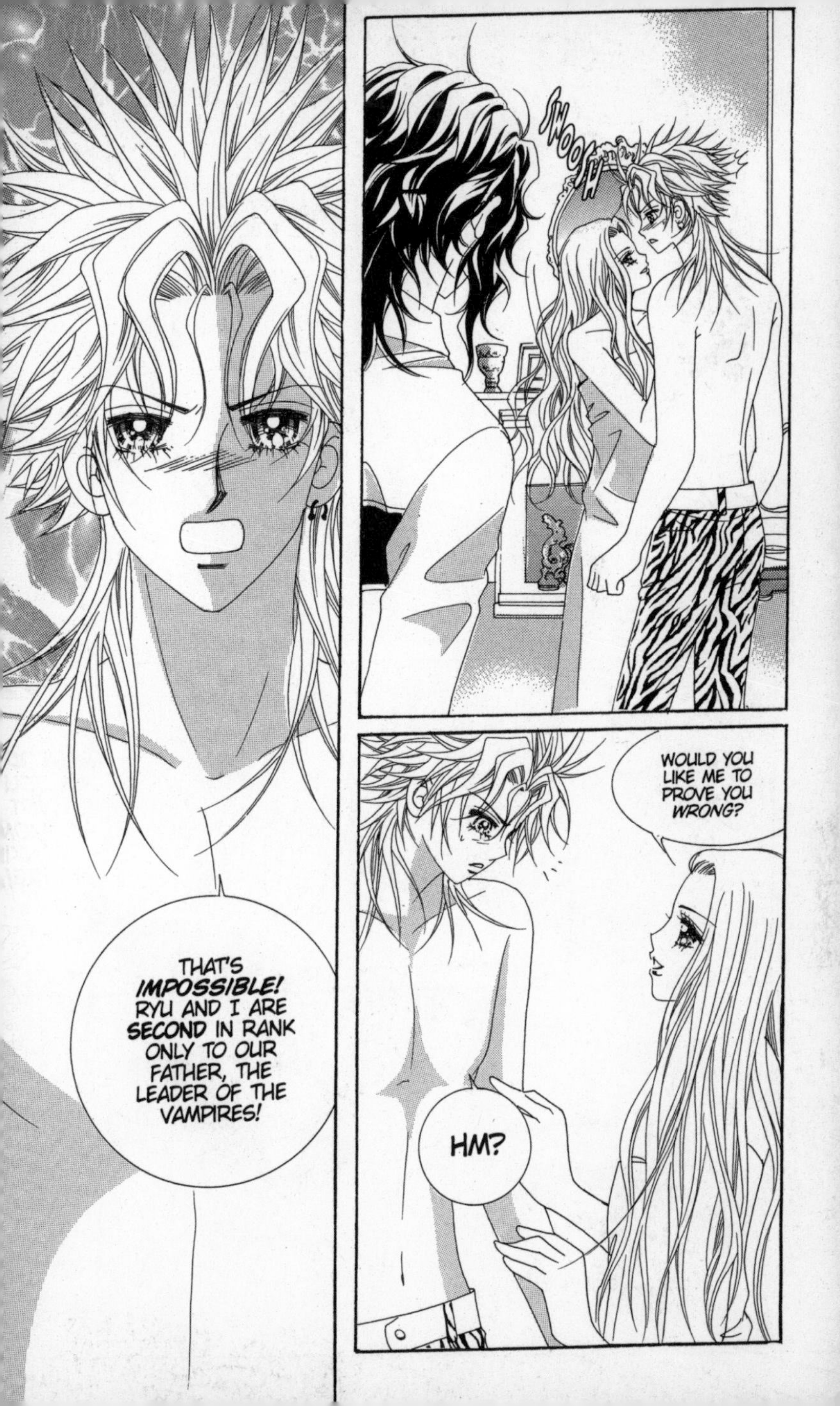
THAT'S *IMPOSSIBLE!* RYU AND I ARE **SECOND** IN RANK ONLY TO OUR FATHER, THE LEADER OF THE VAMPIRES!
SWOOSH
WOULD YOU LIKE ME TO PROVE YOU *WRONG?*
HM?

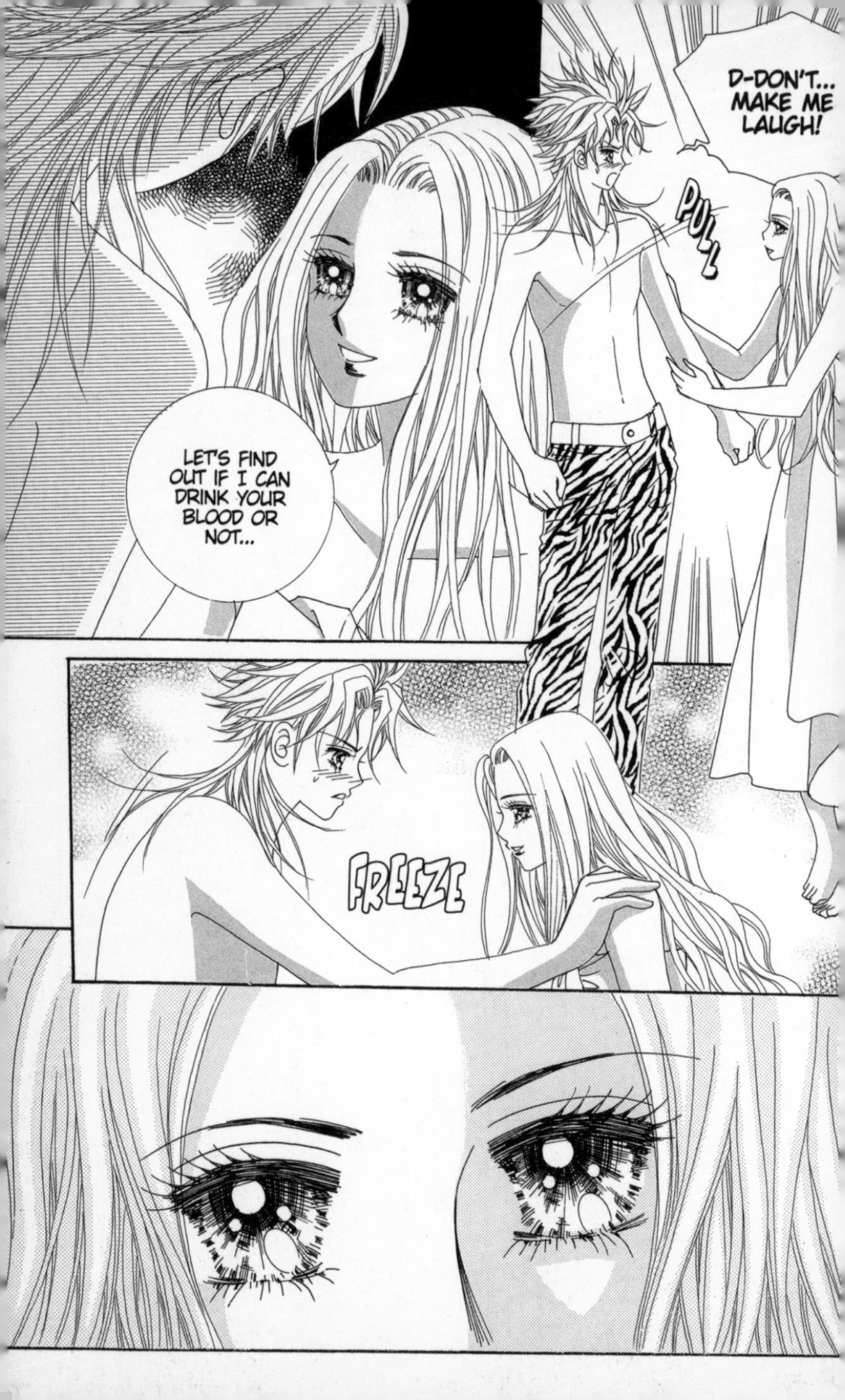
LET'S FIND OUT IF I CAN DRINK YOUR BLOOD OR NOT...
D-DON'T... MAKE ME LAUGH!
PULL
FREEZE

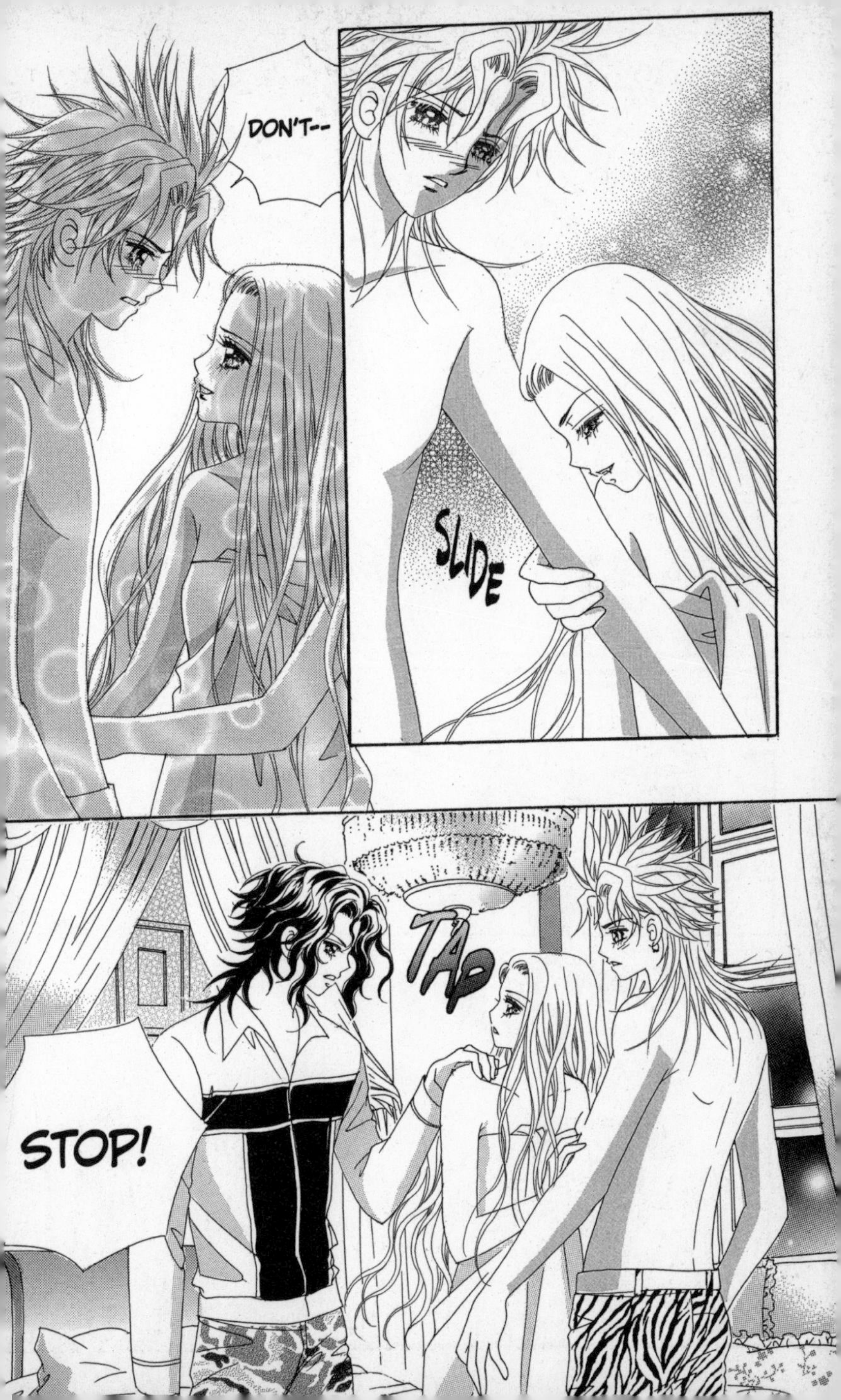
DON'T--
SLIDE
TAP
STOP!

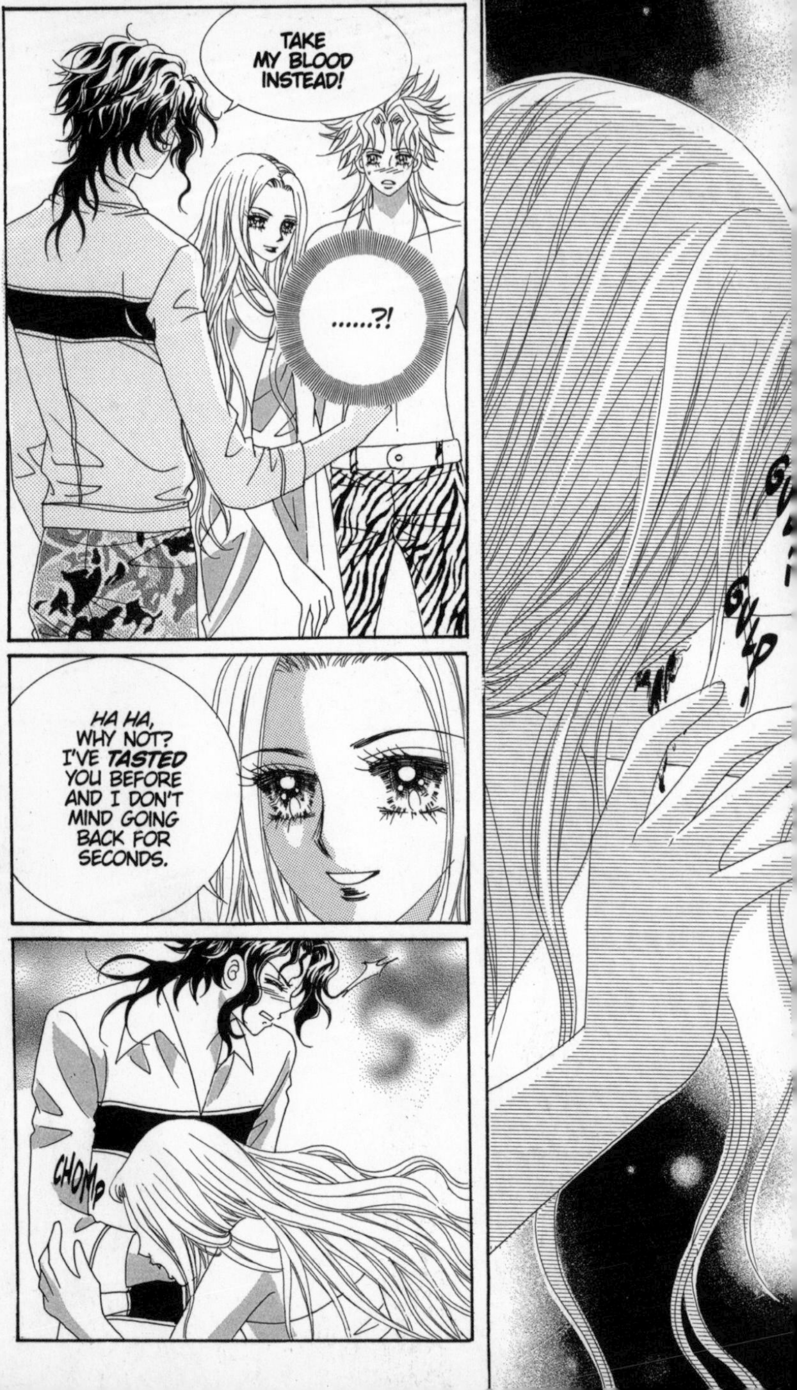
TAKE MY BLOOD INSTEAD!
......?!
HA HA, WHY NOT? I'VE *TASTED* YOU BEFORE AND I DON'T MIND GOING BACK FOR SECONDS.
CHOMP
GULP

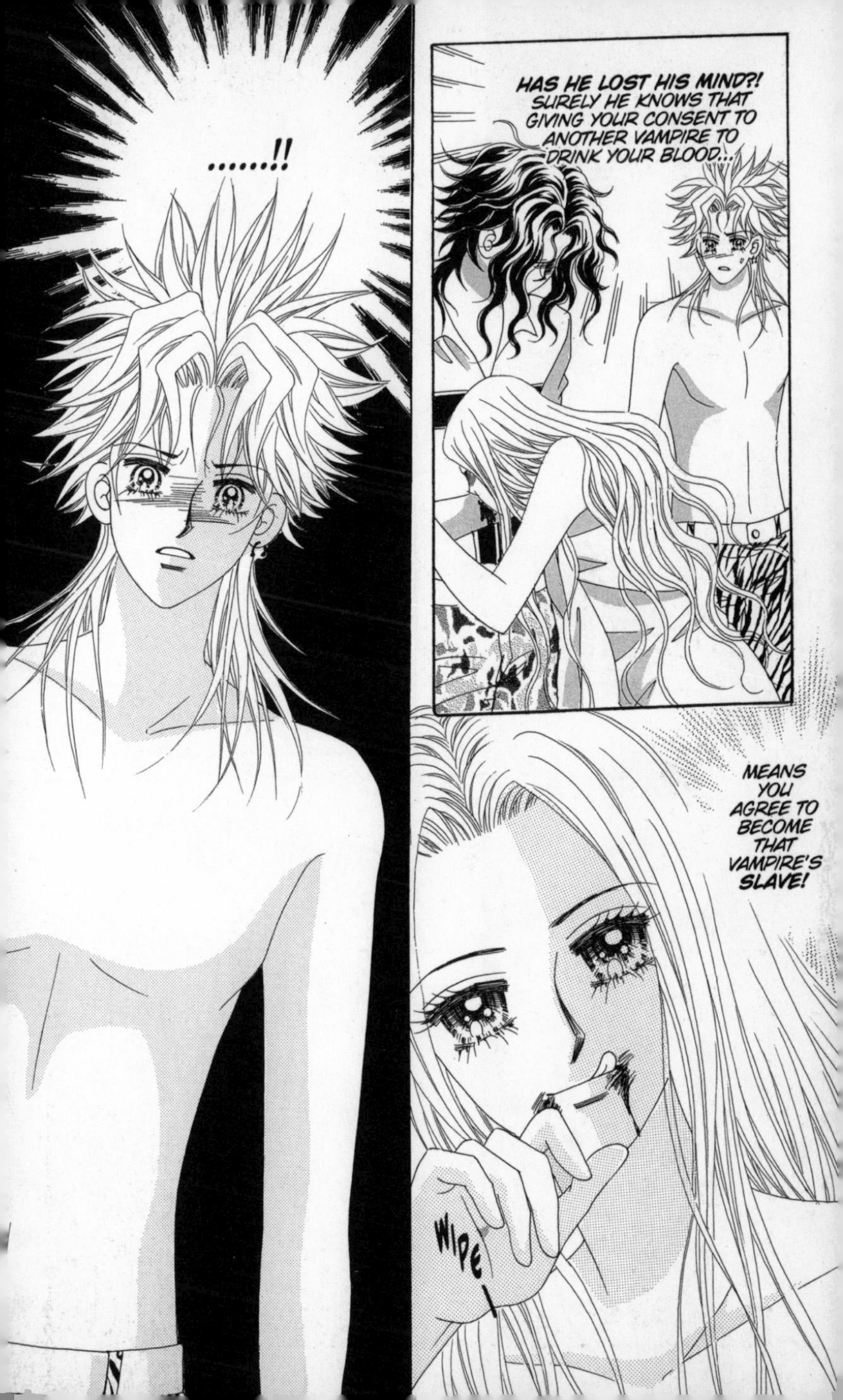
......!!
HAS HE LOST HIS MIND?! SURELY HE KNOWS THAT GIVING YOUR CONSENT TO ANOTHER VAMPIRE TO DRINK YOUR BLOOD...
MEANS YOU AGREE TO BECOME THAT VAMPIRE'S SLAVE!
WIPE

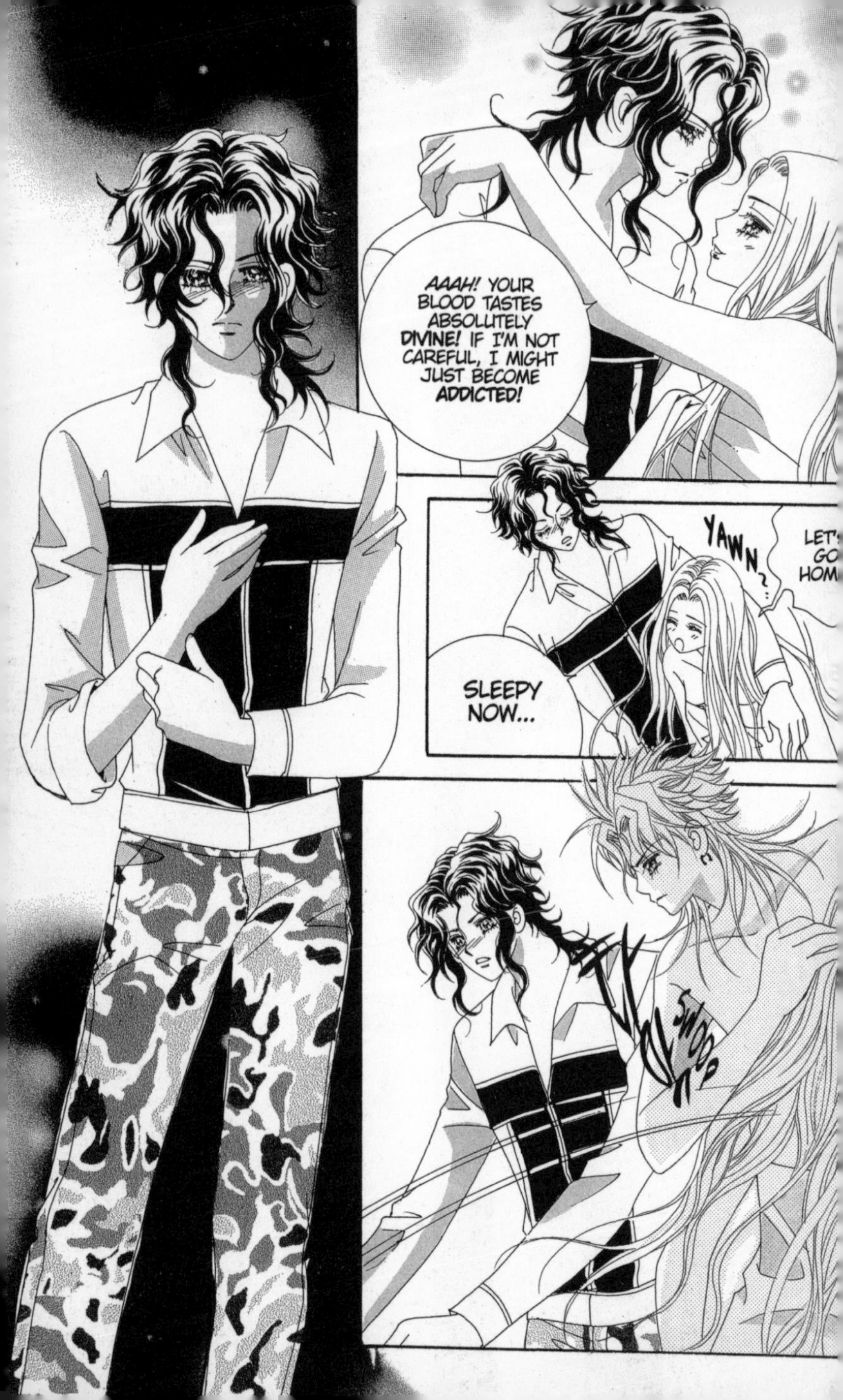
AAAH! YOUR BLOOD TASTES ABSOLUTELY DIVINE! IF I'M NOT CAREFUL, I MIGHT JUST BECOME ADDICTED!
YAWN...
LET'S GO HOM
SLEEPY NOW...
SWOOP

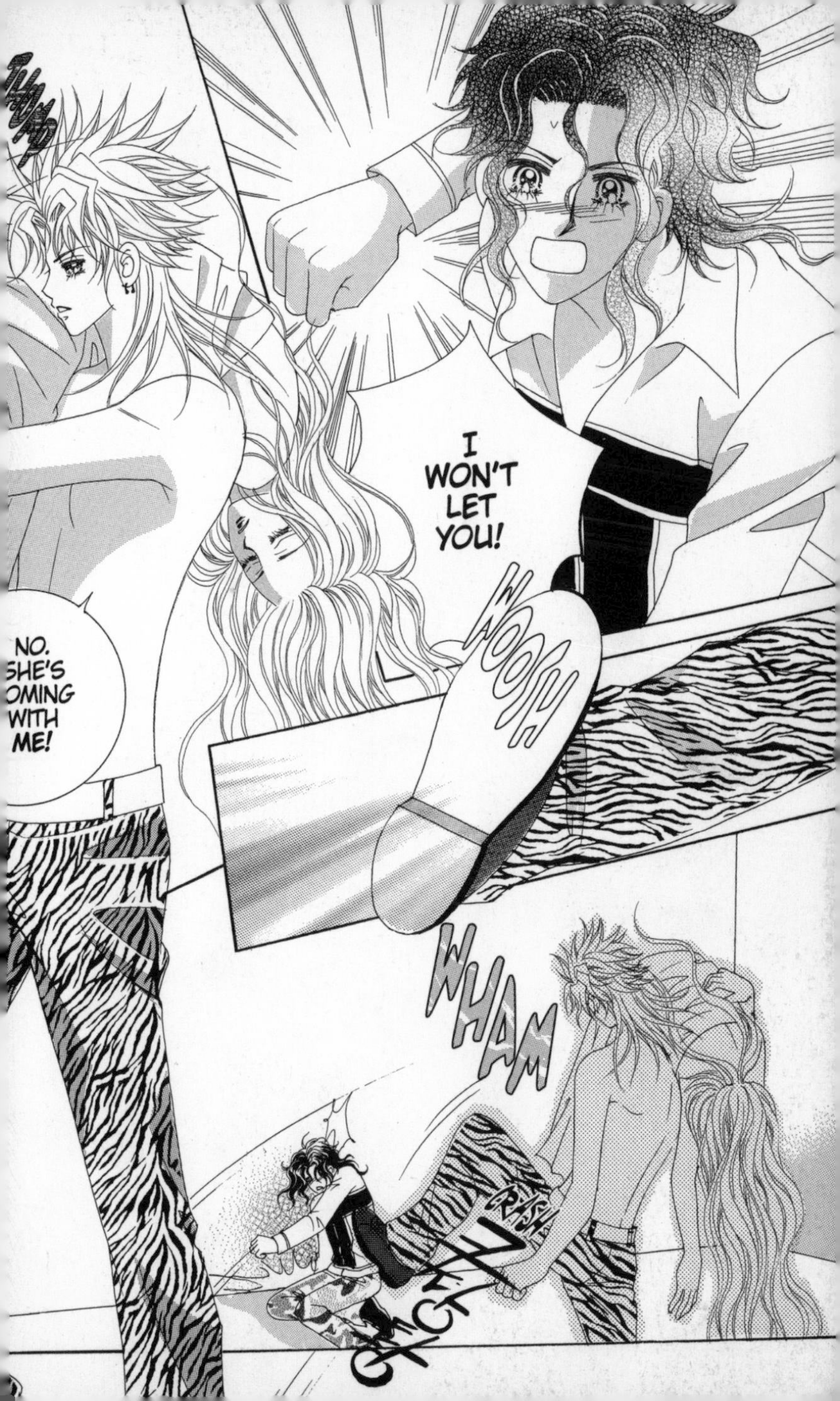
THUMP
I WON'T LET YOU!
NO. SHE'S OMING WITH ME!
WHOOSH
WHAM
CRASH
CRACK

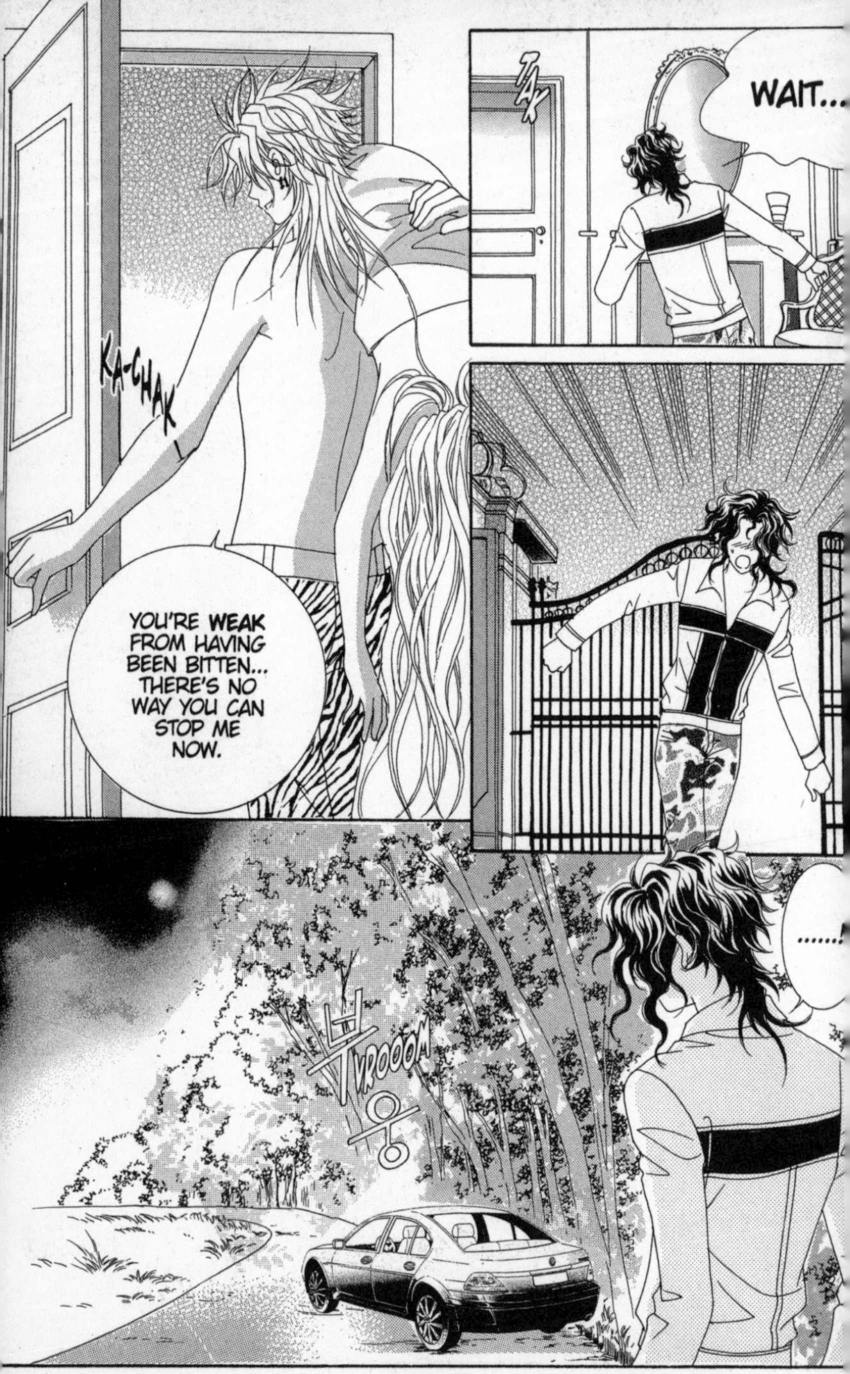
KA-CHAK
YOU'RE WEAK FROM HAVING BEEN BITTEN... THERE'S NO WAY YOU CAN STOP ME NOW.
TAK
WAIT...
VROOOM
......

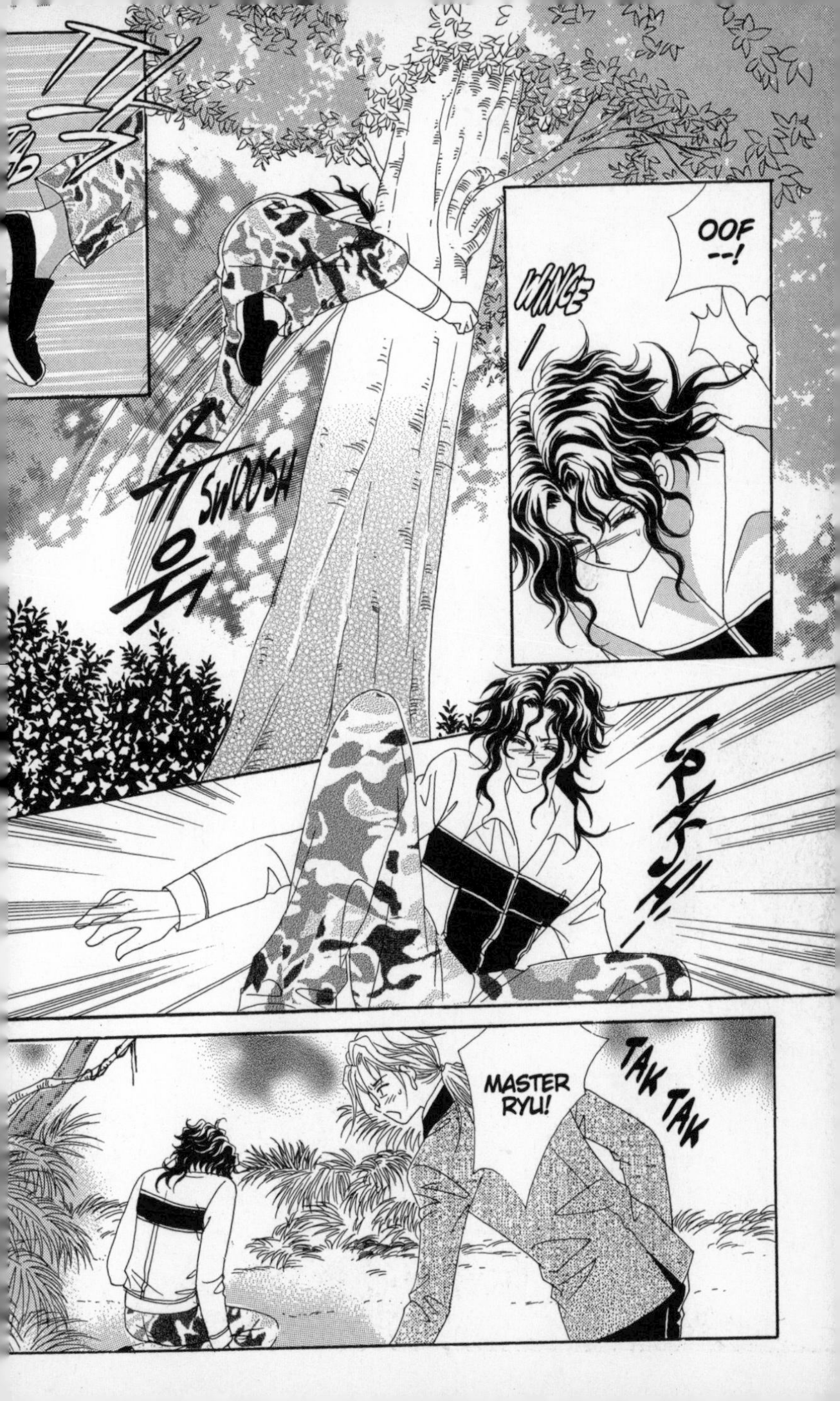
OOF --!
WINCE
SWOOSH
CRASH!!
MASTER RYU!
TAK TAK

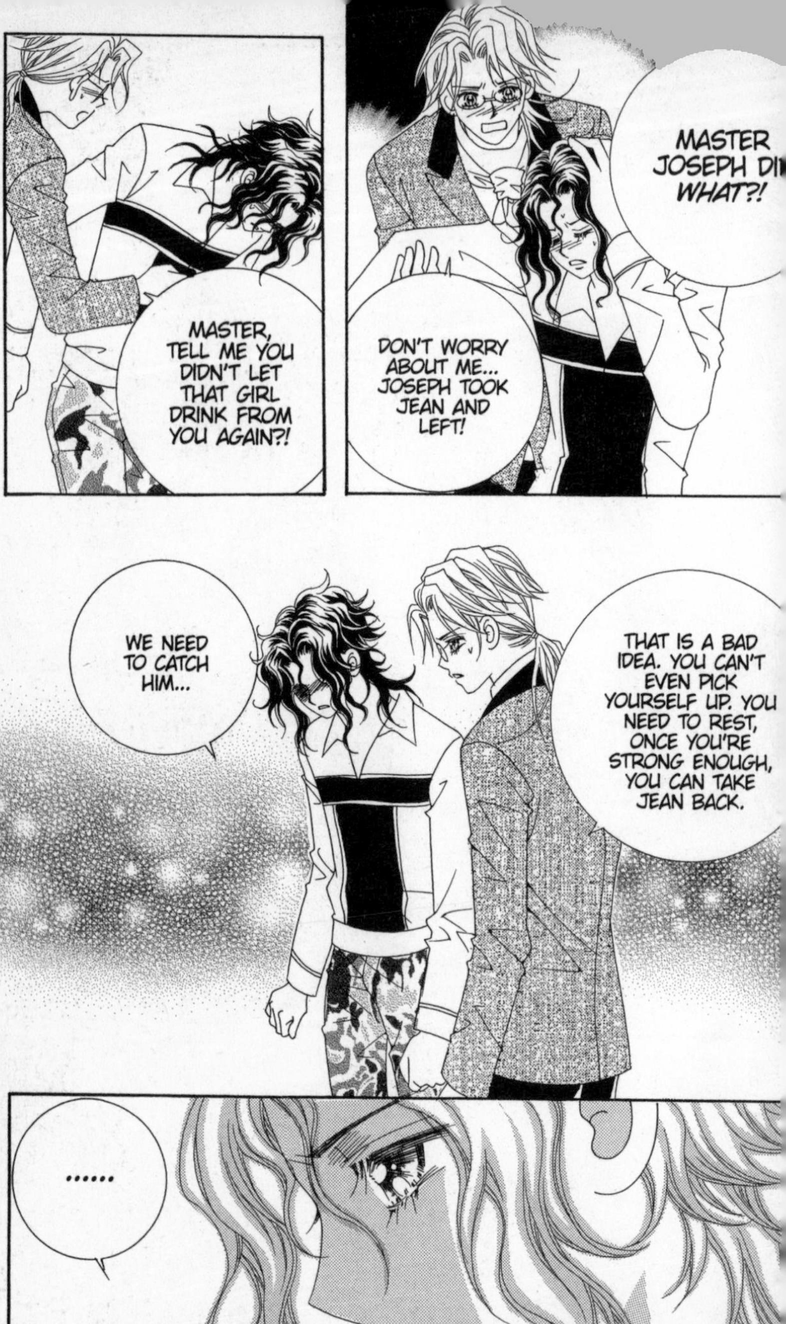
MASTER, TELL ME YOU DIDN'T LET THAT GIRL DRINK FROM YOU AGAIN?!
DON'T WORRY ABOUT ME... JOSEPH TOOK JEAN AND LEFT!
MASTER JOSEPH DI WHAT?!
WE NEED TO CATCH HIM...
THAT IS A BAD IDEA. YOU CAN'T EVEN PICK YOURSELF UP. YOU NEED TO REST, ONCE YOU'RE STRONG ENOUGH, YOU CAN TAKE JEAN BACK.
......

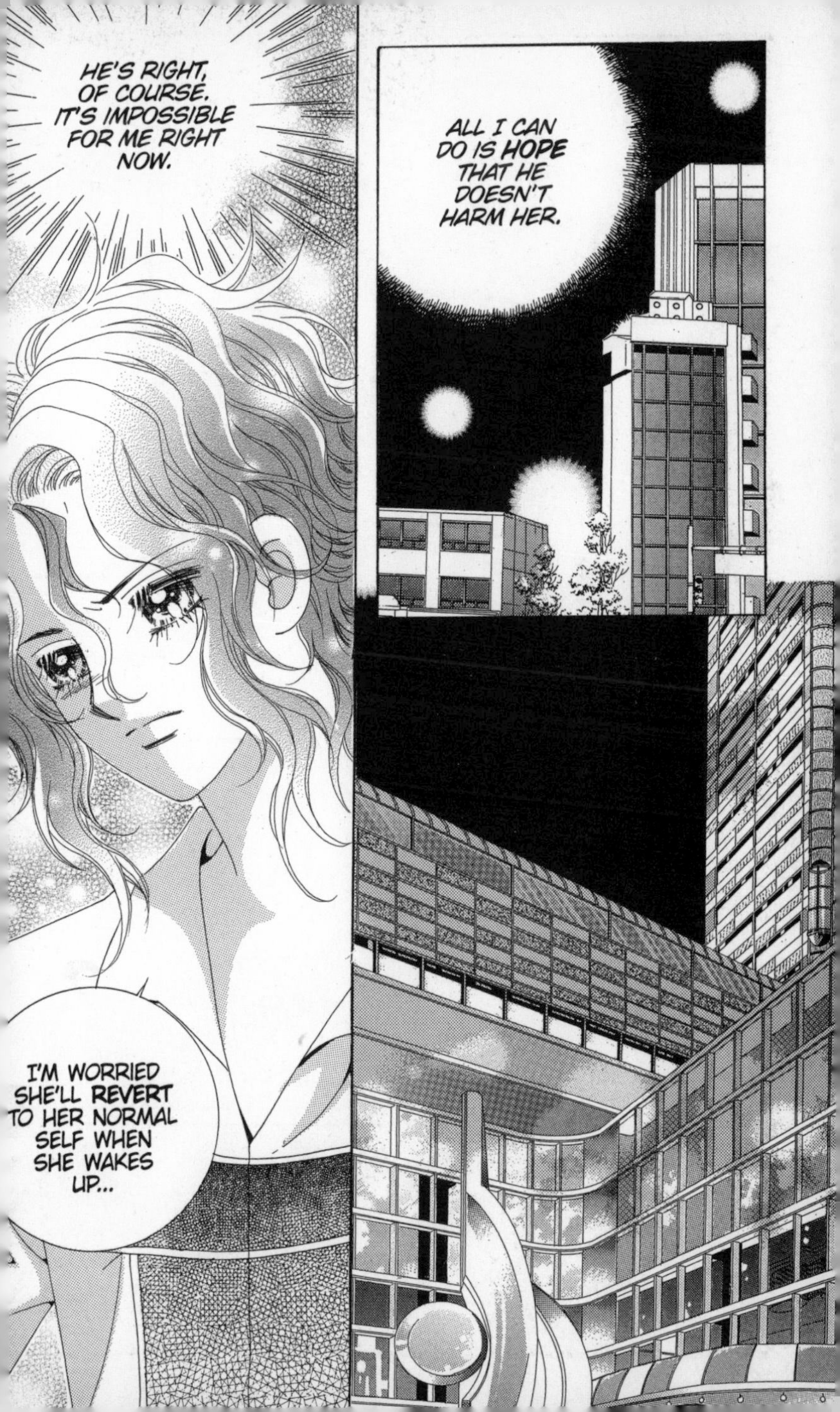
HE'S RIGHT, OF COURSE. IT'S IMPOSSIBLE FOR ME RIGHT NOW.
I'M WORRIED SHE'LL REVERT TO HER NORMAL SELF WHEN SHE WAKES UP...
ALL I CAN DO IS HOPE THAT HE DOESN'T HARM HER.

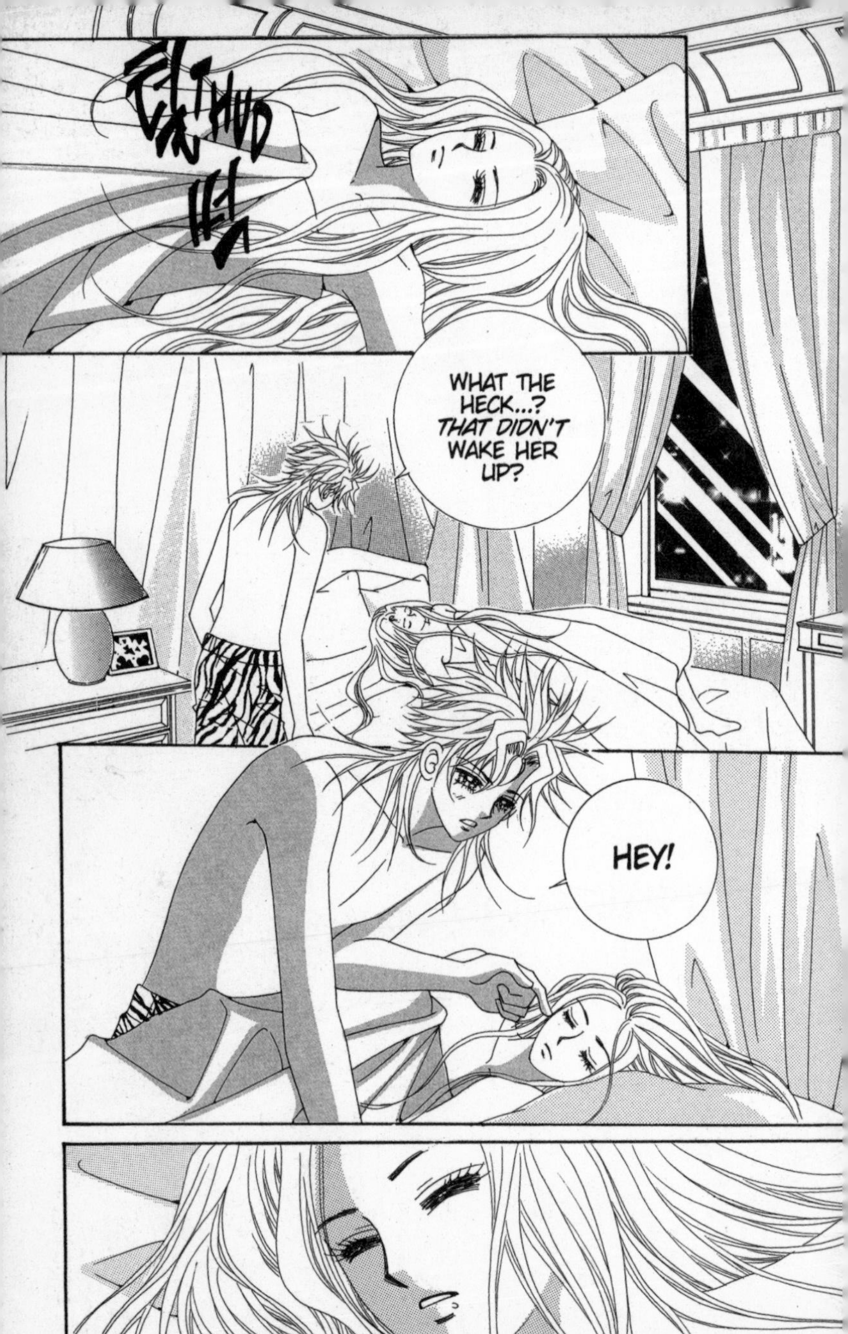
THUD
WHAT THE HECK...? *THAT DIDN'T* WAKE HER UP?
HEY!

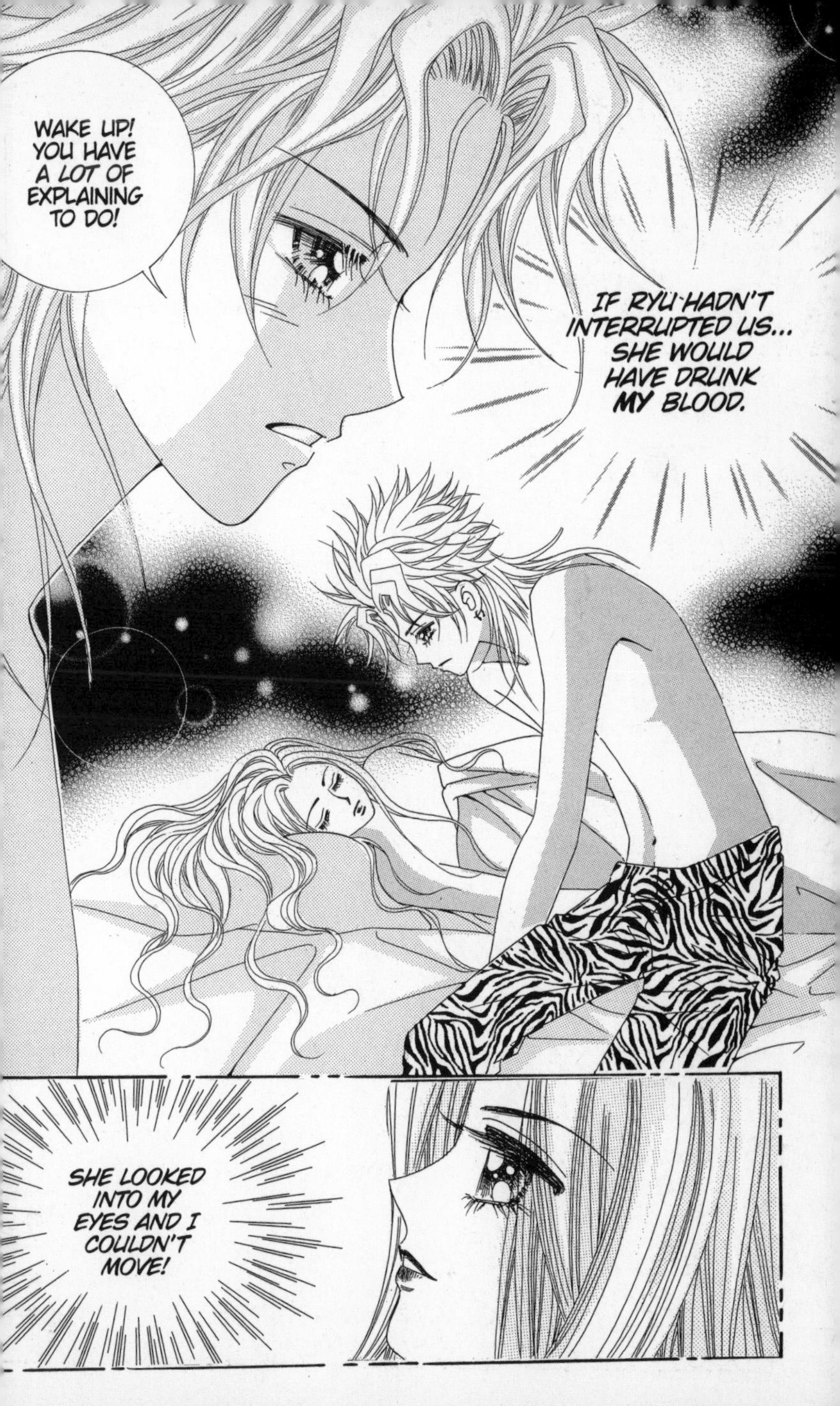
WAKE UP! YOU HAVE A LOT OF EXPLAINING TO DO!
IF RYU HADN'T INTERRUPTED US... SHE WOULD HAVE DRUNK MY BLOOD.
SHE LOOKED INTO MY EYES AND I COULDN'T MOVE!

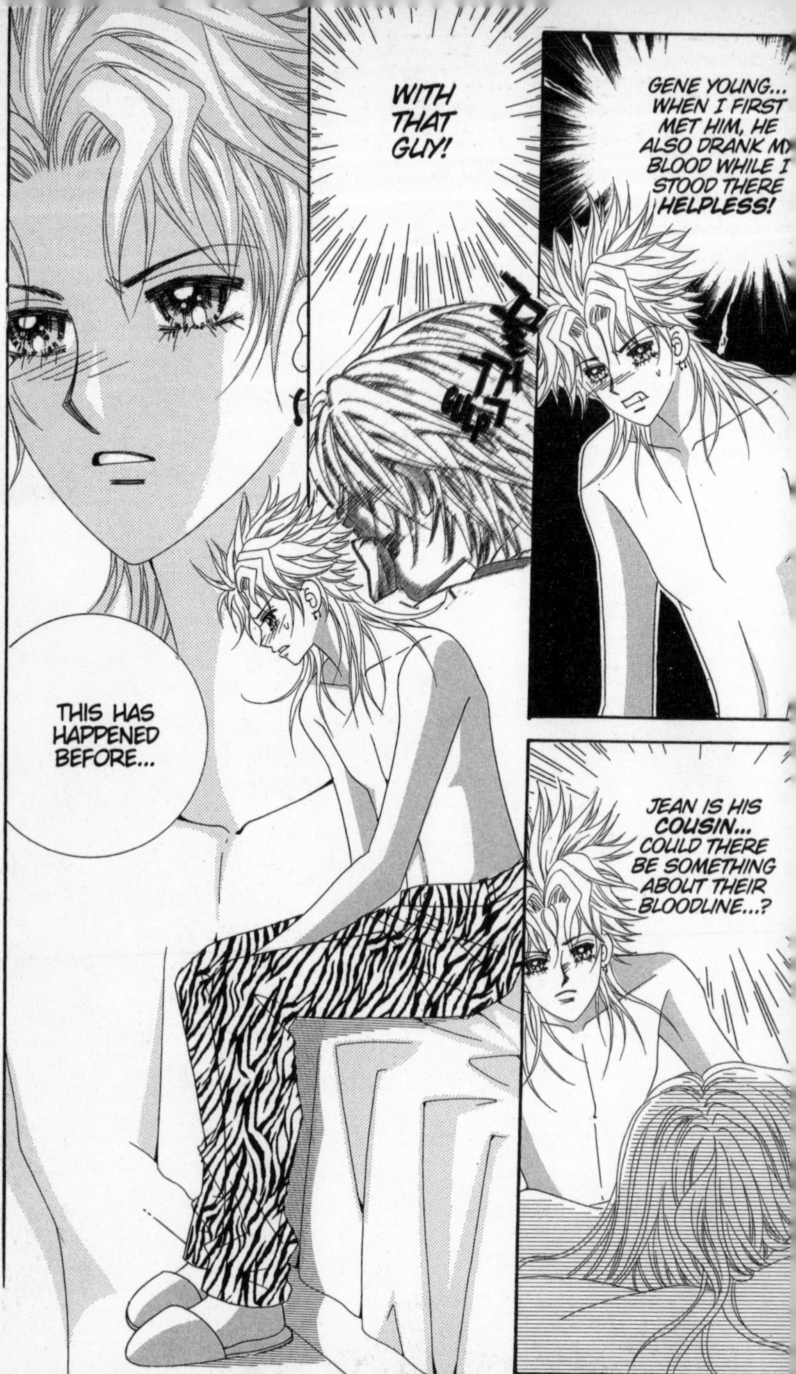
THIS HAS HAPPENED BEFORE...
WITH THAT GUY!
GENE YOUNG... WHEN I FIRST MET HIM, HE ALSO DRANK MY BLOOD WHILE I STOOD THERE HELPLESS!
JEAN IS HIS COUSIN... COULD THERE BE SOMETHING ABOUT THEIR BLOODLINE...?

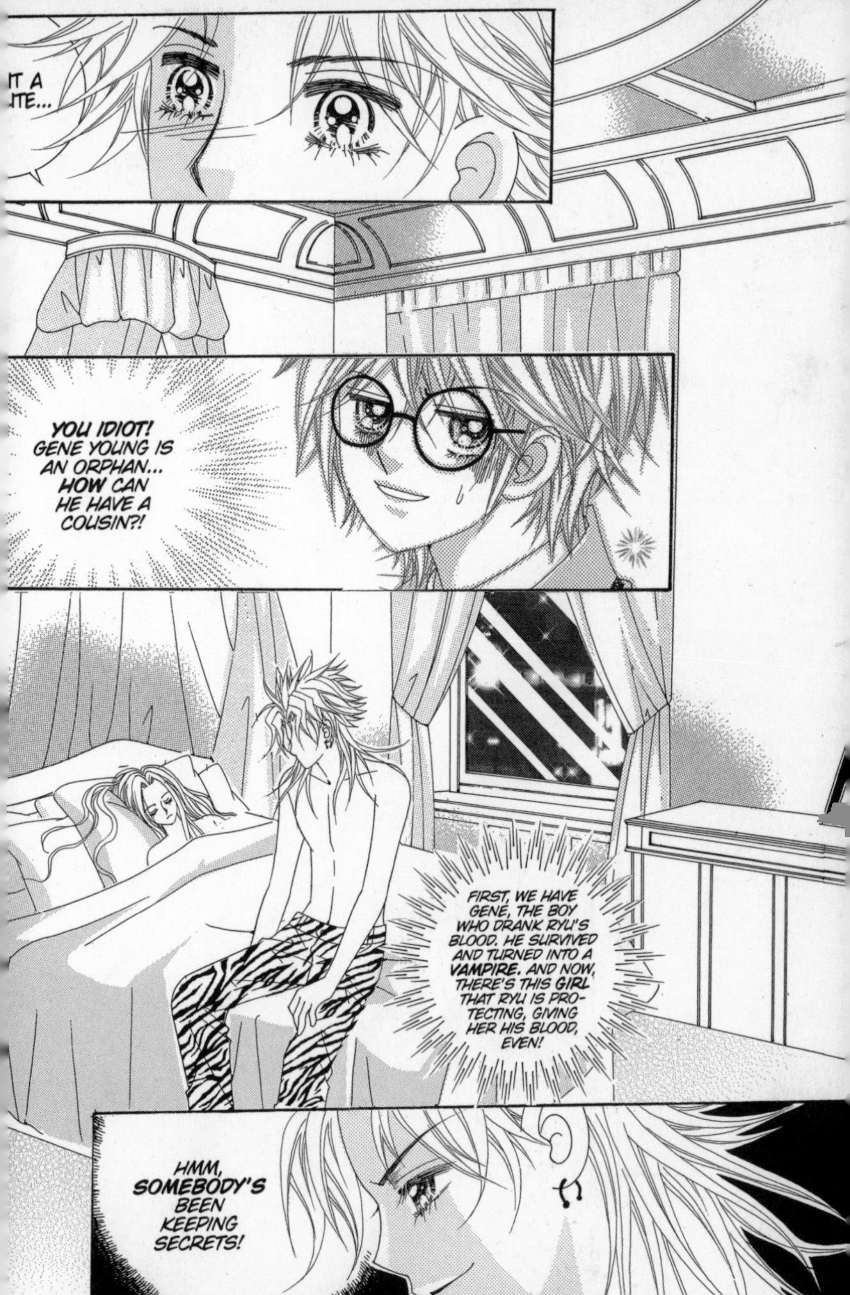
IT A
ITE...
YOU IDIOT! GENE YOUNG IS AN ORPHAN... HOW CAN HE HAVE A COUSIN?!
FIRST, WE HAVE GENE, THE BOY WHO DRANK RYU'S BLOOD. HE SURVIVED AND TURNED INTO A VAMPIRE. AND NOW, THERE'S THIS GIRL THAT RYU IS PRO-TECTING, GIVING HER HIS BLOOD, EVEN!
HMM, SOMEBODY'S BEEN KEEPING SECRETS!

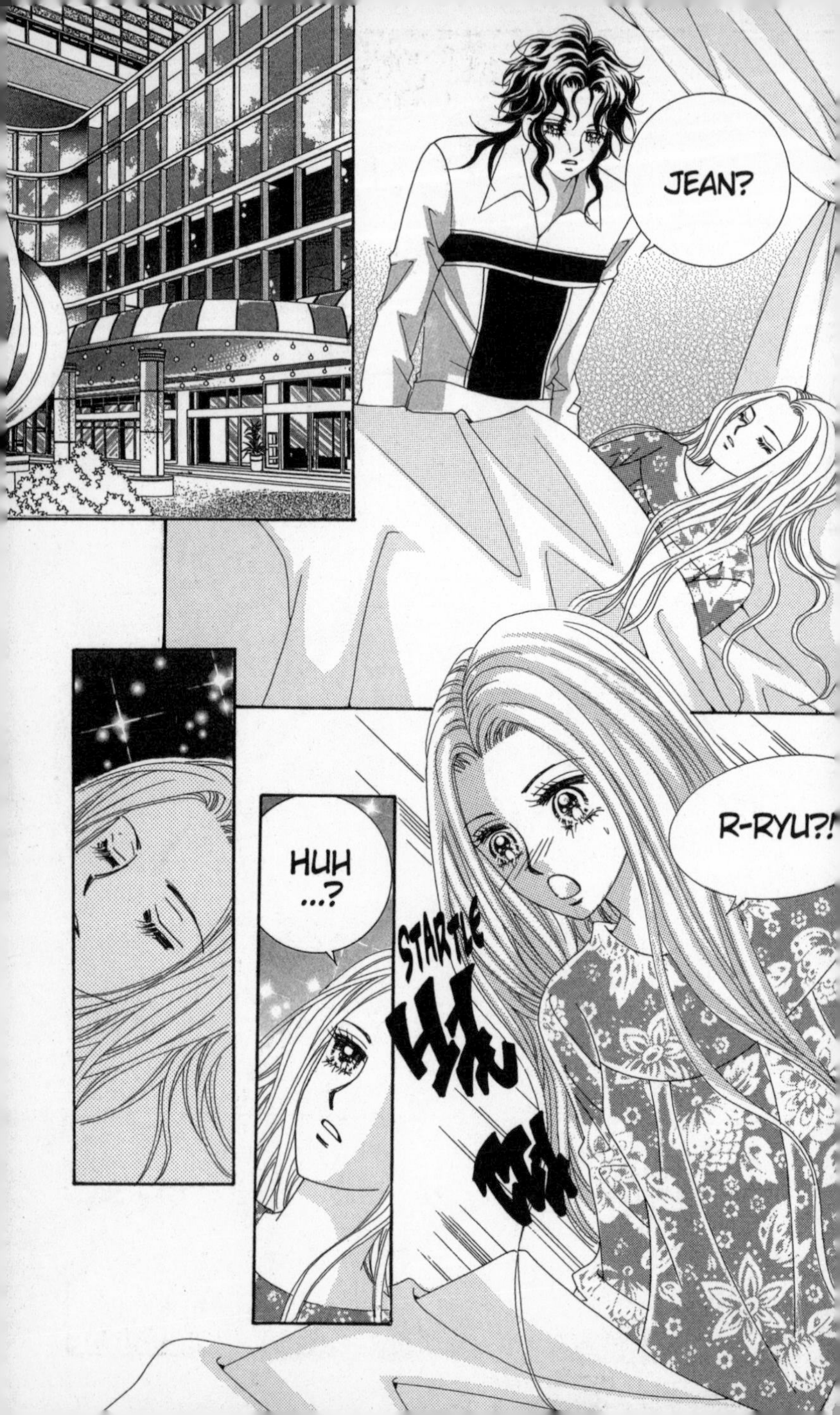
JEAN?
HUH ...?
STARTLE
R-RYU?!

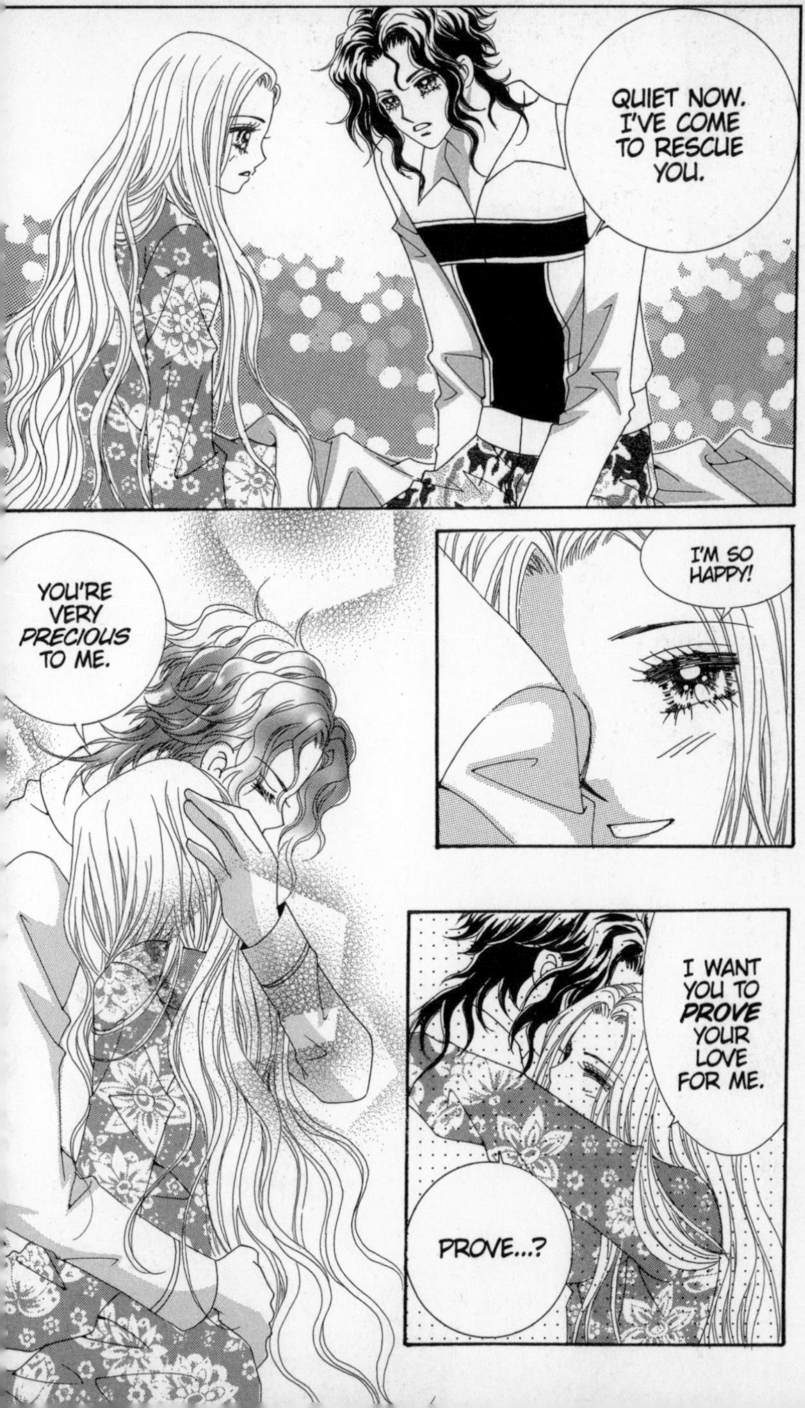
QUIET NOW. I'VE COME TO RESCUE YOU.
YOU'RE VERY *PRECIOUS* TO ME.
I'M SO HAPPY!
I WANT YOU TO *PROVE* YOUR LOVE FOR ME.
PROVE...?

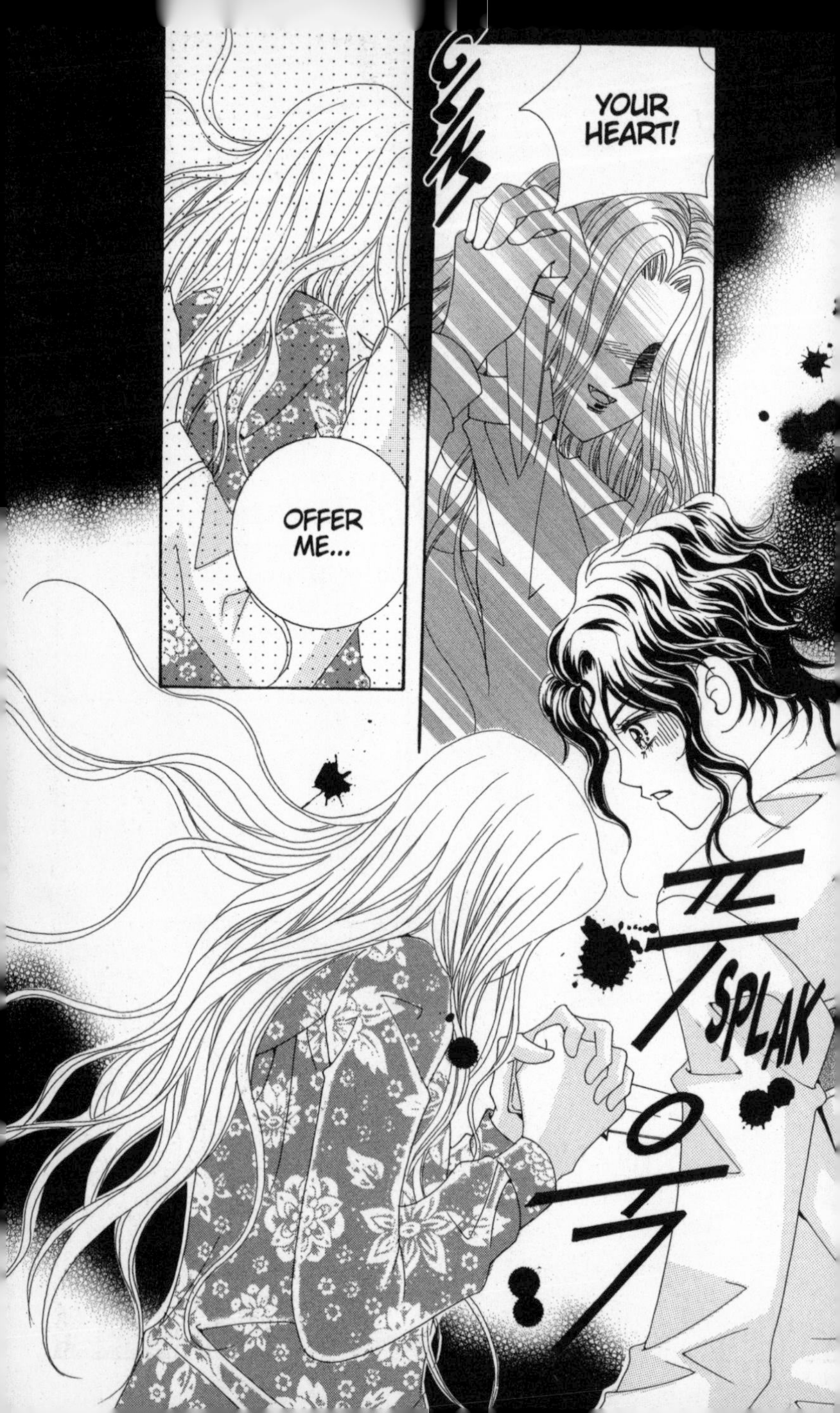
OFFER ME...
GLINT
YOUR HEART!
SPLAK

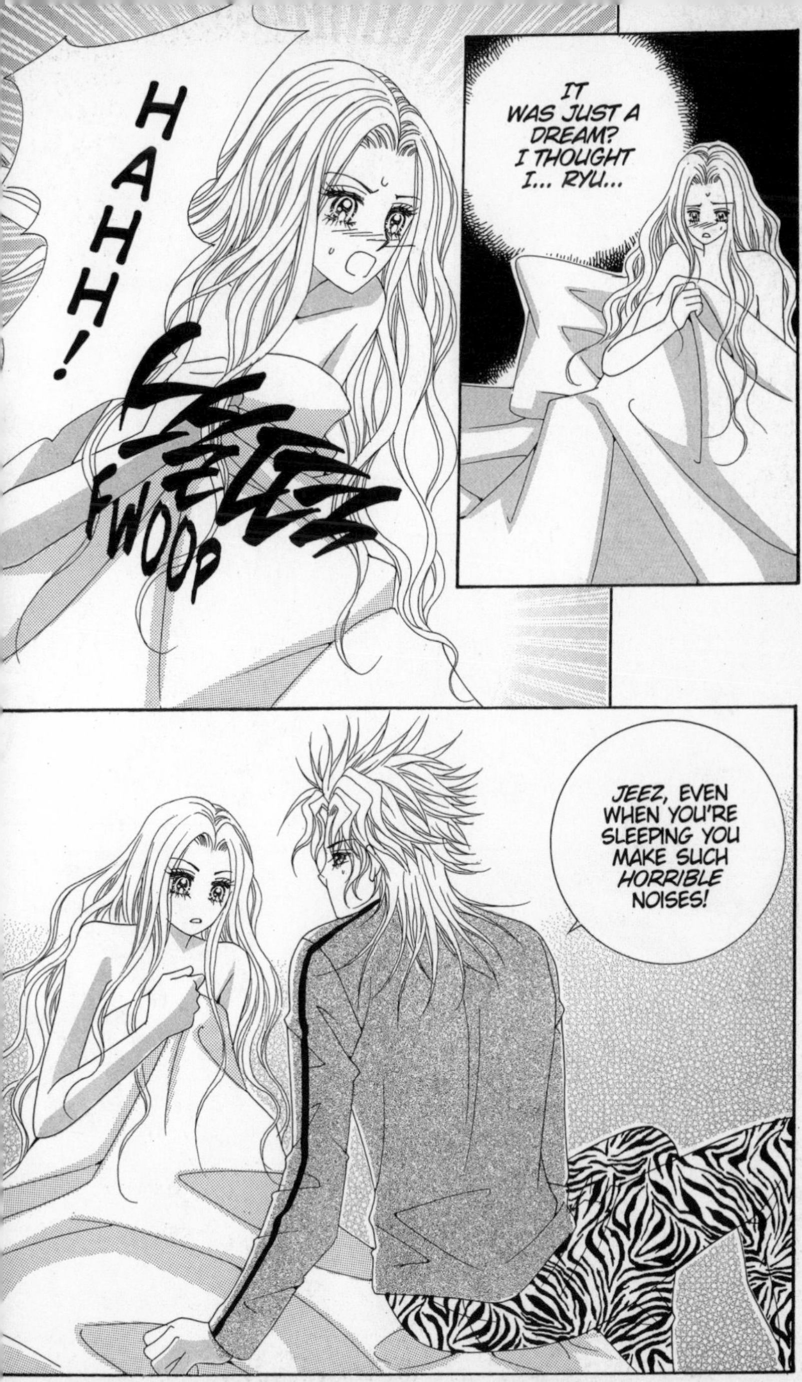
HAHHH!
FWOOP
IT WAS JUST A DREAM? I THOUGHT I... RYU...
JEEZ, EVEN WHEN YOU'RE SLEEPING YOU MAKE SUCH HORRIBLE NOISES!

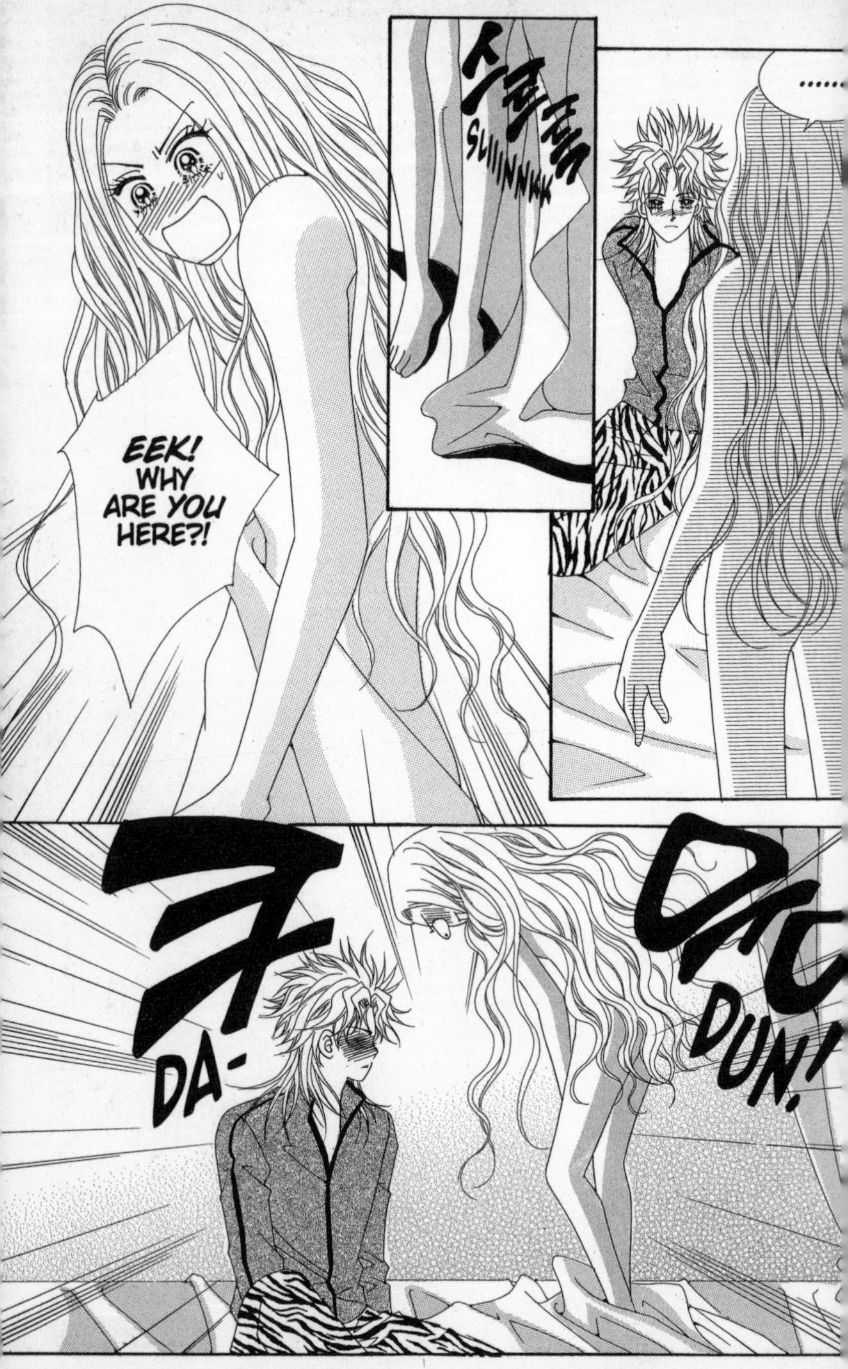
EEK! WHY ARE YOU HERE?!
SLIIIINNKK
......
DA-
DUN!

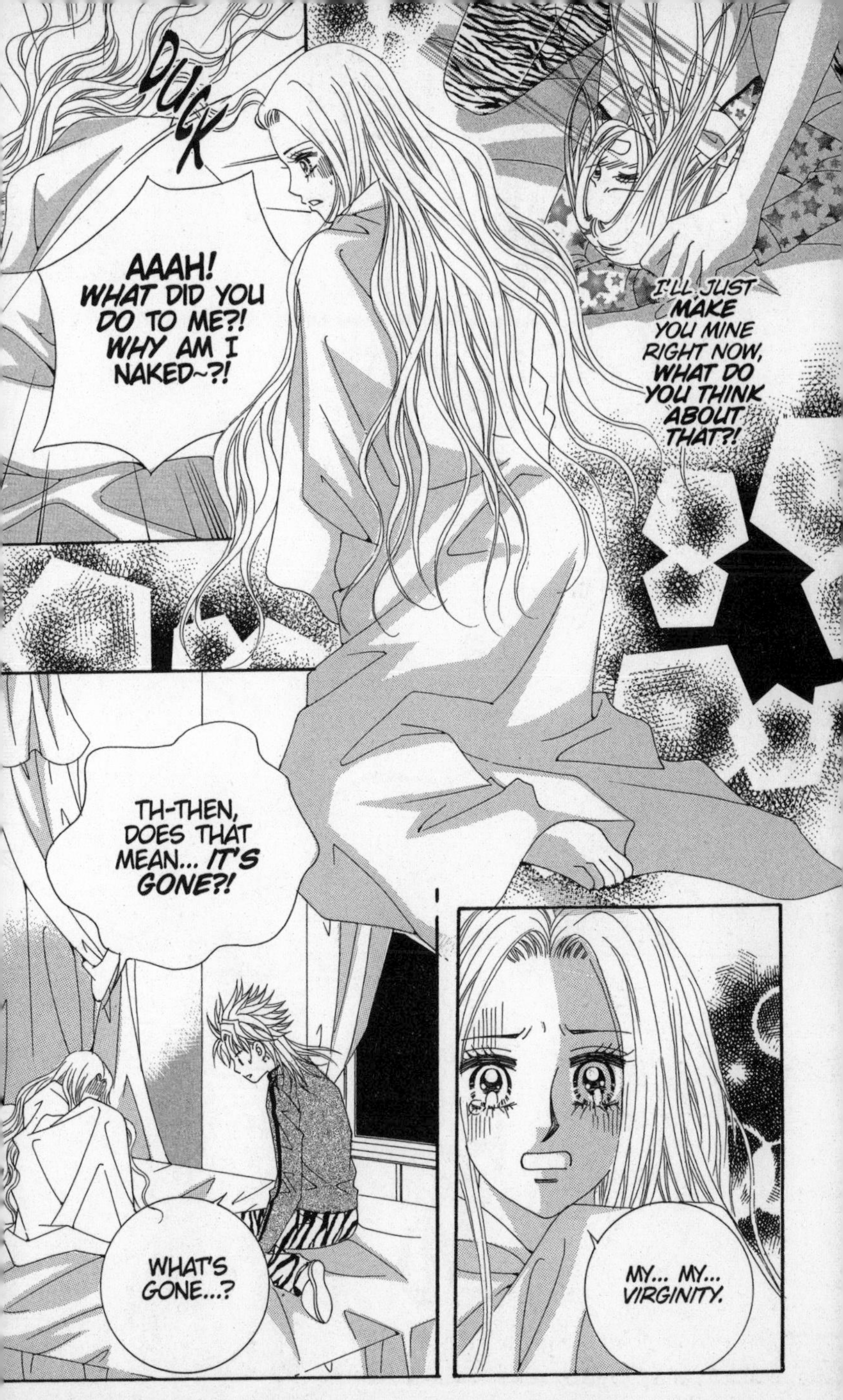
DUCK
AAAH! WHAT DID YOU DO TO ME?! WHY AM I NAKED~?!
I'LL JUST MAKE YOU MINE RIGHT NOW, WHAT DO YOU THINK ABOUT THAT?!
TH-THEN, DOES THAT MEAN... IT'S GONE?!
WHAT'S GONE...?
MY... MY... VIRGINITY.

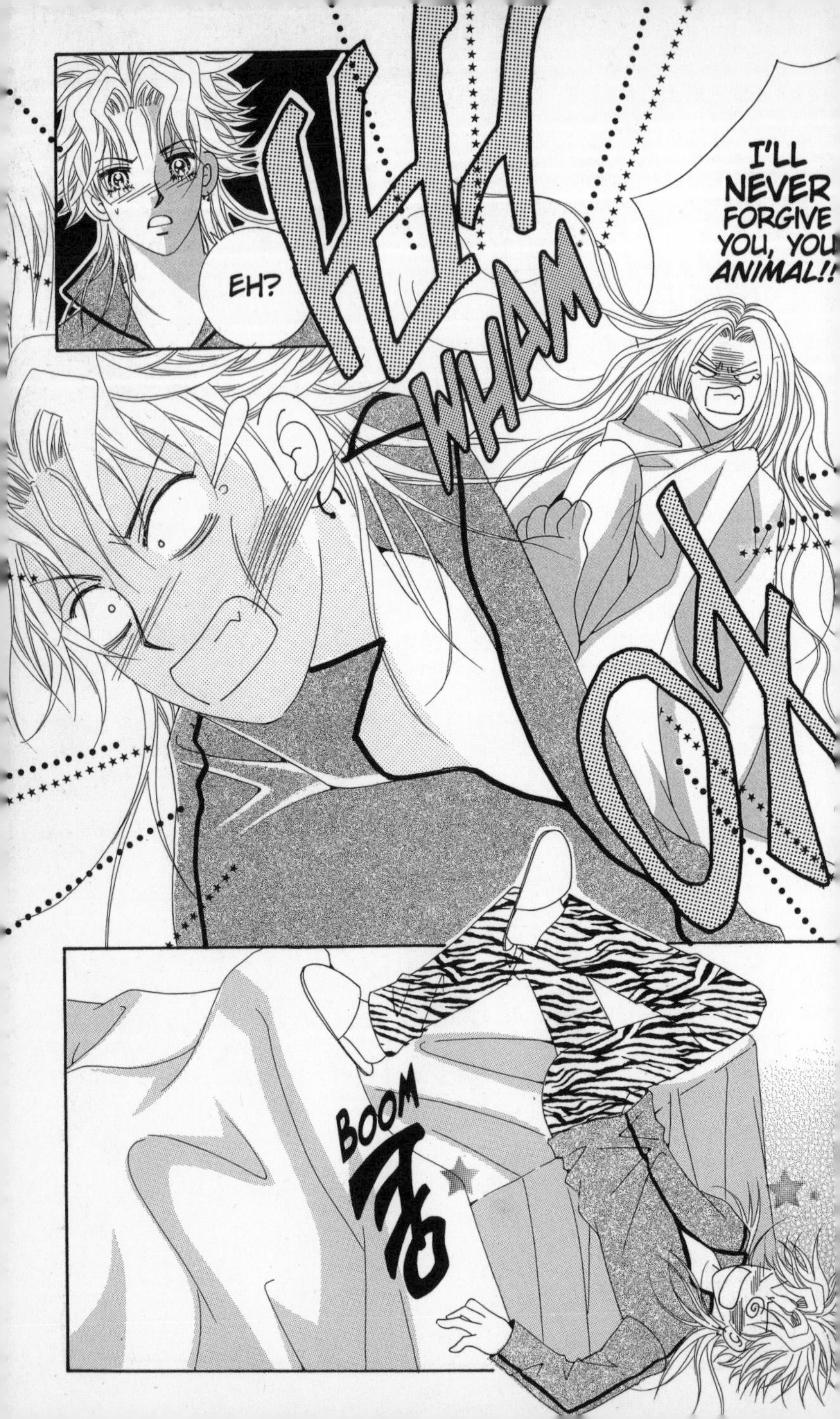
EH?
I'LL NEVER FORGIVE YOU, YOU ANIMAL!!
WHAM
BOOM

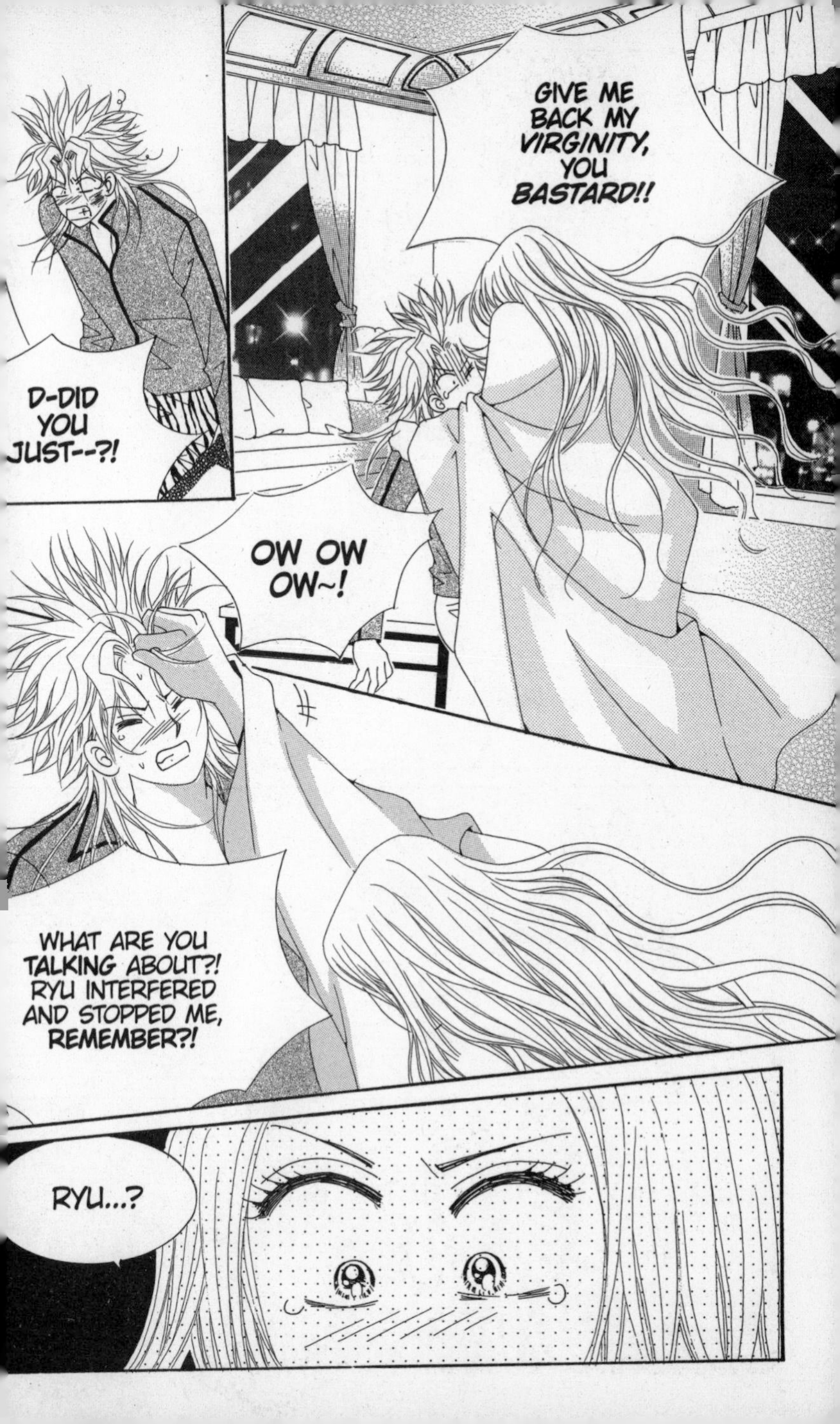
D-DID YOU JUST--?!
GIVE ME BACK MY VIRGINITY, YOU BASTARD!!
OW OW OW~!
WHAT ARE YOU TALKING ABOUT?! RYU INTERFERED AND STOPPED ME, REMEMBER?!
RYU...?

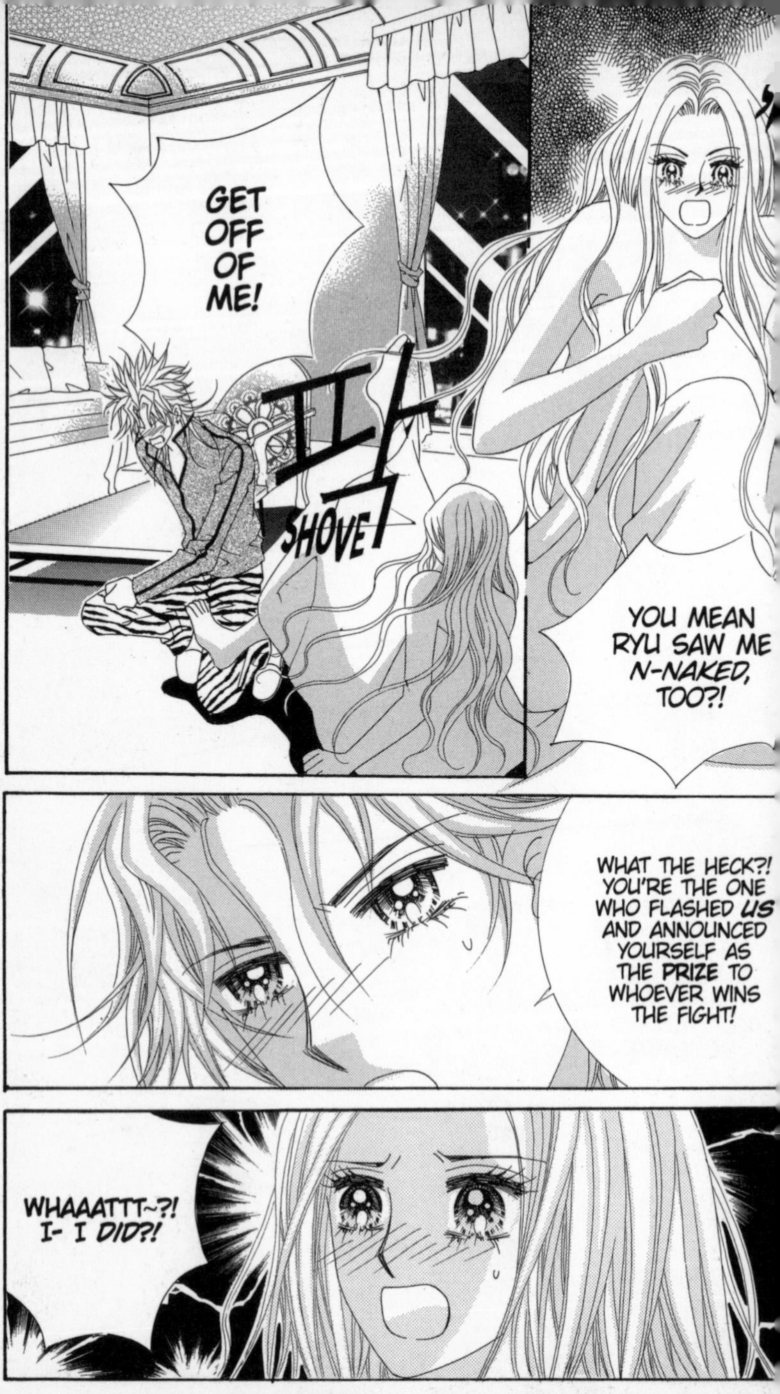
GET OFF OF ME!
SHOVE
YOU MEAN RYU SAW ME N-NAKED, TOO?!
WHAT THE HECK?! YOU'RE THE ONE WHO FLASHED US AND ANNOUNCED YOURSELF AS THE PRIZE TO WHOEVER WINS THE FIGHT!
WHAAATTT~?! I- I DID?!

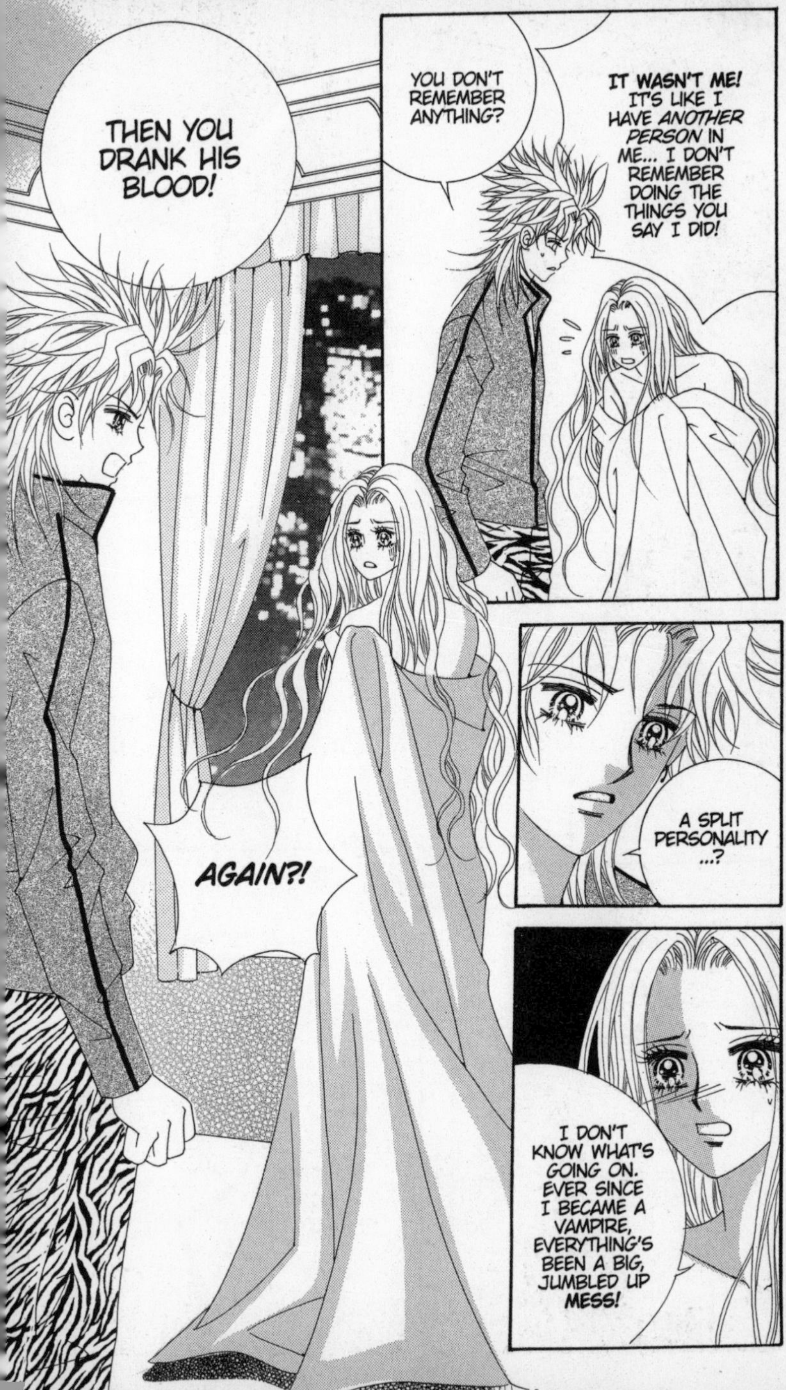
THEN YOU DRANK HIS BLOOD!
AGAIN?!
YOU DON'T REMEMBER ANYTHING?
IT WASN'T ME! IT'S LIKE I HAVE ANOTHER PERSON IN ME... I DON'T REMEMBER DOING THE THINGS YOU SAY I DID!
A SPLIT PERSONALITY ...?
I DON'T KNOW WHAT'S GOING ON. EVER SINCE I BECAME A VAMPIRE, EVERYTHING'S BEEN A BIG, JUMBLED UP MESS!

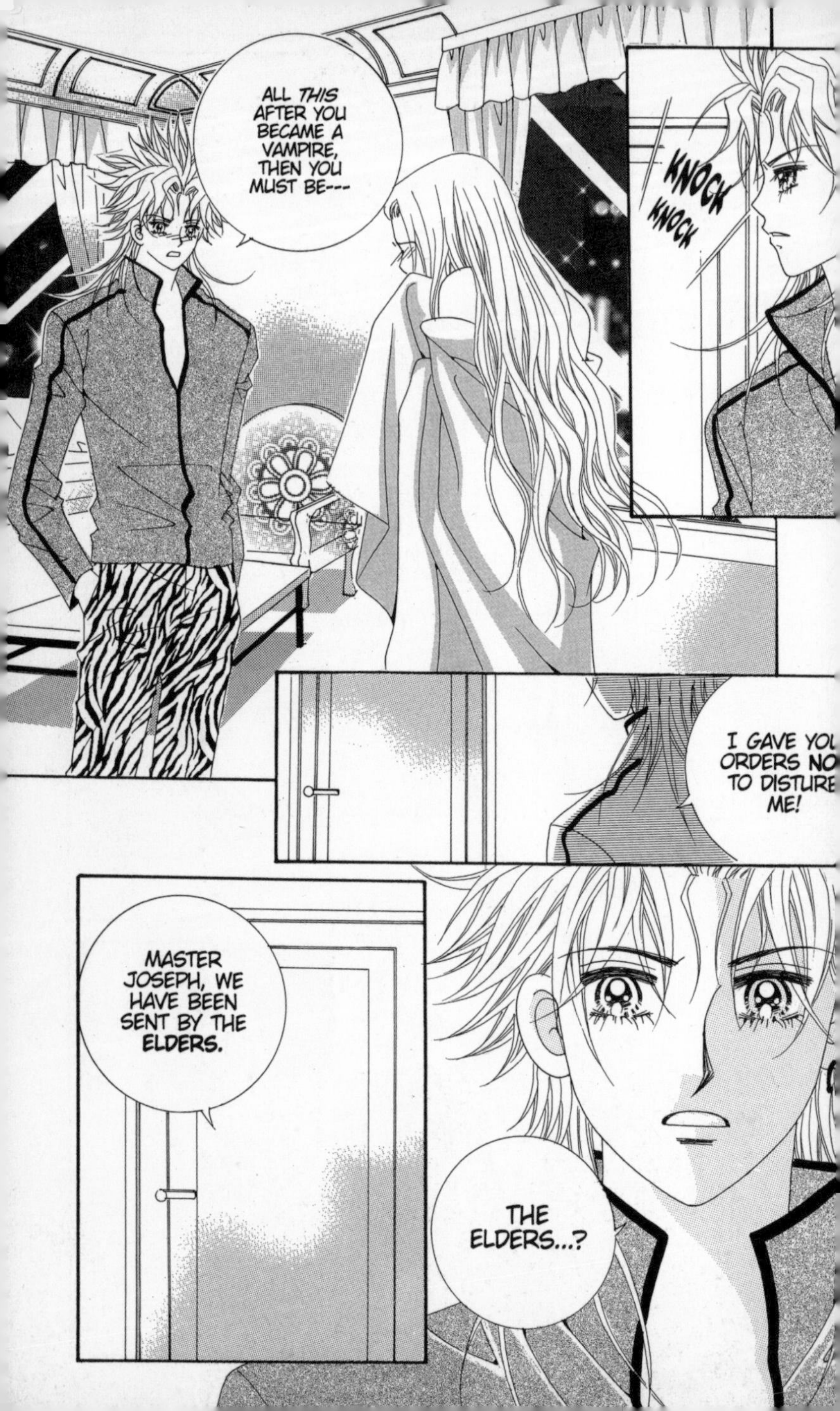
ALL THIS AFTER YOU BECAME A VAMPIRE, THEN YOU MUST BE---
KNOCK KNOCK
I GAVE YOU ORDERS NOT TO DISTURB ME!
MASTER JOSEPH, WE HAVE BEEN SENT BY THE ELDERS.
THE ELDERS...?

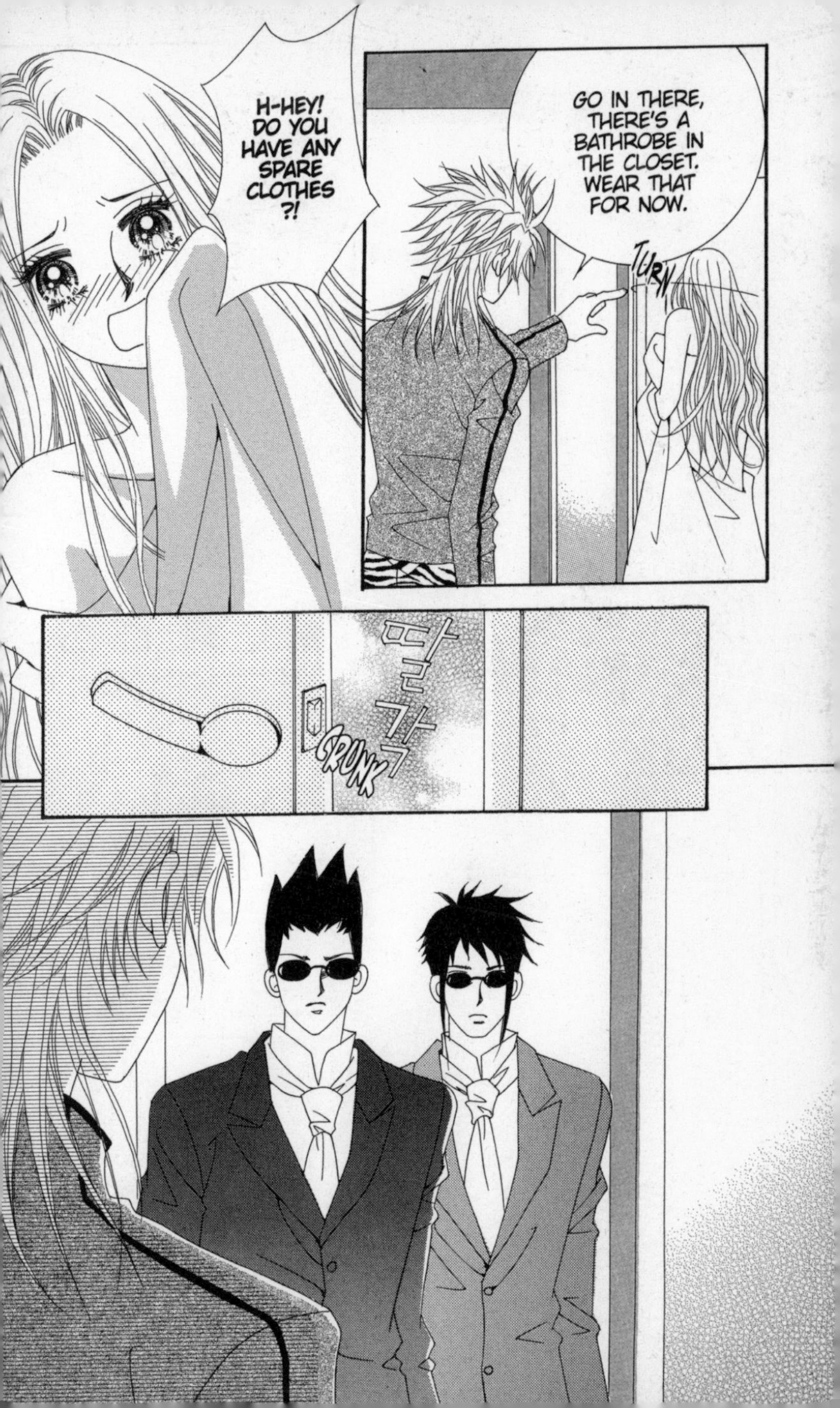

H-HEY! DO YOU HAVE ANY SPARE CLOTHES ?!
GO IN THERE, THERE'S A BATHROBE IN THE CLOSET. WEAR THAT FOR NOW.
TURN
CRUNK

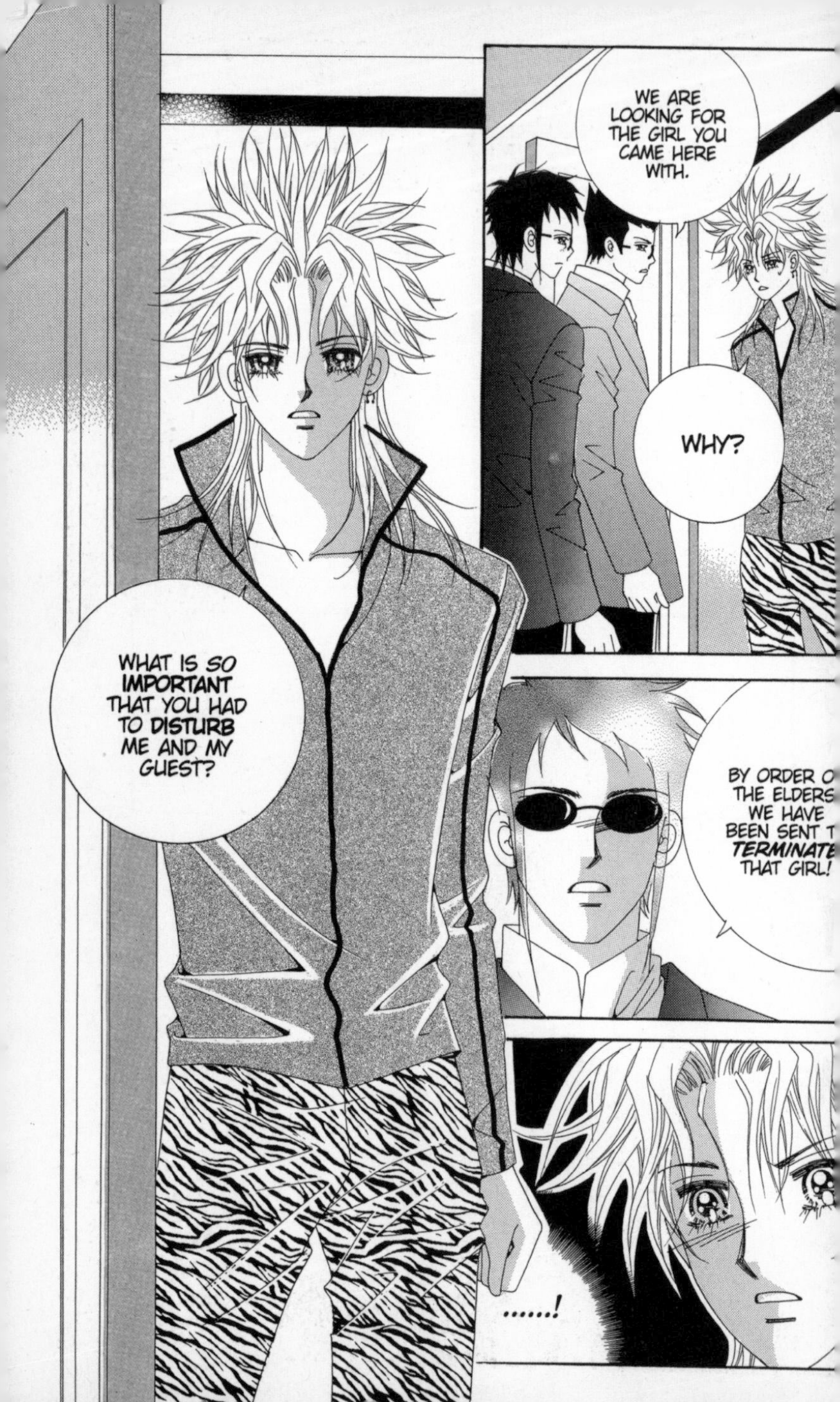
WHAT IS SO IMPORTANT THAT YOU HAD TO DISTURB ME AND MY GUEST?
WE ARE LOOKING FOR THE GIRL YOU CAME HERE WITH.
WHY?
BY ORDER O THE ELDERS WE HAVE BEEN SENT T TERMINATE THAT GIRL!
......!

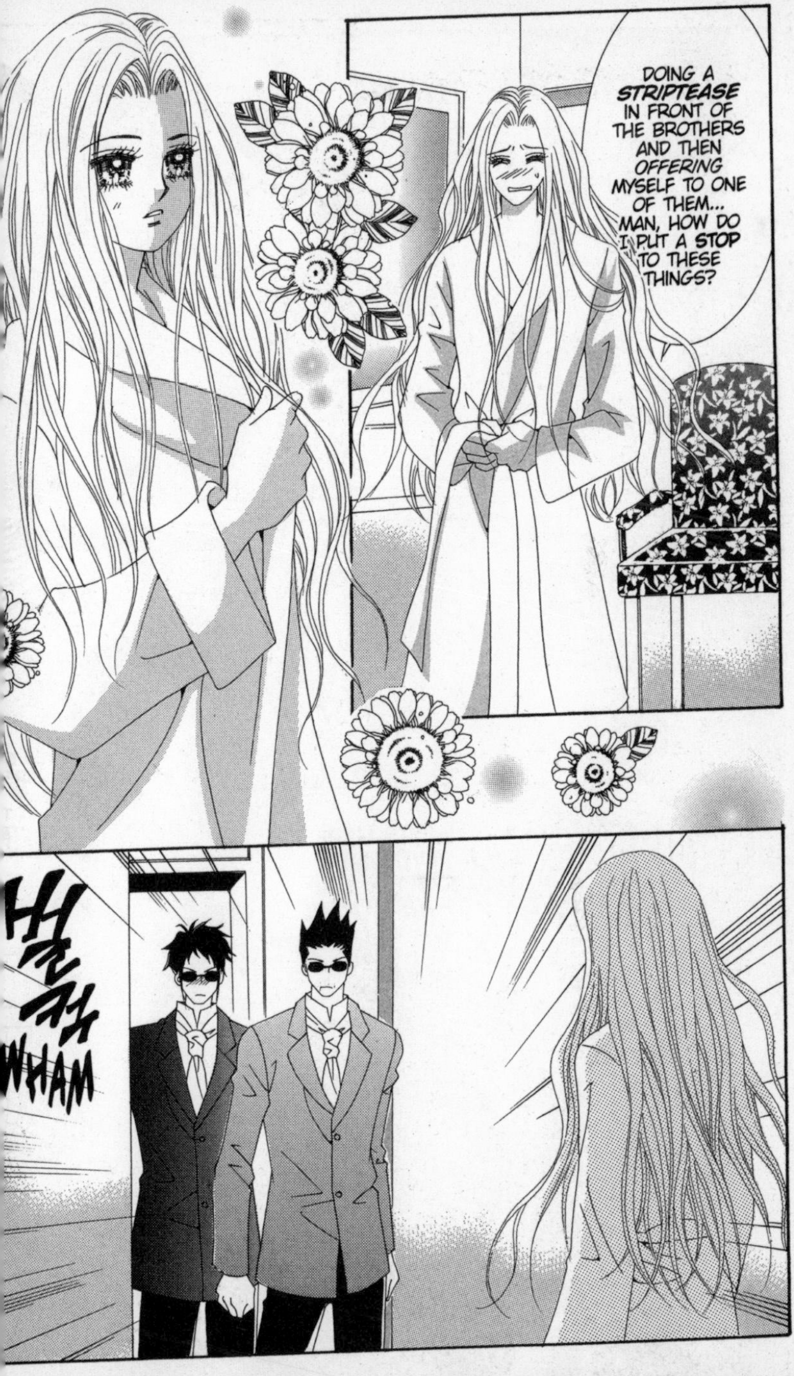
DOING A STRIPTEASE IN FRONT OF THE BROTHERS AND THEN OFFERING MYSELF TO ONE OF THEM... MAN, HOW DO I PUT A STOP TO THESE THINGS?
WHAM

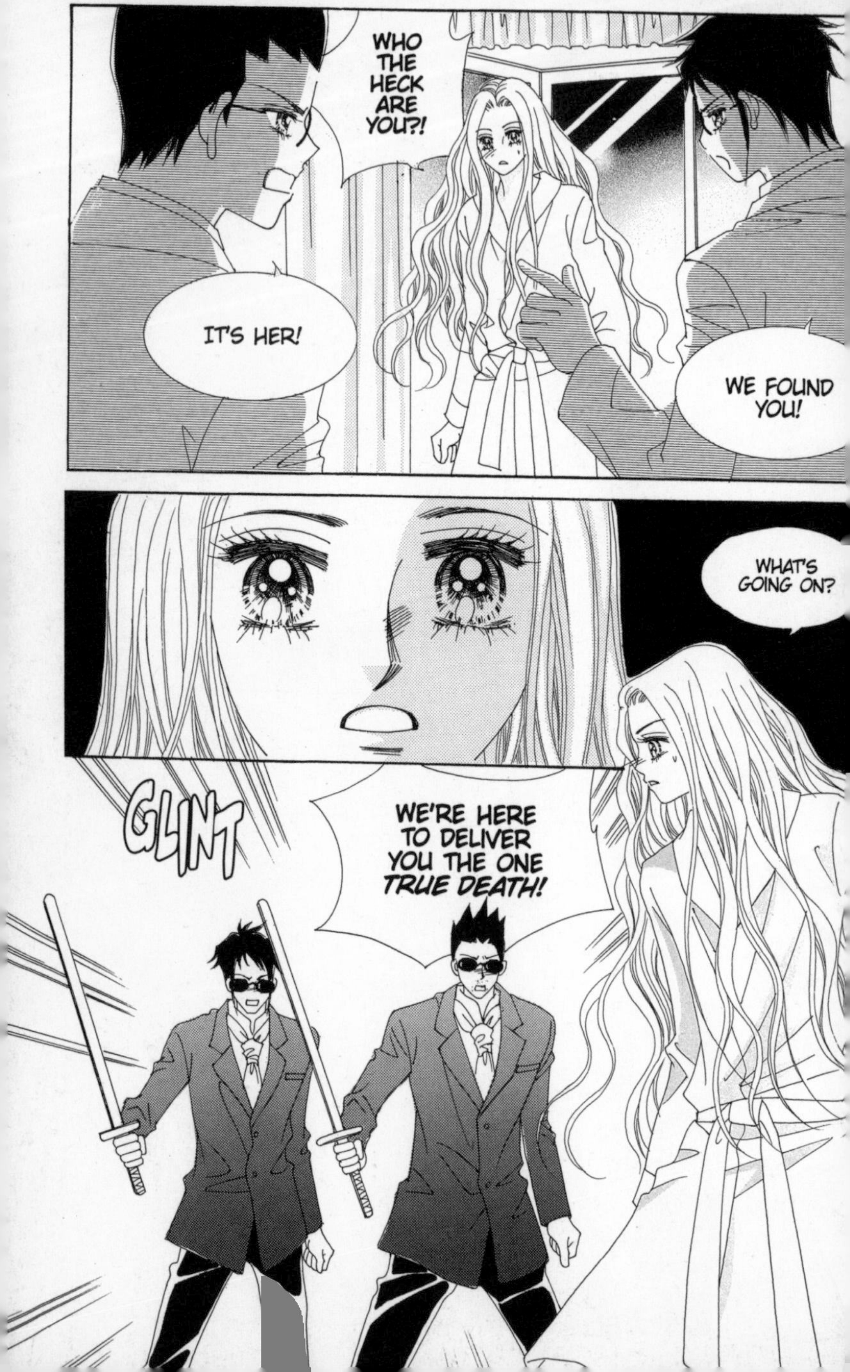
WHO THE HECK ARE YOU?!
IT'S HER!
WE FOUND YOU!
WHAT'S GOING ON?
GLINT
WE'RE HERE TO DELIVER YOU THE ONE TRUE DEATH!

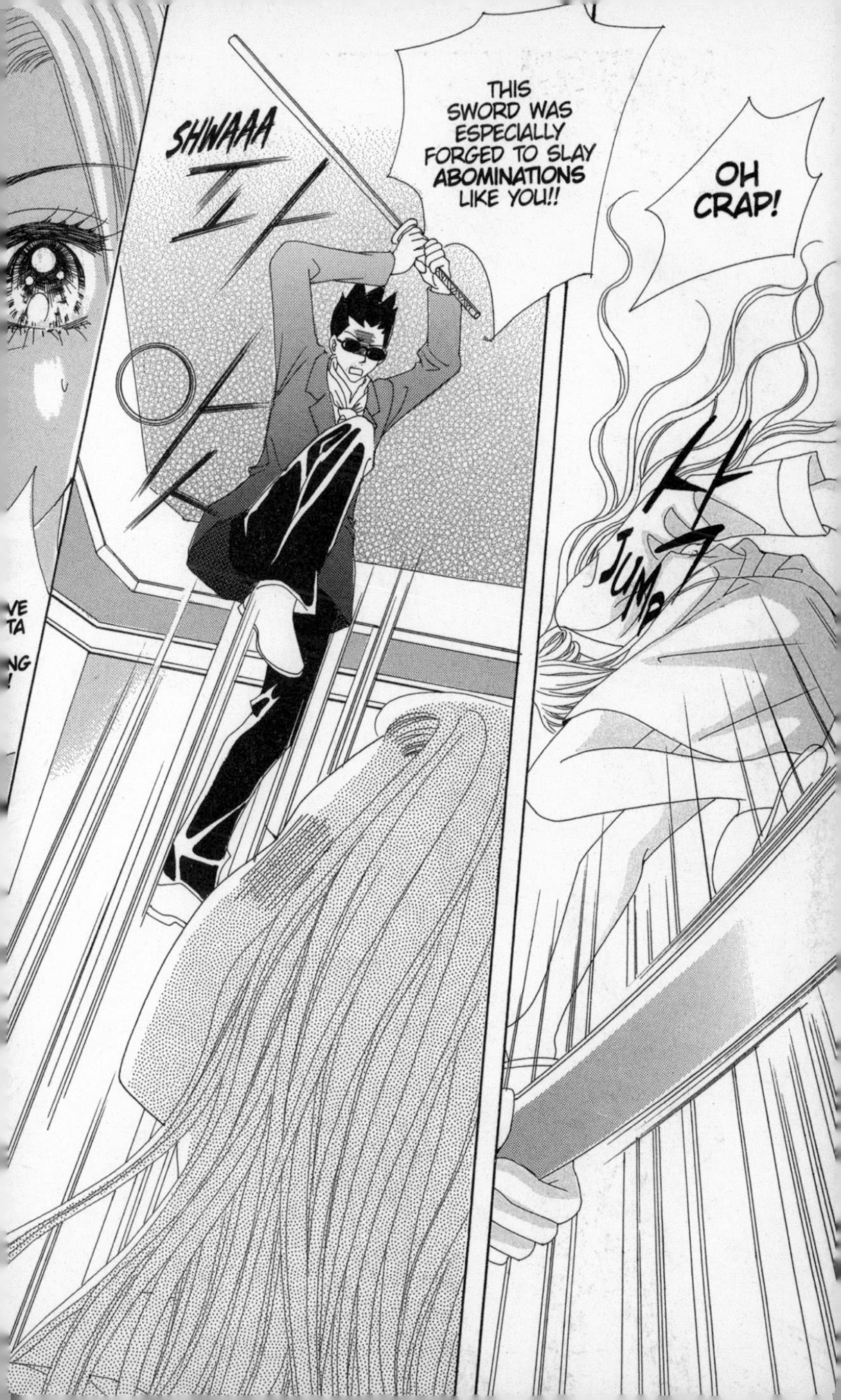
SHWAAA
THIS SWORD WAS ESPECIALLY FORGED TO SLAY ABOMINATIONS LIKE YOU!!
OH CRAP!
JUMP

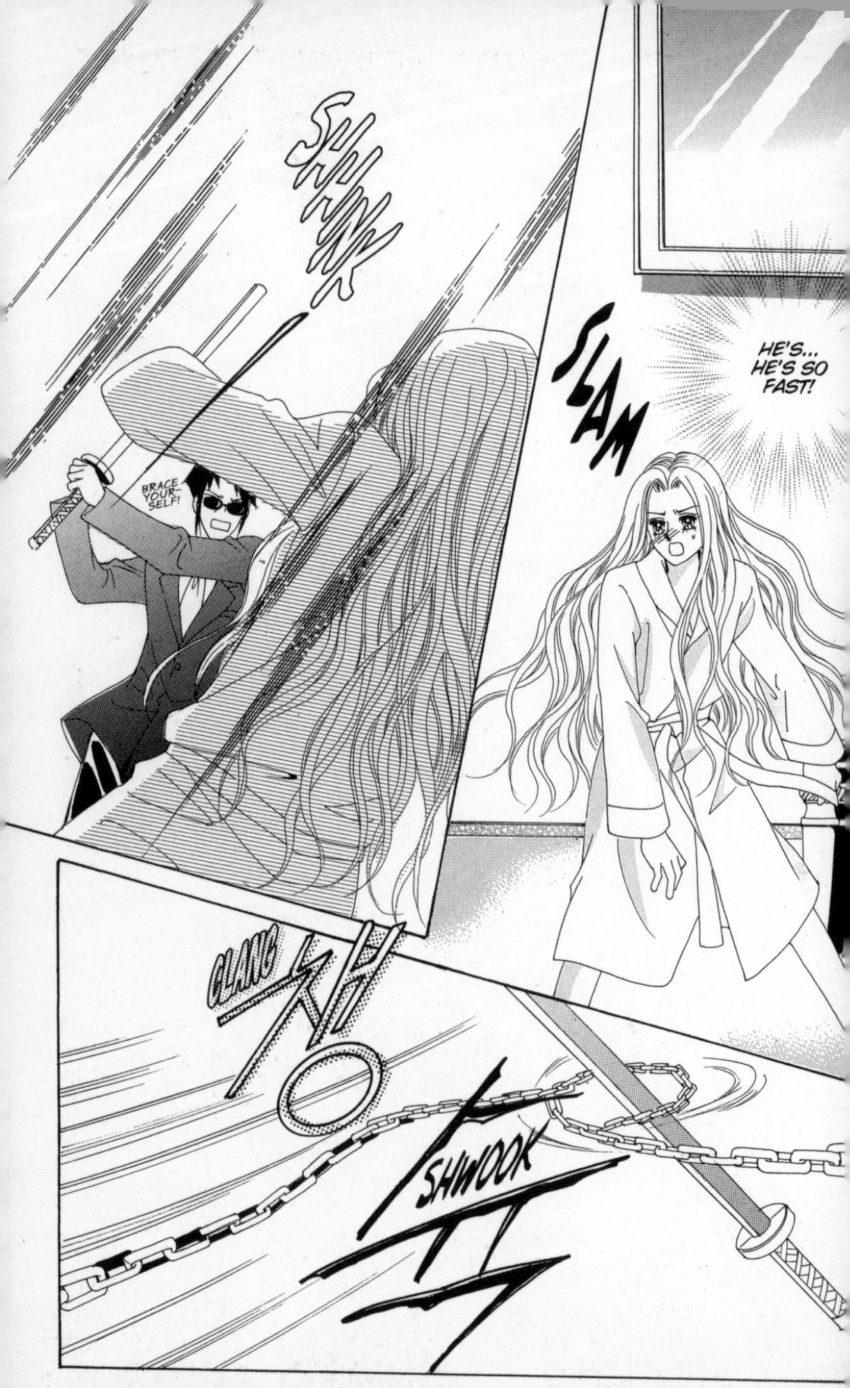
SHUNK
BRACE YOUR-SELF!
SLAM
HE'S... HE'S SO FAST!
CLANG
SHWOOK

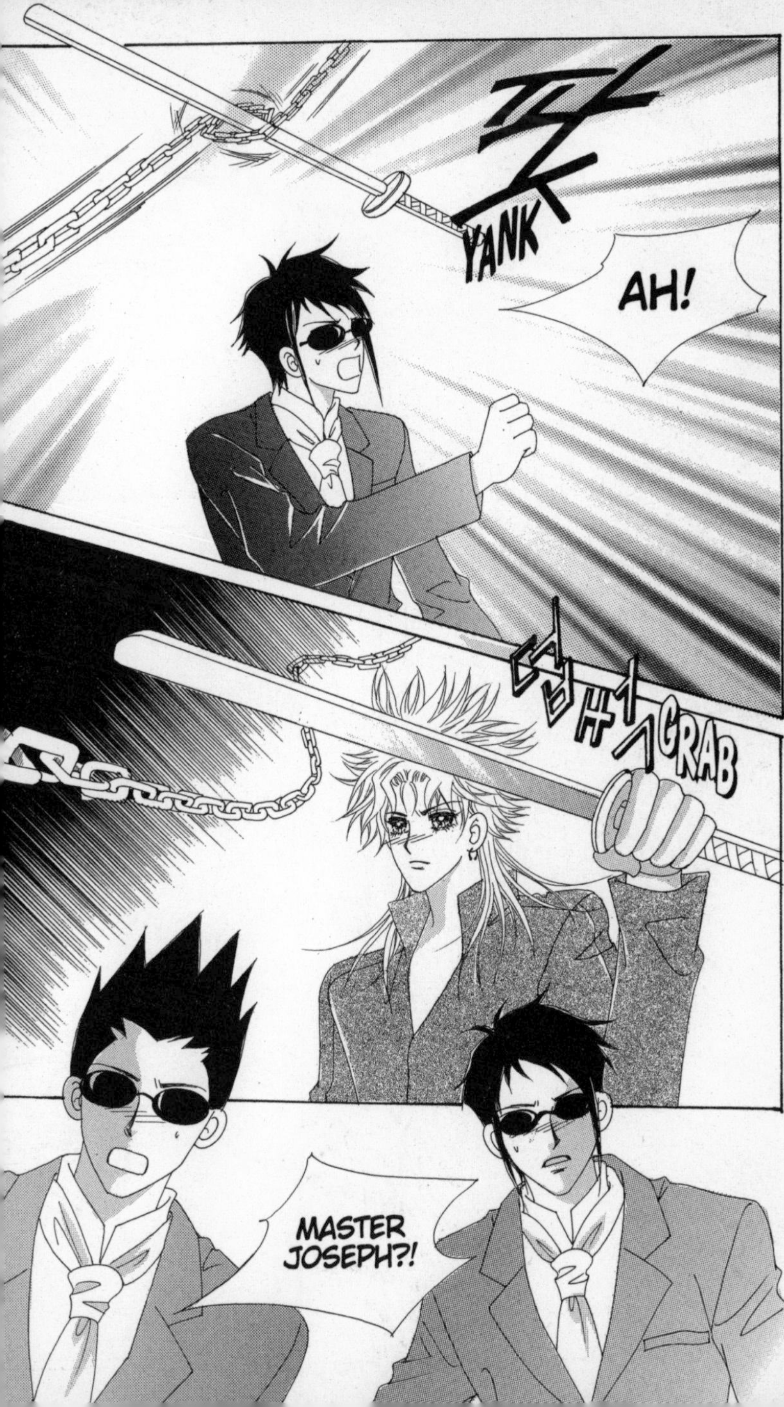
YANK
AH!
덥석
GRAB
MASTER JOSEPH?!

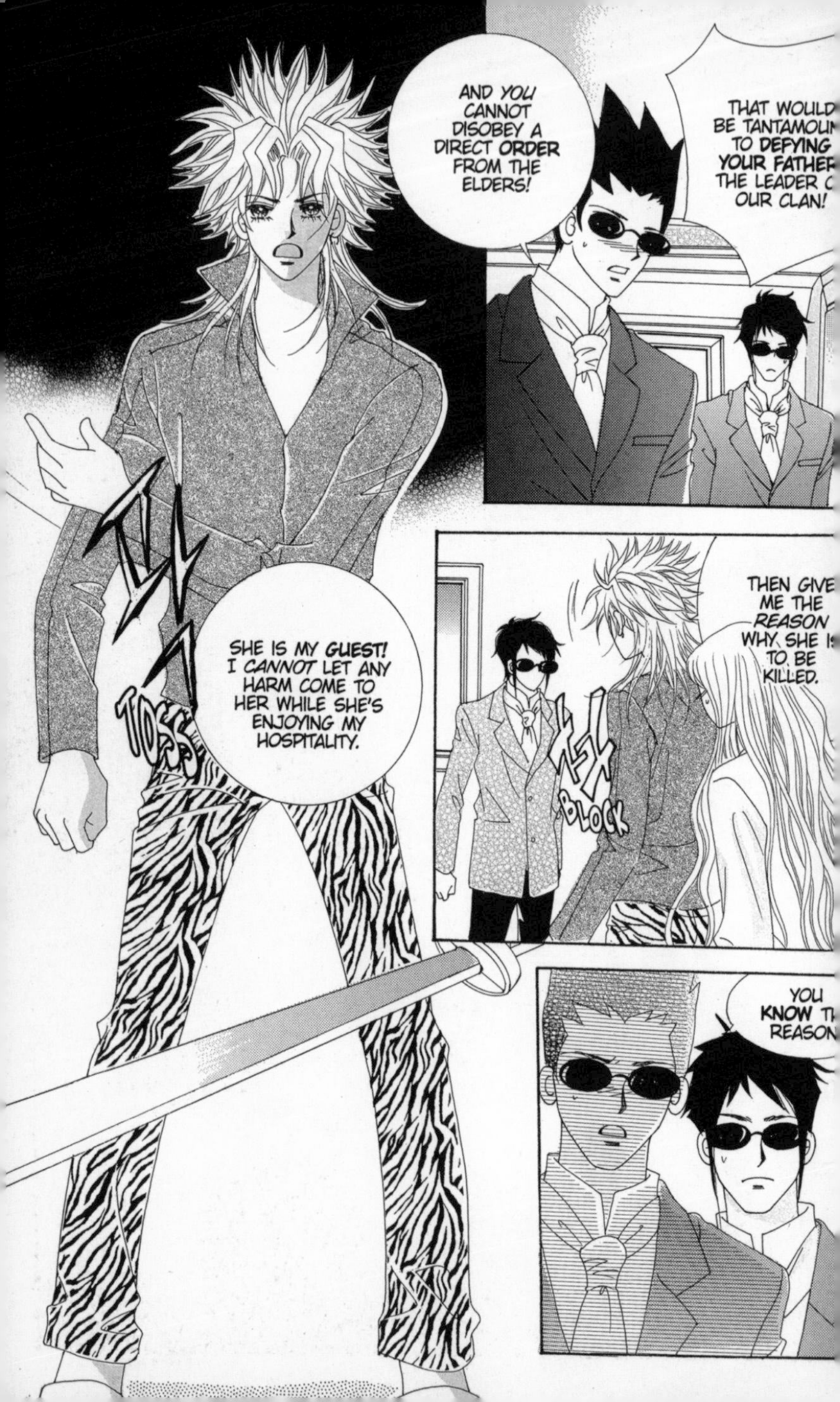
TOSS
SHE IS MY GUEST! I CANNOT LET ANY HARM COME TO HER WHILE SHE'S ENJOYING MY HOSPITALITY.
AND YOU CANNOT DISOBEY A DIRECT ORDER FROM THE ELDERS!
THAT WOULD BE TANTAMOUN TO DEFYING YOUR FATHER THE LEADER O OUR CLAN!
THEN GIVE ME THE REASON WHY SHE IS TO BE KILLED.
BLOCK
YOU KNOW TH REASON

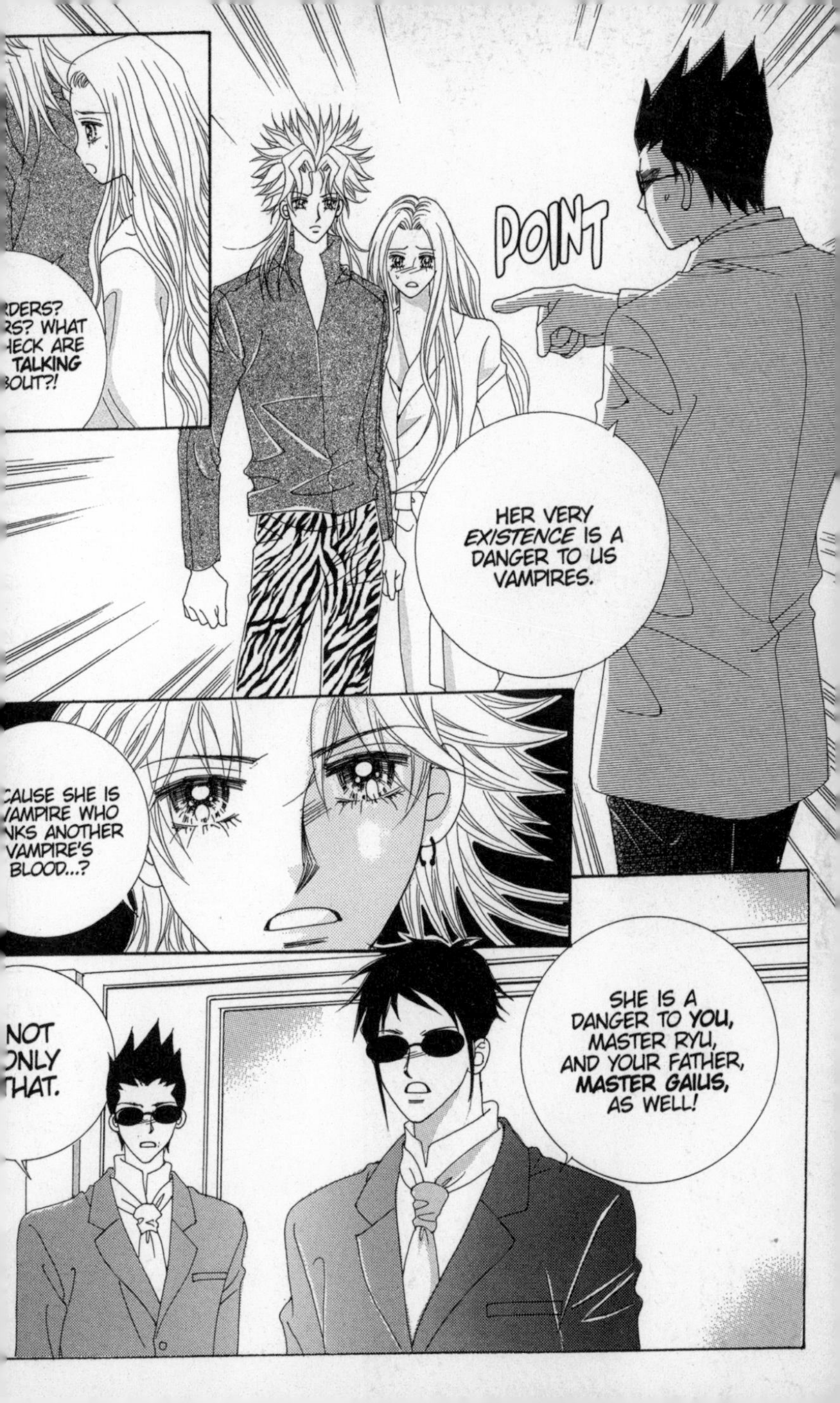

RDERS? RS? WHAT HECK ARE TALKING BOUT?!
POINT
HER VERY *EXISTENCE* IS A DANGER TO US VAMPIRES.
CAUSE SHE IS VAMPIRE WHO NKS ANOTHER VAMPIRE'S BLOOD...?
NOT ONLY THAT.
SHE IS A DANGER TO **YOU**, MASTER RYU, AND YOUR FATHER, **MASTER GAIUS**, AS WELL!

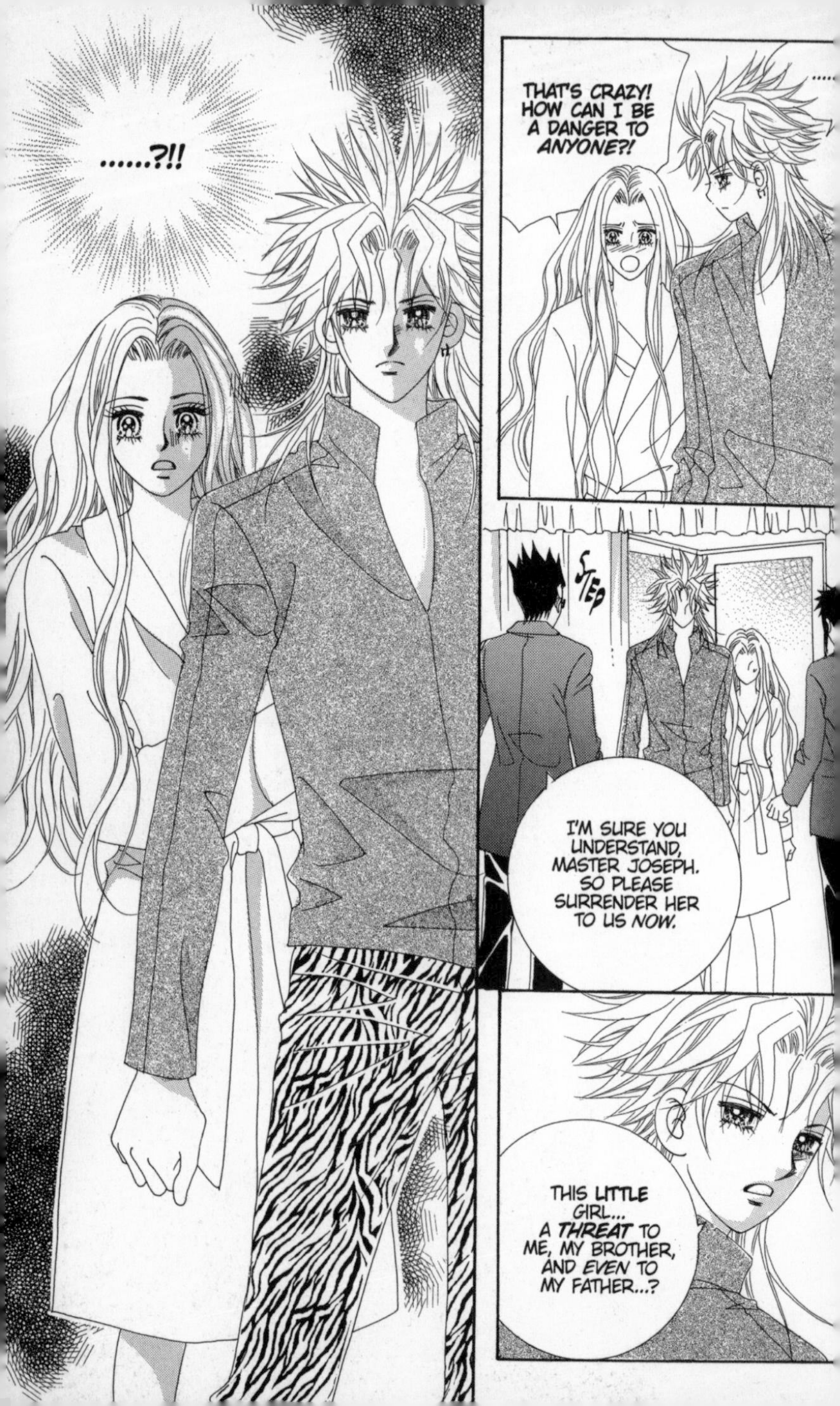
......?!!
THAT'S CRAZY! HOW CAN I BE A DANGER TO *ANYONE*?!
.....
STEP
I'M SURE YOU UNDERSTAND, MASTER JOSEPH. SO PLEASE SURRENDER HER TO US *NOW.*
THIS LITTLE GIRL... A *THREAT* TO ME, MY BROTHER, AND *EVEN* TO MY FATHER...?

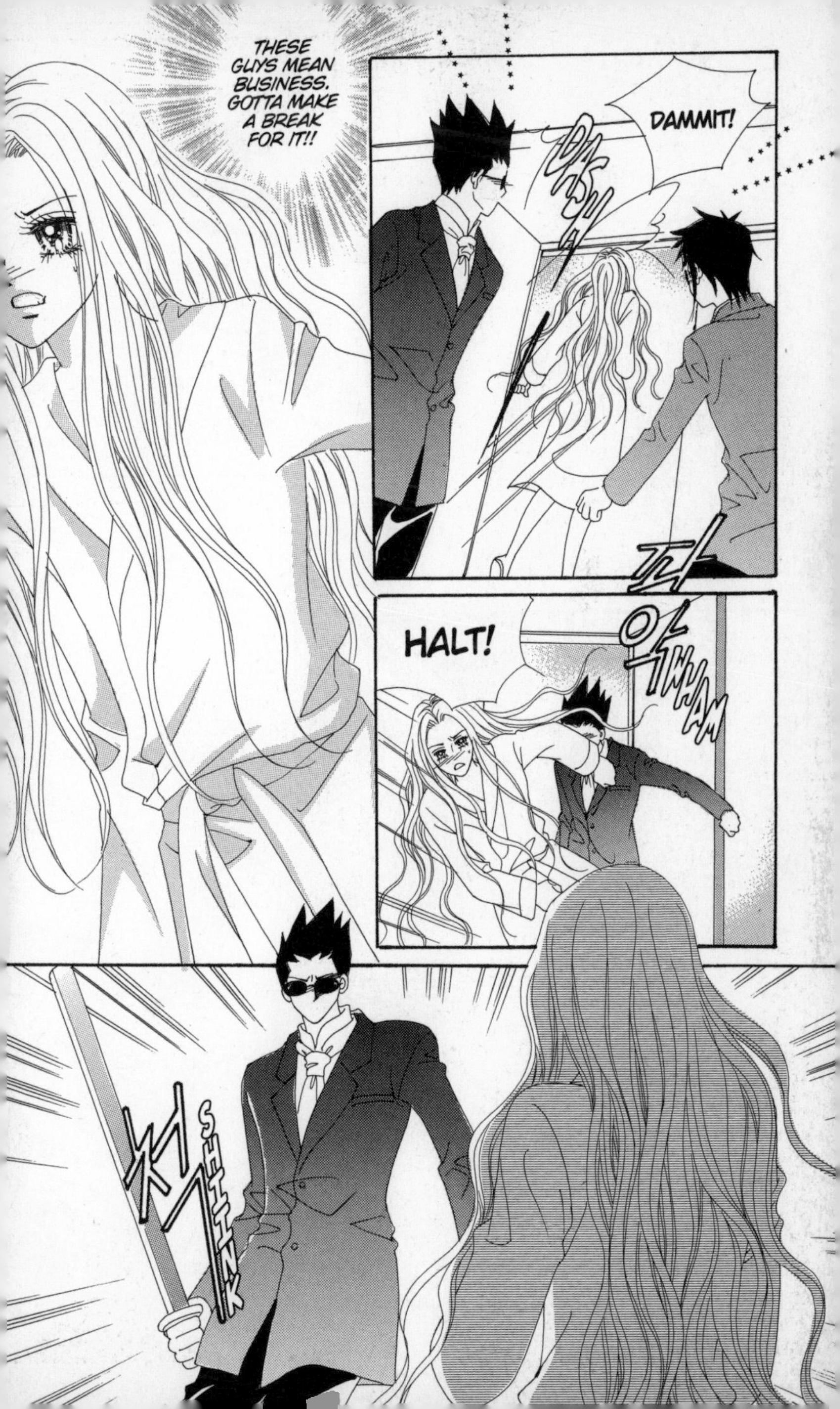
THESE GUYS MEAN BUSINESS. GOTTA MAKE A BREAK FOR IT!!
DAMMIT!
HALT!
WHAM
SHIIINK

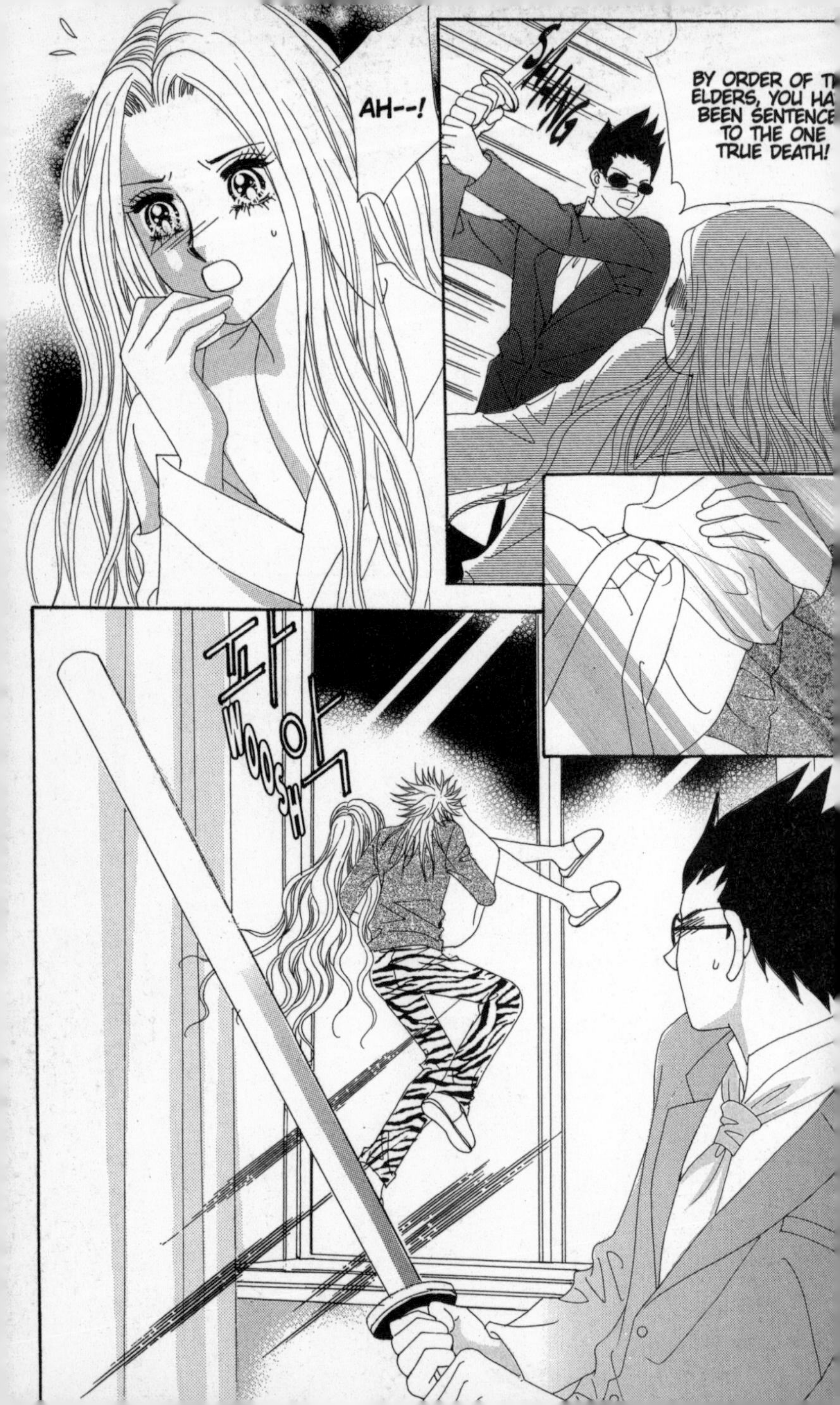
AH--!
SHING
BY ORDER OF T
ELDERS, YOU HA
BEEN SENTENCE
TO THE ONE
TRUE DEATH!
WOOSH

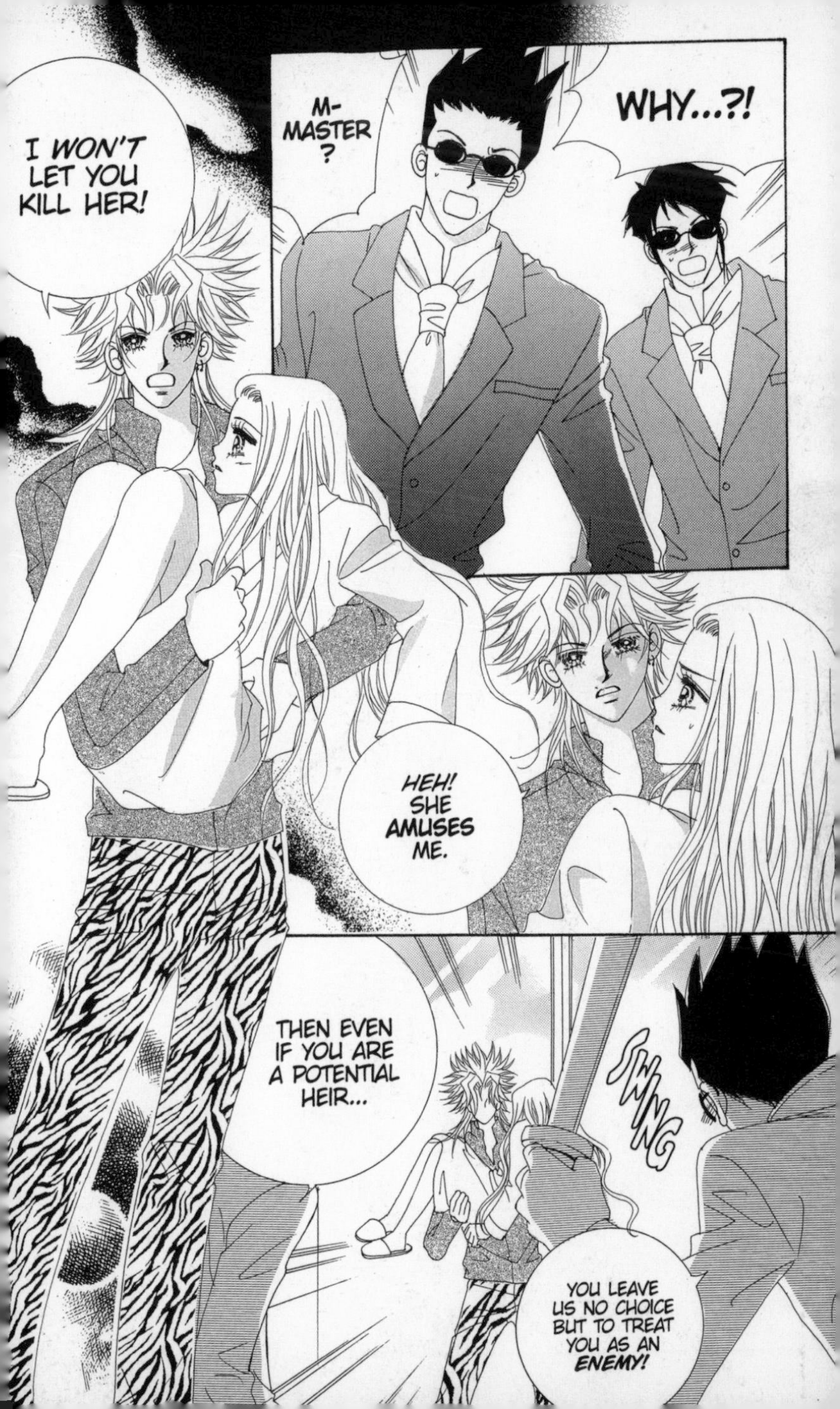

I WON'T LET YOU KILL HER!
M-MASTER?
WHY...?!
HEH! SHE AMUSES ME.
THEN EVEN IF YOU ARE A POTENTIAL HEIR...
SWING
YOU LEAVE US NO CHOICE BUT TO TREAT YOU AS AN ENEMY!

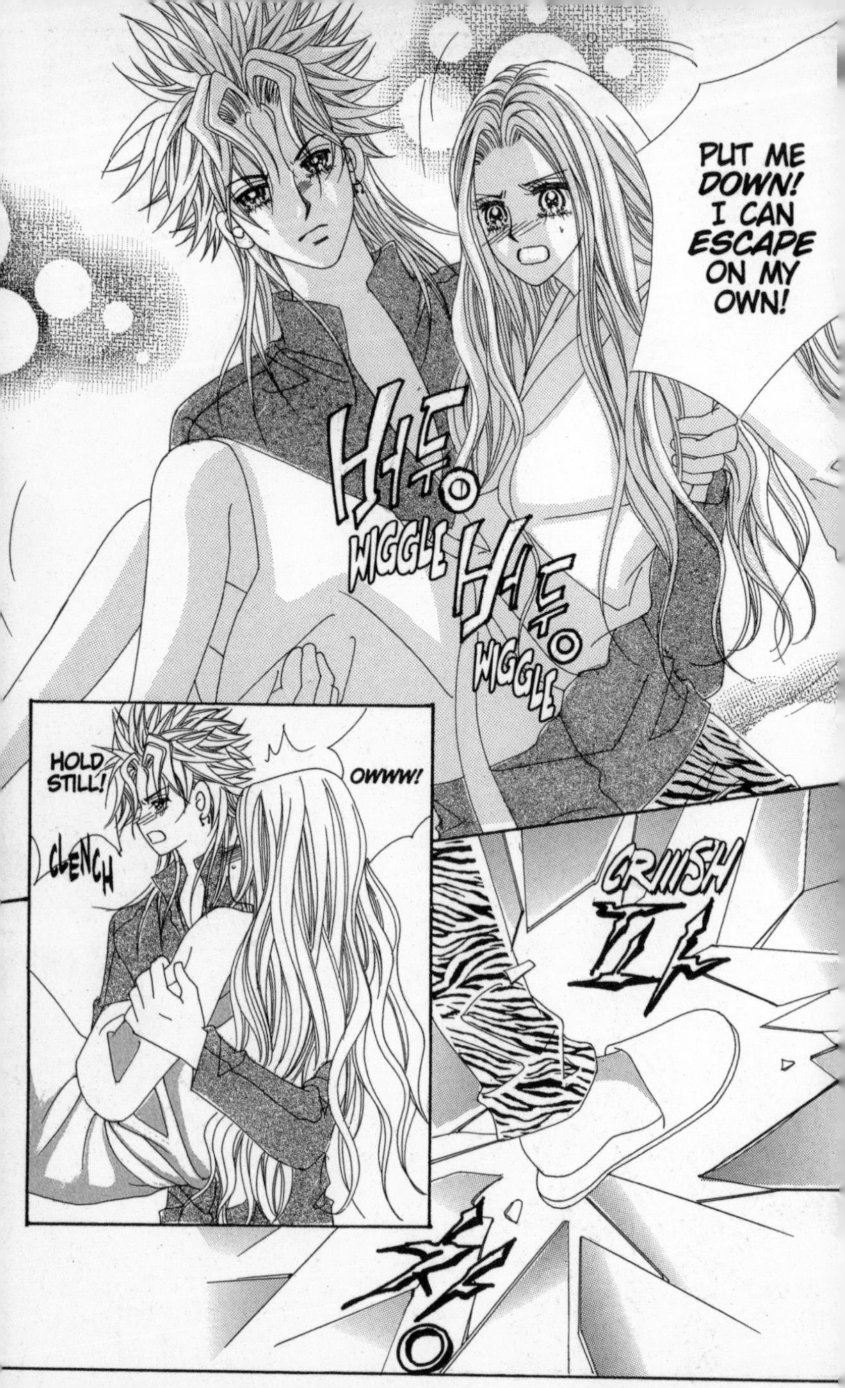
PUT ME DOWN! I CAN ESCAPE ON MY OWN!
WIGGLE
WIGGLE
HOLD STILL!
OWWW!
CLENCH
CRIIISH

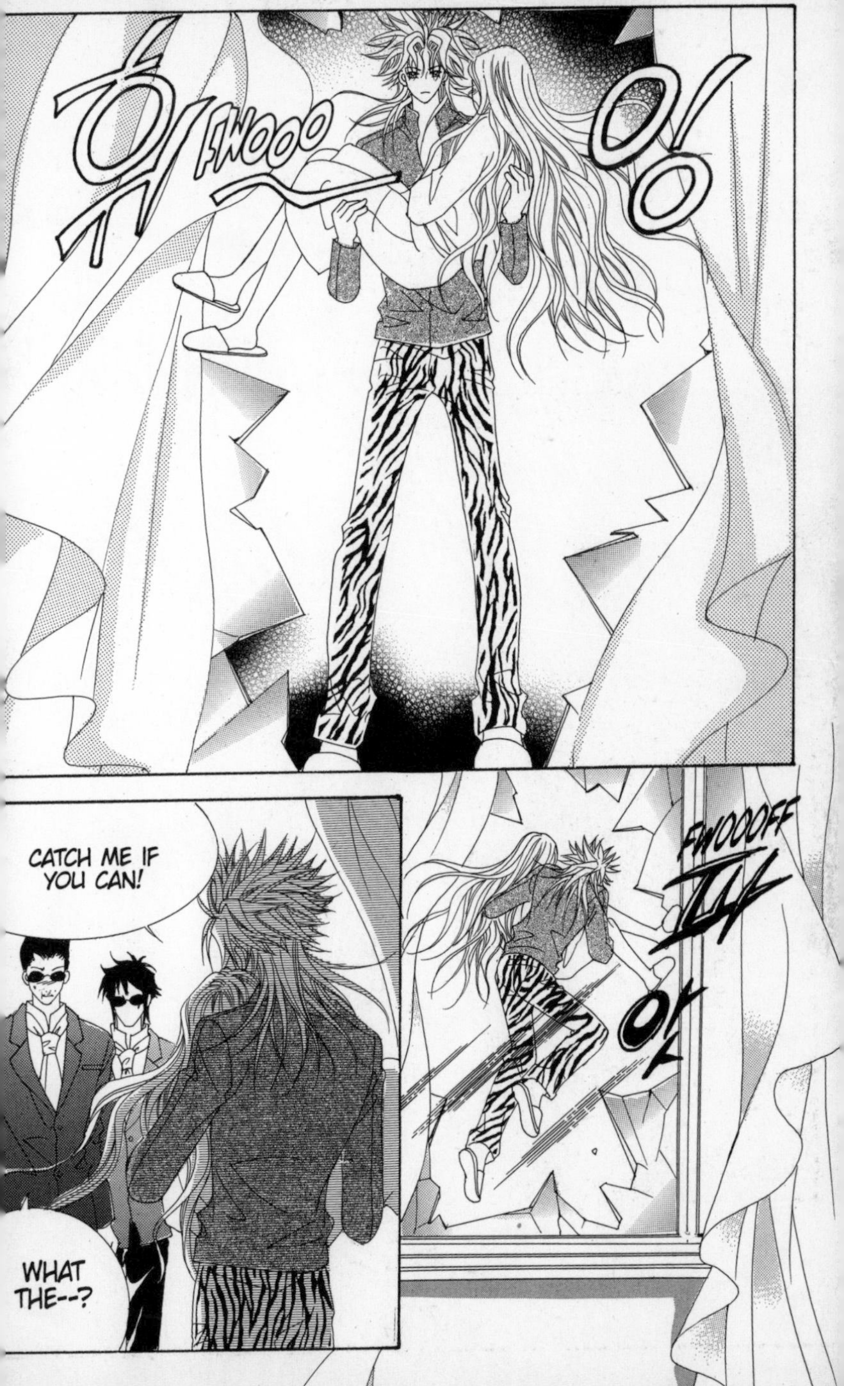
FWOOO
CATCH ME IF YOU CAN!
WHAT THE--?
FWOOOFF

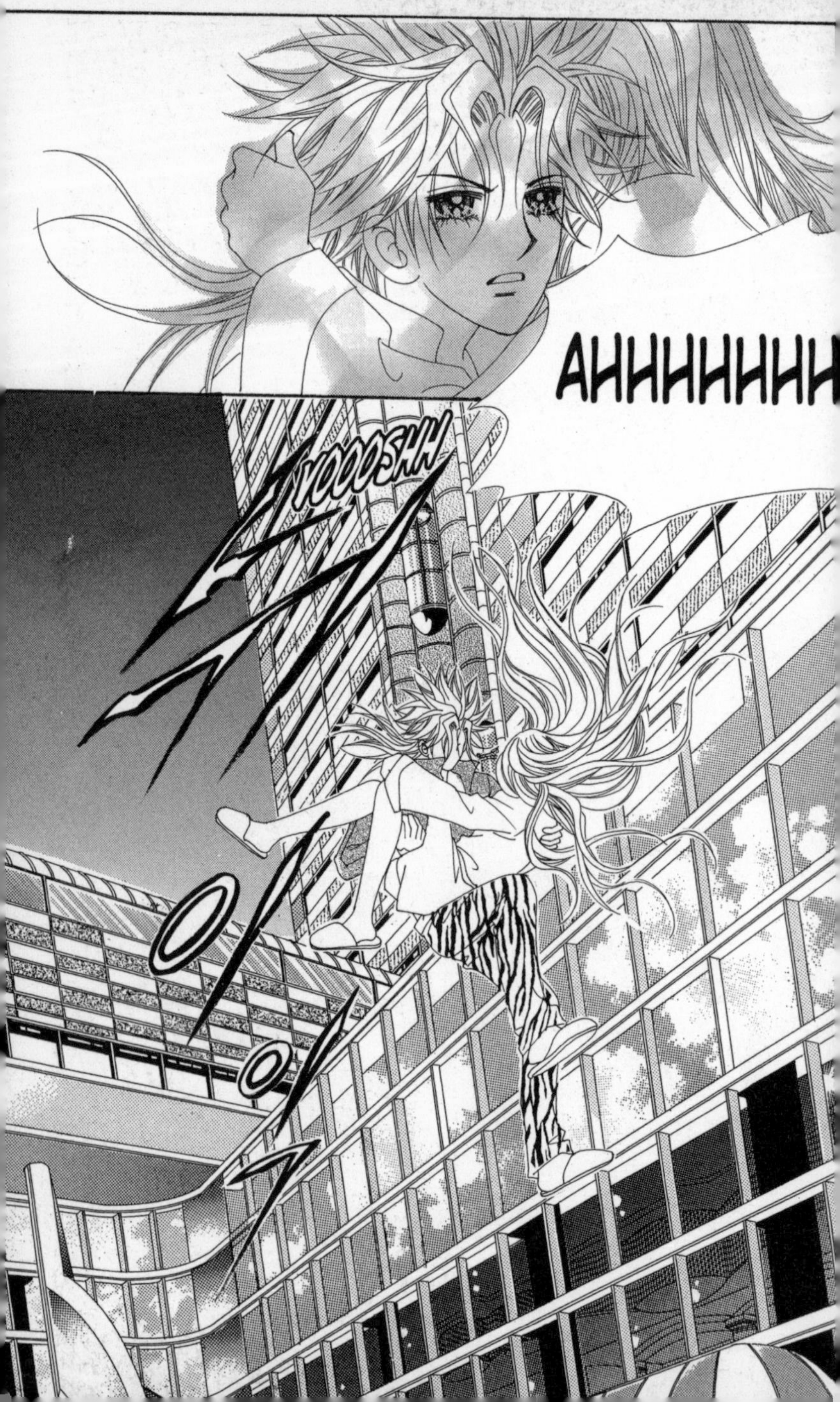
AHHHHHHH
VOOOOSHH

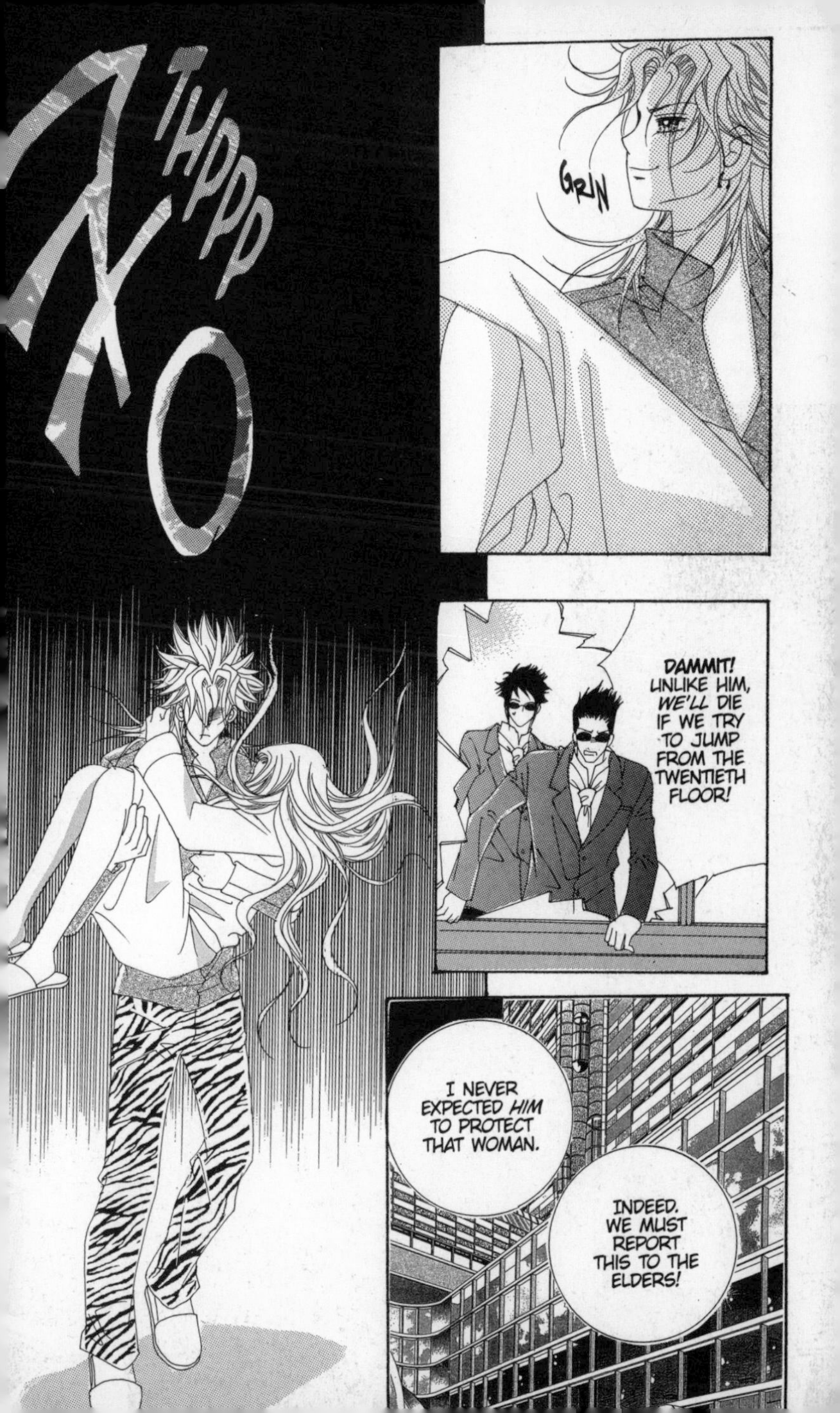
THPPP
GRIN
DAMMIT! UNLIKE HIM, *WE'LL* DIE IF WE TRY TO JUMP FROM THE TWENTIETH FLOOR!
I NEVER EXPECTED *HIM* TO PROTECT THAT WOMAN.
INDEED. WE MUST REPORT THIS TO THE ELDERS!

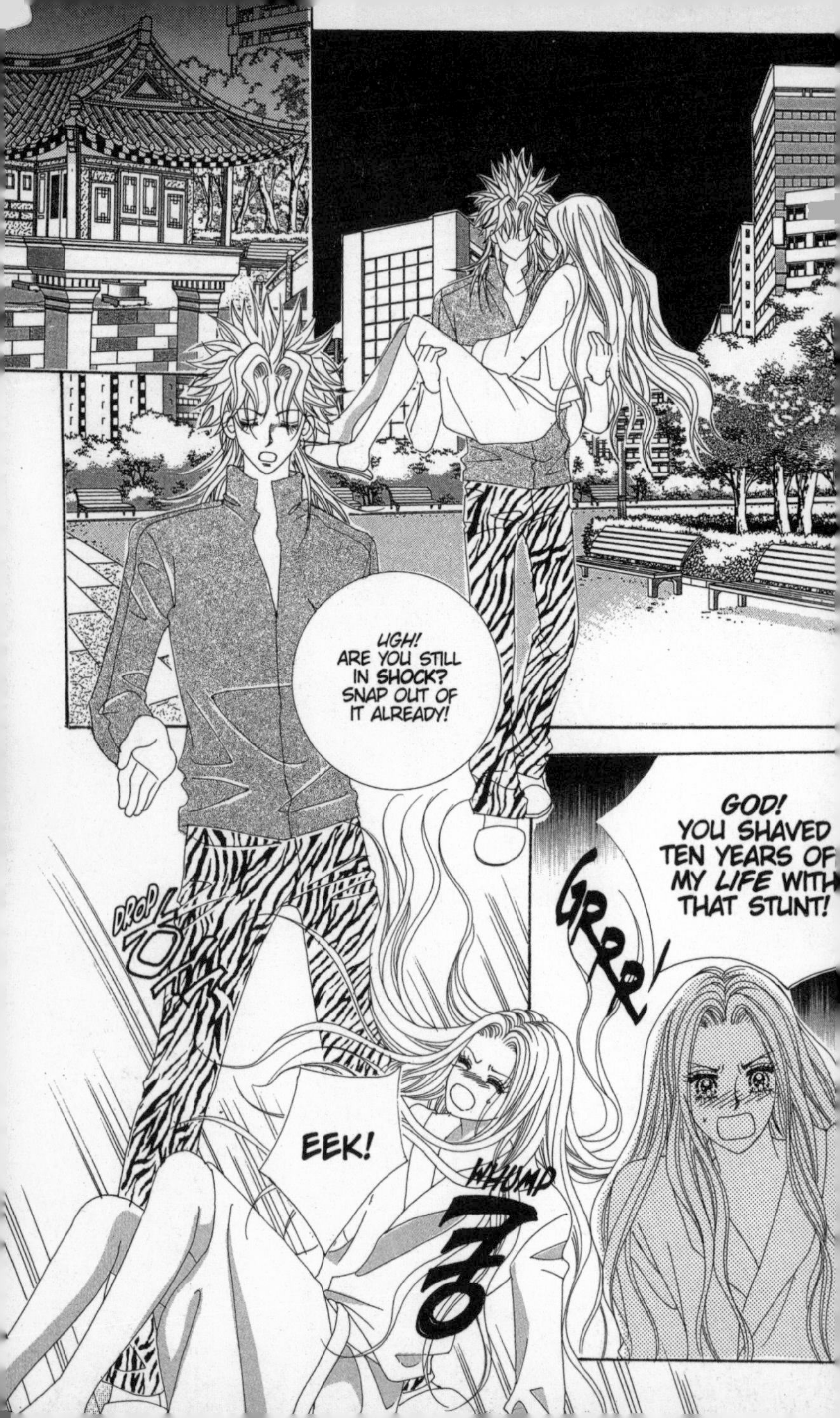
UGH! ARE YOU STILL IN SHOCK? SNAP OUT OF IT ALREADY!
DROP
EEK!
WHUMP
GRRR!
GOD! YOU SHAVED TEN YEARS OF MY LIFE WITH THAT STUNT!

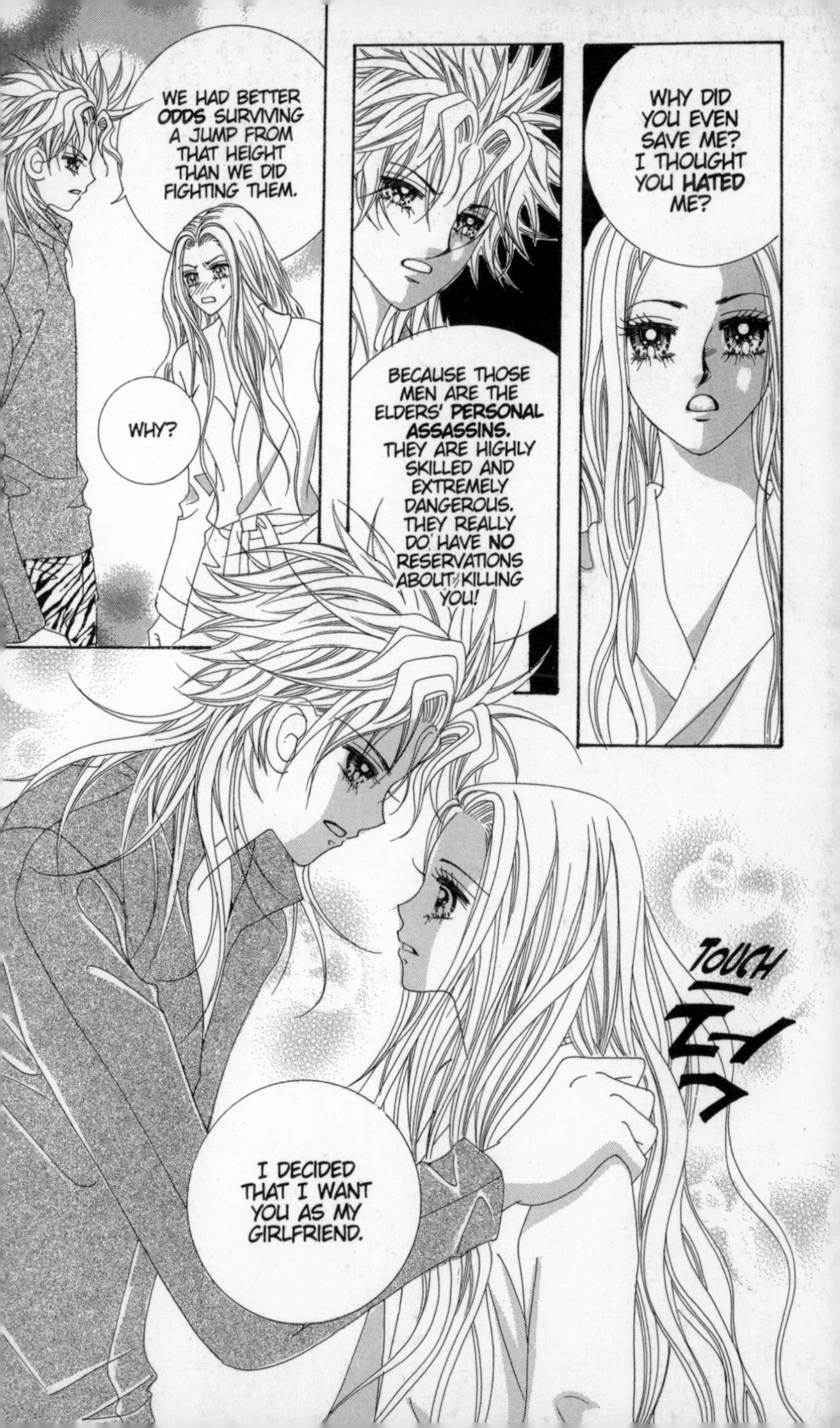
WE HAD BETTER ODDS SURVIVING A JUMP FROM THAT HEIGHT THAN WE DID FIGHTING THEM.
WHY?
BECAUSE THOSE MEN ARE THE ELDERS' PERSONAL ASSASSINS. THEY ARE HIGHLY SKILLED AND EXTREMELY DANGEROUS. THEY REALLY DO HAVE NO RESERVATIONS ABOUT KILLING YOU!
WHY DID YOU EVEN SAVE ME? I THOUGHT YOU HATED ME?
TOUCH
I DECIDED THAT I WANT YOU AS MY GIRLFRIEND.

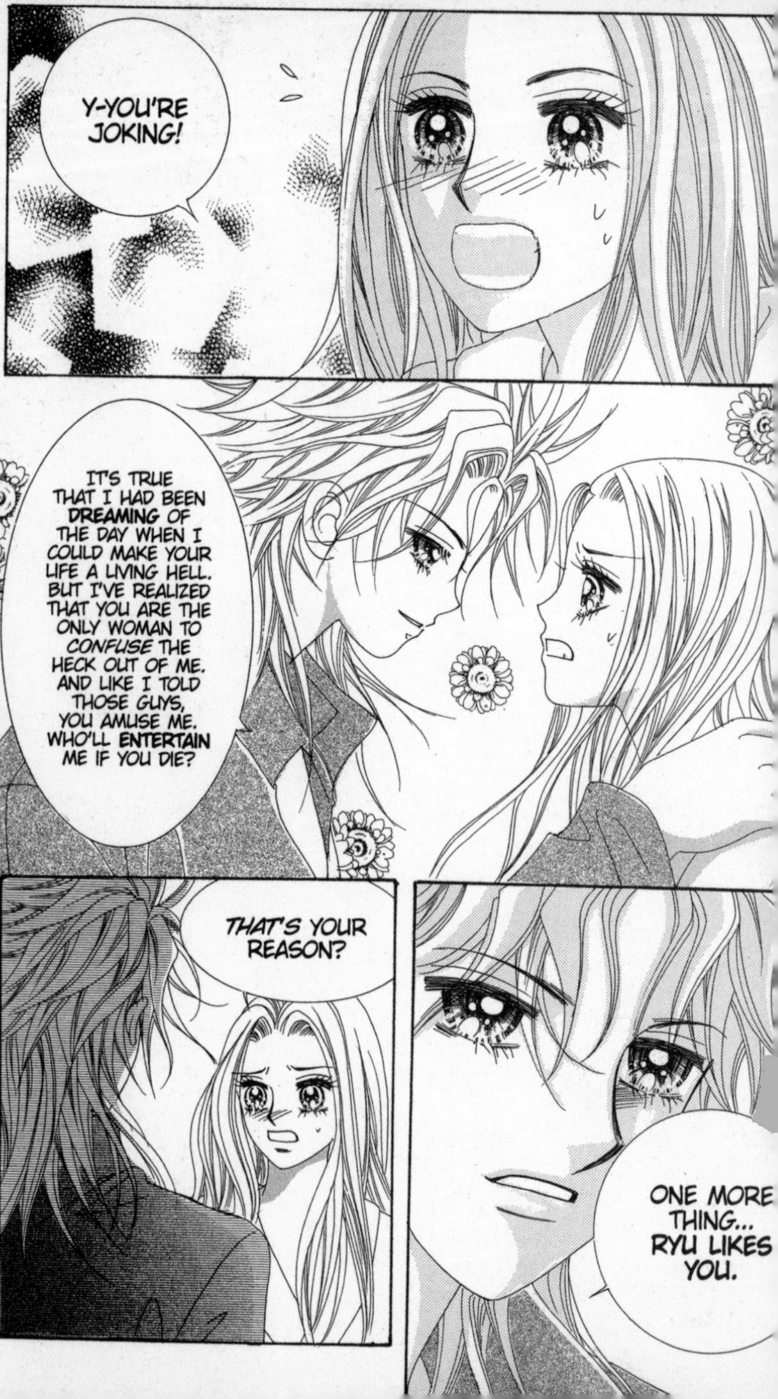
Y-YOU'RE JOKING!
IT'S TRUE THAT I HAD BEEN DREAMING OF THE DAY WHEN I COULD MAKE YOUR LIFE A LIVING HELL. BUT I'VE REALIZED THAT YOU ARE THE ONLY WOMAN TO CONFUSE THE HECK OUT OF ME. AND LIKE I TOLD THOSE GUYS, YOU AMUSE ME. WHO'LL ENTERTAIN ME IF YOU DIE?
THAT'S YOUR REASON?
ONE MORE THING... RYU LIKES YOU.

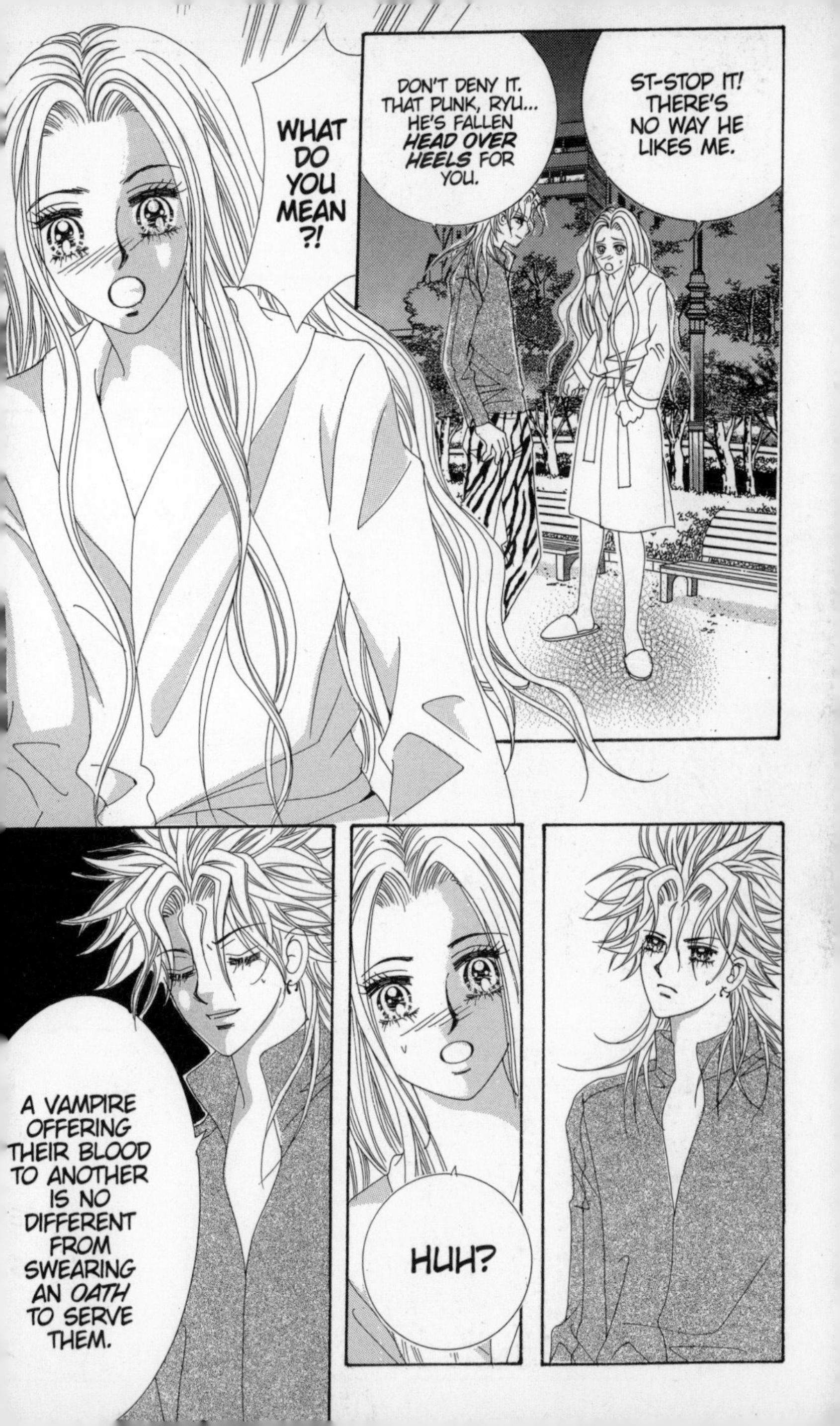
WHAT DO YOU MEAN ?!
DON'T DENY IT. THAT PUNK, RYU... HE'S FALLEN *HEAD OVER HEELS* FOR YOU.
ST-STOP IT! THERE'S NO WAY HE LIKES ME.
A VAMPIRE OFFERING THEIR BLOOD TO ANOTHER IS NO DIFFERENT FROM SWEARING AN *OATH* TO SERVE THEM.
HUH?

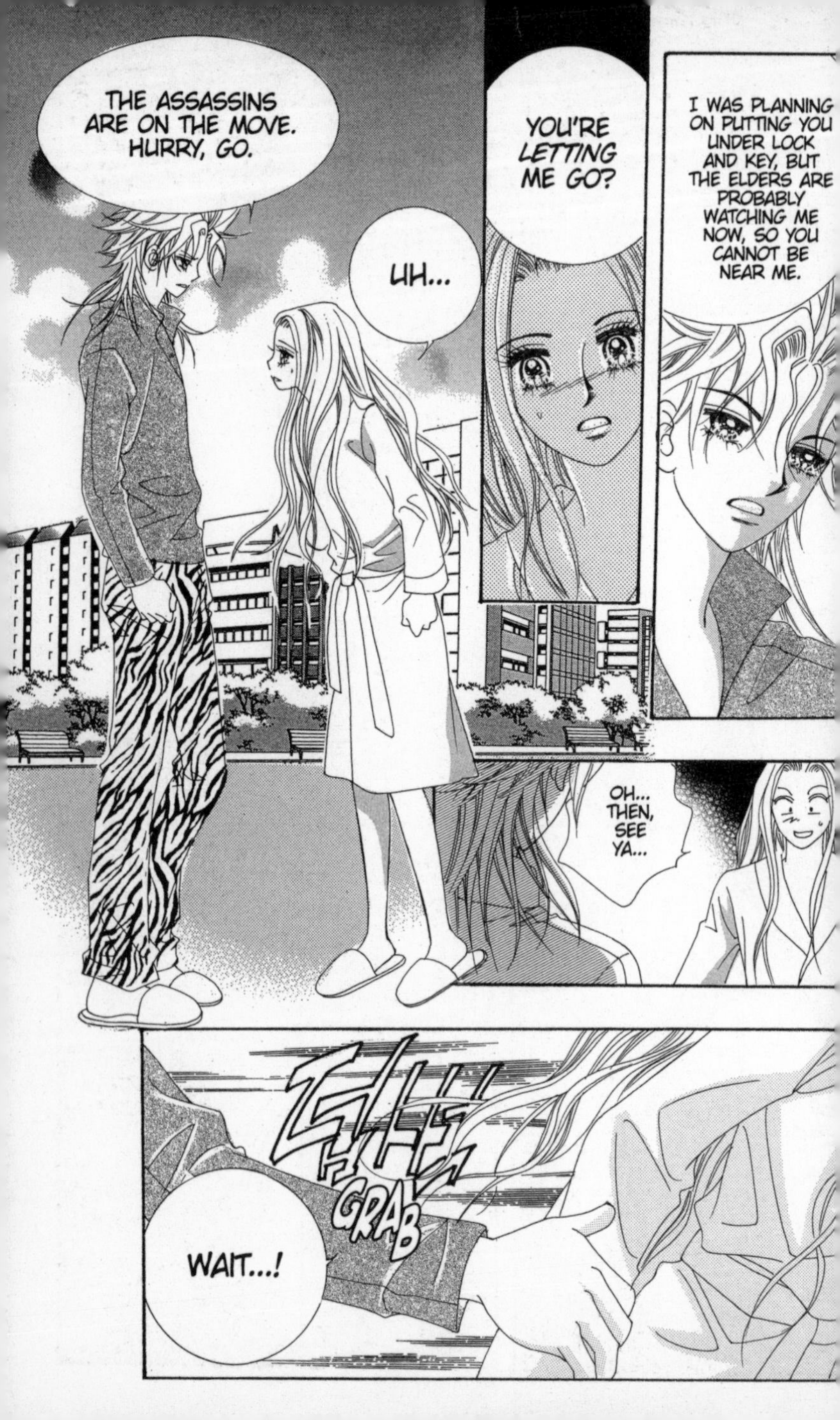
THE ASSASSINS ARE ON THE MOVE. HURRY, GO.
UH...
YOU'RE LETTING ME GO?
I WAS PLANNING ON PUTTING YOU UNDER LOCK AND KEY, BUT THE ELDERS ARE PROBABLY WATCHING ME NOW, SO YOU CANNOT BE NEAR ME.
OH... THEN, SEE YA...
GRAB
WAIT...!

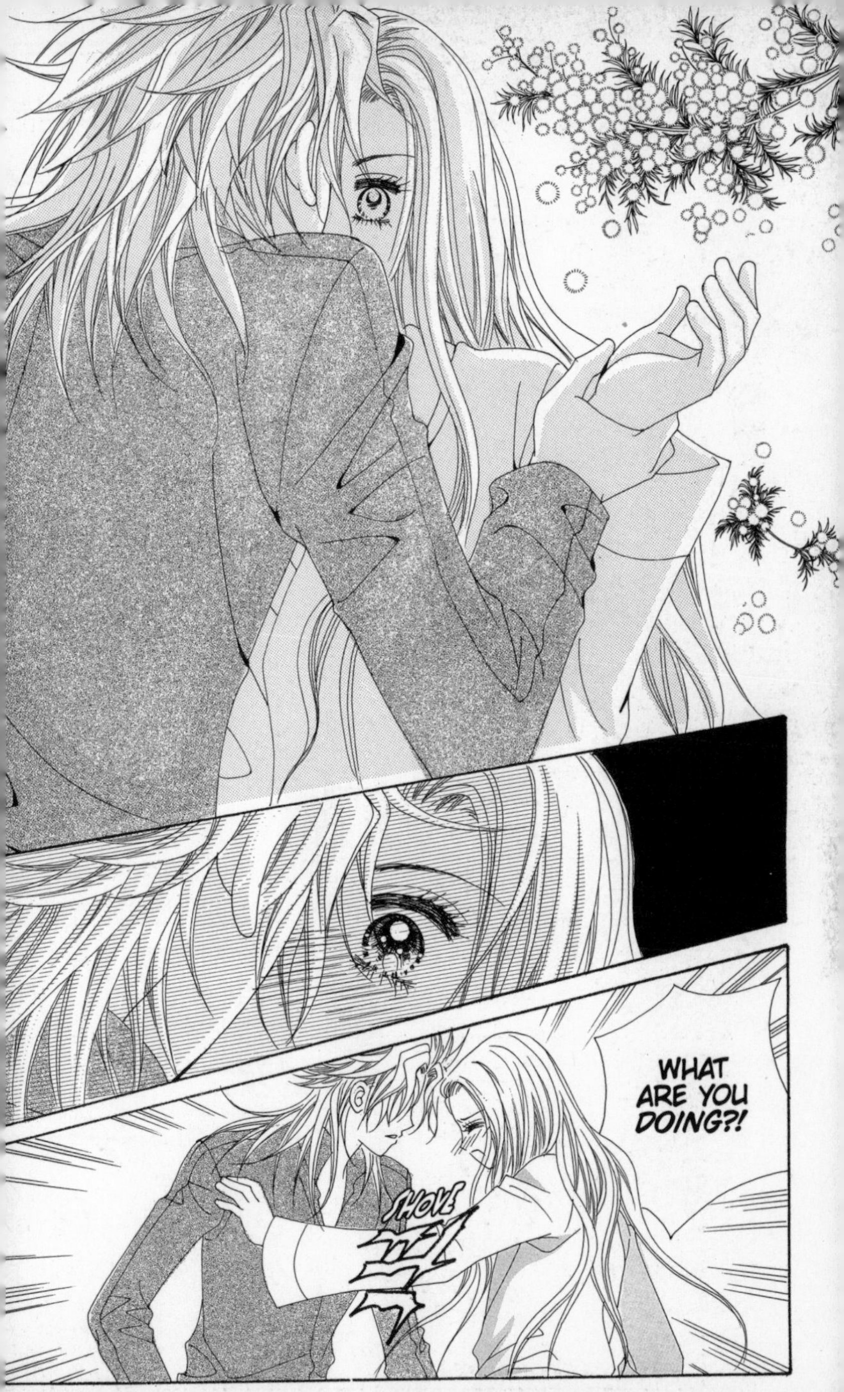
WHAT ARE YOU DOING?!
SHOVE

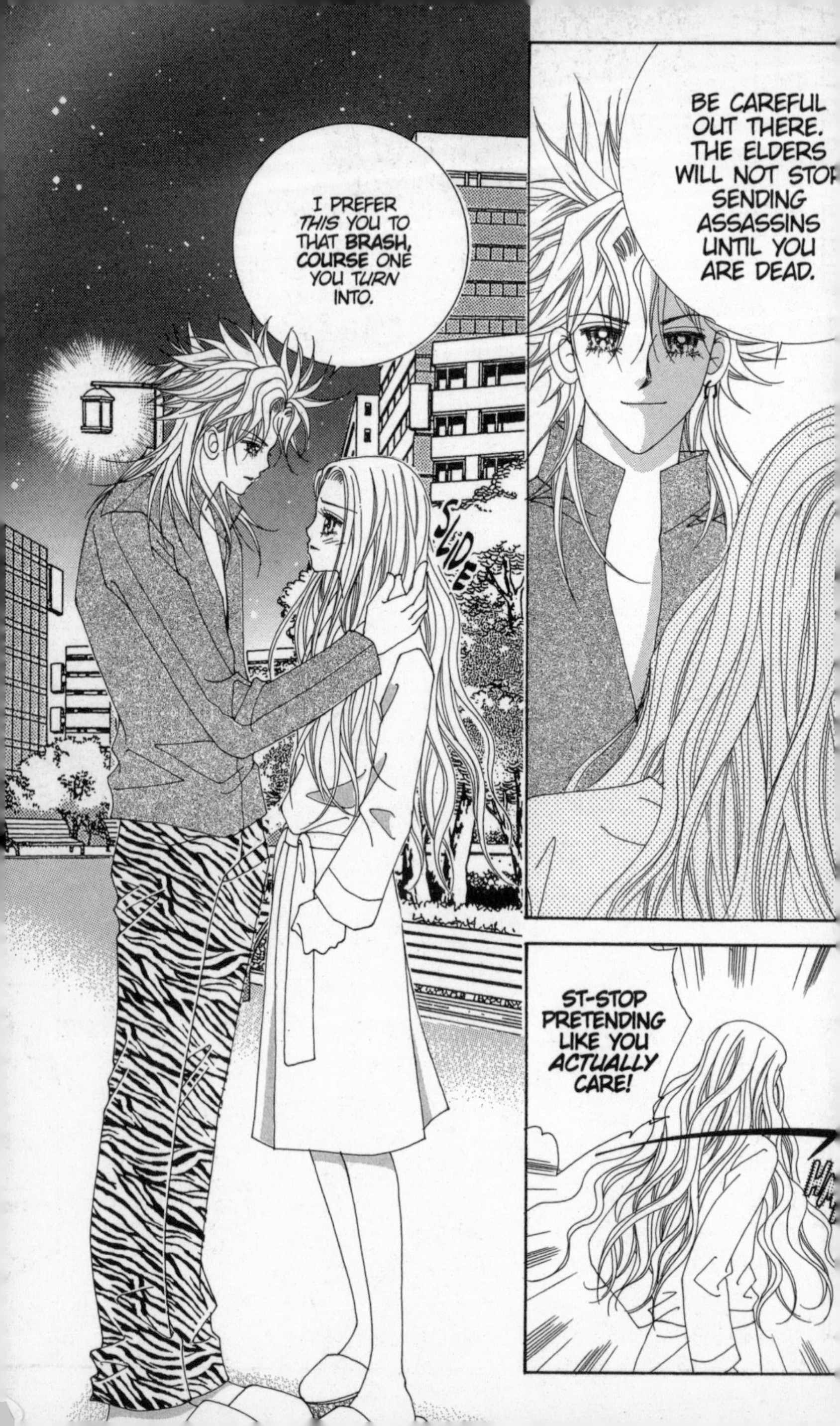
I PREFER *THIS* YOU TO THAT BRASH, COURSE ONE YOU *TURN* INTO.
SLIDE
BE CAREFUL OUT THERE. THE ELDERS WILL NOT STOP SENDING ASSASSINS UNTIL YOU ARE DEAD.
ST-STOP PRETENDING LIKE YOU *ACTUALLY* CARE!

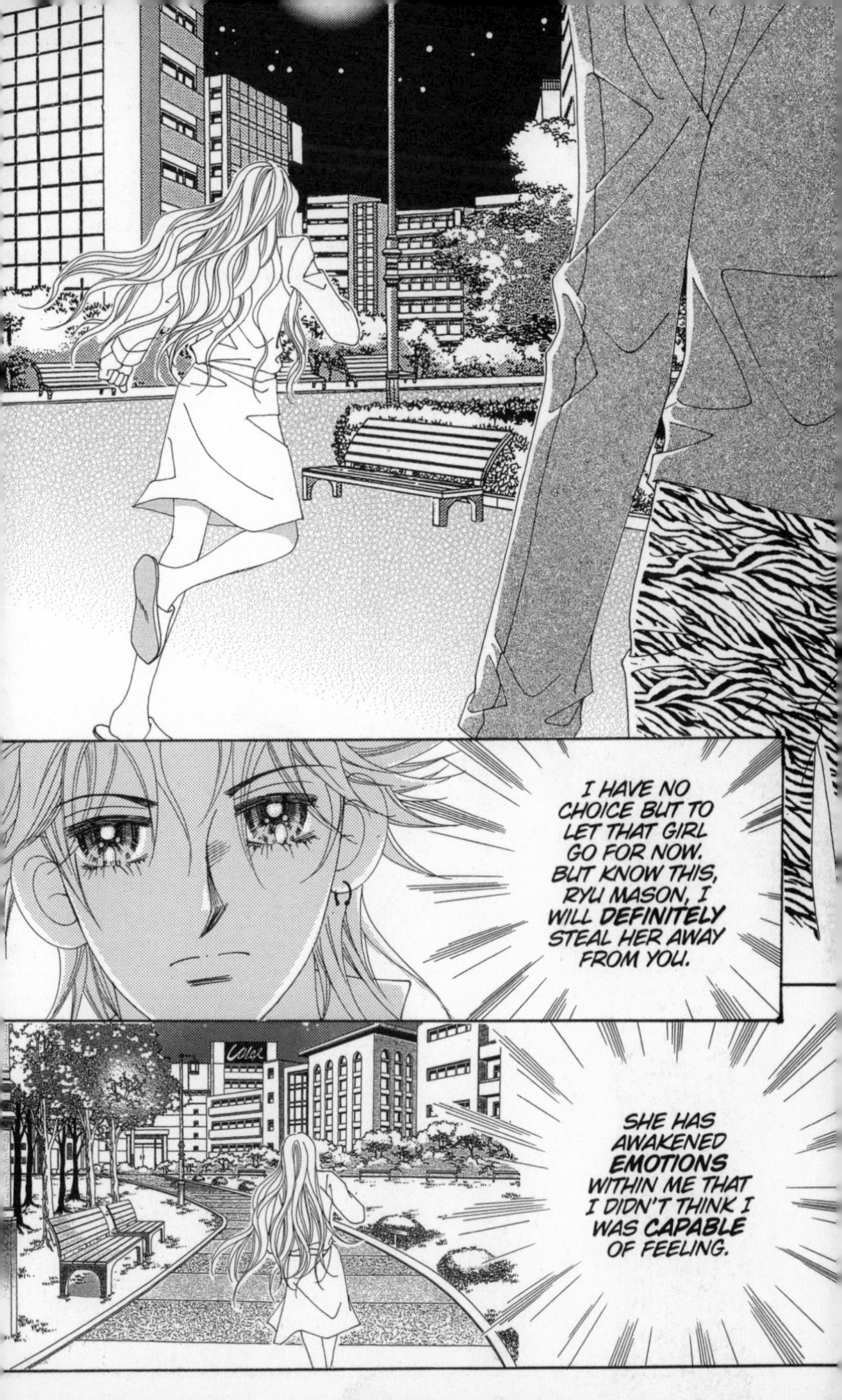
I HAVE NO CHOICE BUT TO LET THAT GIRL GO FOR NOW. BUT KNOW THIS, RYU MASON, I WILL DEFINITELY STEAL HER AWAY FROM YOU.
SHE HAS AWAKENED EMOTIONS WITHIN ME THAT I DIDN'T THINK I WAS CAPABLE OF FEELING.

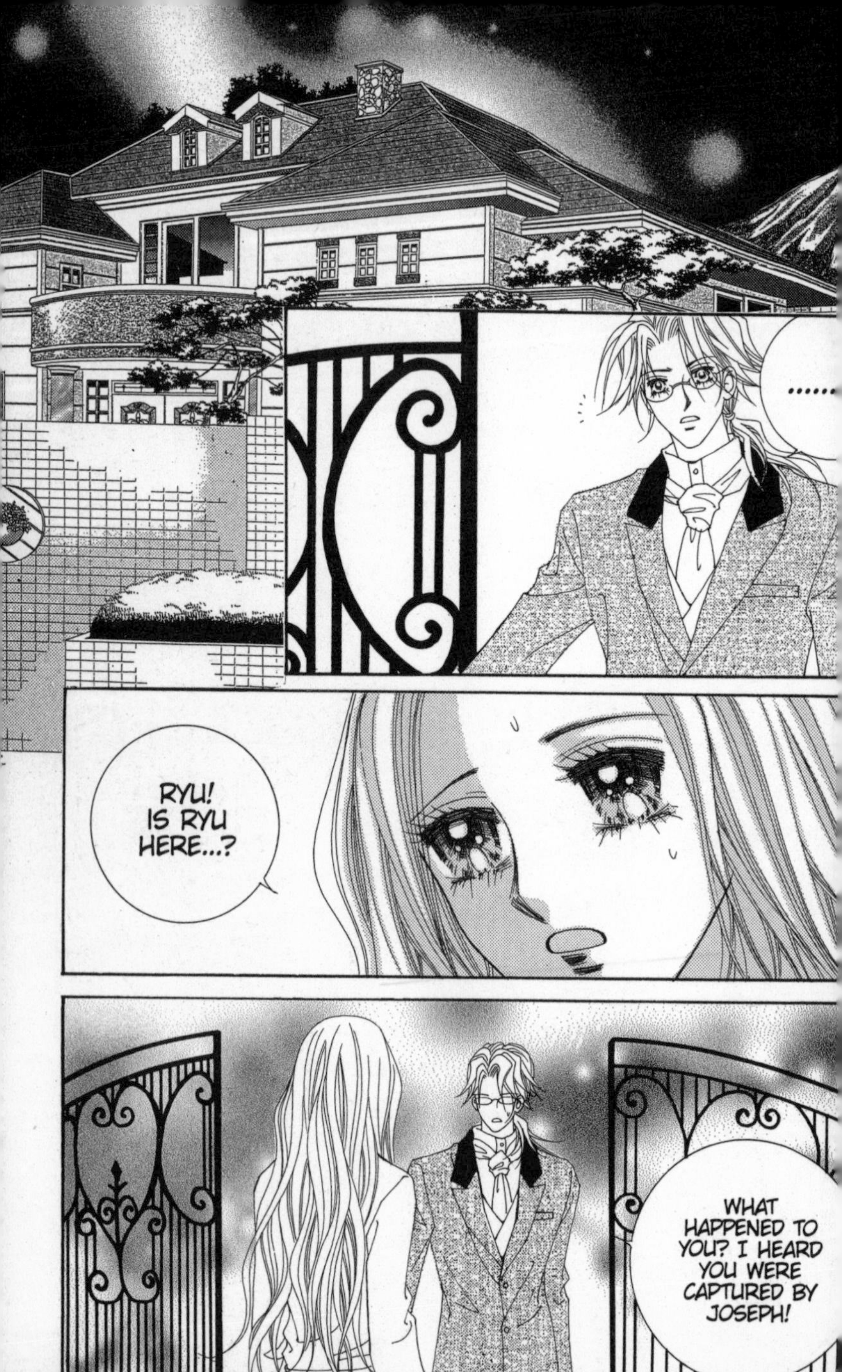
......
RYU! IS RYU HERE...?
WHAT HAPPENED TO YOU? I HEARD YOU WERE CAPTURED BY JOSEPH!

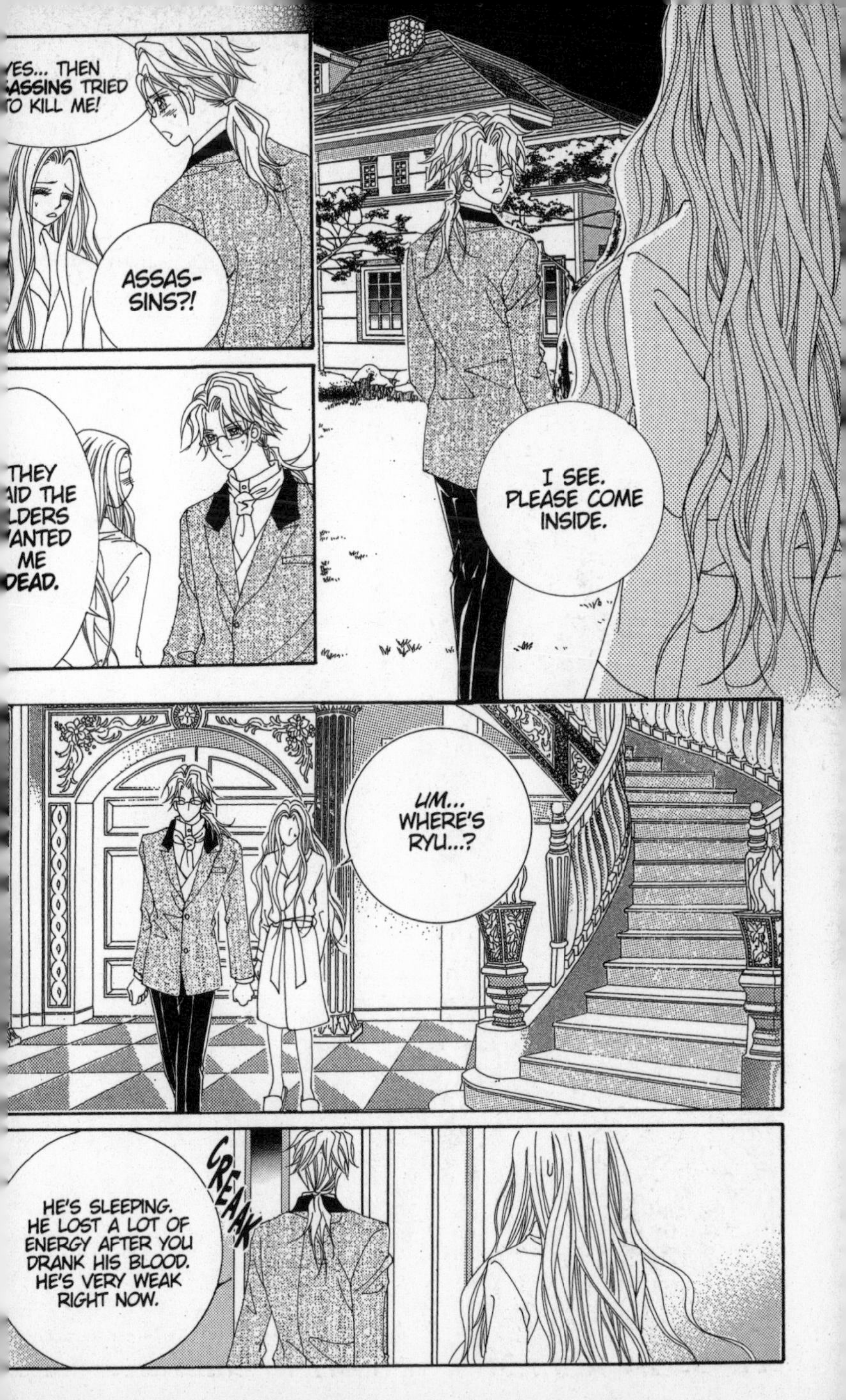
YES... THEN ASSASSINS TRIED TO KILL ME!
ASSAS-SINS?!
THEY SAID THE ELDERS WANTED ME DEAD.
I SEE. PLEASE COME INSIDE.
UM... WHERE'S RYU...?
HE'S SLEEPING. HE LOST A LOT OF ENERGY AFTER YOU DRANK HIS BLOOD. HE'S VERY WEAK RIGHT NOW.
CREAAK

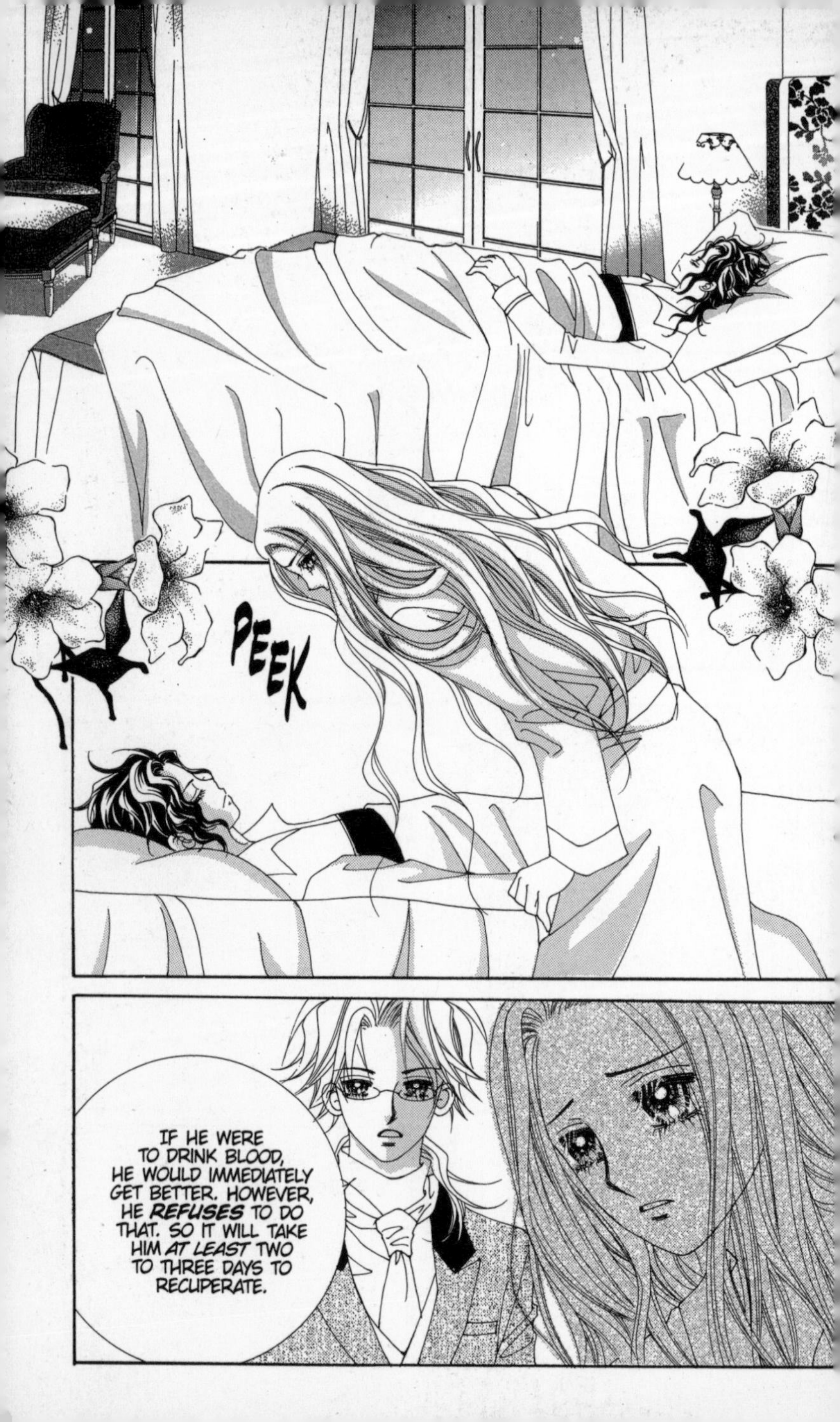
PEEK
IF HE WERE TO DRINK BLOOD, HE WOULD IMMEDIATELY GET BETTER. HOWEVER, HE ***REFUSES*** TO DO THAT. SO IT WILL TAKE HIM ***AT LEAST*** TWO TO THREE DAYS TO RECUPERATE.

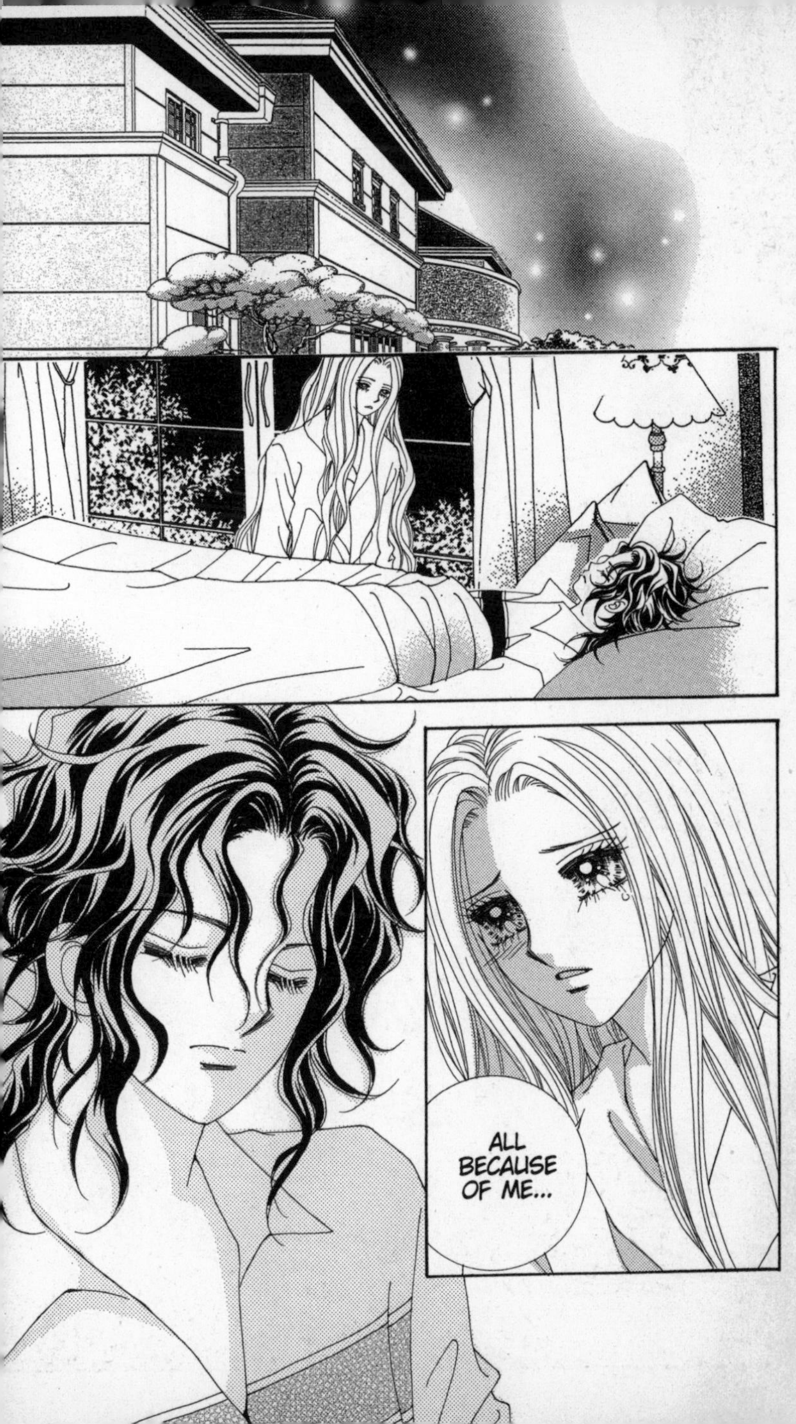
ALL BECAUSE OF ME...

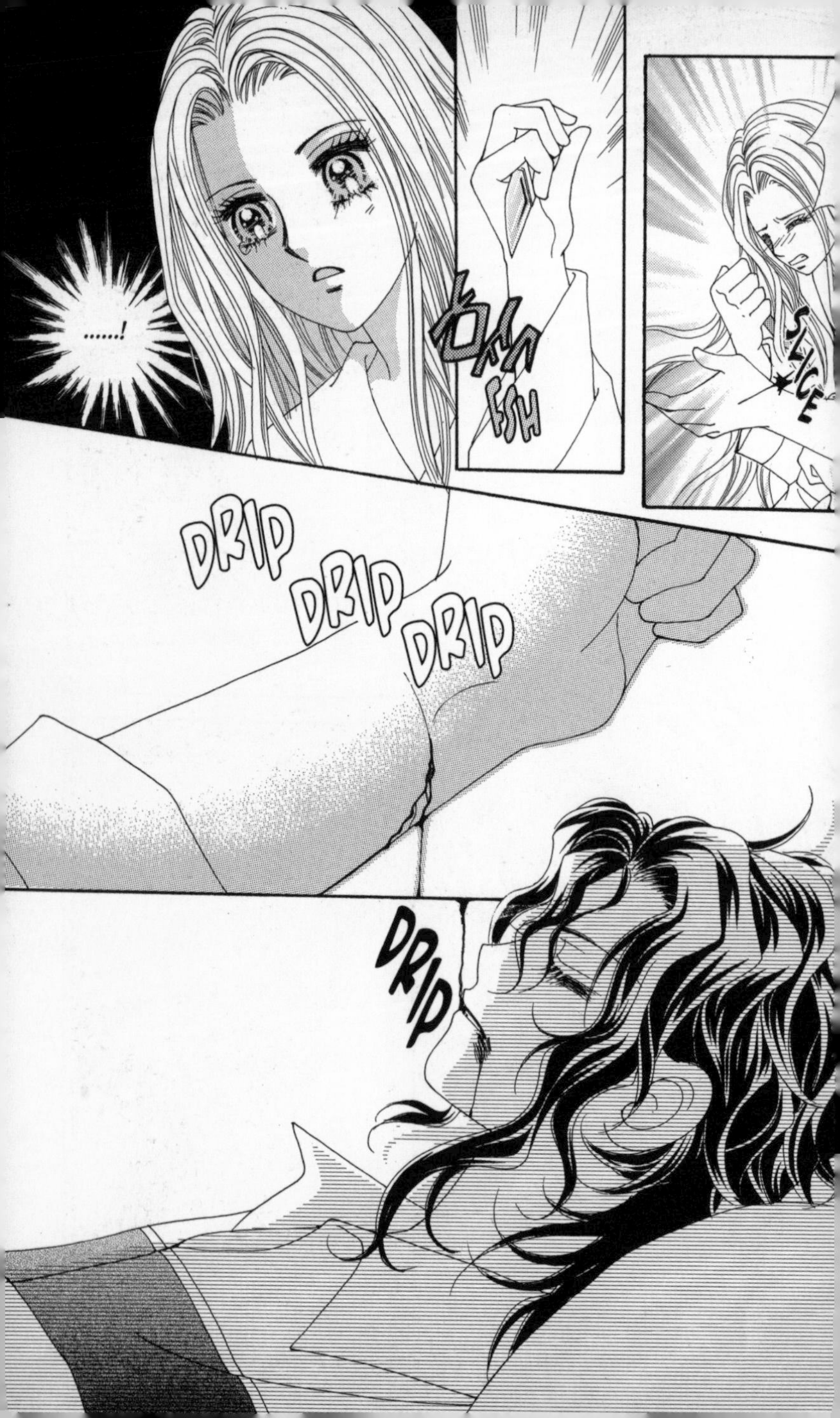
......!
FSH
SLICE
DRIP
DRIP
DRIP
DRIP

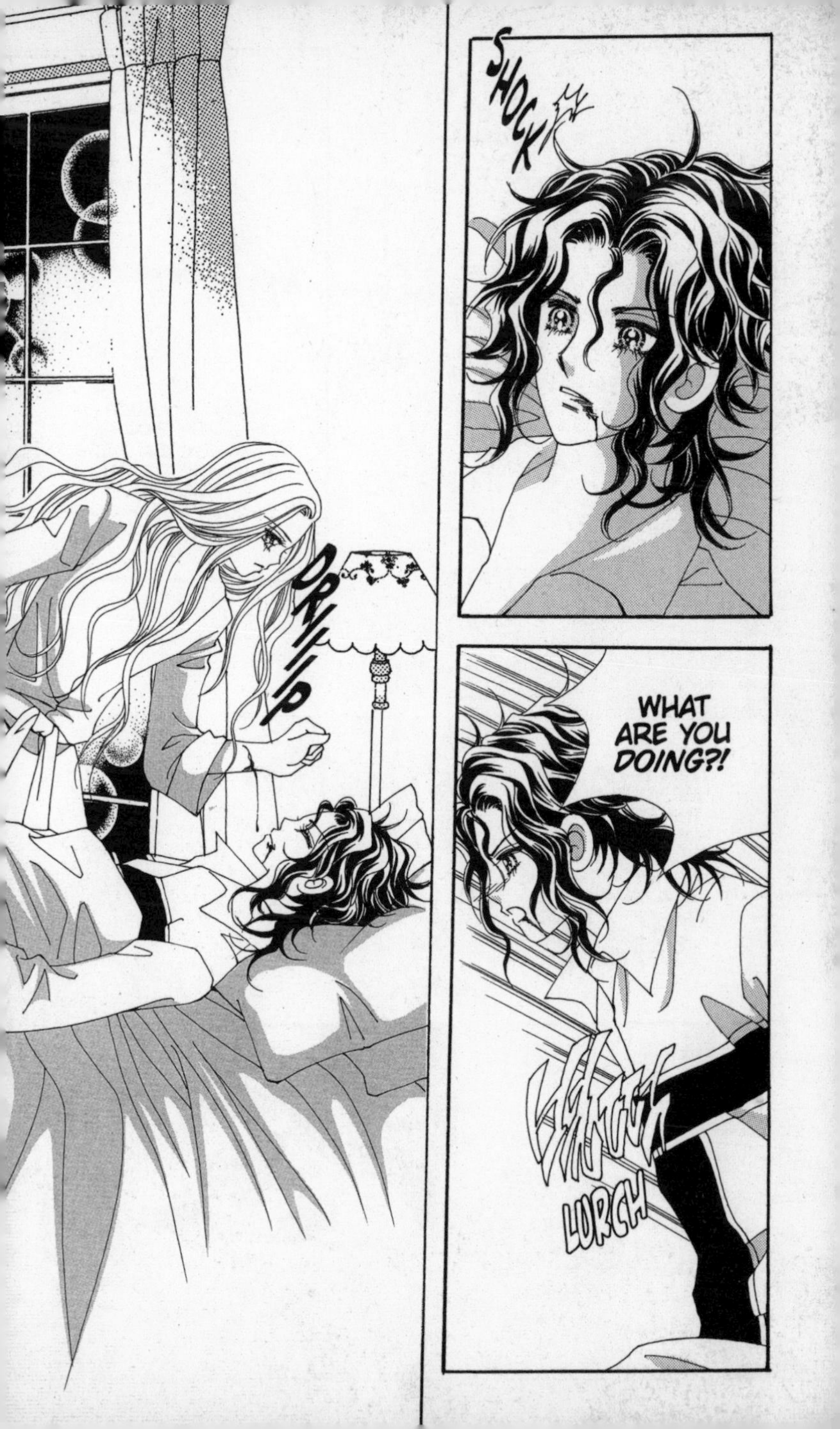
DRIIIP
SHOCK
WHAT ARE YOU DOING?!
LURCH

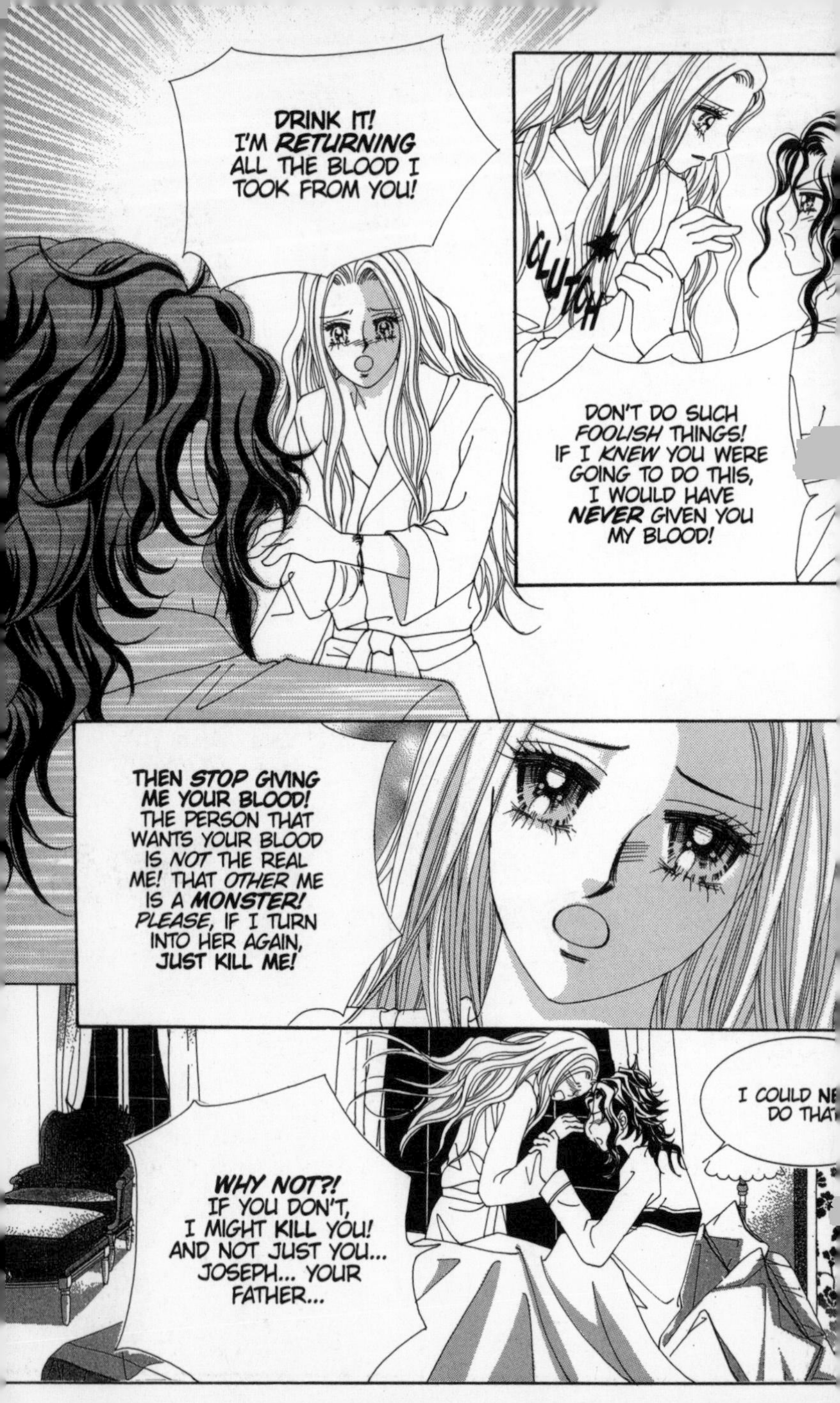
DRINK IT! I'M **RETURNING** ALL THE BLOOD I TOOK FROM YOU!
CLUTCH
DON'T DO SUCH *FOOLISH* THINGS! IF I *KNEW* YOU WERE GOING TO DO THIS, I WOULD HAVE **NEVER** GIVEN YOU MY BLOOD!
THEN *STOP* GIVING ME YOUR BLOOD! THE PERSON THAT WANTS YOUR BLOOD IS *NOT* THE REAL ME! THAT *OTHER* ME IS A **MONSTER!** *PLEASE,* IF I TURN INTO HER AGAIN, JUST KILL ME!
WHY NOT?! IF YOU DON'T, I MIGHT KILL YOU! AND NOT JUST YOU... JOSEPH... YOUR FATHER...
I COULD NE DO THA

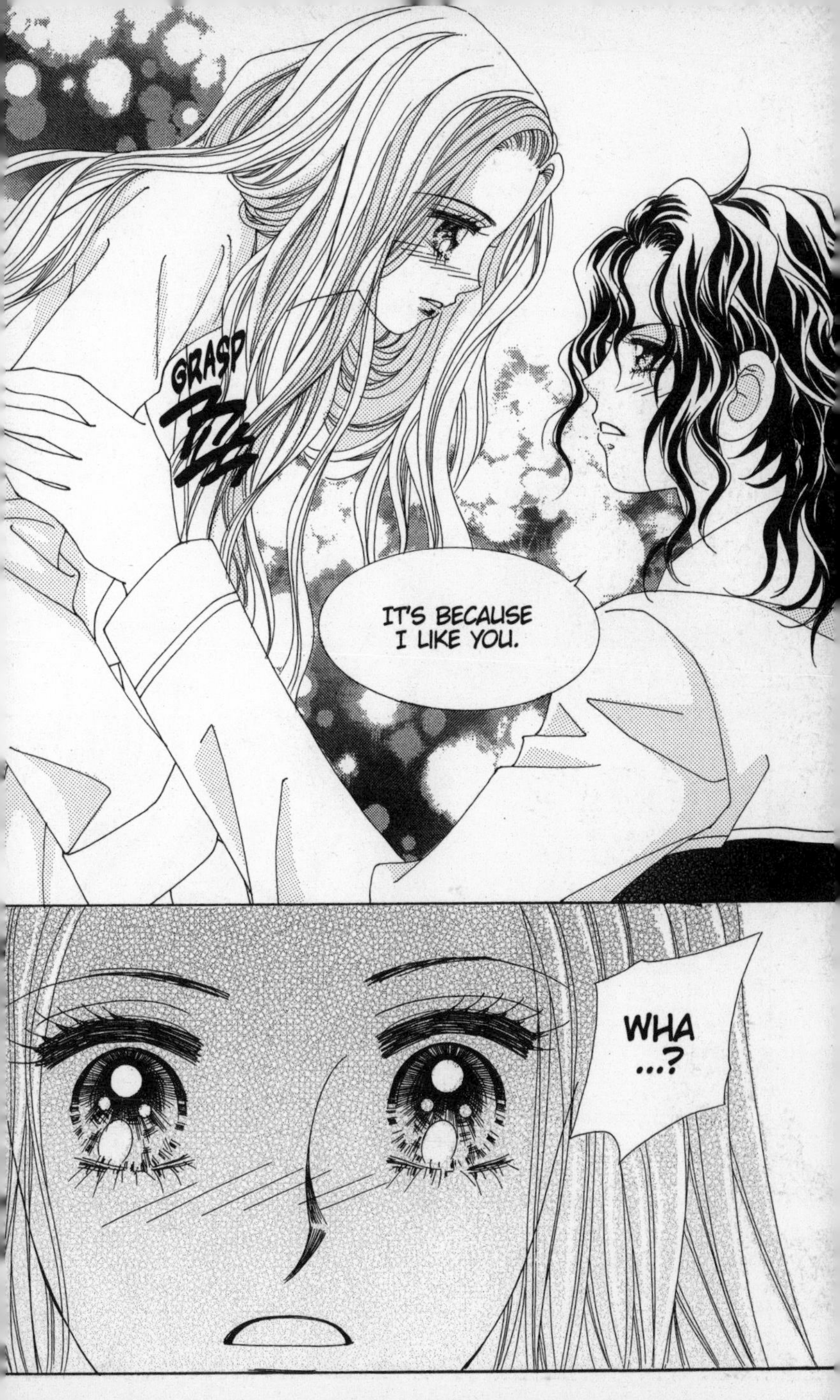
GRASP
IT'S BECAUSE I LIKE YOU.
WHA ...?

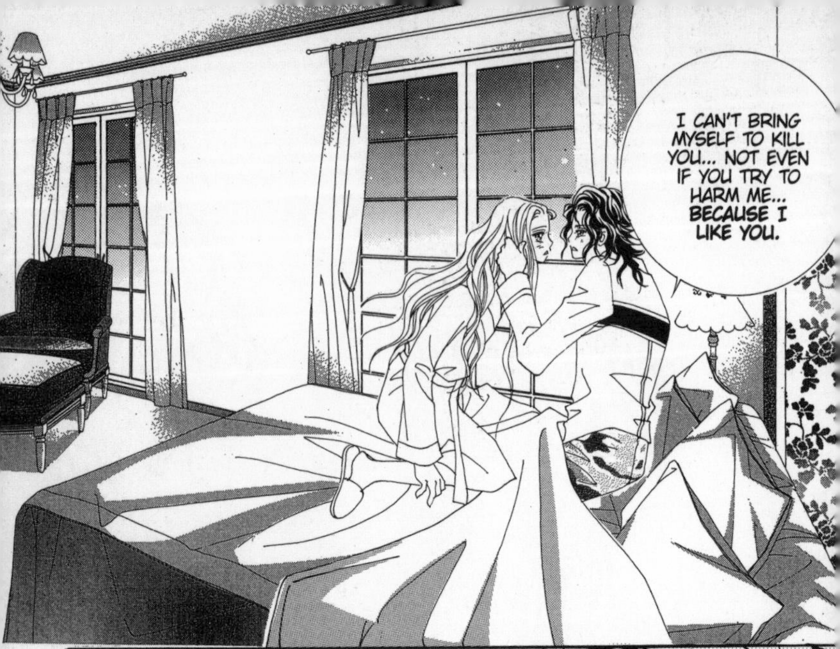
I CAN'T BRING MYSELF TO KILL YOU... NOT EVEN IF YOU TRY TO HARM ME... BECAUSE I LIKE YOU.

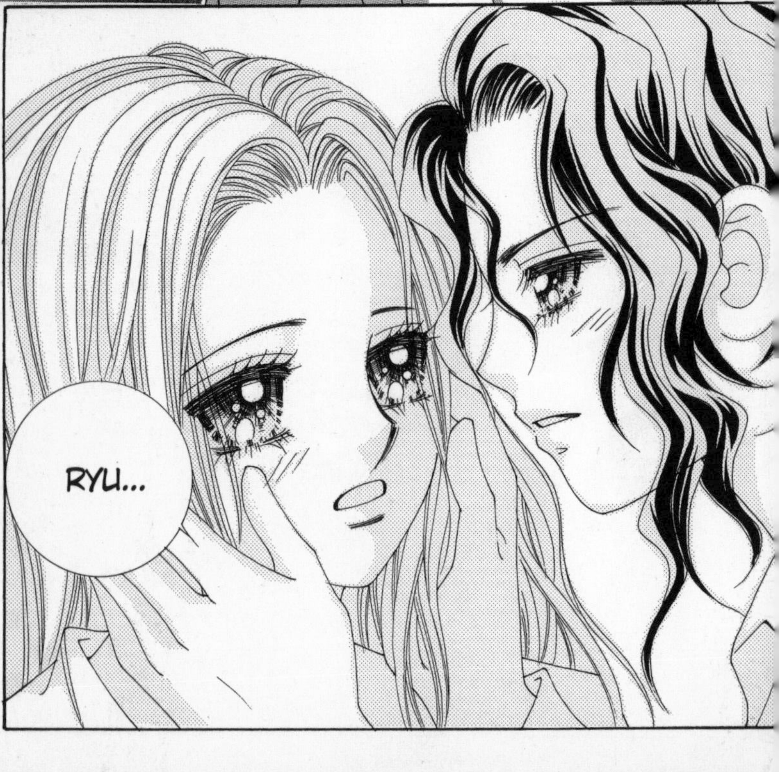
RYU...

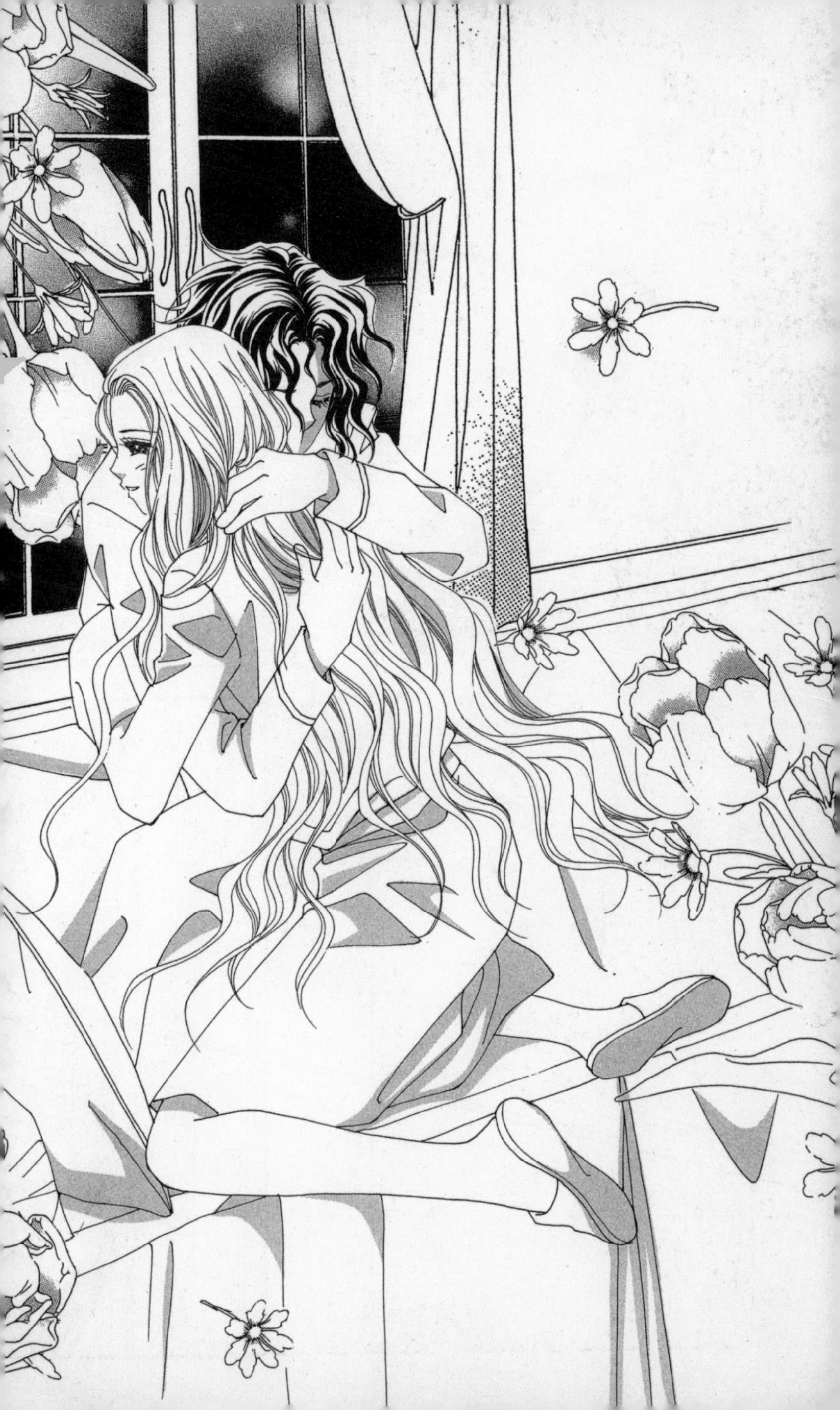

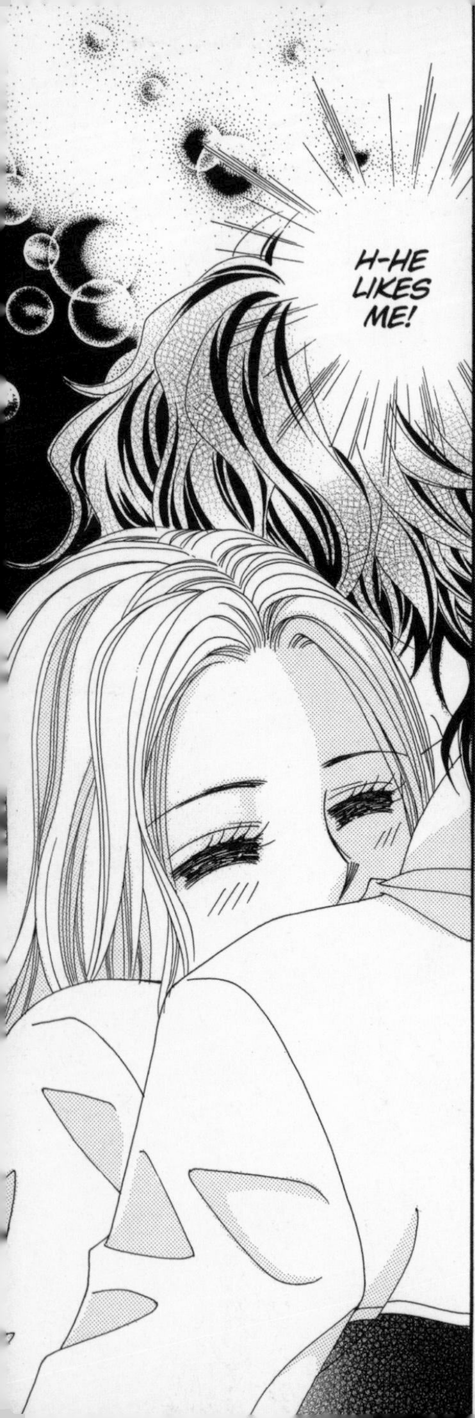
H-HE LIKES ME!
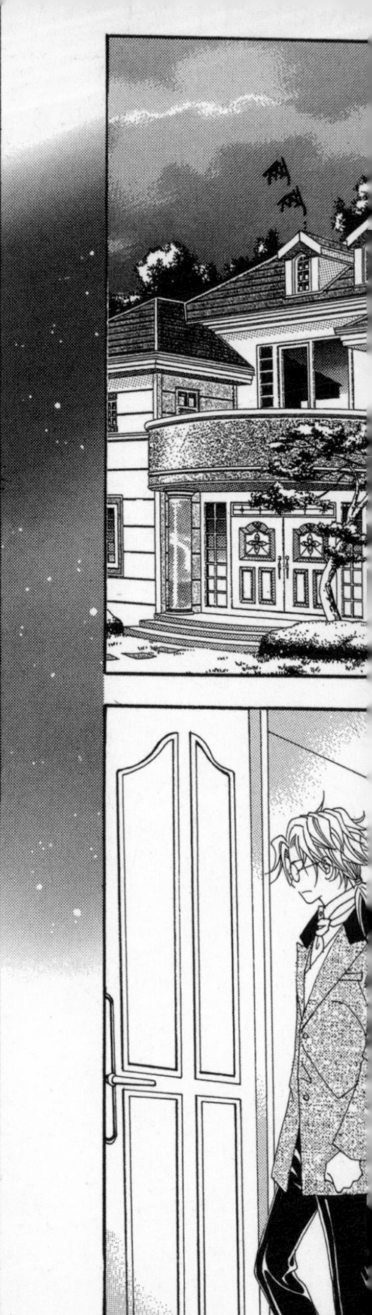

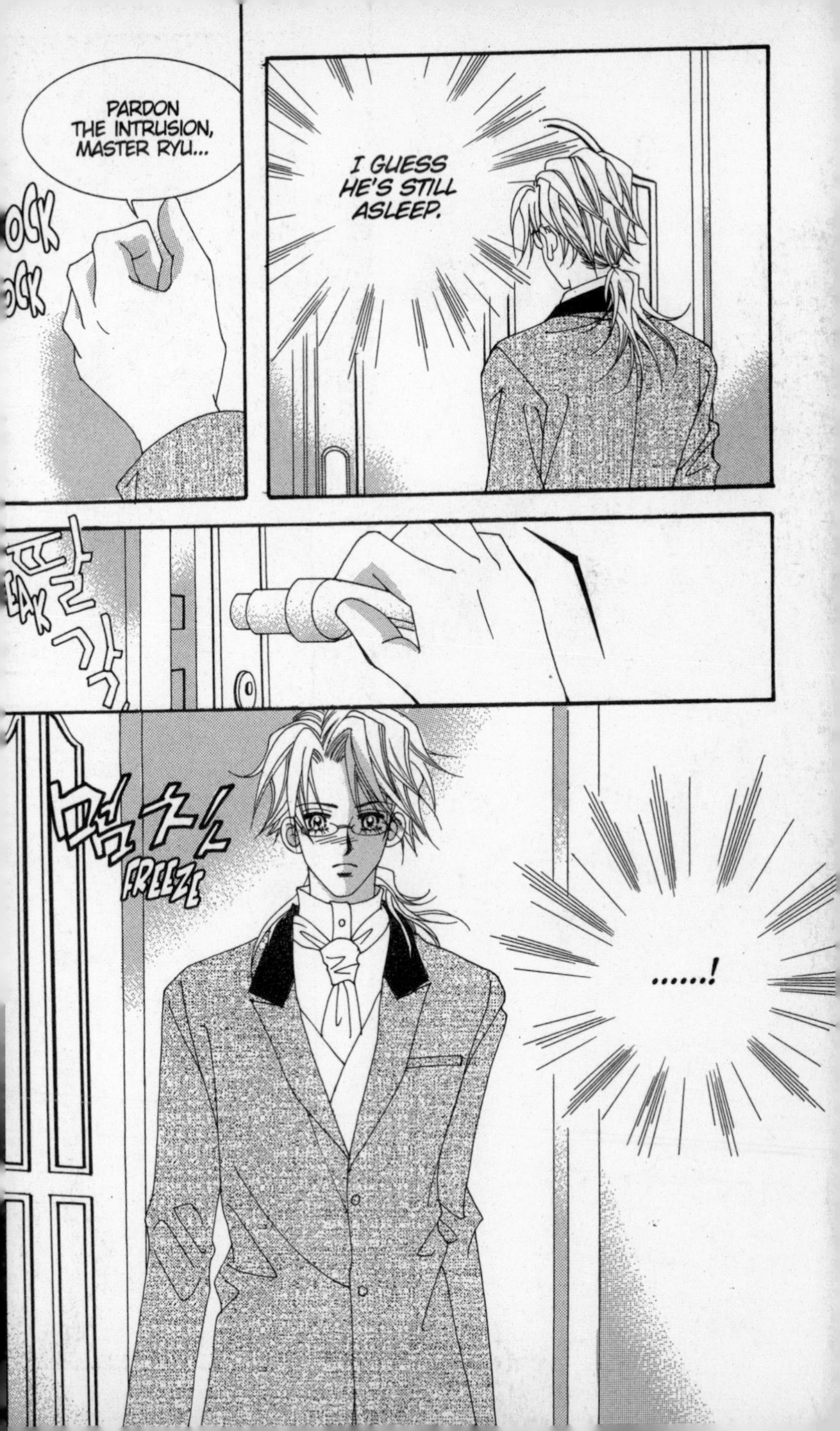
PARDON THE INTRUSION, MASTER RYU...
OCK
OCK
I GUESS HE'S STILL ASLEEP.
EAK
FREEZE
......!

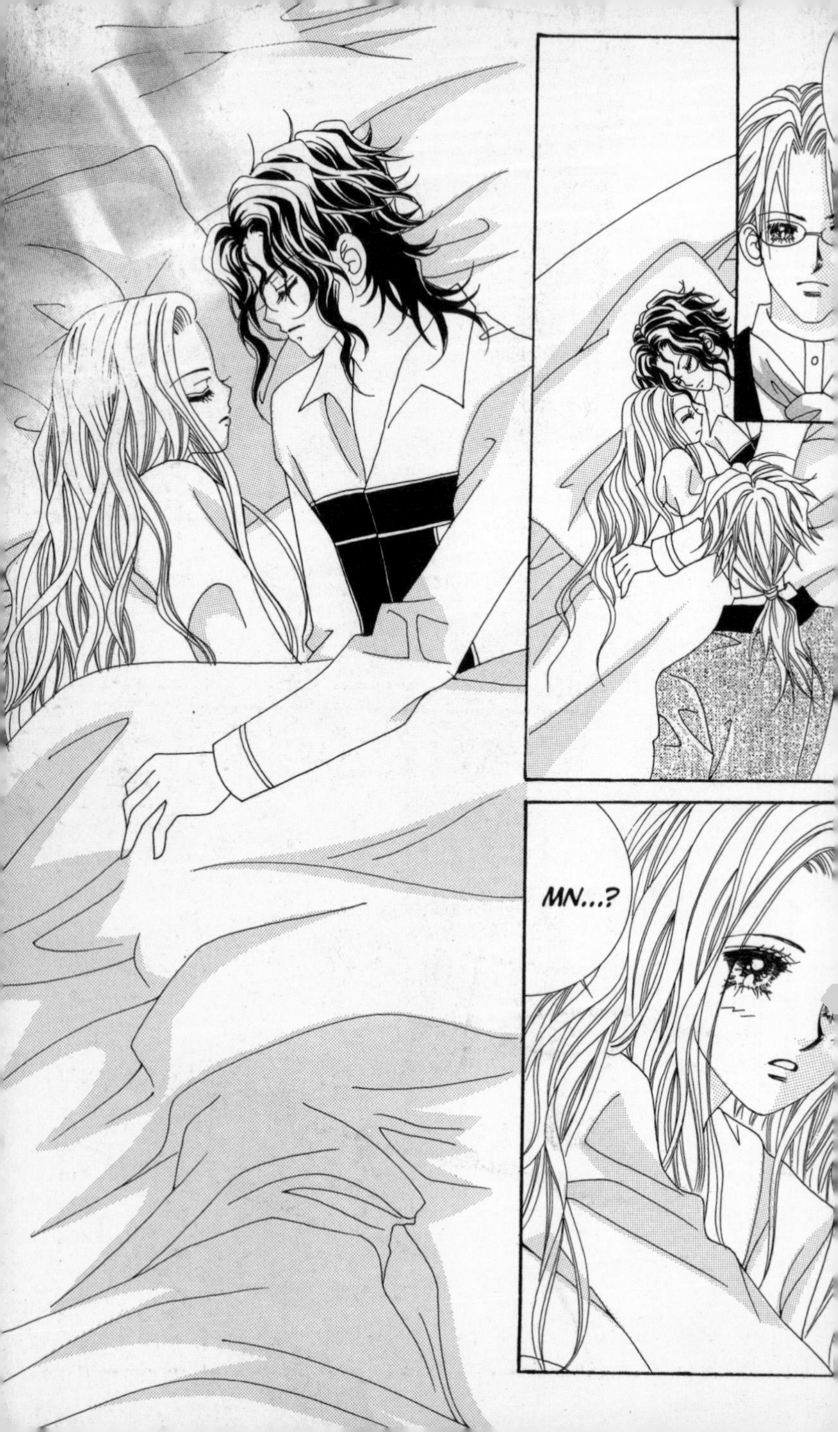
MN...?

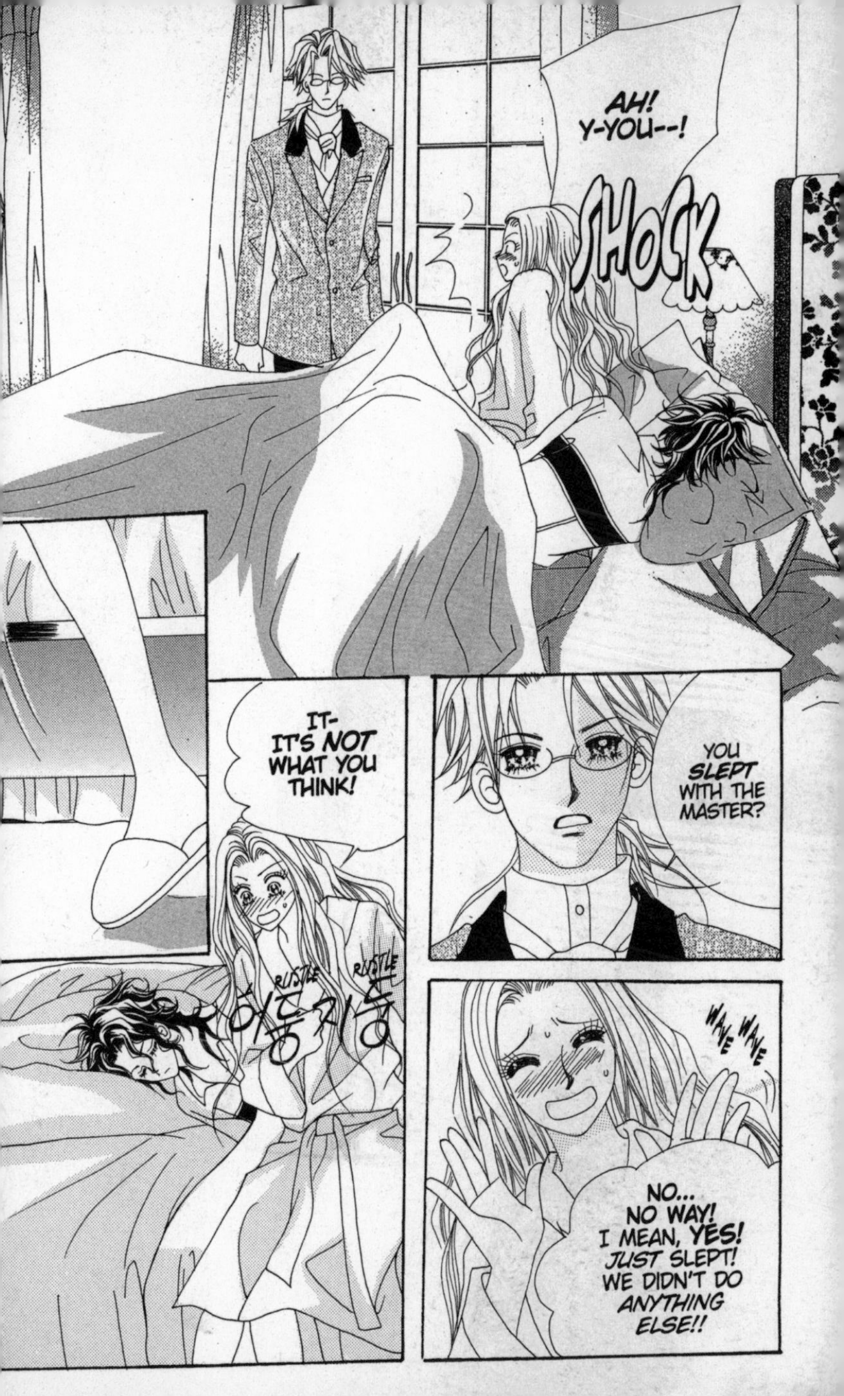
AH! Y-YOU--!
SHOCK
IT- IT'S NOT WHAT YOU THINK!
YOU SLEPT WITH THE MASTER?
RUSTLE RUSTLE
허둥지둥
WAVE WAVE
NO... NO WAY! I MEAN, YES! JUST SLEPT! WE DIDN'T DO ANYTHING ELSE!!

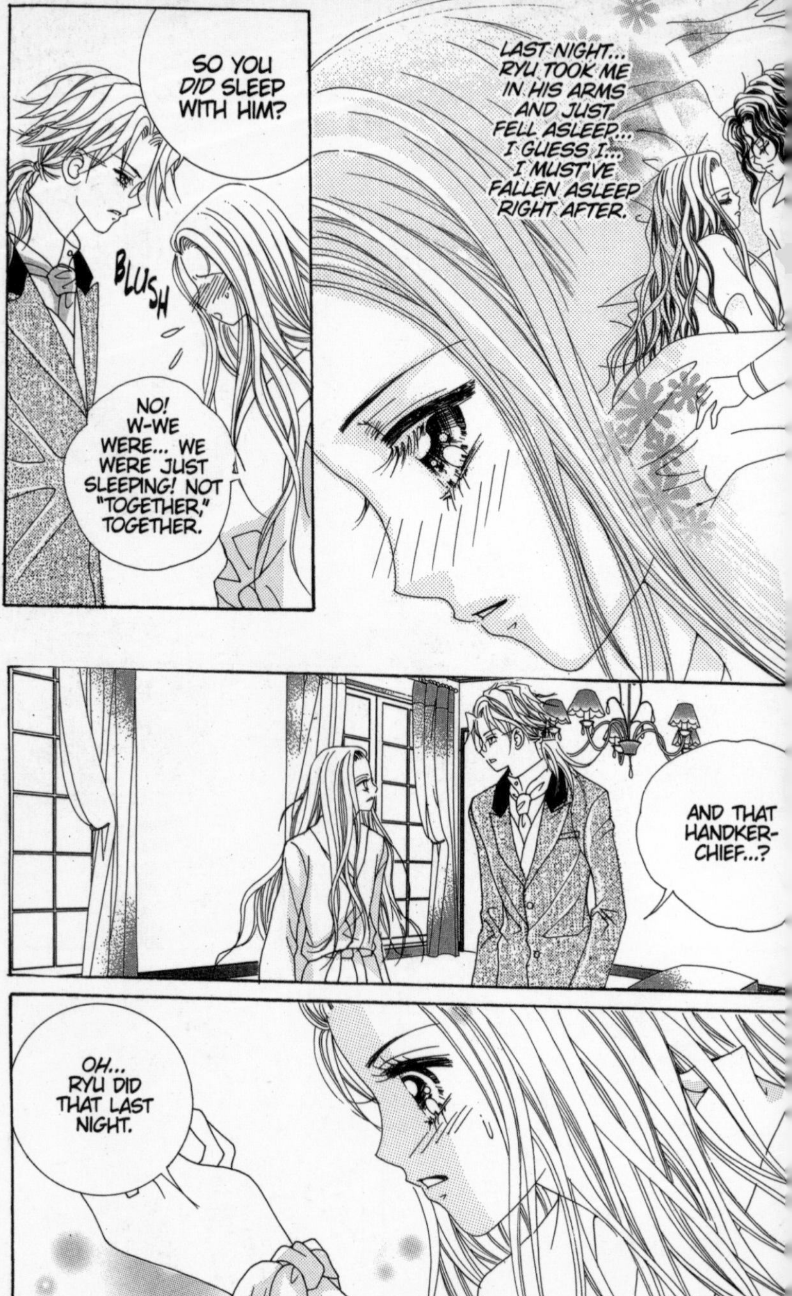
SO YOU DID SLEEP WITH HIM?
BLUSH
NO! W-WE WERE... WE WERE JUST SLEEPING! NOT "TOGETHER," TOGETHER.
LAST NIGHT... RYU TOOK ME IN HIS ARMS AND JUST FELL ASLEEP... I GUESS I... I MUST'VE FALLEN ASLEEP RIGHT AFTER.
AND THAT HANDKERCHIEF...?
OH... RYU DID THAT LAST NIGHT.

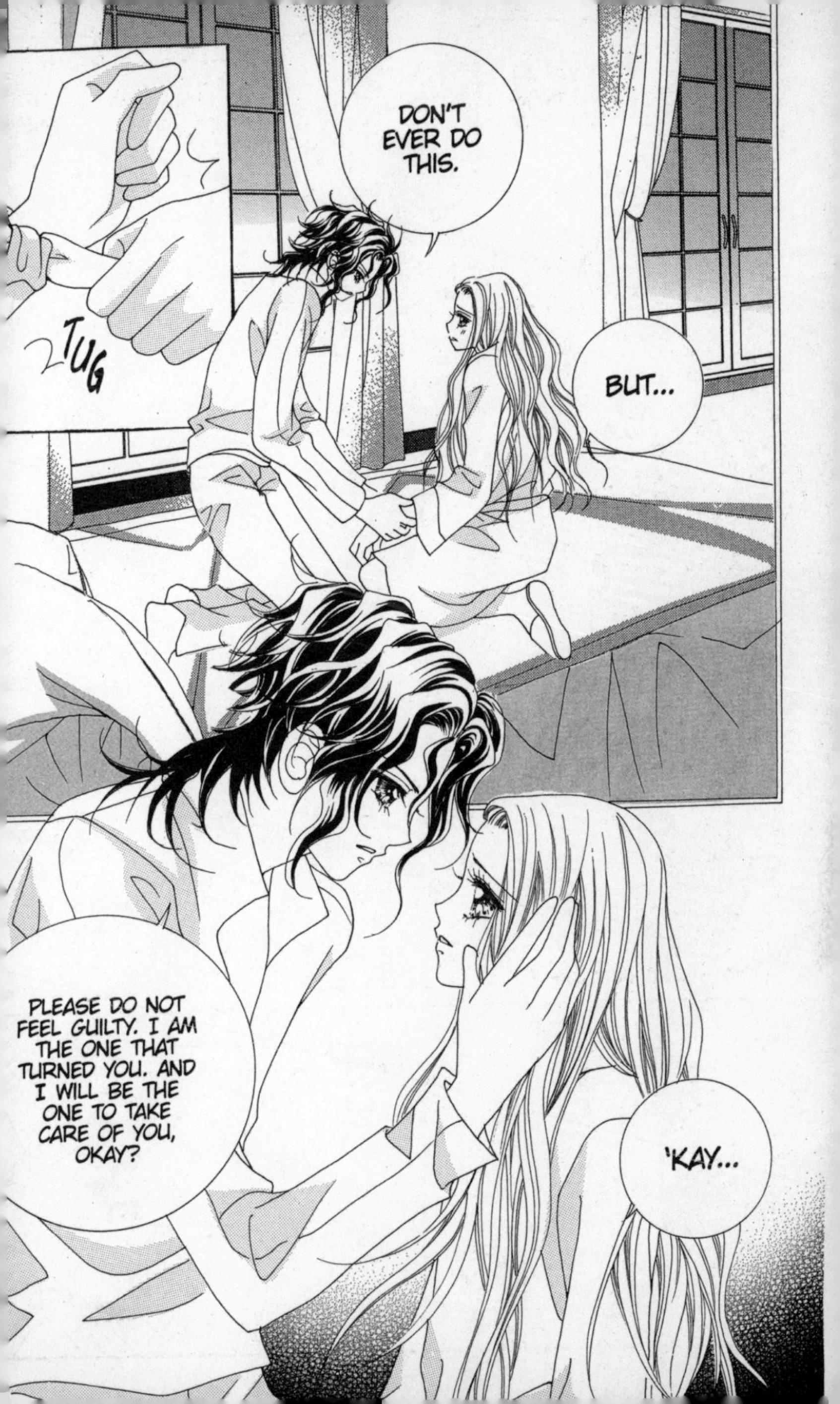
TUG
DON'T EVER DO THIS.
BUT...
PLEASE DO NOT FEEL GUILTY. I AM THE ONE THAT TURNED YOU. AND I WILL BE THE ONE TO TAKE CARE OF YOU, OKAY?
'KAY...

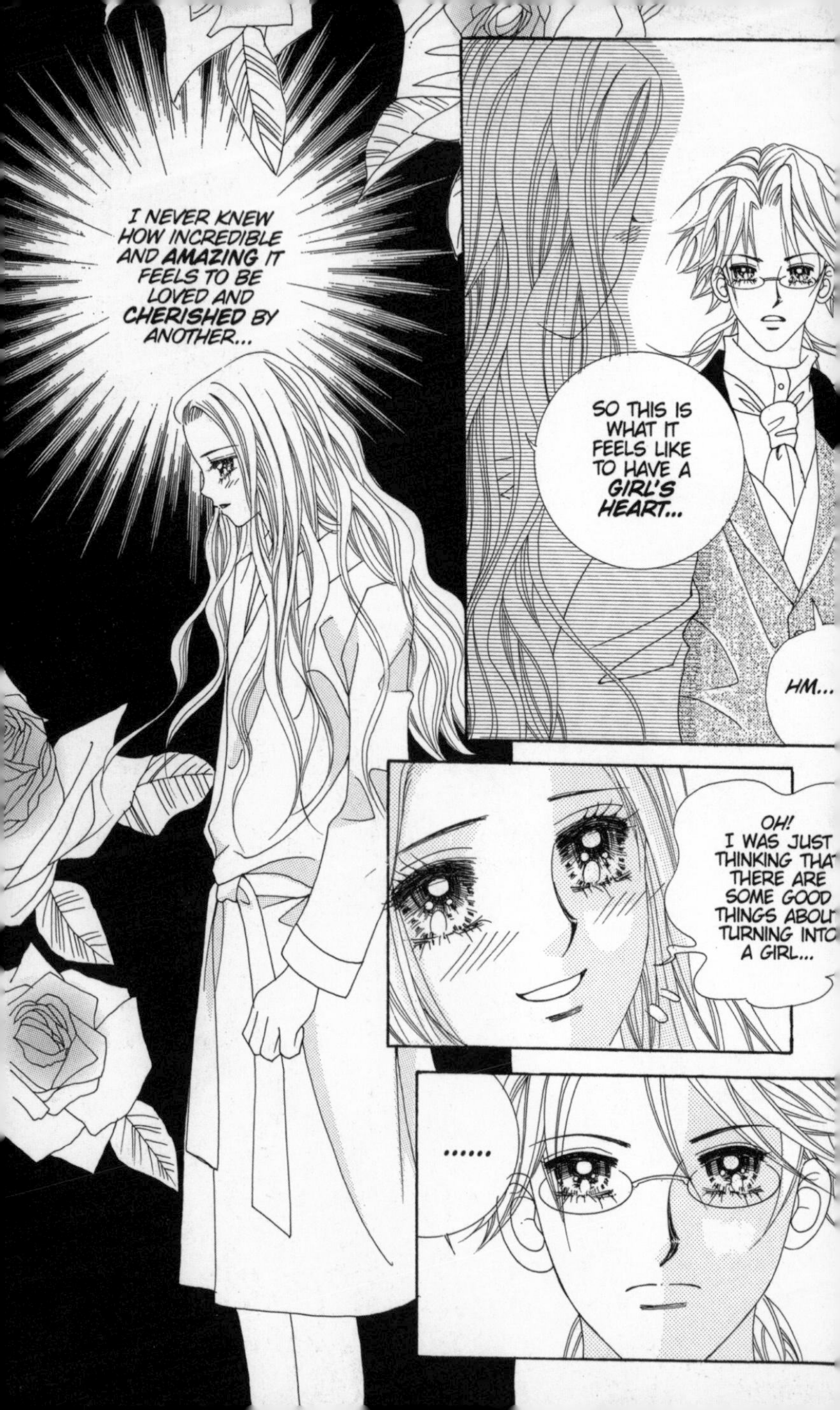
I NEVER KNEW HOW INCREDIBLE AND **AMAZING** IT FEELS TO BE LOVED AND **CHERISHED** BY ANOTHER...
SO THIS IS WHAT IT FEELS LIKE TO HAVE A *GIRL'S HEART*...
HM...
OH! I WAS JUST THINKING THAT THERE ARE SOME GOOD THINGS ABOUT TURNING INTO A GIRL...
......

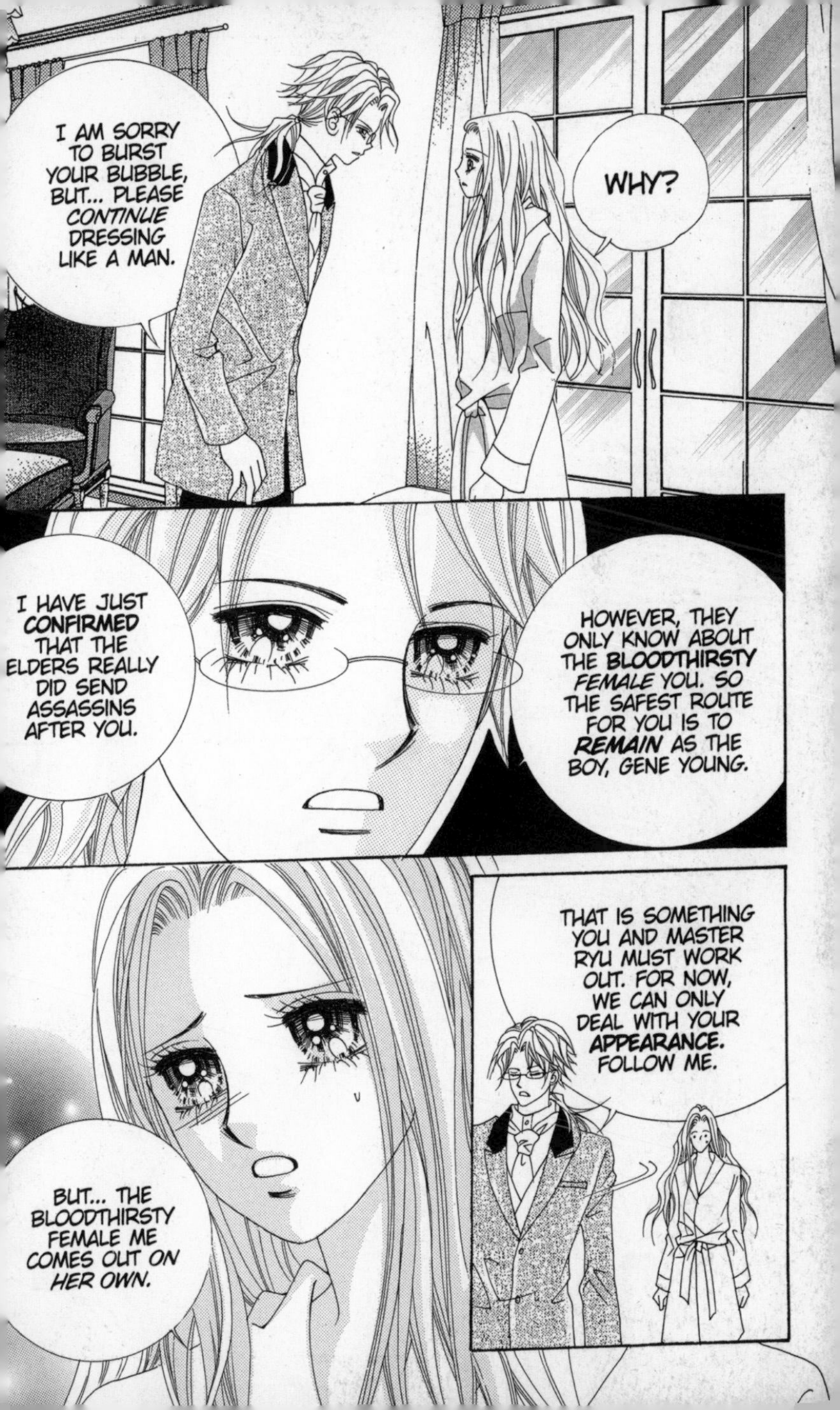
I AM SORRY TO BURST YOUR BUBBLE, BUT... PLEASE *CONTINUE* DRESSING LIKE A MAN.
WHY?
I HAVE JUST **CONFIRMED** THAT THE ELDERS REALLY DID SEND ASSASSINS AFTER YOU.
HOWEVER, THEY ONLY KNOW ABOUT THE **BLOODTHIRSTY** *FEMALE* YOU. SO THE SAFEST ROUTE FOR YOU IS TO ***REMAIN*** AS THE BOY, GENE YOUNG.
BUT... THE BLOODTHIRSTY FEMALE ME COMES OUT ON *HER OWN.*
THAT IS SOMETHING YOU AND MASTER RYU MUST WORK OUT. FOR NOW, WE CAN ONLY DEAL WITH YOUR **APPEARANCE.** FOLLOW ME.

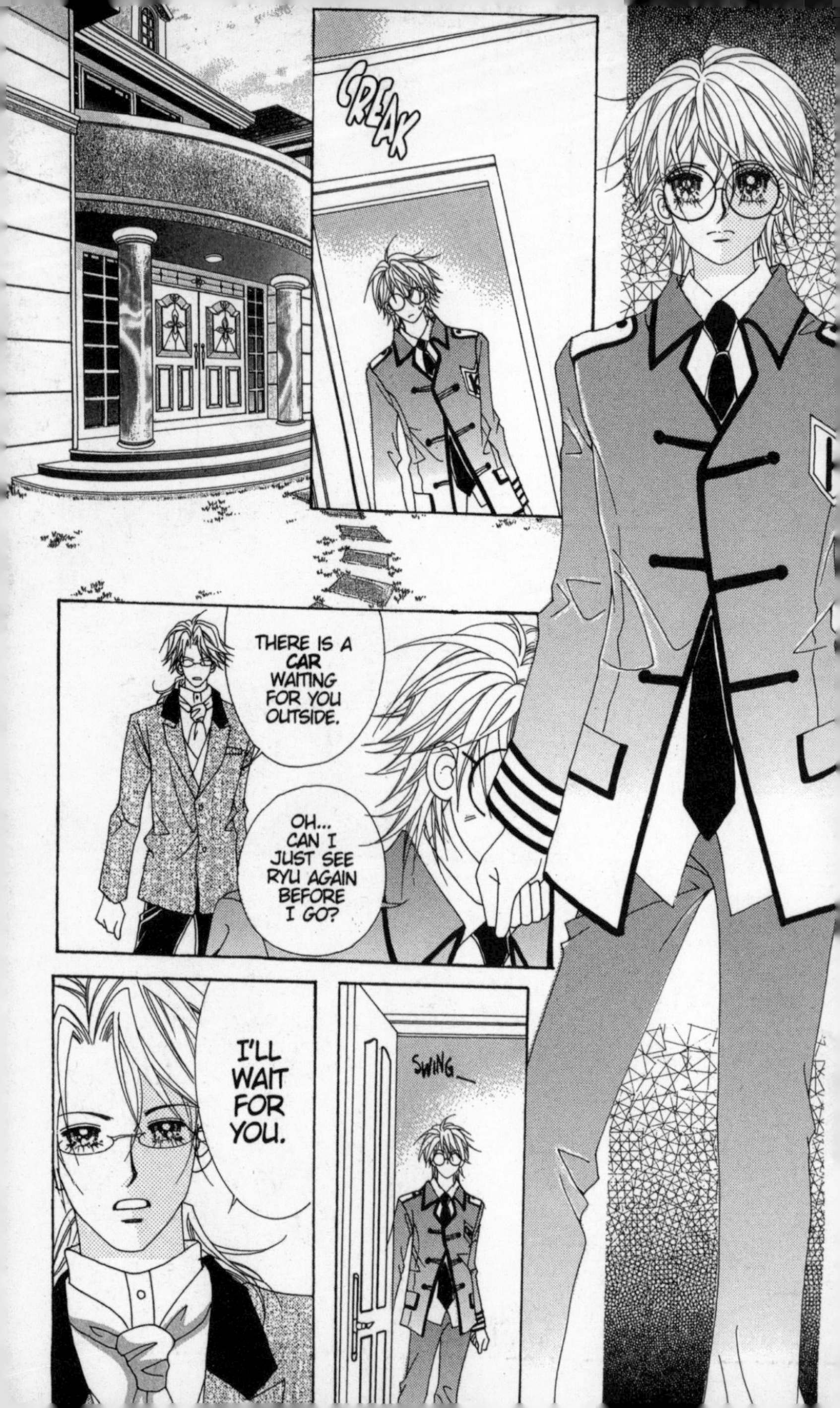
CREAK
THERE IS A CAR WAITING FOR YOU OUTSIDE.
OH... CAN I JUST SEE RYU AGAIN BEFORE I GO?
I'LL WAIT FOR YOU.
SWING

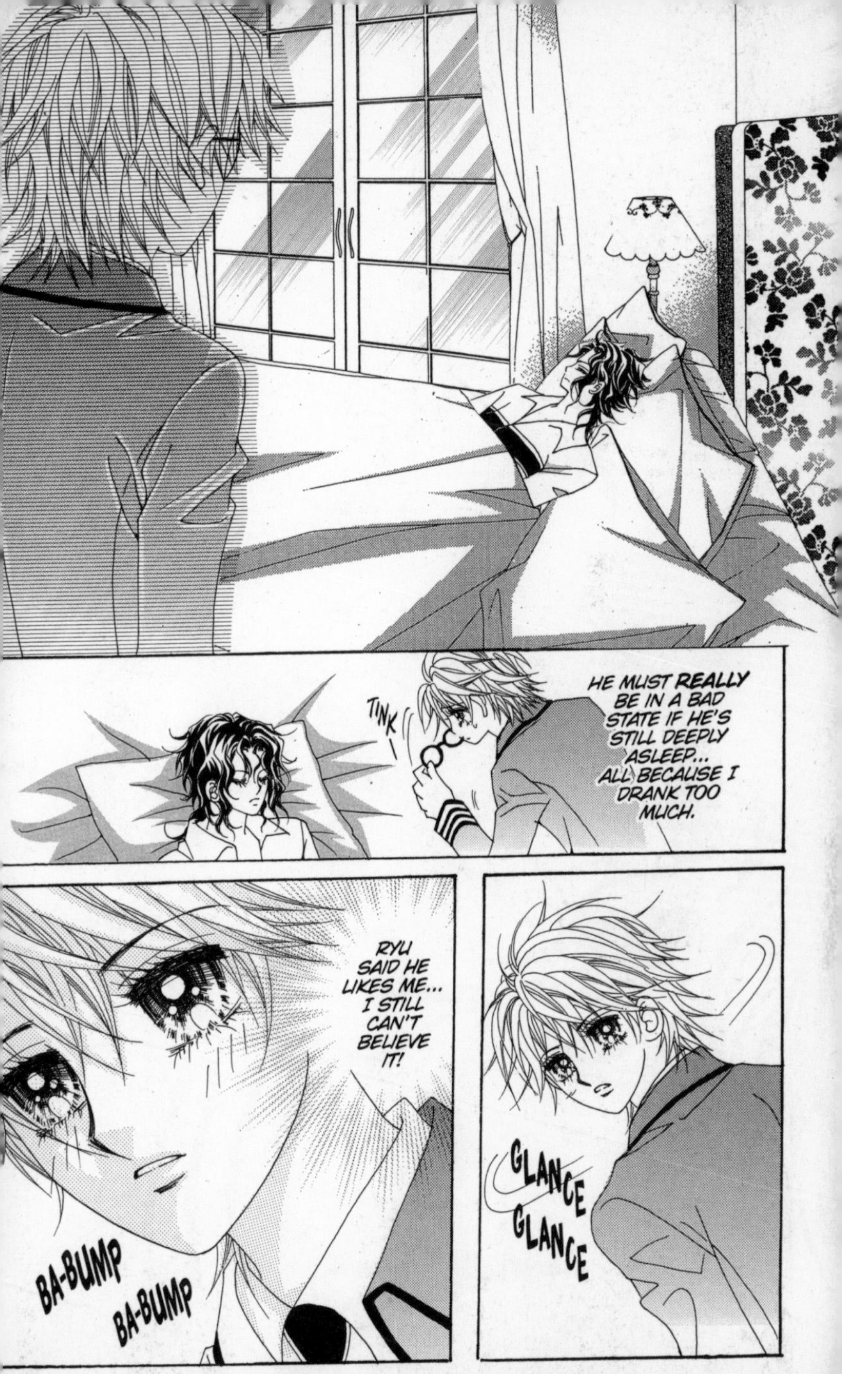
TINK
HE MUST REALLY BE IN A BAD STATE IF HE'S STILL DEEPLY ASLEEP... ALL BECAUSE I DRANK TOO MUCH.
RYU SAID HE LIKES ME... I STILL CAN'T BELIEVE IT!
BA-BUMP
BA-BUMP
GLANCE
GLANCE

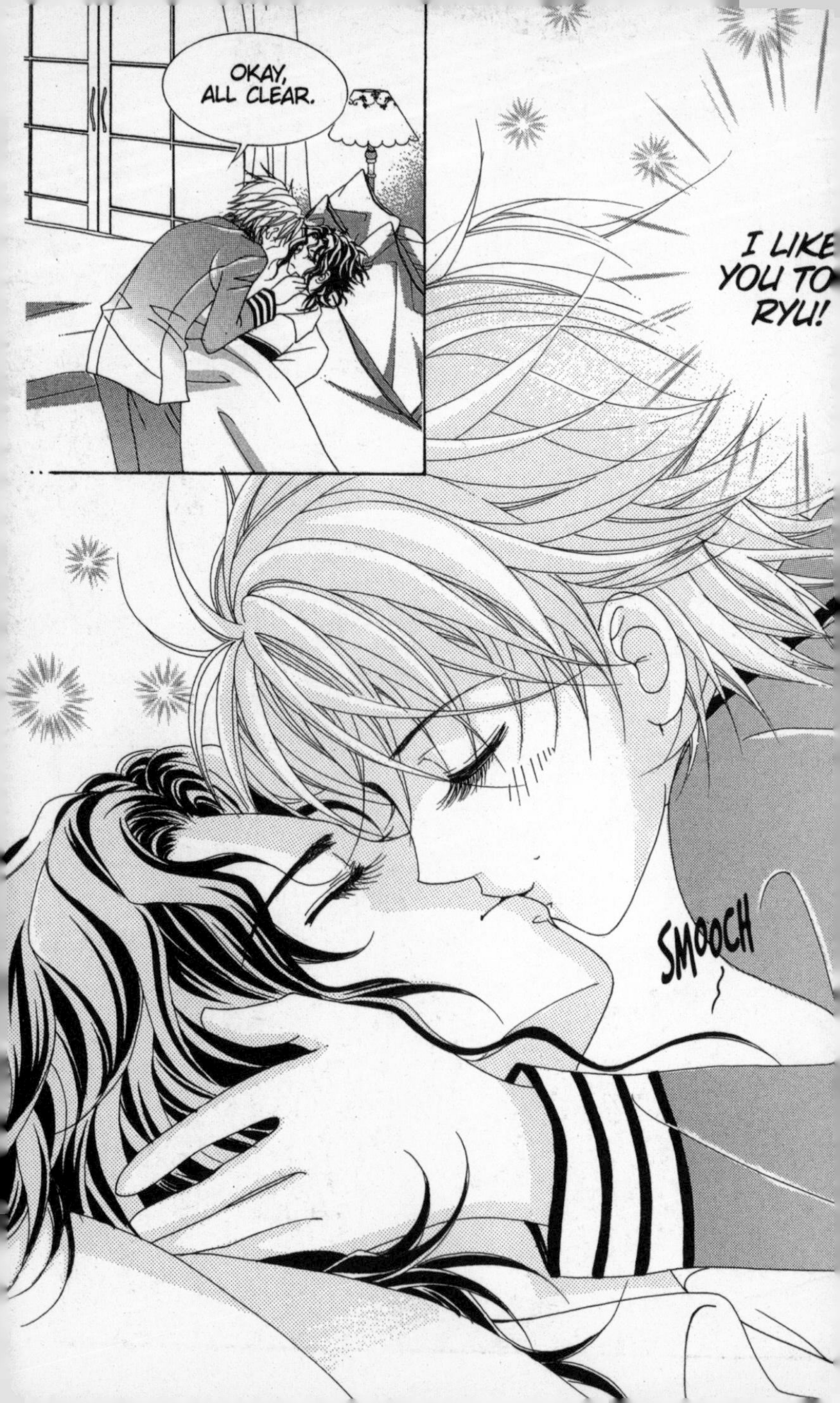
OKAY, ALL CLEAR.
I LIKE YOU TO RYU!
SMOOCH

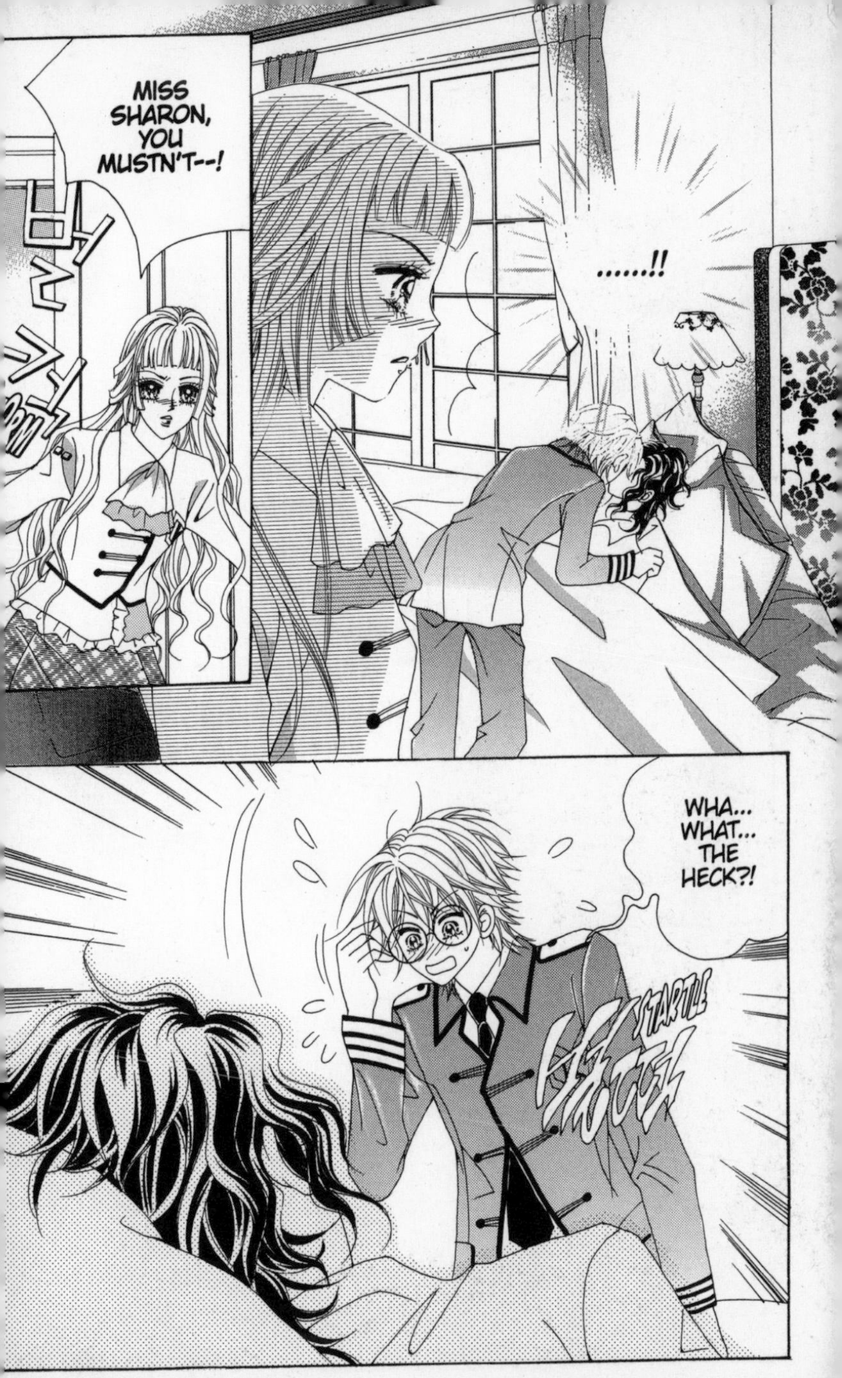
MISS SHARON, YOU MUSTN'T--!
......!!
WHA... WHAT... THE HECK?!
STARTLE

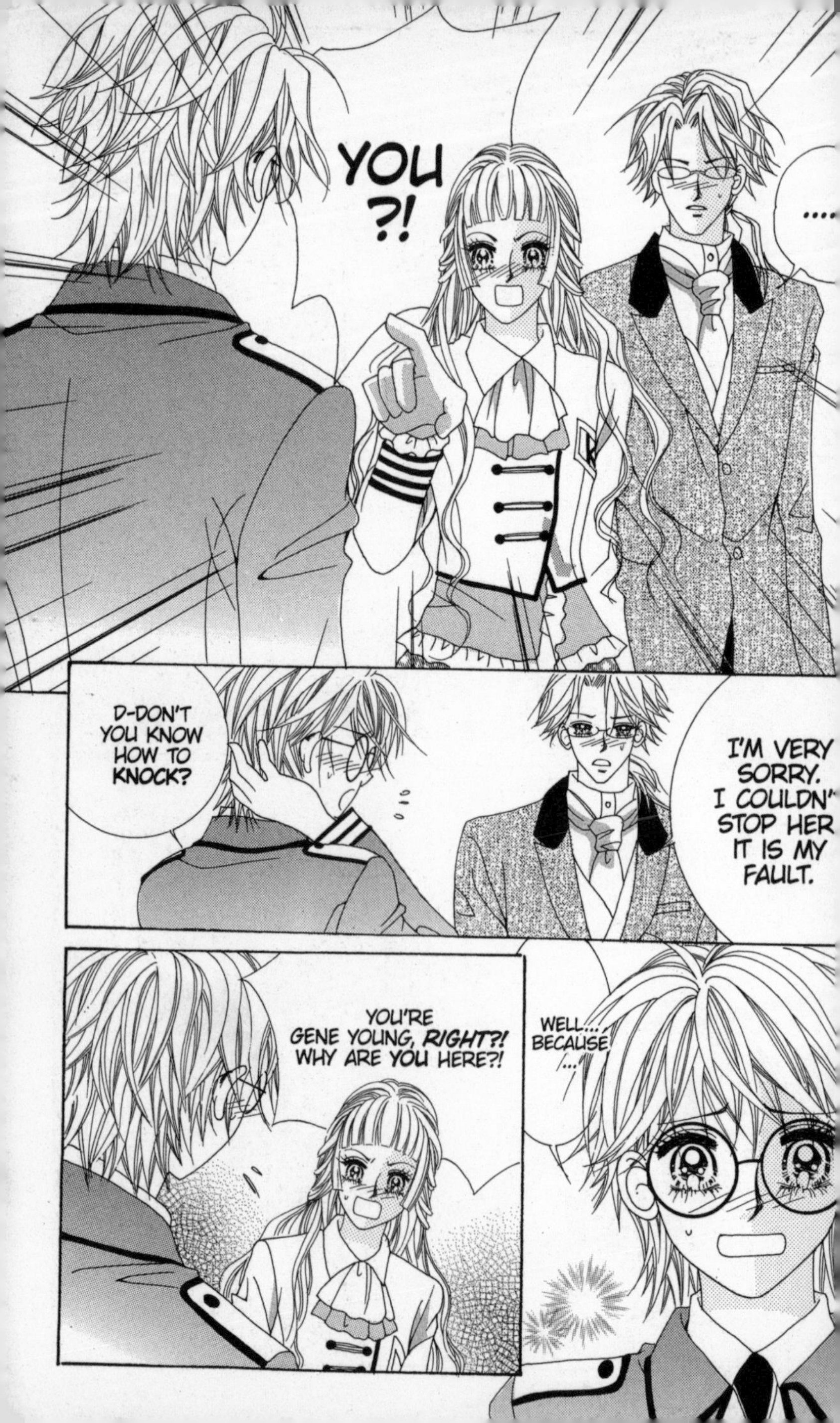

YOU ?!
....
D-DON'T YOU KNOW HOW TO KNOCK?
I'M VERY SORRY. I COULDN' STOP HER IT IS MY FAULT.
YOU'RE GENE YOUNG, *RIGHT?!* WHY ARE YOU HERE?!
WELL.... BECAUSE /...

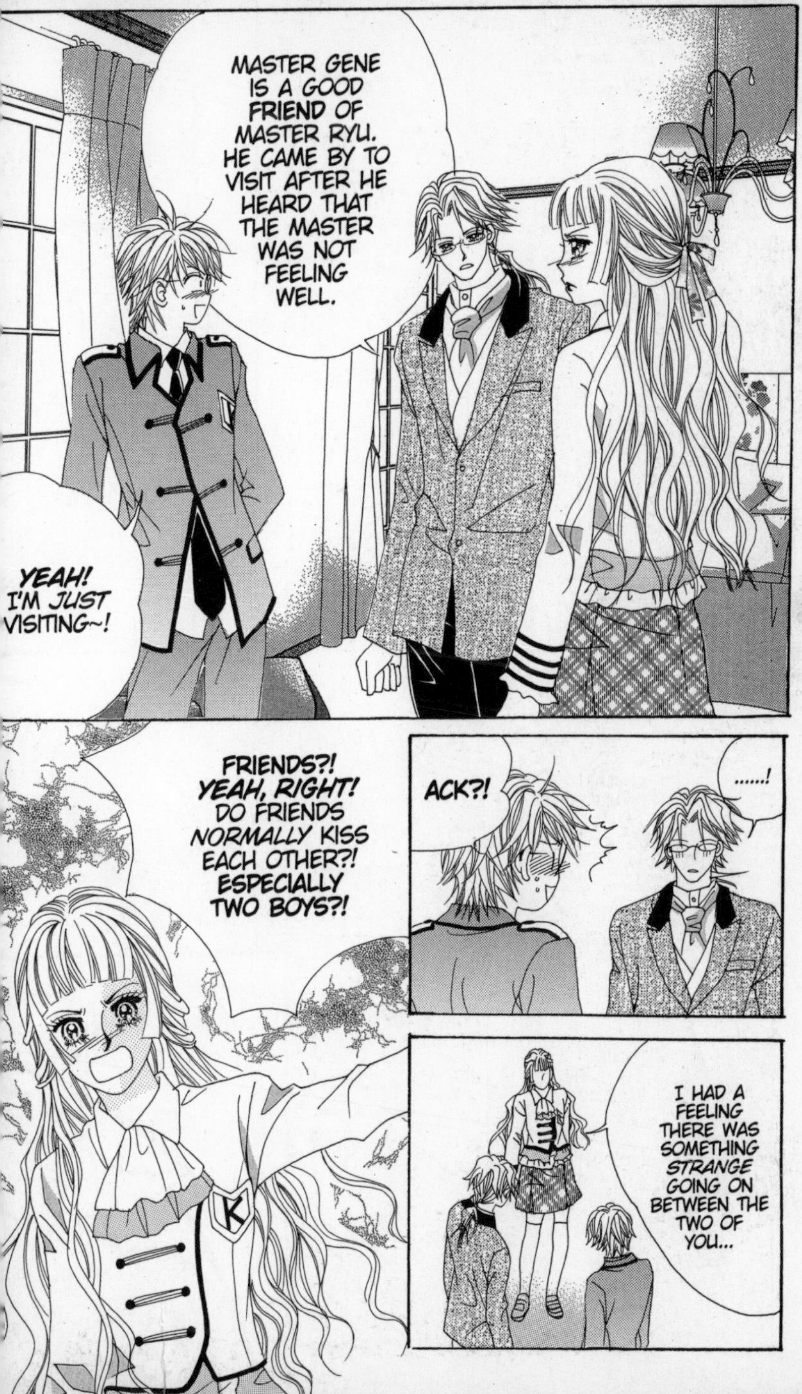
MASTER GENE IS A GOOD FRIEND OF MASTER RYU. HE CAME BY TO VISIT AFTER HE HEARD THAT THE MASTER WAS NOT FEELING WELL.
YEAH! I'M JUST VISITING~!
FRIENDS?! YEAH, RIGHT! DO FRIENDS NORMALLY KISS EACH OTHER?! ESPECIALLY TWO BOYS?!
ACK?!
......!
I HAD A FEELING THERE WAS SOMETHING STRANGE GOING ON BETWEEN THE TWO OF YOU...

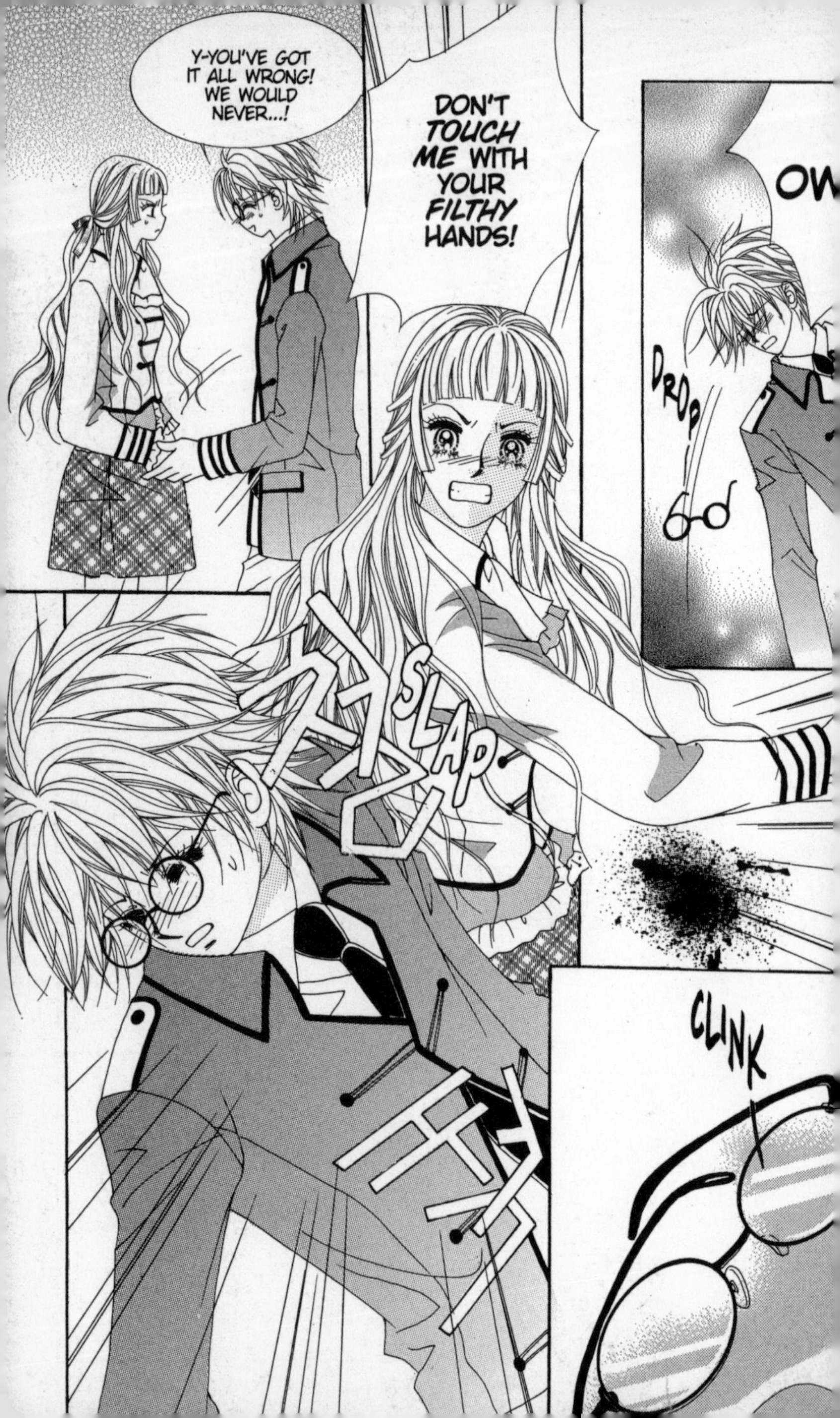
Y-YOU'VE GOT IT ALL WRONG! WE WOULD NEVER...!
DON'T *TOUCH ME* WITH YOUR *FILTHY* HANDS!
OW
DROP
SLAP
CLINK

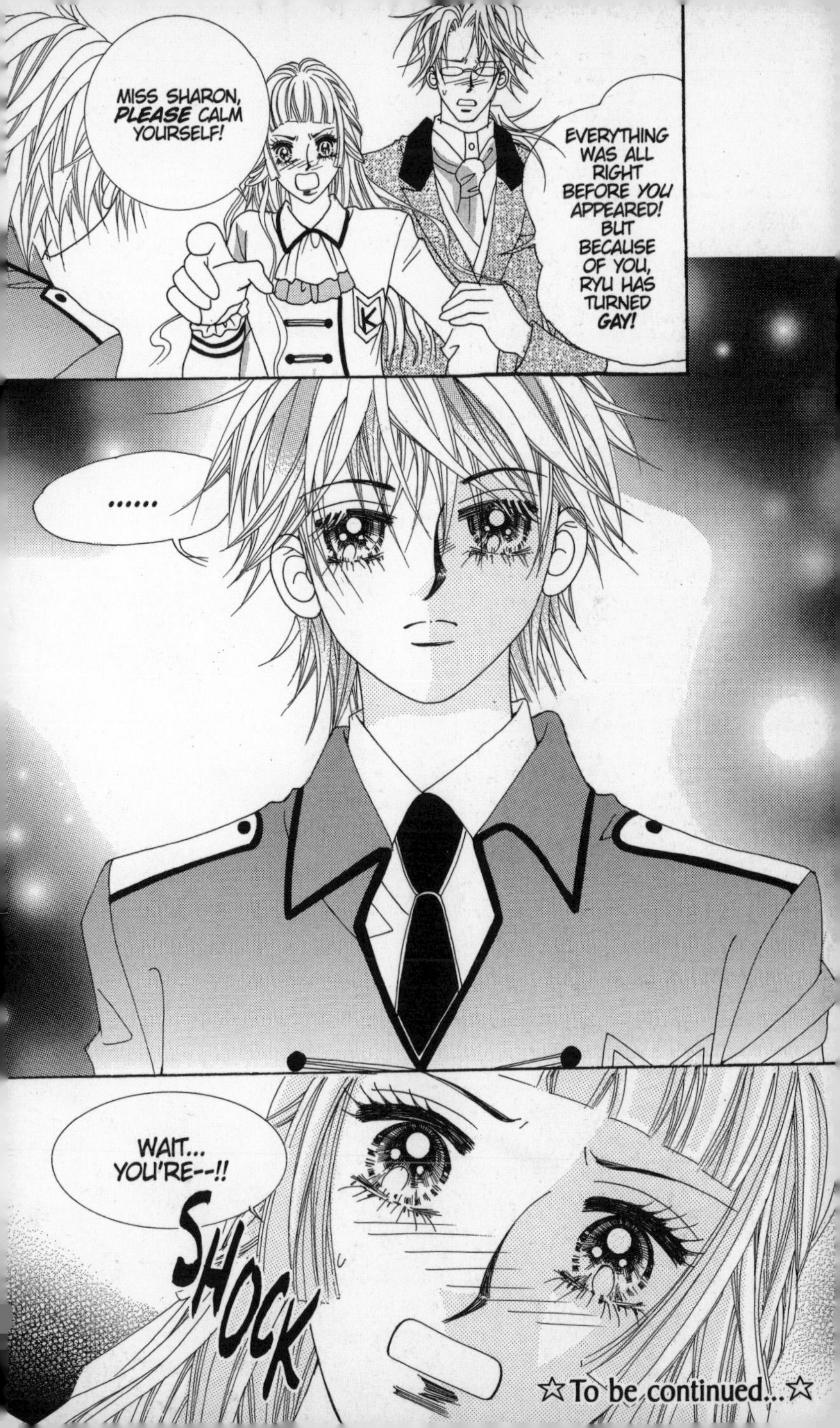
MISS SHARON, PLEASE CALM YOURSELF!
EVERYTHING WAS ALL RIGHT BEFORE YOU APPEARED! BUT BECAUSE OF YOU, RYU HAS TURNED GAY!
......
WAIT... YOU'RE--!!
SHOCK
☆To be continued...☆

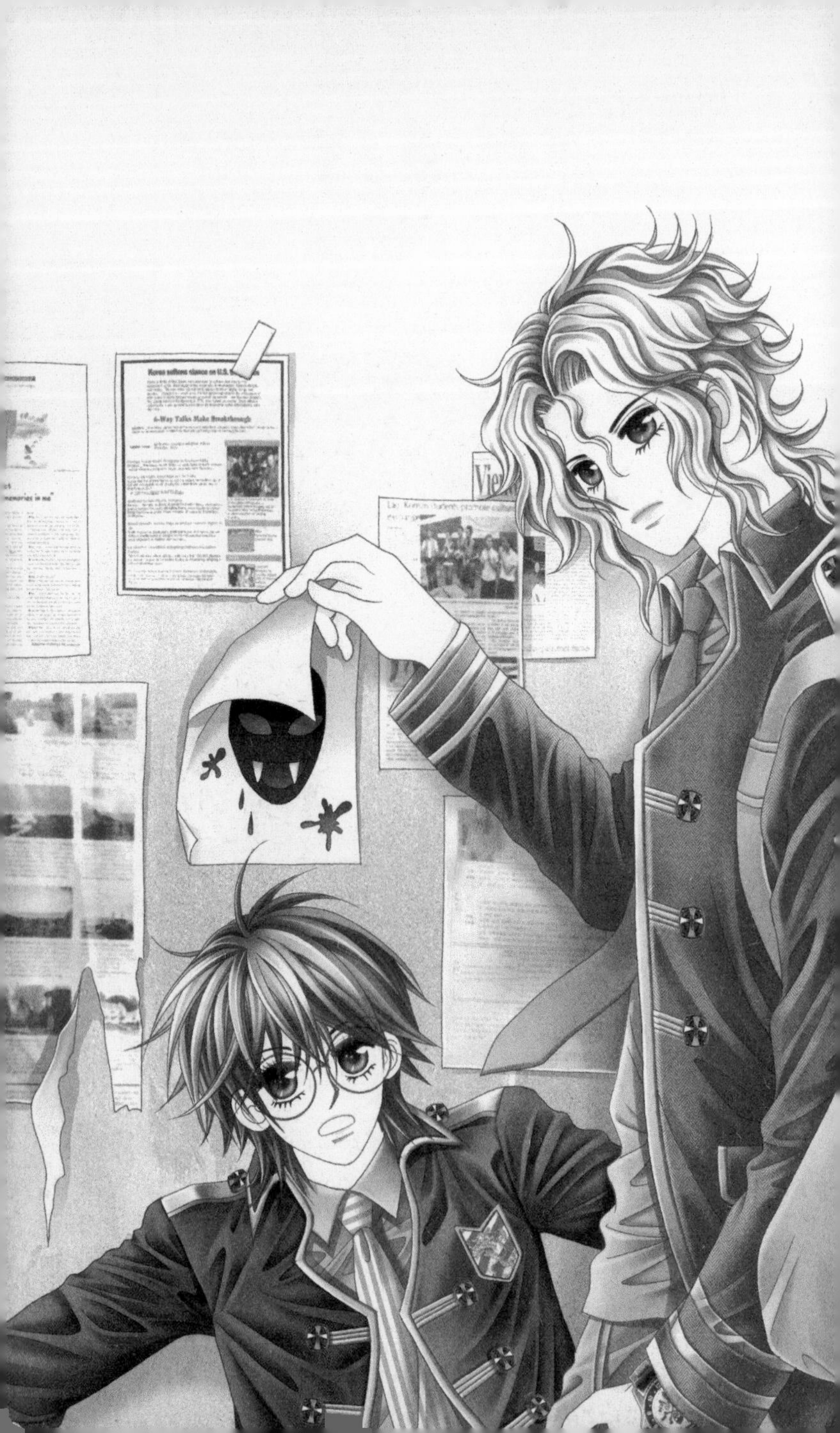

Korea softens stance on U.S.
6-Way Talks Make Breakthrough

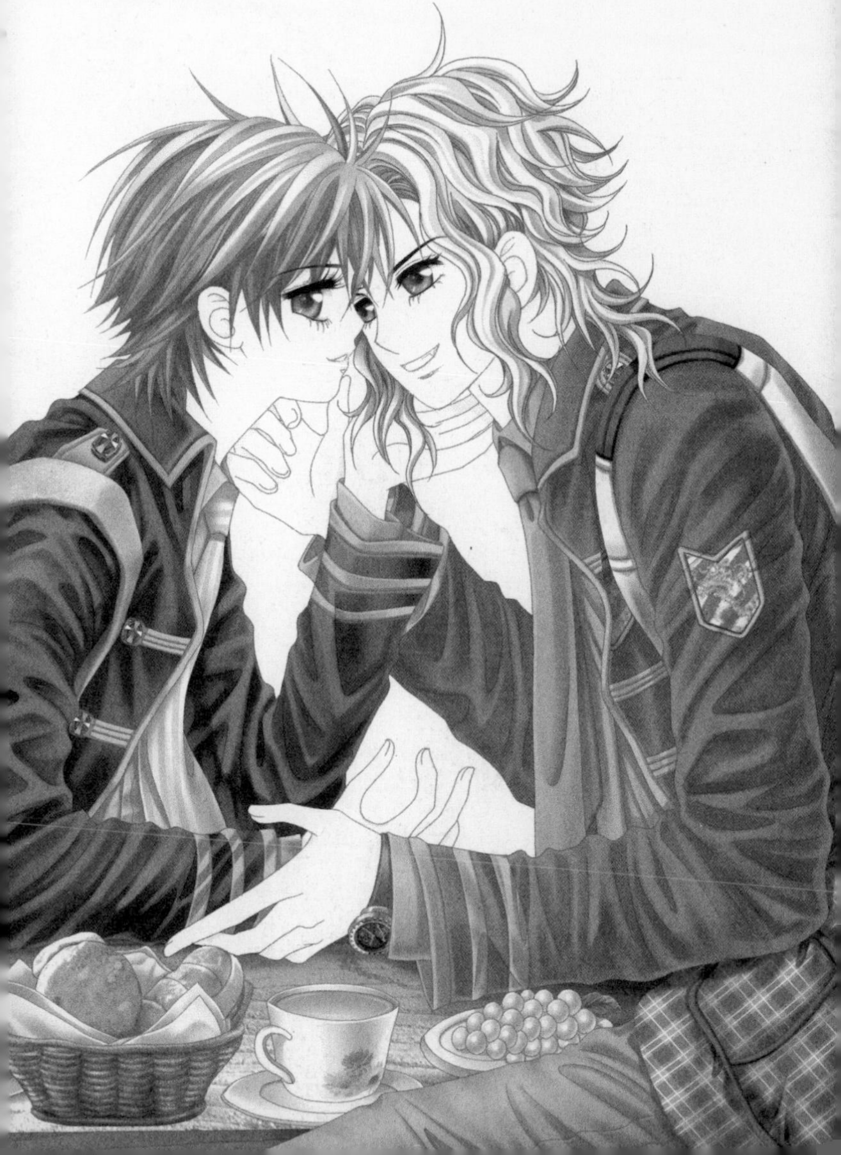

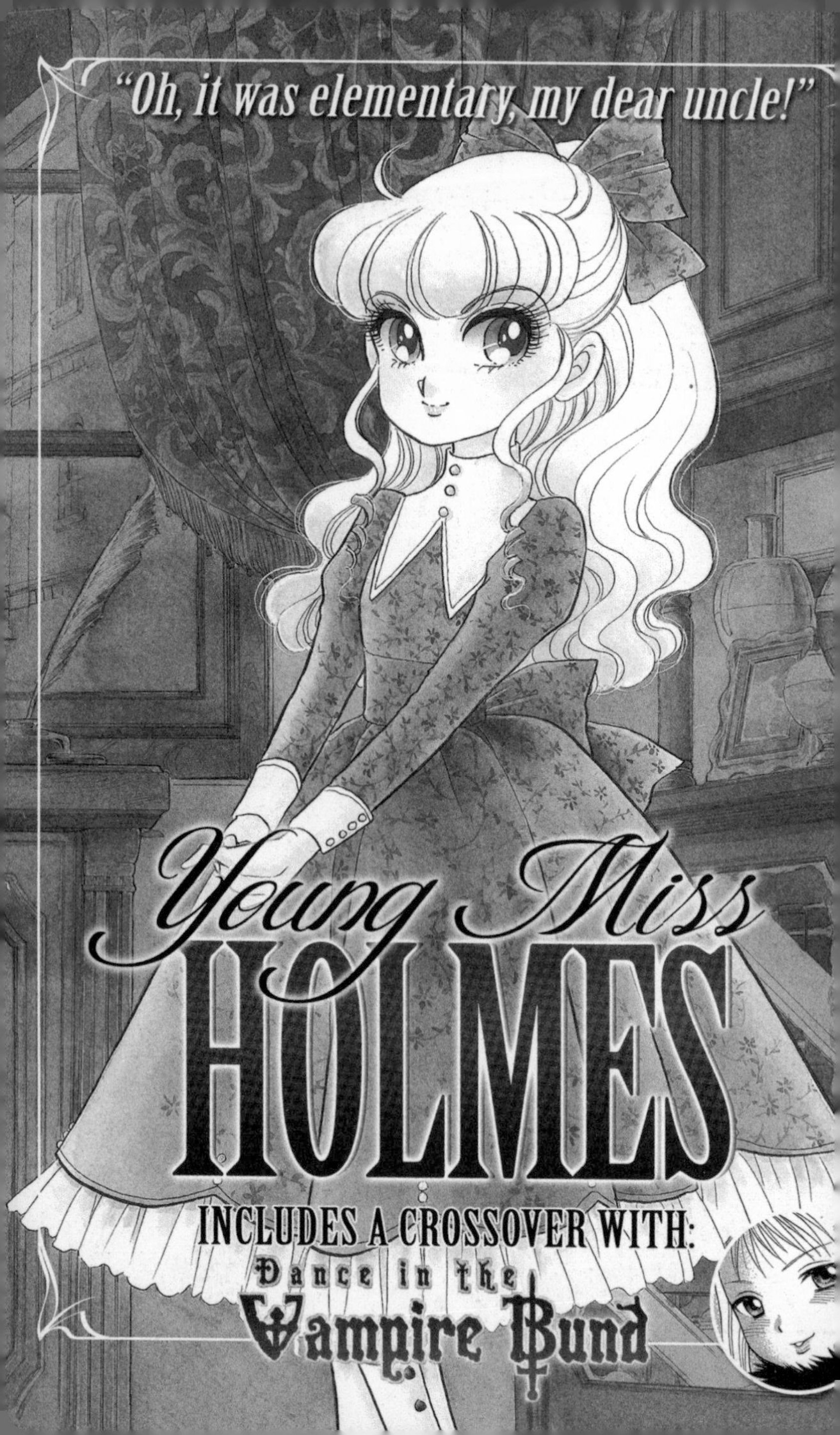
"Oh, it was elementary, my dear uncle!"
Young Miss
HOLMES
INCLUDES A CROSSOVER WITH:
Dance in the
Vampire Bund

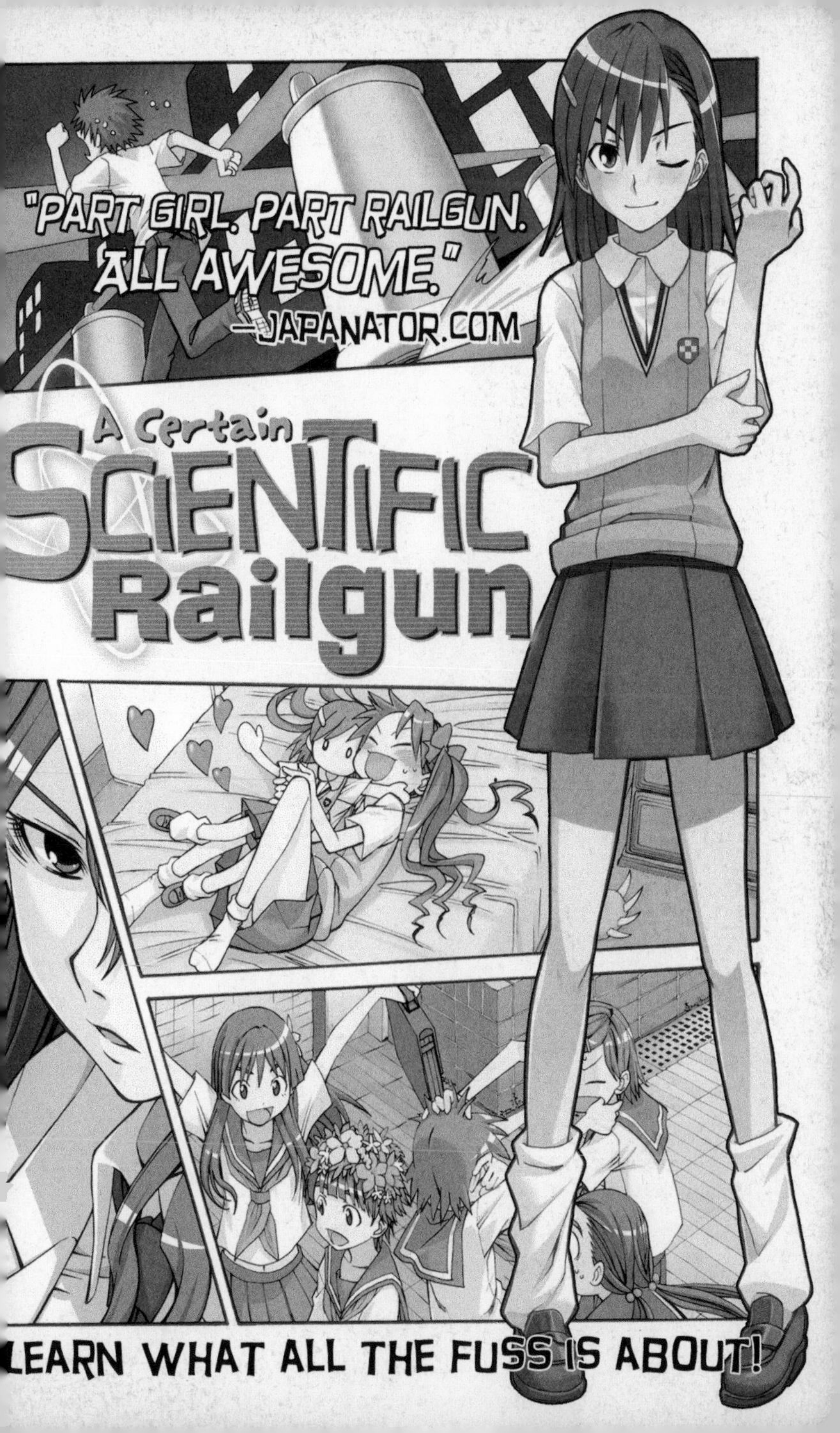

"PART GIRL. PART RAILGUN. ALL AWESOME."
—JAPANATOR.COM
A Certain SCIENTIFIC Railgun
LEARN WHAT ALL THE FUSS IS ABOUT!

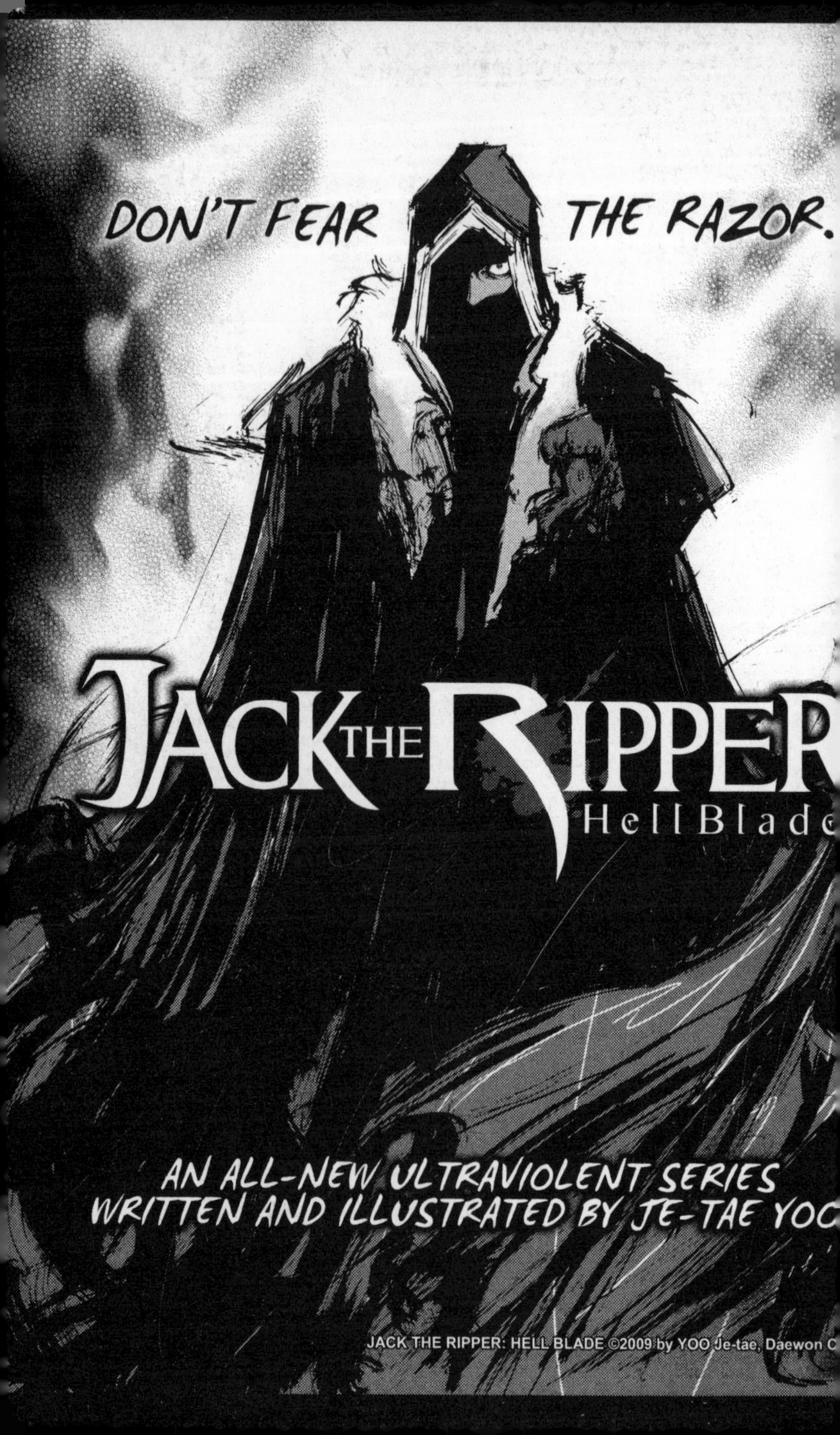
DON'T FEAR THE RAZOR.
JACK THE RIPPER
HellBlade
AN ALL-NEW ULTRAVIOLENT SERIES
WRITTEN AND ILLUSTRATED BY JE-TAE YOO
JACK THE RIPPER: HELL BLADE ©2009 by YOO Je-tae, Daewon C